BIOPSYCHOLOGY 98/99

Fourth Edition

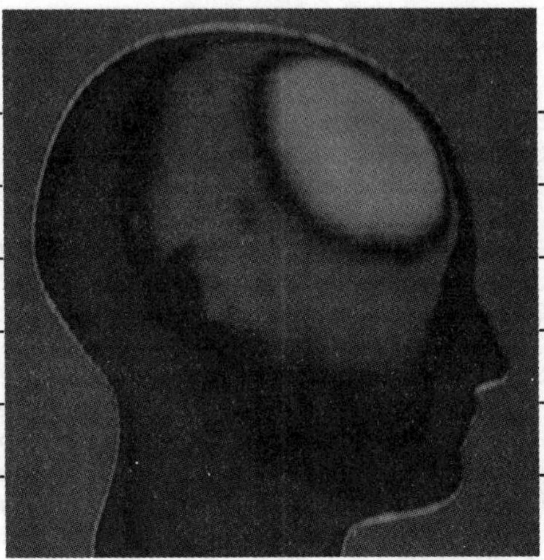

Editor

Boyce M. Jubilan

Allentown College of Saint Francis de Sales

Boyce M. Jubilan is a professor in the Department of Psychology at Allentown College of Saint Francis de Sales. He received his Ph.D. in psychology from Lehigh University and his M.Phil. from the Royal School of Veterinary Medicine, University of Edinburgh, Scotland. He also holds a D.V.M. from the University of the Philippines. His research interests are in the fields of neuroscience, specifically in biopsychology and reproductive physiology, including pheromonal communication.

A Library of Information from the Public Press

Dushkin/McGraw·Hill

Sluice Dock, Guilford, Connecticut 06437

Visit us on the Internet—http://www.dushkin.com/annualeditions

The Annual Editions Series

ANNUAL EDITIONS, including GLOBAL STUDIES, consist of over 70 volumes designed to provide the reader with convenient, low-cost access to a wide range of current, carefully selected articles from some of the most important magazines, newspapers, and journals published today. ANNUAL EDITIONS are updated on an annual basis through a continuous monitoring of over 300 periodical sources. All ANNUAL EDITIONS have a number of features that are designed to make them particularly useful, including topic guides, annotated tables of contents, unit overviews, and indexes. For the teacher using ANNUAL EDITIONS in the classroom, an Instructor's Resource Guide with test questions is available for each volume. GLOBAL STUDIES titles provide comprehensive background information and selected world press articles on the regions and countries of the world.

VOLUMES AVAILABLE

ANNUAL EDITIONS

Abnormal Psychology
Accounting
Adolescent Psychology
Aging
American Foreign Policy
American Government
American History, Pre-Civil War
American History, Post-Civil War
American Public Policy
Anthropology
Archaeology
Astronomy
Biopsychology
Business Ethics
Canadian Politics
Child Growth and Development
Comparative Politics
Computers in Education
Computers in Society
Criminal Justice
Criminology
Developing World
Deviant Behavior
Drugs, Society, and Behavior
Dying, Death, and Bereavement
Early Childhood Education
Economics
Educating Exceptional Children
Education
Educational Psychology
Environment
Geography
Geology
Global Issues
Health
Human Development
Human Resources
Human Sexuality
International Business
Macroeconomics
Management
Marketing
Marriage and Family
Mass Media
Microeconomics
Multicultural Education
Nutrition
Personal Growth and Behavior
Physical Anthropology
Psychology
Public Administration
Race and Ethnic Relations
Social Problems
Social Psychology
Sociology
State and Local Government
Teaching English as a Second Language
Urban Society
Violence and Terrorism
Western Civilization, Pre-Reformation
Western Civilization, Post-Reformation
Women's Health
World History, Pre-Modern
World History, Modern
World Politics

GLOBAL STUDIES

Africa
China
India and South Asia
Japan and the Pacific Rim
Latin America
Middle East
Russia, the Eurasian Republics, and Central/Eastern Europe
Western Europe

Cataloging in Publication Data
Main entry under title: Annual Editions: Biopsychology. 1998/99.
1. Psychobiology—Periodicals. I. Jubilan, Boyce M., *comp.* II. Title: Biopsychology.
ISBN 0-697-39130-2 152.05 ISSN 1092–3683

Fourth Edition

Cover image © 1998 PhotoDisc, Inc.

Printed in the United States of America

Printed on Recycled Paper

Contents

UNIT 1

Methods in Biopsychology

The four articles in this section discuss brain analysis techniques used in assessing the mechanics of brain function.

UNIT 2

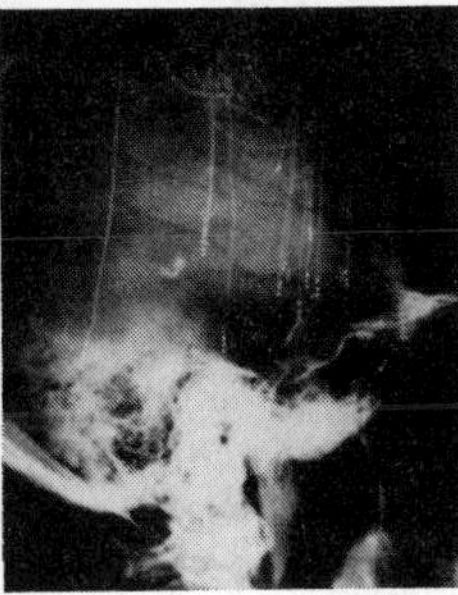

The Neuron and Regions of the Brain

The four articles in this section examine the function of neurotransmitters.

The concepts in bold italics are developed in the article. For further expansion please refer to the Topic Guide and the Index.

UNIT 3

Neural Development and Plasticity

Five articles examine how mental development is affected by psychoactive substances, diet, and other nutritional chemicals.

The concepts in bold italics are developed in the article. For further expansion please refer to the Topic Guide and the Index.

UNIT 4

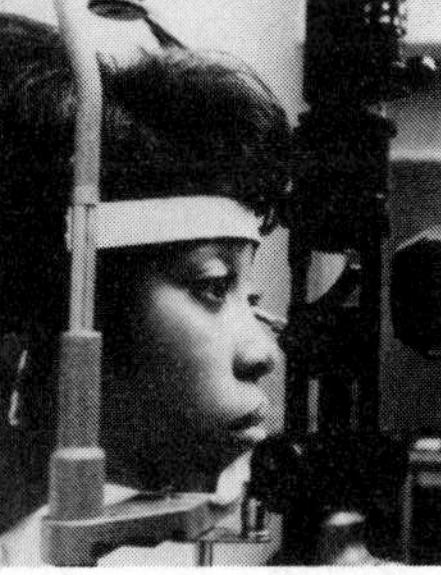

Sensation and Perception

Three unit articles discuss the sensory systems of smell, taste, touch, and hearing and how hormones interact with behavior.

UNIT 5

Motivation: Hunger and Aggression

The three articles in this section examine how hunger and aggression can be motivated by chemicals, hormones, and neurotransmitters.

UNIT 6

Reproductive Behavior

Five articles discuss the underlying mechanisms that control sexual drive.

The concepts in bold italics are developed in the article. For further expansion please refer to the Topic Guide and the Index.

UNIT 7

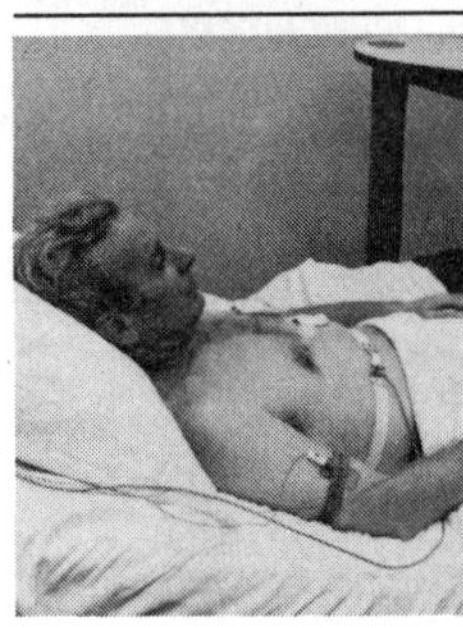

Sleep and Biological Rhythms

Three selections in this section discuss the physiological and environmental variables that influence the daily rhythms of sleep and wakefulness.

UNIT 8

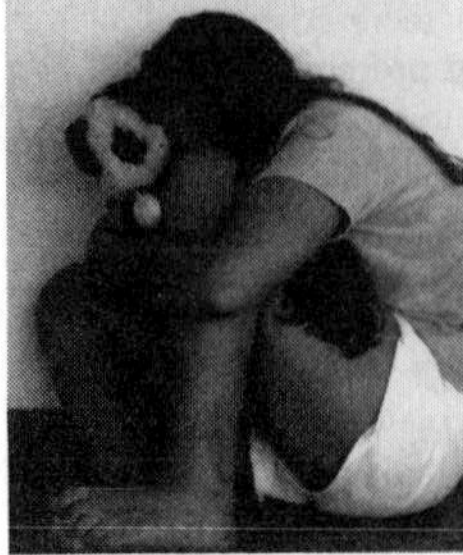

Emotions

Four unit articles examine how emotions and health can be impacted by one's cultural environment, physiology, and level of hostility.

UNIT 9

Learning and Memory

The four articles in this section review how cognitive abilities are developed.

The concepts in bold italics are developed in the article. For further expansion please refer to the Topic Guide and the Index.

UNIT 10

Disorders of Behavior and the Nervous System

Five unit articles examine behavioral disorders that include addiction, Parkinson's disease, dyslexia, and attention deficit disorder.

UNIT 11

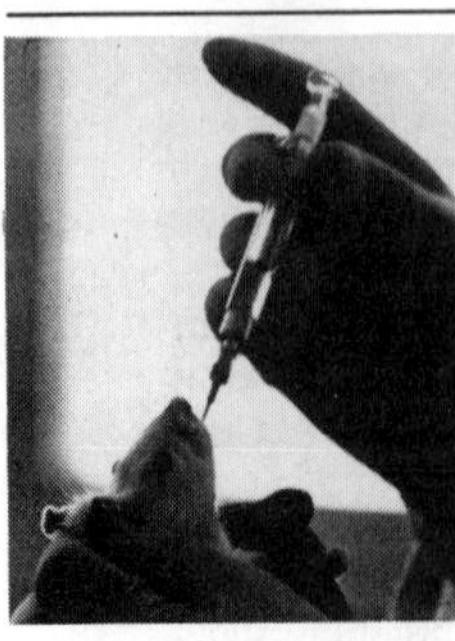

Ethical Issues

Four articles in this section consider the moral and ethical dynamics of clinical trials on humans, nervous tissue transplants, and animal use for scientific inquiry.

The concepts in bold italics are developed in the article. For further expansion please refer to the Topic Guide and the Index.

UNIT 12

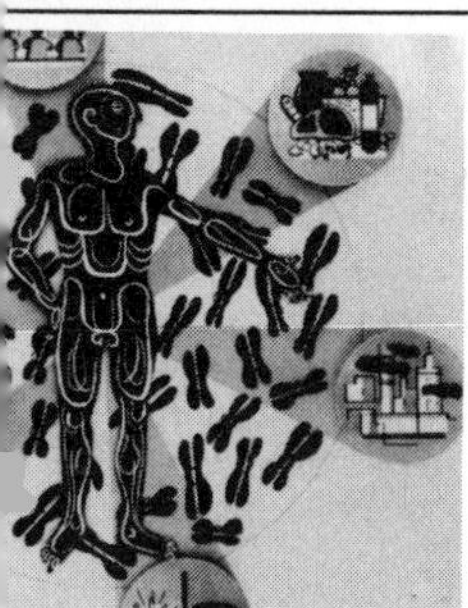

Evolutionary Perspectives

Five articles in this section consider the dynamics of human evolution.

The concepts in bold italics are developed in the article. For further expansion please refer to the Topic Guide and the Index.

Topic Guide

This topic guide suggests how the selections in this book relate to topics of traditional concern to psychology students and professionals It is useful for locating interrelated articles for reading and research. The guide is arranged alphabetically according to topic. Articles may, of course, treat topics that do not appear in the topic guide. In turn, entries in the topic guide do not necessarily constitute a comprehensive listing of all the contents of each selection. **In addition, relevant Web sites, which are annotated on pages 4 and 5, are noted in bold italics under the topic articles.**

TOPIC AREA	TREATED IN
Adrenaline	29. On the Neurobiological Basis of Affiliation ***(21, 22)***
Aggression/ Violence	17. Effects of Alcohol on Human Aggression 19. Aggressive Youth 31. Something Snapped 43. Politics of Biology 49. Male Sexual Proprietariness and Violence against Wives ***(15, 21, 22)***
Alzheimer's Disease	5. Brain's Immune System 13. For the Cortex, Neuron Loss May Be Less than a Thought ***(1, 2, 6, 10, 11)***
Animal Research	42. Trends in Animal Research ***(28)***
Attention Deficit	40. Attention Deficit ***(1, 2, 26)***
Biological Clocks/Rhythms	25. 'Traveling Light" Has New Meaning for Jet Laggards 26. Mouse Helps Explain What Makes Us Tick ***(9, 19, 20)***
Cerebral Cortex	30. Deciding Advantageously before Knowing the Advantageous Strategy 32. Machinery of Thought ***(10, 14, 23)***
Circadian Clocks/Rhythm	25. 'Traveling Light' Has New Meaning for Jet Laggards 26. Mouse Helps Explain What Makes Us Tick ***(19, 20)***
Consciousness	6. Tarzan's Little Brain 11. Studies Show Talking with Infants Shapes Basis of Ability to Think 30. Deciding Advantageously before Knowing the Advantageous Strategy ***(9, 10, 14, 23)***
Dementia	10. Making Our Minds Last a Lifetime 13. For the Cortex, Neuron Loss May Be Less than a Thought ***(8, 9, 10)***
Development	7. Stem Cells in the Central Nervous System 9. Neurotrophins and the Neurotrophic Factor Hypothesis 10. Making Our Minds Last a Lifetime 11. Studies Show Talking with Infants Shapes Basis of Ability to Think 12. Nature, Nurture, Brains, and Behavior 13. For the Cortex, Neuron Loss May Be Less than a Thought 35. Glucose Effects on Declarative and Nondeclarative Memory ***(8, 9, 10, 14, 23)***
Dopamine	36. Addicted 38. Understanding Parkinson's Disease ***(6, 24)***
Dyslexia	39. Looking beyond the Reading Difficulties in Dyslexia ***(24, 26)***
Eating	18. Attenuation of the Obesity Syndrome ***(17)***
Emotions	6. Tarzan's Little Brain 28. Happiness Is a Stochastic Phenomenon 29. On the Neurobiological Basis of Affiliation 30. Deciding Advantageously before Knowing the Advantageous Strategy 31. Something Snapped ***(8, 9, 10, 17, 21, 22)***
Evolutionary Perspectives	2. Evolutions: The Human Cerebral Cortex 45. God's Utility Function 46. Evolution's New Heretics 47. Sex Differences in Social Behavior 48. Sex Differences in Jealousy in Evolutionary and Cultural Perspective 49. Male Sexual Proprietariness and Violence against Wives ***(30, 31)***
Genes	12. Nature, Nurture, Brains, and Behavior 28. Happiness Is a Stochastic Phenomenon 37. Gene Therapy for the Nervous System 41. Science Misapplied 44. Junior Comes Out Perfect 45. God's Utility Function 46. Evolution's New Heretics ***(8, 9, 10, 29)***
Glutamate	8. Why Oligodendrocytes Die in Spinal Cord Injury ***(6, 8, 9)***
Hippocampus	33. How Does the Brain Organize Memories? ***(9, 18, 23)***
Homosexuality	23. Animals' Fancies 43. Politics of Biology
Intelligence/IQ	12. Nature, Nurture, Brains, and Behavior ***(10, 23)***
Learning	32. Machinery of Thought 39. Looking beyond the Reading Difficulties in Dyslexia ***(9, 23)***
Leptin	18. Attenuation of the Obesity Syndrome ***(17)***

TOPIC AREA	TREATED IN
Magnetic Resonance Imaging (MRI)	2. Evolutions: The Human Cerebral Cortex 3. New Imaging Methods *(3, 4, 5)*
Maternal Behavior	20. Natural-Born Mothers *(16)*
Melatonin	25. 'Traveling Light' Has New Meaning for Jet Laggards *(19, 20)*
Memory	10. Making Our Minds Last a Lifetime 32. Machinery of Thought 33. How Does the Brain Organize Memories? 34. Estradiol Is Related to Visual Memory 35. Glucose Effects on Declarative and Nondeclarative Memory *(10, 11, 23)*
Microglia	5. Brain's Immune System *(6, 8, 9)*
Movement	6. Tarzan's Little Brain 38. Understanding Parkinson's Disease *(6, 9, 10)*
Neuroimaging	2. Evolutions: The Human Cerebral Cortex 3. New Imaging Methods *(3, 4, 5)*
Neuropeptide Y	18. Attenuation of the Obesity Syndrome *(17)*
Neuroplasticity	8. Why Oligodendrocytes Die in Spinal Cord Injury 9. Neurotrophins and the Neurotrophic Factor Hypothesis *(6, 7, 8, 9, 10, 11)*
Neurotransmitters	13. For the Cortex, Neuron Loss May Be Less than a Thought 36. Addicted 38. Understanding Parkinson's Disease *(6, 10, 11, 24, 27)*
Neurotrophic Factors	9. Neurotrophins and the Neurotrophic Factor Hypothesis *(10, 11)*
Obesity	18. Attenuation of the Obesity Syndrome *(17)*
Opiates/Opioids	36. Addicted *(27)*
Parkinson's Disease	37. Gene Therapy for the Nervous System 38. Understanding Parkinson's Disease *(6, 24)*
Pheromones	14. Smell of Love 24. Menstrual Synchrony under Optimal Conditions *(14)*

TOPIC AREA	TREATED IN
Positron Emission Tomography (PET)	2. Evolutions: The Human Cerebral Cortex *(3, 4, 5)*
Psychoactive Substances	17. Effects of Alcohol on Human Aggression 36. Addicted 40. Attention Deficit 43. Politics of Biology *(27)*
Reproductive Fitness	22. Subtle, Secret Female Chimpanzees 47. Sex Differences in Social Behavior 48. Sex Differences in Jealousy in Evolutionary and Cultural Perspective 49. Male Sexual Proprietariness and Violence against Wives *(18, 30, 31)*
Sexual Abuse	49. Male Sexual Proprietariness and Violence against Wives *(18, 30, 31)*
Sexual Behavior/ Preference	21. Rethinking Puberty 22. Subtle, Secret Female Chimpanzees 23. Animals' Fancies 47. Sex Differences in Social Behavior 48. Sex differences in Jealousy in Evolutionary and Cultural Perspective *(18)*
Sleep/Wake Cycle	25. 'Traveling Light' Has New Meaning for Jet Laggards 27. Adenosine *(19, 20)*
Smell	14. Smell of Love 15. Senses *(12, 13, 14)*
Spinal Cord Injury	8. Why Oligodendrocytes Die in Spinal Cord Injury *(6, 7, 8, 9)*
Steroid Hormones	21. Rethinking Puberty 34. Estradiol Is Related to Visual Memory *(18)*
Synapse	9. Neurotrophins and the Neurotrophic Factor Hypothesis *(10, 11)*
Taste	15. Senses *(12, 13, 14)*
Techniques	1. Magnet on the Brain 3. New Imaging Methods 4. Creating a Body of Knowledge 37. Gene Therapy for the Nervous System *(3, 4, 5)*
Vision	11. Studies Show Talking with Infants Shapes Basis of Ability to Think 15. Senses 16. Visual Processing 34. Estradiol Is Related to Visual Memory 39. Looking beyond the Reading Difficulties in Dyslexia *(10, 12, 23, 24, 25, 26)*

Selected World Wide Web Sites for *Annual Editions: Biopsychology*

All of these Web sites are hot-linked through the *Annual Editions* home page: *http://www.dushkin.com/annualeditions* (just click on a book). In addition, these sites are referenced by number and appear where relevant in the Topic Guide on the previous two pages.

Some Web sites are continually changing their structure and content, so the information listed may not always be available.

General Sources

1. National Institutes of Health (NIH)—***http://www.nih.gov/***—Consult this site for links to extensive health information and scientific resources. The NIH is one of eight health agencies of the Public Health Service, which is part of the U.S. Department of Health and Human Services.

2. Psychological Associations—***http://foyt.iupui.edu/subjectareas/psychology/assoc.html***—This site is very useful for its links to journals, directors, handbooks, and manuals related to psychology and to some of the most prominent professional associations. These sites, in turn, provide a wealth of information.

Methods in Biopsychology

3. Consortium for Functional Neuroimaging, Human Brain Project—***http://pet.med.va.gov:8080/hbp.html***—Explore this Minneapolis Veterans Affairs Medical Center site that describes the activities of the Consortium for Functional Neuroimaging, whose central research focus is modeling and visualization of spatial and temporal patterns of functional activation in the living human brain.

4. Massachusetts General Hospital/Harvard Medical School—***http://neurosurgery.mgh.harvard.edu/other2.htm***—Not only does this broad-reaching site provide links to general medical sites, but it has links to resources for patients and information of interest regarding neuroscience, neurology, and neurosurgery.

5. National Library of Medicine—***http://www.nlm.nih.gov/***—This site gives you access to the "Visible Man." It also permits you to search a number of databases and electronic information sources such as MEDLINE, learn about research projects and programs, keep up on recent medical news, and peruse medical libraries.

The Neuron and Regions of the Brain

6. Central Nervous System Diseases—***http://www.mic.ki.se/Diseases/c10.228.html***—Consult this Karolinska Institute Library site for useful fact sheets and dozens of links to information about brain injury and diseases of the brain and central nervous system, such as Alzheimer's disease, multiple sclerosis, Parkinson's disease, and epilepsy, as well as new developments in brain disorder research.

7. NeuroTrauma—Law Nexus: Role of the Neurolawyer—***http://www.neurolaw.com/role.html***—For a change of pace, check out this site for neurolawyers, described here as attorneys whose specialty is representing clients with traumatic brain injury or spinal cord injury. The site provides links to information about these injuries, a lengthy glossary, and resources.

8. Scientific American—***http://www.sciam.com/explorations/020397brain/020397explorations.html***—This site will give you access to *Scientific American*'s varied archives. This page discusses neurons, described as "not so simple after all," and leads to interesting links such as a stereoscopic image of a neuron.

9. The Whole Brain Atlas—***http://www.med.harvard.edu/AANLIB/home.html***—This Harvard Medical School site provides extensive links to research and data on the brain. Click onto many varied topics to learn about the brain, from vascular dementia to the structure and function of the brain in normal aging.

Neural Development and Plasticity

10. Brain Dynamics Research Group—***http://www.mhri.edu.au/bdl/***—Examine this Australian site of the Mental Health Research Institute to learn more about brain dynamics. The site provides links to recent papers dealing with such topics as neural networks and the cerebral cortex.

11. Mental Health Net: Disorders and Treatment Index—***http://www.cmhc.com/selfhelp.htm***—This site and its many links are geared to providing information on mental disorders, with an emphasis on self-help. Aging, dementia, Alzheimer's disease, and many other topics, from cancer to depression, are described here.

Sensation

12. Laboratory for Neural Network Modeling in Vision Research—***http://www.voicenet.com/~rybak/nisms.html***—This Web site from the A. B. Kogan Research Institute for Neurocybernetics for Neural Network Modeling in Vision Research in Russia notes the research interests and projects and lists useful links.

13. Mysteries of Odor in Human Sexuality—***http://www.pheromones.com/***—Look into this commercial site to read topics of interest to nonscientists about pheromones. Links to more academic material are included. Check out the diagram of "Mammalian Olfactory-Genetic-Neuronal-Hormonal-Behavioral Reciprocity and Human Sexuality."

14. Sensory Processing Lab—***http://serendip.brynmawr.edu/bbl/Sensorylab.html***—Open this site to do a "lab" in sensory processing. It is intended to illustrate some basic principles of sensory processing by the brain and to give you the background and some incentive to explore them further. When you finish the lab, click onto "Brain and Behavior Links."

Motivation: Hunger and Aggression

15. Crime Times—***http://www.crime-times.org/titles.htm***—This interesting site, which lists research reviews and other information regarding biological causes of criminal, violent, and psychopathic behavior, consists of many articles. It is provided by the nonprofit Wacker Foundation, the publisher of *Crime Times.*

16. Maternal Behavior: Physiological Psaychology Lecture Support Material—***http://www.psy.plym.ac.uk/year2/maternal.htm***—This site presents a summary of a study on maternal behavior as studied in rats. It includes discussions and graphs of such topics as the impact of hormones on maternal

behavior, maternal self-image, and mothers' ability to recognize their babies' smell.

17. Obesity, Leptin, and the Brain—*http://www.nejm.org/public/1996/0334/0005/0324/1.htm*—First read this editorial on obesity. Then click onto the *The New England Journal of Medicine*'s home page to gain access to other materials of interest to those studying the hypothalamus, neuropeptide Y, and leptin.

Reproductive Behavior

18. Bonobo Sex and Society—*http://soong.club.cc.cmu.edu/~julie/bonobos.html*—Julie Waters's site, accessed through Carnegie Mellon University, includes an article explaining how a primate's behavior challenges traditional assumptions about male supremacy in human evolution. Guaranteed to generate spirited debate. Also access *http://data.club.cc.cmu.edu/~julie/brainstuff/index.html* for information on the limbic system, hippocampus, and other topics.

Sleep and Biological Rhythms

19. Society for Light Treatment and Biological Rhythms—*http://www.websciences.org/sltbr/*—Open this SLTBR site for useful links to research and information on circadian rhythms, seasonal affective disorder, melatonin, and sleep disorders.

20. Science News Digest for Physicians and Scientists—*http://genome.eerie.fr/bioscience/news/scientis/obesity2.htm*—This site provides information about neuropeptide Y and its known and suspected functions in regulation of body weight and circadian rhythms, sexual functioning, and anxiety and stress response.

Emotions

21. HighWire Press—*http://highwire.stanford.edu/*—Peruse this site from Stanford University to find valuable links to many sources of materials dealing with physiological aspects of emotions.

22. Institute of HeartMath—*http://www.webcom.com/~hrtmath/IHM/Research/Electrophysiology.html*—What are the effects of stress and emotional states on the electrophysiology of the body? Open this site to find out the impact of emotion on the nervous system and other related topics.

Learning and Memory

23. Resources for Psychology and Cognitive Sciences—*http://www.ke.shinshu-u.ac.jp/psych/index.html*—This frequently updated site of resources for psychology and cognitive science on the Internet provides many links about learning and memory. There are directories of college and university committees and departments, lists of conferences, online library information, and electronic journals.

Disorders of Behavior and the Nervous System

24. Clinical Psychology Resources—*http://www.psychologie.uni-bonn.de/kap/links_20.htm*—This page from Germany's University of Bonn Department of Clinical and Applied Psychology contains Web resources for clinical and abnormal psychology, behavioral medicine, and mental health. There are links to journals, organizations, psychotherapy topics, and discussions of specific disorders.

25. Dr. Ivan's Depression Central—*http://www.psycom.net/depression.central.html*—This extensive site describes itself as the "Internet's central clearinghouse for information on all types of depressive disorders and on the most effective treatments" for these disorders—and it lives up to the billing. Students of biopsychology are likely to turn to this site and its numerous links again and again.

26. National Attention Deficit Disorder Association—*http://www.add.org/*—This site, some of which is under construction, will lead you to information about ADD/ADHD. It has links to self-help and support groups, outlines behaviors and diagnostics, answers FAQs, and suggests books and other resources.

27. National Institute on Drug Abuse—*http://165.112.78.61/*—Use this site index of the National Institute on Drug Abuse to learn more about the possible genetic basis of addiction. Consult it also for NIDA publications and communications, information on drugs of abuse, and links to other related Web sites.

Ethical Issues

28. Ethics—*http://spsp.clarion.edu/RDE3/C1/c1ethics.html*—If you want to examine the ethics of using animals for research purposes, this is a useful site. It provides links to articles considering different facets of the issue and to the American Psychological Association's ethical code.

29. Human Genome Project Information—*http://www.ornl.gov/TechResources/Human_Genome/resource/elsi.html*—This is an excellent site for learning about recent findings in genetic research and to examine the ethical, legal, and social issues and challenges raised by such research. Who, for example, owns and controls genetic information?

Evolutionary Perspectives

30. Long Foreground-Overview of Human Evolution—*http://www.wsu.edu:8001/vwsu/gened/learn-modules/top_longfor/lfopen-index.html*—Washington State University's Web site presents a learning module covering three major topics in human evolution: "Overview," "Hominid Species Timeline," and "Human Physical Characteristics." It also provides a helpful glossary of terms.

31. WWW Virtual Library: Evolution (Biosciences)—*http://golgi.harvard.edu/biopages/evolution.html#internet*—This listing of Internet resources provides dozens of links to sites that will help in expanding your knowledge of human evolution.

We highly recommend that you review our Web site for expanded information and our other product lines. We are continually updating and adding links to our Web site in order to offer you the most usable and useful information that will support and expand the value of your Annual Editions. You can reach us at: *http://www.dushkin.com/annualeditions/*.

Methods in Biopsychology

Biopsychology subscribes to the notion that biological mechanisms underlie mental processes and behaviors, and that these mechanisms are amenable to investigations using practicable techniques. Mental processes are often considered as events associated with thinking, or consciousness, or the mind. Can we prove that the biological basis of the mind is within our brain? And can the brain really control the performance of behaviors? How then can we investigate the biological basis of this mind-brain-behavior interaction?

A number of biopsychological techniques have been developed through the years. Some past attempts were rather ridiculous, if not appalling. Circa 1900, a method known as phrenology endorsed the idea that the size and location of the bumps and depressions on the skull were indicative of personality characteristics and intelligence. It was presumed that these bumps and depressions were caused by the mass of brain tissue lying underneath the skull. An unusually large bump or depression indicated either enhanced or diminished behavioral qualities, respectively.

Modern techniques of brain analysis are more reliable in assessing the morphological and functional status of the brain. Some techniques let us take images of the brain in different states of activity. One technique known as computerized tomography (CT) uses X rays to acquire images of the brain taken from several planes that are later synthesized by a computer. Another technique of brain imaging known as positron emission tomography (PET) uses a scanner to measure radioactivity from parts of the brain that have been exposed to an injected radioactive substance. The areas in the brain that are more active will take more of the radioactive substance and show more radioactivity when measured by the scanner. Pictorial representations or images of radioactivity show the varying degrees of activity across the different areas of the brain.

With the images generated by these techniques, it is now possible to see areas of the brain that have been activated by particular stimuli or situations. For example, scans can be made of the brain while a person is reading words silently, reading words aloud, playing chess, or any other cognitive activity. Brain scans can also differentiate brain activity levels between normal individuals and those suffering from neurological disorders.

Other promising methods in biopsychology are described in this unit. Techniques from other disciplines, such as physics and computer science, have been helpful in developing new strategies for understanding the biological basis of behavior.

Looking Ahead: Challenge Questions

Describe how the following techniques work: computerized tomography, positron emission tomography, magnetic resonance imaging. What are the advantages of each technique? Can these techniques help us understand cognitive processes? How can these techniques assess neurological disorders?

What is the significance of the "Visible Man" project to the sciences? Have you tried accessing the information from the Internet? Do you think computer technology can provide essential tools for biopsychology in the near future?

UNIT 1

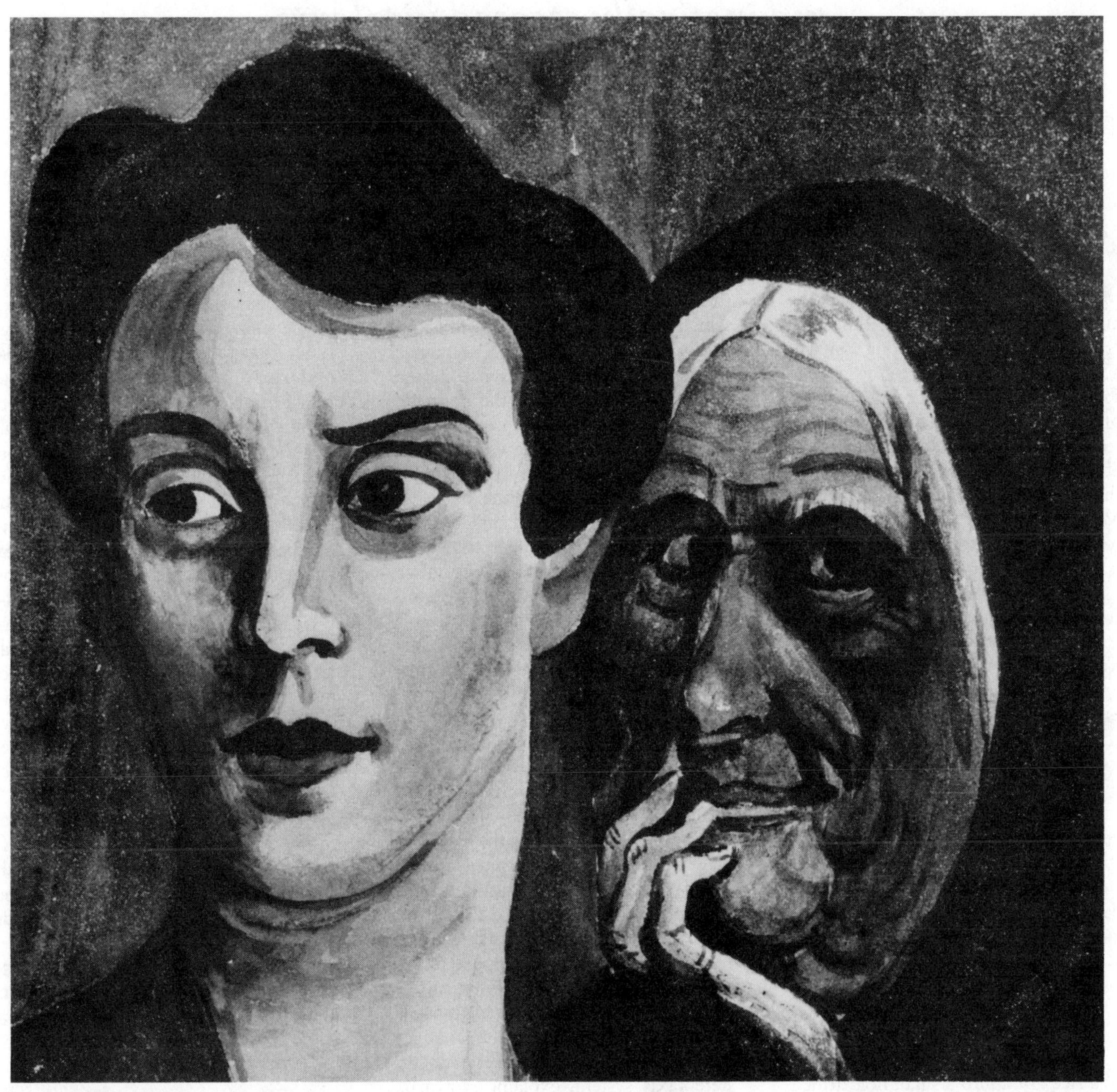

MEDICAL TECHNOLOGY

MAGNET ON THE BRAIN

Safer neurosurgery with magnetically steered implants

Children often learn about magnetism by dragging a paper clip through a paper maze with the aid of a magnet held below. Researchers now hope that before long they will accomplish a similar feat in the maze of the human brain with a refined version of a procedure called stereotaxis. The technique, being tested by workers at Stereotaxis, a firm in St. Louis, and at the Washington University School of Medicine, would allow physicians to reach diseased areas of the brain with the least possible damage to healthy tissue.

Stereotaxis is the procedure in which surgeons plunge, say, needles or electrodes straight through the brain to treat a trouble spot deep within. In the process, they tear healthy and perhaps essential neural tissue—a risk complicated if several needles or electrodes need to be inserted, as is sometimes the case. (For instance, to treat Parkinson's disease stereotaxically, six drug-delivering needles would be inserted in different spots to saturate fully the deep-seated striatum, which contains the defective tissue.) Physicians try to minimize surgical damage by first reviewing a brain-scan image and then avoiding the most crucial areas.

The magnetic version of stereotaxis is in principle less destructive. Surgeons would insert a magnetic pellet the size of a rice grain into a small hole drilled into the skull of a patient. The patient's head would then be placed in a housing the size of a small washing machine, which contains six superconducting magnets. Using a magnetic resonance image as a guide, surgeons would then direct the pellet through the brain by adjusting the forces of the various magnets. The pellet could tow a catheter, electrode or other device to minister to the troublesome neural tissue.

With magnetic steering, surgeons can dodge especially critical neurons. Moreover, they would also be able to move the pellet around within the entire damaged area. A patient being treated for Parkinson's would, therefore, have only one path of neurons damaged, as opposed to six with the conventional method.

The chief obstacle to applying this technique in the past, notes Ralph G. Dacey, Jr., of Washington University, who directs the stereotaxis research team, has been accurately controlling the magnetic fields. A decade ago, however, Matthew A. Howard III, then a physics student at the University of Virginia, realized that the precise instruments physicists use to measure gravity could be applied to the control of magnetic fields. That recognition, coupled with improved computers and brain-imaging devices, enabled investigators to fashion the magnetic stereotaxis system, explains Howard, now a neurosurgeon who assists the researchers in St. Louis from his base at the University of Iowa.

The team has demonstrated the technique on brains from dead mammals and one from a live pig, as well as on a block of gelatin, which has about the same consistency as the human brain. For the moment, other neurosurgeons remain cautious about the system's prospects, and Stereotaxis, which holds the patent on the technique, is the only company committed to this kind of magnetic neurosurgery.

Howard says that although the hardware for magnetic stereotaxis will probably cost more than the conventional technology, it might nonetheless save money by reducing operating time by one half to two thirds. The technology could also be broadened to include use in other parts of the body, such as the liver or blood vessels.

"The challenge," Dacey remarks, "is to find the best complementary use of conventional stereotaxic surgery and specific situations for magnetic stereotaxis." He plans to apply to the Food and Drug Administration before summer's end for approval to start tests with the new method on humans. The first clinical trials, probably for biopsies, could begin next year.

—Philip Yam

Evolutions: The Human Cerebral Cortex

As far back as ancient Greece, the brain has been considered the seat of the mind. Recent research suggests that the human—and indeed, mammalian—cortex is a network of many special-purpose signal processors rather than a single, general-purpose analytical engine.

That behavior arises from the brain was known to the ancient Greeks of the Golden Age. But scientists have been slow to understand which brain structures are involved in specific forms of cognition.

Until recently, researchers relied on brain lesions or on neurological diseases to determine the locations within the brain of specific sensory, motor, and cognitive functions. Today, they are using a variety of imaging and electrophysiological techniques to observe localized brain activity in normal human subjects during specific cognitive tasks. Improvements in laboratory computers have led to high-resolution electroencephalography (EEG), while advances in image-processing hardware and software have contributed to the success of positron emission tomography (PET) and functional magnetic resonance imaging (fMRI) studies. PET scanners monitor the concentration of radioactively labeled substances in the brain, with regions of greater neural activity exhibiting greater uptake of the label because of increased metabolism or increased blood flow (itself an indicator of increased metabolism). The newer technique of fMRI allows monitoring of local cerebral blood flow without the administration of radioactive materials or (in recent versions) magnetic contrast agents.

Electroencephalograms (EEGs) measure the electrical activity in the brain using scalp electrodes. This technique has progressed to systems recording from over 100 electrodes simultaneously. A newer, noninvasive technique for recording brain electrical activity, magnetoencephalography (MEG), uses a helmet containing more than 100 superconducting magnetic sensors to measure the electrical currents produced when large populations of neurons become active simultaneously.

Pre-1800: Although ancient Egyptian physicians described the effects of head injuries in papyri circa 1600 B.C., they believed that the heart was the seat of the intellect. In ancient Greece, Alcmaceon of Crotona (circa 400 B.C.) proposed, on the basis of anatomical dissections, that the brain was the organ of sensation and thought. A follower of Galen's, Nemesius (circa 400 A.D.) located reasoning, imagination, and memory in the cerebral ventricles—which he speculated were filled with "spirits"—rather than in the cerebral cortex.

Vesalius questioned the ventricle hypothesis in 1543, when he noted that the ventricles of animal and human brains were similar in shape, but that animals lacked cognition. A century later, the English anatomist Willis proposed that the cerebral gyri controlled memory and the will.

Starting in the 18th century, animal experiments demonstrated the role of precortical brain structures in sustaining life. In 1760, de Lorry found that damaging the medulla stopped normal respiration in dogs. However, scientists continued to believe that the brain as a whole received and dealt with impressions from the various senses, and that the mind's commands to the body used the same nerves that deliver sensory impressions.

1800–1899: Opposition to the prevailing view that the brain lacked areas with specific functions surfaced early in the 19th century. Bell wrote in 1811: "I have to offer reasons for believing...that the parts of the cerebrum have different functions."

About the same time as Bell, Gall and Spurzheim proposed that the shape of features on the skull indicated the intellectual activities of underlying regions of the brain. The resulting theory—phrenology—became a pseudoscientific fad during the first half of the 19th century, and created deep skepticism among anatomists about the localization of cognitive functions in the brain. Flourens, a vocal critic of phrenology, concluded in 1824 from a series of regional ablation experiments on a variety of animals (mostly birds) that the cerebral cortex acted as a whole, and could not be subdivided as to function.

Localization of specific functions within the cortex received a strong boost in 1861 by Broca, who treated a patient who was known as "Tan" because of a repetitive sound he made. Tan's symptoms included aphasia, or an inability to speak, which had begun 21 years earlier. After Tan's death, an autopsy revealed major damage to the frontal lobe.

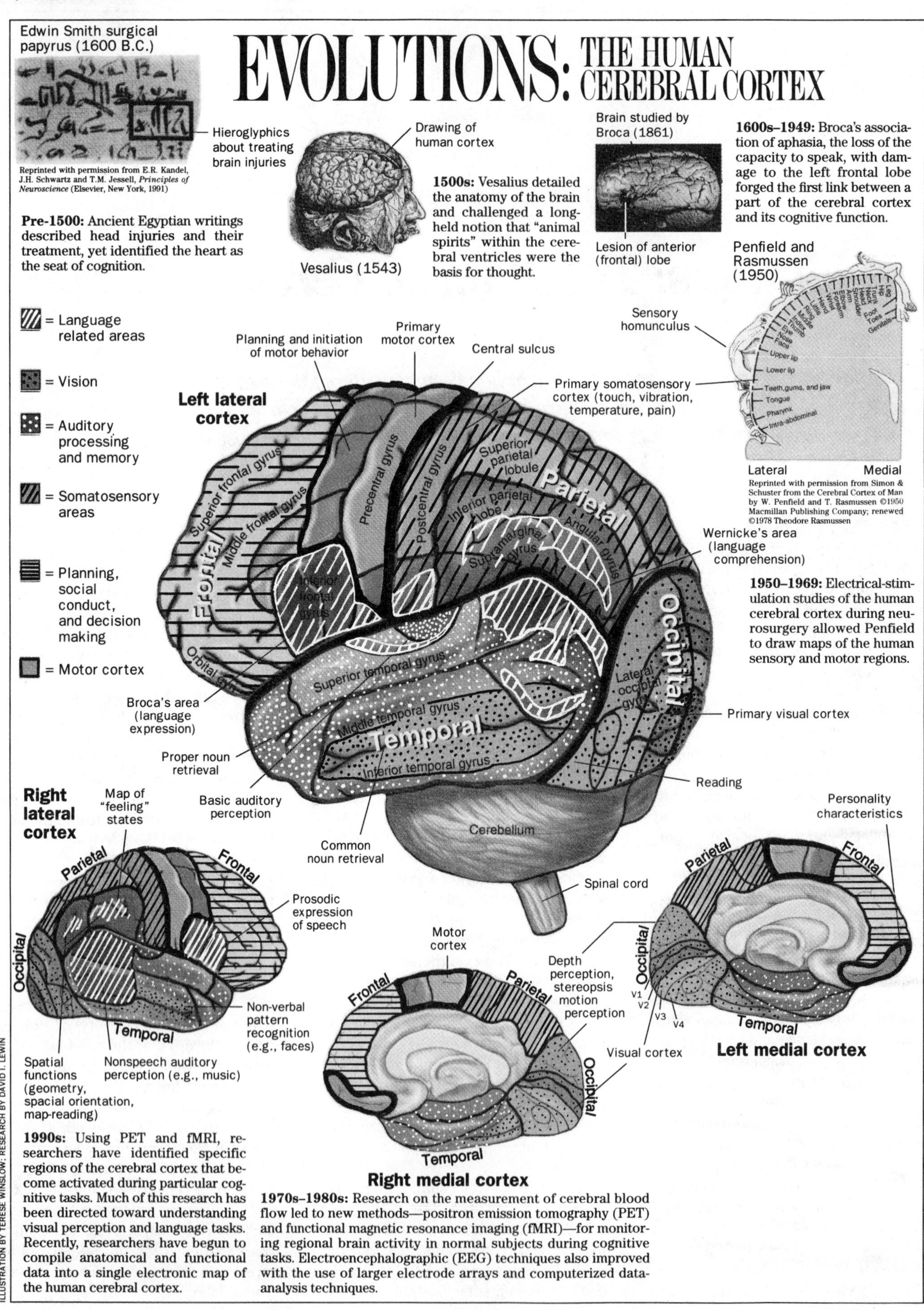
EVOLUTIONS: THE HUMAN CEREBRAL CORTEX
Edwin Smith surgical papyrus (1600 B.C.)
Hieroglyphics about treating brain injuries
Reprinted with permission from E.R. Kandel, J.H. Schwartz and T.M. Jessell, Principles of Neuroscience (Elsevier, New York, 1991)
Pre-1500: Ancient Egyptian writings described head injuries and their treatment, yet identified the heart as the seat of cognition.
Drawing of human cortex
Vesalius (1543)
1500s: Vesalius detailed the anatomy of the brain and challenged a long-held notion that "animal spirits" within the cerebral ventricles were the basis for thought.
Brain studied by Broca (1861)
Lesion of anterior (frontal) lobe
1600s–1949: Broca's association of aphasia, the loss of the capacity to speak, with damage to the left frontal lobe forged the first link between a part of the cerebral cortex and its cognitive function.
Penfield and Rasmussen (1950)
Sensory homunculus
Lateral
Medial
Reprinted with permission from Simon & Schuster from the Cerebral Cortex of Man by W. Penfield and T. Rasmussen ©1950 Macmillan Publishing Company; renewed ©1978 Theodore Rasmussen
1950–1969: Electrical-stimulation studies of the human cerebral cortex during neurosurgery allowed Penfield to draw maps of the human sensory and motor regions.
= Language related areas
= Vision
= Auditory processing and memory
= Somatosensory areas
= Planning, social conduct, and decision making
= Motor cortex
Left lateral cortex
Planning and initiation of motor behavior
Primary motor cortex
Central sulcus
Primary somatosensory cortex (touch, vibration, temperature, pain)
Superior frontal gyrus
Middle frontal gyrus
Frontal
Precentral gyrus
Postcentral gyrus
Superior parietal lobule
Inferior parietal lobe
Parietal
Supramarginal gyrus
Angular gyrus
Inferior frontal gyrus
Orbital gyri
Wernicke's area (language comprehension)
Occipital
Lateral occipital gyri
Primary visual cortex
Superior temporal gyrus
Middle temporal gyrus
Temporal
Inferior temporal gyrus
Broca's area (language expression)
Proper noun retrieval
Basic auditory perception
Common noun retrieval
Reading
Cerebellum
Spinal cord
Right lateral cortex
Map of "feeling" states
Parietal
Frontal
Occipital
Temporal
Prosodic expression of speech
Non-verbal pattern recognition (e.g., faces)
Spatial functions (geometry, spacial orientation, map-reading)
Nonspeech auditory perception (e.g., music)
Motor cortex
Frontal
Parietal
Occipital
Temporal
Right medial cortex
Depth perception, stereopsis motion perception
V1
V2
V3
V4
Visual cortex
Personality characteristics
Parietal
Frontal
Occipital
Temporal
Left medial cortex
1990s: Using PET and fMRI, researchers have identified specific regions of the cerebral cortex that become activated during particular cognitive tasks. Much of this research has been directed toward understanding visual perception and language tasks. Recently, researchers have begun to compile anatomical and functional data into a single electronic map of the human cerebral cortex.
1970s–1980s: Research on the measurement of cerebral blood flow led to new methods—positron emission tomography (PET) and functional magnetic resonance imaging (fMRI)—for monitoring regional brain activity in normal subjects during cognitive tasks. Electroencephalographic (EEG) techniques also improved with the use of larger electrode arrays and computerized data-analysis techniques.
ILLUSTRATION BY TERESE WINSLOW; RESEARCH BY DAVID I. LEWIN

By 1863, Broca had also realized that language is a function of the left hemisphere. Fritsch and Hitzig used a powerful technique for studying the localization of brain function in 1870: direct electrical stimulation of the cerebral cortex. The two scientists laid bare the cerebral cortex of a dog, applied an electrical current to it, and noted any motor responses. In this manner, they confirmed that the frontal cortex includes the motor region, they identified specific control regions for the fore- and hindpaws and the face, and they found that each cerebral hemisphere controls motor activity on an animal's contralateral side.

By the 1880s, a number of researchers were using surgical ablation and electrical stimulation to map the sensory functions in animal brains. Caton reported the first measurement of evoked potentials in a rabbit's brain in 1875.

1900–1949: Using the newly developed techniques of light microscopy and staining, several anatomists detailed the fine anatomy of the cortex (a field of study called cytoarchitectonics) during the early 1900s. In 1909, Brodmann recognized 52 discrete regions in the human cerebral cortex based on differences in cellular architecture.

Mapping the cortex through electrical stimulation, especially in conscious patients investigated during neurosurgery, helped fill in much of what is known about functional localization in the brain beginning in the 1930s. Penfield and his associates used this technique to map the human somatosensory and motor regions. In a 1937 paper, Penfield and Boldrey devised the earliest combined sensory-motor "homunculus" diagram to show the relative size and order of cortical areas related to various parts of the human body.

During the 1930s, researchers also followed up earlier assumptions that the enlarged frontal lobes of humans were the seat of intelligence and creativity. In 1931, Fulton and Jacobsen reported that damage to the chimpanzee frontal lobes produced deficits in tasks requiring delayed responses. This suggested that the function of the frontal region was not general intelligence but rather sequencing actions in time. But five years later, Hebb found that surgical removal of regions of the frontal lobes in patients with epilepsy did not lower the patients' IQs, raising questions about the memory deficit reported by Fulton and Jacobsen.

In 1948, Kety and Schmidt described a technique for measuring blood flow and oxygen consumption in the cerebrum of an unconscious person. This led to further research on cerebral blood flow in conscious patients, and three decades later, to physiological methods for measuring local cortical activity, such as PET and fMRI.

1950–1969: Electrical mapping of the brain continued to dominate localization research during this era. Based on their success in eliciting visual and auditory memories from conscious patients by electrical stimulation during neurosurgery, Penfield and Jasper proposed in 1954 that the temporal lobes had a role in recording the "stream-of-consciousness" as memories. Not everyone was convinced, however. Piercy cautioned in a 1964 review that relying on such patient self-reporting was not sufficient to ensure that memory—rather than hallucination—was involved.

Study of the parietal lobes revealed that they are involved in spatial relationships. In 1955, Semmes and her colleagues demonstrated that damage to either parietal lobe impaired the person's ability to follow tactile or visual maps.

Classical electrical and cytoarchitectural brain mapping of marsupials (pouched mammals such as wallabies and opossums) and monotremes (egg-laying mammals such as the duck-billed platypus) revealed that the functional organization of their brains is far different from that of ordinary (eutherian) mammals. In 1963, Lende reported from the study of 40 opossum and eight wallaby brains that the sensory and motor fields of the opossum cortex coincided, as they did in the wallaby brain. Lende noted that the sensory and motor regions are separate in the advanced (eutherian) mammalian cortex.

The relationship between the two hemispheres of the brain was explored using split-brain experiments by Sperry and his colleagues. In 1962 Gazzaniga, Bogen, and Sperry reported that a patient whose cerebral commissures were severed to treat ongoing epilepsy could use either hand on motor tasks, but could not coordinate the two hands when given a task he had not learned before the surgery.

1970s: Researchers further developed the technologies that led to the imaging revolution of the succeeding two decades. In 1977, Sokoloff and his colleagues, drawing on the earlier work of Kety and Schmidt, reported a technique to visualize regional blood flow—and hence, regional neuronal activity—in the brain. This technique, which monitored positron emissions from ^{14}C-glucose, led to the development of PET.

By the 1880s, a number of researchers were using surgical ablation and electrical stimulation to map the sensory functions in animal brains.

In 1975, Heilman and his colleagues demonstrated that the right hemisphere in humans controls comprehension of the emotional component of speech. When six subjects with right temporoparietal lesions and six with comparable left-hemisphere lesions were asked to judge the mood of the speaker in a series of taped sentences, the subjects with right-hemisphere damage were correct significantly less often.

1980s: Studies of patients with brain lesions continued to localize higher mental functions. In 1981, Kolb and Taylor reported that damage to specific regions of each hemisphere affected the ability to deal with emotions. Damage to the left hemisphere left patients unable to match words to emotional states, while damage to the right hemisphere impaired the ability to match different faces expressing the same emotional states.

Comparative studies of cortical structure and function provided evidence that all mammals share a small number of homologous cortical areas, such as visual areas V1 and V2, and somatosensory area S1. In 1987 Kaas noted that the number of defined cortical regions in eutherian mammals ranges from about 15 in the rat to more than 100 in humans.

Advances in EEG techniques allowed researchers to begin localizing brain function more accurately. In 1983, Gevins and his colleagues reported that they could identify local changes in cortical activity when subjects performed a task that required them to press a button to move an arrow to a target on a video display screen.

In 1987, Gevins and his colleagues used recordings from a set of 26 scalp electrodes to predict accurate and inaccurate performance on a task that required seven right-handed adults to respond with pressure from either their right or left index fingers to a set of visual cues. The researchers found that accurate responses were preceded by preparatory cortical activity in the left frontal lobe.

Throughout the 1980s, researchers used PET scans to localize cortical regions activated in specific cognitive tasks. Scientists including Raichle and Frackowiak observed differences in regional metabolism in the brains of subjects given a control task—which did not require the cognitive function being investigated—and an experimental task.

In 1988, Petersen and his colleagues used PET scans of volunteers who received injections of positron-emitting ^{15}O-water to identify regions of the cortex involved in word recognition. The researchers measured changes in cerebral blood flow in 17 subjects who were asked either to look at a nonverbal image (a crossbar), to look, without reading aloud, at words projected on a screen (a sensory task), to view words with or without saying them aloud (an output task), or to say a use for each of the presented words (an association task). Petersen and his colleagues found that the striate and extrastriate occipital cortex were active when the subjects saw words; the lateral primary auditory cortex, the left-lateral temporoparietal cortex, and the anterior superior temporal cortex were active when the subjects heard words; and the left inferior frontal area and the anterior cingulate gyrus were active when the subjects generated words. The researchers concluded that words presented visually do not need to be translated into sounds for their meaning to be understood.

1990s: Researchers have begun to change their concepts of the relationship between brain structure and cognition. Kaas suggested in 1993 that the human cortex is a network of many specialized processing units rather than a small number of general-purpose areas for abstract thought. In 1994, Ringo and his colleagues concluded that the increase in specialized cortical processing areas in advanced mammals reduces processing time and the number of connections required between each cortical neuron and neurons elsewhere in the brain. Localizing certain functions either to the right or left cerebral hemisphere similarly reduces the need to pass information across the corpus callosum, which links the two hemispheres, the researchers suggested.

In 1991, Felleman and Van Essen published a flattened projection of the cortical sensory and motor regions of the rhesus macaque. Such maps have become a standard means for conveying detailed information about functional specializations within the cortex.

PET imaging and the newer technique of fMRI continue to allow researchers to correlate regional brain activity with specific cognitive tasks in normal volunteers. In 1991, Belliveau and his colleagues used fMRI with an intravenously administered paramagnetic contrast agent to visualize regional blood flow in the human visual cortex during visual stimulation. The experiment, in which seven normal human subjects were exposed to a bright flash of light after they had become acclimated to darkness, demonstrated increased blood flow in the primary visual cortex during the light flash. Subsequent improvements eliminated the need for administering an intravenous contrast agent.

Because fMRI and PET require comparing a baseline condition to an experimental condition, results can differ widely between research groups, depending on the choice of the baseline. In particular, this has led to conflicting reports of the cortical regions involved in processing words. In 1991, Wise and his colleagues used PET to identify the cortical areas used by the human brain to comprehend and retrieve words. Unlike Petersen and his co-workers three years before, Wise and his colleagues observed the activation of Wernicke's area—a part of the left temporal lobe responsible for language comprehension—during semantic tasks such as thinking of verbs appropriate to particular nouns.

In 1995, Spitzer and his colleagues reported that different parts of the human brain are active during the recognition of items from distinct semantic categories, such as fruit, furniture, animals, and tools. Using fMRI, the researchers identified four distinct cortical regions that exhibited increased metabolism when the researchers showed a subject a picture of an item from one of the four semantic categories. The researchers had chosen the categories based on earlier reports that damage to particular parts of the brain could impair the ability to recognize objects from one of these categories but not from others. Damasio and her colleagues reported the following year from a neuropsychological study of patients with specific brain lesions and a PET imaging study of normal human subjects that distinct regions in the temporal lobe link written-word recognition with the names of specific tools and types of animals.

Damage to the left hemisphere left patients unable to match words to emotional states, while damage to the right hemisphere impaired the ability to match different faces expressing the same emotional states.

More recently, in early 1996 Menard and his colleagues repeated Petersen's work using a more complex set of baseline conditions. The researchers found that presenting recognizable words to subjects for silent reading activated Broca's area, the left angular gyrus, and the supramarginal gyrus. But unlike Petersen and his co-workers, they did not find that the left extrastriate cortex was active during the visual processing of words. Instead, Menard and his colleagues observed the activation of Wernicke's area. "We conclude that the results of brain scanning are in fact consistent with results from studies of behavioral deficits following brain lesions," Menard and his colleagues wrote.

Also in 1996, Samelin and his colleagues used whole-head MEG to investigate whether people with dyslexia had impairments in their ability to recognize words presented visually. The researchers used an array of 122 magnetic sensors to measure and localize rapid electrical events in the cortex. They found that the differences in brain activity between dyslexic subjects and normal controls were most dramatic in the left hemisphere. Between 0 and 200 milliseconds after being shown a word, control subjects—but not subjects with dyslexia—exhibited strong activation of the left inferior temporo-occipital cortex. Moreover, unlike controls, between

200 and 400 msec after the stimulus, subjects with dyslexia showed little activation of the left temporal lobe, which contains Wernicke's area—but instead showed activation of the left inferior frontal lobe. The researchers concluded that people with dyslexia have an impaired ability to perceive words as units.

Researchers continue to refine high-resolution EEG. In 1996, Gevins and his colleagues reported localizing the brain regions used for short-term storage and retrieval (working memory) in eight normal subjects using 115 scalp electrodes on each subject. The researchers found that when subjects were asked to determine whether a letter presented to them matched the location or name of a letter presented earlier, a network of cortical regions—some specific for visual or verbal tasks, others common to both tasks—were activated.

Increasingly, researchers are interested in combining the results from several types of noninvasive imaging techniques, but only a few centers are equipped for such multimodal imaging. In 1995, Simpson and his colleagues reported efforts to integrate electrophysiological and functional imaging data to study visual processing in macaques and humans. The researchers localized electrical activity caused by a visual stimulus to a small set of regions on a high-resolution MRI image of a macaque brain.

Researchers are also using a variety of techniques to map cognitive functions in the brain. However, critics such as Sarter and his colleagues caution that strong evidence is needed to conclude that regional activation of a portion of the cortex during cognition reflects the localization of that function to that particular site. Function, they say, reflects the consequences of the output of neural activity. "Despite the fact that [an area] becomes active during happiness, for example, does not imply that happiness is localized to [that area]," they wrote.

—DAVID I. LEWIN

Additional Reading

C. Bell, "Idea of a new anatomy of the brain, submitted for the observations of his friends," *Medical Classics* **1**, 105 (1936) [Original published in 1811].

J.W. Belliveau, D.N. Kennedy Jr., R.C. McKinstry, B.R. Buchbinder, R.M. Weisskoff, M.S. Cohen et al., "Functional mapping of the human visual cortex by magnetic resonance imaging," *Science* **254**, 716 (1991).

J.H. Breasted, *The Edwin Smith Surgical Papyrus* (University of Chicago Press, Chicago, 1930).

P. Broca, "Nouvelle observation d'aphémie produite par une lésion de la moitié postèrieure des deuxième et troisième circonvolutions frontales," *Bull. Mém. Soc. Anat. (Paris)* **6**, 398 (1861). [Transl. as "New observation of aphemia produced by a lesion of the posterior half of the second and third frontal convolutions," in R.H. Wilkins, *Neurosurgical Classics* (American Association of Neurosurgeons, Park Ridge, Ill., 1992).]

K. Brodmann, *Vergleichende Lokalisationlehre der Grosshirnrinde* (Barth, Liepzig, Germany, 1909).

R. Caton, "The electric currents of the brain," *Br. Med. J.* **2**, 278 (1875).

H. Damasio, T.J. Grabowski, D. Tranel, R.D. Hichwa, and A.R. Damasio, "A neural basis for lexical retrieval," *Nature* **380**, 499 (1996).

D.J. Felleman and D.C. Van Essen, "Distributed hierarchical processing in the primate cerebral cortex," *Cereb. Cortex* **1**, 1 (1991).

S. Finger, *Origins of Neuroscience: A History of Exploration Into Brain Function* (Oxford University Press, New York City, 1994).

M.-J.-P. Flourens, *Recherches Expérimental sur les Propriétés et les Fonctions du Systême Nerveaux dans les Animaux vertébrés* (J.B. Ballière, Paris, 1824).

P.T. Fox, H. Burton, and M.E. Richle, "Mapping human somatosensory cortex with positron emission spectroscopy," *J. Neurosurg.* **67**, 34 (1987).

G. Fritsch and E. Hitzig, "Ueber die elektrische Erregbarkeit des Grosshirns," *Arch. Anat. Physiol. wiss. Med.* **37**, 300 (1870). [Transl. as "The Electrical Excitability of the Cerebrum," in R.H. Wilkins, *Neurosurgical Classics* (American Association of Neurosurgeons, Park Ridge, Ill., 1992)]

Galen, *De usu partium* [Transl. by M.T. May as, *On the Usefulness of Parts of the Body* (Cornell Univ. Press, Ithaca, N.Y., 1968)].

M.S. Gazzaniga, J.E. Bogen, and R.W. Sperry, "Some functional effects of sectioning the cerebral commissure in man," *Proc. Natl. Acad. Sci. U.S.A.* **48**, 1765 (1962).

A.S. Gevins, N.H. Morgan, S.L. Bressler, B.A. Cutillo, R.M. White, J. Illes et al., "Human neuroelectricity patterns predict performance accuracy," *Science* **235**, 580 (1987).

A.S. Gevins, R.E. Schaffer, J.C. Doyle, B.A. Cutillo, R.S. Tannehill, and S.L. Bressler, "Shadows of thought: shifting lateralization of human brain electrical patterns during brief visuomotor task," *Science* **220**, 97 (1983).

A. Gevins, M.E. Smith, J. Le, H. Leong, J. Bennett, N. Martin et al., "High resolution evoked potential imaging of the cortical dynamics of human working memory," *Electroencephalogr. Clin. Neurophysiol.* **98**, 327 (1996).

K.M. Heilman, R. Scholes, and R.T. Watson, "Auditory affective agnosia: disturbed comprehension of affective speech," *J. Neurol. Neurosurg. Psychiat.* **38**, 69 (1975).

C.F. Jacobsen, "A study of cerebral function in learning, *J. Comp. Neurol.* **52**, 271 (1931).

J.H. Kaas, "The organization of the neocortex in mammals: implications for theories of brain function," *Annu. Rev. Psychol.* **38**, 129 (1987).

J.H. Kaas, "Evolution of multiple areas and modules within neocortex," *Perspect. Dev. Neurobiol.* **1**, 101 (1993).

S. Kety and C. Schmidt, "Nitrous oxide method for the quantitative determination of cerebral blood flow in man: theory, procedures, and normal values," *J. Clin. Invest.* **27**, 475 (1948).

B. Kolb and L. Taylor, "Affective behavior in patients with localized cortical excisions: role of lesion site and side," *Science* **214**, 89 (1981).

K.K. Kwong, J.W. Belliveau, D.A. Chesler, I.E. Goldberg, R.M. Weisskoff, B.P. Poncelet et al., "Dynamic magnetic resonance imaging of human brain activity during primary sensory stimulation," *Proc. Natl. Acad, Sci. USA* **89**, 5675 (1992).

K.S. Lashley and G. Clark, "The cytoarchitecture of the cerebral cortex of *Ateles*: a critical examination of architectonic studies," *J. comp. Neurol.* **85**, 223 (1946).

N.A. Lassen, D.H. Ingvar, and E. Skinhøj, "Brain function and blood flow," *Sci. Am.* **239**, 50 (1978).

R.A. Lende, "Cerebral cortex: a sensorimotor amalgam in the marsupial," *Science* **141**, 730 (1963).

R.A. Lende, "Representation in the cerebral cortex of a primitive mammal," *J. Neurophysiol.* **27**, 37 (1964).

M.S. Livingstone and D.H. Hubel, "Anatomy and physiology of a color system in the primate visual cortex," *J. Neurosci.* **4**, 309 (1984).

M.T. Menard, S.M. Kosslyn, W.L. Thompson, N.M. Alpert, and S.L. Rauch, "Encoding words and pictures: a positron emission tomographic study," *Neuropsychologia* **34**, 185 (1996).

W. Penfield and E. Boldrey, "Somatic motor and sensory representation in the cerebral cortex of man as studied by electrical stimulation," *Brain* **60**, 389 (1937).

W. Penfield and H. Jasper, *Epilepsy and the Functional Anatomy of the Human Brain* (Little, Brown & Co., Boston, 1954).

S.E. Petersen, P.T. Fox, M.I. Posner, M. Mintun, and M.E. Raichle, "Positron emission tomographic studies of the cortical anatomy of single-word processing," *Nature* **331**, 585 (1988).

M. Piercy, "The effects of cerebral lesions on intellectual function: a review of current research trends," *Br. J. Psychiat.* **110**, 310 (1964).

M.I. Posner, S.E. Petersen, P.T. Fox, and M.E. Raichle, "Localization of cognitive operations in the human brain," *Science* **240**, 1627 (1988).

C.J. Price, R.J.S. Wise, E.A. Warburton, C.J. Moore, D. Howard, K. Patterson et al., "Hearing and saying: the functional neuroanatomy of auditory word processing," *Brain* **119**, 919 (1996).

J.L. Ringo, R.W. Doty, S. DeMenter, and P.Y. Simard, "Time is of the essence: a conjecture that hemispheric specialization arises from interhemispheric conduction delay," *Cereb. Cortex* **4**, 331 (1994).

R. Samelin, E. Service, P. Kiesilä, K. Uutela, and O. Salonen, "Impaired visual word processing in dyslexia revealed with magnetoencephalography," *Ann. Neurol.* **40**, 157 (1996).

M. Sarter, G.G. Berntson, and J.T. Cacioppo, "Brain imaging and cognitive neuroscience: toward strong inference in attributing function to structure," *Amer. Psychol.* **51**, 13 (1996).

W.B. Scoville and B. Miller, "Loss of recent memory after bilateral hippocampal lesions," *J. Neurol. Neurosurg. Psychiat.* **20**, 11 (1957).

J. Semmes, S. Weinstein, L. Ghent, and H.L. Teuber, "Spatial orientation in man after cerebral injury: I. Analysis by locus of lesion," *J. Psychol.* **39**, 227 (1955).

G.V. Simpson, J.J. Foxe, H.G. Vaughan Jr., A.D. Mehta, and C.E. Schroeder, "Integration of electrophysiological source analysis, MRI, and animal models in the study of visual processing and attention," in *Perspectives of Event-Related Potential Research* [*Electroenceph. clin. Neurophysiol. Suppl.* 4] (Elsevier Science, Amsterdam, The Netherlands, 1995).

L. Sokoloff, M. Reivitch, C. Kennedy, M.H. Des Rosiers, C.S. Patlak, K.D. Pettigrew et al., "The [^{14}C] deoxyglucose method for the measurement of local cerebral glucose utilization: theory, procedure, and normal values in the conscious and anesthetized albino rat," *J. Neurochem.* **28**, 897 (1977).

M. Spitzer, K.K. Kwong, W. Kennedy, B.R. Rosen, and J.W. Belliveau, "Category-specific brain activation in fMRI during picture naming," *Neuroreport* **6**, 2109 (1995).

Vesalius, *De humani corporis fabrica*, (J. Oporini, Basilae, 1543).

T. Willis, *Cerebri anatomi: cui accessit nervorum descripto et usus* (J. Martyn, London, 1664).

R. Wise, F. Chollet, U. Hadar, K. Friston, E. Hoffner, and R. Frackowiak, "Distribution of cortical neural networks involved in word comprehension and word retrieval," *Brain* **114**, 1803 (1991).

NEUROBIOLOGY

New Imaging Methods Provide A Better View Into the Brain

For a field that didn't even exist 20 years ago, human brain imaging has developed at a mind-boggling pace. Thanks to one advance after another, neurobiologists can peer into the living human brain and produce pictures that shed new light on brain functions ranging from the processing of sensory information to higher level thinking tasks. But breathtaking as the developments have been, improvements already under way will soon give imagers new perspectives on how the brain goes about its business.

Most of these advances are based on functional magnetic resonance imaging (fMRI), a technique that spots the increases in the blood oxygenation that reflect a boost in blood flow to active brain areas. Because of advantages—including greater speed and higher resolution—in recent years, fMRI has largely eclipsed positron emission tomography (PET), the method that got the imaging field rolling nearly 20 years ago. Now, researchers are devising a whole new wave of modifications, several of which were showcased at a recent conference on brain imaging,* that will allow fMRI to be used to even better advantage.

Some modifications will permit more sophisticated experimental designs that link brain images more closely to a subject's perceptions and behavior. In addition, increased magnet strengths will give even greater spatial resolution of activated brain areas. By combining fMRI with other techniques, researchers are now able to answer previously unaddressable questions about the timing with which brain areas are activated. Those answers will yield insights into how information moves through the brain.

As these advances invigorate the field, a next wave is waiting in the wings: methods that may image neural activity directly by following the flux of sodium ions, or by measuring the scattering of light by brain tissue. These newest directions are as yet unproven, but in a field where methods go from inconceivable to commonplace in a couple of years, researchers have learned never to say never. I hesitate to say [any technique] isn't going anywhere, because I could be writing a grant to try to buy the equipment in 2 years," jokes cognitive neuroscientist George Mangun of the University of California (UC), Davis.

Mangun learned that lesson, he says, from the fast ascent of fMRI. When he heard of an early form of the technique in 1990, Mangun recalls, he thought the technique was "interesting . . . but [would] never go anywhere." Within a year, additional advances had paved the way for it to become the mainstay of the field.

But even as fMRI was catapulting to its position of prominence, researchers using the technique unwittingly handicapped themselves with old habits carried over from PET imaging that have prevented them from taking full advantage of fMRI. PET, which uses radioactive tracers to detect the increased blood flow to activated brain regions, is slow, taking up to a minute to gather the data for a brain image. As a result, neuroscientists using the method do "block trials," in which the subject performs a string of similar short tasks, causing the brain to repeat the same mental process while the data are gathered. Researchers continued to use block trials with fMRI, although that technique takes only 2 seconds to collect an image. "We always assumed if we only looked at one trial, the signal would be so small we wouldn't be able to see it," says neuroimager Randy Buckner of Harvard Medical School in Boston.

That assumption evaporated in 1995, when Robert Savoy and his colleagues at Harvard Medical School reported that fMRI could detect brain activations in response to a visual stimulus lasting only 30 milliseconds. The next year, Buckner and his colleagues did a similar experiment with a cognitive task. They used the word-stem completion test, in which subjects are given three-letter parts of words and asked to complete the word. A single word-stem completion, the researchers found, activated brain areas nearly identical to those activated by a block trial.

Thus was born a new method, "event-related" fMRI, in which researchers collect brain image data from individual trials, which they can then sort and pool as they wish. It opens up many avenues for cognitive experiments, says Buckner. For example, some tests don't work well in block trials, because they involve an element of surprise.

Studies with electroencephalograms (EEGs), which record electrical activity inside the brain, have demonstrated that if you show a person a series of pictures, say, of geometric shapes, and then throw in something different, like a picture of an animal, the oddball picture produces a bigger neural response than the others. Neuroimagers would like to know which brain areas react to the surprise, but they can't find out from a block experiment, says Buckner, because "if you do that kind of surprise three or four times, [the response] goes away." With event-related fMRI, researchers can mix "surprise" trials with other types of trials, and then afterward pool the data from the surprise trials to analyze together.

Research groups have leaped to use the new approach, not only to identify brain areas that react to unusual events, but also to

*"Neuroimaging of Human Brain Function," The Arnold and Mabel Beckman Center of the National Academy of Sciences, Irvine, California, 29–31 May.

relate brain activity directly to subjects' responses or perceptions which can only be determined once the experimental trial is over. For example, the technique allows researchers to sort brain images based on whether a subject got the right or wrong answer in a test, and see how the brain activation differed. Because of its ability to address some of these important questions with imaging for the first time, the technique "is catching on incredibly rapidly," says Buckner.

It is likely to catch on even faster, thanks to some recent troubleshooting done by Buckner and his Harvard colleague Anders Dale. The problem they addressed is this: The fMRI response to a single trial takes more than 10 seconds to run its course, so it seemed that individual trials would have to be separated by 16 seconds or so to be sure the response to one trial was finished before the next one was presented. That is not only time-consuming, but could also alter the results. "Sixteen seconds is a long time to do nothing," says Buckner. "People have more time to work on the problem, more time to prepare." Dale and Buckner have a paper in press in *Human Brain Mapping* showing that trials can be presented as fast as every 2 seconds, and an algorithm can then be used to extract the overlapping brain activation data associated with each trial.

Is bigger better?

Advances like event-related fMRI have opened up countless questions for cognitive neuroscientists to address. Most can be tackled using standard fMRI machines, which have magnetic field strengths of 1.5 or 3 teslas (T) and can distinguish activated brain areas separated by as little as half a centimeter. But "there will be a time when we will definitely have to look beyond" that resolution, says brain imager Kamil Ugurbil of the University of Minnesota, Minneapolis. Ugurbil, who feels that time is rapidly approaching, is leading the charge to higher magnetic fields. The imaging center at Minnesota has a 4-T MRI machine, one of only a handful in the world. With those machines, researchers have revealed multiple strengths of higher fields.

At higher fields, Ugurbil says, event-related fMRI can be developed to its full potential, producing robust images from single trials, and reducing the need for researchers to sort and pool their results. What's more, researchers have already seen two brain features with 4-T machines that have eluded those using lesser magnetic fields. One, the so-called early oxygenation dip, is an apparent drop in blood oxygenation in active brain areas before the rise in blood flow (*Science,* 11 April, p. 196). Researchers using 4 T have also seen ocular dominance columns—columns of neutrons in the visual cortex with diameters on the order of 1 millimeter—which respond selectively to images from one eye or the other. All these effects are sure to be even clearer at fields higher than 4 T, Ugurbil says.

Indeed, neuroimager Roger Tootell, of Harvard Medical School in Boston, calls Ugurbil's sighting of ocular dominance columns a "watershed" in brain imaging. Imagers now focus on activity in whole brain areas, but the opportunity to see the activity of individual columns within those areas promises "a quantum jump in insight," Tootell says. "There are columns all over the brain, and we don't know what they do."

Ugurbil's team hopes to pursue both the oxygenation dip and column resolution with a 7-T human imaging machine they are due to receive in December. It will be the first of its kind in the world. But no human has ever been exposed to a 7-T field, and safety tests on animals, already begun by Ugurbil's group, will be needed before that can be done.

Even if those colossal fields are deemed safe, neuroimager Marcus Raichle of Washington University in St. Louis warns that bigger is not better for everyone, because the bigger machines require an engineering team devoted to tinkering and tuning constantly. "You become hostage to the equipment if you're not careful," he says, likening a high-field magnet to a "Ferrari that needs a $5000 tune-up every year" and isn't really suited to just going for a ride. "A well-equipped, well-running 1.5-T machine, with . . . people who know how to ask the questions, is an enormously powerful piece of equipment," Raichle argues. "There is a tremendous amount of neurobiology that can and will be done on such machines." Nevertheless, he says, someone, preferably with Ugurbil's level of experience, needs to be developing higher field machines to pave the way for a time when the biological questions demand the next wave in resolution. "We may, 5 years from now, say, 'Gosh, we all have to be at 5 T.' "

A timely union

One trick not even the biggest MRI machine can presently pull off on its own is following precisely when brain areas become active during a cognitive process. That's because the neurons themselves respond within 10 milliseconds of a triggering stimulus, while the blood-flow changes measured by fMRI or PET take several seconds to develop. This limitation has been a great frustration for neuroimagers. "Timing is everything in the brain," says UC Davis's Mangun. Without timing information, researchers can only guess about how different brain areas build on each other's work as they perform a task.

To remedy this problem, Mangun's group and others have recently arranged a marriage of convenience between fMRI and PET imaging techniques and a pair of brain-recording methods whose forte is timing: EEG, which measures the electrical fields produced by brain neuron activity, and magnetoencephalography (MEG), which measures neurally generated magnetic fields. Both methods can take readings at more than 100 points on the scalp and can track how neural activity changes with time along the surface of the head. But they have a big weakness: They can't pinpoint the source of the electromagnetic signal.

Mathematical equations can point to brain areas where the activity might be, but the equations yield multiple solutions, with no way to tell which one is right. But "if you can calculate a [candidate] position, and then show that neuroimaging shows that there are active cells in that particular place, then that increases your confidence that you've got it right," says EEG researcher Steven Hillyard of UC San Diego.

Hans-Jochen Heinze at Otto von Guericke University in Magdeburg, Germany, along with Mangun and Hillyard, did just that with a cognitive task in 1994. They presented subjects with pairs of symbols in both their right and left visual fields and directed their attention to either the right or left field by asking them to judge whether the symbols appearing there were the same or different. Earlier work in Hillyard's lab had shown that the EEG wave evoked by the symbols differs, depending on whether the subject is paying attention to them or not: A bump in the wave beginning about 80 milliseconds after the symbols were flashed, known as the P1 component, gets bigger when the subject pays attention.

To find the source of the activity that creates P1, the Heinze team had the subjects do the task once while the researchers took EEG recordings, and again in the PET scanner. The PET data showed two areas in the so-called "extrastriate" portion of the visual cortex that could be the source of P1, and the team then returned to the model to see whether these spots would work as possible sources that would explain the EEG data. Those sites, says Mangun, explained the data very, very well." Mangun has since shown that making the perceptual task easier selectively reduces both P1 and the attention-associated extrastriate activation seen in PET, further support that the two techniques are measuring the same brain function.

That experiment showed that imaging and electromagnetic techniques can work together, says Harvard's Dale. But the math used by the Heinze team could consider only two or three simultaneously active brain areas as possible sources of the EEG signal. And while that was fine in the case they had chosen, Dale points out that in most cognitive processes, many brain areas are activated. Dale is one of several researchers deriving a new generation of mathematical models that can pose thousands of sites of brain activity as potential sources and contain other improvements as well.

Like the model used by the Heinze group, Dale's model begins with electromagnetic data recorded on the scalp and predicts which configuration of active areas in the brain could best explain that activity. But instead of relying just on EEG recordings, it can use MEG and EEG data taken simultaneously. And while older methods model the brain as a sphere inside the skull, Dale's limits the potential sources of activity to the cerebral cortex. Moreover, because each brain is unique in how its cortex is folded, Dale uses a structural MR image to tailor the calculations to the individual brain.

The result is a localized, though fuzzy, estimate of combined activity in the brain that could produce the EEG and MEG signals at any point in time. Dale then takes fMRI data on brain activity during an identical experimental trial and uses those data to "weight" the solutions by having the equations favor areas shown to be active by the fMRI. The end result is a set of crisp images with the spatial resolution of fMRI that show changes in brain activity on a time scale of tens of milliseconds. "You can make a movie animating this," Dale says.

Dale, Tootell, and Jack Belliveau, also of Harvard, have validated the technique by using it to look at the timing of the brain's response to a moving image, and Dale and Eric Halgren of UC Los Angeles have studied the time course with which the brain responds to novel versus repeated words. "It is an important wedding of techniques," says Washington University's Raichle and is likely to become a staple of the field for researchers who want to know the pathways information takes in the course of a thinking process.

Future frontiers

Millisecond movies of neural activity using fMRI, EEG, and MEG might seem visionary enough, but some in the field think such wonders will someday be possible with a single technique—either a new form of fMRI or a much less expensive alternative: imaging with ordinary light beams.

Keith Thulborn's team at the University of Pittsburgh Medical Center is working to devise a way to get images with real-time resolution information directly from fMRI, by measuring changes in the sodium magnetic resonance signal. "Sodium imaging may be a very direct way of looking at neuronal activity," says Thulborn, because sodium ions flow into neurons when they fire. The passage of ions into the neurons changes sodium's magnetic resonance properties in a way that should be detectable by MRI, Thulborn says.

The imaging center at Pittsburgh already uses sodium imaging clinically to assess brain damage in patients with strokes, epilepsy, and tumors. Because the sodium signals are weak, it takes 10 minutes to create a reliable three-dimensional image, says Thulborn. But because MR images are built up from many individual snapshots, Thulborn says it would be possible to construct images that capture the immediate neural response by taking repeated snapshots timed at a very short interval after a repeated stimulus. Thulborn and a team of engineers and physicists have been working for 6 years to improve the MRI machine's ability to detect sodium. Their work has reduced the detection time from 45 minutes to 10, while increasing spatial resolution an order of magnitude, and they plan to test the experimental approach on a 3-T machine within the next few months.

Still other researchers are hoping to image neural activity directly without the $1-million-per-tesla price tag of fMRI. Their preferred medium: light. Studies in living brain slices have shown that the light-scattering properties of neurons change when they become active. Cognitive neuroscientists Gabriele Gratton and Monica Fabiani of the University of Missouri, Columbia, lead one of several labs trying to take advantage of that property by using near-infrared light from a fiber-optic source to image activity changes in living human brains. Their system, which they call EROS, for event-related optical signals, has a bargain-basement cost of less than $50,000.

When a fiber-optic source placed on the scalp shines light into the head, the light penetrates the skull and is scattered by brain tissues before some of it reemerges. EROS uses light sensors placed on the scalp just centimeters from the source to measure the time the light takes to emerge. Because that time is influenced by light scattering, which in turn is affected by neural activity, the system can detect changes induced by an experimental task. And it does it with a temporal resolution similar to that of an EEG. EROS can also locate the source of the scattering changes, based on detector placement and timing of the light's emergence, with spatial resolution of less than a centimeter. Using EROS, Gratton repeated the experiment by which Heinze, Mangun, and Hillyard first showed the power of combining PET with EEG. EROS produced the same results, localizing the effects of attention to the extrastriate cortex.

One limitation of EROS is that the light can only penetrate several centimeters into the head, and so the technique is unable to register activity from deep brain areas. Indeed, some researchers worry that it will not reliably image parts of the cortex that are buried in folds. "If it is limited to the superficial cortex, it will never replace fMRI," says cognitive neuroscientist Steven Luck, of the University of Iowa, Iowa City. But Gratton and Fabiani say they have already imaged cortical areas deep in a fold and have ideas about how to reach even deeper regions.

"My eye is on optical techniques in terms of the next wave," says neuroimager Bruce Rosen, of the magnetic resonance imaging center at Harvard Medical School. "In 10 years, I wonder if we will all be doing optical imaging and throwing away our magnets." While most brain imagers might think that unlikely, this is a field that has learned never to say never.

—Marcia Barinaga

Creating a Body of Knowledge

From the cadaver of an executed murderer, scientists produce digital anatomical images

David L. Wheeler

AFTER A LAST MEAL of two cheeseburgers, Joseph Paul Jernigan sat down in the death chamber in Huntsville, Tex., gazed through the window at his brother and other witnesses, and prepared to die. The convicted murderer, who had chosen to donate his body to science, didn't know that he was about be used as the subject of a highly unusual scientific project.

Mr. Jernigan has become the "Visible Man," a cadaver maintained in cyberspace by the National Library of Medicine. The library needed a body to serve as the basis for an extensive series of anatomical images that could be stored in computers and distributed over the Internet.

The Visible Human Project, which also includes a Visible Woman, is part of an effort by the medical library to give physicians and consumers better information in a visual format. "So much of medicine is what a doctor sees," says Michael J. Ackerman, the head of the project, "but most of medicine is written in books."

Now the tiniest details of Mr. Jernigan's body are regularly displayed on computer monitors around the world, portrayed in commercial CD-ROMS, and manipulated by artists, medical students, and radiologists.

Images of his anatomy have been hung in a gallery in Japan alongside sketches that Leonardo da Vinci made of the human body. The U.S. Army is using the data to simulate the damage caused by shrapnel. Engineers are using the digital cadaver to simulate what happens in car crashes. Scientists at the State University of New York at Stony Brook have created an "interactive fly-through" of his colon.

In its current form—as 15 gigabytes of data—Mr. Jernigan's body may be as close to immortal as one can get.

A high-school dropout, he was kicked out of the Army for using drugs and became a burglar. In 1981, he stabbed and shot a 75-year-old man who he feared might identify him after interrupting a burglary. "I know I did wrong," Mr. Jernigan said in a death-row interview with a wire-service reporter. "I have no one to blame but myself."

On August 5, 1993, he was executed with chemicals that flowed into his body through a catheter attached to his left hand. He was 39 years old, stood at 5 feet and 11 inches and weighed 199 pounds.

'YOU CAN SEE THE ANATOMY'

At the University of Colorado Health Sciences Center, Victor Spitzer was looking for someone like Mr. Jernigan. The researcher didn't care about Mr. Jernigan's life of crime. He was looking for a cadaver from a young, normal body. "In a younger body there is good muscle tone, and you can see the anatomy," explains Mr. Spitzer, head of the university's Center for Human Simulation. "In an older body, things get smaller and harder to see."

But a young, healthy body is hard to find—at least as a cadaver. In Colorado, for example, the average age at death of those who donate their bodies to science is 76. People who die young often do so in accidents, which means their bodies are damaged.

Mr. Spitzer had long been interested in providing scientists with more-detailed anatomical information, based on real bodies. He and his colleagues had been working on a technique of freezing body parts in a gel. Then they shaved fine slices off the blocks of frozen gel and photographed the cross sections of anatomy that were revealed. They tried the method with a knee and with a pelvis.

The Colorado team won the contract from the National Library of Medicine to create the Visible Man and the Visible Woman through a national competition that was a combination of art contest and scientific peer review.

TOUGH COMPETITION

To choose the scientists who would create the visible humans, the library asked finalists to provide cross-sectional pictures of a medium-sized animal, such as a rabbit. A group of reviewers—scientists who regularly use medical images—chose the pictures they liked most without knowing who had made them, or how.

"We were buying the pictures," says the library's Mr. Ackerman. "We weren't buying the method."

After winning the competition, and then waiting two and a half years for suitable cadavers to choose from, Mr. Spitzer learned about Joseph Paul Jernigan through a state board in Texas that distributes bodies for medical use. He arranged for the body to be flown to

Colorado, where ten of his colleagues worked around the clock with an arsenal of modern medical imaging—X-rays, magnetic resonance imaging, and computerized tomography—to get multiple views of the inside of the body.

The scans had two purposes. One was to make sure that the body didn't have any hidden damage that would make it unsuitable. The other was to provide images that could complement actual film of physical cross sections, if the body was to be used as the Visible Man.

Thirty-three hours after Mr. Jernigan died, the scientists froze his body in a block of gel, to minus 70 degrees centigrade. (The freezing point of water is 0 degrees centigrade.)

Other bodies had already arrived from the state boards that collect and distribute cadavers, and received equally intense attention. From three male bodies in the university's freezers that met the standards to become Visible Man, a committee that convened in Colorado chose Mr. Jernigan's.

To fit the body on the cutting equipment, it was sawed into four sections. Then, each morning, the Colorado scientists would slide out a block of frozen gel with a section of Mr. Jernigan in it, pack the sides with dry ice, and place it under an array of three cameras.

The slicing, done with a device resembling a plane used to shave wood, was horizontal, starting with the block taken from the bottom of the body and proceeding in one-millimeter increments. Before each slice, the block was cleaned with compressed air and sprayed with alcohol to give the new surface a uniform look.

1,871 CROSS SECTIONS

As someone interested in human anatomy, Mr. Spitzer says he wasn't repelled by what he saw on the surfaces of the gel blocks. On the contrary, the off-white of bone and fat swirled amid glistening red muscle, framed by the dark blue of the frozen gel. "It was gorgeous," he says.

Each cycle of cutting and filming took six to 10 minutes. "The rhythm was very important," says Mr. Spitzer. "We wanted the top to be the same temperature every time we took a picture."

Four months of work was required to slice the body into 1,871 cross sections and film them. The detail captured in the pictures is so fine that three-dimensional reconstructions, using computer graphics, show even the dragon tattoo that Mr. Jernigan had on his chest.

The Visible Woman, an anonymous 59-year-old Maryland resident who died of a heart attack and donated her body to bio-medical research, was done in even finer slices. The Colorado researchers made more than 5,000 cross-sectional images of her, and the work took a year. Data from that effort became available only late last year, so most of the research with the digital cadavers has been done with the Visible Man.

"This was a raw and fresh perspective that told me things about my own body that I never knew before."

Now that the bodies have been converted to pixels—the smallest unit of a digital image—the National Library of Medicine requires those who want to use a complete data set to obtain a license. Some sample images can be obtained without a license. Mr. Ackerman says the library wants to be able to let taxpayers know if they are getting their money's worth from the $1.4-million the federal government has spent on the project.

About 400 licenses have been issued, to people in more than 25 countries. Scientists from North America can purchase the data on tapes for $1,000. Those from other countries must pay $2,000. Anyone can obtain the data free via the Internet, after both a license and a password have been obtained. (The Visible Human Project can be found on the World Wide Web at http://www.nlm.nih.gov.) But even with a high-speed modem, users have to stay connected for a couple of weeks to get all of the Visible Man's data.

FASCINATION WITH IMAGES

Researchers say the Visible Human Project presents a challenge to those interested in finding the best ways to use high-resolution, three-dimensional data. But many of the computer scientists who have worked with the Visible Man also have become fascinated by the images themselves.

"Medical textbooks give us a highly interpreted view of the human body, emphasizing key organs," says Ben Schneiderman, head of the Human-Computer Interaction Laboratory at the University of Maryland at College Park. "This was a raw and fresh perspective that told me things about my own body that I never knew before."

He was surprised, for instance, by the way the images revealed the strength of the thighs.

A graduate student in Mr. Shneiderman's lab, however, had a different reaction. "The first time I looked at the images, I was grossed out," says Chris North, who has done much of the work to create a program called "Visible Human Explorer," which helps people to find just the view they want.

Although the data were created from two-dimensional cross sections, the program Mr. North created makes it possible to look at the body from any perspective, and to pass through it like a moving wall going through a stationary ghost.

On a powerful computer, the effect is like watching a movie. If a viewer starts at the front of the body and slides toward it, for instance, the outstretched hands appear first, then the stomach, followed shortly by the nose. The chest opens to reveal the lungs and the heart. Then the spine and brain appear, looking like a knobby stick topped by a cauliflower. The shoulder blades and the buttocks are the last things a viewer sees.

NO LABELS

As scientists moved beyond their initial aesthetic reactions and tried to use the images, however, they were quickly confronted with the Visible Man's most important failing. When Mr. Shneiderman's 20-year-old daughter fell while hiking in the mountains of Nepal, he was told that she had broken her talus bone. But he couldn't order the Visible

Man to show him the bone's location. (It is in the ankle.)

The Visible Man and the Visible Woman do not yet have labels showing what organs are where. The Visible Man, says Mr. Spitzer, is "very useful if you already know anatomy. It's difficult to learn any anatomy from him."

COORDINATING INFORMATION

This bothers the project's sponsors. "For a librarian, this is very unsettling," says Mr. Ackerman. "It's like having books lying around all over the place and not indexed or catalogued."

Achieving the ability to coordinate information based on the written word with visual images was, in fact, one of the chief purposes of the project. Researchers at many universities and companies are developing ways to achieve this coordination; eventually, those viewing the visible humans should be able to point to an area on the digital cadavers and get information about it.

Despite the lack of labels on the visible humans, however, physicians already are finding them useful. Carl Jaffe, a professor of diagnostic radiology at Yale University, says the pictures may not usually help in the diagnosis of individual patients, but will help to explain physical abnormalities and disease by providing a good anatomical reference.

Scientists at the State University of New York at Stony Brook have used the Visible Man in an attempt to replace the traditional methods of checking for colon cancer, which can involve considerable discomfort.

Arie E. Kaufman, a professor of computer science and radiology at Stony Brook, has developed a way to reconstruct pictures of the inside of a patient's colon from cross-sectional images obtained from painless scans taken externally. To develop this method, Mr. Kaufman and his colleagues used the Visible Man to simulate what a physician would see while looking at such reconstructed images.

The images, Mr. Kaufman says, give the physician the sensation of steering through the inside of the colon with a camera, and the ability to look closely at potentially cancerous polyps.

Mr. Spitzer has many other ideas about ways to use the Visible Man. He would like to be able to alter the body's age and size. He would like to be able to show people what will happen to their bodies if they don't take care of them.

DOGS AND MICE NEXT?

Some of his colleagues have started working on a surgical simulator. It would allow surgeons to look at a picture of part of the back and to grasp a handle and feel the same resistance they would feel if they were holding a scalpel and cutting into the tissue there.

The success of the Visible Human Project has sparked interest in other digital anatomical maps. Veterinarians want a visible dog and a visible dolphin. Those who work on basic biomedical research want visible mice.

Mr. Ackerman says the library will concentrate on "the human animal." He wants to wait before adding another human cadaver, because he believes researchers are already saturated with data. Eventually, he might like to add a pre-menopausal female.

While scientists debate who, or what else, should join Mr. Jernigan, his body lives on like some Internet angel—grotesque to some, beautiful to others. In his life, he took a life. In death, he may end up saving a few.

The Neuron and Regions of the Brain

It was discovered in the early 1800s that major organs of the body are made up of cells that serve as the basic functional units. Scientists at that time, however, were not sure how the brain was organized. They wondered whether brain cells served as separate functional units similar to those found in other organs, or whether the cells formed a single, continuous structural network. It was not an easy question to resolve due to lack of sophisticated techniques.

A breakthrough occurred during the late 1800s through the works of the Spanish scientist Santiago Ramon y Cajal. Using a staining technique developed earlier by the Italian scientist Camillo Golgi, Cajal found that the brain tissue is composed of cells with branch-like extensions that are morphologically separate from one another. These cells are what we now call neurons. Cajal also noted that these cells touched each other at some sites.

From the studies of Cajal, and with the help of improving technology, the fine structures and functions of the nervous system are now better understood. The brain of an adult person contains a remarkable 180 billion cells, and in spite of the death of thousands of cells each day, the brain can still function effectively. The extensive branching processes of neurons (called axons and dendrites) are used for communication. The point of contact between neurons seen by earlier investigators is a complex system known as the synapse. It is amazing that a tiny neuron can possess as many as 15,000 synapses on its surface, and considering that the brain contains billions of neurons, the total number of connections is astronomical! Neurophysiologists have found that neurons communicate with one another by way of chemical substances known as neurotransmitters.

Neurons are organized as units with designated functions within the brain. For example, a group of neurons in one region of the brain may process visual information, while another set of neurons in another region may process auditory information. A group of neurons located in the brainstem called the reticular activating system regulates our conscious state. The brain is now considered to function by way of several network systems. The earlier idea of the brain as a single, continuous, structural network has been proven erroneous, but such a view anticipated the neural network theory now used to explain brain function.

Looking Ahead: Challenge Questions

Is the brain really deprived of an immune system? Discuss the assumption that microglia serve as the brain's immune apparatus. How do these cells compare with the cells of the immune system present in the blood?

Where in the nervous system is the cerebellum located? What is the function of the cerebellum as we traditionally believe? Discuss the diversity of function of the cerebellum.

What are stem cells in the context of the nervous system? Do you believe that we can develop new neurons in the adult brain? How so? What are the implications of the recent findings concerning stem cells in the nervous system?

What are oligodendrocytes? How can spinal cord injury affect the status of oligodendrocytes in the brain? Discuss the role of glutamate in nervous tissue trauma.

UNIT 2

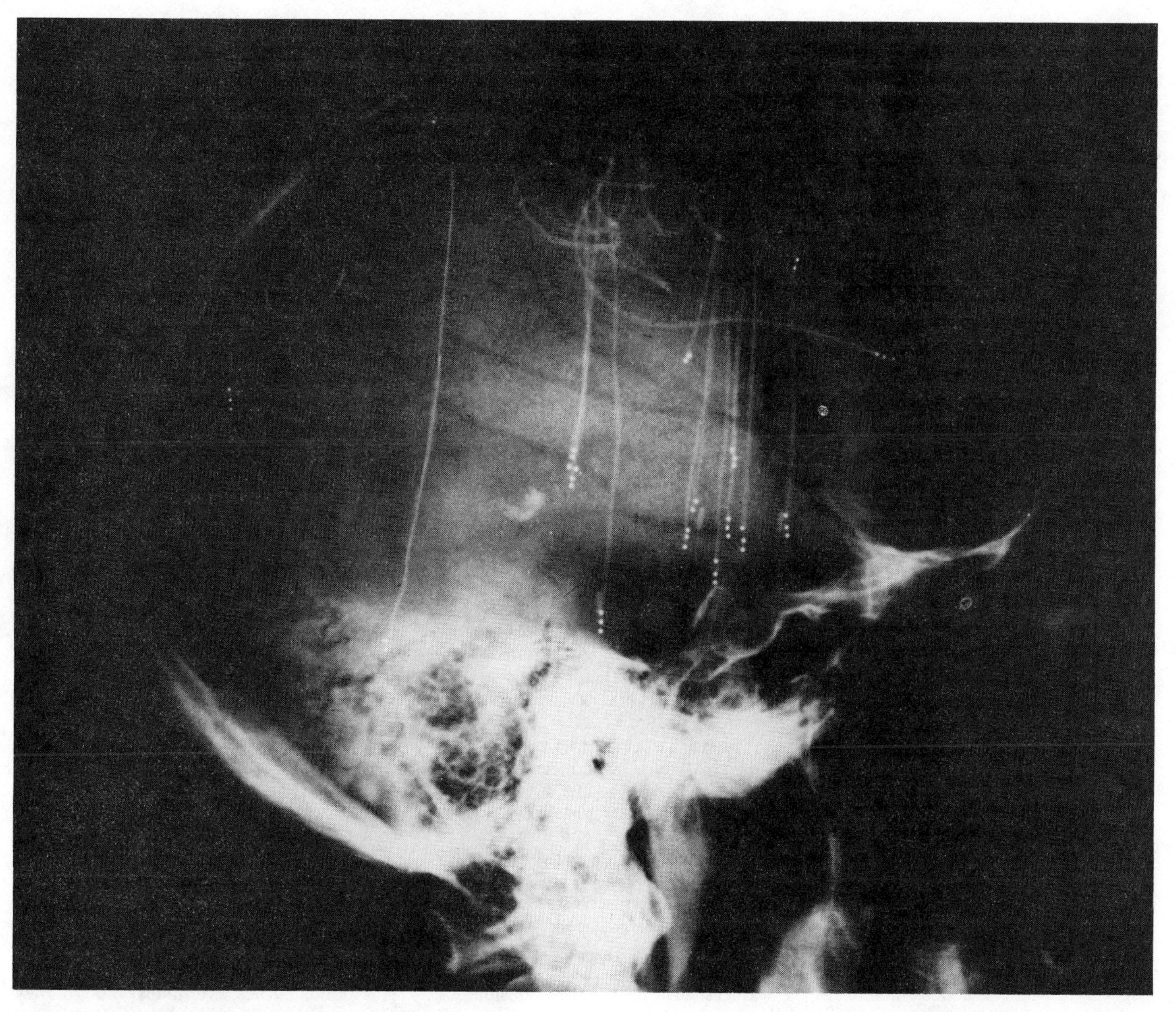

The Brain's Immune System

It consists of cells called microglia that are normally protective but can be surprisingly destructive. The cells may contribute to neurodegenerative diseases and to the dementia of AIDS

Wolfgang J. Streit and Carol A. Kincaid-Colton

WOLFGANG J. STREIT and CAROL A. KINCAID-COLTON conduct separate research programs but have collaborated on developing a symposium on microglia. Streit, who earned his Ph.D. in experimental neuropathology at the Medical University of South Carolina, is associate professor of neuroscience at the University of Florida Brain Institute. He joined the university after working as a staff scientist at the Max Planck Institute for Psychiatry in Martinsried, Germany. Kincaid-Colton is associate professor of physiology and biophysics at the Georgetown University School of Medicine. She holds a doctorate in physiology from Rutgers University and was on staff at the Laboratory of Biophysics at the National Institute of Health before taking her post at Georgetown.

When biologists view healthy tissue from the brain or spinal cord under a microscope, they rarely see white blood cells, the best known sentries of the immune system. And for good reason. Although white blood cells defend against infection and cancer, they also can secrete substances capable of killing irreplaceable nerve cells, or neurons. The body minimizes such destruction by restricting the passage of immune cells out of blood vessels and into the central nervous system; white cells generally escape into the nerve tissue only when blood vessels are damaged by trauma or disease.

Such observations led to the once widespread belief that the central nervous system lacks immune protection. Recently, however, investigators have demonstrated that fascinating cells called microglia form an extensive defensive network there. Most of the time, microglia serve without harming neurons. Yet mounting evidence suggests they occasionally lose their benign character. In fact, there are intimations that the cells can help cause or exacerbate several disabling conditions, among them, stroke, Alzheimer's disease, multiple sclerosis and other neurodegenerative disorders.

Microglia belong to a class of cells—the glia (from Greek, meaning "glue")—that was first recognized in the 1800s. Initially, biologists mistakenly thought of the glia as a single unit that served only as the uninteresting putty between neurons in the brain and spinal cord. But by the 1920s microscopists had identified three kinds of glial cell: astrocytes, oligodendrocytes and microglia. By the 1970s it was evident the first two types, at least, had profound responsibilities.

For instance, the star-shaped astrocyte, which has the largest cell body, had been found to sop up extra neurotransmitter molecules around neurons, thereby protecting nerve cells from receiving too much stimulation [see "Astrocytes," by Harold K. Kimelberg and Michael D. Norenberg; SCIENTIFIC AMERICAN, April 1989]. And the oligodendrocyte, the next largest glial cell, had been shown to produce the myelin sheath that insulates axons (long projections that extend from neuronal cell bodies and carry electrical signals). Some researchers suspected the more diminutive, microglial cell also had a special—immunologic—role, but until the 1980s, the tools needed to validate this speculation were lacking.

The idea grew primarily out of intensive research performed early in the 20th century by Pio del Río-Hortega, a former student of the famous Spanish neuroanatomist Santiago Ramon y Cajal. In 1919 Del Río-Hortega developed a stain, based on silver carbonate, that made it possible to distinguish microglia from neurons, astrocytes and oligodendrocytes in thin slices of the mammalian brain. He then spent more than a decade learning all he could about these odd cells.

He determined that microglia first appear in the developing brain as amorphous bodies. Eventually, though, they differentiate into extensively branched, or ramified, forms that populate every region of the brain and touch neurons and astrocytes (but not one another). He also saw that the cells responded dramatically when the brain was injured severely. For instance, he noted that in reaction to a stab wound, the ramified cells retracted their delicate branches, or processes, and seemed to return to their rounder, immature conformation.

Del Río-Hortega recognized that microglia in this last state resembled macrophages, a form of white blood cell found in tissues outside the brain. He knew as well that when macrophages sensed that tissues were hurt or infected, they usually migrated to the affected areas, proliferated and became highly phagocytic—that is, they became garbage collectors, capable of ingesting and degrading microbes, dying cells and other debris. By 1932 he was able to postulate that the rounding of mature microglia reflected a metamorphosis to a phagocytic state. In other words, he thought microglia functioned as the macrophages of the central nervous system.

Support for an Immune Role

Although del Río-Hortega's ideas made sense, few investigators followed up on them during the next 50 years, largely because his staining method proved unreliable. Without a dependable way of distinguishing microglia from other cells, no one could learn much about their functions. This barrier came down only in the 1980s, after V. Hugh Perry and his colleagues at the University of Oxford began screening monoclonal antibodies for their ability to bind to microglia. Monoclonal antibodies each recognize a highly specific protein target, or antigen. Perry's group knew that if such antibodies found their targets on microglia but not on other cells of the central nervous system, the antibodies could be exploited as a new kind of "stain." The microglia would stand out from other cells if the workers simply linked the bound antibodies to some detectable label, such as a fluorescent compound.

In 1985 Perry's team demonstrated that various monoclonals produced by other groups could indeed pinpoint microglia in brain tissue. Soon, even more antibodies able to serve this purpose became available. Their introduction, together with the advent in the mid-1980s of methods for maintaining pure populations of microglia in culture dishes, finally made it possible to examine the activities of the cells in detail.

The antibodies did more than highlight microglia; they provided strong circumstantial support for the assertion that those cells could operate as immune defenders in the brain and spinal cord. Notably, various antibodies that recognize proteins occurring exclusively on cells of the immune system were able to find their targets on microglia. Further, certain antibodies demonstrated that the cells probably behaved like macrophages.

Macrophages and some of their kin are antigen presenters: they chop up proteins made by invading microbes and display the pieces in molecular showcases known as class II major histocompatibility antigens. Such displays help to induce additional immune cells to launch a full-fledged attack against an invader. Between 1985 and 1989, researchers from around the world demonstrated that monoclonal antibodies able to latch on to class II major histocompatibility antigens often bound well to microglia. This behavior meant that, contrary to prevailing views, microglia produced class II major histocompatibility antigens; hence, they were probably antigen-presenting cells themselves.

The antibody results dovetailed with work by Georg W. Kreutzberg and his colleagues at the Max Planck Institute for Psychiatry in Martinsried. The German group, one of the few with a long-standing interest in microglial function, tested the ability of microglia in the rodent brain to behave like macrophages when confronted with severely injured neurons. At the same time, the workers looked into the contention of some investigators that microglia did not live in the central nervous system at all, that they were nothing more than monocytes that flooded into the brain or spinal cord when blood vessels in the nerve tissue were damaged. This last assertion had been difficult to refute because then, as now, the antibodies and stains that recognized microglia also recognized macrophages derived from blood-borne monocytes.

Kreutzberg and his colleagues applied a simple method to resolve both issues. As a start, they focused on neurons whose cell bodies were located in the brain but whose axons terminated at muscles outside the brain. They injected a toxin into a site near the ends of the axons and allowed the poison to diffuse through—and kill—the neurons without affecting any blood vessels. This maneuver ensured that any macrophagelike cells responding to the damage would be residents of the brain tissue, not interlopers from the blood. Finally, they examined the brain region containing the remains of the affected nerve cells. Analyses of tissue from many animals revealed that microglia do in fact migrate to dead neurons, proliferate and remove dead cells. In short, microglia are, indeed, the brain's own kind of macrophages.

Investigations of cultured microglia and of diseased brains suggest the cells sometimes damage the neurons they are meant to protect.

Experiments on pure populations of microglia in culture have now helped convince even the greatest skeptics that microglia are the immune warriors del Río-Hortega thought them to be. These studies have confirmed that the cells are extremely mobile—a property essential for cells that supposedly move easily to injured areas within the brain. The work has also established that microglia can be induced to produce a wide array of chemicals made by macrophages in other tissues.

How Normal Microglia Behave

It appears, then, that modern research has finally justified del Río-Hortega's belief in the immunologic properties of microglia. The studies have also clarified the operation of the cells in the healthy, as well as the diseased, central nervous system.

Microglia are critical to proper development of the embryo. They may secrete growth factors important to the formation of the central nervous system, but another role has been identified more definitively. The growing fetus generates many more neurons and glial cells than it needs. Over time, the unused cells die, and young microglia, still in their initial, nonramified conformation, remove the dead matter.

As the sculpting of the central nervous system is completed, the need to degrade large numbers of cells disappears, and microglia differentiate into their extensively ramified, resting state. This conformation enables the cells to keep close tabs on the health of many

The Many Guises of Microglia

Microglia (*dark gray in micrographs*) are often found in their resting, highly ramified state (*top*). But when they sense a neuron is in trouble, they begin to retract their branches. They also migrate to the site of danger and take on a new conformation (*middle*). The precise shape usually depends on the architecture of the brain region in which the microglia find themselves. If the cells have enough space, they may become bushy (*left*). If the cells have to fit in among long, thin neuronal projections, they tend to become rodlike (*center*). Other times, they prefer to conform to the surface of injured neurons, as is the case when motor neurons are damaged (*right*). If disordered neurons recover, microglia may revert to their resting state (*gray arrows*). If neurons die, however, microglia progress to a phagocytic state (*bottom*) and assiduously try to remove the dead material.

State 1:
Resting
Ramified microglia constantly monitor the health of cells around them.

State 2:
Newly Activated
Microglia change shape when they first detect a disturbance in their microenvironment, such as injury to a neuron.

State 3:
Phagocytic
Cells in this state are reacting to the death of other cells; they change shape again and attempt to degrade the dead matter.

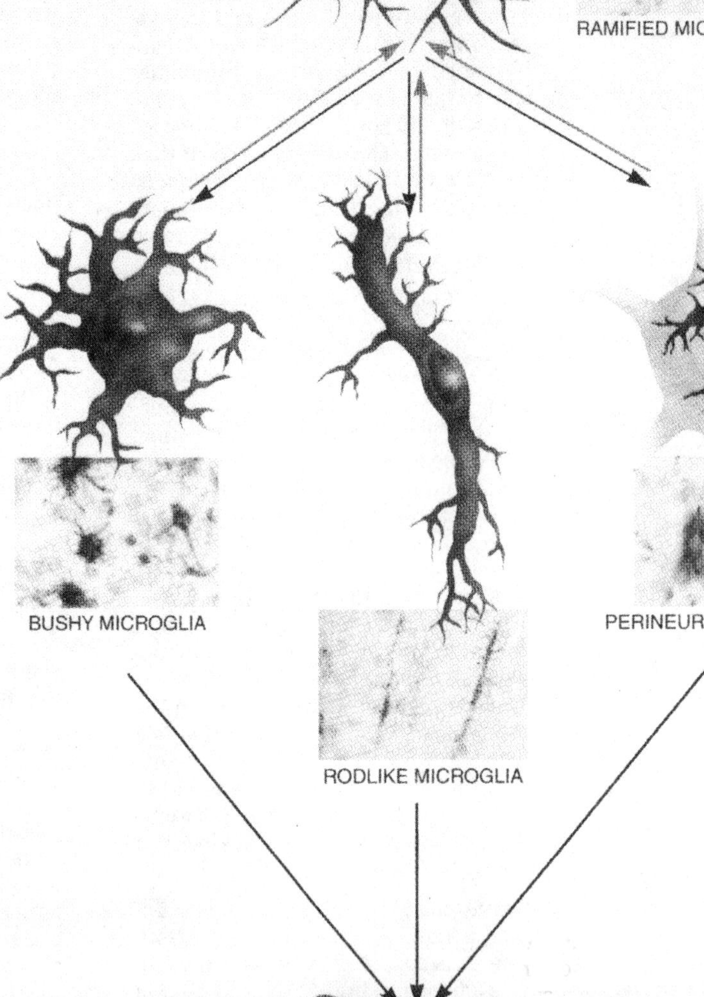

DANA BURNS-PIZER (*drawings*); WOLFGANG J. STREIT (*micrographs*)

cells in their vicinity. No one yet knows much about the other functions of resting microglia, but indirect evidence implies the cells release low levels of growth factors, which at this stage would help mature neurons and glia survive. Those substances may include fibroblast growth factor and nerve growth factor—two proteins that investigators have prodded cultured microglia to secrete.

What is more certain is that resting microglia respond almost instantly (within minutes) to disturbances in their microenvironment and prepare to surround damaged neurons or other cells. The outward signs of such activation are retraction of their branches, other changes in shape, production of proteins not found in the resting state, and stepped-up synthesis of proteins formerly made only in small amounts. For example, expression of major histocompatibility antigens is enhanced markedly. We do not yet know whether the cells release higher amounts of growth factors, but they may well do so in an attempt to repair injured neurons.

The conformation of the newly activated microglia seems to depend a great deal on the architecture of the region in which the cells live. If the area is filled mainly with axons, the cells tend to become long and thin, in order to fit between the cables. If there is room to maneuver, as is the case in much of the brain, the cells often become bushy.

Activated cells do not automatically become phagocytic; they can revert to the resting state if the injury they have detected is mild or reversible. If the injury is severe and kills neurons, however, microglia begin to function as full-fledged, phagocytic macrophages. The ultimate fate of the phagocytes is unclear, but investigations of cultured microglia and of diseased brains suggest the cells sometimes go on to damage the neurons they are meant to protect.

Suspicion that microglia might contribute to neurologic disorders was aroused in part by the discovery, mentioned earlier, that microglia can release many of the same chemicals emitted by macrophages outside the central nervous system. Some of those substances are dangerous to cells and, if made in excessive amounts, could surely kill neurons. For example, one of us (Kincaid-Colton) and her colleagues at Georgetown University have found that when activated microglia in culture are exposed to particular bacterial components, the cells, like other macrophages, generate extremely destructive molecules known as reactive oxygen species. The compounds go by such names as the superoxide anion, the hydroxyl radical (one of the most toxic compounds in the body) and hydrogen peroxide. Along with killing microbes, they can damage membranes, proteins and DNA in neurons and other cells.

Additional, potentially destructive compounds manufactured by strongly activated microglia and other macrophages include enzymes called proteases that digest proteins and can chew holes in cell membranes. They further encompass at least two versatile messenger molecules, or cytokines, that can increase inflammation. That is, these cytokines—among them, interleukin-1 and tumor necrosis factor—often help to recruit other components of the immune system to a site of injury [see "Tumor Necrosis Factor," by Lloyd J. Old; SCIENTIFIC AMERICAN, May 1988]. Inflammation can be important for eradicating infections and incipient cancers, but it can have serious "bystander" effects by which uninfected cells are harmed. Under some circumstances, the cytokines can also damage neurons directly, and tumor necrosis factor can kill oligodendrocytes.

That microglia can synthesize all these substances in culture is not proof that the cells can disrupt the living brain. Indeed, the central nervous system apparently holds microglia on a tight leash, forcing them to keep worrisome secretions to a minimum, even when responding to injury and disease; otherwise no one would survive having microglia everywhere in the brain. Nevertheless, research into a number of neurological disorders suggests that in some patients the leash is loosened, either because a defect exists in the microglia themselves or because some other disease process undermines the normal controls on the behavior of the cells.

Microglia and Disease

Excessive microglial activity has certainly been implicated in the dementia that sometimes arises in patients suffering from AIDS. The human immunodeficiency virus, which causes the disease, does not attack neurons, but it does infect microglia. Such invasion has been shown to spur microglia to make elevated levels of inflammatory cytokines and other molecules that are toxic to neurons.

Disturbed regulation of microglia could play a part in Alzheimer's disease as well. The brains of Alzheimer's patients are marked by large numbers of senile plaques: abnormal regions in which deposits of a protein fragment known as beta amyloid mingle with microglia, astrocytes and the endings of injured neurons. Such plaques are thought to contribute to the neuronal death that underlies the deterioration of the mind. Exactly how they hurt nerve cells is unclear and a matter of heated argument. Many investigators suspect

The Controversial Origin of Microglia

In 1932 Pio del Río-Hortega, the pioneer of microglial research, ignited a controversy that preoccupied most investigators interested in microglia for more than 50 years. In the same paper in which he proposed that microglia were the immune defenders and garbage collectors of the central nervous system, he suggested that the cells did not originate in the same embryonic tissue—the ectoderm—that gives rise to nerve cells. He concluded that microglia derived instead from the mesoderm, the layer of embryonic germ cells that forms the bone marrow, blood, blood vessels and lymphatics. He could not decide, however, on the precise mesodermal lineage of the cells. Did microglia descend from white blood cells called monocytes and enter the brain and spinal cord from the fetal blood circulation? Or did they descend from noncirculating cousins of monocytes and migrate to the central nervous system directly, without passing through the bloodstream?

For a time, the monocytic origin was favored, and the majority opinion held that the precursors of microglia were monocytes attracted to the developing nervous system by neurons that died during the sculpting of the brain and spinal cord. But new findings contradict that view. For instance, Jutta Schnitzer of the Max Delbrück Center for Molecular Medicine in Berlin and Ken W. S. Ashwell of the University of Sydney in Australia have shown that the retina of the eye, a part of the central nervous system, is "seeded" with microglia quite early in development, well before neurons begin to die. In fact, the weight of evidence now favors the "cousin" hypothesis. —*W. S. and C. K.-C.*

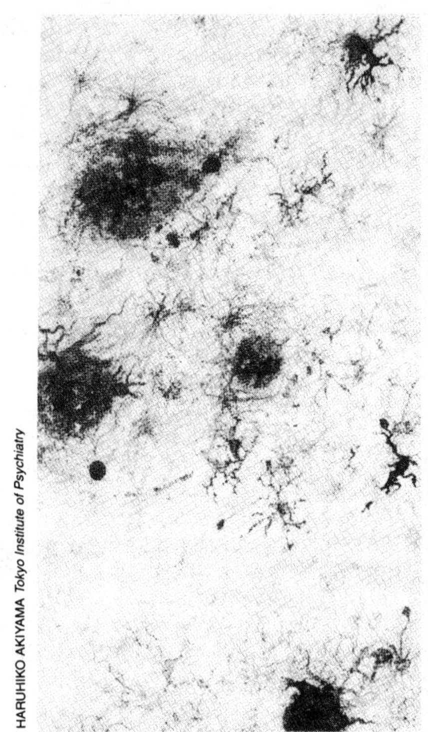

Microglial Products: Double-Edged Swords

Chemical	Beneficial Effects	Harmful Effects
Amyloid precursor protein	Unknown	When cleaved, may give rise to beta amyloid
Cytokines (messenger molecules of the immune system)	Recruit other cells to sites of infection; some promote the survival and repair of astrocytes; some combat tumors	Can harm healthy cells and induce other immune cells to secrete cell-damaging substances
Growth factors	Promote the survival and repair of neurons	Unknown
Protein-cleaving enzymes	Help to degrade microbes and damaged cells	Can degrade membranes of healthy cells; may contribute to formation of beta amyloid
Reactive oxygen species	Can damage membranes, proteins and DNA in microbes	Can damage healthy cells; can promote the aggregation of beta amyloid

SENILE PLAQUES (*round regions in micrograph*) are thought to cause the neuronal damage underlying memory impairment in patients with Alzheimer's disease and Down's syndrome. At their core, the plaques consist mainly of protein fragments called beta amyloid, known to be harmful to neurons, and microglia. The plaques also include other glial cells called astrocytes as well as damaged axons and dendrites (*not visible*). New evidence suggests microglia promote plaque formation. It is also possible that activated microglia disrupt neurons directly, by secreting chemicals that can be toxic to cells. Some of the chemicals made by microglia are listed in the table.

beta amyloid is the agent of trouble. We think beta amyloid might do its mischief by affecting microglia. It is now evident, for instance, that the levels of interleukin-1 and other cytokines known to be made at times by microglia are elevated in senile plaques. Such elevation implies that something—perhaps beta amyloid—pushes the microglia in plaques into a highly active state. In that condition, the cells would presumably also release oxygenated species and protein-degrading enzymes and could thereby disrupt neurons.

Other findings suggest that microglia might even contribute to the formation of plaques. It seems microglia respond to injury in the central nervous system by making one form of the amyloid precursor protein—the molecule that, when cleaved in a particular way, yields beta amyloid. Moreover, studies of cells in culture have shown that interleukin-1 causes various other cells, possibly including neurons, to produce amyloid precursor molecules. Finally, the reactive oxygen species made by activated microglia promote the aggregation of amyloid fragments.

It is easy to imagine that a vicious cycle could ensue after some trigger pushed microglia into a hyperactive state. If the cells made the amyloid precursor protein, their proteases could well cleave the molecule to produce beta amyloid. At the same time, interleukin-1 might induce other cells to make amyloid as well. Then reactive oxygen species could cause the amyloid released by microglia or neighboring cells to clump together. Such clustering, in turn, could lead to activation of additional microglia, production of more amyloid, formation of more plaques, and so on.

People born with Down's syndrome acquire elevated numbers of senile plaques in their brains, albeit earlier than do patients with Alzheimer's disease. Because the brain changes are so alike in the two conditions, Kincaid-Colton and her colleagues have begun exploring the possibility that microglia damage brain tissue in these patients. They have uncovered some support for the concept in studies of mice bearing a genetic defect analogous to that responsible for Down's syndrome in humans. Microglia in such fetuses are unusually reactive and abundant; additionally, the microglia in the "Down's" mice release increased amounts of reactive oxygen species, interleukin-1 and other cytokines that might affect nerve tissue adversely.

Stroke victims, too, might lose neurons to overzealous microglia, according to experiments performed in rats by one of us (Streit) and his co-workers at the University of Florida. When a major blood vessel feeding the forebrain is shut down, the brain tissue dependent on the vessel dies quickly. Over the next several days, particularly vulnerable neurons in a part of the surrounding area—the so-called CA1 region of the hippocampus—die as well. Interestingly, Streit's group has discovered that microglia are activated within minutes after onset of such a stroke, long before the hippocampal neurons die. (This activation is made evident by changes in cell shape and by enhanced stainability.) It is conceivable that the microglia, sensing danger, attempt to protect the neurons, perhaps by initiating or increasing secretion of growth factors potentially able to repair injuries. It is equally likely, however, that the altered chemistry in the region eventually releases the normal brakes on microglial behavior, propelling the cells into a state in which they become dangerous.

Preliminary evidence points as well

to microglia as possible participants in multiple sclerosis, Parkinson's disease and amyotrophic lateral sclerosis (Lou Gehrig's disease). Microglia also change with age, as is evident in the increased display of major histocompatibility antigens. This display could be a sign that the normal inhibitions on progression to the dangerous, highly active state relax with time. Easing of these controls would undoubtedly promote neuronal destruction and could thus contribute to memory declines and senility.

The Good News

A good deal of research into the link between microglia and disorders of the brain casts microglia as villains, but the data do have some encouraging implications. If microglia are indeed central players in neurological diseases, it might be possible to ameliorate these conditions by specifically inhibiting microglia or by blocking the activity of their products. Drug therapies with these aims are already beginning to be tested in patients with Alzheimer's disease. For example, small trials are under way to examine the safety and effectiveness of an anti-inflammatory agent capable of quieting activated microglia. Conversely, scientists might be able to take advantage of the cells' protective aspects and boost microglial production of growth factors.

Ten years ago some investigators denied that microglia even existed. Five years ago most physicians would have laughed if anyone hinted that microglia could be major participants in Alzheimer's disease and other degenerative conditions of the brain. Today the skepticism is evaporating. Indeed, many workers are confident that study of microglia will eventually yield new therapies for some of the most heartbreaking diseases afflicting humankind.

Further Reading

FUNCTIONAL PLASTICITY OF MICROGLIA: A REVIEW. W. J. Streit, M. B. Graeber and G. W. Kreutzberg in *Glia,* Vol. 1, No. 5, pages 301–307; May 1988.

MICROGLIA.Special issue of *Glia.* Edited by M. B. Graeberg, G. W. Kreutzberg and W. J. Streit. Vol. 7, No. 1; January 1993.

NEUGROGLIA.Edited by H. Kettenmann and B. R. Ransom. Oxford University Press, 1995.

Tarzan's Little Brain

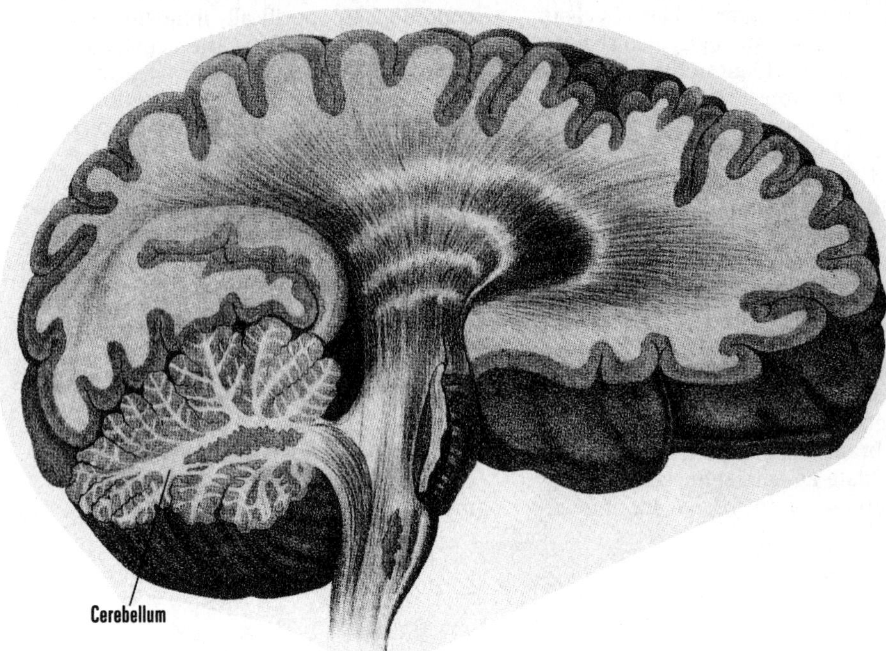

The cerebellum, long regarded as a simple neural middleman, may in fact be a powerful processor that turns the brain into a mind.

BY SARAH RICHARDSON

SPECULATING ABOUT THE EVOLUTION of self-awareness is relatively easy; finding evidence for it is hard. But if Daniel Povinelli's clambering hypothesis is right—if there is indeed a connection between our ancestors' sophisticated tree-negotiating skills and our current capacity for self-awareness—then one might expect to see that development reflected in the anatomy of the human brain. For now, incontestable physical evidence of the linkage isn't even close to being available, but neuroscientists *are* finding that both motor and cognitive tasks may in fact be processed in the same part of the brain. The site of the action consists of two fist-size clumps of tissue at the base of the brain called the cerebellum, from the Latin for "little brain."

Until recently, researchers thought the cerebellum's role was solely to regulate the speed, intensity, and direction of movement. But lately there has been a revolution in thinking about the cerebellum, led by Henrietta and Alan Leiner—two rather unlikely revolutionaries. Both are retired scientists in their eighties, and both were trained in computer science. But back in the 1960s, Henrietta Leiner decided to go to medical school. She was particularly interested in studying the brain. "At that time," she recalls, "it took a roomful of computers to do what the human brain can do in an instant."

While dissecting a human brain in a neuroanatomy class, she began to wonder about the function of a thick cable of fibers running through the cerebellum and up into the cerebral cortex. The received neurological wisdom said that the cerebral cortex—the thin, deeply fissured top layer of the brain, which constitutes its "higher" regions—sent signals through this cable to the cerebellum; the cerebellum processed and coordinated these signals, then fed them back up to the cerebral motor cortex, the region of the brain that controls movement.

What puzzled Leiner was the thickness of the cable. Not only was the cable far bigger in humans than in, say, monkeys, but it seemed outsize even relative to other human structures. It had some 40 million nerve fibers, 40 times as many as are found in the optic tract, which carries the stupendous amount of visual information the human brain receives. Moreover, those 40 million fibers were presumably coming from regions all over the brain. If the cerebellum was involved only in

Ars Medica

movement, Leiner wondered, why did it need so much diverse information?

She began asking more questions. And she learned that over the course of evolution, as the cerebral cortex expanded in apes and humans, so too did the cerebellum. She discovered that a small structure within the cerebellum called the dentate nucleus—the last processing stop in the cerebellum before signals are sent back "upstairs"—had also become relatively larger in apes and humans. Finally, she found that the most evolutionarily recent part of the dentate nucleus—called the neodentate—is present only in humans.

Putting all this together, Leiner began to suspect that the cerebellum might play a role not just in movement but in cognition—that is, in those processes, such as language, by which humans come to know, and make judgments about, themselves and the world around them. The expansion of the dentate nucleus, she reasoned, could have been driven by a need to process the massive amounts of information the cerebral cortex was transmitting. The neodentate, she reasoned further, was found only in the one animal that we know for sure has exceptional cognitive skills. Besides, she thought, if you were going to look for a part of the brain that could allow for high-speed information processing between different brain regions, you could hardly do better than the cerebellum: although it takes up only a tenth of the brain's volume, it contains at least half the brain's neurons. "I thought, 'What a terrific computer!' " Leiner recalls. " 'Now, where does it send its results?' " If the cerebellum was indeed involved in activities other than movement, its information would be sent to other areas besides the motor cortex. At the time, however, no such anatomical pathway had been identified.

Neurologist Robert Dow of Good Samaritan Medical Center in Portland, Oregon, was the first to provide some clinical support for Leiner's ideas, in 1986. He tested a patient with cerebellar damage and found—to his surprise—problems in subtle cognitive functions, such as planning.

Since that finding, several other studies have implicated the cerebellum in nonmotor skills. Among the first was a report of cerebellar activity in word-selection tasks; it was followed by a report of poor performance on similar tasks by a patient with cerebellar damage. In yet another study, researchers asked a normal subject to put rings of different sizes on a pole. If the subject slipped the rings on randomly, the cerebellum showed normal activity. But when the subject had to put the rings on in order from small to large, the cerebellum's activity increased. Most recently, a study detected cerebellar involvement when a subject was asked to judge whether two small, irregularly shaped balls—which he could feel but not see—were the same shape.

Meanwhile, neurologist Jeremy Schmahmann of Harvard Medical School has found that patients with cerebellar injury are often unable to make accurately proportioned line drawings of simple objects. He has also observed a transient but palpable flatness of emotion in such patients. All of this leads him to speculate that the cerebellum regulates a host of complex cognitive tasks, one of which, he suspects, may be the coordination of the physical cues through which nonverbal communication occurs.

"In the past," says Leiner, "the cerebellum was thought to receive signals from the cerebral cortex and send back signals through the dentate nucleus only to the motor cortex. The mistake was in assuming the signals went only to the motor cortex." A recent anatomical finding has finally proved that point. Peter Strick and his colleagues at the Veterans Affairs Medical Center in Syracuse, New York, have traced a pathway in monkeys from the cerebellum back to parts of the brain that are involved in memory, attention, space perception, body positioning, and spatial guidance—all regions that lie outside the motor cortex.

Intriguingly, these diverse findings coincide with one neuroscientist's theory about the origins of autism. Since 1985, Eric Courchesne of the University of California at San Diego has been proposing that autism—a disorder that might well be characterized as an abnormal sense of self—is linked to cerebellar deficits. His own brain-imaging studies have found smaller cerebellums in autistic children; other researchers have found fewer cerebellar neurons. Although Courchesne's theory of autism is directed at humans, it is appealing to speculate that the cerebellum might somehow be involved in the skills that underlie self-awareness in the great apes. "Cerebellar impairments will be an impediment to social language and other kinds of knowledge," Courchesne explains. "And they may affect body-image knowledge as well."

Courchesne has also linked cerebellar damage in humans to an impaired ability to shift attention quickly from one task to another. Like Leiner and Schmahmann, he sees the cerebellum as filtering and integrating the stream of incoming sensory information in ways that permit swift, complex decision making—a skill that, in the end, calls to mind the trait Povinelli thinks distinguishes some seemingly thoughtful apes from their tree-swinging kin.

> One of the cerebellum's many tasks may be to coordinate the physical cues through which nonverbal communication occurs.

Stem Cells in the Central Nervous System

In the vertebrate central nervous system, multipotential cells have been identified in vitro and in vivo. Defined mitogens cause the proliferation of multipotential cells in vitro, the magnitude of which is sufficient to account for the number of cells in the brain. Factors that control the differentiation of fetal stem cells to neurons and glia have been defined in vitro, and multipotential cells with similar signaling logic can be cultured from the adult central nervous system. Transplanting cells to new sites emphasizes that neuroepithelial cells have the potential to integrate into many brain regions. These results focus attention on how information in external stimuli is translated into the number and types of differentiated cells in the brain. The development of therapies for the reconstruction of the diseased or injured brain will be guided by our understanding of the origin and stability of cell type in the central nervous system.

Ronald McKay

Definition of the processes that shape the cellular makeup of the central nervous system (CNS) has relied heavily on three distinct procedures: fate mapping, tissue culture, and transplantation. These traditional tools of embryologists have been significantly improved by the recent incorporation of advanced molecular methods. Fate mapping of neuronal precursors in vertebrates points to the existence of multipotential cells that are precursors to both neurons and glia (*1*). However, this approach does not necessarily reveal the full proliferation and differentiation capability of the cells. In vitro and in vivo manipulations must be used to test the developmental potential of a cell. Tissue culture and transplant techniques, developed in vertebrate systems (*2*), have generated important data on the potential of neural cells (*3*).

The author is in the Laboratory of Molecular Biology, National Institute of Neurological Disorders and Stroke, Bethesda, MD 20892, USA.

Defining a Stem Cell

To be considered a stem cell in the CNS, a cell must have the potential to differentiate into neurons, astrocytes, and oligodendrocytes and to self-renew sufficiently to provide the numbers of cells in the brain. The term "progenitor" refers to a cell with a more restricted potential than a stem cell. "Precursor" is a less stringent term that refers to any cell that is earlier in a developmental pathway than another.

The complete cellular lineage of the nematode *Caenorhabditis elegans* has been described (*4*) and is an influential instance of the power of morphological analysis to define precursor-product relations in vivo. However, in the CNS of mammals, there are too many cells for each to be followed individually. The problem is similar to the technical difficulties biochemists faced in defining metabolic pathways. Without access to pure precursor, it was difficult to

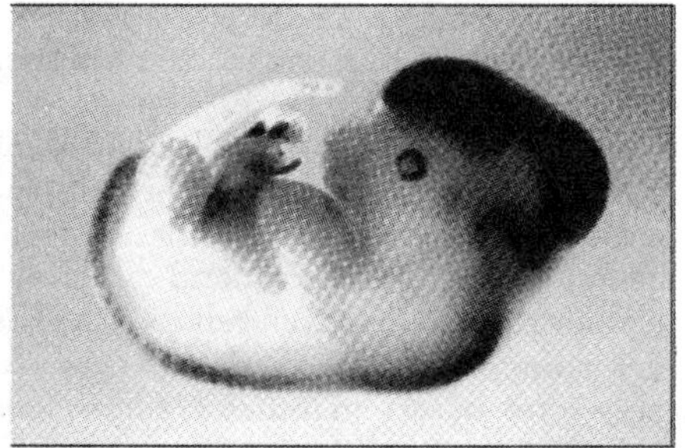

Fig. 1. A transgenic mid-gestation mouse fetus showing the expression (black) in CNS stem cells of a reporter gene under control of 750 base pairs of the second intron of the nestin gene. The approach is described in detail in (*9*).

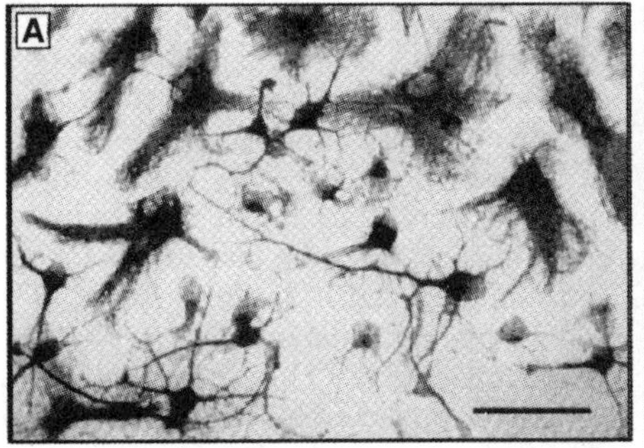

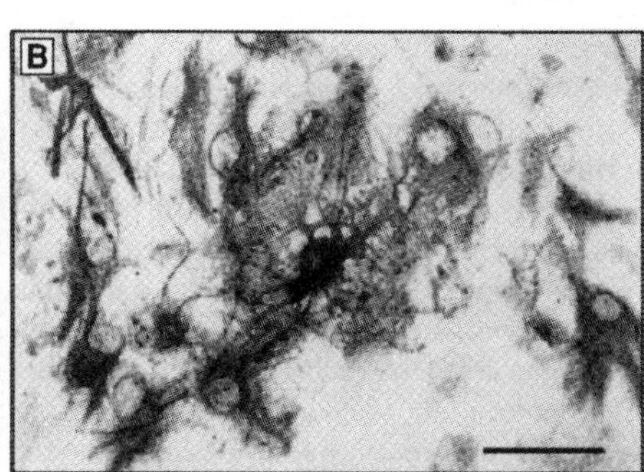

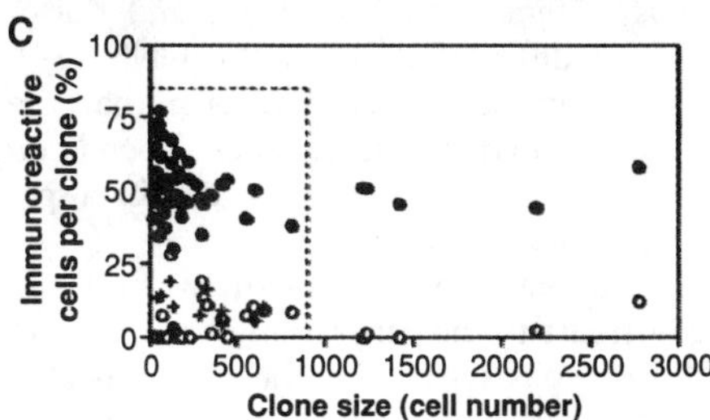

Fig. 2. The differentiation of adult CNS stem cell clones: (**A**) neurons (black) and astrocytes (grey). (**B**) oligodenrocytes (black) and astrocytes (grey). Scale bars: 25 μm. (C) The proportion of cells of different types in fetal stem cell clones: (●) neurons, (O) astrocytes, and (+) oligodendrocytes. The proportion of neurons that differentiates in a clone is constant, independent of clone size. The same proportion of neurons differentiates in adult and fetal stem cell clones. Data taken from (*20*).

establish the catalytic step actually performed by a given enzyme. When this hurdle was overcome, it was recognized that enzymes perform discrete chemical steps, ultimately giving rise to the important concept of one gene–one enzyme (*5*). Similarly, to understand the developing brain, we need to purify the precursor cell types and define their transitions into differentiated progeny. Early work revealed that fetal cells removed from the developing brain and placed in vitro could give rise to differentiated neurons (*6*). For the most part, these neurons were derived from cells that did not divide in tissue culture, although cells that did divide could acquire some features of immature neurons (*7*).

The intermediate filament nestin is a major cytoskeletal protein in neuronal precursors in the mammalian CNS (*8*). Nestin is first detected at the earliest steps in neural plate induction (*9*), and most cells in the neuroepithelium are nestin-positive before neurogenesis (*10*) (Fig. 1). Coincident with their exit from the cell cycle, neurons down-regulate nestin and express distinct intermediate filaments. This transition has also been observed in vitro where precursor cells proliferate and differentiate into neurons (*11–16*) and glia (*17*).

Confirming the results of in vivo fate mapping, lineage experiments in vitro show that neurons and glia can be derived from a common fetal precursor cell (*12, 13, 15, 16, 18–20*) (Fig. 2). The adult nervous system also contains multipotential precursors for neurons, astrocytes, and oligodendrocytes (*13, 16, 18–20*). Cultured cells from both the fetal and adult CNS that have proliferated in vitro can differentiate to show morphological and electrophysiological features characteristic of neurons: regenerative action potentials and synaptic structures (*16, 21*) (Fig. 3). These data show the multipotential nature of cells derived from the CNS.

Quantitative studies have established the homogeneity and stability of multipotent cells derived from the fetal brain (*20*). In vitro these cells divide daily and efficiently generate neurons and glia for at least the first month of culture. These multipotent cells proliferate sufficiently in vitro to account for the large numbers of cells present in the mammalian brain at birth (*10*). These cells can be considered to be stem cells because they fulfill the criteria of multipotency and self-renewal. Asymmetric division, which is sometimes considered to be a property of stem cells (*2*) and may actually occur in the neuroepithelium (*22*), does not appear to be necessary in cultured CNS stem cells (*20*).

Response Mechanisms and Transitions in Vitro

The extraordinary diversity of the adult vertebrate nervous system is generated from a sheet of epithelial cells over a period of several days. Precise numbers of neurons, astrocytes, and oligodendrocytes differentiate in successive waves. The spinal cord, formed from the caudal region of the neural tube, is one of the first sites of neuronal differentiation. Basic fibroblast growth factor (bFGF) is one mechanism that defines rostro-caudal identity in the neural tube (*23*). Neuronal differentiation in the dorso-

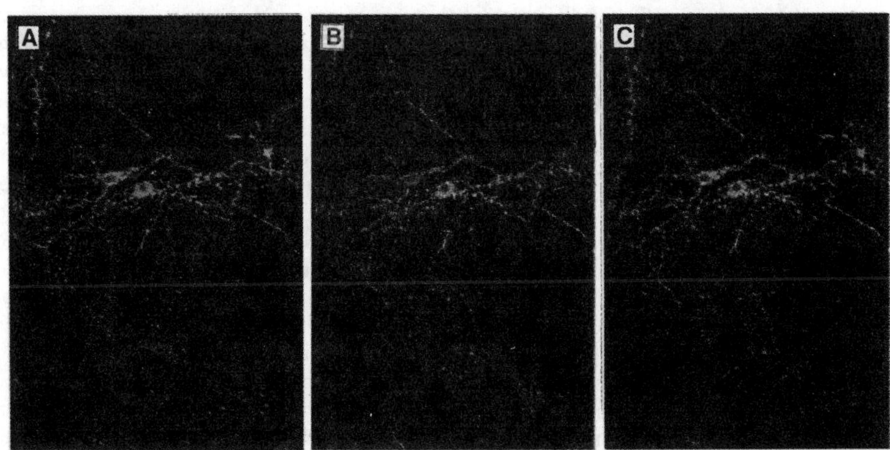

Fig. 3. Neuronal differentiation of CNS stem cells derived from the embryonic day-16 hippocampus. Cells were expanded for 16 days in the presence of bFGF followed by 21 days of differentiation in the presence of BDNF (20 ng/ml). (**A**) Staining with antibody to synapsin (grey), (**B**) staining with antibody to MAP2, and (**C**) the two images superimposed. Synapsin is concentrated in presynaptic terminals, and MAP2, in dendrites. The culture and staining conditions are similar to those reported in (*21*).

ventral axis is a response of uncommitted cells to successive extracellular signals (*24*). Sonic hedgehog and members of the transforming growth factor–β (TGF-β) family influence ventral and dorsal features of development in the caudal neural tube. These signals are used in several cellular contexts. For example, members of the TGF-β family influence segment-specific apoptosis in the neuroepithelium (*25*), astrocyte maturation (*26*), the differentiation of peripheral nervous system stem cells (*27*), and dorsoventral differentiation in the CNS (*24*). These diverse effects emphasize that the action of extracellular ligands depends on the integration of multiple signals by a specific responding cell.

Cell-autonomous mechanisms may also contribute to the generation of cell types in the nervous system. In the hematopoietic system, cell-autonomous stochastic processes are thought to generate all of the mature cell types, and the specificity of differentiation is a consequence of selective mechanisms (*28*). In such a system, specificity is obtained as a consequence of signals acting selectively only after the events that generate the different cell types. There is clear evidence for cell death in the neural tube (*29*) and growing knowledge of extra- and intracellular signals that mediate cell death (*30*). The high rates of apoptosis during neural development are consistent with an important role for selective mechanisms in the CNS.

Instructive mechanisms also occur in both the peripheral (PNS) and central nervous systems. Glial growth factor, a member of the heregulin-neuregulin class of factors, acts instructively on PNS stem cells to direct them to a Schwann cell fate (*31*). Bone morphogenetic proteins (BMP) 2 and 4 stimulate neurogenesis, and TGF-β1 generates smooth-muscle cells from the PNS stem cell (*27*). In the CNS, ciliary neurotrophic factor (CNTF) acts instructively on the multipotential stem cell, directing it to a committed astrocytic fate (*20*).

It has previously been shown that CNTF induces astrocytic differentiation in O2-A cells (*32*). In vitro, CNS stem cells rapidly and efficiently differentiate into astrocytes in the presence of CNTF (*20*). CNTF is not a mitogen for these cells, and a transient exposure (48 hours) to CNTF, even in the presence of mitogen, switches the differentiated state of more than 98% of the uncommitted stem cells. These data suggest that, in the absence of significant cell death, stimulating the Jak-stat system (the effector of CNTF) instructs the stem cell to become an astrocyte. In a recent study, BMPs promoted astrocytic differentiation from cells that had been expanded in vitro in the presence of epidermal growth factor (*26*). It will be interesting to establish whether BMPs and CNTF act through a common pathway at the same stage of astrocyte differentiation.

Thyroid hormone (T3) is also an instructive factor causing stem cells to become lineage-restricted progenitors for oligodendrocytes (*20*). Interestingly, CNTF and T3 are both differentiation and lineage-restriction factors. The differentiation of peripheral and central stem cells can be achieved without selection by the instructive action of extracellular signals. However, it seems likely that a combination of instruction and selection is used in vivo to precisely regulate precursor-product transitions at the cellular level.

The importance of selective mechanisms acting on a defined precursor cell type in brain development is best illustrated by studies on the differentiation of oligodendrocytes. There is evidence from the optic nerve for the existence of a bipotential progenitor in vitro for oligodendrocytes and type-2 astrocytes, the O-2A cell (*33*). In addition, the differentiation of this precursor cell could be controlled by manipulation of extracellular signals. Once the properties of this cell had been established, it became clear that a similar cell existed in the adult optic nerve (*34*). In tissue culture, O-2A cells respond to several factors [bFGF, platelet-derived growth factor, CNTF, neurotrophins, and T3], and many of these factors also act in vivo to increase oligodendrocyte number in the optic nerve (*35*). These in vivo data show that the availability of growth factors is limiting and that cell death is important in regulating oligodendrocyte numbers.

This summary indicates that simple ligands can regulate in vitro the transitions between stem cells and the three major cell types of the adult brain. However, it is not clear how many cell states exist in addition to stem cells and committed progenitors for astrocytes and oligodendrocytes. In some cases precursor-product transitions have been defined, but there are still many aspects of cell-type origins that are unclear and may be advanced by further work in vitro. Epidermal growth factor (EGF) and bFGF have both been used as mitogens to expand CNS stem cells, but EGF may not be the optimal choice for a stem cell mitogen, as there is evidence that EGF favors glial differentiation. In vitro EGF is a stem cell mitogen and a differentiation factor for astrocytes but not a lineage restriction factor, suggesting that the commitment event is distinct from the differentiation mechanism (*20*). However, the in vivo overexpression of EGF receptor may induce a fate shift from neurons to glia rather than simply promote astrocytic differentiation (*36*). It is clearly necessary to define the fundamental biochemical differences between lineage restriction in stem cells and differentiation of progenitor cells.

Another important unresolved question is whether there are proliferating cells capable of giving rise to specific kinds of neuron. There is evidence for a cell of this type in the postnatal cerebellum, but it is not clear whether a committed neuronal progenitor occurs in other brain regions (*37*). The events that generate the pluripotent CNS stem cell from an earlier totipotent embryonic stem cell can also be analyzed in vitro, because embryonic stem cells differentiate through a nestin-positive state to form synaptically active networks of central neurons (*38*). The routine differentiation of functional neurons from propagated stem cells would permit detailed analysis of how early steps in neurogenesis influence later stages of neuronal differentiation. The challenge is to set up experimental systems where the differentiation events of interest can be measured efficiently.

Space and Time

The cortical neuroepithelium is a highly polarized structure. Precursor cells divide at the inner (ventricular) surface of the neural tube, and immature neurons migrate away from the ventricle to specific layers. As different neurons become postmitotic in sequence, their laminar location is a function of the time when the neuron differentiated. Transplants in ferret cortex show that appropriate, layer-specific neuronal differentiation occurs when cells derived from an early time are moved to a later stage (*39*). Conversely, late neuronal precursors transplanted to an earlier stage host do not contribute efficiently to early neuronal fates but rather exhibit laminar positions appropriate for late-generated neurons (*40*). This evidence supports a model where a neuron becomes committed to a particular laminar fate in the ventricular zone at the time of withdrawal from the cell cycle. Thus, it is the timing of the exit from the cycle that is thought to implement two distinct commitment events. In this scenario, the postmitotic neuron is locked into a specific fate, and the remaining precursors are also irrevocably changed.

It is not known what specifies the regional identity of the different areas of the CNS. There are complex patterns of expression of both cell surface signals and transcriptional regulators in the developing neuroepithelium long before neurons themselves differentiate (*41*). But there could be different stem cells for different brain regions. Gene deletion experiments in mice illustrate that whole sections of the brain can be eliminated with relatively little perturbation of the development of adjacent brain regions (42). Although these results are startling, they do not establish whether neuronal precursor cells are irreversibly committed to distinct regional fates. To establish commitment, we must give cells an opportunity to choose another regional fate. In the developing chick, a duplication of a brain region can be obtained by the local application of FGF8 (43). This result suggests that single factors are sufficient to bias the differentiation cascade and establish major regional features of the CNS.

The rhombomeres of the hindbrain are a good example of the compartmental arrangement of the neuroepithelium (44). Although it was first thought that cells were prohibited from crossing the boundaries between rhombomeric compartments, fate mapping in vivo now suggests that cells do move from one compartment to another at a low frequency (45). In other brain regions, neuronal precursors also migrate over great distances (46). When the location of rhombomeres was altered by tissue grafts, rhombomere-specific *Hox* gene expression was respecified by as yet undefined anterior-posterior control systems (47). In these transplant experiments, pieces of tissue were rearranged, making it hard to interpret the responses of single cells. It will be interesting to directly test the plasticity of isolated rhombomeric cells by transplanting dissociated cells from one rhombomere to another.

Grafting experiments with cell lines from the hippocampus support a model in which local signals in the neuroepithelium at the time of neurogenesis give rise to region-specific neuronal subtypes. Immortalized nestin-positive hippocampal cells transplanted to the developing cerebellum differentiated into typical cerebellar neurons (48). Transplants of primary striatal cells into the developing cerebral cortex also showed a switch to the locally appropriate fate (49), suggesting that the plasticity in cell fate shown with immortal cells was not an artifact of immortalization. In conceptually similar experiments, primary cerebellar cells derived from mice expressing the *lacZ* reporter gene under a neuron-specific promoter were grafted into the hippocampus of neonatal rats or wild-type mice. The grafted cells acquired morphological and immunohistochemical features of hippocampal granule neurons (50). The grafted and host neurons also showed kinetics of induction identical to those of the immediate early gene *c-fos* after intraperitoneal injection of neurotransmitter agonists and antagonists (50). These data suggest that immortal and primary neuroepithelial precursor cells grafted to new sites generate region-specific neurons in response to local cues.

A major limitation of postnatal transplantation studies was that heterotopic neuronal integration occurred efficiently only when donor cells were introduced into the few sites that continued to generate neurons in the newborn animal. This limited spectrum of accessible regions was dramatically increased by transplanting neural cells across the uterine wall into the embryonic mammalian brain (49, 51, 52). When genetically labeled mouse telencephalic neuroepithelial cells were simply deposited in the ventricles, large numbers of grafted cells were subsequently found incorporated into many sites in the host brain. The transplanted cells migrated in accordance with known pathways and incorporated into telencephalic, diencephalic, and mesencephalic regions (52). Surprisingly, cells derived from the dorsal and ventral forebrain incorporated into homotopic and many heterotopic brain regions in a similar fashion. After migration, the cells acquired morphological and antigenic features appropriate for neurons in their new environment (Fig. 4). The fact that striatal precursors can give rise to cortical, thalamic, and even tectal neurons illustrates that the regional heterogeneity of the brain results primarily from extracellular signals acting on precursors during neuronal migration and differentiation. These results indicate that the activation of different signaling pathways in uncommitted stem cells generates the spatial heterogeneity of neurons seen in the CNS.

Stem Cells and Disease in the Adult Nervous System

It is important to define the types of precursor cells that give rise to the neurons generated in the adult CNS (53, 54). Cells from the adult brain proliferate and differentiate into neurons and glia in tissue culture (13, 14, 16, 55) with the same efficiency for neuronal differentiation as found in fetal stem cells and the same responses to extracellular ligands (20). For example, 50% of the cells differentiate into neurons, and glial differentiation is strongly enhanced in response to CNTF and T3 in fetal and adult stem cells. Thus, similar general mechanisms control the differentiation of stem cells from fetal or adult brain. In contrast to this apparent homogeneity in vitro, the behavior of cells in the adult proliferative zones in vivo is more difficult to define. Nevertheless, precursor cells in the adult forebrain have been intensely studied (19, 54, 56). The proliferation of these cells can be stimulated by the direct application of mitogenic growth factors in vivo, and in animals treated in this way, proliferating cells in the subventricular zone differentiate into neurons and glia (57). However, in vivo less than 3% of the proliferating cells labeled with bromodeoxyuridine differentiate into neurons. The discrepancy between the efficient neuronal differentiation of adult stem cells in vitro and their inefficient differentiation in vivo is a critical but unresolved question for the field. Thus, the lack of differentiating neurons may not be a consequence of the lack of cells with the appropriate potential but rather a function of the signaling environment in the adult brain. However, a careful analysis of adult stem cells has only just begun, and we cannot yet rule out cell-autonomous restrictions that make the adult stem cells distinct from their fetal counterparts.

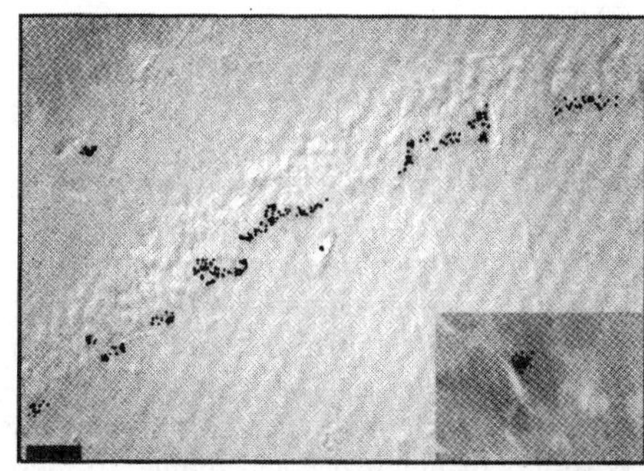

Fig. 4. Genetically labeled cells differentiate into hippocampal CA1 pyramidal neurons. The donor cells were derived from the embryonic day-14 cortical neuroepithelium of a transgenic mouse carrying a *lacZ* reporter gene. They were placed into the telencephalic vesicles of an E18 rat, where they incorporated into the host hippocampus and differentiated into granule and pyramidal neurons. The grafted cells can be identified by the black *lacZ* signal. Data taken from (52). Scale bar: 50 μm.

There is traditionally a close interaction between fundamental and clinical goals in the study of stem cells (58). The identification of extracellular proteins that regulate the differentiation of multipotent cells derived from the adult brain has implications for therapies targeted at neurodegenerative disease. The increased interest in extracellular signals acting on plastic cells during development fits well with the massive effort mounted in the biotechnology community to develop treatments for neurodegenerative disease based on the delivery of neurotrophic proteins. In vitro neuronal survival assays were often used in the initial identification of neurotrophic factors. These factors were then rapidly tested in animal models of neurodegenerative disease. The long-term delivery of proteins in the brain is a major goal in gene therapy. Transplantation of cells engineered to produce growth factors shows the potential of grafted cells as vectors for protein delivery (59). However, the complexity of neurotrophic signals still challenges the technology for gene manipulation and protein delivery in the CNS. There has been encouraging progress in using cell lines derived from the neuroepithelium rather than fibroblasts as cellular vectors in models of CNS disease. Neuroepithelial cells integrate in the host more readily than fibroblasts. This feature is an advantage for distributing a soluble ligand more widely in the diseased brain (60) or correcting a general biochemical deficit in the CNS (61).

It is possible to generate many different immortal cell lines from the developing CNS. These cells can express characteristics of stem cells (48, 62), neurons (63, 64), or glia (17, 65). Immortalized neuroepithelial stem cells can show extensive morphological differentiation into neurons when they are grafted into the developing (48, 62) or adult brain (64). The differentiation of genetically labeled immortal cells into neurons when implanted into the adult brain is notable because it hints that neuronal replacement in the adult is not only possible but might become simple. In most cases, immortalization has been achieved by incorporating oncogenes into a primary cell, which is, of course, not advisable for actual clinical use. However, the CRE-loxP system may be useful for removing the immortalizing oncogene before implantation (66).

More recently, the field has shifted away from the use of oncogene-immortalized cells toward the grafting of primary cells expanded in vitro. An example of this development is an experiment suggesting that primary adult cells derived from the hippocampus and cultured for long periods in vitro can still differentiate into neurons when re-implanted into the migratory pathway used to replenish neurons in the adult olfactory bulb (67). Although this field is still technically demanding, these and other results discussed here suggest that further experimental work should be directed at ambitious cell therapies based on both primary and immortal cells derived from the neuroepithelium. Clinical trials show that neuron replacement therapies for neurodegenerative diseases, such as Parkinson's and Huntington's disease, are feasible (68). Neural grafting is currently limited by a number of factors, including the lack of suitable donor material and the full integration of the grafted cells. In vitro expansion and manipulation of cells from the neuroepithelium will provide a range of well-characterized cells for transplant-based strategies for neurodegenerative disease (69). Experimental grafts in animal models suggest that the integration of grafted neurons into the circuitry of the host may be possible (50, 52, 62, 64, 69). Appropriate pretreatment of the host brain may be required for efficient neuronal differentiation by grafted precursors (70). For clinical applications, cell culture offers an important opportunity to use sophisticated genetics in cell-based therapies for neural disease.

The clinical significance of stem cell biology extends beyond cell-based therapies. The dynamics of cell organization is also critically relevant to a systematic understanding of CNS tumors and of physical injury to the brain. Two examples of nestin expression in the adult brain illustrate this point. In addition to being expressed in adult stem cells, nestin is also found in CNS tumors (71) and reactive astrocytes (72). These observations raise the interesting question of the extent of similarity between these nestin-positive cells and CNS stem cells. The proliferation and migration of CNS tumor cells are their two most damaging features. It is tempting to speculate that the self-renewing cell in a CNS tumor is similar to the stem cells found in the fetal and adult CNS.

These examples illustrate the much more general point that there will be a wide clinical impact resulting from increased knowledge of the mechanisms that control the transitions between cell types in the adult CNS. The clear-cut properties of dissociated CNS stem cells in culture show that in vitro technology can be used to define, at the cellular and molecular levels, the steps in fate choice. The presence in the adult of multipotential cells similar to the fetal stem cell emphasizes the importance of extracellular signals acting on stem cells throughout the mammalian life cycle. As our understanding of the nature of these signals grows, therapies will be developed in which the responses of normal and diseased stem cells will be manipulated to clinically useful ends.

REFERENCES AND NOTES

1. R. Wetts and S. E. Fraser, *Science* **239**, 1142 (1988); C. E. Holt, T. W. Bertsch, H. M. Ellis, W. A. Harris, *Neuron* **1**, 15 (1988); D. L. Turner and C. L. Cepko, *Nature* **328**, 131 (1987); J. Price, D. Turner, C. Cepko, *Proc. Natl. Acad. Sci. U.S.A.* **84**, 156 (1987); G. E. Gray, J. C. Glover, J. Majors, J. R. Sanes, *ibid.* **85**, 7356 (1988); M. B. Luskin, A. L. Pearlman, J. R. Sanes, *Neuron* **1**, 635 (1988).
2. J. Till and E. McCulloch, *Proc. Natl. Acad. Sci. U.S.A.* **51**, 29 (1963); G. J. Spangrude, S. Heimfeld, I. L. Weissman, *Science* **241**, 58 (1988); A. Baroffio, E. Dupin, N. M. LeDouarin, *Proc. Natl. Acad. Sci. U.S.A.* **85**, 5325 (1988); M. Bronner-Fraser and S. E. Fraser, *Nature* **335**, 161 (1988); D. L. Stemple and D. J. Anderson, *Cell* **71**, 973 (1992).
3. The subject of stem cells, with particular reference to the nervous system has also been reviewed recently [D. L. Stemple and N. K. Mahanthappa, *Neuron* **18**, 1 (1997); S. J. Morrison, N. M. Shah, D. J. Anderson, *Cell* **88**, 287 (1997)].
4. S. Brenner, *Genetics* **77**, 71 (1974); J. E. Sulston and H. R. Horvitz, *Dev. Biol.* **56**, 110 (1977); J. E. Sulston, J. Schierenberg, J. White, N. Thomson, *ibid.* **100**, 64 (1983).
5. J. B. S. Haldane, *Trans. Oxford Univ. Sci. Club* **1**, 3 (1920); G. W. Beadle and E. L. Tatum, *Proc. Natl. Acad. Sci. U.S.A.* **27**, 499 (1941).
6. K. Goslin, D. J. Schreyer, J. H. Skene, G. Banker, *Nature* **336**, 672 (1988).
7. K. Unsicker *et al.*, *Proc. Natl. Acad. Sci. U.S.A.* **84**, 5459 (1987); C. Gensburger, G. Labourdette, M. Sensenbrenner, *FEBS Lett.* **8**, 1 (1987).
8. U. Lendahl, L. Zimmerman, R. D. McKay, *Cell* **60**, 585 (1990).
9. L. Zimmerman *et al.*, *Neuron* **12**, 11 (1994).
10. K. Frederiksen and R. D. McKay, *J. Neurosci.* **8**, 1144 (1988).
11. E. Cattaneo and R. D. McKay, *Nature* **347**, 762 (1990); J. Ray and F. H. Gage, *J. Neurosci.* **14**, 3548 (1994).
12. K. Frederiksen, P. S. Jat, D. Levy, N. Valtz, R. D McKay, *Neuron* **1**, 439 (1988).
13. B. A. Reynolds and S. Weiss, *Science* **255**, 1707 (1992).
14. J. Ray, D. A. Peterson, M. Schinstine, F. H. Gage, *Proc. Natl. Acad. Sci. U.S.A.* **90**, 3602 (1993); A. L. Vescovi, B. A. Reynolds, D. D. Fraser, S. Weiss, *Neuron* **11**, 951 (1993).
15. S. Temple, *Nature* **340**, 471 (1989); A. A. Davis and S. Temple, *ibid.* **372**, 263 (1994); T. J. Kilpatrick and P. F. Bartlett, *Neuron* **10**, 255 (1993).
16. A. Gritti *et al.*, *J. Neurosci.* **16**, 1091(1996).
17. G. Alamzan and R. D. McKay, *Brain Res.* **579**, 234 (1992).
18. L. J. Richards, T. J. Kilpatrick, P. F. Bartlett, *Proc. Natl. Acad. Sci. U.S.A.* **89**, 8581 (1992); F. H. Gage *et al.*, *ibid.* **92**, 11879 (1995).
19. C. M. Morshead *et al.*, *Neuron* **13**, 1071 (1994).
20. K. K. Johe, T. G. Hazel, T. Muller, M. M. Dugich-Djordjevic, R. D. McKay, *Genes Dev.* **10**, 3129 (1996).
21. C. Vicario-Abejon, K. K. Johe, T. G. Hazel, D. Collazo, R. D. McKay, *Neuron* **15**, 105 (1995).
22. A. Chenn and S. K. McConnell, *Cell* **82**, 631 (1995); W. M. Zhong, J. N. Feder, M. M. Jiang, L. Y. Jan, Y. N. Jan, *Neuron* **17**, 43 (1996).
23. Reviewed in T. Doniach, *Cell* **83**, 1967 (1995); A. Lumsden and R. Krumlauf, *Science* **274**, 1109 (1996).
24. Y. Tanabe and T. M. Jessell, *Science* **274**, 1115 (1996).
25. A. Graham, P. Francis-West, P. Brickell, A. Lumsden, *Nature* **372**, 684 (1994).
26. R. E. Gross *et al.*, *Neuron* **17**, 595 (1996).
27. N. M. Shah, A. K. Groves, D. J. Anderson, *Cell* **85**, 331 (1996).
28. T. Suda, J. Suda, M. Ogawa, *Proc. Natl. Acad. Sci. U.S.A.* **80**, 6689 (1983); M. Ogawa, *Blood* **81**, 2844 (1993).
29. K. A. Wood, B. Dipasquale, R. J. Youle, *Neuron* **11**, 621 (1993); L. Li *et al.*, *Proc. Natl. Acad. Sci. U.S.A.* **92**, 9771 (1995); H. Yaginuma *et al.*, *J. Neurosci.* **16**, 3685 (1996); A. J. Blaschke, K. Staley, J. Chun, *Development* **122**, 1165 (1996).
30. J. M. Frade, A. Rodriguez-Tebar, Y. A. Barde, *Nature* **383**, 166 (1996); T. M. Miller and E. M. Johnson Jr., *J. Neurosci.* **16**, 7487 (1996); J. Ham *et al.*, *Neuron* **14**, 927 (1995); P. Casaccia-Bonnefil, B. D. Carter, R. T. Dobrowsky, M. V. Chao, *Nature* **383**, 716 (1996).
31. N. M. Shah, M. A. Marchionni, I. Isaacs, P. W. Stroobant, D. J. Anderson, *Cell* **77**, 349 (1994).
32. L. E. Lillien, M. Sendtner, H. Rohrer, S. M. Hughes, M. C. Raff, *Neuron* **1**, 485 (1988).
33. M. C. Raff, R. H. Miller, M. Noble, *Nature* **303**, 390 (1983); M. C. Raff, *Science* **243**, 1450 (1989).
34. G. Wolswijk and M. Noble, *Development* **105**, 387 (1989).
35. B. A. Barres, R. Schmid, M. Sendnter, M. C. Raff, *ibid.* **118**, 283 (1993); B. Barres and M. Raff, *Neuron* **12**, 935 (1994); B. A. Barres, M. A. Lazar, M. C. Raff,

Development **120**, 1097 (1994); B. A. Barres *et al.*, *Nature* **367**, 371 (1994).
36. L. E. Lillien, *Nature* **377**, 158 (1995).
37. J. Alder, N. K. Cho, M. E. Hatten, *Neuron* **17**, 389 (1996).
38. G. Bain, D. Kitchens, M. Yao, J. E. Huettner, D. I. Gottlieb, *Dev. Biol.* **168**, 342 (1995); S. Okabe, K. Forsberg-Nilsson, A. C. Spiro, M. Segal, R. D. McKay, *Mech. Dev.* **59**, 89 (1996).
39. S. K. McConnell, *J. Neurosci.* **8**, 945 (1988).
40. G. D. Frantz and S. K. McConnell, *Neuron* **17**, 55 (1996).
41. J. L. Rubenstein and L. Puelles, *Curr. Top. Dev. Biol.* **29**, 1 (1994); J. L. R. Rubenstein, S. Martinez, K. Shimamura, L. Puelles, *Science* **266**, 578 (1994).
42. K. R. Thomas and M. R. Capecchi, *Nature* **346**, 847 (1990); A. P. McMahon and A. Bradley, *Cell* **62**, 1073 (1990); S. Xuan *et al.*, *Neuron* **14**, 1141 (1995).
43. P. H. Crossley, S. Martinez, G. R. Martin, *Nature* **380**, 66 (1996).
44. R. Keynes and A. Lumsden, *Neuron* **4**, 1 (1990).
45. S. Fraser, R. Keynes, A. Lumsden, *Nature* **344**, 431 (1990); S. Guthrie and A. Lumsden, *Development* **112**, 221 (1991); A. Lumsden, J. D. Clarke, R. Keynes, S. Fraser, *ibid.* **120**, 1581 (1994).
46. E. F. Ryder and C. L. Cepko, *Neuron* **12**, 1011 (1994); S. A. Arnold-Aldea and C. L. Cepko, *Dev. Biol.* **173**, 148 (1996); J. A. Golden and C. L. Cepko, *Development* **122**, 65 (1996).
47. A. Grappin-Botton, M. A. Bonnin, L. A. McNaughton, R. Krumlauf, N. M. Le Douarin, *Development* **121**, 2707 (1995).
48. P. Renfranz, M. Cunningham, R. D. McKay, *Cell* **66**, 713 (1991).
49. G. Fishell, *Development* **121**, 803 (1995).
50. C. Vicario-Abejon, M. G. Cunningham, R. D. McKay, *J. Neurosci.* **15**, 6351 (1995).
51. K. Campbell, M. Olsson, A. Bjorklund, *Neuron* **15**, 1259 (1995).
52. O. Brustle, U. Maskos, R. D. McKay, *ibid.*, p. 1275.
53. J. Altman , *J. Comp. Neurol.* **137**, 433 (1969); S. Goldman and F. Nottebohm, *Proc. Natl. Acad. Sci. U.S.A.* **80**, 2390 (1983); M. S. Kaplan, N. A. McNelly, J. W. Hinds, *J. Comp. Neurol.* **239**, 117 (1985).
54. C. Lois and A. Alvarez-Buylla, *Proc. Natl. Acad. Sci. U.S.A.* **90**, 2074 (1993); M. B. Luskin, *Neuron* **11**, 173 (1993); H. A. Cameron, C. S. Wooley, B. S. McEwen, E. Gould, *Neuroscience* **56**, 337 (1993); C. Lois and A. Alvarez-Buylla, *Science* **264**, 1145 (1994).
55. T. D. Palmer, J. Ray, F. H. Gage, *Mol. Cell. Neurosci.* **6**, 474 (1995); J. Ray *et al.*, in *Isolation, Characterization and Utilization of CNS Stem Cells*, F. H. Gage and Y. Christen, Eds. (Springer, Berlin, 1996), pp. 129–150.
56. C. M. Morshead and D. Van der Kooy, *J. Neurosci.* **12**, 249 (1992); T. Seki and S. Arai, *Neuroreport* **6**, 2479 (1995); H. G. Kuhn, H. Dickinson-Anson, F. H. Gage, *J. Neurosci.* **16**, 2027 (1996).
57. C. G. Craig *et al.*, *J. Neurosci.* **16**, 2649 (1996).
58. I. L. Weissman, in *Isolation, Characterization and Utilization of CNS Stem Cells*, F. H. Gage and Y. Christen, Eds. (Springer, Berlin, 1996), pp. 1–8. This volume contains more extensive discussion of many topics that can only be briefly considered here.
59. These references illustrate this point by reference to the discovery and use of GDNF: A. Beck *et al.*, *Nature* **373**, 339 (1995); A. Tomac *et al.*, *ibid.*, p. 335; M. W. Moore *et al.*, *ibid.* **382**, 76 (1996).
60. A. Martinez-Serrano, W. Fischer, A. Bjorklund, *Neuron* **15**, 473 (1995); A. Martinez-Serrano *et al.*, *J. Neurosci.* **15**, 5668 (1995); A. Martinez-Serrano and A. Bjorklund, *ibid.* **16**, 4604 (1996); A. Martinez-Serrano, W. Fischer, S. Soderstrom, T. Ebendal, A. Bjorklund, *Proc. Natl. Acad. Sci. U.S.A.* **93**, 6355 (1996).
61. E. Y. Snyder, R. M. Taylor, J. H. Wolfe, *Nature* **374**, 367 (1995); J. H. Wolfe *et al.*, *Gene Ther.* **1** (suppl. 1), S55 (1994).
62. E. Y. Snyder *et al.*, *Cell* **68**, 33 (1992). The application of immortalized cells in neurobiology is reviewed in S. R. Whittemore and E. Y. Snyder, *Mol. Neurobiol.* **12**, 13 (1996).
63. L. A. White *et al.*, *J. Neurosci.* **14**, 6744 (1994); J. S. Rudge, M. J. Eaton, P. Mather, R. M. Lindsay, S. R. Whittemore, *Mol. Cell. Neurosci.* **7**, 204 (1996).
64. L. S. Shihabuddin, J. A. Hertz, V. R. Holets, S. R. Whittemore, *J. Neurosci.* **15**, 6666 (1995).
65. J. C. Louis, E. Magal, D. Muir, M. Manthorpe, S. Varon, *J. Neurosci. Res.* **31**, 193 (1992); J.-C. Louis, E. Magal, S. Takayama, S. Varon, *Science* **259**, 689 (1993); J. Trotter, A. J. Crang, M. Schanchner, W. F. Blakemore, *Glia* **9**, 25 (1993).
66. K. A. Westerman and P. Leboulch, *Proc. Natl. Acad. Sci. U.S.A.* **93**, 8971 (1996).
67. J. O. Suhonen, D. A. Peterson, J. Ray, F. H. Gage, *Nature* **383**, 624 (1996).
68. O. Lindvall, in *Functional Neural Transplantation*, B. Dunnett and A. Bjorklund, Eds. (Raven, New York, 1993); O. Lindvall *et al.*, *Ann. Neurol.* **35**, 172 (1994); J. H. Kordower *et al.*, *N. Engl. J. Med.* **332**, 1118 (1995).
69. In addition to the several examples cited above, there have been several important studies that illustrate the use of in vitro manipulated donor cells that differentiate in vivo into oligodendrocytes: U. Tonsch, D. R. Archer, M. Dubois-Dalcq, I. D. Duncan, *Proc. Natl. Acad. Sci. U.S.A.* **91**, 11616 (1994); A. K. Groves *et al.*, *Nature* **362**, 453 (1993).
70. C. S. Hernit-Grant and J. D. Macklis, *Exp. Neurol.* **139**, 131 (1996); J. D. Macklis, *J. Neurosci.* **13**, 3848 (1993).
71. T. Valtz, T. Norregaard, T. Hayes, S. Liu, R. D. McKay, *New Biol.* **3**, 364 (1991); J. Dahlstrand, V. P. Collins, U. Lendahl, *Cancer Res.* **52**, 5334 (1992); V. A. Florenes, R. Holm, O. Myklebost, U. Lendahl, O. Fodstad, *ibid.* **54**, 354 (1994); O. Brustle and R. D. McKay, *J. Neuro-oncology* **24**, 57 (1995).
72. S. R. Clarke, A. K. Shetty, J. L. Bradley, D. A. Turner, *Neuroreport* **5**, 1885 (1994); R. C. Lin, D. F. Matesic, M. Marvin, R. D. McKay, O. Brustle, *Neurobiol. Dis.* **2**, 79 (1995); J. Frisen, C. B. Johansson, C. Torok, M. Risling, U. Lendahl, *J. Cell Biol.* **131**, 453 (1995).
73. I thank the members of the Laboratory of Molecular Biology and S. Landis for their comments. Thanks also to Cell Press and Cold Spring Harbor Laboratory Press for permission to reproduce data.

Why Oligodendrocytes Die in Spinal Cord Injury

BY JOHN W. MCDONALD, M.D., PH.D., AND DENNIS W. CHOI, M.D., PH.D.

We have been studying the mechanisms underlying spinal cord damage after traumatic insults, in the hope of contributing to the development of new treatments. We have recently identified a new mechanism that may help explain why certain cells, called oligodendrocytes, die after spinal cord trauma.

Oligodendrocytes are a class of supportive cells (glia) in the brain and spinal cord; they are responsible for insulating nerve cells with a substance called myelin. Like the plastic insulation that surrounds electrical wires, myelin forms a sheath around nerve cell projections (axons), permitting the axons to pass nerve impulses over long distances, such as the distance from the brain to spinal cord neurons in the lower back.

Trauma to the spinal cord can disrupt axons, blocking this flow of signals downward from brain to the periphery to control muscle movements, or upward from the periphery to the brain to convey sensory information. However, there is evidence that some nerve impulses may be lost, not because axons are physically disrupted, but because oligodendrocytes die and axon myelin is lost. Thus achieving the preservation of oligodendrocytes, both after initial injury, and perhaps in the future after restorative manipulations, may be a prerequisite for optimal functional recovery.

Working together with another researcher at Washington University, Dr. Mark Goldberg, we found that oligodendrocytes can be killed by a substance called glutamate. Glutamate is used routinely as a chemical messenger by nerve cells in the brain and spinal cord; however, after brain injury, glutamate is released in large amounts. When this occurs, it can become toxic to nerve cells by overstimulating docking proteins (glutamate receptors) on the outside of the cells — a process called excitotoxicity. Excessive glutamate receptor activation opens pores in the cells' surface membranes, causing a rapid influx of calcium into cells. A sustained rise in intracellular calcium triggers a cascade of molecular events that disrupt normal processes and lead to cell death.

The prevailing view of excitotoxicity is that nerve cells alone are vulnerable to being killed by glutamate. However, recent evidence indicates that oligodendrocytes also have the docking proteins for glutamate, called AMPA receptors. The normal function of these AMPA receptors on oligodendrocytes is unclear. By examining the effect of exposure to glutamate or similar compounds on oligodendrocytes grown in cultures from mouse brain, we tested the possibility that overactivation of oligodendrocytes' own AMPA receptors could lead to the fatal injury of these cells. Surprisingly, exposure to low levels of glutamate or other compounds that activate AMPA receptors produced rapid oligodendrocyte swelling, followed by death 24 hours later. Drugs that prevented the activation of AMPA glutamate receptors blocked this oligodendrocyte death.

Lastly, we predicted that, if glutamate excitotoxicity is indeed an important mechanism of oligodendrocyte death, then excitotoxic oligodendrocyte death would also occur if cells were deprived of nutrients and oxygen (as occurs after a stroke or after trauma), since glutamate levels rise outside cells in this condition. In fact, oligodendrocytes were as vulnerable to death induced by oxygen-glucose deprivation as neurons, and again this oligodendrocyte death could be blocked by drugs that prevented AMPA receptor activation.

Achieving the preservation of oligodendrocytes may be a prerequisite for optimal functional recovery.

Therefore, oligodendrocytes may share with neurons the property of a high vulnerability to glutamate excitotoxicity. Our observations suggest that oligodendrocytes may die, at least in part, an excitotoxic death after spinal cord insults. This raises the intriguing possibility that drugs capable of blocking glutamate toxicity may be useful in preserving oligodendrocytes — and therefore possibly nerve axon myelin — after such insults. Since only 5 to 10 percent of spinal cord axons are required for movement, functional preservation of a small subset of axons may translate into important changes in functional recovery.

Prevention of oligodendrocyte death may also lessen later damage to bare axons, denuded of their protective myelin sheath. Finally, it is possible that preservation of oligodendrocytes might help facilitate new axonal regeneration, by maintaining a scaffolding that could guide new axons as they grow in. We hope that these and other studies of the mechanisms underlying spinal cord injury will lead to the development of more effective treatments for the human condition.

John McDonald is Instructor, Neurology, at Washington University in St. Louis; Dennis Choi is Andrew B. and Gretchen P. Jones Professor and Neurologist-in-Chief at Barnes Hospital, St. Louis.

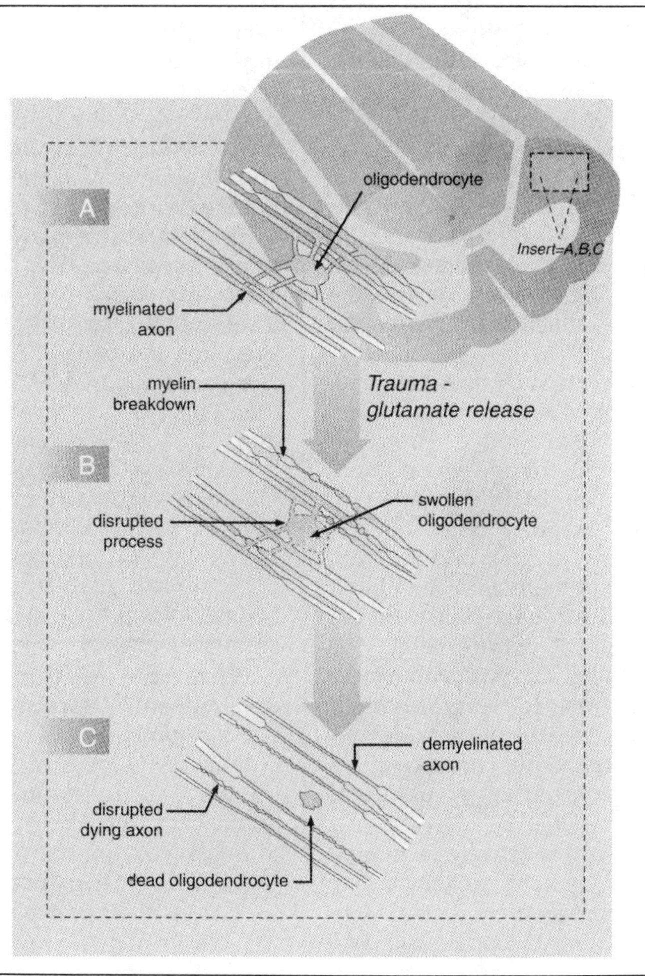

How glutamate-induced death of oligodendrocytes seems to occur in spinal cord trauma: **(A)** *Normal spinal cord white matter. The lines represent myelinated axons running parallel along the length of the spinal cord. The cell is an oligodendrocyte with several processes that are simultaneously ensheathing multiple axons.* **(B)** *Initial phase of spinal cord trauma, which induces the toxic accumulation of glutamate that overstimulates AMPA receptors on the surface of oligodendrocytes, producing massive influx of ions and cell swelling. Excessive calcium influx orchestrates a cascade of molecular events that lead to oligodendrocyte death.* **(C)** *Oligodendrocyte death causes demyelination and dysfunction of neuronal axons. Demyelination may also render "nude" axons more vulnerable to secondary injury from later inflammatory changes.*

Neural Development and Plasticity

Brain development follows a pattern similar to that of other organs of the body: it starts relatively small at conception, then gradually increases in size as the individual grows older. The human brain weighs about 400 grams at birth and up to 1,400 grams at maturity. It is tempting to correlate the progress in brain size with changes in cognitive functions. After all, infants possessing smaller brains exhibit elementary forms of intelligence, whereas adults with larger brains are capable of processing complex cognitive concepts.

Brain size alone, however, cannot account for differences in cognitive abilities. Dolphins have somewhat larger brains than humans relative to body size. These animals acquired the larger brains much earlier in the course of evolution than humans. In spite of their larger brain size, the cognitive abilities of dolphins obviously do not approximate that of humans. Furthermore, wild species of animals have larger brains than their domestic counterparts, as in the case of wildcats versus domestic cats, but the difference in brain size cannot account for quantitative differences in their cognitive abilities. Other factors besides brain size must be relevant during the course of development that can influence the formation of cognitive abilities.

Brain development includes events such as neurogenesis, division of neuronal precursor cells; migration of precursor cells to target areas; differentiation of precursor cells into neurons; and formation of synapses among neurons. The neurons in the mammalian brain are unique in development compared to cells in other organs of the body. As a general rule, neurons do not undergo cell division after birth. The tendency of the mammalian brain is to lose these neurons by cell death later in life. By the time a person reaches the age of 75, approximately 100 grams of brain tissue is gone. There are, however, exceptions to the rule. Some precursor cells to neurons present in an adult mammalian brain are capable of neurogenesis when placed in a suitable environment. These cells are also capable of migration to designated target areas and of differentiating into neurons.

During brain development, neurons actively form connections or synapses with other neurons so that a tiny neuron can possibly receive approximately 15,000 synapses. The extension of arm-like axons to bodies and dendrites of other neurons to make a synapse is not a random process, but a calculated mechanism. Neurons are believed to be instructed by the genes when forming synapses. Compounds present in the environment of neurons, such as the neurotrophic factors, can also direct synapse formation. The same factors are necessary for the survival of neurons.

In spite of the sophisticated internal programming of neuronal development, extraneous factors can significantly influence the course of brain development. Exposure to psychoactive substances such as alcohol, nicotine, and opiates during development adversely affects the development of certain brain structures. Damage to the morphology of the brain often translates as deficiencies in cognitive functioning. Some children exposed to crack cocaine while still in the mother's womb are born with physical deformities and grow up retarded intellectually. Thus it appears that the normal development of the brain requires a proper set of experiences as early as infancy.

The remarkable plasticity of the brain can be exploited to our advantage. This is exemplified by a group of nuns living in a convent in Minnesota. The group is unique in a sense that these nuns tend to live longer and healthier lives than the general population. The average age in the convent is 85, and of the 150 retired nuns, 25 are older than 90. The incidence of Alzheimer's disease among the nuns is also lower than that of the general population of the same age group. The secret, they declare, is to expose the mind to constant challenges. The nuns regularly write spiritual meditations, keep in touch with current world events, and do puzzles to stimulate the mind.

Looking Ahead: Challenge Questions

What is the significance of neurotrophic factors in brain development? Describe some of these factors. What are some of their possible clinical uses?

Discuss the role of the genes in the development of the brain. Can early infancy experiences affect the development of the brain and its cognitive ability? If so, through what mechanisms?

Do you believe that drugs can enhance memory? If so, discuss their possible mechanisms. If not, explain why you disagree.

UNIT 3

Neurotrophins and the Neurotrophic Factor Hypothesis

Eric C. Yuen, Yiwen Li, Rebecca E. Mischel, Charles L. Howe, David M. Holtzman and William C. Mobley*
Departments of Neurology, Pediatrics and the Neurosciences Program, University of California, San Francisco

Introduction

Neurotrophic factors are polypeptides that support the growth, differentiation and survival of neurons in the developing nervous system and maintain neurons in the mature nervous system (1,2). Recent data support the view that some neurotrophic factors also may be involved in the modification of neuronal connections in the developing brain (3). Though certain neurotrophic factors act predominantly on neurons, others affect both neuronal and non-neuronal cells. In recent years, a number of neurotrophic factors have been identified. A partial listing of these factors is provided in Table 1.

Neurotrophins are an important family of neurotrophic factors. Nerve growth factor (NGF) was the first neurotrophin discovered and is the best characterized member of this family. Other neurotrophins include brain-derived neurotrophic factor (BDNF), neurotrophin-3 (NT-3), and neurotrophin-4/5 (NT-4/5) (2). These molecules exert their effects by binding to and activating specific cell surface receptors of the Trk gene family. Activated receptors initiate a cascade of intracellular events, which ultimately induce gene expression and modify neuronal morphology and function. This article addresses primarily the expression and actions of neurotrophins and their receptors.

The *Neurotrophic Factor Hypothesis*

NGF was discovered during early investigations of the interaction between developing neural centers (i.e., ganglia or neuronal nuclei) and their targets of innervation. By the late 1940s, it was known that modifying the size of the target had a marked effect on the size of the corresponding neural center. Thus, removing a limb resulted in hypoplasia of the developing neural center, whereas transplanting an extra limb produced hyperplasia (4). Hamburger and Levi-Montalcini discovered that cell death occurred normally during neuronal development and that the hypoplasia of neural centers following limb bud extirpation was associated with increased degeneration of cells in the centers that would normally supply the extirpated limb. Significantly, during normal development, neurons died at the time that their processes entered the target. These studies were important because they identified the target as playing a key role in neuronal development. Moreover, these studies suggest that the target determines the size of its neural center by regulating cell death among neurons. To explain these data, Hamburger and Levi-Montalcini proposed a "metabolic exchange between the neurite and the substrate in which it grows" (4). The nature of this "metabolic exchange" was eventually demonstrated in experiments in which a very large and relatively homogeneous target was created by implanting mouse sarcoma fragments into the body wall of chick embryos. Confirming earlier studies by Bueker (1948), Levi-Montalcini and Hamburger discovered enlargement of dorsal root sensory ganglia (DRGs) and sympathetic ganglia with no increase in the growth of motor neurons. Importantly, they noted marked ganglion hyperplasia—including ganglia distant from the tumor—and abnormal innervation of certain viscera (5,6). These findings suggested that the neoplastic cells released a soluble, diffusible agent that acted on sympathetic and sensory neurons. The putative factor was named nerve growth factor. Subsequent studies showed that when DRGs or sympathetic ganglia were explanted *in vitro* adjacent to the mouse sarcoma, a halo of outgrowing nerve fibers developed (7). This *in vitro* bioassay was instrumental in the eventual purification of NGF (8,9). In recent

Table 1. Partial Listing of Neurotrophic Factors

FAMILY	MEMBER	SIGNALING RECEPTOR
Neurotrophins	Nerve growth factor (NGF)	TrkA
	Brain-derived neurotrophic factor (BDNF)	TrkB
	Neurotrophin-3 (NT-3)	TrkC, less so TrkA and TrkB
	Neurotrophin-4/5 (NT-4/5)	TrkB
Neuropoietins	Ciliary neurotrophic factor (CNTF)	CNTF receptor complex (CNTFRα, gp130, LIFRβ subunits)
	Leukemia inhibitory factor (LIF or CDF/LIF)	LIF receptor complex (gp130, LIFRβ subunits)
Insulin-like growth factors	Insulin-like growth factor-I (IGF-I)	IGF Type I receptor (IGF1R), less so insulin receptor (IR)
	Insulin-like growth factor-II (IGF-II)	IGF1R, less so IR
Transforming growth factor beta	Transforming growth factor β ($TGF\beta_1$, $TGF\beta_2$, $TGF\beta_3$)	TGFβ type I, II and III receptors
	Glial cell line-derived neurotrophic factor (GDNF)	Unknown
Fibroblast growth factors	Acidic fibroblast growth factor (aFGF or FGF-1)	FGF receptors 1–4 (FGFR-1–4)
	Basic fibroblast growth factor (bFGF or FGF-2)	FGFR-1–3
	Fibroblast growth factor-5 (FGF-5)	FGFR-1, FGFR-2
Other growth factors	Transforming growth factor alpha (TGF-α)	EGFR
	Platelet-derived growth factor (PDGF: AA, AB and BB isoforms)	PDGF α- and β-receptors
	Stem cell factor (mast cell growth factor)	c-kit

years, highly purified NGF has made possible many studies to examine its structure and actions, and to identify its receptors. Over the past 45 years, these studies have confirmed the findings of Levi-Montalcini and Hamburger and extended considerably our understanding of NGF actions on the survival, differentiation and growth of specific neurons.

The discovery of NGF was instrumental to the formulation of the *Neurotrophic Factor Hypothesis,* which postulates that *...once a developing neuron has grown its process into its target, it competes with other developing neurons of the same type for a limited supply of a neurotrophic factor provided by the target.* Successful competitors survive; unsuccessful ones die. Under this hypothesis, a neurotrophic factor should be diffusible and act on specific cell surface receptors localized on the processes of innervating neurons. It also predicts that a neurotrophic factor(s) will be present at a concentration lower than that necessary to maintain the viability of all innervating neurons. Logical extensions of the hypothesis are that: i) the target would produce one or only a limited number of neurotrophic factors for each innervating population; ii) correspondingly, there would be a specific neurotrophic factor for each neuronal population, raising the possibility that literally thousands of such factors would exist to act on the many thousands of different neuronal populations in the nervous system; iii) neurons would be the only cells to respond to a neurotrophic factor; and iv) like survival, measures of neuronal differentiation also would be regulated by limiting concentrations of neurotrophic factors. Although important aspects of neurotrophic factors and their signaling biology were accurately predicted by the *Neurotrophic Factor Hypothesis,* there is considerably more complexity and diversity than was initially anticipated.

Complexity and Diversity in Neurotrophic Factor Expression and Actions

The discovery of a number of neurotrophic factors has considerably broadened our concepts about the actions of such factors. In a significant departure from the original *Neurotrophic Factor Hypothesis,* factors can act on non-neuronal as well as neuronal cells. Even for the neurotrophins, whose actions are relatively restricted to neurons, much was not predicted by the hypothesis. For example, recent studies on the expression and actions of neurotrophins indicate that, in addition to target-derived factor acquisition, autocrine and non-target-derived paracrine modes of neurotrophin presentation are likely to be important (10) (Figure 1). BDNF has been shown to participate in an autocrine loop in adult DRGs (11). In addition, BDNF and NT-3 may serve an autocrine or paracrine role in the hippocampus, where neurons appear to produce mRNAs for BDNF and NT-3, as well as for their respective receptors, TrkB and TrkC (12-14). In fact, certain hippocampal neurons contain both BDNF and TrkB mRNA (15). In that exogenous BDNF induces *c-fos* in cultured hippocampal pyramidal and dentate granule cells (16), BDNF does appear to act on these neurons. Adding to the complexity is the possibility that hippocampal neurons produce BDNF to act on innervating basal forebrain cholinergic neurons. These neurons contain TrkB mRNA (13); and BDNF increases choline acetyltransferase (ChAT) activity in these cells (17). It is intriguing that an individual neuron may produce

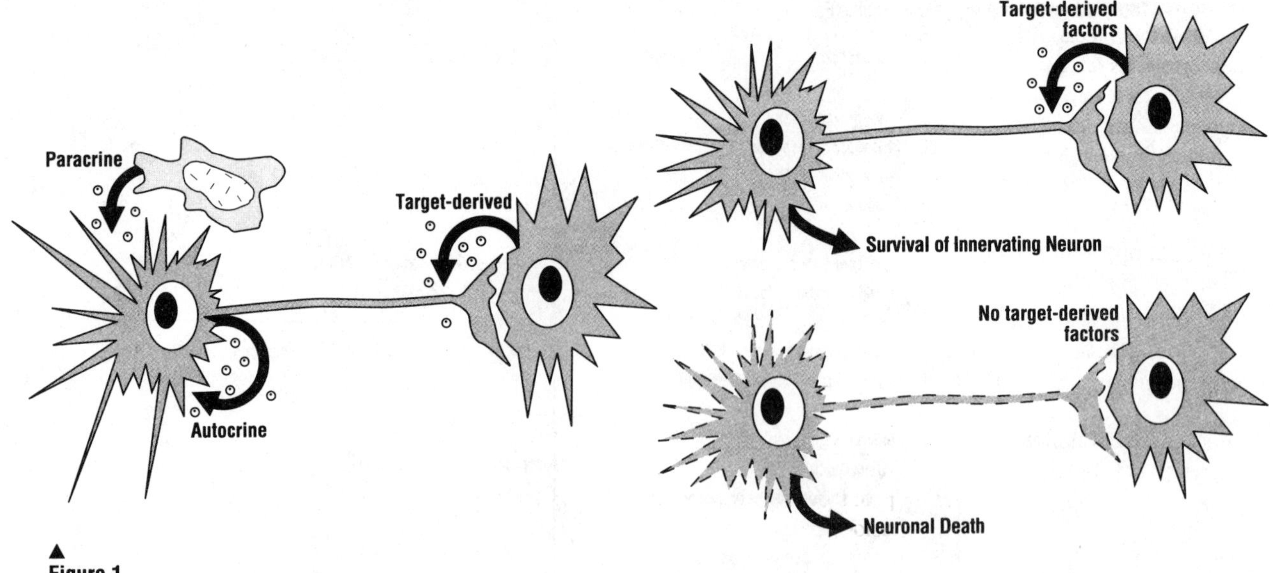

Figure 1.

Target-derived, autocrine and paracrine modes of neurotrophin presentation. At right, the survival of an innervating neuron is shown to be dependent on target-derived neurotrophic factors.

neurotrophins to engage in both local and target-derived relationships. Clearly, there is much to learn about *in vivo* neurotrophin presentation.

In another departure from the original *Neurotrophic Factor Hypothesis*, it appears that a given population of neurons can respond to many different neurotrophic factors. For example, motor neurons respond to at least 13 different factors (18). How many of these have a physiological role in enhancing survival is not certain. If no single factor does, then it is possible that factors do not act alone to control neuron survival. In contrast, if individual factors do enhance survival, this will suggest that the level of several factors acting together determines whether motor neurons live or die. An interesting correlate to the finding that a single population of neurons responds to many neurotrophic factors is data that demonstrates that a single factor can act on many different neuronal populations. NGF, for example, acts on DRG sensory and sympathetic neurons in the peripheral nervous system and at least nine distinct CNS populations (19). Thus, it appears that the survival and differentiation of neurons may, in many instances, involve the collaboration of several neurotrophic factors. The expectation that thousands of neurotrophic factors are used to direct the development of an equally large number of neuronal populations may be incorrect. Rather, it is likely that precise combinations of a relatively limited number of factors may be important in regulating neuronal development and survival.

Diversity also is apparent in the receptors activated by neurotrophic factors. For example, the neurotrophins have two receptors. Each of the neurotrophins binds to $p75^{NTR}$ (low affinity neurotrophin receptor) and to a member(s) of the Trk gene family. $p75^{NTR}$ is a single transmembrane glycoprotein that has a role in modulating neurotrophin signaling through Trk receptors (2). The members of the Trk family are TrkA, TrkB, and TrkC. Each is a receptor tyrosine kinase with a preferred neurotrophin ligand (i.e., NGF binds TrkA, BDNF and NT-4/5 bind TrkB, and NT-3 binds TrkC). Nevertheless, some crosstalk may occur—in the case of NT-3, TrkA and TrkB receptors also can be activated (3). Further documenting receptor diversity, a number of isoforms of TrkB and TrkC exist that lack the tyrosine kinase domain or contain inserts in the intracellular domain which influence signaling (2,14).

Recently, it has become apparent that the actions of neurotrophic factors are not restricted to developing post-mitotic neurons. Indeed, these factors can act on dividing neuroblasts as well as mature neurons that have established stable synaptic contacts. For example, NT-3 enhances the survival of dividing sympathetic neuroblasts as well as young sympathetic neurons (20). Mature sympathetic neurons subsequently switch their survival dependence to NGF. This change correlates with a switch in neurotrophin receptor expression from TrkC to TrkA. Thus, the development of certain neuronal populations appears to require the sequential actions of multiple neurotrophins (21). With respect to a role for NGF in mature neurons, local infusion of NGF antibodies into the rat footpad produced a reduction in axonal diameter and neurofilament levels and an increase in the number of neurons with eccentric nuclei in lumbar DRG neurons. Finally, in a line of investigation that was not predicted by the original *Neurotrophic Factor Hypothesis* but followed logically from it, the neurotrophins have been shown to protect against neuronal dysfunction and death in animal models of injury and neurologic disease (18). These data raise the exciting possibility that neurotrophins may act to protect neurons in diseased as well as normal neurons.

The *Neurotrophic Factor Hypothesis* addresses the role of neurotrophic factors in enhancing the survival of developing neurons. In addition to this important function, recent data point to a role for neurotrophins in regulating reinforcement of synapses in the developing cortex (reviewed in reference 3). The development of visual cortex is changed significantly by the administration of exogenous neurotrophins (22,23) or by reagents that sequester them (24-26). These new data give exciting hints to neurotrophin involvement in modifying the structure and function of synaptic connections, a role not anticipated by the original *Neurotrophic Factor Hypothesis.*

NGF actions in the CNS: NGF and Basal Forebrain Cholinergic Neurons

The discussion above describes the potential complexity of neurotrophic relationships. It follows that simply documenting expression of a neurotrophic factor and its receptor does not prove the existence of such a relationship. In fact, although neurotrophins and their receptors are widely expressed in the CNS, relatively little data exists for the physiological significance of neurotrophin signaling in CNS neurons. Approaches to define a physiological role for these factors include: i) documenting localization of gene expression; ii) characterizing regulation of gene expression; iii) demonstrating the effect of a given neurotrophin on a specific population of neurons *in vitro* and *in vivo*; iv) examining the effect of giving antibodies to sequester a neurotrophin; and v) evaluating the result of disrupting the gene for the neurotrophin or its receptors. Studies in the CNS have been most informative for NGF. Most NGF actions appear to be mediated by TrkA. NGF acts on a number of forebrain and brainstem neurons (19), but most attention has been focused on basal forebrain cholinergic neurons (BFCNs). These projection neurons send their axons to innervate the hippocampus and neocortex (Figure 2) and play a role in learning, memory and attention (27). Several lines of evidence have suggested that NGF is a target-derived neurotrophic factor for developing BFCNs. NGF is produced in the hippocampus and neocortex (12, 28-32). Exogenous NGF enhances the neurochemical differentiation of BFCNs, inducing expression of a number of developmentally regulated genes (33-35). There is close temporal correspondence during development between endogenous NGF levels in the hippocampus and neocortex and the activity in the basal forebrain of ChAT, the specific cholinergic neurotransmitter synthetic enzyme (36,37). Recent studies demonstrated that TrkA is expressed in these cells and that the pattern during development of the regulation of the *trk*A gene was very similar to that for ChAT (35). Three lines of evidence were developed to support the view that NGF acts to regulate the differentiation of BFCNs. First, NGF injections induced activation of TrkA in the developing basal forebrain. Second, exogenous NGF induced an increase in both TrkA and ChAT mRNA levels and in the size of BFCNs. Third, administration of specific anti-NGF antibodies decreased expression for both genes and suppressed the normal developmental increase in BFCN cell size (35). These findings indicate that NGF is a neurotrophic factor for developing BFCNs. Disruption of the genes for NGF and TrkA provided results consistent with these findings. In the case of NGF gene disruption, BFCNs were present but were smaller and more lightly immunostained for ChAT (38). BFCNs were also present

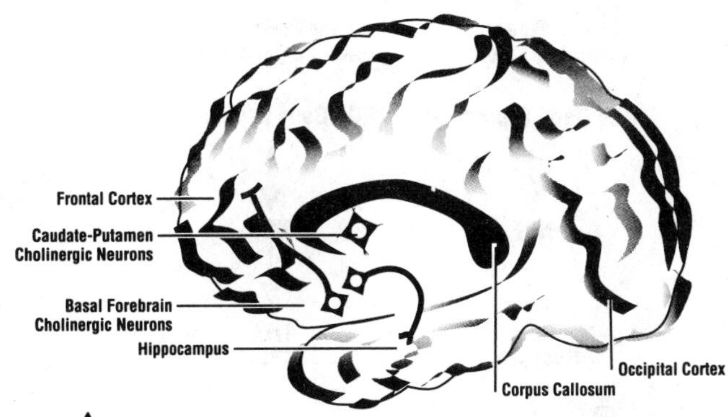

Figure 2.

Schematic of basal forebrain and caudate-putamen cholinergic neurons. Basal forebrain cholinergic neurons are projection neurons; they send their axons to innervate the hippocampus and neocortex. These cells play a role in learning, memory and attention. Caudate-putamen cholinergic neurons, on the other hand, are interneurons that are involved in controlling movement.

following *trk*A gene disruption but demonstrated decreased staining for acetylcholinesterase in the hippocampus and cortex (39). These results provide strong evidence that endogenous NGF acts on developing BFCNs to enhance gene expression and cellular differentiation.

NGF and Caudate-putamen Cholinergic Neurons

NGF also acts on developing caudate-putamen cholinergic neurons (CPCNs) which play an important role in the control of movement. Unlike BFCNs, CPCNs are interneurons and their axons ramify entirely within the caudate-putamen. Therefore, the caudate-putamen not only contains cholinergic neurons, it also serves as their target (40). In earlier studies, it was shown that NGF is produced in the developing caudate-putamen and that exogenous NGF enhances neurochemical differentiation of these cells. Interestingly, and distinct from the findings on BFCNs, it was discovered that the level of endogenous NGF was poorly correlated with differentiation of CPCNs. Rather, the amount of NGF binding to high-affinity receptor was correlated (41). In recent studies, we have extended the analysis to show that: i) TrkA expression is localized in developing CPCNs; ii) TrkA mRNA and protein are present throughout the postnatal period; iii) TrkA can be activated by NGF during the postnatal period; and iv) TrkA and ChAT gene expression are well correlated with each other and with the increase in neuron size that occurs during the postnatal period. The latter findings suggested the possibility that gene expression for TrkA and ChAT and neuron size were regulated by the same factor(s). NGF is known to increase ChAT and TrkA mRNA and to increase the size of these neurons in adult animals (42). We asked if NGF would produce similar changes in developing CPCNs. We found that exogenous NGF upregulated the expression of ChAT. Also, NGF induced hypertrophy of TrkA positive cells in the caudate-putamen and modestly increased the level of TrkA mRNA. However, as indicated, NGF levels in the developing caudate-putamen were not correlated with differentiation. Thus, the significance of studies examining exogenous NGF is unclear. To address whether endogenous NGF regulated CPCN differentia-

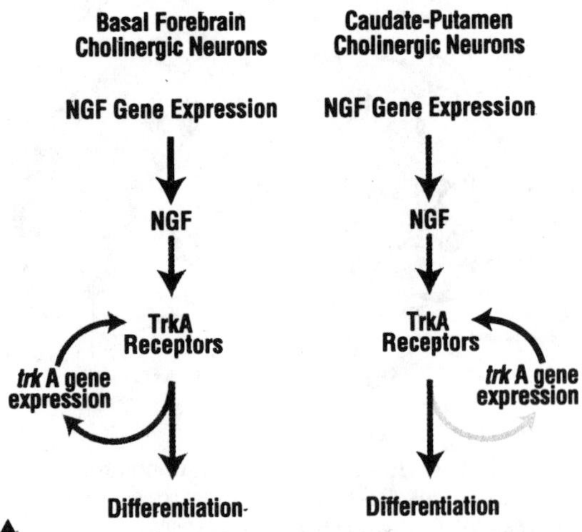

Figure 3.

Different levels of regulation in basal forebrain and caudate-putamen cholinergic neurons. The primary regulatory step is each pathway is represented with a dark arrow.

tion, we examined the size of these neurons in animals in which one copy of the NGF gene was disrupted. There was no difference. Remarkably, there was a clear difference in the size of BFCNs in the same animals. Given the tight linkage of *trk*A and ChAT gene expression, we next asked whether TrkA was critical for CPCN differentiation; in animals in which the *trk*A gene was disrupted, the CPCNs were clearly smaller. This result indicates that TrkA expression is critical for normal CPCN development. Since NGF is the most likely neurotrophin to act through TrkA to enhance CPCN development, NGF is important as well. However, the data suggests that CPCN differentiation is determined by the level of TrkA receptors and not by the NGF level.

Neuronal Differentiation—Controls at Many Levels

Studies on BFCNs and CPCNs suggest that the actions of neurotrophins and their receptors can be regulated at two or more levels (Figure 3). In one case, as in the case of BFCNs, it is the level of the factor that dictates downstream events. Regulation of differentiation is controlled by the availability and the concentration of the neurotrophin. This logical extension of the *Neurotrophic Factor Hypothesis* emphasizes target availability of the neurotrophin. In the second case, it is the receptor whose level of expression regulates subsequent events. Significantly, a factor(s) other than the neurotrophin regulates receptor expression. The identity of this other factor is yet to be discovered. However, it is possible that another target-derived neurotrophic factor is responsible. Assuming that TrkA is not a receptor for this factor, this would be an example of neurotrophic factor crosstalk, wherein one such factor prepares a neuron to respond to another factor. In the case of CPCNs, NGF must be present to activate the receptor, but its absolute level is unimportant. Such regulation at the level of the receptor for a neurotrophic factor is a clear departure from the original *Neurotrophic Factor Hypothesis*. It is noteworthy that BFCNs are projection neurons and CPCNs are interneurons. Perhaps different levels of regulation are appropriate for neurons with different physiological roles.

Conclusion

The discovery of NGF and the formulation of the *Neurotrophic Factor Hypothesis* have been extraordinarily important in directing efforts at discovering neurotrophic factors and characterizing their actions. As our knowledge increases, it is apparent that there is considerable diversity and complexity in neurotrophic relationships. Future efforts are likely to expand on these themes. It is hoped that they will provide us with important new insights for understanding the development and maintenance of the nervous system and in treating neurological diseases.

References

1. Longo, F.M. *et al.* (1993) In: *Neurotrophic Factors*, Fallon, J. and Loughlin, S., eds., Academic Press, 209.
2. Bothwell, M. (1995) *Annu. Rev. Neurosci.* **18**, 223.
3. Thoenen, H. (1995) *Science* **270**, 593.
4. Hamburger, V. and Levi-Montalcini, R. (1949) *J. Exp. Zool.* **111**, 457.
5. Levi-Montalcini, R. and Hamburger, V. (1951) *J. Exp. Zool.* **116**, 321.
6. Levi-Montalcini, R. (1987) *Science* **237**, 1154.
7. Levi-Montalcini, R. and Hamburger, V. (1953) *J. Exp. Zool.* **123**, 233.
8. Cohen, S. and Levi-Montalcini, R. (1956) *Proc. Natl. Acad. Sci. USA* **42**, 571.
9. Cohen, S. (1960) *Proc. Natl. Acad. Sci. USA* **46**, 302.
10. Schecterson, L.C. and Bothwell, M. (1992) *Neuron* **9**, 449.
11. Acheson, A. *et al.* (1995) *Nature* **374**, 450.
12. Phillips, H.S. *et al.* (1990) *Science* **250**, 290.
13. Merlio, J.P. *et al.* (1992) *Neurosci.* **51**, 513.
14. Barbacid, M. (1994) *J. Neurobiol.* **25**, 1386.
15. Kokaia, Z. *et al.* (1993) *Proc. Natl. Acad. Sci. USA* **90**, 6711.
16. Collazo, D., Takahashi, H. and McKay, R.D. (1992) *Neuron* **9**, 643
17. Alderson, R.F. *et al.* (1990) *Neuron* **5**, 297.
18. Yuen, E.C. and Mobley, W C. (1995) *Mol. Med. Today* **1**, 278.
19. Holtzman, D.M. *et al.* (1995) *J. Neurosci.* **15**, 1567.
20. DiCicco-Bloom, E., Friedman, W.J. and Black, I.B. (1993) *Neuron* **11**, 1101.
21. Verdi, J.M. and Anderson, D.J. (1994) *Neuron* **13**, 1359.
22. Maffei, L., *et al.* (1992) *J. Neurosci.* **12**, 4651.
23. Cabelli, R.J., Hohn, A. and Shatz, C.J. (1995) *Science* **267**, 1662.
24. Domenici, L. *et al.* (1994) *Neuroreport* **5**, 2041.
25. Berardi, N. *et al.* (1994) *Proc. Natl. Acad. Sci. USA* **91**, 684.
26. McMahon, S.B. *et al.* (1995) *Nature Med.* **1**, 774.
27. Olton, D. *et al.* (1991) *Adv. Exp. Med. Biol.* **295**, 353.
28. Korsching, S. *et al.* (1985) *EMBO J.* **4**, 1389.
29. Shelton, D.L. and Reichardt, L.F. (1986) *Proc. Natl. Acad. Sci. USA* **83**, 2714.
30. Whittemore, S.R. *et al.* (1986) *Proc. Natl. Acad. Sci. USA* **83**, 817.
31. Ayer-LeLievre, C. *et al.* (1988) *Science* **240**, 1339.
32. Ernfors, P. *et al.* (1990) *Proc. Natl. Acad. Sci. USA* **87**, 5454.
33. Gnahn, H. *et al.* (1983) *Dev. Brain Res.* **9**, 42.
34. Mobley, W.C. *et al.* (1986) *Mol. Brain Res.* **387**, 53.
35. Li, Y. *et al.* (1995) *J. Neurosci.* **15**, 2888.
36. Large, T.H. *et al.* (1986) *Science* **234**, 352.
37. Auburger, G. *et al.* (1987) *Dev. Biol.* **120**, 322.
38. Crowley, C. *et al.* (1994) *Cell* **76**, 1001.
39. Smeyne, R.J. *et al.* (1994) *Nature* **368**, 246.
40. Mobley, W.C. *et al.* (1985) *Science* **229**, 284.
41. Mobley, W.C. *et al.* (1989) *Neuron* **3**, 655.
42. Holtzman, D.M. *et al.* (1993) *Neurology* **43**, 2668.

Making Our Minds Last a Lifetime

While it may not be possible to completely age-proof our brains, a brave new world of anti-aging research shows that our gray matter may be far more flexible than we thought. So no one, no matter how old, has to lose their mind.

By Katharine Greider

The brain has often been called the three-pound universe. It's our most powerful and mysterious organ, the seat of the self, laced with as many billions of neurons as the galaxy has stars. No wonder the mere notion of an aging, failing brain—and the prospect of memory loss, confusion, and the unraveling of our personality—is so terrifying. About a third of all people age 60 and over have recall problems that are noticeable to them and measurable with testing. At least a quarter of people age 85 and up suffer from dementia—the loss of memory and cognitive function and an inability to understand words, carry out motor activities, and recognize or identify objects. As Mark Williams, M.D., author of *The American Geriatrics Society's Complete Guide to Aging and Health,* says, "The fear of dementia is stronger than the fear of death itself."

Yet the degeneration of the brain is far from inevitable. "Its design features are such that it should continue to function for a lifetime," says Zaven Khachaturian, Ph.D., director of the Alzheimer's Association's Ronald and Nancy Reagan Research Institute. "There's no reason to expect it to deteriorate with age, even though many of us are living longer lives." In fact, scientists' view of the brain's potential is rapidly changing, according to Stanford University neuroscientist Robert Sapolsky, Ph.D. "Thirty-five years ago we thought Alzheimer's disease was a dramatic version of normal aging. Now we realize it's a disease with a distinct pathology. In fact, some people simply don't experience any mental decline, so we've begun to study them." Antonio Damasio, M.D., Ph.D., head of the Department of Neurology at the University of Iowa and author of *Descartes' Error,* concurs. "Older people can continue to have extremely rich and healthy mental lives."

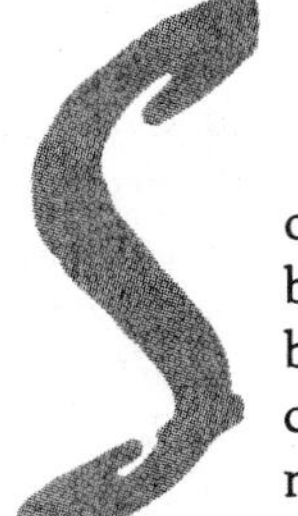

Successful Aging

So what's the secret to keeping our brains agile and fit? Activity seems to be the key. In fact, mental and physical challenges are both strongly connected to cerebral fitness. This finding springs in large part from a decade of research sponsored by the MacArthur Foundation Network on Successful Aging. Fifteen scientists across the nation have been studying the genetic, psychological, social, and environmental factors that contribute to mental fitness. In one study, Marilyn Albert, Ph.D., of Harvard Medical School, and colleagues from Yale, Duke, and Brandeis Universities and the Mt. Sinai School of Medicine examined 1,192 healthy and mentally fit individuals between the ages of 70 and 80. Twenty-two different variables were measured. "We looked at them in great detail," Albert says, "measuring everything from their blood pressure and cholesterol levels to psychiatric symptoms and whether they smoked."

The seniors were tested in 1988 and again in 1991. Four factors were found to be related to their mental fitness: levels of education and physical activity, lung function, and feelings of self-efficacy. "Each of these elements alters the way our brain functions," says Albert, who hypothesizes that regular exercise may actually stimulate blood flow to the brain and nerve growth, both of which create more densely branched neurons, rendering the neurons stronger and better able to resist disease. Moderate aerobic exercise, including long brisk walks and frequently climbing stairs, will accomplish this.

Animal studies confirm that both mental and physical activity boost brain fitness. At the Beckman Institute for Advanced Science and Technology in Urbana, Illinois, psychologist William Greenough, Ph.D., let some rats play with a profusion of toys. These rodents developed about 25 percent more connections between their neurons than did rats that didn't get any mentally stimulating recreation. In addition, rats that exercised on a treadmill developed more capillaries in specific parts of their brains than did their sedentary counterparts. This increased the blood flow to their brains. "Clearly the message is to do as many *different* things as possible," Greenough says.

Education also seems to enhance brain function. People who have challenged themselves with at least a college education may actually stimulate the neurons in their brains. Moreover, native intelligence may protect our brains. It's possible that smart people begin life with a greater number of neurons, and therefore have a greater reserve to fall back on if some begin to fail. "If you have a lot of neurons and keep them busy, you may be able to tolerate more damage to your brain before it shows," says Peter Davies, M.D., of the Albert Einstein College of Medicine in the Bronx, New York. That may explain why the progression of Alzheimer's disease in people who have big heads—craniums with a circumference of more than 24 inches—is slower. These people may simply have more brain tissue and more neurons.

Early linguistic ability also seems to help our brains later in life. A recent study in the *New England Journal of Medicine* looked at 93 elderly nuns and examined the autobiographies they had written 60 years earlier, just as they were joining a convent. The nuns whose essays were complex and dense with ideas remained sharp into their eighties and nineties.

Finally, personality seems to play an important role in protecting our mental prowess. A sense of self-efficacy may protect our brain, buffeting it from the harmful effects of stress. According to Albert, there's evidence that elevated levels of stress hormones may harm brain cells and cause the hippocampus—a small seahorse-shaped organ that's a crucial moderator of memory—to atrophy. A sense that we can effectively chart our own course in the world may retard the release of stress hormones and protect us as we age. "It's not a matter of whether you experience stress or not," Albert concludes, "it's your attitude toward it."

Reducing stress by meditating on a regular basis may buffer the brain as well. It also increases the activity of the brain's pineal gland, the source of the antioxidant hormone melatonin, which regulates sleep and may retard the aging process. Studies at the University of Massachusetts Medical Center and the University of Western Ontario found that people who meditated regularly had higher levels of melatonin than those who took 5-milligram supplements. Another study, conducted jointly by Maharishi International University, Harvard University, and the University of Maryland, found that seniors who meditated for three months experienced dramatic improvements in their psychological well-being, compared to their non-meditative peers.

Modern Alchemy and Brain Chemistry

Like professional sleuths, neuroscientists have been hard at work discovering just what happens to brain cells when their power begins to fade. What they've uncovered may eventually lead to an astonishingly wide range of chemical approaches to preserving and enhancing cognitive function. Substances as diverse as nicotine, prednisone, ibuprofen, estrogen, and a whole host of new drugs that seem to fine-tune brain chemistry may have a potent impact on our gray matter. According to James L. McGaugh, Ph.D., who's been working on memory-enhancing drugs for 40 years, there's extensive laboratory evidence that animal recall is improved with drugs as well as hormones. But McGaugh notes that we're still a long way from safely and accurately fine-tuning the brain with chemicals. The first generation of memory-improving drugs may be a breakthrough, yet their effect may be modest.

Here are the most promising chemical substances and their potential impact on cognition:

- **Estrogen may increase cognitive ability, specifically short-term memory and the capacity to learn new tasks.** Richard Mayeux, M.D., a professor at Columbia University's School of Public Health, and his colleagues studied over 1,000 women age 70 and up. Those who had taken estrogen for just a year were significantly less likely to develop Alzheimer's disease than women who had never taken the hormone. Dr. Mayeux estimates that women who take estrogen for a decade may reduce their risk for the illness by about 40 percent. Researchers theorize that estrogen may stimulate neurons to grow more branches. The National Institutes of Health (NIH) is now launching a study on the impact of estrogen on Alzheimer's disease at 38 medical centers across the country. Eight thousand healthy women who are 65 years old or older and who are already taking estrogen will be studied.

- **Anti-inflammatory drugs may be just as promising as estrogen when it comes to warding off Alzheimer's disease.** According to Khachaturian, "our body's reaction to inflammation can cause cells to die." The role of inflammation was first recognized when scientists discovered that arthritis sufferers—who usually take anti-inflammatory drugs—have lower rates of Alzheimer's disease than those who don't take drugs. A recent review of 17 studies by researchers at the University of British Columbia found that people taking anti-inflammatory drugs reduced their risk of Alzheimer's disease by nearly half.

Feed Your Head?

Why wait decades for science to hand us "smart" drugs and nutrients that supposedly enhance brain function when we may already have them at hand? That's the philosophy of Steven Fowkes, the 44-year-old editor of the newsletter *Smart Drug News.* These medications include deprenyl (for Parkinson's disease), vasopression (used to treat diabetes), piracetam (for learning disabilities), and others that are available only in Mexico and Europe. Also on the list of smart drugs are a host of amino acids that are building blocks for neurotransmitters—such as tryptophan, tyrosine, and choline—as well as dimethylaminoethanol (DMAE) and nicotinamide adenine dinucleotide (NADH), nutrients that seem to enhance cognitive function.

Fowkes, who devised his own smart drug regimen, says it has changed the way he works and sleeps. "I used to be a night owl. But as soon as I began taking piracetam, that changed. I woke up spontaneously at dawn, got a load of work done in the morning, and stopped drinking caffeine. Piracetam gives me all the benefits of caffeine without the feeling of being wired or overstimulated." Piracetam is available by prescription from a few special pharmacies (Apothecure [800-203-2158] and College Pharmacy [800-888-9358]). Fowkes also takes deprenyl, which he imports—and which does not have Federal Drug Administration approval. And he uses a vitamin-and-mineral formula called Extend, which he says has about 40 different nutrients.

Fowkes's colleague John Morgenthaler, the 36-year-old co-author of *Smart Drugs & Nutrients,* the book that may have launched the entire cognitive-enhancement movement, says he's developed his own nutrient regimen, which includes such substances as pregnenolone (a precursor of DHEA), melatonin (an antioxidant hormone), and antioxidants that combat free radicals (highly reactive molecules that damage cells and contribute to aging). "I want to feel good 25 years from now," Morgenthaler says. "You have to think ahead."

Although the 3,000 subscribers to *Smart Drug News* would probably agree with Morgenthaler, most experts advise caution. All drugs have side effects, and we don't know the long-term risks of taking drugs for enhancement rather than to treat disease.

—*Jill Neimark*

Both steroids and nonsteroidal drugs, like aspirin and ibuprofen, were included in this review. The National Institute on Aging is now studying the effect of the powerful anti-inflammatory drug prednisone on Alzheimer's disease. And two other drugs—the gout medication colchicine and the antimalarial drug chloroquine—are under consideration to be studied, according to neurologist Douglas Galasko, M.D., of the San Diego Veterans Administration Medical Center at the University of California.

•Nicotine, which mimics some of the effects of acetylcholine, a major neurotransmitter, may enhance brain function. "Acetylcholine is quite important for cognitive function and memory," notes Edward Levin, Ph.D., of the NeuroBehavioral Research Laboratory at Duke University Medical Center in Durham, North Carolina. "Several studies have shown that nicotine will improve cognitive performance in Alzheimer's disease patients," Levin says, adding that it also seems to be effective in treating adults with attention-deficit disorder. Additionally, smokers have lower rates of Alzheimer's disease, though Levin is quick to assert that smoking's health hazards far outweigh its benefits as an antidote to failing memory.

•Studies looking into the effects of 20 new "cognition enhancing" drugs on humans began last year. According to the Dana Alliance for Brain Initiatives, a nonprofit association of neuroscientists, many of these drugs increase the action of acetylcholine or mimic its effect.

•A new class of drugs, called ampakines, may immediately enhance our ability to learn or create new memories. Developed by Gary Lynch, Ph.D., a neuroscientist at the University of California at Irvine, the safety of these drugs has been tested in humans in a small pilot study with no side effects so far. But much research on their safety and efficacy remains to be done.

•An antibody that enhances learning has been found. "When we put this molecule into the brains of rabbits they learned more quickly," says Jan Leestma, M.D., of the discovery he and his colleagues at the Chicago Institute of Neurosurgery and Neuroresearch made.

At the Corner Store: Vitamins and Nutrients

It's not just scientists who are catching anti-aging fever. Walk into any health food store, and you'll find nutritional formulas—with names like Brainstorm and Smart ALEC—that claim to sharpen mental ability. The book *Smart Drugs & Nutrients*, by Ward Dean, M.D., and John Morgenthaler, was self-published in 1990 and has sold over

120,000 copies worldwide. It has also spawned an underground network of people tweaking their own brain chemistry with nutrients and drugs—the latter sometimes obtain from Europe and Mexico (see "Feed Your Head?). Sales of ginkgo—an extract from the leaves of the 200-million-year-old ginkgo tree, which has been shown in published studies to increase oxygen in the brain and ameliorate symptoms of Alzheimer's disease—are up by 22 percent in the last six months alone, according to Paddy Spence, president of SPINS, a San Francisco–based market research firm.

Indeed, products that increase and preserve mental performance are a small but emerging segment of the supplements industry, says Linda Gilbert, president of HealthFocus, a company that researches consumer health trends. While neuroscientists like Khachaturian liken the use of these products to the superstition of tossing salt over your shoulder, the public is nevertheless gobbling up nutrients that promise cognitive enhancement. For example:

- **Antioxidants offer a promising approach to safeguarding the brain.** They protect cells from attack by free radicals—highly reactive substances that damage cells and contribute to aging. According to Dr. Galasko, small studies in the United States, Canada, and Scandinavia have hinted that two substances with powerful antioxidant properties—vitamin E and deprenyl, a drug used to treat Parkinson's disease—may indeed stem free-radical damage in the brain. Results from a study pairing the two substances, sponsored by the National Institute on Aging, should be available next year.
- **Acetyl-L-carnitine, a derivative of the amino acid L-carnitine, protects brain cells in animals.** L-carnitine aids the process by which a cell turns fat into energy, but on its own it does not reach the brain. Acetyl-L-carnitine does. It's available by mail order and in some health food stores. However, studies on the impact of this nutrient on Alzheimer's disease patients have not shown promise.
- **Choline is a building block for acetylcholine, a major brain neurotransmitter.** Evidence that it actually stimulates acetylcholine production is slim, and choline supplements have not helped Alzheimer's disease patients. But some studies indicate that this may be because damaged brain cells can no longer absorb the choline. If supplements of choline are taken at a younger age, the theory goes, it may help prevent the brain's decline.

Underestimating the Obvious

Despite being a neuroscientist who works with drugs, McGaugh believes that for most people the way to maintain high brain function will not be found in chemicals. "There's growing neurobiological evidence that supports the common sense notion of 'use it or lose it,' " he says. "The brain may be more like a muscle than we ever thought."

Psychiatrist James Gordon, M.D., a professor at the Georgetown University School of Medicine and author of *Manifesto for a New Medicine,* takes that insight a step further. "I wish people would be more concerned with wisdom and less concerned about cognition," he says. "Why not spend some time meditating, dancing, or performing tai chi every day? These activities will work on your brain chemistry, too." Dr. Gordon recalls a dinner he shared with the now-71-year-old painter Robert Rauschenberg in 1992. "All over his studio there were these huge canvasses. After we finished eating, Rauschenberg said it was time for him to get back to work. My friend asked him if he ever took any time off. 'Honey,' he said, 'I don't want more time off. I want more time on.' "

With an ever-increasing number of anti-aging drugs, nutrients, and hormones available, and new insight into the impact lifestyle has on the brain, we may all have a lot more time to think. However, it will still be up to us to grow wise.

Katharine Greider is a freelance journalist living in New York City.

Studies Show Talking With Infants Shapes Basis of Ability to Think

By SANDRA BLAKESLEE

When a White House conference on early child development convenes today, one of the findings Hillary Rodham Clinton will hear from scientists is that the neurological foundations for rational thinking, problem solving and general reasoning appear to be largely established by age 1—long before babies show any signs of knowing an abstraction from a pacifier.

Furthermore, new studies are showing that spoken language has an astonishing impact on an infant's brain development. In fact, some researchers say the number of words an infant hears each day is the single most important predictor of later intelligence, school success and social competence. There is one catch—the words have to come from an attentive, engaged human being. As far as anyone has been able to determine, radio and television do not work.

"We now know that neural connections are formed very early in life and that the infant's brain is literally waiting for experiences to determine how connections are made," said Dr. Patricia Kuhl, a neuroscientist at the University of Washington in Seattle and a key speaker at today's conference. "We didn't realize until very recently how early this process begins," she said in a telephone interview. "For example, infants have learned the sounds of their native language by the age of six months."

This relatively new view of infant brain development, supported by many scientists, has obvious political and social implications. It suggests that infants and babies develop most rapidly with caretakers who are not only loving, but also talkative and articulate, and that a more verbal family will increase an infant's chances for success. It challenges some deeply held beliefs—that infants will thrive intellectually if they are simply given lots of love and that purposeful efforts to influence babies' cognitive development are harmful.

If the period from birth to 3 is crucial, parents may assume a more crucial role in a child's intellectual development than teachers, an idea sure to provoke new debates about parental responsibility, said Dr. Irving Lazar, a professor of special education and resident scholar at the Center for Research in Human Development at Vanderbilt University in Nashville. And it offers yet another reason to provide stimulating, high quality day care for infants whose primary caretakers work, which is unavoidably expensive.

Environmental factors seem to take over for genetic influence.

The idea that early experience shapes human potential is not new, said Dr. Harry Chugani, a pediatric neurologist at Wayne State University in Detroit and one of the scientists whose research has shed light on critical periods in child brain development. What is new is the extent of the research in the field known as cognitive neuroscience and the resulting synthesis of findings on the influence of both nature and nurture. Before birth, it appears that genes predominantly direct how the brain establishes basic wir-

TIMETABLE

The Growing Brain: What Might Help Your Infant

Dr. William Staso, an expert in neurological development, suggests that different kinds of stimulation should be emphasized at different ages. At all stages, parental interaction and a conversational dialogue with the child are important. Here are some examples:

FIRST MONTH: A low level of stimulation reduces stress and increases the infant's wakefulness and alertness. The brain essentially shuts down the system when there is overstimulation from competing sources. When talking to an infant, for example, filter out distracting noises, like a radio.

MONTHS 1 TO 3 Light/dark contours, like high-contrast pictures or objects, foster development in neural networks that encode vision. The brain also starts to discriminate among acoustic patterns of language, like intonation, lilt and pitch. Speaking to the infant, especially in an animated voice, aids this process.

MONTHS 3 TO 5 The infant relies primarily on vision to acquire information about the world. Make available increasingly complex designs that correspond to real objects in the baby's environment; motion also attracts attention. A large-scale picture of a fork, moved across the field of vision, would offer more stimulation than just an actual fork.

MONTHS 6 TO 7 The infant becomes alert to relationships like cause and effect, the location of objects and the functions of objects. Demonstrate and talk about situations like how the turning of a doorknob leads to the opening of a door.

MONTHS 7 TO 8 The brain is oriented to make associations between sounds and some meaningful activity or object. For example, parents can deliberately emphasize in conversation that the sound of water running in the bathroom signals an impending bath, or that a doorbell means a visitor.

MONTHS 9 TO 12 Learning adds up to a new level of awareness of the environment and increased interest in exploration; sensory and motor skills coordinate in a more mature fashion. This is the time to let the child turn on a faucet or a light switch, under supervision.

MONTHS 13 TO 18 The brain establishes accelerated and more complex associations, especially if the toddler experiments directly with objects. A rich environment will help the toddler make such associations, understand sequences, differentiate between objects and reason about them.

ing patterns. Neurons grow and travel into distinct neighborhoods, awaiting further instructions.

After birth, it seems that environmental factors predominate. A recent study found that mice exposed to an enriched environment have more brain cells than mice raised in less intellectually stimulating conditions. In humans, the inflowing stream of sights, sounds, noises, smells, touches—and most importantly, language and eye contact—literally makes the brain take shape. It is a radical and shocking concept.

Experience in the first year of life lays the basis for networks of neurons that enable us to be smart, creative and adaptable in all the years that follow, said Dr. Esther Thelen, a neurobiologist at Indiana University in Bloomington.

The brain is a self-organizing system, Dr. Thelen said, whose many parts co-operate to produce coherent behavior. There is no master program pulling it together but rather the parts self-organize. "What we know about these systems is that they are very sensitive to initial conditions," Dr. Thelen said. "Where you are now depends on where you've been."

The implication for infant development is clear. Given the explosive growth and self-organizing capacity of the brain in the first year of life, the experiences an infant has during this period are the conditions that set the stage for everything that follows.

In later life, what makes us smart and creative and adaptable are networks of neurons which support our ability to use abstractions from one memory to help form new ideas and solve problems, said Dr. Charles Stevens, a neurobiologist at the Salk Institute in San Diego. Smarter people may have a greater number of neural networks that are more intricately woven together, a process that starts in the first year.

The complexity of the synaptic web laid down early may very well be the physical basis of what we call general intelligence, said Dr. Lazar at Vanderbilt. The more complex that set of interconnections, the brighter the child is likely to be since there are more ways to sort, file and access experiences.

Of course, brain development "happens" in stimulating and dull environments. Virtually all babies learn to sit up, crawl, walk, talk, eat independently and make transactions with others, said Dr. Steven Petersen, a neurologist at Washington University School of Medicine in St. Louis. Such skills are not at risk except in rare circumstances of sensory and social deprivation, like being locked in a closet for the first few years of life. Subject to tremendous variability within the normal range of environments are the abilities to perceive, conceptualize, understand, reason, associate and judge. The ability to function in a technologically complex society like ours does not simply "happen."

One implication of the new knowledge about infant brain development is that intervention programs like Head Start may be too little, too late, Dr. Lazar said. If educators hope to make a big difference, he said, they will need to develop programs for children from birth to 3.

Dr. Bettye Caldwell, a professor of pediatrics and an expert in child development at the University of Arkansas in Little Rock, who supports the importance of early stimulation, said that in early childhood education there is a strong bias against planned intellectual stimulation. Teachers of very young children are taught to follow "developmentally appropriate practices," she said, which means that the child chooses what he or she wants to do. The teacher is a responder and not a stimulator.

Asked about the bias Dr. Caldwell described, Matthew Melmed, executive director of Zero to Three, a research and training organization for early childhood development in Washington, D.C., said that knowing how much stimulation is too much or too little, especially for infants, is "a really tricky question. It's a dilemma parents and educators face every day," he said.

In a poll released today, Zero to Three found that 87 percent of parents think that the more stimulation a baby receives the better off the baby is, Mr. Melmed said. "Many parents have the concept that a baby is something you fill up with information and that's not good," he said.

"We are concerned that many parents are going to take this new information about brain research and rush to do more things with their babies, more activities, forgetting that it's not the activities that are important. The most important thing is connecting with the baby and creating an emotional bond," Mr. Melmed said.

There is some danger of overstimulating an infant, said Dr. William Staso, a school psychologist from Orcutt, Calif., who has written a book called "What Stimulation Your Baby Needs to Become Smart." Some people think that any interaction with very young children that involves their intelligence must also involve pushing them to excel, he said. But the "curriculum" that most benefits young babies is simply common sense, Dr. Staso said. It does not involve teaching several languages or numerical concepts but rather carrying out an ongoing dialogue with adult speech. Vocabulary words are a magnet for a child's thinking and reasoning skills.

This constant patter may be the single most important factor in early brain development, said Dr. Betty Hart, a professor emeritus of human development at the University of Kansas in Lawrence. With her colleague, Dr. Todd Ridley of the University of Alaska, Dr. Hart recently co-authored a book—"Meaningful Differences in the Everyday Experience of Young American Children."

Challenging the deep belief that lots of love is enough.

The researchers studied 42 children born to professional, working class or welfare parents. During the first two and a half years of the children's lives, the scientists spent an hour a month recording every spoken word and every parent-child interaction in every home. For all the families, the data include 1,300 hours of everyday interactions, Dr. Hart said, involving millions of ordinary utterances.

At age 3, the children were given standard tests. The children of professional parents scored highest. Spoken language was the key variable, Dr. Hart said.

A child with professional parents heard, on average, 2,100 words an hour. Children of working-class parents heard 1,200 words and those with parents on welfare heard only 600 words an hour. Professional parents talked three times as much to their infants, Dr. Hart said. Moreover, children with professional parents got positive feedback 30 times an hour—twice as often as working-class parents and five times as often as welfare parents.

The tone of voice made a difference, Dr. Hart said. Affirmative feedback is very important. A child who hears, "What did we do yesterday? What did we see?" will listen more to a parent than will a child who always hears "Stop that," or "Come here!"

By age 2, all parents started talking more to their children, Dr. Hart said. But by age two, the differences among children were so great that those left behind could never catch up. The differences in academic achievement remained in each group through primary school.

Every child learned to use language and could say complex sentences but the deprived children did not deal with words in a conceptual manner, she said.

A recent study of day care found the same thing. Children who were talked to at very young ages were better at problem solving later on.

For an infant, Dr. Hart said, all words are novel and worth learning. The key to brain development seems to be the rate of early learning—not so much what is wired but how much of the brain gets interconnected in those first months and years.

Nature, Nurture, Brains, and Behavior

Scientists are beginning to unravel the complex processes by which genetics and environment interact to determine brain development and human potential.

Kenneth J. Mack

Kenneth J. Mack is a child neurologist and molecular biologist at the Waisman Center on Mental Retardation, University of Wisconsin, Madison. His research interests deal with how seizures and learning affect gene expression.

The genetic makeup of a child seems to have a direct effect on that child's development. Yet anyone who has spent time around children has to acknowledge that the environment also has a large impact on development. The question that has puzzled many a researcher, philosopher, psychologist, and parent is, what role does each factor play, and how do these two factors interact to determine our brain development?

Advances in understanding how genes affect neural development offer the hope that science may one day be able to explain how genes affect behavior, and conversely, how environment and behavior affect genes.

Genetic effects on nervous-system development

Our genes are coded instructions for making a rich variety of protein molecules, with one gene corresponding roughly to one protein. These genetic instructions are contained in a DNA language consisting of bits of nucleic acids called basepairs. The human genome, containing approximately 3.3 billion basepairs, is transcribed or expressed into about 100,000 different units of messenger RNA, which in turn are used to generate about 100,000 different proteins. Hence we say that the human genome consists of about 100,000 different genes.

Some researchers have estimated that approximately 30,000–50,000 of these genes are expressed in the central nervous system, and about two-thirds of these are expressed only in the brain. The specific RNA messages that a cell expresses will help determine its structure, function, and activity level. A nerve cell's specific pattern of gene expression, for example, may help make it unique among the nervous system's one trillion total cells.

In simplified form, gene expression may be thought of as a two-step process in which the message contained within the DNA is first "transcribed" into another nucleic-acid language, an RNA form. In the second step, the RNA message is "translated" into protein. Most gene expression is controlled at the level of transcription. Proteins known as transcription factors bind to a gene's regulatory region at the front end of a gene and either promote or repress transcription. Typically, a single transcription factor is not enough to start transcription. Oftentimes the combined action of three or more factors is needed to promote transcription. Hence these transcription factors help determine which of our genes are expressed and to what degree.

It is estimated that there are approximately 5,000 transcription factors in humans, and these are classified into at least 12 different families based on their protein structure. Some families of transcription factors, such as homeodomains and paired boxes, have been implicated in development, whereas transcription factors of the leucine-zipper and zinc-finger type have roles in learning.

In the nervous system, much of gene expression is preprogrammed and independent of environment. An example of this preprogrammed process is the determination of whether a cell will survive through development

This article originally appeared in *The World & I*, July 1996, pp. 194-201. Reprinted by permission of *The World & I*, a publication of The Washington Times Corporation. © 1996.

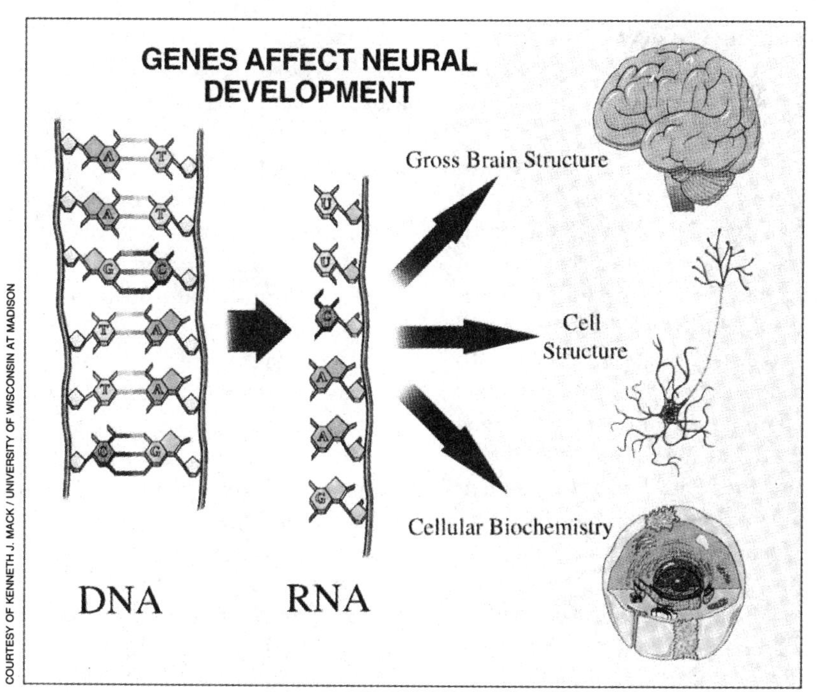

■ **Genes affect nervous-system development at many different levels via a two-step process. First, the genetic codes of DNA are "transcribed" into RNA, which is then "translated" into protein molecules that perform myriad functions.**

or undergo a process called "programmed cell death." For instance, the nematode *C. elegans* (a type of wormlike creature) produces exactly 1,090 cells during its growth to adulthood. Of these 1,090 cells, exactly 131 are destined to die as part of the animal's normal development. Most (80 percent) of the cells "destined to die" are nerve cells.

Cells that express programmed-cell-death genes undergo an active process of suicide unless these cells also express genes that specifically protect them from programmed cell death. This normal developmental process also occurs in humans. However, many researchers now believe that aberrations in programmed cell death may be responsible for diseases such as amyotrophic lateral sclerosis (Lou Gehrig's disease) and certain muscular diseases of childhood.

Across many animal species, certain transcription factors produced by key developmental genes determine the formation of specific brain regions. Present also in humans, these genes include those of the homeobox (Hox), homeodomain, zinc finger, and paired box (Pax) families. Many of these genes are specifically expressed in certain brain regions and have an important role in determining the structure of that region. For example, studies in the embryonic development of the mouse have revealed that the Pax and the Hox genes are expressed in spatially and temporarily restricted patterns during the development of the nervous system. Pax transcription factors seem to play a role in the dorsal-ventral (back to front) positioning of cells, whereas Hox genes are more likely to play a role in the positioning along the rostral-caudal (head to toe) axis. Hence these transcription factors specify the position for the cell in the nervous system.

Pax and Hox genes producing Pax and Hox transcription factors are examples of how structural aspects of brain development are genetically determined. Mutations in these developmental genes have already been identified in human clinical syndromes of developmental abnormalities. Craniosynostosis is a condition where premature closure of an infant's skull sutures occurs. Recently this abnormality has been associated with Pax-2 mutations in one family. Pax-3 mutations are found in patients with Waardenburg's syndrome, which consists of deafness and partial albinism. Pax-6 mutations are found in aniridia (complete or partial absence of the iris) in humans.

Regulatory genes may assist in determining not only the position of the cell but also the specific attributes of the cell. The Hox-type gene Gtx is specifically expressed in glial cells (support cells in the nervous system). The gene for transcription factor SCIP is expressed in layer 5 pyramidal neurons. These genes demonstrate the cell-type specificity of many of these factors. Certainly, what genes a cell expresses will predetermine whether it will survive development and what type of cell it will become.

Importance of gene expression in intelligence

Most of us are born with "normal" intelligence. Of the 30,000–50,000 genes that are expressed in our nervous system, most seem to function well and allow us to survive in a complex world. Our environment can presumably help, or hinder, our genetic substrate and determine our current intellect. Perhaps the clearest examples of environmental influences on intellect are demonstrated in disease states or in extreme conditions.

Three percent of all children are mentally retarded. The roles of environment and education become critical to optimize their final developmental level. Mental retardation can result from more than 500 genetic conditions, as well as innumerable "acquired" mental-retardation syndromes, such as head trauma and prematurity. Although the molecular etiology of many mental-retardation syndromes is diverse, a basic problem to all these syndromes is the difficulty in learning. In some forms of mental retardation, the neural substrates of learning—the cerebral cortex and the hippocampus—may be absent or severely malformed. In other conditions, the basic neuronal architecture and connections seem to be present, and the mechanisms for the cognitive problems remain more elusive.

How can one make learning more efficient and effective? Part of the difficulty in answering this question is that only a superficial understanding of the mechanisms of learning is known. In animal models, multiple biochemical and structural changes occur after learning and during critical periods in development. It is generally believed that many important aspects of learning take place in the connections between nerve cells, called synapses, and many of these changes are dependent on gene expression. A more focused question then becomes, how does learning cause changes in gene expression?

Does experience affect nervous-system development?

Despite a beautifully complex and exact role for predetermined gene regulation in neuronal development, environment also plays a major role. Yet, at a scientific level, it is difficult to ask directly how environmental influences change the circuitry and molecular biology of the brain. Some researchers maintain that a complex environment that promotes learning will excite specific groups of nerve cells, resulting in changes specific to learning. Thus, investigators often study nerve-cell excitation as a model of learning.

One important function of neuronal excitation is to support the survival of developing neurons. In a fetus, the number of nerve cells, as well as the number of connections or "synapses" between cells, continues to expand. However, starting after infancy, the number of nerve cells and synapses decreases as a normal part of development. As mentioned above, much of this "programmed cell death" is determined genetically. Yet studies have shown that whenever cells are excited, or "depolarized," they are much less likely to die. When excitation is blocked, the nerve cells are more likely to die. One may infer from these studies that neuronal activity will promote neuronal cell survival. The nervous system almost seems to follow a "use it or lose it" rule during development.

Prevention of programmed cell death in the central nervous system of a young animal or human is important. In the visual system, the blocking of optic-nerve activity from the eye leads to increased cell death in visual areas of the brain. Restoration of this visual activity is followed by decreased cell death.

Perhaps some of the most compelling examples of the effects of experience on gene expression come from observations made in the behavioral sciences. In the 1940s, Rene Spitz observed two groups of orphans. One group was taken care of in a foundling home, with one nurse per seven children. These children were kept relatively isolated in a crib with a white sheet over it. A second group of orphans was raised in a nursing home attached to a women's prison. These orphans received more "one on one" attention from the women prisoners and were raised in cribs where they could see more of their environment.

At 4 months of age, the foundling infants were slightly more advanced than the nursing-home infants. However, at 2 years of age, the nursing-home infants were significantly more advanced than the foundling infants. The nursing-home infants were normal, while only 2 of 26 foundling infants could walk by 24 months (normally children walk before 15 months of age). Most of the foundling infants used very few words at this age, while many normal infants use 100 or more words. These studies show that an impoverished environment can result in long-term developmental delays.

Related observations in a more controlled animal experiment were made by Harry Harlow and coworkers at the University of Wisconsin in the late 1950s. Harlow observed that if monkeys were raised in isolation (typical laboratory conditions for that time), they showed poor social interaction as adults. However, the presence of a mother, or other peer monkeys, would increase the skills of the observed monkeys. Harlow's studies suggested that early experience may have a permanent effect on behavior.

What are the structural and biochemical changes that underlie the behavioral changes? The visual system has been a useful model in trying to sort out these effects. As early as 1932, Marius von Senden noted that children with cataracts removed at 10–20 years of age would be able to recognize color but had difficulty recognizing form. Presumably some early activation of specific visual pathways was necessary to develop this pattern recognition.

Nobel laureates David Hubel and Torsten Weisel of Harvard University, in a set of now classic studies, were able to demonstrate that connections from the thalamus (a relay nucleus for visual input) to the primary visual cortex (where basic visual perception is perceived) were arranged in columns, with input from each eye controlling alternate columns of cells. If the vision from one eye were disrupted during development, then the relative size of its representation in the cortex would change. It is now well known that early visual deprivation will produce gross alterations in visual cortex organization. Hubel and Weisel's experiments helped demonstrate that experience affects the gross morphology of the brain.

William Greenough at the University of Illinois has asked if experience can affect the structure of individual nerve cells. In Greenough's experiments, rats were raised in an either "enriched" or "impoverished" environment. These experiments focused on a part of the neuron called a dendrite, whose function is to receive input from other cells. Greenough noted that the complexity of dendrites is positively correlated with experience, with the more experienced animals having a much more complex and elegant dendritic system. Interestingly, a parallel observation occurs in humans with mental retardation. Individuals with some forms of mental retardation have a much simpler set of dendrites than do normal subjects.

Experience affects gene expression

The above studies suggest that visual experience during development affects the viability and structure of the nerve cell. However, experience affects not only the morphology of nerve cells but also their molecular biology. Stewart Hendry and Edward Jones, of the University of California at Irvine, have looked at how visual experience affects expression of the protein glutamic acid decarboxylase (GAD), the rate-limiting enzyme involved in the synthesis of the neurotransmitter GABA. Hendry and Jones demonstrated that depriving a visual system of input would cause a decrease in its GAD levels. In contrast, restoring visual activity to the system leads to restoration of GAD expression.

If deprivation can cause a decrease in gene expression, then can an increase in activity cause an increase in gene expression? To answer this question, multiple investigators have studied the rodent barrel cortex system, another excellent model for studying the effects of experience. The barrel cortex receives information from the animal's whiskers, or vibrissae. Many animals use their whiskers in the same way humans use their fingers to touch and explore objects. The information encoded in the barrel cortex seems not to represent simple touch but rather information about the form of an object. A rodent uses this barrel information to understand if a touched object is food, another animal, or some structure. It is superficially comparable to stereognosis in humans, where an individual is able to recognize an object (such as a coin, paper clip, or rock) by form.

Hendrik VanderLoos and colleagues of the University of Lausanne, Switzerland, used the barrel cortex to ask if new experience can result in an increase in gene expression. They observed that stimulating a rat's whiskers resulted in an increase of GAD expression, suggesting that environmental stimuli are important for maintaining GAD expression by nerve cells. More sensory experience increases the levels of this synaptic protein, whereas deprivation decreases this level. Since GAD is regulated in an experience-dependent manner, and since GAD-containing neurons constitute 25–30 percent of the neuronal population in the cortex, it has been suggested that this system plays a major role in cortical plasticity and learning.

My own research at the University of Wisconsin has asked what biochemical steps occur between a learning type of experience and the final synaptic changes that take place in nerve cells. After a learning experience, nerve cells are "excited," or activated, and they express many of the same transcription factors seen in development. These factors can then interact with the regulatory regions of genes for several synaptic proteins, including GAD. The end result of these changes is seen in the biochemistry and structure of the synapse, where learning is presumed to be based. Anatomical studies looking at synaptic morphology would suggest that experience results in long-lasting biochemical and structural changes.

Opportunities for gene therapy

If we can identify molecular pathways that are involved in experience and learning, then can we effectively change these pathways? Can one make these pathways more efficient and thereby facilitate learning? Unfortunately, the answer is probably not, given the technology of 1996.

In the best scenario, one could envision that the addition of a single gene (such as the gene for a transcription factor specific to learning) could optimize "learning" and therefore improve the lot of the mentally retarded, or even of normal children. Unfortunately, gene therapeutic approaches for single gene/protein defects have been wanting. Even in the area of Parkinson's disease, where the pathology is relatively limited and the biochemistry is relatively well understood, gene-therapy techniques have not been able to facilitate upregulation of tyrosine hydroxylase (the deficit involved in Parkinson's disease) in a long-term and side effect–free manner.

Some researchers have speculated on a pharmaceutical approach to gene transcription. It is theoretically possible to have compounds that directly interact with transcription factors. These pharmaceutical compounds may then specifically up-or down-regulate gene transcription. Transcription factors are prime candidates for this type of pharmaceutical development, because of their specificity, diversity, and importance in human disease.

A third approach may be to optimize the benefits obtained from a learning experience. Given the molecular complexity of developmental plasticity and learning, it may be wisest to use the neuronal pathways that are already in place. Although technically not very exciting, this relies on the beautifully complex nature of the nervous system to reinforce itself. The combination of a well-structured educational approach, as well as medically keeping these children healthy (free of seizure activity, and well nourished), may be the most efficacious "molecular" approach we have to facilitate learning in the normal as well as mentally retarded child.

Programs that facilitate experience in young children

The largest experiment to optimize human potential within developing children is certainly the Head Start program. Started in the 1960s, this program has allowed children from disadvantaged backgrounds to improve their educational experience and optimize their potential. Many investigators have studied the results of Head Start, and the summary of its effectiveness is certainly controversial. It seems that children who go through the program show gains in achievement through at least the early elementary years, but beyond that the achievements are harder to document. In a more comprehensive early intervention program, the Perry Preschool Project, researchers were able to demonstrate benefits of the program into young adulthood.

For children at risk for cognitive disabilities, federally mandated early intervention programs are provided by local school districts. From zero to three years of age, the children are provided with a variety of positive interventions, including physical therapy, occupational therapy, and speech therapy. The children then go into a classroom situation from age three until kindergarten. Studies have shown benefits in measures of development and IQ in select populations. Anecdotally, parents seem to be extremely supportive of the role that these programs play in their children's education.

Perhaps the most interesting long-term effect of childhood education is evidenced by a study from Shanghai, China. This study provided evidence that education may help prevent Alzheimer's disease. People who were formally educated through only early grade school years are almost 10 times more likely to develop Alzheimer's than people who were educated through at least high school. An additional positive effect is seen with further postsecondary education. Although the purpose of early education programs is not to prevent Alzheimer's disease, these data do point out that early education results in long-lasting changes in the central nervous system.

The challenges for researchers in this area are innumerable. The specific genetics of neuronal development, and the effects of learning on gene expression, are at best superficially understood. Even if we can identify single gene abnormalities that result in poor learning, medicine is years to decades away from developing effective gene-therapy approaches for neurological diseases. The challenge for behavioral scientists is to understand when an educational approach will make a difference. For example, should structured educational situations be offered for all four-year-olds? For infants? Even those from nondisadvantaged backgrounds? Perhaps an even more formidable challenge is to understand what type of educational approach is optimal. We haven't yet answered that question for most elementary or secondary education.

Conclusion

Like a complex musical score, the nervous system exhibits an intricate program of gene expression during development. However, similar to the way a conductor directs that musical score, the environment exerts a strong influence on how that genetic potential is expressed. It is still too early to incorporate the above information into specific useful suggestions for educators and parents. In general, however, it seems that positive interpersonal interactions encourage positive developmental and behavioral changes in children. Additionally, exposure to learning situations in the early childhood years results in long-term effects on brain growth, development, and achievement.

THE AGING BRAIN

For the Cortex, Neuron Loss May Be Less Than Thought

Nearly everyone fears the changes that advanced age will bring to his or her mind. And some change is almost inevitable: As people get older, they become more forgetful and find learning new things more difficult. But careful study reveals that for healthy brains, as opposed to those beset by Alzheimer's disease, age-related changes are selective and hardly incapacitating. Movie plots are remembered, for example, even as their details are lost. Facts can still be learned, although their source may vanish. And now, in a departure from what was previously thought, several groups of neurobiologists are proposing that the biological changes in the healthy aging brain are similarly subtle—and possibly correctable.

Just a decade ago, almost all experts thought that widespread cell death in the brain caused the cognitive changes of normal aging. But in the past few years, better methods of telling normal subjects from those with neurodegenerative diseases and more sophisticated techniques for examining the brain have started to yield results challenging that notion—especially for the neocortex, the brain area governing much of human cognition. A similar picture may also be emerging for the hippocampus, a structure important in memory (*Science*, 1 March, p. 1229). "The field of [brain] aging is undergoing a major reassessment," says neuropsychologist Mark Moss of Boston University School of Medicine. "It's an exciting time."

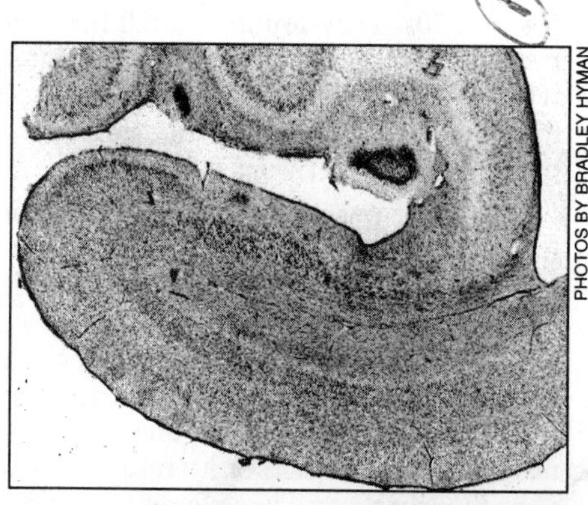

PHOTOS BY BRADLEY HYMAN

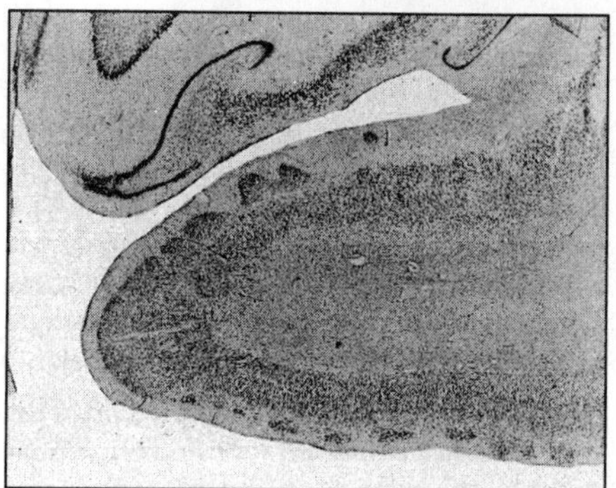

Normal versus diseased. An Alzheimer's brain *(above)* shows extensive neuronal loss in the entorhinal cortex compared to a normal brain *(below)*.

That reassessment is still incomplete, as not everyone thinks that the new data, some of which haven't yet been published, have proved that cortical neurons are preserved during aging. "There's no definitive study on cell loss and normal aging," says neurobiologist Paul Coleman of the University of Rochester School of Medicine and Dentistry in New York. "It's a messy area." But if the new findings are correct, they might have implications for developing drugs that bolster aging memories.

That's because it might be possible to compensate for some of the other brain changes being considered as contributors to the cognitive deficits of age. They include, for example, a decrease in the density of certain of the receptor proteins through which neurons respond to neurotransmitter signals and a breakdown of myelin, the fatty sheath that insulates nerve fibers and thereby facilitates their ability to transmit signals. Such alterations, unlike actual neuronal loss, might be remedied with drugs. "If the brain is preserved structurally, there's hope that we'll be able to reconstitute its function [with drugs]," says Bradley Hyman, a neuroscientist at Massachusetts General Hospital in Boston.

The long-standing belief that neurons are lost during aging got its major impetus in 1955, when anatomist Harold Brody at the State University of New York, Buffalo, published the first study correlating neuronal counts in the neocortex with age. Studying brains from 20 human subjects, from newborns to 95-year-olds, Brody saw extensive cell loss in a number of neocortical areas, including the cognitive areas of the frontal and temporal cortex. Follow-up studies by Brody's own group, as well as by several others, indicated that the cortex could lose up to 40% of its neurons during aging.

Although no one knew for sure how such massive cell death related to mental ability, experts thought it could cause rather dramatic declines in cognitive abilities in the normal, healthy elderly. Additionally, it was assumed that these changes were inevitable and almost impossible to reverse. In any case, the belief that the cortex loses neurons with age went without a serious challenge until 1984.

In that year, anatomist Herbert Haug and his colleagues at the Medical University of Lübeck in Germany published results suggesting that a common method of preparing brain tissue for microscopic study causes young cortical tissue to shrink more than old tissue. This raised the possibility that the earlier studies, which were based on cell density measures, showed higher densities in young brains simply because the tissue had shrunk more. Indeed, taking this shrinkage into account, Haug's group found no evidence of cortical neuron loss with age in a study of 120 normal human brains.

At the time, that conclusion was roundly criticized. The critics pointed out that differential shrinkage should not have been a problem for all the earlier studies, as some investigators had also noticed the problem and attempted to correct for it, while others used tissue preparation methods that didn't cause shrinkage. But in 1987, results obtained by neuropathologist Robert Terry of the University of California, San Diego, and his colleagues suggested that something else might have led the older studies astray. Because the methods used to screen for brain pathologies were not as sensitive as those developed later, Terry suggested, earlier researchers may have inadvertently included brains with Alzheimer's disease or other dementias known to cause rampant cell death.

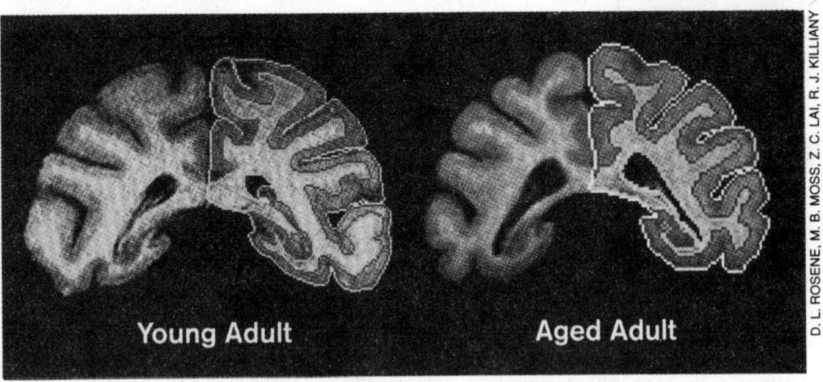

No shades of gray. These MRI images show loss of white, but not gray, matter in the brain of a 32-year-old rhesus monkey *(right)*. The young adult is 5 years old.

Consistent with that idea, when Terry and his colleagues examined 51 normal brains, carefully screened to eliminate those showing signs of Alzheimer's or other pathologies, they saw a decrease with age in the number of large neurons, but they also found an equal increase in the number of small neurons. The conclusion: Neurons shrink but don't disappear. "Brody is an excellent scientist, but I'm confident that he included Alzheimer's cases and that these lowered his cell counts," Terry says.

Since then, other results have buttressed the idea that normal brains, unlike those of Alzheimer's patients, show little loss of cortical neurons. Some of these come from Alan Peters, Mark Moss, Doug Rosene, and their colleagues at Boston University School of Medicine, who have been studying rhesus monkeys. Although these animals don't develop Alzheimer's disease, they do suffer a humanlike cognitive decline with age—but with no apparent loss of cortical neurons.

In work begun about 10 years ago, the Boston workers found no relation between either cell counts and age or cell counts and cognitive function in areas of the neocortex as diverse as the visual cortex, motor cortex, and prefrontal cortex, a region involved in problem-solving tasks that require holding complex information in mind and manipulating it. "When we first began looking at monkeys, we assumed there'd be a loss of neurons from the cortex," Peters recalls. "It took a long time to find out there isn't."

And human work that is just now being published also finds little or no loss of cortical neurons in normal aging. In a study that began 16 years ago and is still continuing, John Morris, Leonard Berg, and their colleagues at Washington University Medical School in St. Louis have been following more than 200 subjects who were all healthy when they entered the study. The researchers test the cognitive abilities of the participants annually and also interview their close relatives, looking for subtle signs of mental slippage that augur early dementia. When the subjects die, Hyman's team at Mass. General examines their brains for evidence of pathology, including cell loss.

Results on the first 10 normal subjects, which will appear in the 15 July issue of the *Journal of Neuroscience*, show no age-related differences in cell numbers between ages 60 and 90 in the entorhinal cortex, a structure critical to memory and a way station for signals passing from the neocortex to the hippocampus. And, in as yet unpublished work on 28 normal brains, the Mass. General team detected no cell losses between the ages of 57 and 98 in an area of the neocortex called the superior temporal sulcus that is involved in a number of cognitive functions.

In contrast, a group of age-matched patients with early dementia had lost half the cells in the entorhinal cortex, and a third group with more advanced Alzheimer's disease was missing up to 65% of the cells in both of the brain structures examined. "If one thing seems clear," says Dennis Dickson, a neuropathologist at Albert Einstein College of Medicine in the Bronx, New York, "it's that normal aging is different from Alzheimer's disease."

Nevertheless, because so much older data supports the idea of extensive neuronal loss, even in normal aging, many researchers want more evidence before they discard the idea. For example, some experts think that more areas of the brain need to be sampled in healthy people. "Additional work is needed to map out the locus of the most salient age-related changes in carefully screened subjects," says Mony de Leon, who studies brain aging at New York University School of Medicine.

Skeptics also point out that all studies based on neuronal counts suffer from uncertainties. One problem is that tissue can undergo structural changes after death but before it is scientifically scrutinized. Another is that researchers can perform only one count—at the age of death—from any given individual. As a result, they don't have a baseline for telling whether that particular brain lost neurons. "If a neuron left behind a signpost when it died, then we could directly measure cell loss," says Dickson. Instead, scientists must infer a loss of cells by comparing the brains of subjects who die at different ages—a tricky comparison because individuals can vary in the number of cells they start with.

What's more, imaging studies have shown that the brain shrinks with age, and many people interpret that shrinkage as cell loss. For example, in work published 4 years ago, Stanley Rapoport, chief of the neuroscience laboratory at the National Institute on Aging, used magnetic resonance imaging (MRI) on the brains of healthy men and saw a 10% drop in total brain volume in men over 60 versus that of men more than 25 years younger. Rapoport's team also has data suggesting that some of the shrinkage is occurring in gray matter, which contains neuronal cell bodies, although his data point most clearly to loss in subcortical nuclei.

"There likely is a real loss of neurons that occurs with healthy aging," Rapoport maintains. De Leon's team saw something similar when comparing images of the cortex from young adults in their 20s and 30s with those from people in their 60s and 70s. They found a small but significant loss of both gray matter and white matter, which contains the axons, the long nerve projections that carry electrical messages between neurons.

But other imaging studies indicate that brain shrinkage might be due almost exclusively to loss of white matter. In an MRI study of 70 healthy human brains reported 3 years ago, Marilyn Albert of Harvard Medical School and her colleagues found almost no change in the gray matter, but an 8% drop in white matter, between the ages of 30 and 80. "It used to be thought that we lose neurons every day of our lives. That's just not true—at least for the cortex," says Albert.

Peters and his colleagues go one step further: They have evidence that changes in white matter may account for the cognitive changes in aging rhesus monkeys. They originally got this idea 5 or 6 years ago when they saw a breakdown of the fatty sheaths of myelin that insulate axons in old monkey brains, but not in young ones. Then, over the last 2 years, the researchers followed up on this observation, examining how the change might relate to the animals' cognitive status.

Using preserved tissue from seven old monkey brains from their previous work, they ranked the degree of myelin erosion in one small part of the neocortex. In work not yet published, they discovered that the extent of disorder paralleled the monkeys' degree of cognitive impairment. "We're beginning to think that myelin breakdown might be bringing about most of the changes with age," Peters says. Now the researchers also have indirect clues using MRI that this breakdown occurs throughout the cerebral hemispheres, which include the neocortex, resulting in a 10% shrinkage in white matter in old monkeys. At the same time, they reported at last fall's Society of Neuroscience meeting, they found no age-related differences in the volume of the animals' gray matter.

Myelin loss might contribute to the cognitive deficits of aging because it is necessary for the rapid conduction of impulses along an axon. While the Boston University biologists theorize that myelin breakdown slows neural traffic everywhere in the brain, it may have its greatest impact in the prefrontal cortex because speed may be most critical to the problem-solving tasks performed there. Indeed, it is these types of tasks that elderly people perform less quickly and accurately than do young adults. "Changes in white matter could have significant effects on the brain," says Peter Rapp, a neuroanatomist at the State University of New York, Stony Brook. "But [the Boston group's] observations need to be confirmed in larger numbers of animals" and with quantitative measures of myelin pathology.

Myelin is not the only neuronal component that may atrophy with age, possibly leading to a decline in nerve cell function. In one of the few quantitative, molecular studies of normal brain aging, John Morrison and Adam Gazzaley at Mount Sinai School of Medicine in New York City and their colleagues have discovered evidence for an age-related drop of about 30% in the density of the *N*-methyl-D-aspartate (NMDA) receptor for the neurotransmitter glutamate, which is thought to play a critical role in learning and memory. The receptor loss occurs in nerve cells at the end of the perforant path, a critical neural circuit that funnels information from the neocortex to the hippocampus and is "extremely vulnerable to aging," Morrison says. Moreover, the perforant-path nerve terminals and the neurons to which they connect were both intact, suggesting that the NMDA receptor decrease occurs without associated structural degeneration of nerve cells.

Not only the receptors but the neurotransmitters themselves may decline with age, impairing nerve cell function. Although cells may not die off in large numbers in the cortex, they are lost in other parts of the brain, such as the brainstem, and the loss changes brain chemistry. For example, some brainstem neurons produce dopamine, a neurotransmitter whose levels decline with age in the monkey neocortex, and that drop, Amy Arnsten, Patricia Goldman-Rakic, and their colleagues at Yale University have shown, contributes to the kind of memory deficits seen in normal aging.

But as long as cortical neurons remain alive, there may be ways to boost their function and stave off mental decline in old age. This might be accomplished, for example, by drugs that compensate for neurotransmitter deficiencies, or provide an extra tweak for the remaining receptors, or help prevent myelin loss, if that is indeed contributing to neuronal dysfunction. And those prospects raise hopes that one day, even the subtle memory deficits of old age will become a distant memory.

–Ingrid Wickelgren

Additional Reading

M. Albert, "Neuropsychological and neurophysiological changes in healthy adult humans across the age range," *Neurobiology of Aging* **14**, 623 (1993).

A.F.T. Arnsten *et al.*, "Dopamine D1 receptor mechanisms in the cognitive performance of young adult and aged monkeys," *Psychopharmacology* **116**, 143 (1994).

A. H. Gazzaley *et al.*, "Circuit-specific alterations of *N*-methyl-D-aspartate receptor subunit 1 in the dentate gyrus of aged monkeys," *Proceedings of the National Academy of Sciences* **93**, 3121 (1996).

A. Peters *et al.*, "The effects of aging on area 46 of the frontal cortex of the rhesus monkey," *Cerebral Cortex* **6**, 621 (1994).

Ingrid Wickelgren is a free-lance writer in Brooklyn, New York.

Sensation and Perception

One of the ways that prisoners of war were induced to reveal secrets was by keeping them in isolation, deprived of most sensory stimulation. Prisoners who survived to report such treatment expressed severe psychological discomfort, such as hallucinations and emotional turmoil. They considered the experience to be as bad as physical torture.

These reports suggest that sensory stimulation is important in maintaining a healthy psychological state. Between 1950 and 1970, systematic investigations were conducted to examine the effects of sensory deprivation in humans. One experimental setup consisted of a tiny boxlike room without windows, with a mattress on the floor on which the subject had to lie down. Extraneous sounds were eliminated and the room temperature was held constant. The subject's eyes were covered and hands were wrapped in gloves. Another experimental setup consisted of an opaque tank that looked like a coffin filled with warm saline water. The subject was asked to lie floating inside the tank. With the lid of the tank down, sound and light stimuli were eliminated. Both contraptions were designed to deprive the subjects of sensory stimulation.

Most of the subjects quit the study within 2 days in spite of the fair monetary incentive given for participating. Subjects reported unbearable psychological discomfort similar to that experienced by prisoners of war. Although sensory deprivation studies are not popular anymore, they did confirm the hypothesis that sensory stimulation is essential for our well-being.

Organisms possess a variety of sensory systems, such as the systems for vision, smell, and touch. Some sensory systems are highly developed in certain species. For example, eagles have acute vision, enabling them to fly hundreds of feet above ground hunting for prey. Cats have acute night vision that is adapted to a nocturnal lifestyle. Humans do not have these attributes simply because we do not need them—our habitat and lifestyle are different.

The human visual system is still remarkably sophisticated compared to other sensory systems. Much more is known about the visual system than of other sensory modalities, possibly because scientists consider the visual system to be the most relevant. Some people who are deprived of the sense of sight are able to adapt to their environment by utilizing the functions of other sensory systems, such as the sense of touch.

The sense of smell is the most important sensory modality for a number of mammalian species. Dogs and cats, for example, investigate the environment by way of olfaction. The olfactory system uses odors as a means of communication. These odors are processed by specialized cells in the nasal cavity and neurons in the brain.

Is olfaction critically important in humans? Certainly it is annoying not to be able to smell anything when you have a cold, but apparently it is not a life-threatening condition. The olfactory bulb, which contains neurons that process olfactory information, is tiny in humans compared to the analogous structure in other mammals relative to the overall brain size. Does this mean that the olfactory system in humans has become irrelevant through the course of evolution? If so, how do we explain the phenomenal success of the perfume industry?

Looking Ahead: Challenge Questions

Discuss the neural pathway for olfaction. How do we perceive odors? What are pheromones? Can you cite examples of pheromones in animals? Do you believe that humans also communicate by way of pheromones? If so, cite some situations in humans.

Describe the neural pathway involved in processing visual stimuli. Which part of the brain is specialized to process visual information? Differentiate visual sensation from visual perception. Where in the central nervous system do these events happen?

UNIT 4

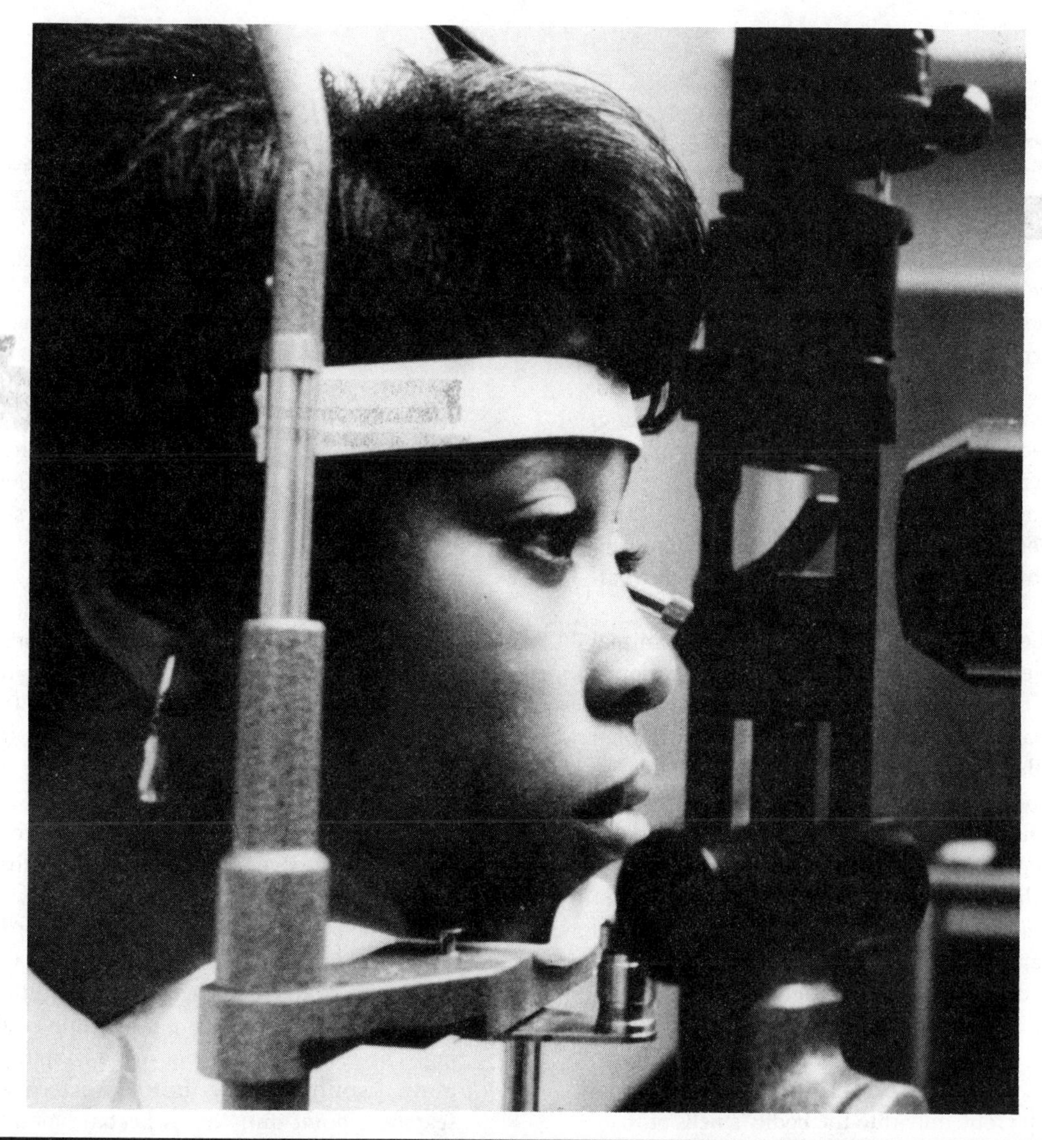

The Smell of Love

After long dismissing the search for a human pheromone as folly, scientists have begun to take a second look at how human body odor influences sexual attraction. The magic scent is not some romantic elixir but the aromatic effluence of our immune system. The only trouble is we don't give it half a chance. By F. Bryant Furlow

How do we humans announce, and excite, sexual availability? Many animals do it with their own biochemical bouquets known as pheromones. "Why do bulls and horses turn up their nostrils when excited by love?" Darwin pondered deep in one of his unpublished notebooks. He came to believe that natural selection designed animals to produce two, and only two, types of odors—defensive ones, like the skunk's, and scents for territorial marking and mate attracting, like that exuded by the male musk deer and bottled by perfumers everywhere. The evaluative sniffing that mammals engage in during courtship were clues that scent is the chemical equivalent of the peacock's plumage or the nightingale's song—finery with which to attract mates.

In the following century, a rich array of animal pheromones were documented for seals, boars, rodents, and all manner of other critters. But not for human beings.

Some of Darwin's contemporaries embraced human uniqueness in this regard as evidence of our inevitable ascendance, as if Nature's Plan somehow called for the evolution of a nearly naked two-legged primate with a poor sense of smell to conquer the Earth. The French physician Paul Broca—noting that primates' social olfactory abilities are diminished compared to those of other mammals—asserted that monkeys, apes, and humans represent ascending steps from four-legged sniffing beasts to sight-oriented bipeds.

Monkeys, he argued, have smaller "smell brains" than other mammals, and apes' brains are even smaller than that. Among humans, only the tribal "primitives," Broca wrote, could still attach erotic import to the bodily smells of man.

More enlightened researchers dismissed such views as racist tripe. But they still noted that humans engage in very little scent-driven socializing—compared to, say, the urine-washing displays of monkeys (during which urine is rubbed on the feet to attract mates).

To make matters worse, humans seemed to lack the hardware for communicating by scent. Pheromone reception in other species is the business of two little pits (one in each nostril) known collectively as the vomeronasal organ (VNO). Few scientists of the time claimed to have been able to locate a human VNO. Those who did complained that the VNO is so small that they could detect it only rarely.

But most scientists, without bothering to look, simply dismissed the idea of a VNO in humans. It's been scientific dogma for most of this century that humans do not rely on scent to any appreciable degree, and that any VNOs found are vestigial throwbacks. Then, in the 1930s, physiologists declared that humans lack the brain part to process VNO signals, firmly closing the book on any role for body odor in human sexual attraction. Even if we had a VNO, the thinking was, our brains wouldn't be able to interpret its signals.

Recent discoveries suggest, however, that the reports of our olfactory devolution have been greatly exaggerated.

Some suspected as much the whole time. Smell researchers Barbara Sommerville and David Gee of the University of Leeds in England observed that smelling one another's hands or faces is a nearly universal human greeting. The Eskimo kiss is not just a rubbing of noses but a mutual sniffing. "Only in the Western world," the researchers point out, "has it become modified to a kiss."

Overall, women prefer those scents **exuded by men whose immune system** genes vary most from their own.

Hands and faces may be significant choices for these formalities—they are the two most accessible concentrations of scent glands on the human body besides the ears.

✿ Scent and Sentiment

Curiously, remembering a smell is usually difficult—yet when exposed to certain scents, many people—of whom Proust is the paragon—may suddenly recall a distant childhood memory in emotionally rich detail. Some aromas even affect us physiologically. Laboratory researchers exploring human olfaction have found that:

✿ A faint trace of lemon significantly increases people's perception of their own health.

✿ Lavender incense contributes to a pleasant mood—but it lowers volunteers' mathematical abilities.

✿ A whiff of lavender and eucalyptus increases people's respiratory rate and alertness.

✿ The scent of phenethyl alcohol (a constituent of rose oil) reduces blood pressure.

Such findings have led to the rapid development of an aromatherapy industry. Aromatherapists point to scientific findings that smell can dramatically affect our moods as evidence that therapy with aromatic oils can help buyers manage their emotional lives.

Mood is demonstrably affected by scent. But scientists have found that, despite some extravagant industry promises, the attraction value in perfumes resides strictly in their pleasantness, not their sexiness. So far, at least, store-bought scent is more decoration than mood manager or love potion. A subtle "look this way" nudge to the nose, inspiring a stranger's curiosity, or at most a smile, is all perfume advertisers can in good conscience claim for their products—not overwhelming and immediate infatuation.

Grandiose claims for the allure of a bottled smell are not new. In their haste to mass-market sexual attraction during the last century, perfumers nearly drove the gentle musk deer extinct. In Victorian England, a nice-smelling young lady with financial savvy could do a brisk business selling handkerchiefs scented with her body odor.

So it should come as no surprise that when physiologists discovered a functioning vomeronasal organ inside the human nose, it was a venture capitalist intent on cashing in on manufactured human pheromone who funded the team's research. That was less than a decade ago. Using high-tech microscope probes that were unavailable to VNO hunters earlier in the century, a team led by Luis Monti-Bloch of the University of Utah found a tiny pair of pits, one in each nostril, snuggled up against the septum an inch inside the nose.

The pits are lined with receptor cells that fire like mad when presented with certain substances. Yet subjects report that they don't smell a thing during such experiments. What they often do report is a warm, vague feeling of well-being.

And the olfactory bulb that neurophysiologists couldn't find in the 1930s isn't absent in human brains at all, researchers recently discovered. It's just so enveloped by the massive frontal cortex that it's very difficult to find. This finding, coupled with the discovery of a functional human VNO, has ushered in a new chapter of the story of a human pheromone.

Get a Whiff of the Myths!

Humans have smaller "smell brains" than the rest of the animal kingdom.

Oops. The olfactory bulb has been there all along. It's just that it's hard to find, buried in folds and folds of the frontal cortex.

Okay, but we're above scent-driven socialization.

Left to its own devices, body scent plays a large and very clever role in mate attraction.

The sexiest smells humans produce are related to the sex hormones.

Actually, the body scents important in mate attraction are—this even surprised researchers—aromatic byproducts of the immune system.

Each of us has a unique "smellprint" that is equally appealing to all others.

How pleasant and sexy our body odors are is a totally relative matter. We smell best to a person whose genetically based immunity to disease differs most from our own.

The notion that animal senses play a role in personal attraction diminishes our humanity.

Scientific understanding of the role of smell in our lives leads only to conclusions that our tastes and emotions are highly sophisticated, the product of many inputs.

THE GREAT PHEROMONE HUNT

FOR AN ANIMAL whose nose supposedly plays no role in sexual attraction or social life, human emotions are strongly moved by smells. And we appear to be profoundly overequipped with smell-producing hardware for what little sniffing we have been thought to be up to. Human sweat, urine, breath, saliva, breast milk, skin oils, and sexual secretions all contain scent-communicating chemical compounds. Zoologist Michael Stoddart, author of *The Scented Ape* (Cambridge University Press, 1991), points out that humans possess denser skin concentrations of scent glands than almost any other mammal. This makes little sense until one abandons the myth that humans pay little attention to the fragrant or the rancid in their day-to-day lives.

Part of the confusion may be due to the fact that not all smells register in our conscious minds. When those telltale scents were introduced to the VNO of human subjects, they didn't report smelling anything—but nevertheless demonstrated subtle changes in mood.

What could be a source of what might be our very own pheromone?

Humans possess three major types of skin glands—sebaceous glands, eccrine (or sweat) glands, and apocrine glands. Sebaceous glands are most common on the face and forehead but occur around all of the body's openings, including eyelids, ears, nostrils, lips, and nipples. This placement is particularly handy, as the secretions of these glands kill potentially dangerous microorganisms. They also contain fats that keep skin supple and waterproof—and, on the downside, cause acne. Little is known, however, about how sebaceous glands contribute to human body odor.

The sweat glands exude water and salt and are nonodorous in healthy people. That leaves the third potential source of a human pheromone—the apocrine gland. Apocrine glands hold special promise as the source of smells that might affect interpersonal interactions. They do not serve any temperature-managing functions in people, as

HOW TO SMELL A MATE

How does body odor affect a woman's sexiness? Scientists don't know for sure, but they do know that a man's allure depends in part on how many immune system genes he shares with a potential mate.

Since it's known that women can detect genetic compatibility by smell—it's not that men can't but that so far no one knows—the onus is on females to sniff out a suitable squire.

Choosing a genetically compatible partner can be difficult in today's perfume rich postindustrial jungle, and getting your immune system genes profiled can be expensive. Before you run to a doctor for blood work to see whether your mate is a suitable match—and sire for your future children—try listening to your nose. (Unfortunately, the sniff test will only work if you're not taking birth control pills.)

• 1. Declare a deception-free day for the nostrils. Have your beau shower with fragrance-free soap and wear clean cotton clothing for a day, away from smokers and the perfumed masses. Be sure you don't have a cold, and that you yourself haven't been around smokers for a few days.

• 2. After he spends a day and a night in his cotton clothes, before he tosses them in the direction of the hamper, wrestle them form him and have a "smell-down." Make it a romantic experience. If your man's shirt doesn't offend, you should be safe. (Find the scent alluring or sexy? Even better! That attraction is nature's way of telling you he's a safe contributor to your offspring's genetic ensemble.)

• 3. If your man's odor reminds you of your father or of a brother, you may want to consider getting in touch with your doctor and ask about genetic tests before trying to conceive a child. Tell the doctor you're concerned that you may share a close MHC or "HLA" profile. (HLA, for human leukocyte antigen, is a technical tag for human MHC.) Meanwhile, a deceptively pleasing gift of cologne might be in order.

• 4. Genetic incompatibility is not the only reason you may find his odor offensive. Does his body scent seem unusually intense? He might have a medical condition that explains the smell. Ask him to bring it up at his next medical checkup. A very sweet scent is sometimes evidence of diabetes or schizophrenia—both of which appear to be heritable. It is wise to discuss these issues with each other, and with a doctor, before having kids.

• 5. Before you decide that your relationship stinks, check your mate's diet. A taste for spicy foods or an overindulgence in garlic can cause strong body odors.

• 6. If your mate still offends, don't head for the hills just yet. Some clothing detergents can prove to be a bad mix with a fella's scent. Ask that the next time he visits the laundry, he change brands—and give the stinker a second chance!—F.B.F.

they do in other animals. They occur in dense concentrations on hands, cheeks, scalp, breast areolas, and wherever we possess body hair—and are only functional after puberty, when we begin searching for mates.

Men's apocrine glands are larger than women's, and they secrete most actively during times of nervousness or excitement. Waiting colonies of bacteria turn apocrine secretions into the noxious fumes that keep deodorant makers in business. Hair provides surface area from which apocrine smells can diffuse—part of the reason why hairier men smell particularly pungent. (Is it any coincidence that hair at the arm pit and the genitals sprouts at puberty, when apocrine glands start producing food for our skin bacteria?)

Most promising of all, apocrine glands exude odorous steroids known to affect sexual behavior in other mammals. Androsterone—a steroid related to the one that nearly doomed the hapless musk deer—is one such substance. Men secrete more androsterone than women do, and most men become unable to detect the stuff right around the time they start producing it themselves—at puberty.

In 1986, the National Geographic Society organized the World Smell Survey to investigate whether people from all cultures experience odor in the same fashion. They distributed over a million scratch-and-sniff cards and questionnaires about subjects' detection and perceptions of intensity of smells, from banana to the sulfur compounds added to natural gas as a warning agent. Included in the survey was the scent of human androsterone.

The steroid itself is not pleasant to smell. Worldwide, those who could smell it rated it second to last in pleasantness—just ahead of the sulfur compounds put in natural gas. A foul-smelling pheromone? It's hardly what scientists expected to find.

✿ Anti-Pheromones?

DESPITE THE poor showing of androsterone in smell ratings, Karl Grammer of Austria's Institute for Human Biology thought it might be the sought-after human pheromone and studied women's reactions to it. He expected to find that women have a strong, favorable reaction to the smell of androsterone around ovulation, when their sense of smell becomes more acute and when they are most likely to conceive. Changes in their bodies' estrogen levels around ovulation, Grammer suspected, may change how women react to androsterone's smell.

He found that women's reactions to androsterone indeed change around ovulation—but not in the manner he expected. Instead of attraction, Grammer's ovulating volunteers shrugged their shoulders and reported indifference. Androsterone, it seems, offers little hope to men looking for a $19.95 solution to their dating slumps.

If your man's odor reminds you of Dad or your brother, you may want genetic tests before trying to conceive a child.

✿ Of Mice and Men

THE EMPIRICAL proof of odor's effect on human sexual attraction came out of left field. Medical geneticists studying inheritance rules for the immune system, not smell physiologists, made a series of crucial discoveries that nobody believed were relevant to human mate preferences—at first.

Research on tissue rejection in organ transplant surgery patients led to the discovery that the body recognizes an alien presence (whether a virus or a surgically implanted kidney) because the body's own cells are coated with proteins that our immune system recognizes as "self." But the immune system gets a lot more subtle about recognizing "nonself" intruders. It can recognize specific types of disease organisms, attach protein identifiers to them, and muster antibodies designed specifically for destroying that particular disease. And it can "remember" that particular invader years later, sending out specific antibodies to it.

A segment of our DNA called the major histocompatibility complex (MHC) codes for some of these disease-detecting structures, which function as the immune system's eyes. When a disease is recognized, the immune system's teeth—the killer T cells—are alerted, and they swarm the intruders, smothering them with destructive enzymes.

Unlike many genes, which have one or two alternative versions (like the genes that code for attached or unattached ear lobes), MHC genes have dozens of alternatives. And unlike earlobe genes, in which the version inherited from one parent dominates so that the version inherited from the other parent is not expressed, MHC genes are "co-dominant." This means that if a lab mouse inherits a version of an MHC gene for resistance to Disease A from its mother and a version lending resistance to Disease B from its father, that mouse will be able to resist both diseases.

When a female mouse is offered two suitors in mate

Females' superior sense of smell **may be due to their need to more carefully** evaluate a potential mate's merits.

choice trials, she inevitably chooses to mate with the one whose MHC genes least overlap with her own. It turns out that female mice evaluate males' MHC profile by sniffing their urine. The immune system creates scented proteins that are unique to every version of each MHC gene. These immune by-products are excreted from the body with other used-up chemicals, allowing a discerning female to sniff out exactly how closely related to her that other mouse is.

By choosing MHC-dissimilar mates, a female mouse makes sure that she doesn't inbreed. She also secures a survival advantage for her offspring by assuring that they will have a wider range of disease resistance than they would had she mated with her brother.

It's not that she seeks out diverse MHC genes for her young on purpose, of course. Ancestral females who preferred the smell of closely related males were simply outrun through evolutionary time by females who preferred the scent of unrelated sires.

✿ Can You Smell That Smell?

SINCE HUMANS show little interest in one another's urine, few researchers thought that the story of MHC in rodent attraction could shed light on human interactions. But then someone made an eyebrow-raising discovery: Human volunteers can discriminate between mice that differ genetically only in their MHC. If human noses could detect small differences in the immune systems of mice (mice!) by giving the critters a sniff, excited researchers realized, we may well be able to detect the aromatic by-products of the immune system in human body odor as well!

A team led by Claus Wedekind at the University of Bern in Switzerland decided to see whether MHC differences in men's apocrine gland secretions affected women's ratings of male smells. The team recruited just under 100 college students. Males and females were sought from different schools, to reduce the chances that they knew each other. The men were given untreated cotton T-shirts to wear as they slept alone for two consecutive nights. They were told not to eat spicy foods; not to use deodorants, cologne, or perfumed soaps; and to avoid smoking, drinking, and sex during the two-day experiment. During the day, their sweaty shirts were kept in sealed plastic containers.

And then came the big smell test. For two weeks prior, women had used a nasal spray to protect the delicate mucous membranes lining the nose. Around the time they were ovulating (when their sense of smell is enhanced), the women were put alone in a room and presented with boxes containing the male volunteers' shirts. First they sniffed a new, unworn shirt to control for the scent of the shirts themselves. Then the women were asked to rate each man's shirt for "sexiness," "pleasantness," and "intensity of smell."

✿ Sexy Genes

IT WAS FOUND, by Wedekind and his team, that how women rate a man's body odor pleasantness and sexiness depends upon how much of their MHC profile is shared. Overall, women prefer those scents exuded by men whose MHC profiles varied the most from their own. Hence, any given man's odor could be pleasingly alluring to one woman, yet an offensive turnoff to another.

Raters said that the smells they preferred reminded them of current or ex-lovers about twice as often as did the smells of men who have MHC profiles similar to their own, suggesting that smell had played a role in past decisions about who to date. MHC-similar men's smells were more often described as being like a brother's or father's body odor...as would be expected if the components of smell being rated are MHC determined.

Somewhat more surprising is that women's evaluations of

When a Kiss Is Not a Kiss!

The Eskimo kiss is a rubbing of noses.

In reality it is a case of mutual sniffing of bodily smells. Only in the Western world has mutual sniffing been reprogrammed to a kiss.

We humans are smell poor, possessing less hardware for smelling than other animals.

Recent findings demonstrate that we have lots of scent-related equipment.

People pay little attention to the fragrant or the rancid in their everyday lives.

Human sweat, urine, breath, saliva, breast milk, skin oils, and sexual secretions all contain scent-laden chemical compounds. Part of the problem is that not all smells register in our conscious mind—although they may nonetheless influence mood.

body odor intensities did not differ between MHC-similar and MHC-dissimilar men. Body scent for MHC-dissimilar men was rated as less sexy and less pleasant the stronger it was, but intensity did not affect the women's already low ratings for MHC-similar men's smells.

That strong odor turned raters off even with MHC-dissimilar men may be due to the fact that strong body odor is a useful indicator of disease. From diabetes to viral infection to schizophrenia, unusually sweet or strong body odors are a warning cue that ancestral females in search of good genes for their offspring may have been designed to heed. (In the case of schizophrenia, the issue is confounded—while some schizophrenics do actually have an unusually sweet smell, many suffer from delusions of foul smells emanating from their bodies.)

Nobody yet knows what roles MHC may play in male evaluations of female attractiveness. Females' superior sense of smell, however, may well be due to their need to more carefully evaluate a potential mate's merits—a poor mate choice for male ancestors may have meant as little as a few minutes wasted, whereas a human female's mistake could result in a nine-month-long "morning after" and a child unlikely to survive.

Perfumers who really want to provide that sexy allure to their male customers will apparently need to get a genetic fingerprint of the special someone before they can tailor a scent that she will find attractive. But before men contemplate fooling women in this way, they should consider the possible consequences.

✿ Fooling Mother Nature

THE SWISS researchers found that women taking oral contraceptives (which block conception by tricking the body into thinking it's pregnant) reported reversed preferences, liking more the smells that reminded them of home and kin. Since the Pill reverses natural preferences, a woman may feel attracted to men she wouldn't normally notice if she were not on birth control—men who have similar MHC profiles.

The effects of such evolutionary novel mate choices can go well beyond the bewilderment of a wife who stops taking her contraceptive pills and notices her husband's "newly" foul body odor. Couples experiencing difficulty conceiving a child—even after several attempts at tubal embryo transfer—share significantly more of their MHC than do couples who conceive more easily. These couples' grief is not caused by either partner's infertility, but to an unfortunate combination of otherwise viable genes.

Doctors have known since the mid-1980s that couples suffering repeated spontaneous abortions tend to share more of their MHC than couples for whom pregnancies are carried to term. And even when MHC-similar couples do successfully bring a pregnancy to term, their babies are often underweight.

The Swiss team believes that MHC-related pregnancy problems in humans are too widespread to be due to inbreeding alone. They argue that in-couple infertility problems are due to strategic, unconscious "decisions" made by women's bodies to curtail investment in offspring with inferior immune systems—offspring unlikely to have survived to adulthood in the environments of our evolutionary past.

When Broca and other social Darwinists pointed out that "uncivilized races" were more sensitive to body odor, they may have been correct—insofar as Europeans tend to go to greater lengths to perfume and wash away their natural scents. But this is hardly evidence of European superiority over "less evolved" peoples, as Broca insisted. Paying careful attention to the health of others and their suitability as sires to one's offspring in the disease-rich tropics, whose cultures Broca derided, actually makes exceedingly good sense.

Perfume; daily, soapy showers; convenient contraceptive pills—all have their charms. But they also may be short-circuiting our own built-in means of mate choice, adaptations shaped to our unique needs by millions of years of ancestral adversities. The existence of couples who long for children they cannot have indicates that the Western dismissal of body scent is scarcely benign.

Those who find offensive the notion that animal senses play a role in their attraction to a partner need not worry. As the role of smell in human affairs yields to understanding, we see not that we are less human but that our tastes and emotions are far more complex and sophisticated than anyone ever imagined.

THE SENSES

They delight, heal, define the boundaries of our world. And they are helping unlock the brain's secrets

To the 19th-century French poet Charles Baudelaire, there was no such thing as a bad smell. What a squeamish, oversensitive bunch he would have deemed the denizens of 20th-century America, where body odors are taboo, strong aromas are immediately suppressed with air freshener, and perfume—long celebrated for its seductive and healing powers—is banned in some places to protect those with multiple chemical sensitivities.

Indeed, in the years since Baudelaire set pen to paper, civilization has played havoc with the natural state of all the human senses, technology providing the ability not only to tame and to mute but also to tease and overstimulate. Artificial fragrances and flavors trick the nose and tongue. Advertisers dazzle the eyes with rapid-fire images. Wailing sirens vie with the beeping of pagers to challenge the ears' ability to cope.

Yet even as we fiddle with the texture and scope of our sensibilities, science is indicating it might behoove us to show them a bit more respect. Growing evidence documents the surprising consequences of depriving or overwhelming the senses. And failing to nurture our natural capabilities, researchers are discovering, can affect health, emotions, even intelligence. Hearing, for example, is intimately connected to emotional circuits: When a nursing infant looks up from the breast, muscles in the middle ear reflexively tighten, readying the child for the pitch of a human voice. The touch of massage can relieve pain and improve concentration. And no matter how we spritz or scrub, every human body produces a natural odor as distinctive as the whorls on the fingertips—an aroma that research is showing to be a critical factor in choosing a sexual partner.

Beyond their capacity to heal and delight, the senses have also opened a window on the workings of the human brain. A flood of studies on smell, sight, hearing, touch and taste in the last two decades have upended most of the theories about how the brain functions. Scientists once believed, for example, that the brain was hard-wired at birth, the trillions of connections that made up its neural circuits genetically predetermined. But a huge proportion of neurons in a newborn infant's brain, it turns out, require input from the senses in order to hook up to one another properly.

Similarly, scientific theory until recently held that the sense organs did the lion's share of processing information about the world: The eye detected movement; the nose recognized smells. But researchers now know that ears, eyes and fingers are only way stations, transmitting signals that are then processed centrally. "The nose doesn't smell—the brain does," says Richard Axel, a molecular biologist at Columbia University. Each of our senses shatters experience into fragments, parsing the world like so many nouns and verbs, then leaving the brain to put the pieces back together and make sense of it all.

In labs across the country, researchers are drafting a picture of the senses that promises not only to unravel the mysterious tangle of nerves in the brain but also to offer reasons to revel in sensuous experience. Cradling a baby not only feels marvelous, scientists are finding, but is absolutely vital to a newborn's emotional and cognitive development. And the results of this research are beginning to translate into practical help for people whose senses are impaired: Researchers in Boston last year unveiled a tiny electronic device called a retinal chip that one day may restore sight to people blinded after childhood. Gradually, this new science of the senses is redefining what it means to be a feeling and thinking human being. One day it may lead to an understanding of consciousness itself.

SIGHT

Seeing is believing, because vision is the body's top intelligence gatherer, at least by the brain's reckoning. A full quarter of the cerebral cortex, the brain's crinkled top layer, is devoted to sight, according to a new estimate by neuroscientist David Van Essen of Washington University in St. Louis—almost certainly more than is devoted to any other sense.

SIGHT

Cells in the retina of the eye are so sensitive they can respond to a single photon, or particle of light.

It seems fitting, then, that vision has offered scientists their most powerful insights on the brain's structure and operations. Research on sight "has been absolutely fundamental" for understanding the brain, says neurobiologist Semir Zeki of University College in London, in part because the visual system is easier to study than the other senses. The first clues to the workings of the visual system emerged in the 1950s, when Johns Hopkins neurobiologists David Hubel and Torsten Wiesel conducted a series of Nobel Prize–winning experiments. Using hair-thin electrodes implanted in a cat's brain, they recorded the firing of single neurons in the area where vision is processed. When the animal was looking at a diagonal bar of light, one neuron fired. When the bar was at a slightly different angle, a different nerve cell responded.

Hubel and Wiesel's discovery led to a revolutionary idea: While we are perceiving a unified scene, the brain is dissecting the view into many parts, each of which triggers a different set of neurons, called a visual map. One map responds to color and form, another only to motion. There are at least five such maps in the visual system alone, and recent work is showing that other senses are similarly encoded in the brain. In an auditory map, for example, the two sets of neurons that respond to two similar sounds, such as "go" and "ko," are located near each other, while those resonating with the sound "mo" lie at a distance.

Though we think of sensory abilities as independent, researchers are finding that each sense receives help from the others in apprehending the world. In 1995, psycholinguist Michael Tanenhaus of the University of Rochester videotaped people as they listened to sentences about nearby objects. As they listened, the subjects' eyes flicked to the objects. Those movements—so fast the subjects did not realize they'd shifted their gaze—helped them understand the grammar of the sentences, Tanenhaus found. Obviously, vision isn't required to comprehend grammar. But given the chance, the brain integrates visual cues while processing language.

The brain also does much of the heavy lifting for color vision, so much so that some people with brain damage see the world in shades of gray. But the ability to see colors begins with cells in the back of the eyeball called cones. For decades, scientists thought everyone with normal color vision had the same three types of cone cell—for red, green and blue light—and saw the same hues. New research shows, however, that everybody sees a different palette. Last year, Medical College of Wisconsin researchers Maureen Neitz and her husband, Jay, discovered that people have up to nine genes for cones, indicating there may be many kinds of cones. Already, two red cone subtypes have been found. People with one type see red differently from those with the second. Says Maureen Neitz: "That's why people argue about adjusting the color on the TV set."

HEARING

Hearing is the gateway to language, a uniquely human skill. In a normal child, the ears tune themselves to human sounds soon after birth, cementing the neural connections between language, emotions and intelligence. Even a tiny glitch in the way a child processes sound can unhinge development.

About 7 million American children who have normal hearing and intelligence develop intractable problems with language, reading and writing because they cannot decipher certain parcels of language. Research by Paula Tallal, a Rutgers University neurobiologist, has shown that children with language learning disabilities (LLD) fail to distinguish between the "plosive" consonants, such as *b, t* and *p*. To them, "bug" sounds like "tug" sounds like "pug." The problem, Tallal has long argued, is that for such kids the sounds come too fast. Vowels resonate for 100 milliseconds or more, but

HEARING

At six months, a baby's brain tunes in to the sounds of its native tongue and tunes out other languages.

plosive consonants last for a mere 40 milliseconds—not long enough for some children to process them. "These children hear the sound. It just isn't transmitted to the brain normally," she says.

Two years ago, Tallal teamed up with Michael Merzenich, a neurobiologist at the University of California–San Francisco, to create a set of computer games that have produced stunning gains in 29 children with LLD. With William Jenkins and Steve Miller, the neurobiologists wrote computer programs that elongated the plosive consonants, making them louder—"like making a yellow highlighter for the brain," says Tallal. After a month of daily three-hour sessions, children who were one to three years behind their peers in language and reading had leaped forward a full two years. The researchers have formed a company, Scientific Learning Corp., that could make their system available to teachers and professionals within a few years. (See their Web site: *http://www.scilearn.com* or call 415-296-1470.)

An inability to hear the sounds of human speech properly also may contribute to autism, a disorder that leaves children unable to relate emotionally to other people. According to University of Maryland psychophysiologist Stephen Porges, many autistic children are listening not to the sounds of human speech but instead to frightening noises. He blames the children's fear on a section of the nervous system that controls facial expressions, speech, visceral feelings and the muscles in the middle ear.

These muscles, the tiniest in the body, allow the ear to filter sounds, much the way muscles in the eye focus the eyeball on near or distant objects. In autistic children, the neural system that includes the middle ear is lazy. As a result, these children attend not to the pitch of the human voice but instead to sounds that are much lower: the rumble of traffic, the growl of a vacuum cleaner. In the deep evolutionary past, such noises signaled danger. Porges contends that autistic children feel too anxious to interact emotionally, and the neural system controlling many emotional responses fails to develop.

Porges says that exercising the neural system may help autistic kids gain language and emotional skills. He and his colleagues have begun an experimental treatment consisting of tones and songs altered by computer to filter out low sounds, forcing the middle ear to focus on the pitches of human speech. After five 90-minute sessions, most of the 16 children have made strides that surprised even Porges. Third grader Tomlin Clark, for example, who once spoke only rarely, recently delighted his parents by getting in trouble for talking out of turn in school. And for the first time, he shows a sense of humor. "Listening to sounds seems so simple, doesn't it?" says Porges. "But so does jogging."

TOUCH

The skin, writes pathologist Marc Lappé, "is both literally and metaphorically 'the body's edge' . . . a boundary against an inimical world." Yet the skin also is the organ that speaks the language of love most clearly—and not just in the erogenous zones. The caress of another person releases hormones that can ease pain and clear the mind. Deprive a child of touch, and his brain and body will stop growing.

This new view of the most intimate sense was sparked a decade ago, when child psychologist Tiffany Field showed that premature infants who were massaged for 15 minutes three times a day gained weight 47 percent faster than preemies given standard intensive care nursery treatment: as little touching as possible. The preemies who were massaged weren't eating more; they just processed food more efficiently, says Field, now director of the University of Miami's Touch Research Institute. Field found that massaged preemies were more alert and aware of their surroundings when awake, while their sleep was deeper and more restorative. Eight months later, the massaged infants scored better on mental and motor tests.

TOUCH

People with "synesthesia" feel colors, see sounds and taste shapes.

SIXTH SENSES

Wish you had that nose?

Folklore abounds with tales of animals possessing exceptional sensory powers, from pigs predicting earthquakes to pets telepathically anticipating their owners' arrival home. In some cases, myth and reality are not so far apart. Nature is full of creatures with superhuman senses: built-in compasses, highly accurate sonar, infrared vision. "Our worldview is limited by our senses," says Dartmouth College psychologist Howard Hughes, "so we are both reluctant to believe that animals can have capabilities beyond ours, and we attribute to them supernatural powers. The truth is somewhere between the two."

In the case of Watson, a Labrador retriever, reality is more impressive than any fiction. For over a year, Watson has reliably pawed his owner, Emily Ramsey, 45 minutes before her epileptic seizures begin, giving her time to move to a safe place. Placed by Canine Partners for Life, Watson has a 97 percent success rate, according to the Ramsey family. No one has formally studied how such dogs can predict seizure onset consistently. But they may smell the chemical changes known to precede epileptic attacks. "Whatever it is," says Harvard University neurologist Steven Schachter, "I think there's something to it."

Scientists have scrutinized other animals for decades, trying to decipher their sensory secrets. Birds, bees, moles and some 80 other creatures are known to sense magnetic fields. But new studies indicate birds have two magnetic detection systems: One seems to translate polarized light into visual patterns that act as a compass; the other is an internal magnet birds use to further orient themselves.

Dolphin sonar so intrigued government researchers that they launched the U.S. Navy marine Mammal Program in 1960, hoping it would lead to more-sophisticated tracking equipment. But the animals still beat the machines, says spokesman Tom LaPuzza. In a murky sea, dolphins can pinpoint a softball two football fields away. A lobe in their forehead focuses their biosonar as a flashlight channels light, beaming 200-decibel clicks.

It took night-vision goggles for humans to replicate the infrared vision snakes come by naturally: A cameralike device in organs lining their lips lets them see heat patterns made by mammals. And humans can only envy the ability of sharks, skates and rays to feel electric fields through pores in their snouts—perhaps a primordial skill used by Earth's earliest creatures to scout out the new world.

BY ANNA MULRINE

SMELL

A woman's sense of smell is keener than a man's. And smell plays a larger role in sexual attraction for women.

Being touched has healing powers throughout life. Massage, researchers have found, can ease the pain of severely burned children and boost the immune systems of AIDS patients. Field recently showed that office workers who received a 15-minute massage began emitting higher levels of brain waves associated with alertness. After their massage, the workers executed a math test in half their previous time with half the errors.

While such findings may sound touchy-feely, an increasing volume of physiological evidence backs them up. In a recent series of experiments, Swedish physiologist Kerstin Uvnas-Moberg found that gentle stroking can stimulate the body to release oxytocin, sometimes called the love hormone because it helps cement the bond between mothers and their young in many species. "There are deep, deep, physiological connections between touching and love," Uvnas-Moberg says. Oxytocin also blunts pain and dampens the hormones release when a person feels anxious or stressed.

For the babies of any species, touch signals that mother—the source of food, warmth and safety—is near. When she is gone, many young animals show physiological signs of stress and shut down their metabolism—an innate response designed to conserve energy until she returns. Without mother, rat pups do not grow, says Saul Schanberg, a Duke University pharmacologist, even when they are fed and kept warm. Stroking them with a brush in a manner that mimics their mother licking them restores the pups to robust health. "You need the right kind of touch in order to grow," says Schanberg, "even more than vitamins."

SMELL

Long ago in human evolution, smell played a prominent role, signaling who was ready to mate and who ready to fight. But after a while, smell fell into disrepute. Aristotle disparaged it as the most animalistic of the senses, and Immanuel Kant dreamed of losing it. Recent research has restored the nose to some of its former glory. "Odor plays a far more important role in human behavior and physiology than we realize," says Gary Beauchamp, director of Philadelphia's Monell Chemical Senses Center.

A baby recognizes its mother by her odor soon after birth, and studies show that adults can identify clothing worn by their children or spouses by smell alone. In 1995, Beauchamp and colleagues at Monell reported that a woman's scent—genetically determined—changes in pregnancy to reflect a combination of her odor and that of her fetus.

The sense of smell's most celebrated capacity is its power to stir memory. "Hit a tripwire of smell, and memories explode all at once," writes poet Diane Ackerman. The reason, says Monell psychologist Rachel Herz, is that "smells carry an emotional quality." In her latest experiment, Herz showed people a series of evocative paintings. At the same time, the subjects were exposed to another sensory cue—an orange, for example—in different ways. Some saw an orange. Others were given an orange to touch, heard the word "orange" or smelled the fruit. Two days later, when subjects were given the same cue and were asked to recall the painting that matched it, those exposed to the smell of the orange recalled the painting and produced a flood of emotional responses to it.

Herz and others suspect that an aroma's capacity to spark such vivid remembrances arises out of anatomy. An odor's first way station in the brain is the olfactory bulb, two blueberry-sized lumps of cortex from which neurons extend through the skull into the nose. Smell molecules, those wafting off a cinnamon bun, for example, bind to these olfactory neurons, which fire off their signals first to the olfactory bulb and then to the limbic system—the seat of sexual drive, emotions and memory. Connections between the olfactory bulb and the neocortex, or thinking part of the brain, are secondary roads compared to the highways leading to emotional centers.

Scientists once thought all smells were made up of combinations of seven basic odors. But in an elegant series of experiments, research teams led by Columbia's Axel and Linda Buck of Harvard have shown the mechanics of smell to be much more complicated. In 1991, the scientists discovered a family of at least 1,000 genes corresponding to about 1,000 types of olfactory neurons in the nose. Each of these neuronal types responds to one—and only one—type of odor molecule.

The average person, of course, can detect far more than 1,000 odors. That's because a single scent is made up of more than one type of molecule, perhaps even dozens. A rose might stimulate neurons A, B and C, while jasmine sets off neurons B, C and F. "Theoretically, we can detect an astronomical number of smells." says Axel—the equivalent of 10 to the 23rd power. The brain, however, doesn't have the space to keep track of all those possible combinations of molecules, and so it focuses on smells that were relevant in evolution, like the scent of ripe fruit or a sexually receptive mate—about 10,000 odors in all.

Axel and Buck have now discovered that the olfactory bulb contains a "map," similar to those the brain employs for vision and hearing. By implanting a gene into mice, the researchers dyed blue the nerves leading

ARE YOU A SUPERTASTER?

All tongues are not created equal. How intense flavors seem is determined by heredity. In this test, devised by Yale University taste experts Linda Bartoshuk and Laurie Lucchina, find out if you are a **nontaster,** an **average taster** or a **supertaster.** Answers on next page.

TASTE BUDS. Punch a hole with a standard hole punch in a square of wax paper. Paint the front of your tongue with a cotton swab dipped in blue food coloring. Put wax paper on the tip of your tongue, just to the right of center. With a flashlight and magnifying glass, count the number of pink, unstained circles. They contain taste buds.

SWEET. Rinse your mouth with water before tasting each sample. Put ½ cup of sugar in a measuring cup, and then add enough water to make 1 cup. Mix. Coat front half of your tongue, including the tip, with a cotton swab dipped in the solution. Wait a few moments. Rate the sweetness according to the scale shown below.

SALT. Put 2 teaspoons of salt in a measuring cup and add enough water to make 1 cup. Repeat the steps listed above, rating how salty the solution is.

SPICY. Add 1 teaspoon of Tabasco sauce to 1 cup of water. Apply with a cotton swab to first half inch of the tongue, including the tip. Keep your tongue out of your mouth until the burn reaches a peak, then rate the pain according to the scale.

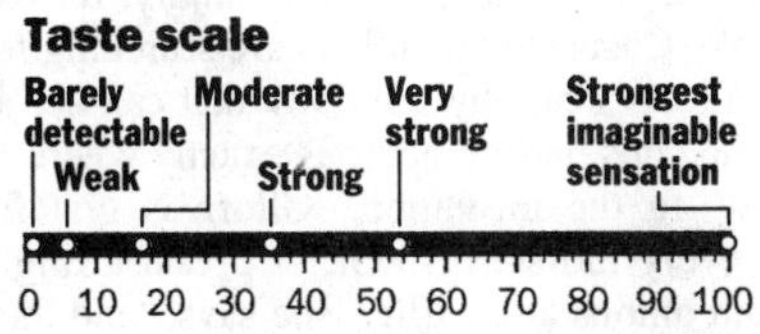

from the animals' olfactory bulbs to their noses. Tracing the path of these neurons, the researchers discovered that those responsible for detecting a single type of odor molecule all led back to a single point in the olfactory bulb. In other words, the jumble of neurons that exists in the nose is reduced to regimental order in the brain.

Smell maps may one day help anosmics, people who cannot smell. Susan Killorn of Richmond, Va., lost her sense of smell three years ago when she landed on her head while in-line skating and damaged the nerves leading from her nose to her brain. A gourmet cook, Killorn was devastated. "I can remember sitting at the dinner table and begging my husband to describe the meal I'd just cooked," she says. Killorn's ability to detect odors has gradually returned, but nothing smells quite right. One possibility, says Richard Costanzo, a neurophysiologist at Virginia Commonwealth University, is that some of the nerves from her nose have recovered or regenerated but now are hooked up to the wrong spot in her smell map.

Though imperfect, recoveries like Killorn's give researchers hope they may one day be able to stimulate other neurons to regenerate—after a spinal cord injury, for example. Costanzo and others are searching for chemicals made by the body that can act as traffic cops, telling neurons exactly where to grow. In the meantime, Killorn is grateful for every morsel of odor. "I dream at night about onions and garlic," she says, "and they smell like they are supposed to."

TASTE

TASTE

Human beings are genetically hard-wired to crave sweetness; sugar on the lips of a newborn baby will bring a smile.

Human beings will put almost anything into their mouths and consider it food, from stinging nettles to grubs. Fortunately, evolution armed the human tongue with a set of sensors to keep venturesome members of the species from dying of malnutrition or poison. The four simple flavors—sweet, salty, bitter and sour—tell human beings what's healthy and what's harmful. But as researchers are finding, the sense of taste does far more than keep us from killing ourselves. Each person tastes food differently, a genetically determined sensitivity that can affect diet, weight and health.

In a quest for novelty, people around the world have developed an affinity for foods that cause a modicum of pain. "Humans have the ability to say, 'Oh, that didn't really hurt me—let me try it again,' " says Barry Green, a psychologist at the John B. Pierce Laboratory in New Haven, Conn. Spicy food, Green has found, gives the impression of being painfully hot by stimulating the nerves in the mouth that sense temperature extremes. The bubbles in soda and champagne feel as if they are popping inside the mouth; in reality, carbon dioxide inside the bubbles irritates nerves that sense pain.

One person's spicy meatball, however, is another's bland and tasteless meal. Researchers have long known that certain people have an inherited inability to taste a mildly bitter substance with a tongue-twisting name: propylthiouracil, or PROP, for short. About a quarter of Caucasians are "nontasters," utterly insensitive to PROP, while the vast majority of Asians and Africans can taste it. Now, researchers at Yale University led by psychologist Linda Bartoshuk have discovered a third group of people called "supertasters." So sensitive are supertasters' tongues that they gag on PROP and can detect the merest hint of other bitter compounds in a host of foods, from chocolate and saccharin to vegetables such as broccoli, "which could explain why George Bush hates it," Bartoshuk says. She has recently discovered that supertasters have twice as many taste buds as nontasters and more of the nerve endings that detect the feel of foods. As a consequence, sweets taste sweeter to supertasters, and cream feels creamier. A spicy dish can send a supertaster through the roof.

In an ongoing study, Bartoshuk's group has found that older women who are nontasters tend to prefer sweets and fatty foods—dishes that some of the supertasters find cloying. Not surprisingly, supertasters also tend to be thinner and have lower cholesterol. In their study, the researchers ask subjects to taste cream mixed with oil, a combination Bartoshuk confesses she finds delicious. "I'm a nontaster, and I'm heavy," she says. "I gobble up the test." But tasting ability is not only a matter of cuisine preference and body weight. Monell's Marcia Pelchat and a graduate student recently completed a study indicating that nontasters also may be predisposed to alcoholism.

RESULTS OF TASTE TEST ON PREVIOUS PAGE

	SUPER-TASTERS	NON-TASTERS
No. of taste buds	25 on average	10
Sweet rating	56 on average	32
Tabasco rating	64 on average	31

Average tasters lie in between. Bartoshuk and Lucchina lack the data to rate salt.

The human senses detect only a fraction of reality: We can't see the ultraviolet markers that guide a honeybee to nectar; we can't hear most of the noises emitted by a dolphin. In this way, the senses define the boundaries of mental awareness. But the brain also defines the limits of what we perceive. Human beings see, feel, taste, touch and smell not the world around them but a version of the world, one their brains have concocted. "People imagine that they're seeing what's really there, but they're not," says neuroscientist John Maunsell of Baylor College of Medicine in Houston. The eyes take in the light reflecting off objects around us, but the brain only pays attention to part of the scene. Looking for a pen on a messy desk, for example, you can scan the surface without noticing the papers scattered across it.

The word "sentience" derives from the Latin verb *sentire,* meaning "to feel." And research on the senses, especially the discovery of sensory mapping, has taken scientists one step further in understanding the state we call consciousness. Yet even this dramatic advance is only a beginning. "In a way, these sexy maps have seduced us," says Michael Shipley, director of neurosciences at the University of Maryland–Baltimore. "We still haven't answered the question of how do you go from visual maps to recognizing faces, or from an auditory map to recognizing a Mozart sonata played by two different pianists." The challenge for the 21st century will be figuring out how the brain, once it has broken the sensory landscape into pieces, puts them together again.

BY SHANNON BROWNLEE
WITH TRACI WATSON

Visual Processing: More Than Meets The Eye

"YOU WON'T BELIEVE YOUR EYES!" shout those irritating ads enticing you to take a gander at everything from the two-headed sheep in the circus sideshow to the rock-bottom prices at a holiday wall-to-wall carpeting sale. But as any magician can tell you, we do tend to believe what we see. Or at least what our brains tell us we see.

With the help of millions of neurons in the human visual system that respond to shapes, colors, and movement, our brains assemble workable snapshots of the world that surrounds us. But how does the brain turn simple data on the wavelength, intensity, and direction of incoming light into the image of a red Chevy Nova tooling down the street at 15 miles per hour? And where in the brain do the individual brush strokes come together to paint a detailed portrait of the visual scene?

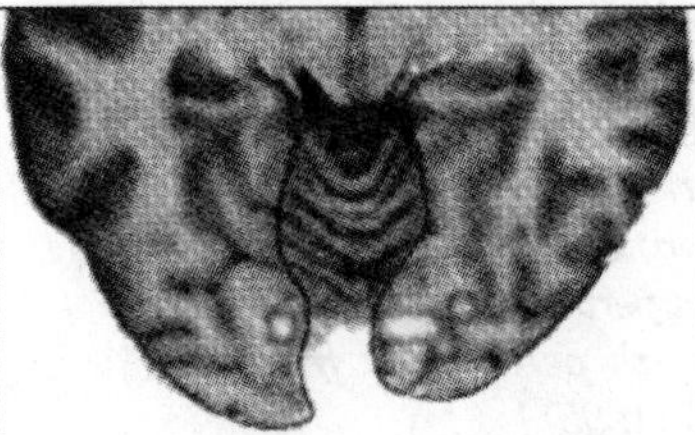
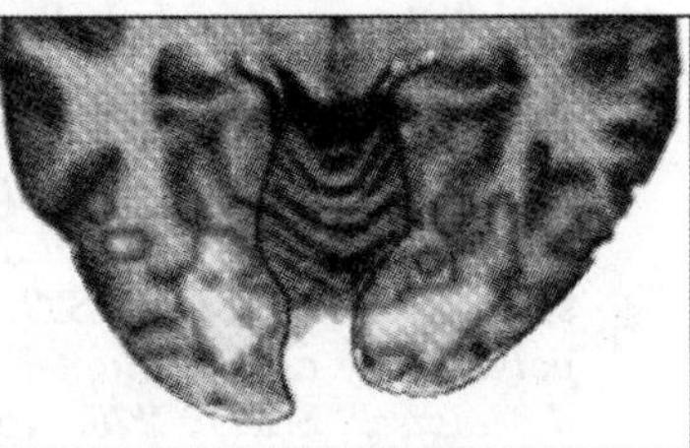

Functional magnetic resonance images show how attention to a visual task enhances neuronal activity *in the human occipito-temporal cortex. Lightest grey areas indicate activity when researchers asked the subject to passively look at a checkerboard pattern (left), or to look at the same pattern, watch for the appearance of a target somewhere on the same background, and report on its position or movement (right). [Courtesy Edgar DeYoe, Medical College of Wisconsin, Milwaukee.]*

For years, researchers have believed that the eyes take in everything and that only later do the brain regions concerned with cognitive processes select the bits of visual information that are important. Now, several studies in monkeys suggest that even neurons near the beginning of the visual-processing pathway can tell whether an animal is paying attention to a particular visual stimulus. Attention to visual detail such as color or motion may provide the brain with a spotlight it can use to draw a particular stimulus to center stage. Understanding how and when the brain uses attention to react to selected items in the visual field is central to understanding how humans process and act on visual information.

Meanwhile, other researchers are examining how neurons in the cat visual cortex chat with one another, sharing information. Recent results suggest that lateral connections may allow individual cells, which only see a fragment of the visual field, to piece together the bigger picture.

Finally, a number of researchers are developing techniques that allow them to see how and when the brain regions in humans interact to process visual input and generate an image of the surroundings—and to see what happens when we shift our focus from the forest to the trees.

It wasn't until the early 1960s that David Hubel, who is now at Harvard University Medical School in Boston, and Torsten Wiesel, who is now at Rockefeller University in New York City, demonstrated that neurons in the visual cortex operate as "feature detectors," each responding to a different aspect of a stimulus. In studies that led to their sharing the 1981 Nobel Prize in Physiology or Medicine with Roger Sperry, Hubel and Wiesel found that some neurons respond best to a thin bar of light, some to an edge and others to a line with a particular orienta-

From *The Journal of NIH Research,* November 1996, pp. 36-41.

tion. Still others respond most strongly to stimuli of a particular wavelength, texture, or direction of motion.

As information proceeds along the visual-processing pathway, it passes from the visual cortex at the back of the brain forward to the cognitive areas that couple images with meaning. At each successive anatomical level, the area of the visual scene that each neuron responds to, called its receptive field, grows larger and the cells recognize more complex features of the stimulus. Accordingly, at higher levels, neurons might increase their firing rate more readily in response to a face than a line.

Though neuroscientists don't believe in a "grandmother cell"—the single neuron that allows someone to recognize the familiar face of grandma—neither do they believe that individual neurons respond only to one thing, such as the color blue or a horizontal line. Instead, neurons at various levels show preferences; a neuron might fire most vigorously in response to the color red and to stimuli that are moving slowly southward.

Red or blue, north or south, it all starts in the eye. Neurons in the retina respond to stimuli in their receptive fields by sending a signal to neurons in a small region of the thalamus called the lateral geniculate nucleus (LGN). Some of these retinal neurons respond more readily to color contrasts, others to abrupt changes in the visual field, such as flashing lights.

Neurons in the LGN serve as relays, sending axonal projections to the primary visual cortex, which is also called V1. Neurons in this first layer of the visual cortex—which is sometimes called the striate cortex because of its striped appearance—process information about orientation, movement, and color.

Once past V1, information about "what" an object is and "where" it is located diverges, with spatial details flowing toward the parietal cortex and information on color, texture, and shape heading toward the temporal cortex. Along the way, connections are made through the extrastriate areas, V2 through V4, and the middle temporal area (MT) for processing and assembly. The parietal and temporal systems then pass along their take on the world to the prefrontal cortex and the frontal cortex, which are considered the seats of higher cognitive processing.

But the information doesn't flow in only one direction. Higher areas send input back to neurons in the lower areas of the visual cortex. What might this feedback accomplish? Scientists postulate that it helps to focus attention. Imagine looking for a pen on a cluttered desktop. "We bring in a lot of information during a visual search," says Brad Motter of the Veterans Affairs Medical Center in Syracuse, N.Y. "But we then filter it based on what we want to look at. The question is, where is the information being filtered?"

In the September 1993 issue of the *Journal of Neuroscience*, Motter reported that attention begins to influence neuronal activity as early in the process as V1. In his studies of rhesus macaques, Motter found that neurons in the cortical V1, V2, and V4 regions responded more vigorously to certain visual stimuli when the monkeys were first cued to look for them.

Although Motter remains the only researcher to have found that attention influences neuronal activity in the monkey primary visual cortex, many scientists fancy the idea. "I'm a critic of the concept that attention doesn't affect visual processing until late in the pathway," says Charles Schroeder of the Albert Einstein College of Medicine in New York City and the Nathan Kline Institute for Psychiatric Research in Orangeburg, N.Y. "Unfortunately, at this point our evidence does not indicate any clear attentional effects at the level of the LGN or V1."

Schroeder and his graduate student Ashesh Mehta reported at the Society for Neuroscience meetings in

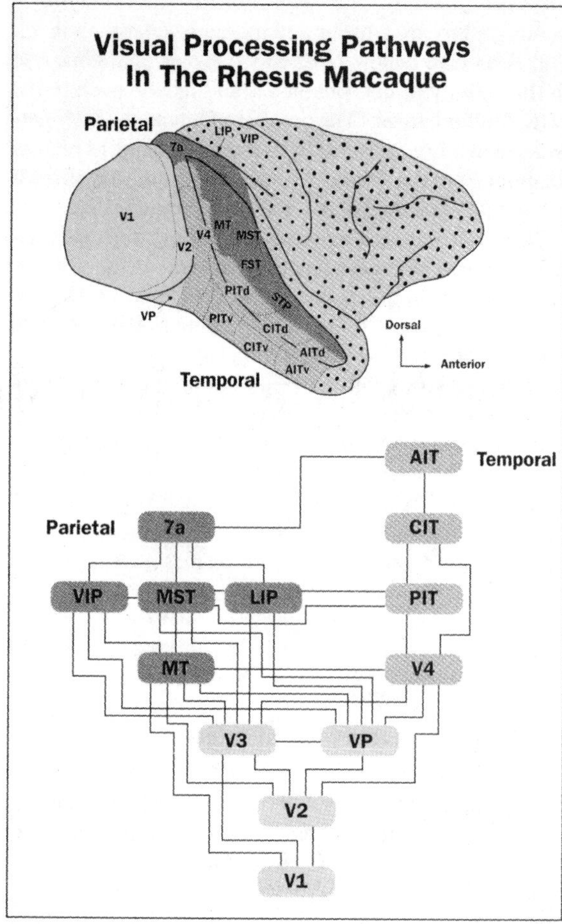

Road map of the visual-processing system of the rhesus macaque. *Visual information enters the primary visual cortext (V1) from the lateral geniculate nucleus (not shown). Information on an object's motion, shape, and color pass through V1, V2, V3, and VP (light grey) and then separate. At that point, information about "where" an object is flows through the parietal pathway (dark grey) and information about "what" an object is flows through the temporal pathway (medium grey). Abbreviations: V1 through V4, visual areas 1 through 4; VP, ventral posterior area; MT, middle temporal area; VIP, ventral intraparietal area; MST, medial superior temporal area; LIP, lateral intraparietal area; 7a, Brodmann's area 7a; PIT, posterior inferotemporal area; AIT, anterior inferotemporal area; CIT, central inferotemporal area; FST, fundus of the superior temporal area; STP, superior temporal polysensory area. [Adapted with permission from J. Maunsell, Science* ***270,*** *765 (1995).]*

1994 and 1995 that attention affects neuronal activity in V2 more than in V1. In their experiments, the researchers presented a long-tailed macaque with both auditory and visual stimuli—a series of tones, one a different pitch, and a series of circles, one brighter than the others—at the same time. They primed the animal to monitor one type of stimulus or the other by presenting an auditory or visual cue before starting the experimental trial. Electrodes placed in the monkey's brain recorded the activity of neurons in V1 and V2 while the animal responded to the stimuli.

When the monkey attended to the visual stimulus, he released a bar when he saw the brighter circle. Then the researchers presented the same series of visual stimuli, but cued the monkey to respond to the odd sound rather than the bright circle. By comparing the activity of neurons in both cases, in which identical visual stimuli are either being monitored or ignored, the researchers determine how attention affects visual processing.

Schroeder and Mehta have found that neurons in the V2 region are less active when a monkey is not paying attention to the visual stimulus. Not only do the V2 neurons fire less frequently, but their membranes are hyperpolarized, suggesting that a lack of attention actually inhibits the activity of neurons in V2. The same applies to area V4, says Schroeder.

"The brain has an intrinsic mechanism for shutting down inputs when you're ignoring something, which makes sense," says Schroeder. Attention operates by removing the inhibition and allowing the visual information to pass through to higher processing levels, he speculates.

Schroeder and Mehta find similar effects in V1, although they are smaller and more irregular than in V2. Still, Schroeder believes that attention may play some role in the activity of neurons in V1, and maybe even in the LGN. Motter agrees. "The number of inputs the LGN gets as feedback from the cortex is nearly six times as high as its input from the retina," he says. "Why are they there if not to influence the behavior of cells [in the LGN]?"

Less controversy surrounds the finding that attention affects neuronal processing in areas outside the primary visual cortex. In the Aug. 8 issue of *Nature*, John Maunsell of the Baylor College of Medicine in Houston and Stefan Treue of the University of Tübingen in Germany described a strong influence of attention on visual processing in the MT area of monkeys.

Neurons in the MT respond to motion and each neuron exhibits a preferred direction. In their experiment, Maunsell and Treue examined how neurons in the MT of rhesus macaques reacted when the animal simultaneously viewed two dots, one moving in the preferred direction, the other going the opposite way. The researchers found that if a particular neuron responded best to upwards motion and the monkey was cued before the experiment to pay attention to the dot moving north, the activity of the neuron was strong. But if they cued the monkey to pay attention to the southbound dot, the same neuron responded poorly, even though the actual visual stimulus remained the same.

"The most striking thing to me about the study is the sheer magnitude of the effect," says Michael Paradiso of Brown University in Providence, R.I., who studies visual processing. "The response of individual cells would double or triple [when the animal was paying attention to the stimulus preferred by the neuron being monitored]. That's a much larger effect than people have found previously."

Robert Desimone of the National Institute of Mental Health in Bethesda, Md., finds that attention also enhances the processing of another visual feature—color. Desimone and colleagues Steven Luck of the University of Iowa in Iowa City, Leonardo Chelazzi of the University of Verona in Italy, and Steven Hillyard of the University of California at San Diego, presented rhesus macaques with two or more competing visual stimuli that fell within the receptive field of a particular neuron. Their setup was similar to Maunsell's and Treue's, only Desimone and his colleagues trained the monkeys to pay attention to stimuli that varied in color.

In a paper in press at the *Journal of Neurophysiology*, the researchers report that neurons in the V2 and V4 regions responded most vigorously when the animals were paying attention to a stimulus of a preferred color. Like the neurons in the MT, which exhibit a preferred direction, neurons in these regions exhibit preferred colors.

In addition, Desimone and his colleagues found that just cuing a monkey to direct his attention to the region of the visual field where a stimulus would appear activated neurons in V2 and V4, even before the visual target was present. "It's like the cells are primed and prepared for the task you've given them," he says. "This is a signature of feedback from higher regions to the visual cortex, because there's nothing coming into the visual cortex to turn it on."

Desimone suspects the prefrontal cortex, the brain region thought to store working memory, influences how neurons in the earlier stages of visual processing respond to the colors or visual locations to which a monkey is cued to pay attention. "The general feeling is developing that the prefrontal cortex is playing a more important role in all sorts of visual operations than people have generally given it credit for," says Desimone.

In humans, John Marshall of the Radcliffe Infirmary in Oxford, England, finds evidence that the temporal and parietal areas influence attention early in visual processing. Marshall—with Gereon Fink and Richard Frackowiak and their colleagues at the Institute of Neurology in London—used positron emission tomography (PET) scans to monitor the neuronal activity of subjects asked to describe either the global or the local composition of a complex figure, such as a large "S" formed by a snaking string of "F"s.

In the Aug. 15 issue of *Nature*, the researchers confirmed earlier observations that the left hemisphere of the brain tends to process local details—in this case the individual "F"s—and that the right hemisphere processes the big picture, a large "S." Further, the researchers observed neuronal activation in areas at the beginning of the visual-processing pathway, V2 and V3. Marshall attributes such early effects to feedback from the temporal and parietal cortices. "These areas modulate the representation of the visual world that's computed in the early visual cortex," he says.

Other groups of researchers are also trying to track visual processing in humans using imaging techniques, like PET scanning, that are noninvasive. Edgar DeYoe at the Medical College of Wisconsin in Milwaukee asks subjects to locate visually a target that periodically appears somewhere on a checkerboard background; he then monitors the neural activity in their brains with functional magnetic resonance imaging (fMRI), a technique that uses rapidly changing magnetic fields to detect changes in the amount of oxygen carried by blood vessels in the brain.

In the Mar. 19 issue of the *Proceedings of the National Academy of Sciences (PNAS)*, DeYoe and his colleagues mapped the locations of the V1, V2, V3, V4,

Brains In The Bronx

Monkeys are more than happy to work for juice; maybe too happy, say neuroscientists at the Albert Einstein College of Medicine in New York City. **Charlie Schroeder** and his student Ashesh Mehta often find themselves at the mercy of long-tailed macaques who perform visual tasks for hours, pressing a bar in response to the proper stimuli—all for a shot of apple juice. But it's hard to say which the animals enjoy more, the work or the juice. "It's like they get some kind of satisfaction from performing the tasks," says Schroeder, who allows the animals to work until they decide on their own they've had enough for one day. Maybe it's some kind of simian power trip. "When they're down here in the lab, the monkeys pretty much run the show," says Schroeder.

Like Schroeder, **Greg Simpson** started his stint at Einstein as a postdoctoral fellow and decided to stick around. His interest in visual attention stretches back to his early graduate school days, when he worked with Steve Hillyard of the University of California at San Diego. Simpson then moved to the University of California at Berkeley, where he studied sensory processing in humans and rats with Robert Knight.

How does a California boy find contentment in the Big Apple? Roses. After a long search, Simpson managed to land an apartment with a deck, where he has established a garden with a view. Now Simpson spends his spare time pruning the roses and tending the lavender.

The Beaten Path

After spending almost eight years in Milwaukee at the Medical College of Wisconsin, **Ted DeYoe** says he still doesn't "feel like a Wisconsinite....Probably spent too much time in New York and California," he says. A self-described "monkey man in a previous life," DeYoe now uses functional magnetic resonance imaging (fMRI) to map out visual processing pathways in humans.

The DeYoe road to vision research began in Rochester, N.Y., where he completed his Ph.D. in neuroscience and experimental psychology with Bob Doty at the University of Rochester. DeYoe then went on to do his postdoctoral training with David Van Essen when he was at the California Institute of Technology in Pasadena.

As DeYoe touched down in Pasadena, Van Essen's graduate student, John Maunsell, headed in the opposite direction, to the Massachusetts Institute of Technology in Cambridge and then on to the University of Rochester. "There were a lot of serious and talented people in computer science there who help bridge experimental and computational neuroscience." Which is where it's at, as far as Maunsell can see. "The brain is like a big parallel computer," he says. "To understand how the brain does its thing, we need to understand what it means to have sparsely distributed coding moving across parallel networks of 10^{10} processors."

But Maunsell has no complaints about Baylor College of Medicine in Houston, where he takes advantage of the "excellent facilities and colleagues" he has in the division of neuroscience. Well, maybe one. "Parking is a problem," he says. The medical complex supports between 40,000 and 80,000 employees in an area of roughly six square blocks.

Deeper Than Philosophy

"To look at my brain, press this button," invites **Christof Koch**'s Web page at the California Institute of Technology in Pasadena *(http://www.klab.caltech.edu)*. A click of the mouse reveals an MRI image of Koch's brain. "Cool, eh?" he asks.

Almost as cool as Koch's 10-year collaboration with Francis Crick of the Salk Institute for Biological Studies in La Jolla, Calif. After spending a solid week discussing visual attention with Crick in the mid-1980s, Koch struck up a relationship with the Nobel Prize–winning scientist that has taken him down a pathway toward understanding how neurons work together to generate awareness.

In the past decade, Koch has noticed some changes. "Ten years ago it was a no-no to discuss consciousness, at least during the day," he says. "Now it's okay to talk about awareness, even among card-carrying neuroscientists."

Koch's interests range from pinning down the physiology of consciousness to understanding how neurons integrate and propagate information—quite a change from his earlier studies in philosophy. "In Germany, you have to study Nietzsche, and Heidegger, and Wittgenstein," says Koch. "But they really cannot help you answer the big questions. I mean, Wittgenstein is all very nice and heroic, but do we know anything more after reading him than before?" Science, on the other hand, provides precise answers as well as questions, he says.

But Koch, who once danced classical ballet and enjoys dancing the night away at scientific meetings, still waxes philosophical now and again. Among the "major intellectual interests" he lists on his Web page: "Trying to find out where I came from, where I will go to, and what I am doing here."

—K.H.

and MT regions in humans. "Functional MRI has been the first technology to let you go in and run an individual subject on multiple visual tasks and really see what the brain is doing," he says.

DeYoe and his colleague Michael Beauchamp also have found that attention affects the activity of neurons in the MT region during motion-detection tasks, findings they will present this month at the Society for Neuroscience meeting in Washington, D.C. When the researchers asked a subject to pay attention to the motion of a particular visual stimulus, the subject's MT region was active. But when they presented the same visual stimulus and asked the subject to watch for a change in its brightness rather than its motion, the MT grew quiet. "This suggests that attention effects may not be so subtle," says DeYoe. "They may be able to shut down entire brain regions."

The problem with the fMRI data, says DeYoe, is that it's hard to tell whether the active regions are working in parallel or whether they process information independently and then relay data back and forth. The activation and deactivation of individual brain regions occur too rapidly for information about timing to be teased out of the fMRI images.

That's where Greg Simpson of Albert Einstein comes in. Simpson and his colleagues Herbert Vaughn, John Foxe, and Seppo Ahlfors combine fMRI with more dynamic and quicker measurements, called event-related electric potentials (ERPs) and event-related magnetic fields (ERFs). Using these techniques, Simpson can examine the activity of the entire visual system in space and time (see "Multimodal Imaging Reveals Cerebral Dynamics").*

To record ERPs, which are similar to electroencephalograms, Simpson and his colleagues attach 128 surface electrodes to the subjects' scalps. To measure ERFs, the researchers place a 122-channel magnetometer, which Simpson says resembles an old-fashioned hair dryer, over the subjects' heads. The magnetometer measures changes in magnetic fields that reflect neural activity in the brain.

The beauty of these techniques lies in their ability to record changes in neural activity from moment to moment. PET scans and fMRIs provide more precise pictures of the locations of activity, but present an average activation over time. ERPs and ERFs permit researchers to monitor neural activity in real time.

Combined with fMRI, these dynamic neuroimaging methods should allow Simpson and his collaborators to determine when attention modulates neural activity. His preliminary results, presented at the First International Conference on Functional Mapping of the Human Brain in June 1995, suggest that V1 and V2 aren't simply switched on and turned off, but remain active for hundreds of milliseconds (ms)—quite a bit of time in terms of visual processing. In addition, his data suggest that V1, V2, and other extrastriate areas communicate back and forth with higher cortical areas—including the frontal and parietal cortices—in waves of activity that oscillate at different rates.

To combine the fMRI recordings with the ERP and ERF data, Simpson collaborates with Jack Belliveau of the Massachusetts General Hospital in Boston, Risto Ilmoniemi of the Helsinki University Central Hospital in Finland, John George at Los Alamos National Laboratory in Los Alamos, N.M., and their respective colleagues. The researchers fly their subjects from center to center to perform visual tasks while they're monitored by the various pieces of equipment.

When it comes to visual processing, Simpson and his colleagues find that people don't necessarily think alike. Some subjects show attentional effects as early as V1; others do not. Among those subjects who show V1 effects, one might show that attention alters the activation of V1 beginning at 50 ms after the onset of a stimulus, suggesting that attention directly affects activity in V1. Another might not show a V1 effect until 150 ms after the stimulus appears, suggesting that the V1 neurons in that subject receive feedback from higher cortical areas. The difference may reflect strategy. "When we debrief people, some say they're on autopilot; others are trying to look at the stimulus without actually looking at it," says Simpson.

"Advances in imaging techniques have really made a big difference in the study of visual processing," says Michael Posner of the University of Oregon in Eugene, a pioneer in the study of how attention affects visual perception. "Of course, that doesn't mean that everyone agrees about the results," he adds, referring to the ongoing debate over how early in visual processing attention exerts its effects.

Even if attention did adjust the activity of neurons in the primary visual cortex, causing certain objects to be highlighted and others to be ignored, which neurons are responsible for making humans aware of what they're seeing? Christof Koch of the California Institute of Technology in Pasadena and Francis Crick of the Salk Institute for Biological Studies in La Jolla, Calif., are looking into the visual system for clues to the cellular basis of visual awareness—a search they feel might lead to an understanding of consciousness.

Koch and Crick think that awareness comes into play only after processing has passed the primary visual cortex. They base their conclusion on experimental evidence from studies of a temporary condition called induced blindsight. Using a computer, scientists can present subjects with an image hidden on a background of moving dots. Although the subjects report that they cannot see the image, they can often correctly "guess" its position. Because the scientists use images that activate the primary visual cortex, but not extrastriate areas, Koch says that neurons in V1 must not be responsible for visual awareness.

In the Sept. 26 issue of *Nature*, Sheng He and his colleagues at Harvard University in Cambridge, Mass., offer further evidence that awareness arises outside the primary visual cortex. The researchers took advantage of a visual after-effect illusion that is mediated by neurons in V1. When human subjects stare at a circle filled with a fine, horizontal grating pattern, and then immediately look at a screen covered with faint horizontal grating, they have trouble seeing the pattern on the screen.

In their experiment, He and his colleagues added several more finely patterned circles to the visual field. The circles were grouped so closely together that the subjects could no longer see that the pattern in the center circle was a horizontal grating. Yet the after-effect, a difficulty in seeing a horizontal pattern on a second screen, remained the same. Because this after-effect is generally thought to occur in the primary visual cortex, Koch says this region cannot be involved in visual awareness.

Although the primary visual cortex is necessary for visual awareness, Koch says it's not where awareness resides. "It's tricky," he admits. "I mean, you need your eyes, right? If I take away your eyes, you don't see anything. But that doesn't mean that the retina is where consciousness arises," says Koch.

For his part, Paradiso is willing to entertain the notion that perception kicks in as early as the primary visual cortex. In their studies in cats, Paradiso and his colleagues find that neurons in the V1 area respond to the apparent brightness of an object—a feature that can be altered simply by adjusting the shading of the background that surrounds it.

Look, for example, at the optical illusion at left on the opposite page. Although the horizontal bar is uniform in brightness, the contrasting surroundings make the left side of the bar appear to be brighter than the right. (If you're in doubt, cover the background.)

The illusion also fools neurons in the primary visual cortex of cats. In their experiment, Paradiso and his colleagues presented a similar illusion, which used identically shaded discs rather than the uniformly shaded bar, to anesthetized cats and recorded the response of neurons in V1. In the Aug. 23 issue of *Science*, the researchers reported that neurons' response to the discs depended on the background. When the researchers changed the background from darker to lighter during the experiment, neurons in V1 altered their activity as if the intensity of the center disc had changed.

These results suggest that brightness perception may occur in the primary visual cortex. But how? Because neurons in V1 have very small receptive fields, a single neuron could not possibly "see" outside the border of the disc to register the change in background shading that makes the disc appear brighter. Mriganka Sur of the Massachusetts Institute of Technology in Cambridge is placing his bets on long-range connections within V1.

Sur says that many neurons in the primary visual cortex send axons across 4 or 5 millimeters to contact other neurons within V1. These cross-connections might permit V1 neurons to stitch together their individual swatches of the visual field, allowing them to detect and react to context, Sur hypothesizes.

For example, in the Sept. 17 issue of *PNAS*, Sur and his colleagues describe how neurons in the cat primary visual cortex may participate in a visual phenomenon called "filling in." When human subjects are presented with a patterned visual field that is missing a piece, they often visually fill in the blank patch and report seeing an uninterrupted pattern (see figure, above). To examine the cellular basis for this perceptual phenomenon, Sur and his colleagues went back to the cat—a favorite animal model for studying the mammalian visual system.

The researchers exposed anesthetized cats to a fill-in illusion and then measured the activity of neurons in each cat's primary visual cortex using a combination of optical imaging, similar to fMRI, and electrophysiological recordings from individual neurons. When they presented the stimulus to a cat, the researchers found that the neurons in V1 that responded to the patterned background were active. But many of the neurons that responded to the blank portion of the field were active as well, some as active as the cells that responded directly to the background. Such a mechanism could explain how neurons in V1 could fill in a visual blank spot to match a patterned background.

In the same paper, Sur and his colleagues show how the visual illusion known as "pop out" might be caused

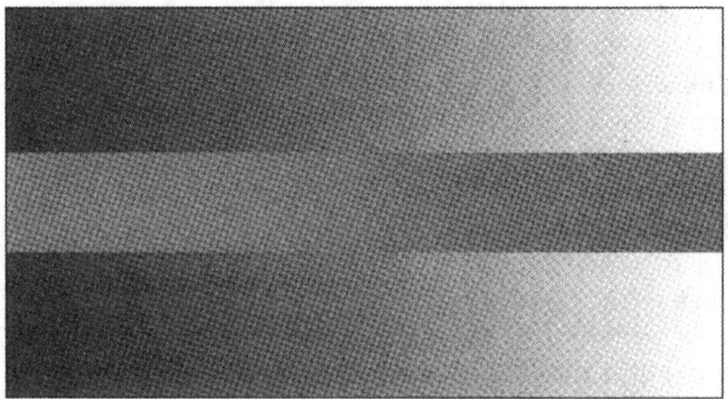

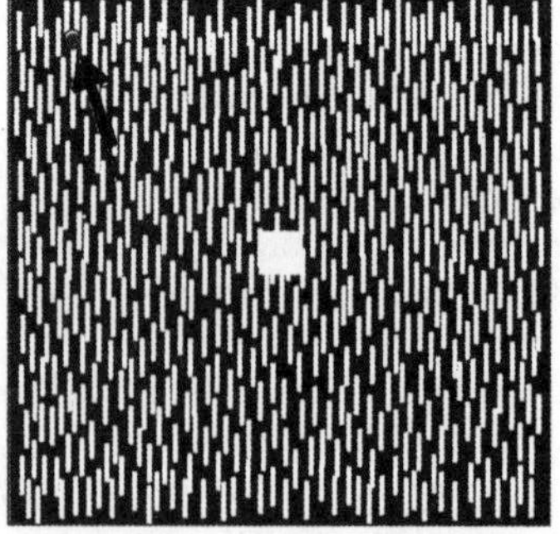

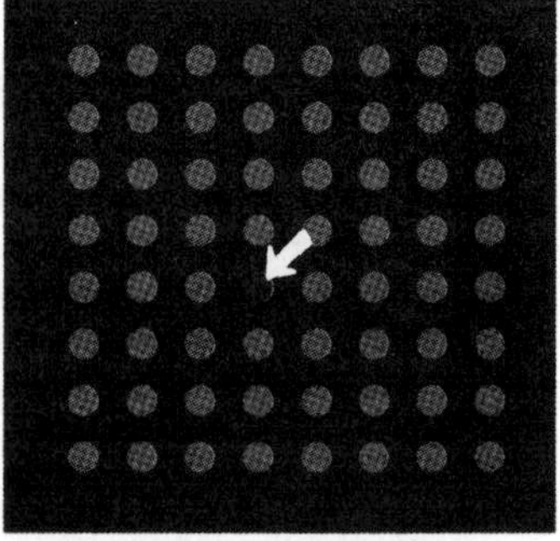

Optical illusions provide clues about visual perception. *Although the central bar (left panel) appears to progress from light to dark, it's actually a uniform shade of blue. A recent study in cats suggests that this illusion might fool neurons in the primary visual cortex, V1. In a separate study, researchers found that long-range connections between neurons in V1 may also account for visual phenomena called "filling in" and "pop-out." In the center panel, stare at the dot (arrow), and neurons in V1 may "fill in" the blank patch with the pattern from the background. In the right panel, communication between neurons in V1 may allow the dark circle (arrow) to "pop out" without a lengthy search. [Center panel adapted with permission from P. De Weerd et al., Nature 377, 731 (1995).]*

by an inverse mechanism. In humans, the "pop-out" phenomenon enables subjects to locate instantly a single red circle in a field of blue circles (see arrows in figure, previous page). The viewers need not search through the array, circle by circle, until they find the red target.

Again in cats, Sur finds that long-range connections in the primary visual cortex may also contribute to "pop out." In this instance, though, neurons that responded to a central target (such as a solitary red circle) initially displayed vigorous activity. When the researchers added a surrounding pattern (in our example, the blue circles), the activity of the neurons responding to the central target dropped. According to Sur, long-range inhibitory connections probably precipitate this loss of activity, which, paradoxically, makes a central target, such as the red circle, "pop out." Although the cats cannot confirm that they perceive "fill in" or "pop out," Sur believes that the long-range connections in V1 certainly play a role in these visual illusions.

Sur doesn't rule out effects from higher cortical areas, but he stands by his results in the primary visual cortex. "In the past few years, we've gotten a much richer understanding of the local processing that happens in V1," he says. "So our results are not really shocking, but they're just starting to be accepted and appreciated."

With so much left to be learned about the neurobiology that allows us to use our eyes to distinguish between a loved one and a head of lettuce, theories of vision should continue to evolve. As long as particular neurons in the monkey visual cortex respond equally strongly to human faces and to toilet brushes, the visual processing system will continue to challenge scientists in many fields.

The good news is that plenty of researchers have set their sights on understanding how we see the world. And they even get funding to do it. "Now you can even put the word 'awareness' right in the front of your grant application," says Koch. "Well...I'll let you know if it works."

—KAREN HOPKIN

******The Journal of NIH Research,* **November 1996, Vol. 8, p. 22.**

Motivation: Hunger and Aggression

Have you ever wondered what made you do certain things or behave in certain ways? We perform some behaviors willfully, but others we do without apparent reason. An underlying psychological force called motivation arouses, directs, and maintains the performance of these behaviors.

Withdrawing your finger from a hot stove after accidentally touching it is not necessarily a motivated behavior. It is a simple sensory-motor reflex that does not require higher cognitive processing. But touching the stove again just after you have burned your finger is certainly a motivated behavior. Perhaps you wanted to test the speed of your reflex or maybe your endurance of heat!

In the past, many people attributed their behavior to supernatural forces, such as the motion of heavenly bodies. A remnant of that practice is the belief in horoscopes. They also made attributions to supernatural forces such as curses and evil spirits. Some people who were condemned as witches or said to be possessed of evil spirits were burned at the stake because of the prevailing superstition. Archival data show that the unusual behaviors of those condemned people were probably due to insanity or other organic disorders. Nowadays, it is common for some people to attribute their behavior to certain biological factors, such as genetics and hormones. Some of these attributions are made toward behaviors that are socially, morally, or legally unacceptable.

How do we identify the sources of motivations, and why is there a shift in the kind of attribution people make through the years? Regardless of the kind of attributions we make, there appears to be a tendency to seek out motivations beyond our control when we are held accountable for unwarranted behaviors. Perhaps it is a form of the Freudian defense mechanism. The shift in the kind of attributions people make coincides with progress in science. Since science has discredited the existence of supernatural forces, it has become unenlightened and legally unacceptable to consider such forces as justifiable sources of motivation.

The public finds certain behaviors more interesting to understand than others. For example, nowadays much attention is given to eating behavior. This interest is reflected in the obsession of many to control their eating habits. During recent years, diet centers, clubs, spas, self-help groups, and publications have mushroomed all over the country to address this obsession. In spite of such concern about eating, recent statistics show that one-third of the American population is technically obese. If obesity is a disease, an epidemic is occurring!

The biological basis of motivation for eating is hunger. Hunger is a physiological state of discomfort experienced when the caloric energy supply of the body is low. Receptors for nutrients such as glucose and fat exist in some parts of the body and are responsible for sensing fluctuations in key metabolites. Eating behavior is partly controlled by the hypothalamus. On the basis of previous animal studies, lesions applied to some discrete areas of the brain can either induce overeating that can lead to obesity or completely inhibit the behavior, which can lead to emaciation. A chemical messenger implicated in the regulation of eating behavior is neuropeptide Y. Injection of neuropeptide Y into the hypothalamus stimulates eating in laboratory animals. In addition, a gene associated with the hormone leptin has also been reported to play a significant role in obesity.

Aggression or violence is another behavior that concerns our society. Federal and local governments consider it a priority to curb crimes associated with violence. This is one behavior wherein "nurture" or the environment is considered as the primary source of motivation. Socioeconomic factors and early childhood experiences may provide the motivations for violent behavior.

Does "nature" or biology play a role in aggression or violence? Recent studies give evidence for the biological

UNIT 5

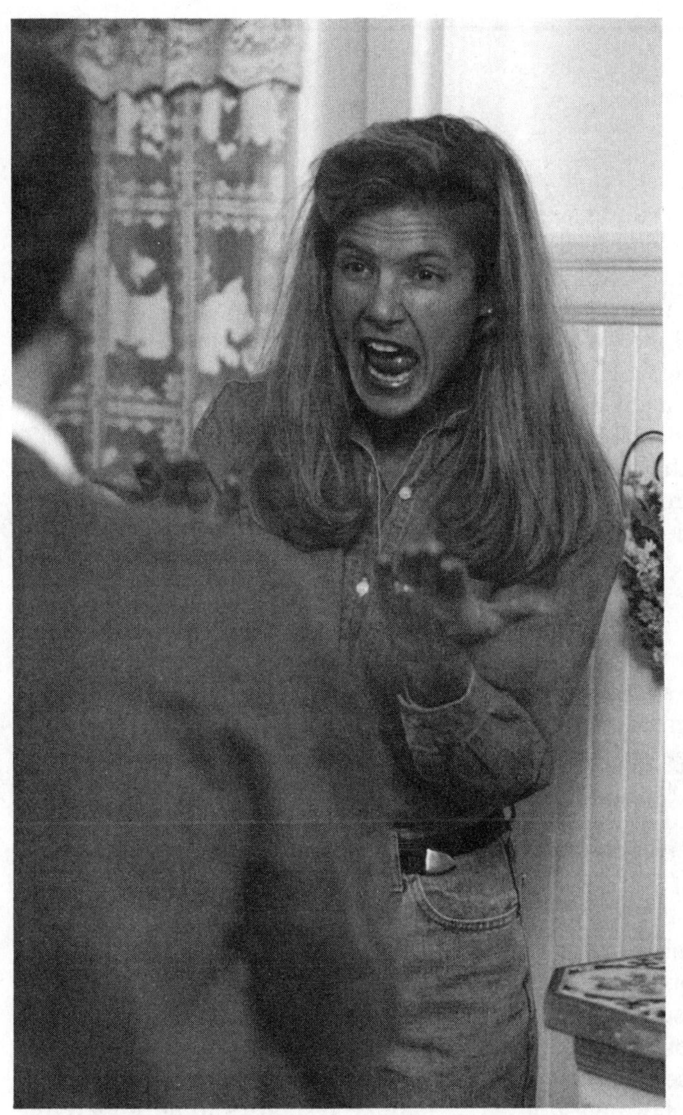

basis of aggression. For example, a report identifying a possible gene that can account for violent behavior in a Dutch family suggests the heritability of this behavior. Other studies reveal an abnormal brain neurotransmitter profile of violent individuals when compared to normal ones. Furthermore, on the basis of animal studies, lesioning or stimulation of certain hypothalamic areas abolishes or elicits aggressive behaviors, respectively.

The attribution of motivation for violent behavior to biological factors has important implications. It can be misconstrued that violent behavior cannot be avoided since it is biologically motivated. The effects of biological factors on behavior, however, are not necessarily inevitable, since the environment is equally effective in modifying behaviors. Certainly there are crimes that are legitimately attributable to some organic disorders in humans, but a judicious examination is necessary for this kind of attribution. The study of violent behavior is one field in which scientists and lawmakers need to integrate their knowledge for the welfare of society.

Looking Ahead: Challenge Questions

What regions of the brain regulate eating behavior? Differentiate the functions of different nuclei found in the hypothalamus. What is neuropeptide Y, and what is the significance of this compound on eating behavior? What are *ob/ob* mice? What do these creatures reveal to us in terms of our understanding of eating behavior?

What biological systems control aggressive or violent behavior? Describe the role of neurotransmitters in the regulation of aggressive behavior. What evidence supports the idea of a genetic basis for violent behavior? How can alcohol influence aggressiveness in people?

Effects of Alcohol on Human Aggression

Validity of Proposed Explanations

Brad J. Bushman

Abstract. In the present review, meta-analytic procedures were used to test the validity of three explanations of alcohol-related aggression: physiological disinhibition, expectancy, and indirect cause. According to the physiological disinhibition explanation, alcohol increases aggression directly by anesthetizing the center of the brain that normally inhibits aggressive responding. According to the expectancy explanation, alcohol increases aggression because people expect it to. According to the indirect cause explanation, alcohol increases aggression by causing changes within the person that increase the probability of aggression (e.g., by reducing intellectual functioning). The results from the review were inconsistent with the physiological disinhibition and expectancy explanations, but were consistent with the indirect cause explanation. Experimental manipulations that increased aggression (e.g., provocations, frustrations, aggressive cues) had a stronger effect on intoxicated participants than on sober participants.

1. Introduction

Violent crime is the issue of greatest concern to Americans today.[1–3] There is probably good reason for this concern, because the US violent crime rate has been increasing over the past several years (see Fig. 1). One violent crime occurs every 16 seconds in the United States.[4] Although it is not the only factor that contributes to violent crime, alcohol intoxication does make a significant contribution. Numerous correlational studies have found a strong relation between alcohol intoxication and violent crime. These studies generally find that over 50% of the assailants were intoxicated at the time the violent crimes were committed.[5–11]

Unfortunately, it is difficult to draw causal inferences about the relation between alcohol and aggression from correlational data. Some of the complications surrounding correlational studies of alcohol-related aggression are these: The aggressor may misreport alcohol ingestion as an excuse or to avoid punishment; alcohol consumption may accompany participation in group events that could lead to violence; alcohol containers (e.g., bottles, beer glasses) may be used as weapons; alcoholism may force people into a social stratum where crime is more probable; some alcoholics involve themselves in crimes to support their habits; alcohol-related bungling of crimes may increase the probability of capture; and alcohol and violent crime may be responses to an underlying

From *Recent Developments in Alcoholism,* edited by Marc Galanter, Volume 13, 1997, Chapter 10, pp. 227-243.

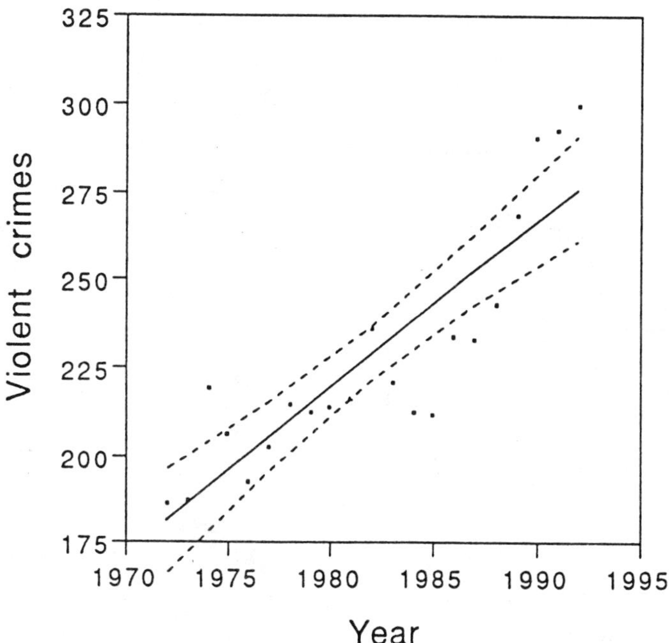

Figure 1. United States violent crime rate per 100,000 inhabitants, 1971–1992. NOTE: Data from US Department of Justice.[27] According to the FBI, violent crimes are offenses of murder, forcible rape, aggravated assault, and robbery. A regression line (solid line) and 95% confidence limits (dashed lines) were fit to these data. The least-squares regression line was −9136.53 + 4.73(year), the coefficient of determination was r^2 = .79, and the coefficient of correlation was r = .89.

social malaise.[12] The experimental method avoids these and many other pitfalls because the researcher controls the occurrence of events and randomly assigns participants to conditions. Consequently, it is much easier to draw causal inferences about the effects of alcohol on aggression from experimental data than from correlational data. It also is much easier to test explanations of alcohol-related aggression with experimental studies than with correlational studies. The data base for the present review was therefore limited to experimental studies of alcohol-related human aggression.[13,14]

2. Prototypical Methods of Administering Alcohol and Measuring Aggression in Experimental Studies

Although each experimental study of alcohol-related aggression has unique components, many experimental studies have common features. The typical laboratory procedures for administering alcohol and measuring aggression are described in the following sections.

2.1. *Administration of Alcohol*

To evaluate the effects of alcohol on aggression in humans, most researchers use a placebo design, in which all participants are told that they will receive alcohol. Only half the participants, however, are actually given alcohol; the other half are given a placebo. To enhance the credibility of the placebo drink, experimenters have poured the beverage from "legitimate" bottles and have placed a small amount of alcohol on the surface of the drink. Sometimes an additional group is added to the placebo design, in which participants are told that they will not receive alcohol and they are not given alcohol. This group serves as a control because participants receive neither alcohol nor the expectancy of alcohol. The major problem with comparing participants in the alcohol group with participants in the placebo or control groups is that the psychological (e.g., expectancy) and pharmacological effects of alcohol are confounded in these studies.

The balanced placebo design overcomes this confounding problem.[15] In the balanced placebo design, half of the participants are told that they will receive alcohol and half are told that they will not receive alcohol. Within each of these groups, half of the participants are given alcohol and half are not (see Fig. 2). To enhance the credibility of the antiplacebo drink, experimenters have poured the beverage from "legitimate" bottles, diluted the alcohol, used false Breathalyzer readings, and required participants to complete tasks that distract them from focusing on the interoceptive signs of intoxication. The pure pharmacological effects of alcohol on aggression can be determined by comparing the antiplacebo group with the control group. The pure effects of alcohol-related expectancies on aggression can be determined by comparing the placebo group with the control group. Because the balanced placebo design crosses level of alcohol with level of expectancy, the interaction of these two factors also can be tested. It is difficult, however, to use the balanced placebo design with large alcohol doses because participants become suspicious when they notice the physiological effects of alcohol.

		Expect alcohol	
		Yes	No
Given alcohol	Yes	Alcohol	Antiplacebo
	No	Placebo	Control

Figure 2. Balanced placebo design.

2.2. *Measurement of Aggression*

Buss[16] defined aggression as "a response that delivers noxious stimuli to another organism" (p. 1). Green[17] clarified this definition by adding two elements: (1) the aggressor delivers the noxious stimuli with the intent to harm the victim, and (2) the aggressor expects that the noxious stimuli will have their intended effect. Buss further proposed that acts of human aggression can be classified using combinations of three dichotomous variables: physical versus verbal, direct versus indirect, and active versus passive. Although there are eight possible combinations of the three dichotomous variables proposed by Buss, none of the four "passive" types of aggression are common in experimental studies of alcohol-related aggression. This chapter therefore focuses on the four "active" types of human aggression. In physical aggression the noxious stimuli delivered to the victim are pain and injury, whereas in verbal aggression the noxious stimuli delivered to the victim are rejection and threat. In direct aggression the aggressor is easily identified by the victim, whereas in indirect aggression the aggressor is not easily identified by the victim. There are two ways in which an aggressive act can be indirect. First, the victim is not present and the noxious stimuli are delivered via the negative reactions of others. Second, the victim is not injured or threatened, but his or her belongings are stolen or damaged.

In the "real world," most extreme acts of aggression are violent crimes, which the FBI classifies as murder, forcible rape, aggravated assault, and robbery. According to Buss's framework, murder, forcible rape, and aggravated assault are examples of direct physical aggression, whereas robbery is an example of indirect physical aggression. Table I gives real world and laboratory examples of each of the four types of active aggression proposed by Buss (i.e., direct physical, indirect physical, direct verbal, indirect verbal). Prototypical procedures for measuring each type of active aggression are given below.

2.2.1. Direct Physical Aggression. The aggression machine paradigm has been the primary laboratory procedure used to measure direct physical aggression, although it is used less frequently now than it was in the past.[16] In this procedure, a participant and a confederate are generally told that the study is concerned with the effects of alcohol on teaching and learning abilities. Using a rigged lottery, the real participant is selected to be the teacher and the confederate is selected to be the learner. The participant presents stimulus materials to the confederate who attempts to master them. Before the learning task begins, the participant is sometimes angered by the confederate. When the confederate makes an incorrect response on a trial, the participant is told to punish him or her by means of electric shock. By using different buttons, the participant can control the intensity and duration of shock given to the confederate. The shocks, for example, may range in intensity from "just perceptible" (e.g., button 1) to "excruciatingly painful" (e.g., button 10). In some experiments, shock duration is controlled by holding down the shock button for the desired duration. The dependent variables are the intensity and the duration of shock given to the confederate. Some researchers have used noxious stimuli other than electric shocks, such as noise blasts.

The competitive reaction-time paradigm is another method commonly employed to study the effects of alcohol on direct physical aggression.[18] In this procedure, a participant and a confederate are generally told that the study is concerned with the effects of alcohol on perceptual motor skills. The participant competes with the confederate on a reaction-time task in which the slower-responding person receives electric shock. At the beginning of

Table I. "Real World" and Laboratory Examples of the Direct and Indirect Types of Physical and Verbal Aggression

Type of aggression	"Real world" examples	Laboratory examples
Physical-Direct	Assaulting someone with body parts (e.g., limbs, teeth) or weapons (e.g., clubs, knives, guns).	Using intense shocks to punish a confederate whenever he or she makes an error on a task Using shocks to evaluate a confederate's solution to a problem Delivering intense shocks to a confederate on a competitive reaction-time task.
Physical-Indirect	Stealing or damaging someone's property Setting a booby trap for someone Hiring an assassin to kill someone	Subtracting money from a confederate in an experiment
Verbal-Direct	Criticizing, derogating, or cursing someone Making obscene gestures to someone Threatening someone	Making negative verbal statements to a confederate
Verbal-Indirect	Spreading vicious rumors about someone	Negatively evaluating someone on a questionnaire

each trial, the participant sets the level of shock he or she wants the confederate to receive if the confederate's response is slower. At the end of each trial, the participant is informed of the level of shock the confederate set for him or her to receive on the trial. The slower-responding person then receives the indicated intensity of shock. In actuality, the experimenter determines who wins and loses and the feedback/shocks delivered. Sometimes provocation is manipulated by increasing the intensity of shock set by the "opponent" across trials on the reaction-time task. The dependent measure is the intensity of shock the participant sets for the opponent. Some researchers have used noise blasts rather than electric shocks as noxious stimuli.

2.2.2. Indirect Physical Aggression. The laboratory paradigms used to measure direct physical aggression also have been modified to measure indirect physical aggression. In one study, for example, male college students were given $2.00 and course credit for their participation.[19] Participants were told to subtract between zero cents (button 0) and nine cents (button 9) from a confederate whenever he made a mistake on a trial. This paradigm measures indirect physical aggression because the participant takes the confederate's belongings (i.e., his money).

The free-operant paradigm is another method commonly employed to study the effects of alcohol on indirect physical aggression.[20] In this procedure, the participant can press one of two buttons on an apparatus. Pressing button A results in the accumulation of points exchangeable for money. Pressing button B results in the subtraction of points from a fictitious second participant. Sometimes provocation is manipulated by subtracting points from the participant; the point loss is attributed to the fictitious second participant. The fixed ratios associated with each button also can be manipulated (e.g., a fixed-ratio of 100 responses might be required for button A, whereas a fixed-ratio of 10 responses might be required for button B).

2.2.3. Direct Verbal Aggression. In the laboratory, direct verbal aggression is measured by recording a participant's vocal comments to one or more confederates and counting the frequency of attacks or other negative verbal statements. In one study, for example, male participants were told that they would be participating in a study of alcohol's effect on creativity with five other participants whom they would not know.[21] Two of the group members were confederates. One confederate was a social facilitator who tried to develop cohesiveness among group members by initiating conversation and telling jokes. The other confederate tried to antagonize participants by complaining and insulting their intelligence (e.g., he said that this was the dumbest group of people he had ever encountered). The experimental sessions were video-taped and later coded for verbally aggressive statements made by the participants.

2.2.4. Indirect Verbal Aggression. Indirect measures of verbal aggression are more common in laboratory experiments than are direct measures of verbal aggression. Generally, a confederate or experimenter first provokes the participant. Rather than confronting the confederate or experimenter face-to-face, the participant uses a pencil-and-paper measure to evaluate him or her. The participant is led to believe that negative ratings will harm the confederate or experimenter in some way. In one study, for example, a male participant was told to trace a circle as slowly as possible.[22] After this task was completed, a male experimenter burst in the room, introduced himself as the supervisor who had been observing through a one-way mirror, and contemptuously stated, "Obviously, you don't follow instructions. You were supposed to trace the circle as slowly as possible without stopping but you clearly didn't do this. Now I don't know if we can use your data." The experimenter paused, then continued (interrupting the participant if he or she tried to respond), "Do it over again." After the experiment, the participant completed an evaluation form for each member of the lab staff, including the obnoxious experimenter. The form asked the participant to rate each staff member on 7-point scales as to whether he or she was effective in performing duties, was a capable employee, was likeable, made the participant feel comfortable, showed respect for the participant, and should be rehired. The evaluations were placed in a sealed envelope and were allegedly sent to the principal investigator to be used in future hiring decisions.

3. Explanations of Alcohol-Related Aggression

Although several explanations have been proposed to account for alcohol-related aggression, most can be placed into one of three categories depending on the role each assigns to alcohol: physiological disinhibition, expectancy, and indirect cause.

3.1. Physiological Disinhibition

Normally, people have strong inhibitions against behaving aggressively, because society strongly sanctions such behavior. According to the physiological disinhibition explanation, alcohol increases aggression directly by anesthetizing the center of the brain that normally inhibits aggressive responding. Disinhibition theorists argue that alcohol facilitates aggression "not by 'stepping on the gas' but rather by paralyzing the brakes" (p. 40).[23]

If alcohol directly causes aggression by reducing inhibitions, then participants in the antiplacebo group should behave more aggressively than participants in the control group. The antiplacebo versus control comparison provides the best test of the validity of the physiological disinhibition explanation of intoxicated aggression because it gives the pure pharmacological effects of alcohol on aggression (i.e., the effects of alcohol-related expectancies on aggression are removed).

3.2. Expectancy

According to the expectancy explanation, alcohol increases aggression because people expect it to. Those who behave aggressively while intoxicated can therefore "blame the bottle" for their actions. According to MacAndrew and Edgerton,[24] violence and other antisocial behaviors occur when alcohol is consumed because, in many societies, drinking occasions are culturally agreed-on "time-out" periods when people are not held accountable for their actions.

If alcohol-related expectancies cause aggression, then participants in the placebo group should behave more aggressively than participants in the control group. The placebo versus control comparison provides the best test of the validity of the expectancy explanation of intoxicated aggression because it gives the pure effects of alcohol-related expectancies on aggression (i.e., the pharmacological effects of alcohol on aggression are removed).

3.3. Indirect Cause

According to the indirect cause explanation, alcohol increases aggression by causing certain cognitive, emotional, and physiological changes that increase the probability of aggression. For example, some of the cognitive changes that accompany alcohol consumption are impaired intellectual functioning, inaccurate assessment of risks, and reduced self-awareness.

If alcohol indirectly causes aggression, then manipulations that increase aggression in laboratory experiments, such as provocations, frustrations, and aggressive cues, should have a greater effect on intoxicated participants than on sober participants. Support for the indirect cause explanation of intoxicated would be provided by a significant Alcohol × Manipulation interaction, followed up by contrasts that show that the experimental manipulation increased aggression more in participants who were given alcohol than in participants who were not given alcohol.

4. Present Review

The primary purpose of the present review was to test the validity of the physiological disinhibition, expectancy, and indirect cause explanations of intoxicated aggression. There are two general approaches to reviewing the literature: the narrative (or qualitative) approach and the meta-analytic (or quantitative) approach. In the traditional narrative review, the reviewer uses "mental algebra" to integrate the findings from a collection of studies and describes the results in a narrative manner. In the meta-analytic review, the reviewer uses statistical procedures to integrate the findings from a collection of studies and describes the results using numerical effect size estimates. Traditional narrative reviews are more likely than meta-analytic reviews to depend on the subjective judgments, preferences, and biases of the reviewer.[25] In the present review, meta-analytic procedures were used to test the validity of the proposed explanations of intoxicated aggression.

5. Method

5.1. Literature Search Procedures

All experimental studies retrieved in previous meta-analytic reviews of alcohol and aggression by Bushman and his colleagues were included.[13,14] To obtain more recent experimental studies, the PsycLIT computer data base was searched from January 1992 to March 1995. The terms used to describe aggression (aggression, agonistic, anger, attack, dominant, fight, hostility, violence) were the same descriptors used by the International Society for Research on Aggression in their journal, *Aggressive Behavior.* The aggression keywords were paired with three alcohol terms: alcohol, ethanol, and intoxicant. Various forms of the keywords also were used (e.g., aggress, aggression, aggressive, aggressor). The search was restricted to studies that used human participants. The literature review retrieved 60 research reports that included 66 independent samples of participants.*

5.2. *Criteria for Relevance*

Because the primary purpose of this review was to determine the validity of causal explanations of intoxicated aggression, two exclusion criteria were used. First, correlational studies were excluded from the review. Second, studies that used aggressive state measures were excluded unless they also used behavioral measures of aggression. An aggressive state is a combination of thoughts, feelings, behavioral tendencies, and physiological arousal levels that are elicited by stimuli capable of evoking aggression. Although an aggressive state should heighten the likelihood of aggression, it would not be classified by most psychologists as aggressive "behavior."

5.3. *Coding Frame*

The information listed in the Appendix was extracted from the report of each study. These data were divided into three categories: participant characteristics, experiment characteristics, and primary study results. (For a detailed description of the source, participant, and experiment characteristics that moderate the relation between alcohol intoxication and aggression, see the meta-analysis by Bushman and Cooper.[13,14])

5.4. *Meta-Analytic Procedures*

The effect size estimate used in this review was the standardized mean difference, d (see Appendix). The standardized mean difference gives the number of standard deviation units between the sample means of two groups (e.g., placebo and control). According to Cohen,[28] a "small" d is 0.20, a "medium" d is 0.50, and a "large" d is 0.80. The average weighted sample standardized mean differences, where each standardized mean difference was weighted by the inverse of its variance, was used to estimate the common population standardized mean difference, δ. (Average standardized mean differences, 95% confidence intervals, and moderator tests were calculated using the procedures described in Hedges and Olkin.[29]) A 95% confidence interval also was calculated for δ.[29] If studies did not provide enough information to compute an effect size estimate, but did report the direction or statistical significance of results, vote-counting procedures were used to obtain an effect size estimate.[30] The procedure proposed by Bushman and Wang[31] was then used to combine the estimates based effect size and vote-counting procedures.

One problem that arises in estimating average effect size estimates is deciding what constitutes an independent hypothesis test. The present review used a shifting unit of analysis.[32] Each statistical test was coded as if it were an independent event. For example, if a single study contained two measures of aggression (e.g., intensity of shock given to a confederate and amount of money subtracted from a confederate), two effect size estimates would be coded. For the estimate of alcohol's overall effect on aggression, the two effect size estimates would be averaged so that the study would contribute only one effect size estimate. For an analysis in which the effects of alcohol are compared for different measures of aggression, the study would contribute two effect size estimates (e.g., direct physical aggression and indirect physical aggression). Thus, the shifting unit of analysis retains as much data as possible without violating too greatly the independence assumption that underlies the validity of meta-analytic procedures.

6. Results

6.1. *Sex Differences in Intoxicated Aggression*

The results showed that alcohol increased aggression more in men than in women. χ^2 $(1, k = 65) = 4.64$, $p < 0.05$, where k is the number of independent samples of participants.[29] The average weighted effect size estimate for the 59 samples of male participants was 0.50 with 95% confidence interval [0.41, 0.58]. The average weighted effect size estimate for the six samples of female participants was 0.13 with 95% confidence interval [−0.20, 0.45]. Because alcohol increased aggression more in men than in women, subsequent analyses were based on the results from men only.

6.2. *Measurement of Aggression*

The type of aggression measure used (i.e., direct physical, indirect physical, direct verbal, indirect verbal) did not significantly influence the results reported in this review. Thus, the four types of aggression

* Extreme outliers were removed from the data set. In the study by Zeichner and Pihl,[26] the noise intensity standardized mean estimates were 6.64 and 6.81 for the alcohol versus placebo comparisons, respectively. In the study by Zeichner and Pihl,[27] the noise intensity standardized mean estimates were 11.63 and 7.00 for the alcohol versus control and alcohol versus placebo comparisons, respectively.

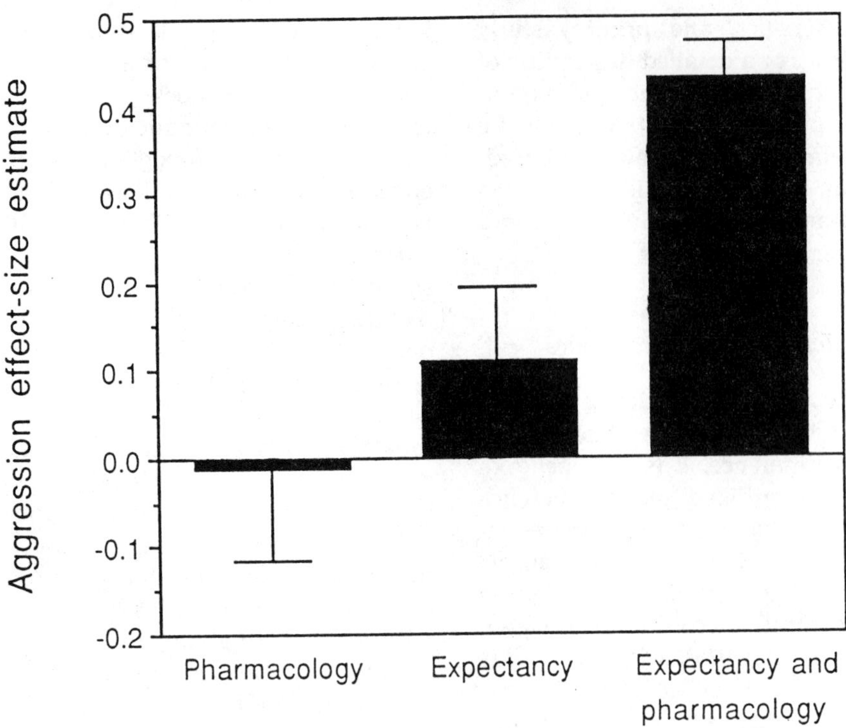

Figure 3. Psychological and pharmacological effects of alcohol on human aggression. NOTE: Capped vertical bars denote 1 standard error. Pharmacology, antiplacebo versus control comparison. Expectancy, placebo versus control comparison. Expectancy and pharmacology confounded, alcohol versus placebo and alcohol versus control comparisons combined.

measures were pooled for subsequent analyses.

6.3. Validity of Proposed Explanations of Alcohol-Related Aggression

6.3.1. Physiological Disinhibition. If alcohol directly causes aggression by reducing inhibitions, then the level of aggression should be higher for participants in the antiplacebo group than for participants in the control group. The average weighted effect size estimate for the 13 antiplacebo versus control comparisons was −0.01, with 95% confidence interval [−0.21, 0.19]. Because the confidence interval contains the value zero, it appears that alcohol does not directly cause aggression.

6.3.2. Expectancy. If alcohol-related expectancies cause aggression, then the level of aggression should be higher for participants in the placebo group than for participants in the control group. The average weighted effect size estimate for the 20 placebo versus control comparison was 0.11, with 95% confidence interval [−0.06, 0.28]. Because the confidence interval contains the value zero, it appears that alcohol-related expectancies do not cause aggression.

As can be seen in Fig. 3, the effects of alcohol on aggression cannot be attributed solely to the pharmacological effects of alcohol nor to the effects of alcohol-related expectancies. Figure 3 also shows the results from studies in which the psychological and pharmacological effects of alcohol are confounded (i.e., alcohol versus placebo and alcohol versus control comparisons combined). In the real world, of course, the pharmacological and psychological effects of alcohol are confounded. For these confounded studies, the level of aggression was significantly higher for intoxicated participants than for sober participants. The average weighted effect size estimate based on 75 comparisons was 0.43 with 95% confidence interval [0.44, 0.62]. As can be seen in Fig. 3, the pharmacological and psychological effects of alcohol on aggression are not additive nor are they multiplicative. Thus, alcohol-related aggression cannot be explained by the independent or joint pharmacological and psychological effects of alcohol; another explanation is required.

6.3.3. Indirect Cause. If alcohol indirectly causes aggression by producing internal changes that increase the probability of aggression, then experimental manipulations that increase aggression should have a greater impact on intoxicated participants than on sober participants. Eighty-two percent of the studies included in this review used such manipulations. For this subset of studies, raters coded whether the Alcohol × Manipulation interaction was significant or nonsignificant. If the manipulation increased aggression, raters coded whether the effect was stronger for participants who received alcohol than for participants who did not receive alcohol.

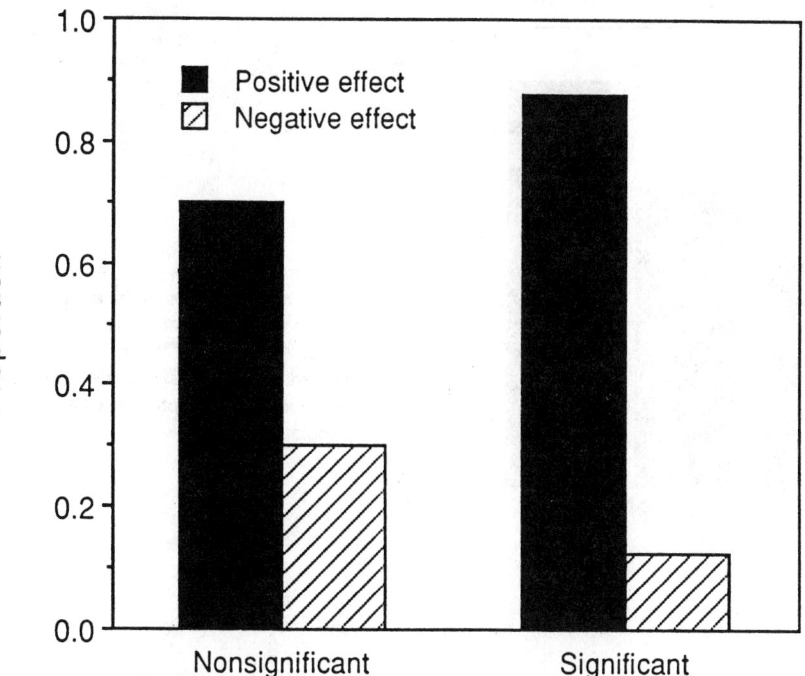

Figure 4. Effects of experimental aggression manipulations on intoxicated and sober participants. NOTE: Positive effect, aggression-eliciting manipulation was stronger for participants who received alcohol than for participants who did not receive alcohol. Negative effect, aggression-eliciting manipulation was stronger for participants who did not receive alcohol than for participants who received alcohol.

The results from studies with nonsignificant and significant Alcohol × Manipulation interactions are shown in Fig. 4* For nonsignificant interactions, 36 results were positive (i.e., in the predicted direction) and 14 results were negative (i.e., in the opposite direction). A sign test showed that the proportion of positive results was significantly greater than .5, $p < 0.05$. The corresponding effect size estimate was $g = .22$, a value close to Cohen's[28] conventional value for a "large" effect (i.e., $g = .25$). For significant interactions, 14 results were positive and 2 results were negative. A sign test showed that the proportion of positive results was significantly greater than .5, $p < 0.05$. The corresponding effect size estimate was $g = .38$, a value greater than Cohen's conventional value for a large effect. These results are entirely consistent with the indirect cause explanation of intoxicated aggression.

7. Conclusions

Does alcohol cause aggression? The results from this review suggest that it does. In experimental studies, intoxicated participants were more aggressive, on average, than were sober participants. Larger effects might be obtained for higher alcohol doses on human aggression. The effects of alcohol on aggression are as large as the effects of other independent variables on aggression (e.g., media violence, anonymity, hot temperatures).[33] Alcohol also influences aggressive behavior as much as it influences other social (e.g., risk taking, moral judgment, sexual interest) and nonsocial (e.g., information processing, self-reported mood, physiological arousal) behaviors.[34]

Why does alcohol increase aggression? The results from this review suggest that intoxicated aggression cannot be solely attributed to the pharmacological or expectancy effects of alcohol. Another possibility, however, is that the null effects for the antiplacebo versus control and placebo versus control comparisons are due to methodological problems associated with the antiplacebo and placebo groups. These groups both involve deception. Participants in the antiplacebo group do not expect to receive alcohol and might become suspicious when they taste, smell, and notice the physiological effects of alcohol. Participants in the placebo group expect to receive alcohol and might become suspicious when they do not experience the physiological effects of alcohol. When participants in the antiplacebo and placebo groups realize that the experimenter has attempted to deceive them concerning the contents of their beverage, they also might become suspicious about other facets of the experiment and become more aware of their behavior. Because aggression is not a so-

* Four studies manipulated variables that decreased aggression (i.e., nonaggressive norms, nonaggressive cues, pain feedback). The Alcohol × Manipulation interaction was significant for one of the four studies. All four studies found that aggression reducing manipulations had a weaker effect on intoxicated participants than on sober participants.

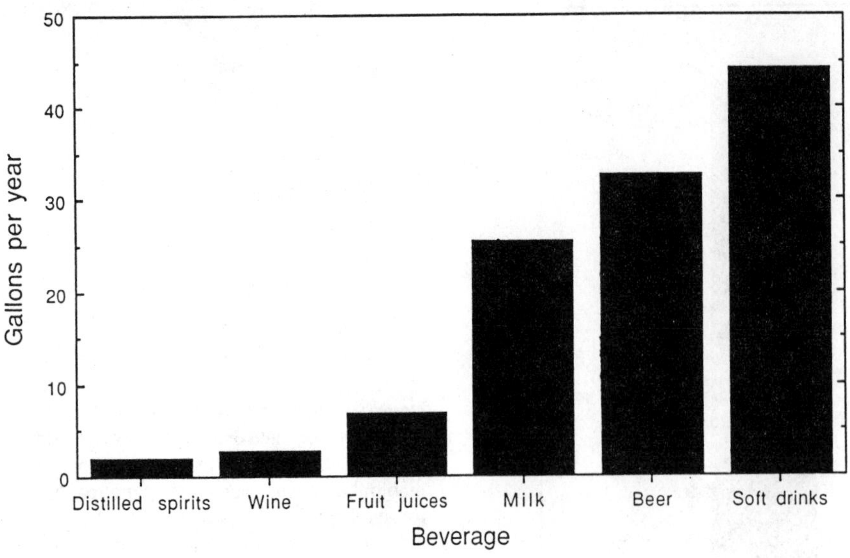

Figure 5. United States per capita consumption of selected beverages. NOTE: Data from US Department of Agriculture.[28] Milk includes plain and flavored. Fruit juices excludes vegetable juices. Alcoholic consumption rates are for the adult population.

cially desirable response, participants in the antiplacebo and placebo groups might inhibit their behavior consciously.

The results from this review are consistent with the idea that alcohol indirectly causes aggression by producing changes within the person that increase the probability of aggression. Experimental manipulations that facilitate aggression, such as provocations, frustrations, and aggressive cues, were shown to have a stronger effect on intoxicated participants than on sober participants. This may explain why "barroom brawls" are so common. Bars often are crowded, noisy, smoky, and provocative environments.

The relation between alcohol and aggression would be of little concern if people rarely drank alcohol. But in the United States, alcohol is the beverage of choice for many people. As can be seen in Fig. 5, the average American adult drinks more beer than milk each year. What would happen to violent crime rates in the United States if people drank less alcohol? A study by Cook and Moore[35] reported that if alcohol consumption per capita decreased by just 10%, there would be a corresponding 1% decrease in murders, 6% decrease in forcible rapes, 6% decrease in aggravated assaults, and 9% decrease in robberies.* Thus, one way to obtain a kinder, gentler society would be to decrease alcohol consumption.

8. Appendix

8.1. Participant Characteristics

1. Sex of participants.
2. Number of participants.

8.2. Experiment Characteristics

1. Type of comparison (i.e., antiplacebo versus control, placebo versus control, alcohol versus placebo, alcohol versus control).

2. Type of aggression (i.e., direct physical, indirect physical, direct verbal, indirect verbal).

3. If the study contained an experimental manipulation that was expected to influence aggression, was the Alcohol × Experimental manipulation significant or nonsignificant at the $\alpha = 0.10$ level? (Due to low statistical power, the $\alpha = 0.10$ level was used rather than the $\alpha = 0.05$ level) What was the direction of the contrast analysis (i.e., *positive,* if the manipulation increased aggression, the effect was stronger for participants who received alcohol than for participants who did not receive alcohol; *negative,* if the manipulation increased aggression, the effect was stronger for participants who did not receive alcohol than for participants who received alcohol; *null,* the effect was the same for participants who did and did not receive alcohol)?

8.3. Primary Study Results

1. Direction of effect (i.e., positive, negative, null effect).

2. Significance of effect (i.e., significant, nonsignificant at the $\alpha = 0.05$ level).

3. Magnitude of effect (i.e., standardized mean differences estimate, *d*). The standardized mean difference estimate was defined as $d = (M_1 - M_2)/SD$, where M_1 and M_2 are the respective sample means for groups 1 and 2, and SD is the pooled standard deviation. When means and standard deviations were not reported, but *t* tests or *F* tests with 1 degree of freedom in the numerator were reported, *d* was calculated us-

* Cook and Moore[35] calculated these estimates using regression analysis from US violent crime rates from 1979 to 1988.

ing Friedman's formula.[29] If F tests with multiple degrees of freedom in the numerator were reported, means and standard deviations were requested from authors.

References

1. Adler J: Kids growing up scared. *Newsweek* 43–50, 1994. January 10.
2. Lacayo R: Lock 'em up! *Time* 50–53, 1994, February 7.
3. Shannon E: Crime: Safer streets, yet greater fear. *Time* 63–65, 1995, January 30.
4. Shannon E: Crime: Safer streets, yet greater fear. *Time* 63–65, 1995, January 30.
5. Beck AJ: *Profile of Jail Inmates, 1989.* Washington, DC, Bureau of Justice Statistics, 1991.
6. Beck AJ, Kline SA, Greenfield LA: *Survey of Youth in Custody, 1987.* Washington, DC, Bureau of Justice Statistics, 1988.
7. Greenberg SW: Alcohol and crime: A methodological critique of the literature, in Collins JJ (ed): *Drinking and Crime: Perspectives on the Relationships between Alcohol Consumption and Criminal Behavior.* New York, Guilford, 1981.
8. Innes CA: *Drug Use and Crime.* Washington, DC, US Department of Justice, 1988.
9. MacDonald JM: *The Murderer and His Victim.* Springfield, IL, Charles C. Thomas, 1961.
10. Murdoch D, Pihl RO, Ross D: Alcohol and crimes of violence: Present issues. *Int J Addict* 25:1065–1081, 1990.
11. Pernanen K: *Alcohol in Human Violence.* New York, Guilford Press, 1991.
12. Brain PF: Multidisciplinary examinations of the "causes" of crime: The case of the link between alcohol and violence. *Alcohol Alcohol* 21:237–240, 1986.
13. Bushman BJ: Human aggression while under the influence of alcohol and other drugs: An integrative research review. *Curr Direct Psychol Sci* 2:148–152, 1993.
14. Bushman BJ, Cooper HM: Effects of alcohol on human aggression: An integrative research review. *Psychol Bull* 107:341–354, 1990.
15. Ross S, Krugman AD, Lyerly SB, Clyde DJ: Drugs and placebos: A model design. *Psychol Rep* 10:383–392, 1962.
16. Buss AH: *The Psychology of Aggression.* New York, Wiley, 1961.
17. Green RG: *Human Aggression.* Pacific Grove, CA, Brooks/Cole, 1990.
18. Taylor SP: Aggressive behavior and physiological arousal as a function of provocation and the tendency to inhibit aggression. *J Pers* 35:297–310, 1967.
19. Barnett RK: The effects of alcohol, expectancy, provocation, and permission to aggress upon aggressive behavior. *Dissertation Abstracts International* 40:4993B (University Microfilms No. ADG8O-09229, 0000), 1979.
20. Cherek DR, Spiga R, Egli M: Effects of response requirement and alcohol on human aggressive responding. *J Exp Anal Behav* 58:577–587, 1992.
21. Murdoch D, Pihl RO: Alcohol and aggression in a group interaction. *Addict Behav* 10:97–101, 1985.
22. Rohsenow DJ, Bachorowski J: Effect of alcohol and expectancies on verbal aggression in men and women. *J Abnorm Psychol* 93:418–432, 1984.
23. Muehlberger CW: Medicolegal aspects of alcohol intoxication. *Mich State Bar J* 35:38–42, 1956.
24. MacAndrew C, Edgerton RB: *Drunken Comportment: A Social Explanation.* Chicago, Aldine, 1969.
25. Cooper H, Rosenthal R: Statistical versus traditional procedures for summarizing research findings. *Psychological Bulletin* 87:442–449, 1980.
26. Zeichner A, Pihl RO: Effects of alcohol and behavior contingencies on human aggression. *J Abnorm Psychol* 88:153–160, 1979.
27. Zeichner A, Pihl RO: Effects of alcohol and instigator intent on human aggression. *J Stud Alcohol* 41:265–276, 1980.
28. Cohen J: *Statistical Power Analysis for the Behavioral Sciences,* 2nd ed. Hillsdale, NJ, Lawrence Erlbaum, 1988.
29. Hedges LV, Olkin I: *Statistical Methods for Meta-analysis.* New York, Academic Press, 1985.
30. Bushman BJ: Vote-counting procedures in meta-analysis, in Cooper H, Hedges LV (eds): *The Handbook of Research Synthesis.* New York, Russell Sage Foundation, 1994, pp 193–213.
31. Bushman BJ, Wang MC: A procedure for combining sample standardized mean differences and vote counts to estimate the population standardized mean difference in fixed effects models. *Psychol Methods* 1:66–80.
32. Cooper HM: Integrating research: *A Guide for Literature Reviews,* 2nd ed. Hillsdale, NJ, Erlbaum, 1989.
33. Anderson CA, Bushman BJ: External validity of "trivial" experiments: The case of laboratory aggression. *General Psychology Review,* in press.
34. Steele CM, Southwick L: Alcohol and social behavior I: The psychology of drunken excess. *J Pers Soc Psychol* 48:18–34, 1985.
35. Cook PJ, Moore MJ: Violence reduction through restrictions on alcohol availability. *Alcohol Health Res World* 17:151–156, 1993.
36. Maguire K, Pastotre AL (eds): *Sourcebook of Criminal Justice Statistics, 1993.* US Department of Justice, Bureau of Justice Statistics. Washington, DC, US Government Printing Office, 1994.
37. US Bureau of the Census: *Statistical Abstract of the United States:* 1994, 114th ed. Washington, DC, US Government Printing Office, 1994.
38. Friedman H: Magnitude of an experimental effect and a table for its rapid estimation. *Psychol Bull* 70:194–197, 1968.

Attenuation of the Obesity Syndrome of *ob/ob* Mice by the Loss of Neuropeptide Y

Jay C. Erickson, Gunther Hollopeter, Richard D. Palmiter*

The obesity syndrome of *ob/ob* mice results from lack of leptin, a hormone released by fat cells that acts in the brain to suppress feeding and stimulate metabolism. Neuropeptide Y (NPY) is a neuromodulator implicated in the control of energy balance and is overproduced in the hypothalamus of *ob/ob* mice. To determine the role of NPY in the response to leptin deficiency, *ob/ob* mice deficient for NPY were generated. In the absence of NPY, *ob/ob* mice are less obese because of reduced food intake and increased energy expenditure, and are less severely affected by diabetes, sterility, and somatotropic defects. These results suggest that NPY is a central effector of leptin deficiency.

The circulating hormone leptin informs the brain about the abundance of body fat, thereby allowing feeding behavior, metabolism, and endocrine physiology to be coupled to the nutritional state of the organism. Leptin promotes weight loss by suppressing appetite and stimulating metabolism, and is required for normal endocrine function (*1–3*). Consequently, mutant mice that lack leptin or functional leptin receptors, such as *ob/ob* and *db/db* mice, respectively, are profoundly hyperphagic, massively obese, hypometabolic, hypothermic, diabetic, and infertile (*4, 5*).

The mechanisms by which alterations in circulating leptin levels trigger changes in feeding behavior, metabolism, and endocrine function are unknown. Neuropeptide Y (NPY), a neuromodulator abundant in regions of the hypothalamus that participate in energy balance and neuroendocrine signaling, has been implicated as a mediator of the response to leptin deficiency (*3, 6, 7*). The expression and release of hypothalamic NPY are inhibited by leptin (*6, 7*); consequently, NPY signaling is elevated in the hypothalamus of leptin-deficient rodents (*6, 8*). In addition, chronic administration of NPY into the hypothalamus of normal animals mimics the phenotype of leptin deficiency, including obesity, hyperphagia, reduced thermogenesis, decreased fertility, and inhibition of growth hormone production (*9*). In light of these findings, our observation that mice deficient in NPY have normal body weight, body adiposity, and food intake was unexpected (*10*).

To investigate the role of NPY in the obesity syndrome resulting from the absence of leptin, we generated mice deficient in both leptin and NPY by breeding the mutant NPY allele onto the *ob/ob* background (*11*). The double mutants ($NPY^{-/-}$ *ob/ob* mice) could be distinguished from *ob/ob* mice by their narrower bodies and improved grooming (Fig. 1A). This physical difference was evident at ~6 weeks and became more pronounced with increasing age. However, double mutants were clearly larger than normal mice at all ages after weaning.

As expected from differences in body shape, $NPY^{-/-}$ *ob/ob* mice weighed less than *ob/ob* mice but more than normal mice (Fig. 1B). The difference in body weight between double mutants and *ob/ob* mice was significant after 10 weeks of age in males and 6 weeks of age in females. At 16 weeks of age, double mutant males

A

OB/OB | *ob/ob* | *ob/ob* $NPY^{-/-}$

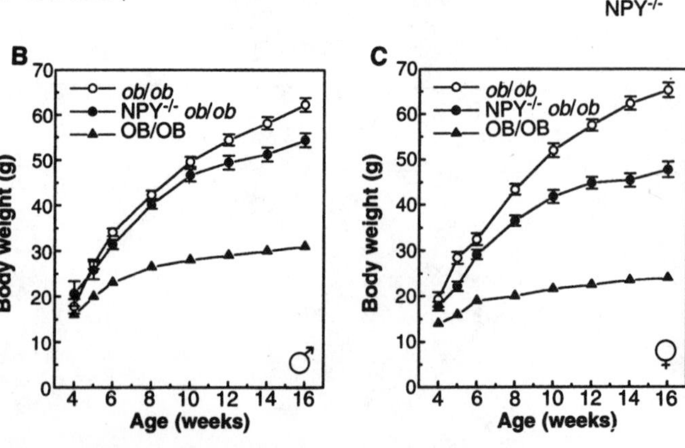

Fig. 1. Physical appearance and body weights of normal (OB/OB), *ob/ob*, and $NPY^{-/-}$ *ob/ob* mice. (**A**) Representative body shapes of male mice at 15 weeks of age. Photo was cropped at mid-tail level. (**B** and **C**) Body weights of male and female mice at various ages. Values are the mean ± SEM; $n > 10$ for each group. Body weight of $NPY^{-/-}$ *ob/ob* females was significantly lower than that of *ob/ob* females at all ages after 6 weeks ($P < 0.01$). Body weight of $NPY^{-/-}$ *ob/ob* males was significantly lower than that of *ob/ob* males at all ages after 10 weeks ($P < 0.02$).

Howard Hughes Medical Institute and Department of Biochemistry, University of Washington, Box 357370, Seattle, WA 98195-7370, USA.

*To whom correspondence should be addressed.

weighed 13% less than *ob/ob* males ($P <$ 0.002) and double mutant females weighed 27% less than *ob/ob* females ($P <$ 0.001), reflecting a ~25% and ~40% correction of the excess weight of *ob/ob* mice, respectively.

Double mutants were not as obese as *ob/ob* mice. Whole-mouse magnetic resonance imaging (*12*) revealed that $NPY^{-/-}$ *ob/ob* mice had less fat throughout their bodies than *ob/ob* mice, although they were more obese than normal mice (Fig. 2A). In addition, the lipid:water ratio, indicative of percent body fat, for 12- to 14-week-old double mutants was ~40% less than that for *ob/ob* mice (Fig. 2B). We confirmed the lower fat content of $NPY^{-/-}$ *ob/ob* mice at 16 weeks of age by weighing discrete fat pads. The weights of inguinal, reproductive (epididymal in males, parametrial in females), retroperitoneal, and scapular fat pads were lower in double mutant mice than in *ob/ob* mice. The fat depots showing the biggest weight differences were the scapular fat pad [0.28 ± 0.05 g in normal, 7.5 ± 0.5 g in *ob/ob*, and 2.3 ± 0.4 g in double mutant mice ($P < 0.001$ compared to *ob/ob*)], and the inguinal fat pads [0.38 ± 0.05 g in normal, 7.5 ± 0.4 g in *ob/ob*, and 3.2 ± 0.3 g in double mutant mice ($P < 0.001$ compared to *ob/ob*)]. The average combined weight of the four fat pads was 51% less in $NPY^{-/-}$ *ob/ob* mice than in *ob/ob* mice (Fig. 2C).

The obesity of *ob/ob* mice is accompanied by extensive deposition of fat in liver, resulting in hepatomegaly. Histological examination revealed that double mutants had fatty livers, but the hepatic lipid deposits were smaller and fewer in number than in *ob/ob* mice. The average liver weight was 1.32 ± 0.05 g for normal mice, 3.72 ± 0.18 g for *ob/ob* mice, and 2.71 ± 0.15 g for $NPY^{-/-}$ *ob/ob* mice ($P < 0.001$ compared to *ob/ob*).

Body weight and adiposity are influenced by the rate of food consumption and the rate at which energy is expended metabolically. To determine whether reduced food intake or increased energy expenditure was responsible for the decreased obesity of $NPY^{-/-}$ *ob/ob* mice relative to *ob/ob* mice, we compared their rates of food and oxygen consumption. Whereas *ob/ob* mice ate 62% more food than normal mice, double mutants ate only 35% more, corresponding to a ~40% suppression of hyperphagia (Fig. 3A). In addition, basal oxygen consumption was significantly higher in double mutant mice than in *ob/ob* mice (Fig. 3B). Thus, both reduced food intake and increased metabolic rate help to normalize energy balance in $NPY^{-/-}$ *ob/ob* mice. The increased oxygen consumption of $NPY^{-/-}$ *ob/ob* mice was due in part to the maintenance of a higher body temperature (Fig. 3C). Energy expenditure of double mutants was further enhanced by increased physical activity as indicated by 24-hour ambulation (Fig. 3D). No significant differences in any of these metabolic parameters were detected between wild-type mice and $NPY^{-/-}$ mice.

The *ob/ob* mice develop a form of diabetes similar to human type-II diabetes (*5*), a condition commonly associated with obesity. To determine whether development of diabetes was delayed in $NPY^{-/-}$ *ob/ob* mice, we monitored urine glucose. Between 4 and 6 weeks of age, 42% of *ob/ob* mice, but only 20% of double mutants, had detectable levels of glucose

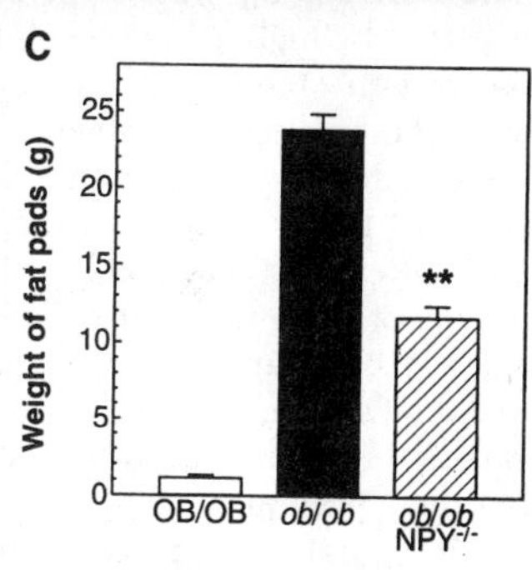

Fig. 2. Adiposity of normal, *ob/ob*, and $NPY^{-/-}$ *ob/ob* mice. (**A**) Fat-selective magnetic resonance images (MRIs) of male mice at 14 weeks of age (*12*). Images are 3-mm thick, body length, horizontal sections. Adipose tissue appears white. Images are oriented such that the head of each mouse is at the top. The sides of the *ob/ob* image are straight because the mouse was pressed against the walls of the MR tube. (**B**) Average lipid:water ratios of 12- to 15-week-old mice obtained from MR spectra (*12*). Values are the mean ± SEM. Each group consisted of four males and three females. *$P < 0.001$ compared to *ob/ob* mice; unpaired *t*-test. Some *ob/ob* mice, but not double mutants, could not be analyzed by this technique because they were too large to fit into the 4.2-cm-diameter coil. Consequently, the adiposity of *ob/ob* mice was slightly underestimated. (**C**) Combined weights of inguinal, retroperitoneal, scapular, and reproductive pads, measured when mice were 16 weeks of age. Values are the mean ± SEM. The *ob/ob* group consisted of 19 males and 15 females; the double mutant group consisted of 12 males and 10 females. **$P < 0.001$ compared to *ob/ob* mice, unpaired *t*-test.

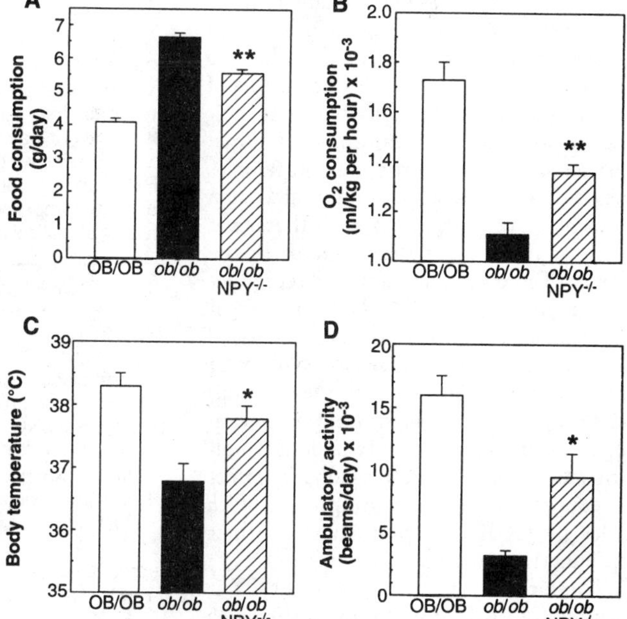

Fig. 3. Energy balance in normal, *ob/ob*, and $NPY^{-/-}$ *ob/ob* mice. (**A**) Average daily food consumption. Food intake was determined by measuring 5-day intake in mice at 6, 8, 12, and 14 weeks of age; $n > 25$ for each genotype. **$P < 0.001$ compared to *ob/ob* mice. (**B**) Basal oxygen consumption of 12- to 14-week-old mice as measured by indirect calorimetry (*20*); $n = 12$ for each genotype. **$P < 0.001$ compared to *ob/ob* mice. (**C**) Body temperature of 14- to 16-week-old mice. Core temperature was measured with a rectal thermister (Yellow Springs Instruments, Yellow Springs, Ohio). $n \geq 14$ for each genotype. *$P < 0.01$ compared to *ob/ob* mice. (**D**) Ambulatory activity of 10- to 14-week-old mice (*21*); $n > 10$ for each genotype. *$P < 0.01$ compared to *ob/ob* mice. All values are the mean ± SEM. Approximately equal numbers of males and females were included in all measurements. No significant differences were detected between $NPY^{-/-}$ and wild-type mice, so their values were combined and used as the values for normal mice.

in their urine. Between 8 and 14 weeks of age, the fraction of *ob/ob* mice with glucosuria increased to 70%, whereas the fraction of double mutants with glucosuria was only 23% (Table 1). We also measured serum glucose and insulin levels in mice at 16 weeks of age. Serum glucose levels were close to normal in double mutants but were elevated in *ob/ob* mice (Table 1). Although serum insulin levels were high in $NPY^{-/-}$ *ob/ob* mice, they were ~50% lower than the levels in *ob/ob* mice (Table 1). The decreased incidence and severity of diabetes in $NPY^{-/-}$ *ob/ob* mice is most likely related to the reduced obesity.

The hypothalamic-pituitary axis is also impaired in *ob/ob* mice as manifested by sexual immaturity and reduced secretion of growth hormone (*2*, *13*). The somatotropic axis of double mutant mice was more active than that of *ob/ob* mice, as suggested by higher liver levels of insulin-like growth factor–I (IGF-I) mRNA and longer body length, parameters that positively correlate with growth hormone production (Table 1). In addition, the absolute difference in combined fat pad weights of *ob/ob* males and double mutant males (10.1 g) and the difference in their total body fat mass estimated from MRI analysis (15 g) exceeded the difference in their body weights (7.9 g), indicating that double mutant mice have greater lean body mass than *ob/ob* mice.

The fertility of *ob/ob* mice was also improved by the absence of NPY (Table 1). One-third of double mutant males, but only 5% of *ob/ob* males, were fertile. Surprisingly, 2 of 10 double mutant females were fertile whereas *ob/ob* females were always infertile (Table 1) (*2*, *5*). The two fertile $NPY^{-/-}$ *ob/ob* females had litters of normal size and successfully nurtured their pups to weaning. In addition, the seminal vesicles in males and the uteri in females weighed more in double mutant mice than in *ob/ob* mice, suggesting that there was greater stimulation by sex steroids in the former (Table 1). The improved reproductive function of $NPY^{-/-}$ *ob/ob* mice, especially females, is likely due to enhanced pituitary hormone release, as *ob/ob* mice are pituitary-insufficient and exogenous NPY suppresses gonadotropin secretion (*2*, *5*, *9*). Increased fertility of double mutant males may also be a secondary effect of reduced adiposity, as thinning of *ob/ob* males by food restriction improves their reproductive capacity (*14*).

These results demonstrate that NPY is required for full manifestation of the *ob/ob* phenotype and thereby implicate NPY-containing neural pathways as mediators of the hyperphagia, hypometabolism, and endocrine alterations resulting from chronic leptin deficiency. Although NPY is found throughout the mammalian nervous system, its actions in mediating the effects of leptin deficiency probably occur in the hypothalamus, where NPY is synthesized by neurons of the arcuate nucleus and secreted from their terminals in the paraventricular nucleus and ventromedial hypothalamus (*15*). The leptin receptor is expressed by arcuate neurons (*7*, *16*) and leptin inhibits both the expression and release of hypothalamic NPY (*6*, *7*). Leptin also decreases sensitivity to NPY's appetite-stimulating effect in the brain (*17*). Our study provides evidence that antagonism of the hypothalamic NPY system is a critical element of leptin's regulatory actions on body weight.

Why does the loss of NPY attenuate the obesity syndrome of *ob/ob* mice without any discernible effect on feeding, body weight, or the response to fasting of normal mice (*10*)? The requirement of NPY in the response to leptin deficiency most likely reflects the striking elevation in hypothalamic NPY activity in this condition. Although compensatory mechanisms may substitute for the loss of NPY in normal mice, these mechanisms may be inadequate in *ob/ob* mice. Furthermore, although both *ob/ob* mice and fasted mice exhibit an increased drive to eat and a decreased metabolic rate, the loss of energy reserves in the latter is a significant threat to survival and may recruit signaling pathways in addition to those activated by leptin deficiency alone.

The involvement of other neuromodulators in the hypothalamic response to leptin deficiency is suggested by the observation that elimination of NPY did not completely reverse the phenotype of *ob/ob* mice. Localization of leptin receptor expression to brain regions outside the arcuate nucleus (*7*, *16*) supports this proposition. Melanin-concentrating hormone and corticotropin-releasing hormone are strong candidates for additional leptin-sensitive regulators of energy balance (*7*, *18*).

The high levels of leptin detected in obese humans and rodents suggests that leptin "resistance" may underlie obesity (*19*). Because NPY mediates some of the hyperphagia and hypometabolism resulting from complete absence of leptin action in *ob/ob* mice, it might also contribute to forms of obesity associated with impaired leptin signaling.

REFERENCES AND NOTES

1. J. L. Halaas *et al.*, *Science* **269**, 543 (1995); L. A. Campfield, F. J. Smith, Y. Guisez, R. Devos, P. Burn, *ibid.*, p. 546; M. A. Pelleymounter *et al.*, *ibid.*, p. 540; D. S. Weigle *et al.*, *J. Clin. Invest.* **96**, 2065 (1996).
2. F. F. Chehab, M. E. Lim, R. Lu, *Nature Genet.* **12**, 318 (1996); I. A. Barash *et al.*, *Endocrinology* **137**, 3144 (1996).

Table 1. Indices of endocrine function in normal, *ob/ob*, and $NPY^{-/-}$ *ob/ob* mice. The presence of glucose in urine (glucosuria) was tested in mice between 8 and 14 weeks of age on three separate occasions using Chemstrip urine test strips (Boehringer Mannheim). Insulin and glucose concentrations were measured in serum from ~16-week-old mice (n = 7 OB/OB, n = 11 *ob/ob*, n = 9 $NPY^{-/-}$ *ob/ob*) by radioimmunoassay using a human insulin standard and the glucose oxidase method (Glucose Analyzer II, Beckman), respectively. IGF-I mRNA was quantitated in the livers of four males and four females of each group by solution hybridization (*22*). Fertility was tested by housing each mouse with a proven breeder of the opposite sex for 3 weeks beginning at 8 weeks of age. The presence of copulatory plugs was checked daily and animals were considered fertile if a litter was subsequently born. Seminal vesicle weight was measured in ~16-week-old males (n = 19 OB/OB, n = 19 *ob/ob*, n = 12 $NPY^{-/-}$ *ob/ob*). Uterine weight was measured in ~16-week-old females (n = 12 OB/OB, n = 15 *ob/ob*, n = 10 $NPY^{-/-}$ *ob/ob*). Values are the mean ± SEM. Two-tailed Fisher exact test and χ^2 analysis were used for statistical comparison of fertility rates and incidence of glucosuria, respectively. Unpaired t-test was used for statistical comparison of all other measurements.

Endocrine parameter	OB/OB	*ob/ob*	$NPY^{-/-}$ *ob/ob*	*P* value*
Diabetes				
Glucosuria (%)	0/6 (0%)	12/17 (70%)	6/26 (23%)	<0.01
Serum glucose (mg/dl)	205 ± 17	382 ± 38	261 ± 12	<0.01
Serum insulin (μU/ml)	40 ± 18	2820 ± 392	1460 ± 372	<0.05
Somatotropic axis				
Liver IGF-I mRNA (molecules per cell)	399 ± 6.3	238 ± 9.6	343 ± 14	<0.001
Nasal–anal length (cm)				
Males	10.30 ± 0.07	10.02 ± 0.09	10.49 ± 0.10	<0.002
Females	9.95 ± 0.05	9.85 ± 0.09	10.09 ± 0.11	<0.10
Reproductive axis				
Fertility (%)				
Males	ND†	1/20 (5%)	5/15 (33%)	<0.05
Females	ND	0/15 (0%)	2/10 (20%)	<0.15
Seminal vesicle weight (mg)	279 ± 15	195 ± 24	325 ± 33	<0.005
Uterine weight (mg)	131 ± 16	30 ± 3	62 ± 24	<0.2

*Refers to the difference between *ob/ob* mice and $NPY^{-/-}$ *ob/ob* mice. †ND, not determined.

3. R. S. Ahima *et al.*, *Nature* **382**, 250 (1996).
4. Y. Zhang *et al.*, *ibid.* **372**, 425 (1994); H. Chen *et al.*, *Cell* **84**, 491 (1996); G. H. Lee *et al.*, *Nature* **379**, 632 (1996); S. C. Chua Jr. *et al.*, *Science* **271**, 994 (1996).
5. D. L. Coleman, *Diabetologia* **14**, 141 (1978); G. A. Bray and D. A. York, *Physiol. Rev.* **59**, 719 (1979).
6. T. W. Stephens *et al.*, *Nature* **377**, 530 (1995); M. W. Schwartz *et al.*, *Diabetes* **45**, 531 (1996).
7. M. W. Schwartz, R. J. Seeley, L. A. Campfield, P. Burn, D. G. Baskin, *J. Clin. Invest.* **98**, 1101 (1996).
8. J. P. H. Wilding *et al.*, *Endocrinology* **132**, 1939 (1993).
9. C. Catzeflis *et al.*, *ibid.*, p. 224; N. Zarjevski, I. Cusin, R. Vetter, F. Rohner-Jeanrenaud, B. Jeanrenaud, *ibid.* **133**, 1753 (1993); D. D. Pierroz, C. Catzeflis, A. C. Aebi, J. E. Rivier, M. L. Aubert, *ibid.* **137**, 3 (1996); B. G. Stanley, S. E. Kyrkouli, S. Lampert, S. F. Leibowitz, *Peptides* **7**, 1189 (1986).
10. J. C. Erickson, K. E. Clegg, R. D. Palmiter, *Nature* **381**, 415 (1996).
11. Because the NPY and *ob* genes are genetically linked on mouse chromosome 6, three crosses were required to generate *ob/ob* mice homozygous for the inactivated NPY allele. First, $NPY^{+/-}$ males (129Sv strain) were mated with *ob*/+ females (C57Bl strain, Jackson Laboratory) to generate compound heterozygotes. Next, compound heterozygotes were mated and $NPY^{+/+}$ *ob*/+ and $NPY^{-/-}$ *ob*/+ recombinant offspring were identified. Finally, $NPY^{-/-}$ *ob*/+ mice and $NPY^{+/+}$ *ob*/+ mice were inbred to produce $NPY^{-/-}$ *ob/ob* mice and $NPY^{+/+}$ OB/OB mice, respectively. Approximately 5 males and 10 females were used as breeders for each group to ensure diversity of the hybrid genetic background. The genotyping strategy was based on the fact that the *ob* mutation generates a Dde I restriction site. A ~160-bp region spanning the site of the *ob* mutation was amplified by the polymerase chain reaction using oligonucleotides 5′-TGTC-CAAGATGGACCAGACTC-3′ and 5′-ACTGGTCT-GAGGCAGGGAGCA-3′, digested with Dde I, and the products resolved on a 2% NuSeive agarose gel. Animals were weaned between 3 and 4 weeks of age and housed individually. Mice had free access to standard rodent chow (Teklad) and were treated in accordance with University of Washington guidelines.
12. D. T. Stein, E. E. Babcock, C. R. Malloy, J. D. McGarry, *Int. J. Obes. Relat. Metab. Disord.* **19**, 804 (1995); D. E. Cummings *et al.*, *Nature* **382**, 622 (1996).
13. B. A. Larson, Y. N. Sinha, W. P. Vanderlaan, *Endocrinology* **98**, 139 (1976).
14. P. W. Lane, M. M. Dickie, *J. Hered.* **45**, 56 (1954).
15. B. G. Stanley, in *The Biology of Neuropeptide Y and Related Peptides*, W. F. Colmers and C. Wahlestedt, Eds. (Humana Press, Totowa, NJ, 1993), pp. 457–509.
16. J. G. Mercer *et al.*, *FEBS Lett* **387**, 113 (1996).
17. F. J. Smith, L. A. Campfield, J. A. Moschera, P. S. Bailon, P. Burn, *Nature* **382**, 307 (1996).
18. D. Qu *et al.*, *ibid.* **380**, 243 (1996).
19. R. C. Frederich *et al.*, *Nature Med.* **1**, 1311 (1995); M. Maffei *et al.*, *ibid.*, p. 1155; R. V. Considine *et al.*, *N. Engl. J. Med.* **334**, 292 (1996); R. C. Frederich *et al.*, *J. Clin. Invest.* **96**, 1658 (1996).
20. We measured oxygen consumption of individual mice with an Oxymax apparatus (Columbus Instruments, Columbus, OH). Each mouse was placed in a sealed chamber with an air flow of 1 liter per minute for ~4 hours. The O_2 levels in air going into and out of the chamber were measured every minute. Basal oxygen consumption was the average at low plateaus, which coincided with periods of inactivity.
21. We measured ambulatory activity of individual mice in their transparent plastic, home cage (28 cm × 17 cm × 11.5 cm) over 24 hours with an Opto-varimex mini activity meter (Columbus Instruments). The distance between infrared beams was 2.65 cm.
22. L. S. Mathews *et al.*, *Endocrinology* **123**, 2827 (1988).

23. Special thanks to E. Shankland and M. Kushmerick for MRIs and spectra; G. Froelick for histology; the laboratory of S. Woods for help with indirect calorimetry; the Metabolism Laboratory of the Puget Sound Veterans Affairs Medical Center for serum insulin and glucose determinations; and M. Schwartz and D. Cummings for discussion and suggestions. J.C.E. is a Merck fellow.

4 September 1996; accepted 8 October 1996

Aggressive Youth: Healing Biology with Relationship

J. ERIC VANCE

North Carolina State Willie M. Program For Aggressive Youth
Raleigh, North Carolina 27695

Aggressive behavior as a trait is among the most stable conditions in the human behavioral repertoire, and aggressive disorders among youth often herald a long course of violent behaviors. Current psychophysiologic research suggests that many of the known risk factors for the development of aggressive disorders may relate to the interactive effects of autonomic hyperarousal[1,2] and disturbances in the normal processing of fearful or painful stimuli,[3,4] in the absence of effective cortical modulation (TABLE 1).

It is apparent from various outcome studies that the existence or creation of close social relationships with high-risk youth can result in dramatic prevention or attentuation of many aggressive disorders.[5–7] It is obvious that secure relationships serve as the primary antidote for fearful or painful experiences, as well as attenuating states of hyperarousal from infancy through the life cycle. Current understanding of the psychophysiologic effects of social relationships provides a means to explain the likely neurobiologic mechanisms underlying the potent moderating effect of relationships on the risk factors promoting aggression. For example, in secure maternal-infant attachment, that repeated gratification of psychophysiologic needs in the infant likely results in entrainment of the plastic autonomic system to decrease sympathetic arousal, increase vagal tone, and promote vagal flexibility; effects that decrease the likelihood of aggressive behavior.[1] Release of oxytocin through warm physical contact may offset the androgen-mediated aggression effects of vasopressin by increasing vagal tone via the dorsal motor nucleus, and it promotes the exclusivity of a relationship bond, explaining why infant distress and youthful aggression abate only in the context of specific and chosen relationships rather than in response to just any social relationship.[8] Trigeminal sensory afferents, which sense the autonomic facial expressions of pleasure associated with proximity of a loved one, connect to vagal nuclei, increasing vagal tone.[1]

Close relationships and social support also decrease the risk of affective illness, possibly by increasing available CNS serotonin, which might therefore increase behavioral tendencies towards "harm avoidance" and decrease

From *Annals of the New York Academy of Sciences,* December 1996, pp. 1704-1707.

TABLE 1. Risk Factors for Aggressive Disorders[a]

Autonomic dysregulation
Difficult temperament
Attention deficit/hyperactivity disorder (ADHD)
Abuse effects
Antisocial PD, Conduct disorder
Monoamine oxidase a deficiency
Cognitive oversight
Substance abuse
Dyslexia
Lead exposure
Head injury
Fetal substance exposure
Fear/Pain processing disorders
Poor maternal-infant attachment
Neglect/abandonment
Physical/sexual abuse
Witness to domestic violence
Cultural exposure to violence
Lesch-Nyhan syndrome
Antisocial PD, Conduct disorder
Borderline personality
Paranoid disorders
Affective illness
Substance abuse

[a]In relation to growing knowledge in developmental psychophysiology, risk factors for aggression can be conceptually integrated based on their effects on autonomic nervous system functioning, disturbances in the normative processing of fear and pain, or disruption of cognitive oversight of the limbic system structures responsible for aggressive behavior.

the likelihood of aggressive or suicidal behavior.[9,10] In the absence of these direct psychophysiologic effects of relationships on CNS functioning, it is difficult to explain the profound and lasting protective effect of secure maternal attachment or the dramatic behavioral changes of aggressive youth in the context of close mentor relationships. The effectiveness of intensive relationship therapies in older youth suggests that many of these neurodevelopmental pathways may remain somewhat plastic well into later childhood, challenging the common wisdom that all but early intervention comes "too late" for aggressive youth. Intensive relationship therapy, with the specific goal of creating close affectional bonds with aggressive youth,[11] holds promise which far exceeds the narrow effects of symptom-targeted pharmacologic interventions, context-bound cognitive-behavioral therapies, or correctional approaches currently used in the management of aggressive disorders in youth.

References

1. Porges, S. W. *et al.* 1994. Monogr. Soc. Res. Child Dev. **59:** 167–186.
2. Charney, D. S. *et al.* 1993. Arch. Gen. Psychiatry **50:** 294–305.
3. Raine, A. *et al.* 1995. Am. J. Psychiatry **152:** 1595–1600.
4. Hare, R. D. 1978. Psychopathic Behav.: Approaches Res.: 107–144.
5. Tierney, J. P. *et al.* 1995. Public/Private Ventures. Philadelphia, PA.
6. Werner, E. E. 1989. Am. J. Orthopsychiatry **59:** 72–81.
7. Borduin, C. M. *et al.* 1995. J. Consult. Clin. Psychol. **63:** 569–578.
8. Carter, C. S. 1995. Neurosci. Biobehav. Rev. **19:** 303–314.
9. Blazer, D. G. *et al.* 1992. J. Nerv. Ment. Dis. **180:** 172–178.
10. Cloninger, C. R. 1987. Arch. Gen. Psychiatry **44:** 573–588.
11. Vance, J. E. & H. Sanchez. 1994. Delivering Resiliency to Those at Risk. Unpublished manuscript.

Reproductive Behavior

From fairest creatures we desire increase,
That thereby beauty's rose might never die,
But as the riper should by the time decease,
His tender heir might bear his memory;
But if thou live rememb'red not to be,
Die single, and thine image dies with thee.
—William Shakespeare

These lines from Shakespeare's sonnet present a rationale for sexual behavior, which is to reproduce. It assumes a perspective akin to the evolutionary view that sexual behaviors allow the perpetuation of the genes for posterity. In sexually dimorphic species, engaging in sexual behavior is the only way to reproduce.

There are other ways of investigating the biological basis of sexual behavior. One approach is to examine the role of circulating hormones. Steroid hormones secreted by the gonads can influence motivation and performance of sexual behaviors. Damage to or removal of the steroid-secreting organs can lead to loss of libido or inhibition of sexual motoric responses. Systemic steroid hormone replacement can reinstate lost functions.

Steroid hormones secreted by the gonads act on the brain to elicit sexual behavior. An area of the brain involved in the regulation of sexual behavior is the hypothalamus. On the basis of animal studies, lesioning or stimulation of certain hypothalamic areas can abolish or enhance the performance of particular sexual behaviors, respectively. Steroid hormones act in conjunction with the neurotransmitters in the brain in facilitating these behaviors.

Can we find a biological mechanism to account for sexual behaviors not motivated by reproduction? For example, reproduction is virtually impossible in homosexual behavior. Is there a biological basis for homosexuality? The steroid hormone concentration in the blood of homosexual and heterosexual individuals is not significantly different. If the brain regulates sexual behavior, are there differences in brain structure between homosexual and heterosexual individuals?

A few years ago, researcher Simon LeVay published a report that sparked many controversies. LeVay found that an area in the hypothalamus in heterosexual men is significantly larger than that in homosexual men. There was no significant difference in size of this hypothalamic area between homosexual men and heterosexual women. Since the hypothalamus plays a major role in regulating sexual behavior, it is speculated that brain organization varies according to sexual preference. It is difficult to identify which factor is the "cause" or the "effect."

Biological mechanisms for sexual behavior are relatively easy to demonstrate in animal studies, but they are not straightforward in humans. Such difficulty goes to prove that biological mechanisms cannot completely account for human sexuality. In order to achieve a better understanding of human sexual behavior, the analysis must include both social and cognitive factors.

Looking Ahead: Challenge Questions

When does puberty occur? What are some important behavioral events associated with puberty? Discuss the onset of sexual attraction in humans. Does is occur at puberty? What is the current understanding of the mechanism underlying the emergence of sexual attraction?

How significant is the role of females in maintaining reproductive success as observed in nonhuman primates? Discuss the phenomenon of menstrual synchrony as reported in human females. What is the possible significance of this phenomenon?

Describe manifestation of maternal behaviors in different species of mammals, including humans. What is the biological basis of maternal behavior? How is maternal behavior in humans affected by external factors?

Is homosexual behavior observed in animals? If so, under what conditions does this behavior occur? What is the proposed sociobiological significance of homosexuality?

UNIT 6

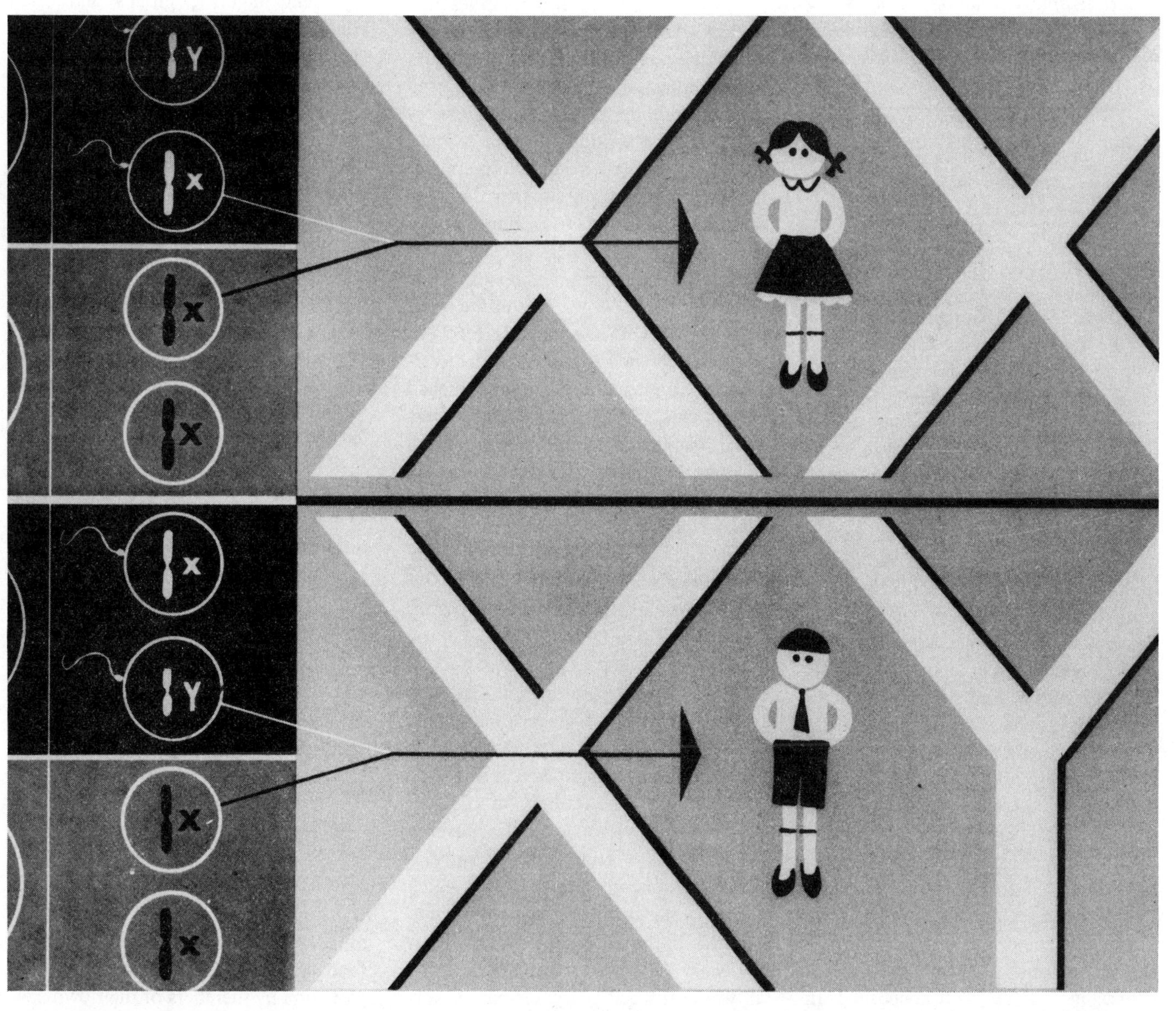

Natural-born Mothers

Motherhood is not as straightforward a matter as just turning on the milk.

Sarah Blaffer Hrdy

Sarah Blaffer Hrdy is an anthropologist at the University of California-Davis, a middle-aged mother of three, an ardent advocate of breast-feeding, and one of five children. As such, she has had considerable firsthand experience observing maternal fitness trade-offs. One of her various hobbies is allomaternal caretaking (aka, being a mother's helper).

On the day that the eleventh-century Italian saint Peter Damian was born, his mother was ready to call it quits. According to the saint's biography, written by his associate John of Lodi, his mother was "worn out by childbearing" and further disheartened by the reproach of an adolescent son who took her to task for bringing into the world yet another mouth to feed and one more son to add to her already existing "throng of heirs." In despair, the mother refused to nurse. The fledgling saint was on the verge of starvation when a neighbor, the kindly concubine of a local priest, intervened, reminding her that even a savage beast, a tigress or a mother lion, would suckle her own young. Could a Christian woman do less?

Five hundred years later, Italian poet Luigi Tansillo echoed similar sentiments in response to the widespread use of wet nurses—the main alternative to maternal breast-feeding in the days before the baby bottle. In a poem entitled "La Balia" (The Nurse), Tansillo wrote, "What fury, hostile to our common kind,/First led from nature's path the female mind . . . [resulting in] a babe denied its mother's breast?" In the following centuries, tens of thousands of babies in Europe were deposited in foundling homes or shipped to middlemen who contracted for a lactating woman to suckle them. In urban centers like Paris, the majority of babies were suckled by strangers. This traffic in babies led to staggering rates of infant mortality.

Reaction against wet-nursing reached a peak during the Enlightenment. In 1793, the French National Convention decreed that only mothers who nursed their own children would be eligible for state aid. The writings of Jean Jacques Rousseau inspired many reformers (although the great philosopher sent his own five children to foundling homes). Almost always, reformers invoked "natural laws," encouraging mothers to follow their instinctive urges to nurture their babies. "Look to the animals for your example," French physician and moralist Jean Emmanuel Gilibert admonished his patients. "Even though the mothers have their stomachs torn open. . . . Even though their offspring have been the cause of all their woes, their first care makes them forget all they have suffered. . . . They forget themselves, little concerned with their own happiness. . . . Woman, like all animals, is under the sway of this instinct."

For further support of their beliefs, reformers could turn to Carolus Linnaeus, the father of modern taxonomy. A physician and the father of seven children, Linnaeus was an ardent advocate of maternal breast-feeding. In 1752 he set down his views in *Nutrix noverca* (Step-Nurse), a widely read denunciation of commercial wet-nursing (which Gilibert translated from Latin into French). In the 1758 edition of his opus *Systema Naturae*, Linnaeus subsumed all warm-blooded, hairy, viviparous vertebrates into a single group—the class Mammalia—identified with milk-secreting glands of the female. (The Latin term for breasts, *mammae*, derives from the plaintive cry "mama," spontaneously uttered by young children from widely divergent linguistic groups and often conveying a single, urgent message, "suckle me.")

Linnaeus's nomenclature underscored a natural role for women based on a salient homology between women and other animals that nursed their young. Mother mammals are alchemists able to transform available fodder—grass, insects, even toxic leaves—into biological white gold. Lactation allows a mother to stockpile resources while they are available, repackage them in digestible form, and then parcel them out to growing infants at her own pace. Able to rely on its mother for food, an immature can stay safe either attached to the mother or stashed in hiding places she chooses, buffered from the vagaries and hazards of foraging in the wide world.

For most mammals, the art of reproduction is to survive poor conditions and breed again under better ones.

But motherhood is not as straightforward a matter as just turning on the milk. Mothers have to factor in recurring food shortages, predators, and social exploitation by members of their own species. Faced with poor conditions, a mother must weigh babies in hand against her own well-being, long-term survival, and—most important—the possibility of breeding again under better circumstances. Behavioral ecologists are only beginning to understand how mother mammals respond to such natural dilemmas, called fitness trade-offs.

Most mammals are iteroparous: breeding more than once, they produce offspring, either singly or in litters, over a breeding career that may last several years—twenty-five or more in the case of a woman. (A very few mammals—primarily some marsupial mice—are semelparous, breeding in one fecund burst followed by death.) In an evolutionary sense, the bottom line for iteroparous females is not the success of any particular birth but reproductive output over a lifetime. The art of iteroparity, therefore, is generally to survive poor conditions and breed again under better ones. By drawing on help from others, however, some mothers manage to breed under circumstances that would otherwise be impossible.

Consider the case of the cotton-top tamarins. Although the birth of twins is rare among primates, the pint-sized tamarins and marmosets of South America are exceptions. Adapted

Hormonal Cocktails for Two

Sarah Blaffer Hrdy and C. Sue Carter

When first presented with pups, a virgin female laboratory rat generally ignores them; she may appear afraid of the tiny, squirming, naked creatures and, occasionally, may even eat them. Only after being introduced to pups many times over several days can a virgin rat be conditioned to tolerate and care for them—licking them, crouching protectively over them, retrieving them when they stray from her side. In contrast, a pregnant rat responds within minutes to pups, even prior to delivery of her own.

The idea that physiological changes might prepare the expectant mother for her new role led to a now classic experiment. In 1968 Joseph Terkel and Jay Rosenblatt, of Rutgers University, injected blood from a rat that had just given birth into a virgin female. The result was a dramatic reduction in the time it took virgins to nurture pups.

Since 1968, we have learned a great deal about what goes inside female mammals as they prepare for motherhood. During the last third of pregnancy, a cascade of endocrinological events readies and motivates mothers. Prominent in this maternal cocktail are the steroid hormones estrogen and progesterone, manufactured by the placenta and essential to maintaining pregnancy. But since the placenta is delivered along with the baby, progesterone and, a little later, estrogen levels fall around the time of birth. By themselves, these hormones cannot account for maternal responsiveness.

Enter prolactin and oxytocin, hormones essential for milk production and nursing. Prolactin is a very ancient molecule whose original function was to maintain salt and water balance in early vertebrates such as fish. Over evolutionary time, this hormone has proved very versatile and now performs diverse physiological functions in many kinds of animals. In mammals it is associated with caretaking behavior in both females and males.

But perhaps the quintessential mammal hormone is oxytocin. A muscle contractor, oxytocin (from the Greek for "swift birth") evolved in mammals and produces the uterine contractions of birth and milk ejection during lactation. Present when the mother first greets her emerging offspring, it continues to be released whenever she nurses. Oxytocin released into the brain is known to promote calming and positive social behaviors, such as pair bonding.

Studies of domestic sheep by Barry Keverne, Keith Kendrick, and their colleagues at the University of Cambridge provide the most complete picture we have of the behavioral effects of oxytocin. As a lamb moves down the birth canal, nerves stimulated during the passage trigger the release of oxytocin in the mother's nervous system. Only if oxytocin is present at birth or injected so that it reaches the brain at the same time a mother meets her newborn, will she bond with her offspring. If release of oxytocin is blocked, the ewe rejects her lamb. High levels of oxytocin also are found in mother's milk, raising the possibility that this hormone plays a role in making the mother-infant attachment mutual.

As important as these hormones can be in determining how responsive a mother will be, they do not act in a deterministic fashion. They both affect and are affected by a mother's behavior and her experience. Exposure to pups, for instance, can lead to reorganization of neural pathways in a mother rat's brain, making her respond faster to pups in the future, even with lower hormone levels. And some recent studies suggest that the hormones of breastfeeding may benefit a mother's mental health and increase her ability to deal with stress.

In many mammals, males, as well as adoptive virgin females, can be primed to exhibit parental behaviors. Prairie vole males, for instance, typically respond to a newborn pup by retrieving it and huddling over it. Geert De Vries, of the University of Massachusetts, found that such nurturing is facilitated by vasopressin, a hormone that in other contexts is associated with aggressive, territorial behavior.

for fluctuating habitats, these monkeys have the potential to breed at a staggering pace, sometimes giving birth as often as twice a year to twins whose combined weight totals up to 20 percent of the mother's. Only the help of other group members—fathers, older offspring, and transient adults—makes the mother's feat of fecundity possible. Helpers carry the offspring most of the time, except when the mother is suckling. Near weaning, helpers also provide infants with crickets and other tidbits.

Working with captive cotton-tops, Lorna Johnson, of the New England Primate Center, revealed how important helpers can be. (This species is endangered in the wild but is still well represented in research colonies.) In her analysis of breeding records over an eighteen-year period, Johnson focused on experienced parents that had already successfully reared offspring. She found that among these veterans, fully 57 percent of parents without help abandoned their young, nearly five times the rate at which parents with helpers voted "no-go."

Among marmosets and tamarins, it is usual for only one female in the group to reproduce during a breeding season. A similar situation prevails among the communally breeding dwarf mongooses of the Serengeti. Studying what keeps the other females from breeding, Purdue University biologist Scott Creel discovered that estrogen levels of these nonbreeders remained only one-third as high as in the breeding female, below that necessary for ovulation. Creel speculates that in species producing large litters, heavy young, or young designed to grow rapidly after birth, the cost of gestation and lactation is just too high for any but the most advantaged female to hazard giving birth. Often harassed and less well fed, a subordinate has such a slim chance of producing young that survive to weaning that she is better off deferring reproduction, helping instead to rear the offspring of her kin—occasionally even suckling them—and generally doing her best to be tolerated in the group and to stay alive until she can become a breeder in her own right.

While studying a closely related subspecies of dwarf mongoose, O. Anne E. Rasa, of Bonn University, learned that subordinate females have an even more pressing reason to postpone reproduction. The dominant female may destroy the pups of any rival that does breed. Earlier this year, Duke University's Leslie Digby reported that there appears to be the same pattern among wild common marmosets in Brazil. In a rare instance when a subordinate female gave birth, one of her infants was killed; the other disappeared at about the same time. For marmosets and dwarf mongooses, then, most subordinate females make the best of a grim lot by temporarily shutting down their ovaries. With luck, their time to breed does come.

Suppression of ovulation is only one of the many means for mothers to adjust the timing of their reproductive effort. In a diverse array of mammals—including bats, skunks, minks, and armadillos—ovulation occurs, but implantation of the fertilized egg in the uterine wall is delayed so as to insure birth of the offspring at the optimal season. As soon as a kangaroo mother ceases to suckle one joey, levels in her blood of the nursing hormone prolactin fall. At this signal, a tiny blastocyst (a nearly hollow globe of cells, produced by the fertilized egg, inside of which the embryo will develop) emerges from diapause (a period of developmental dormancy) and begins to grow again. In the European badger, this blastocyst-in-waiting continues to grow, but ever so slowly. Embryonic slowdown or diapause can persist for days in rodents or even months in larger mammals, until some cue signals the embryo to attach to the uterine wall and resume development. American black bears breed from May to July, but not until the female repairs to her den for winter does implantation occur, so that birth takes place to a lethargic mother in the snug safety of her winter refuge. Yet if the berry crop that year had failed, and the mother, as a result, was not in good condition, implantation might well have failed, too.

Planned parenthood primate style revolves around breast-feeding. In almost all monkeys and apes, as well as in people still living in traditional settings where infants enjoy nearly continuous contact with their mothers, babies nurse on demand. Emory University anthropologists Mel Konner and Carol Worthman report that the !Kung San of the Kalahari suckle their babies for two minutes or so as often as four times every hour, even while they sleep at night.

In eighteenth-century France, many poor mothers would give up their own babies and hire themselves out as wet nurses.

Throughout most of human evolution, mothers suckled their children on demand from infancy to the age of three or four—in some circumstances, even longer. A series of studies of hunter-gatherers from Central Africa, Botswana, and New Guinea, as well as of housewives in New England, have documented the dynamic interaction between a woman's nutritional status, her workload, and her fertility—what Harvard anthropologist Peter Ellison likes to call the ecology of the ovaries. Nipple stimulation from nearly continuous "Pleistocene style" suckling causes the pituitary to secrete more prolactin, the body's "work order" for more milk production. Through a complex and as yet poorly understood series of mediating effects involving the hypothalamus, ovulation is somehow inhibited when prolactin levels are high. The result is birth intervals as long as five years in long-suckling people like the !Kung. According to Ellison, the link between the intensity of suckling and postpartum infertility prevents a nursing mother, already energetically burdened by metabolizing for two, from being saddled with another pregnancy and the even more daunting task of metabolizing for three. (Unless, that is, she happens to be particularly well fed. Worthman and others have recently discovered that among well-nourished

Milk: It Does a Baby Good

Virginia Hayssen

A complex fluid with a long history, milk feeds us, protects us from disease, and even directs aspects of our behavior and physiology. The nutritional value of milk varies greatly from species to species. Cow's milk and human milk, for example, are both about 88 percent water and 4 percent fat, with 165 calories in an eight-ounce glass. Cow's milk, however, has 30 percent less sugar and three times more protein. For a low-fat milk, try that of black rhinos: their milk has only 0.2 percent fat. As a source of energy for their developing young, rhinos and horses use sugars instead of fats. The result is milk with only two-thirds the calories of human milk.

The cream of the crop is hooded seal milk, which is 61 percent fat, with about 1,400 calories in an eight-ounce glass. Small wonder the pups can gain forty-five pounds during their very short (four-day) nursing period. Hooded seals give birth on ice floes and must wean their pups before the ice breaks up or melts. The high-fat, low-protein milk is well suited to provide seal pups with the most important thing they need: a thick layer of blubber to insulate them against cold polar oceans.

The milk of chimpanzees living in tropical environments provides a striking contrast. There, where a mother may carry her suckling offspring with her everywhere for many months, mother's milk is very dilute, low in both fat and protein.

Mother hares, whose first priority is to provide a safe hideaway for their vulnerable babies and to keep its location a secret from predators, can only afford to let their young suckle once a day and, even then, for no more than five minutes. Not surprisingly, the milk of hares is rich in fat and protein.

Milk composition in many species changes over the course of lactation. Milk delivered in the early stages, and again as weaning approaches, often has more protein and less sugar than that produced during the interim stages. The kinds of fat in milk vary with the mother's diet. In fact, milk has different flavors depending on what mothers eat. Those flavors may later direct the food likes and dislikes of offspring.

Kangaroos are a special case in that mothers frequently suckle young of very different sizes and ages simultaneously. The youngest joey is attached to a tiny teat within the pouch and suckles constantly, while its older sibling, who may be 5,000 times larger, intermittently pokes its head into the pouch to suck on a much more elongated nipple. The milk from these adjacent teats is very different in composition.

The extent to which young mammals depend on milk for nutrition is also variable. Voles and mice rely completely upon milk for their well-being until weaning, while the young of many hoofed animals, such as deer and antelope, may begin eating grass only a few days after birth, well before weaning occurs. Mother koalas excrete a yellow-green ooze of partly digested eucalyptus leaves that their young energetically eat. The opening of the mother's pouch is directed backward, allowing the baby easy access to the nutritious slime.

In addition to nutrients, milk contains hormones and growth factors that can regulate the behavior and physiology of both mother and baby. As a mother nurses her young, subtle manipulations may be at work. Studies of rats, monkeys, and other animals have shown that nursing releases natural opiates in the mother's brain, perhaps rendering her more pliant to her baby's demands. Opiates are also present in milk, making the baby feel content, as well as well fed.

Lactation also acts as a fertility control. By suppressing ovulation, it tends to lengthen the interval between births, thus helping insure that each offspring (or litter) receives its mother's undivided attention. And experiments with rodents suggest that at least one component of milk delays puberty in female offspring by retarding ovarian development.

Another of milk's functions is immunological. Colostrum, the protein-rich fluid produced right after birth, is an important source of antibodies that confer immunity to various diseases. The protection provided by some other milk proteins, such as lysozyme and interleukin, may last throughout lactation.

The origins of milk and lactation will always remain somewhat mysterious. Without a time machine, reconstructing the early stages of any complex organ or process is difficult. As the English biologist St. George J. Mivart asked in 1871, "Is it conceivable that the young of any animal was ever saved from destruction by accidentally suckling a drop of scarcely nutritious fluid from an accidentally hypertrophied cutaneous gland of its mother?"

Nevertheless, we know that milk did evolve, and one of the proteins specific to milk—alpha-lactalbumin—may provide some clues as to how. Today, alpha-lactalbumin helps in the synthesis of lactose, but it evolved from another protein, lysozyme, common in blood and other body fluids, as well as in certain glandular secretions, including milk. Lysozyme kills bacteria and fungi, protecting animals from infection. It also protects milk from microbial attack.

Since lysozyme occurs in so many mammalian body fluids and milk, and since it gave rise to alpha-lactalbumin, this protein very likely was present in ancestral fluids that evolved into milk. The first mammals laid eggs, as the platypus and echidnas still do, and the early protomilk may have protected eggs or newly hatched young from bacterial or fungal attack. Because lysozyme is also a protein, neonates who lapped up the fluid from their mothers' bodies may have received a nutritional bonus. Eventually, the value of the fluid as a source of food and water became more important than its original, antibacterial function.

Prenatal Power Plays

David Haig

The most intimate human relationship is that between a mother and her unborn young. A fetus obtains all its nutrients and disposes of all of its wastes via its mother's blood. It shares every breath that its mother takes, every meal she eats, and draws on her fat reserves when food is scarce. What is the nature of this relationship? Do mother and fetus form one body and one flesh, a harmonious union with each attentive to the other's needs? Or is the fetus an alien intruder, a parasite that takes what it can without concern for its maternal host?

Neither the idyllic nor the parasitic vision adequately captures the complexities of pregnancy. Because they share half their genes, mother and fetus have common genetic interests, but sometimes their interests conflict because each also carries genes absent from the other. In particular, maternal and fetal genes are predicted to "disagree" over how a pregnant mother should allocate energy, time, and resources between her own needs and those of the fetus.

Mammal species vary markedly in the ability of the fetus to influence the amount of food it receives from its mother. Bush babies, for example, are small African primates with a placenta that simply absorbs uterine "milk" secreted by the glands of the mother's uterus. Other nutrients diffuse directly from the mother's blood to fetal blood across the thin layer of maternal and placental tissues that separates the two bloodstreams. A bush baby mother is probably able to control the flow of nutrients to her fetus by contracting or relaxing the blood vessels supplying the lining of her uterus. Similar arrangements occur in a variety of animals, including pigs, cows, and whales.

By contrast, the human placenta is invasive (as are the placentas of mice, bats, sloths, and armadillos). Uterine milk is a significant source of nutrients only during the earliest stages of pregnancy. As the embryo implants within the lining of the uterus, it sends out cells that invade the blood vessels supplying the uterine lining. These invasive cells destroy the muscular wall and greatly expand the diameter of the blood vessels. The result is that the fetus has direct access to its mother's blood, and the mother, unable to constrict the vessels, cannot regulate the flow of nutrients to the placenta without starving her own tissues.

Direct access to the mother's blood also enables the placenta to release a variety of hormones into her circulatory system. These hormones probably evolved to manipulate maternal physiology for fetal benefit. For example, human placental lactogen is produced in larger quantities than any other human hormone. One of its effects is to make maternal tissues less sensitive to the effects of insulin. If this effect went unopposed, maternal blood sugar would rise higher after meals and would remain elevated for a longer period, allowing the fetus to take a greater share of each meal. The mother is not completely powerless, however, and responds by increasing insulin production. Mothers usually maintain control of their blood sugar during pregnancy, but when they do not, gestational diabetes develops and is relieved only with the delivery of the baby and its placenta.

An appreciation of the genetic conflicts of pregnancy may help doctors understand other medical complications of pregnancy. Sometimes the placenta has inadequate access to maternal blood. One way for the placenta to compensate is to increase the flow of blood by increasing maternal blood pressure. When accompanied by excessive protein in the mother's urine, this high blood pressure can be a symptom of a life-threatening condition called preeclampsia.

Both mother and fetus, of course, share one overriding interest: the successful outcome to pregnancy. To reach that goal, the mother-child relationship appears from the very start to be marked by negotiation and compromise, although negotiations sometimes break down.

mothers, the inhibition of ovulation by suckling is less effective.)

Like delayed implantation, lactational suppression of ovulation provides made-to-order birth control. No system is foolproof, however. Saddled with an inopportune conception, a mother mammal may resort to remedies that although unmotherly to modern tastes, are nonetheless utterly natural. Possible options depend on what type of mammal she is. Untimely fetuses may be reabsorbed, spontaneously aborted, abandoned after birth, or under some circumstances, killed and even eaten.

Golden hamsters, for instance, are highly flexible breeders adapted to the irregular rainfall and erratic food supplies in their native habitat in the arid regions of the Middle East. In addition to building a nest, licking their pups clean, protecting and suckling them—all pleasantly conventional maternal pursuits—these hamster moms may also recoup maternal resources otherwise lost in the production of pups by eating a few.

For hamsters, to quote Canadian psychologists Corinne Day and Bennett Galef, cannibalizing pups is an "organized part of normal maternal behavior which allows an individual female to adjust her litter size in accord with her capacity to rear young in the environmental conditions prevailing at the time of her parturition." Quality control can also be an issue. Among mice (but not hamsters), pups below median weight are the ones most likely to be rejected when mothers cull very large litters.

The cues mothers respond to may derive from prevailing conditions or their own internal state.

Another "rule of paw" might read: abort poor prospects sooner rather than later and, if possible, recoup resources. Recall how the mother bear's body factors in the latest update on food supplies before either canceling implantation or committing to gestation. The cues mothers respond to may derive from prevailing conditions or their own internal state. Biologist John Hoogland spent sixteen years monitoring a population of black-tailed prairie dogs in South Dakota. Mothers attempt to rear 91 percent of all litters produced; the rest of the time, they abandon their pups at birth and allow other group members to eat them, sometimes even joining in. Under closer examination, Hoogland found that the mothers that gave up on their litters weighed less. He speculated that abandonment was an adaptive response to poor body condition.

Deteriorating social conditions can also alter maternal commitment. Across a broad spectrum of animals from mice to lions, the appearance of strange males on the horizon can present a danger to unweaned infants sired by other, rival males. By killing these infants, the newcomers subvert the mother's control over the timing of her own reproduction. To minimize her loss, she breeds again sooner than she would have if she had continued to suckle her babies. Although this revised schedule of breeding is detrimental to the mother (not to mention her babies), she may ovulate again while the killer is still in the vicinity. Had the killer waited until her infants were weaned, his own window of opportunity might have long since shut, for he too is bound to be replaced by another male.

Among the strains of house mice studied by Frederick von Saal, at the University of Missouri, and by Robert Elwood, at Queen's University in Belfast, Northern Ireland, roving males that have failed to mate in the preceding seven weeks (equivalent to a three-week pregnancy, followed by four weeks of lactation) attack babies in any nest they bump into. By contrast, males that have mated during that crucial period are statistically more likely to behave "paternally," retrieving pups that have slipped out of the nest, keeping them warm, and licking them clean. Some behavioral switch accompanying ejaculation (especially if he remains near the female) transforms this potential killer into a kinder, gentler rodent. This transformation (Elwood calls it a "switch in time") saves the male from mistakenly destroying his own progeny (although, depending on circumstances, it may occasionally lead him to tolerate offspring of another male).

Male mice can also have a devastating effect on unborn young, for a pregnant mouse that encounters a strange male may reabsorb her budding embryos. This form of early abortion avoids the even greater misfortune of losing a full-term litter later on. It has become known as "the Bruce effect," after biologist Hilda Bruce, who first reported the phenomenon for laboratory mice in 1959 (at the time, its function was unclear). The Bruce effect has since been reported for deer mice, collared lemmings, and several species of voles. Elwood and others have shown that pregnant mice are especially likely to block pregnancies when confronted with males known to be infanticidal.

As bizarre as it may seem, when a mammal mother thwarts her own pregnancy, she is behaving—in strictly biological terms—just like a mother.

From the female's point of view, losing a pregnancy is scarcely an ideal strategy. Rather, her body is making the best of dismal circumstances. As bizarre as it may seem, when a mammal mother thwarts her pregnancy, she is behaving—in strictly biological terms—just like a mother. For she may soon conceive again, perhaps with a male who will stick around to help or at least keep other males away. Bruce had discovered a natural, spontaneous form of energy-conserving, early-stage abortion.

Mice are not the only animals that have to cope with infanticidal males. Among the lean and graceful langur monkeys that I studied at Mount Abu, Rajasthan, India, males pose serious threats to infants. My colleagues S. M. Mohnot and Volker Sommer, whose team has monitored the langur population at nearby Jodhpur for more than twenty years, learned that one-third of all infants born are killed by males coming into the group. Mothers initially avoid such usurpers or even fight back, but once a new male becomes ensconced in the group, he has the advantage of being able to try to kill the babies again and again, day after day.

Confronted with discouraging odds, a mother may try to deposit a nearly weaned infant with former resident males, now ousted and roving about the vicinity. This strategy rarely works. The infant will usually wend its way back to its mother, placing itself right back in harm's way. Especially if she is young with many fertile years ahead of her, a mother under persistent assault may simply stop defending her infant, leaving more intrepid kin—usually old females that have not reproduced for years—to intervene. And so it was that I once observed an aged and stiff twenty-pound female, assisted by another older female, wrest a wounded infant from the sharp-toothed jaws of a forty-pound male. The far stronger and healthier young mother watched from the sidelines. Just days before, the same young mother had made no effort to intervene when her infant fell from a jacaranda tree branch and was grabbed up by the male. Again, it was the old female who rushed to the rescue.

In the last weeks of pregnancy, langurs may respond to a usurping male by aborting rather than continuing to expend energy on a reproductive venture so unlikely to end well. Similar late-pregnancy variations on the Bruce effect have been reported for an odd assortment of large mammals, including wild horses. University of Nevada's Joel Berger, an animal behaviorist who studied wild horses in the Great Basin, watched what happens when one stallion successfully challenges another for possession of his harem. During the disruption following the changeover, 82 percent of the mares that had been impregnated in the last six months by the deposed stallion aborted their fetuses.

Infanticide, abortion, cannibalism, these are altogether natural lapses from imagined "natural laws." Why is it only in the last two decades that researchers have begun to view such behaviors as other than aberrations? Opinions, even scientific ones, are often influenced by received wisdom. As late as the 1960s, when animal behaviorists set up labs to study the maternal activities of rats, monkeys, and dogs, the categories devised to describe their behavior took for granted that mothers were instinctively nurturing. In her pioneering studies of dogs, for example, comparative psychologist Harriet Rheingold separated mothers and their pups from all other animals and then recorded behaviors that fell into her preconceived protocol of maternal activities: contact, nursing, licking, play, and so forth.

Indeed, much of the time mother mammals do carry, groom, and suckle their young. The types of maternal activities Rheingold and others investigated were those that insured that mothers passed on their genes to future generations—the primary focus of the time. Such a view of what it means to be a mother could fairly be classified as essentialist.

But the study of animal behavior has changed. With the emergence of sociobiology in the 1970s, researchers began to focus on individuals and the idiosyncratic social and environmental circumstances of each. With this new perspective, it not only became clear that one mother is not the same as another but also that not all females would be mothers. Far from essentialist or biologically determinist, most biologists today think context is critically important. Researchers like Scott Creel and Carol Worthman combined fieldwork with laboratory measures to search for the cues—inside and out—that prompt a female to opt for one reproductive strategy rather than another.

Across her life course, both a mother and her circumstances are constantly changing—as she ages, finds a new mate, loses a potential helper, stockpiles fat. In a world of leisure, plenty, and supportive social groups or in realms where offspring cost their parents little to rear, trade-offs fade from view. In contrast, overpopulation, social oppression, scarcity, bad times—none of these have ever been conducive to the development of the sort of mother characterized in Marge Piercy's poem "Magic mama" as "an aphid enrolled to sweeten the lives of others. The woman who puts down her work like knitting the moment you speak."

Real mamas must not only be magic but also multifaceted. Motherhood is more than all the licking, tending, suckling, and awe-inspiring protectiveness for which mother mammals are so justly famous. Such indeed is the art—and the tragedy—of iteroparity: offspring born at one time may be more costly to a mother or less viable than offspring born at another. Far from invalidating biological bases for maternal behavior, the extraordinary flexibility in what it means to be a mother should merely remind us that the physiological and motivational underpinnings of an archetypically pro-choice mammal are scarcely new.

Rethinking Puberty: The Development of Sexual Attraction

Martha K. McClintock and Gilbert Herdt[1]

Department of Psychology, The University of Chicago, Chicago, Illinois

A youth remembers a time when he was sitting in the family room with his parents watching the original "Star Trek" television series. He reports that he was 10 years old and had not yet developed any of the obvious signs of puberty. When "Captain Kirk" suddenly peeled off his shirt, the boy was titillated. At 10 years of age, this was his first experience of sexual attraction, and he knew intuitively that, according to the norms of his parents and society, he should not be feeling this same-gender attraction. The youth relating this memory is a self-identified gay 18-year-old in Chicago. He also reports that at age 5 he had an absence of sexual attractions of any kind, and that even by age 8 he had not experienced overt awareness of sexual attraction. By age 10, however, a profound transformation had begun, and it was already completed by the time he entered puberty; sexual attraction to the same gender was so familiar to him (Herdt & Boxer, 1993) that it defined his selfhood.

Recent findings from three distinct and significant studies have pointed to the age of 10 as the mean age of first sexual attraction—well before puberty, which is typically defined as the age when the capacity to procreate is attained (Timiras, 1972). These findings are at odds with previous developmental and social science models of behavioral sexual development in Western countries, which suggested that *gonadarche* (final maturation of the testes or ovaries) is the biological basis for the child's budding interest in sexual matters. Earlier studies postulated that the profound maturational changes during puberty instigate the transition from preadolescent to adult forms of sexuality that involve sexual attraction, fantasy, and behavior (Money & Ehrhardt, 1972). Thus, adult forms of sexuality were thought to develop only after gonadarche, typically around ages 12 for girls and 14 for boys, with early and late bloomers being regarded as "off time" in development (Boxer, Levinson, & Petersen, 1989). But the new findings, which locate the development of sexual attraction before these ages, are forcing researchers to rethink the role of gonadarche in the development of sexual attraction as well as the conceptualization of puberty as simply the product of complete gonadal maturation.

Many researchers have conflated puberty and gonadarche, thinking that the two are synonymous in development. The new research on sexual orientation has provided data that invalidate the old model of gonadarche as the sole biological cause of adult forms of sexuality. To the extent that sexual attraction is affected by hormones, the new data indicate that there should be another significant hormonal event around age 10. Indeed, there is: the maturation of the adrenal glands during middle childhood, termed *adrenarche.* (The adrenal glands[2] are the biggest nongonadal source of sex steroids.) This biological process, distinctively different from gonadarche, may underlie the development not only of sexual attraction, but of cognition, emotions, motivations, and social behavior as well. This observation, in turn, leads to a redefinition of prepubertal and pubertal development.

GONADARCHE IS NOT A SUFFICIENT EXPLANATION

Previous biopsychological models of sexual development have attributed changes in adolescent behavior to changes in hormone levels accompanied by gonadarche (Boxer et al., 1989), presumably because of a focus on the most dramatic features of gonadal development in each gender: menarche in girls and spermarche in boys. If gonadarche were responsible for first sexual attractions, then the mean age of the development of sexual attractions should be around the age of gonadarche. Moreover, one would expect a sex difference in the age of first attraction, corresponding to the sex difference in age of gonadarche: 12 for girls and 14 for boys. Neither of these predictions, however, has been borne out by recent data.

In three studies attempting to illuminate the sources of sexual orientation, adolescents have been asked to recall their earliest sexual thoughts; their answers are surprising. One study (Herdt & Boxer, 1993) investigated the development of sexual identity and social relations in a group of self-identified gay and lesbian teenagers (ages 14–20, with a mean age of 18) from Chicago. The mean age for first same-sex attraction was around age 10 for both males and females. Moreover, sexual attraction marked the first event in a developmental sequence: same-sex attraction, same-sex fantasy, and finally same-sex behavior (see Table 1).

This evidence provides a key for understanding sexuality as a process of development, rather than thinking of it as a discrete event, which emerges suddenly at a single moment in time. Virtually all models of adolescent sexual development, from Anna Freud and Erik Erikson up to the present, have been based on the gonadarche model (Boxer et al., 1989). It conceptualizes the development of sexuality as a precipitous, singular, psychological event, fueled by intrinsic changes in hormone levels. Gonadarche is seen as a "switch," turning on desire and attraction, and hence triggering the developmental sequelae of adult sexuality.

Instead, the new data suggest a longer series of intertwined erotic and gender formations that differentiate beginning in middle childhood. Indeed, the psychological sequence of attraction, fantasy, and behavior may parallel the well-known Tanner stages, which are routinely used by clinicians to quantify the process of physical development during puberty (Timiras, 1972). For example, in girls, onset of sexual attraction may co-occur with Tanner Stage II (development of breast buds); sexual fantasy may co-occur with Tanner Stage III (enlargement of mammary glands); and sexual behavior may co-occur with Tanner Stage IV (full breast development), with each psychosexual stage reflecting a different stage of hormonal development. If so, then we may begin to look for a biological mechanism for psychosexual development in the physiological basis for these early Tanner stages that occur prior to the final gonadal maturation that enables procreation.

The generality of these psychological findings is substantiated by two other recent studies that also reported the age of first sexual attraction to be around 10 (see Fig. 1). Pattatucci and Hamer (1995) and Hamer, Hu, Magnuson, Hu, and Pattatucci (1993) asked similar retrospective questions of two distinctive samples of gay- and lesbian-identified adults in the United States. Unlike the Chicago study (Herdt & Boxer, 1993), these studies gathered information from subjects throughout the United States and interviewed adults who were mostly in their mid-30s (range from 18 to 55). They also used different surveys and interview methodologies. Nevertheless, all three studies pinpointed 10 to 10.5 as the mean age of first sexual attraction. Admittedly, none of the studies was ideal for assessing early development of sexuality; the age of first recalled sexual attraction may not be the actual age. Nonetheless, this work is an essential part of the systematic investigation of same-gender attractions in children.

The question then arises whether there is a similar developmental pattern among heterosexuals. We know of no reason to assume that heterosexuals and homosexuals would have different mechanisms for the activation of sexual attraction and desire. Fortunately, we could test this hypothesis because both Pattatucci's and Hamer's samples had comparison groups of heterosexuals. Indeed, the reported age of first attraction was the same for heterosexually as for homosexually identified adults (only the attraction was toward the opposite sex). Thus, regardless of sexual orientation or gender, the age of initial sexual attraction hovered just over age 10. In sum, the switch mechanism responsible for "turning on" sexual attraction seems to be operating at the same time both for boys and for girls, and regardless of whether their sexual orientation is toward the same or opposite gender.

Thus, we surmise that the maturation of the gonads cannot explain the data found independently by these three studies in different samples and geographic areas. There is no known mechanism that would enable the gonads to supply sufficient levels of hormones at that age to cause sexual attraction, because they are not fully developed. The mean age of sexual attraction is the same in both genders and in both structural forms of sexual orientation; therefore, the biological counterpart in both genders and in both structural forms of sexual orientation of sexual attraction is probably the same. These constraints effectively eliminate gonadarche as a candidate to explain the observed findings.

Table 1. *Ages (years) at which males and females recall having their first same-sex attraction, fantasy, and activity (from Herdt & Boxer, 1993)*

	Males			Females		
Developmental event	*M*	*SD*	*n*	*M*	*SD*	*n*
First same-sex attraction	9.6	3.6	146	10.1	3.7	55
First same-sex fantasy	11.2	3.5	144	11.9	2.9	54
First same-sex activity	13.1	4.3	136	15.2	3.1	49

ADRENARCHE IN MIDDLE CHILDHOOD

In the pediatric literature, it is well recognized that children between the ages of 6 and 11 are experiencing a rise in sex steroids. These hormones come from the maturing adrenal glands. Adrenarche is clinically recognized primarily by the onset of pubic hair, but it also includes a growth spurt, increased oil on the skin, changes in the external genitalia, and the development of body odor (New, Levine, & Pang, 1981; Parker, 1991). Nonetheless, both the psychological literature and the institutions of our culture regard this period of middle childhood as hormonally quiescent. Freud's (1905/1965) classic notion of a "latency" period between ages 4 to 6 and puberty perhaps best distills the cultural prejudices. In contrast, we have hypothesized that the rise in adrenal steroid production is critical for understanding interpersonal and intrapsychic development in middle childhood.

Both male and female infants have adult levels of sex steroids during the first days of life, and their adrenal androgens also approach the adult range (see Fig. 2). After a few months, the sex hormone levels begin to fall to a very low level and then remain low until the maturation of the adrenal glands and gonads. When children are between 6 and 8 years of age, their adrenal glands begin to mature. Specifically, the adrenal cortex begins to secrete low levels of androgens, primarily dehydroepiandrosterone (DHEA; see Fig. 2) (Parker, 1991). The metabolism of DHEA leads to both testosterone and estradiol, the primary sex steroids in men and women.

It is noteworthy that both girls and boys experience a rise in androgens, although androgens are typically misidentified as male hormones. Moreover, there is no sex difference in the age at which these androgens begin to rise or the rate at which they do so. After adrenarche, an individual's level of androgens plateaus until around 12 years of age in girls and 14 years of age in boys, whereupon gonadarche triggers a second hormonal rise into the adult range (Parker, 1991).

In adults, the androgens that are produced by the adrenal cortex and their metabolites are known to have psychological effects in a variety of developmental areas relating to aggression, cognition, perception, attention, emotions, and sexuality. Although adult levels of DHEA are not reached until after gonadarche, levels of this hormone do increase significantly around age 10 (see Fig. 2; De Peretti & Forest, 1976), when they become 10 times the levels experienced by children between 1 and 4 years or age. It is plausible that this marked increase in androgen levels alters the brain, and thus behavior, either by modifying neural function or by permanently altering cellular structure.

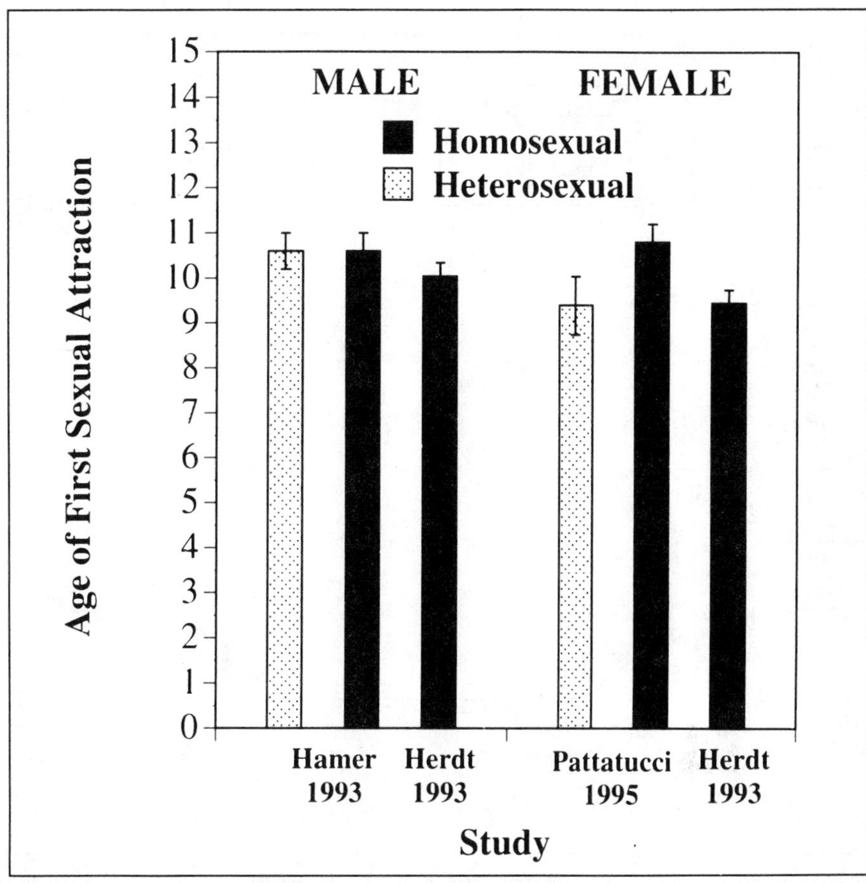

Fig. 1. Mean age (±*SEM*) of first sexual attraction reported by males and females, both homosexual and heterosexual. The data are reported in three studies: Herdt and Boxer (1993), Pattatucci and Hamer (1995), and Hamer, Hu, Magnuson, Hu, and Pattatucci (1993).

WHAT IS SPECIAL ABOUT THE FOURTH GRADE?

We considered the hypothesis that the age of first sexual attraction is similar for boys and girls, both homosexual and heterosexual, because there is some marked change in environmental stimuli, socialization, or cognitive abilities around the age of 10. If so, then the 10-fold rise in DHEA would be only correlated with the emergence of sexuality and should not be considered its direct cause.

A major weakness of the idea that environmental stimuli lead to the emergence of sexual attraction at age 10 is the fact that, in the United States, there is no marked cultural prompt for sexuality in a 10-year-old. Children this age are typically in fourth grade. To our knowledge, there is no overt change in social expectations between Grades 3 and 4, or between Grades 4 and 5, that might account for the developmental emergence of sexual attraction at age 10. In U.S. culture, the typical ages for the so-called rites of passage are 12 to 13, when the adolescent becomes a "teenager," or around 15 to 16, when the driver's license is issued. Perhaps between Grades 5 and 6 (or, depending on the school system, between Grades 6 and 7), we might identify a critical change during the transition from elementary to middle school. Yet all of these culturally more prominent transitions occur later than age 10. Other subtle changes, such as girls wearing ornate earrings or boys forming preteenage groups, may occur around age 10, but these social factors seem too weak to adequately explain the sudden emergence of sexual attraction before anatomical changes are noteworthy in the child.

We also considered the possibility that although the social environment does not change at age 10, sexual attraction arises at this age because of an increase in the child's cognitive capability to perceive and understand the sexual and social environment. When the child becomes cognitively capable of understanding sexual interactions among adults, the child is capable also of imitating and putting into action the behaviors he or she has observed. This may be a plausible explanation for development of an awareness of sexual attraction in heterosexuals, and no doubt plays a role in the development of sexuality (after all, people typically do not develop sexuality in a vacuum). But does the explanation hold for children who are sexually attracted to the same gender?

The simple social-learning hypothesis predicts that as soon as children become aware of a strong cultural taboo on the expression of homosexual feelings, they should inhibit or even extinguish these desires in subsequent sexual development. We would therefore expect to find that homosexuals would reveal same-sex attraction significantly later than the age when heterosexuals reveal opposite-sex attraction. But this is not the case.

If 10-year-old children are simply mimicking the sexual behavior most commonly seen in adults (and the biological ability to actually carry out the behavior will arise only with gonadarche), then, given the predominant culture, all 10-year-old boys should demonstrate sexual attraction toward females, and all 10-year-old girls should show sexual attraction toward males. However, this also is not the case.

Other criticisms of simple learning-theory hypotheses regarding sexual development are well known and need not be repeated here (Abramson & Pinkerton, 1995). However, the Sambia of Papua New Guinea (Herdt, 1981) provide particularly compelling counterevidence to a simple learning theory model. The Sambia provide powerful reinforcement for same-gender relations by institutionalizing the practice of men inseminating boys over a period of many years beginning at age 7 to 10. The goal of the men is to masculinize and "grow" the youths into competent reproductive adult men. This intensive training and reinforcement of sexual relationships between males does not result in exclusive homosexuality in adulthood. Instead, adult Sambia men reveal marked bifurcation of their sexual interest; they generality stop all same-gender relations after marriage and enjoy sexual relations with women.

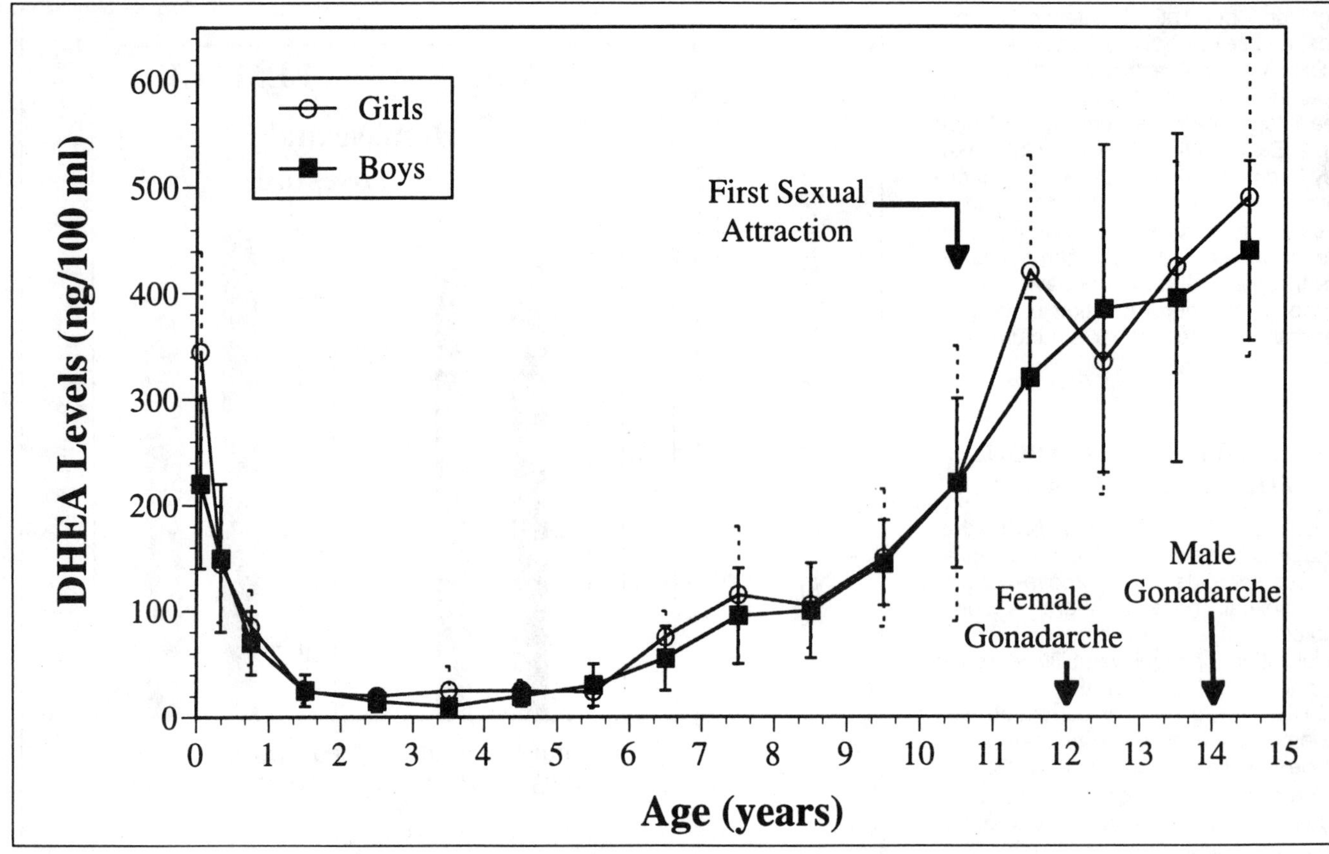

Fig. 2. Mean levels (±*SEM*) of the primary adrenal androgen dehydroepiandrosterone (DHEA) from birth through gonadarche in boys (solid error bars) and girls (dashed error bars). (Data redrawn from De Peretti & Forest, 1976.)

THE RELATIONSHIP BETWEEN ADRENARCHE AND SEXUALITY: CAUSE OR CORRELATION?

Does the inability of the hypotheses of gonadarche and social learning to explain the data imply that adrenarche is the key to the emergence of sexual attraction at age 10? That question cannot yet be answered conclusively. It is entirely possible that the sequential changes in attraction, fantasy, and behavior result from major structural changes in the brain that have their etiology in sources other than sex steroids. However, there has been no documented evidence for such neural structures as of yet. Moreover, if structural changes in the brain do prove to be the cause of the emergence of sexual attraction, modification of all current sexual developmental models and theories will still be needed because they assume that adult desires and behaviors develop from gonadarche.

A change in the nervous system that results from hormones released at adrenarche does took like the most likely developmental mechanism for several reasons. First, girls and boys experience their first sexual attraction, but not gonadarche, at the same age. Second, DHEA, the primary androgen released by the adrenal, is intimately linked with testosterone and estradiol, the major adult sex hormones. Their dynamic relationship is based on the fact that they share many of the fundamental features of steroid function: metabolic pathways that produce the steroids, binding proteins in the blood that carry them to their target tissue, and receptors that enable the cells in the target tissue, including the brain, to change their function in response to the hormonal information. Third, these androgens are known to affect the sexual fantasies and behavior of adolescents and adults, and it is plausible that the same hormones would have similar effects at an earlier age.

RETHINKING PUBERTY: IMPLICATIONS FOR MANY DOMAINS

Given the strong possibility that the currently popular model of puberty is limited, if not incorrect, researchers need to rethink puberty and test the new models in a wide range of psychological disciplines. Adrenarche clearly raises androgens to significant levels, and if these hormones are responsible for the effects seen in sexual attraction, then they are likely to affect a wide range of other behaviors: aggression, cognition, perception, attention, arousal, emotions, and, of course, sexual identity, fantasy, and behavior.

Even if it turns out that hormones released from the adrenal glands are not responsible for the onset of sexual attraction, the behavioral data themselves demonstrate that the concept of puberty must be greatly elaborated and its various stages unpacked. Indeed, Freud's idea of a latency period is seriously flawed. The current behavioral work reinforces the well-established clinical understanding that puberty is composed of at least two separate maturational processes: adrenarche and gonadarche. Any psychosocial research that uses puberty as a stage in development needs to break down the relevant developmental and social behaviors into these two different stages. Researchers need to take into account the hormonal fact that the start of puberty in normal individuals is around ages 6 to 8 and the end of puberty is not until around ages 15 to 17.

The idea of sexuality developing in stages is nothing new to social scientists. But the idea that sexuality is a continuous process that begins from the inside, well before gonadarche, and extends into adulthood is a conceptual advance. These new data from sexual orientation research force a reevaluation of the social and health models of sexual development. No longer can the brain at puberty be treated as a black box, which is suddenly able to process sexual stimuli *de novo* at the time of gonadal change.

Although adrenarche may not be the answer to all the riddles of sexual development, the new data from the developmental and social study of sexual identity have triggered a major conceptual advance in the understanding of both puberty and sexual development as psychobiological phenomena.

Acknowledgements—We extend our profound thanks to Colin Davis, who coordinated the data and helped substantially with manuscript preparation; to Ruvance Pietrz, who edited text and figures; and to Amanda Woodward for her insightful and constructive comments. This work was supported by National Institute of Mental Health MERIT Award R37 MH41788 to Martha K. McClintock.

Notes

1. Address correspondence to Martha K. McClintock, 5730 Woodlawn Ave., Chicago, IL 60637; e-mail: mkml@midway.uchicago.edu.
2. The adrenal glands are small, pyramidal glands located above the kidneys. They produce hormones that affect metabolism, salt regulation, response to stress, and reproductive function, in part by binding in the brain and altering neural function.

References

Abramson, P., & Pinkerton, S. (Eds.). (1995). *Sexual nature, sexual culture.* Chicago: University of Chicago Press.

Boxer, A., Levinson, R. A., & Petersen, A. C. (1989). Adolescent sexuality. In J. Worell & F. Danner (Eds.), *The adolescent as decision-maker* (pp. 209–244). San Diego: Academic Press.

De Peretti, E., & Forest, M. G. (1976). Unconjugated dehydroepiandrosterone plasma levels in normal subjects from birth to adolescence in humans: The use of a sensitive radioimmunoassay. *Journal of Clinical Endocrinology and Metabolism, 43,* 982–991.

Freud, S. (1965). *Three essays on the theory of sexuality.* New York: Basic Books. (Original work published 1905)

Hamer, D. H., Hu, S., Magnuson, V. L., Hu, N., Pattatucci, A. M. L. (1993). A linkage between DNA markers on the X chromosome and male sexual orientation. *Science, 261,* 321–327.

Herdt, G. (1981). *Guardians of the flutes.* New York: McGraw-Hill.

Herdt, G., & Boxer, A. (1993). *Children of horizons.* New York: Beacon Press.

Money, J., & Ehrhardt, A. (1972). *Man, woman, boy, girl.* Baltimore: Johns Hopkins University Press.

New, M. I., Levine, L. S., & Pang, S. (1981). Adrenal androgens and growth. In M. Ritzen (Ed.), *The biology of normal human growth: Transactions of the First Karolinska Institute Nobel Conference* (pp. 285–295). New York: Raven Press.

Parker, L. N. (1991). Adrenarche. *Endocrinology and Metabolism Clinics of North America, 20(1),* 71–83.

Pattatucci, A. M. L., & Hamer, D. H. (1995). Development and familiality of sexual orientation in females. *Behavior Genetics, 25,* 407–420.

Timiras, P. S. (1972). *Developmental physiology and aging.* New York: Macmillan.

Recommended Reading

Becker, J. B., Breedlove, S. M., & Crews, D. (Ed.). (1992). *Behavioral endocrinology.* London: MIT Press.

Boxer, A., & Cohler, B. (1989). The life-course of gay and lesbian youth: An immodest proposal for the study of lives. In G. Herdt (Ed.), *Gay and lesbian youth* (pp. 315–335). New York: Harrington Park Press.

Korth-Schütz, S. S. (1989). Precocious adrenarche. In F. G. Maguelone (Ed.), *Pediatric and adolescent endocrinology* (pp. 226–235). New York: Karger.

Rosenfield, R. L. (1994). Normal and almost normal precocious variations in pubertal development: Premature pubarche and premature thelarche revisited. *Hormone Research, 41,* (Suppl. 2), 7–13.

Subtle, Secret Female Chimpanzees

Richard W. Wrangham

PHOTOS: R. WRANGHAM

Around three decades ago, the myth of the passive female primate was at its height, bolstered by two assumptions. All females were assumed to be uniformly successful at reproduction, because "all females breed." And social evolution was thought to proceed mainly by sexual selection, in which female-female relationships played a small part. So when female cercopithecines—animals such as baboons and macaques—were found to have highly variable levels of success in breeding, correlated with an individual's lifelong rank in the female hierarchy (her dominance status), the myth took a beating (*1*). From then on, female strategies were seen to have their own logic independent of males, and the ecology of female primate relationships became a vigorous research area that was crucial to understanding social evolution. But there were a few holdouts. In some well-studied species—the great apes, for example—there seemed to be little variance in female reproduction. Selection on female reproductive strategies appeared particularly weak in these species, allowing females to be considered as relatively passive pawns of male maneuvering. A new study on page 828 of this issue suggests that this view was simply the result of our ignorance (*2*) and that dominant female chimpanzees are indeed more reproductively successful than their lower-ranked associates.

Better on top. Among female chimpanzees, as among males, rank in the dominance hierarchy determines reproductive success.

Pusey, Williams, and Goodall (*2*) show that female chimpanzees in Gombe National Park, Tanzania, vary in their fitness and that fitness is correlated with dominance. If it seems odd that it has taken 37 years for Jane Goodall's Gombe studies to yield data on female reproductive success, consider that the chimpanzee social community contains only 10 to 15 females at any one time, with a mean interbirth interval of 5 years between surviving offspring. Half of the breeding females are immigrants, often of unknown age. Many females meet each other rarely, and even then clear-cut dominance interactions are infrequent, so that it can take several years for observers to detect the dominance relationship of any given pair. But by indexing the dominance ranking of the females over 2-year periods, Pusey *et al.* found that status correlated with at least three measures of fitness for breeding females. The effects are weak enough that if an infertile female is included in the data, the correlations disappear. Nevertheless the results gain strength from parallel correlations of female rank with infant production, infant survival, and offspring maturation rate. Indeed, the rate of production of weaned offspring by dominant females was almost twice as fast as by subordinate females, for whom it was 9 to 10 years.

It is too early to say why rank has these effects, or why, if rank is as important as the new data suggest, females challenge each other so little. At Gombe, each mother's foraging is concentrated in her own core area within a larger community range defended by natal males. Escalated aggression among females is rare, but Pusey *et al.* speculate that such competition as there is, including infanticide by high-ranking females, may serve to acquire or retain the best core areas. What makes this reasonable is that in extreme circumstances female chimpanzees can compete as intensively as males. Thus captive females, meeting for the first time as adults, can use male-like behavioral strategies to gain rank, including opportunistic coalitions and frequent reconciliations (*3*). It may be that occasional female tactics, still seen too rarely for observers to assess their significance, stabilize ranks in adolescence and underwrite a lifetime of covert rivalry.

Covert behavior by female chimpanzees may be important in the sexual realm as well. In the most substantial analysis yet of chimpanzee paternity, Gagneux *et al.* (*4*) genotyped 13 infants in Taï National Park, Ivory Coast, together with their mothers and all the males of their community. Seven of the infants (54%) proved to have been fathered outside the community, a proportion far higher than anyone anticipated. In Taï, although females normally sleep together with the whole community, individual females sometimes disappear for days or weeks at a time. One of the cuckolding females was unseen by observers for only 1 day and another for 2 days during the months in which they conceived. Intense territorial competition means that male intrusions occur only in large subgroups, with fights but no matings, and are therefore rarely surreptitious. Gagneux *et al.* accordingly believe that extra-group paternity is a result of females visiting neighboring communities. The implication: Females are highly motivated to travel a long distance in search of the neighboring males.

Again, the small sample size implies caution. But even if the rate of extra-group paternity proves generally lower than 54%, a detectable rate of cuckoldry is remarkable and raises two significant points. First, female chimpanzees typically copulate several hundred times per baby, and only a small proportion of their copulations can occur with the neighbors. The data imply that females can select fertile times to cuckold their home-group males, suggesting they are choosing genes.

Second, the costs to females of sneaky matings appear substantial, implying that they bring major benefits. Females risk severe aggression not only from the neighboring males, but also from males who are known to kill infants fathered from other communities. Yet it is hard to imagine how the genetic benefits can be very high, because females mate multiply. This means that even when a fecund female chooses to

The author is in the Department of Anthropology, Harvard University, Cambridge, MA 02138, USA. E-mail: wrangham@fas.harvard.edu mate in a neighboring community, she could not, so far as we know, select a specific male as father. The phenotypic benefit thought to account best for multiple mating in chimpanzees is infanticide prevention, on the theory that males forgo aggression toward infants of mothers with whom they remember mating (5). In the Taï case, mating with the neighbors could provide an insurance against future encounters with them when she is accompanied by her offspring.

But why should the female ever encounter the neighboring males in the future? Males have been dying at a high rate in the Taï study community. Could the cuckolding copulations be a preemptive safeguard against a take-over by neighbors? This might explain the curious observation that no neighboring females have been seen mating with the males of the study community. If so, the Gagneux *et al.* result may prove to be a rare phenomenon even among chimpanzees, specific to an unusual historical moment. Or is she insuring herself against a bad fruit-season in her own range, when she might need to eat in a neighboring range? That would suggest extra-group matings will be found commonly in other populations. Genetic data are being compiled quickly in other chimpanzee sites and should soon show whether high rates of extra-group paternity are common.

Until this year, no one suspected that female chimpanzees were so active in pursuit of their reproductive interests, yet they are probably doing still more than we appreciate. Chimpanzee and human social systems differ importantly in the characteristics of the female relationships, so there are certainly no direct analogies for human sociobiology. But these studies remind us that even where females interact rarely or subtly, female initiative can be a major force in the evolution of social systems. Selective impact doesn't necessarily correspond with social power.

References

1. S. B. Hrdy and G. C. Williams, in *Social Behavior of Female Vertebrates*, S. K. Wasser, Ed. (Academic Press, New York, 1983), pp. 3–17.
2. A. E. Pusey *et al., Science* **277**, 828 (1997).
3. K. C. Baker and B. B. Smuts, in *Chimpanzee Cultures*, R. W. Wrangham, W. C. McGrew, F. B. M. de Waal, P. G. Heltne, Eds. (Harvard Univ. Press, Cambridge, MA, 1994), pp. 227–242.
4. P. Gagneux *et al., Nature* **387**, 358 (1997).
5. R. W. Wrangham, *Hum. Nat.* **4**, 47 (1993).

Animals' Fancies

Why members of some species prefer their own sex

By TINA ADLER

Courtship in the barnyard usually puts a smile on farmers' faces and dollar signs in their eyes. That good cheer quickly sours, however, when the the two lovebirds happen to be of the same sex. The problem isn't a moral one, of course. Strictly financial.

Many domestic and wild animals engage in sexual activity with members of both the same and the opposite sex; a smaller number have eyes only for their own sex. Some of these homosexual activities appear to boost reproduction. Female cows often mount each other, thereby signaling any bulls in sight that they are ready to reproduce. In other cases, same-sex affairs may help reproduction indirectly, by promoting the general fitness of a group or individual. For example, in some species, animals are more willing to share food with a member of their own sex after sexual activity with him or her.

Indeed, researchers interested in animal behavior and sexual selection have long held that the main function of homosexual endeavors is to ensure, in a roundabout way, that one's genes get passed along.

The sheep farmer who paid big bucks for a ram's mating abilities and finds the animal ignoring his ewes would certainly question this theory. Besides failing at their jobs, high-libido homosexual rams cause havoc in the sheep pens by disrupting other males mating with females.

Carole Gauthier/Univ. of Montreal

Homosexual liaisons among Japanese macaques don't appear to interfere with reproduction, researchers say.

A few scientists are now siding with the farmers. Recent studies indicate that homosexual behavior in some species may have much more to do with sexual gratification than with reproduction. Studies are also revealing biological differences between straight and gay animals. These findings may lead to screening tests to help prevent the wrong animals from getting hired for mating jobs. They may also shed light on the possible roots of human homosexuality, some researchers argue.

For the most part, homosexual behaviors in domestic animals are considered normal and helpful for the development of reproduction. "This is not always the case," animal behaviorist Anne Perkins of Carroll College in Helena, Mont., and James A. Fitzgerald of Oregon State University in Corvallis assert in *Sexual Orientation* (Westport, Conn.: Praeger, in press). Perkins' research on sheep supports this argument.

Scientists have studied the sex drive and sexual orientation of domesticated and wild rams. A heterosexual ram with a strong sex drive will mount either other males or ewes. However, a significant proportion of domesticated males—up to 16 percent—never mate with females during a breeding season, Perkins says.

About 6 percent seem uninterested in any sexual activity. Another 10 percent are homosexual, choosing males even when females are available. Domesticated rams resemble their wild relatives, which scientists have also observed participating in homosexual relations. Ewes rarely engage in such activities.

To try to determine whether rams will service their ewes, farmers simply watch the animals' behavior. They'd like a more foolproof, efficient system, however. Encouraged by new findings on the brain chemistry of homosexual and low-libido sheep, Perkins and her colleagues hope that in the future they'll be able to offer farmers a blood or genetic test.

Estradiol, a form of estrogen, is the bewitching compound that piques a heterosexual ram's interest in females. Ewes and homosexual rams can store a similar amount of estradiol in a brain structure called the amygdala; heterosexual rams accumulate significantly more, Perkins and her colleagues reported in the March 1995 HORMONES AND BEHAVIOR.

Compared to their heterosexual counterparts, homosexual rams have a low concentration of testosterone in their blood, the result of testes that fail to synthesize the hormone as efficiently, Perkins, John A. Resko of Oregon Health Sciences University in Portland, and their colleagues report in the July BIOLOGY OF REPRODUCTION. Homosexual rams also have lower aromatase activity in a part of the brain, the preoptic area, that helps control sexual behavior in many species. Aromatase, an enzyme, converts testosterone to estrogen.

Though these differences may arise in part during fetal development, a ram's sexual activities may help maintain regions of the amygdala and the preoptic area that mediate sexual behavior, Perkins speculates. Abstinence may cause them to atrophy.

"It's a use-it-or-lose-it kind of thing," she explains.

The idea that animals may have sex just because it feels good proves difficult for some people to accept, says primatologist Paul L. Vasey of the University of Montreal. The Japanese macaques he studies, which are hardly anomalies in the animal kingdom, might change the minds of some of these reluctant scientists.

Both wild and captive males occasionally mount each other, but they almost always pick their mates from the pool of available feminine companions. The females frequently engage in same-sex consortships but aren't exclusively homosexual. Females in a captive group that Vasey studies average seven partners each during their breeding season, about half of them male. Among the monkeys' wild relatives, female homosexuality is most common in troops with a relatively low proportion of males.

The captive females' homosexual liaisons occur only during the breeding season and last from an hour to more than a week, Vasey finds. During that time, they mount only each other, and they do so repeatedly. They remain by each other's side, foraging, grooming, and resting. Males, in contrast, usually take off after copulating.

Female couples fail to fall for flirtatious males and will, 90 percent of the time, either ignore or attack them, Vasey found in a recent study of 14 females in his coed group of Japanese macaques. He reported his findings in October at a meeting of the Canadian Association for Physical Anthropologists in Kingston, Ontario.

Some researchers have argued that animals engage in homosexual activities to associate with dominant same-sex members of their clan and thereby boost their social standing. This theory does not apply to his macaques, Vasey reports in the September ANIMAL BEHAVIOUR.

For 2 years, he collected data on the mating habits of three macaque families, made up of 18 adult females, 5 adult males, and 14 youngsters. Of the mature females, 15 engaged in homosexual consortships.

In over 75 percent of the homosexual couples, one or both partners regularly supported the other in fights. Dominant and subordinate members paired up and came to each other's aid, seemingly blind to rank. Moreover, consorts took the unusual step of siding with their partners over their kin during squabbles.

The homosexual relationships also altered social structures. "During homosexual consortships, over half of the subordinate female partners increased in dominance," Vasey reports. The dominant animal's position remained stable.

However, the monkeys didn't choose their same-sex partners on the basis of their potential as allies, otherwise big-shots would have had little interest in their subordinates, he argues. Also, the dominant animals did most of the grooming, and low- and high-ranking members of a couple mounted each other at a similar rate.

"Mutual sexual attraction was the impetus for the formation and maintenance of homosexual consortships," he contends. Sexual selection theory holds that animals pick partners that will increase their chances of passing on their genes, but this doesn't apply to homosexual macaques.

"I'm not saying Darwin was wrong, but there's room for working on the theory so it can accommodate observations of homosexual behavior," he asserts.

Although homosexual relations appear to have little reproductive value for species such as macaques and rams, examples exist of animals ingeniously partnering with the same sex to improve their chances of passing along their genes.

In the wild, when male ring-billed and California gulls are scarce, up to 5 percent of females raise their young with a female partner. They court each other as they would a male and set up a nest together. One or both then copulate with males that already have mates, research by Michael R. Conover of Utah State University in Logan and others has shown. Two-parent families are a necessity in gull communities. One parent stays home and guards the nest from egg-hungry neighbors, while the other goes in search of food.

Females may remain with their same-sex partner for several years, although about half find a male companion by the following mating season, reports Conover.

Because different species of gulls look so similar, scientists had wondered how female gulls select males that belong to their species. In an experiment, researchers put herring gull eggs in the nests of wild ring-billed gulls. When ready for breeding, the female offspring sought out ring-billed mates. This suggests that the birds pick males that resemble their fathers—or in this case, their adoptive fathers, says Conover.

This finding recently led him and his colleagues to begin investigating how birds raised by same-sex, same-species couples select their mates. They have banded several thousand chicks and plan to monitor their mate choice for 5 years. Of the first four gulls that they've observed with mates, all had picked members of their own species. Two had partnered with females, and the others had picked males.

Research into the benefits and origins of homosexuality in animals is important to furthering understanding of animal behavior. However, people can't help wondering what the findings say about, well, people. Growing numbers of human studies are now linking homosexuality to unique biological traits (SN: 8/10/96, p. 88).

The discovery of estradiol differences in homosexual and heterosexual rams "complements recent reports regarding the genetic and anatomical correlates of homosexual orientation described in humans," Perkins and her colleagues proposed in the 1995 HORMONES AND BEHAVIOR.

However, Perkins and Fitzgerald "leave it up to each reader [of *Sexual Orientation*] to determine whether mechanisms mediating sexual orientation in sheep could help explain similar mechanisms involved in humans." Perkins does note that humans and sheep have more similar reproductive systems than do humans and other laboratory animals, such as rats.

What does the macaque research say about human sexuality? It raises the possibility that human homosexuality has no "evolutionary or reproductive benefits and that it's just for pleasure also," contends Vasey.

The making of a homosexual

While some researchers examine what benefits animals may derive from same-sex sexual activities, others are trying to pinpoint straightforward biological causes of the behavior. They find that dosing pregnant animals with certain hormones greatly increases the mothers' odds of producing homosexual offspring and that among fruit flies, a genetic mutation leads male flies to choose other males (SN: 12/14/96, p. 373).

Animal experiments also reveal that castrating males or giving them drugs to inhibit their production of the enzyme aromatase causes them to fancy members of their own sex, Viveka Mansukhani and her colleagues at Cornell University explain in the December HORMONES AND BEHAVIOR. Testosterone or estradiol treatments make females likely to consort with other females.

In their study, Mansukhani and her coworkers tampered with the sexual orientation of animals that choose one mate for life—a group whose sexual preferences have drawn little attention from other researchers. They gave female zebra finches estradiol during their first 2 weeks of life, then put them in either all-female or coed cages for up to 100 days. Next, they gave them testosterone and observed their mate preferences.

In environments intended to replicate a natural colony, the female birds that grew up in unisex housing were more likely to prefer females than were those in the coed group, they report. As juveniles, the birds may need to see males in order to learn to choose them as mates, speculates coauthor Elizabeth Adkins-Regan.

Because of the great importance of having a partner and the finite supply of males in cages, some captive female zebra finches select a same-sex companion even without any hormone treatments, says Adkins-Regan. In cages, "there's always a chance that they may get left out—that nobody wants them," she says. In the wild, they can usually go in search of other males to court and probably don't hook up with females.

Menstrual Synchrony Under Optimal Conditions: Bedouin Families

Aron Weller and Leonard Weller
Bar-Ilan University

Ovarian cycles of females living and interacting together have been shown to synchronize in a number of species. In humans, the related phenomenon of menstrual synchrony has been reported among roommates and best friends. Menstrual data were collected prospectively for 3 months from 27 Bedouin nuclear families living under conditions optimally conducive for synchrony: (a) women living together for many years, (b) a highly sexually segregated society, (c) standard living conditions, and (d) minimal use of oral contraceptives. Results show unequivocally the existence of menstrual synchrony: A 20%–25% shift toward synchrony was found for sisters–roommates, sisters–roommates who are close friends, and the family (all women in the family between 13 and 50 years of age).

Many biological rhythms undergo a process of social synchronization. For example, bees synchronize their daily foraging patterns to those of other bees (Medugorac & Lindauer, 1967), and feeding rhythms of restrained rhesus monkeys (*Macaca mulatta*; Rohles, 1971) can become socially synchronized. The ovarian cycles of female rats (*Rattus norvegicus*; McClintock, 1978) and golden hamsters (*Mesocricetus auratus*; Handelmann, Ravizza, & Ray, 1980) that live and interact together have also been shown to synchronize. Ovarian synchrony apparently requires three to four cycles to develop and is not perfect: A portion of the groups (and of the individuals in the groups) does not synchronize (McClintock, 1983). In a number of species of mammals, including nonhuman primates, estrous synchrony has been shown to be mediated by olfactory cues (Graham, 1991; McClintock, 1983; Wallis, 1985). As an instance of biological synchronization, ovarian synchrony has been described according to the mathematical framework of mutual entrainment, or coupling, of a set of oscillators (McClintock, 1983; Schank & McClintock, 1992; Strogatz & Stewart, 1993).

Human menstrual and ovarian cycles are endogenous rhythms, affected by various exogenous, social, and environmental stimuli. For example, time-zone transition (Preston, Bateman, Short, & Wilkinson, 1974), stress (e.g., Asso, 1983; Matteo, 1987; Sommer, 1978), and frequency of sexual activity (Burleson, Gregory, & Trevathan, 1995; Cutler, Preti, Huggins, Erickson, & Garcia, 1985) are associated with menstrual cycle length, regularity, and the induction of anovulatory cycles (i.e., ovulatory suppression). Although ovarian synchrony has not been documented directly in humans, its expression as menstrual synchrony has been studied. The measure of change and synchrony in these studies is the date of the menstrual onset, which may be an imprecise index of ovulatory synchrony, especially if some anovulatory cycles are included (as discussed by Graham, 1991). The adaptive function of ovarian synchrony in animals and humans is unclear, although various possibilities have been proposed (Graham, 1991; Kiltie, 1982; McClintock, 1981, 1983).

Menstrual synchrony, the convergence of the onset dates of the menstrual flow, was first documented 25 years ago among women living in a college dormitory and among close friends (McClintock, 1971). The majority of the research since then has continued to examine menstrual synchrony among women living together (mostly in dormitories, but also in private residences) and among close friends (L. Weller & Weller, 1993a). Menstrual synchrony has also been studied among women who work together (Matteo, 1987; A. Weller & Weller, 1995b), between a mother and her daughter (A. Weller & Weller, 1993; L. Weller & Weller, 1993b), and among women basketball players (A. Weller & Weller, 1995a).

The phenomenon of menstrual synchrony appears to be a clear demonstration in humans of social interactions influencing the patterning of neuroendocrinological activity. Two possible mechanisms have been proposed for human menstrual synchrony: pheromonal and common environmental influences. Pheromones are chemical substances produced by one individual that affect the behavior or physiology of another. Common environmental influences include such factors as similar food, stress, and light–dark cycles. McClintock (1971) ruled out the effect of these common environmental influences and explained synchrony as resulting from the women's living together. She suggested that this effect was mediated by pheromones. Because there is no direct evidence that pheromonal communication exists among humans, the phenomenon of menstrual synchrony, combined with evidence that common environmental influences do not affect it, may be the best, albeit indirect, evidence for the existence of pheromonal communication in humans.

Aron Weller, Department of Psychology, and Leonard Weller, Department of Sociology, Bar-Ilan University, Ramat-Gan, Israel.

This research was supported by the Committee for Research Advancement of Bar-Ilan University. We are deeply indebted to Hegar Kabia for collecting the data. We also thank Orli Turgeman Goldschmidt for her assistance.

Correspondence concerning this article should be addressed to Aron Weller, Department of Psychology, Bar-Ilan University, Ramat-Gan 52900, Israel. Electronic mail may be sent to weller@popeye.cc.biu.ac.il.

For a period of almost 20 years the accumulated research, almost unequivocally, continued to confirm the original findings (Graham, 1991). In the last 5 years the picture has changed. Negative findings have been reported (Trevathan, Burleson, & Gregory, 1993; L. Weller, Weller, & Avinir, 1995; Wilson, Kiefphaber, & Gravel, 1991), in addition to the previously reported negative findings (Goldman & Schneider, 1987; Jarett, 1984), plus the reanalysis of one of the classical studies (Quadagno, Shubeita, Deck, & Francoeur, 1981) whose findings have now been shown not to have demonstrated synchrony (Wilson, 1992, p. 579). Furthermore, Wilson (1992) criticized the original procedure for calculating synchrony, in which the initial onset differences of pairs are compared with their final onset differences several months later, on the grounds that over the short period in which the participants lived together, about half of the sample would have synchronized anyway by chance.

In an alternative approach for assessing menstrual synchrony, pairs of women who have lived together for a considerable length of time are asked to record their onset dates. The distribution of onset differences between pairs of women are compared with the probability distribution expected if onset dates were randomly distributed. Whereas some of these studies have reported synchrony (A. Weller & Weller, 1992, 1993; L. Weller & Weller, 1993b), others have not (A. Weller & Weller, 1995a, 1995b; L. Weller et al., 1995).

In the last 5 years a number of methodological issues have been raised, making it difficult to assess the extent or perhaps even the existence of this phenomenon (Graham, 1991; L. Weller & Weller, 1993a, 1995, in press; Wilson, 1992). One issue is the inclusion of samples of women who used oral contraceptives. Owing to the fact that the day a woman starts taking oral contraceptives determines the timing of her menstruation, the inclusion of women who use them could potentially confound the results. Three approaches have been used to study women who use oral contraceptives: include them, exclude them, or include them when only one woman of the couple uses oral contraceptives.

Theoretically, if the sample is large enough, no harm would be done by including couples for which both women use oral contraceptives, as they would be randomly distributed among the synchronous and nonsynchronous couples. However, there is no benefit in including them, the samples are not always large enough, and the empirical distribution does not always behave according to the desired theoretical distribution.

The inclusion of couples in which only one of the partners uses oral contraceptives may be regarded as a conservative approach to testing synchrony. Synchrony would only occur if the nonuser alters her menstrual cycle, whereas when neither woman takes the contraceptive, either or both women could alter their menstruation dates. This approach seems reasonable. Yet, it implicitly assumes that each woman in the couple changes her cycle to the same degree as her partner. But we do not know if this is indeed so; quite possibly, one of the women does most of the changing or would do most of the changing were she not using the oral contraceptive.

Although it would be best to study synchronization among women who do not use oral contraceptives, groups (or even dyads) in which no woman uses them may be hard to find. In a 1992 survey of almost 7,000 American women, 52% of the unmarried women reported using them (Forrest & Fordyce, 1993).

A second concern is the use of retrospective reporting in some samples. Although we are not aware of any study that compared prospective and retrospective reporting of menstrual dates, the reliability of retrospective reporting in general (Nisbett & Wilson, 1977) and of menstrual information in particular (McFarland, Ross, & DeCourville, 1989) has been seriously criticized.

A third issue concerns the low (less than 50%) response rate in most prospective studies, raising the concern of sample bias (L. Weller & Weller, 1993a, 1995). It is not known whether women who participated in these studies differed in their menstrual synchrony from women who did not agree to participate and, if so, which of the two groups of women would be more synchronous. It is known, however, that college women's readiness to participate in research varies with the stage of their menstrual cycle (Doty & Silverthorne, 1975). Substantial evidence has accumulated showing that volunteers for psychological experiments differ in a number of ways from nonvolunteers. Among others, volunteers are higher in the need for social approval, have more unconventional personalities, tend to be firstborn, are less well-adjusted, and have a higher need for achievement (Jung, 1971).

A fourth concern is the failure of most studies to recognize that because women's menstrual cycles are inherently variable (e.g., Treloar, Boynton, Borghild, & Brown, 1967; Vollman, 1977), menstrual synchrony should be determined on the basis of more than 1 month at the terminal point of the study. As a measure of reliability, we have recommended using at least 2, or preferably 3, consecutive months (L. Weller & Weller, in press).

There are additional issues that may account for some of the negative findings. These refer to conditions that may not have been adequately controlled. One, the degree of sexual exposure to men, may have a confounding effect on menstrual synchrony, because frequency of sexual activity has been shown to be associated with ovulation and cycle length (Cutler, Garcia, & Kreiger, 1979; Cutler et al., 1985; Veith, Buck, Getzlaf, Van Dalfsen, & Slade, 1983). Thus, some of the negative findings reported in the literature may be the result of different cycle lengths of each woman in a couple, caused by different degrees of sexual activity.

Two, in some studies the conditions necessary for synchrony to occur might not exist. In many of the prospective studies, the participants were college students who lived together for one semester. This may not have been long enough for synchrony to become established. And even if the study had been undertaken for the entire academic year (about 8 months), it must be remembered that the academic year is interrupted by long vacations. Furthermore, another critical question regarding roommates is how many nights per week both women sleep in the same room. Only one study (L. Weller et al., 1995) has reported such information.

Three, the need to control for physical conditions must be taken into consideration. This may not be a major problem; most of the research has centered on women living in college dormitories, so that the physical conditions may have been similar. Yet dormitory housing is not identical, sometimes even within the same university. For example, in some dormitories, accommodations are centered around a common lounge, so that the women in this cluster are most likely to socialize among themselves.

Outside of dormitories it would be useful to examine the effects of different physical conditions of menstrual synchrony. No study has yet done this. This would be a most difficult undertaking, for many variables would have to be manipulated, such as the number of bedrooms, size of the bedrooms, distance between beds, whether the blankets are acrylic or cotton (to allow for possible pheromonal transmissions), whether bathrooms are shared, and of course, whether both women are together in the room a sufficiently long period of time.

It is noted that virtually all studies of dormitory roommates were of women who were young (about 19 years of age) and of women with similar if not identical ages. L. Weller and Weller (1995) raised the question whether menstrual synchrony would occur among women of diverse ages.

In the present study, we examined families who live under optimal conditions for menstrual synchrony to occur and meet the methodological requirements discussed above. The menstrual data of 27 Bedouin families were studied. They have all lived together in their houses for many years. In this society, the nuclear families (parents and children) live in separate houses and form a separate household but live close to their extended families. Bedouin norms preclude the possibility of men and women intermingling, because the purpose of an encounter between men and women is defined as sexual (Kressel, 1992). Premarital sexual behavior is strictly prohibited in their culture. If a girl is known not to be a virgin, she may never get married. Although there is some change among the younger generation, the society remains highly sexually segregated; that is, women form their own female network interacting almost totally among themselves. Even among preadolescents, boys and girls must avoid having contact with one another. In addition, women do not leave the village much. Women do not discuss worldly matters or anything remotely intimate with their brothers or fathers. No hugging or embracing occurs between brothers and sisters. We were told of one instance in which the brother embraced his sister—they had not seen one another for 10 years. Privacy in the Western sense does not exist. Women with the same social network know when each one has her menstrual period. Tampons are not used. Our interviewer was not allowed to sleep in a university dormitory while studying to be a nurse but was required to return home every day. The fact that her father agreed to let her travel to a university was in itself an exception. Thus, the physical and social conditions appear to be most relevant for critical examination of synchrony.

We examined whether menstrual synchrony occurs among sisters living in the same room, among sisters living in the same room and who are also close friends, and among all the women between 13 and 50 years of age in the family. The research hypothesis is that menstrual synchrony will be observed in these three groups.

This is the first time that menstrual synchrony in complete families with multiple daughters has been studied. Because the living unit for a dormitory woman is her room, researchers sought synchrony among women sharing the same room. However, among the Bedouins, the living unit seems not to be the bedroom but the house (Ben-David, 1988), and because of the intensive interactions among the women, one might well expect synchrony for the entire family. It is even possible that synchrony occurs within the family but not among the roommates, because the living unit is the house and not the bedroom. In addition, in this particular study, not only was there a wide variety of ages because of the mother–daughter comparisons (minimum difference = 18 years; maximum difference = 41 years; mean difference = 27.4 years), but there was also, in many families, a fairly wide age discrepancy among the sisters themselves (minimum difference = 2 years; maximum difference = 19 years; mean difference = 5.9 years).

Another objective of the study was to examine the impact of social interaction, joint activity, and menstrual-related factors on menstrual synchrony. A number of studies have examined whether women who engage in more joint activities would be more synchronous (Jarett, 1984; A. Weller & Weller, 1992, 1993, 1995a, 1995b; L. Weller & Weller, 1993b; L. Weller et al., 1995), because women who spend more time together would also be expected to be exposed to greater mutual pheromonal influences.

It has been suggested that women who are good friends would be more likely to synchronize than women who are not (Goldman & Schneider, 1987; Graham, 1991; McClintock, 1971; A. Weller & Weller, 1992, 1993, 1995a, 1995b; L. Weller & Weller, 1993a, 1993b, 1995; L. Weller et al., 1995). Two noncompeting explanations have been offered as to why friends show greater synchrony than nonfriends. One, research has shown that friendship is an indicator of time spent together, closeness, and exposure. Specifically, increased friendship is associated with closer personal space (defined as the area individuals maintain around themselves into which others cannot intrude without arousing discomfort), and there is a positive linear relationship between frequency of contact and strength of liking (Bell, Kline, & Barnard, 1998; Ebbesen, Kjos, & Konecni, 1976; Hayduk, 1983). Two, it has been suggested that friendship may induce physiological changes (Jarett, 1984). Emotional involvement may result in physiological changes in heart rate, blood pressure, galvanic skin response, and free fatty-acid levels. Emotional involvement between close friends may then lead to physiological changes which, in turn, could increase the participants' sensitivity to factors that alter the timing of their biological clocks.

A parallel field of research, emotional contagion, has also shown friendship to affect synchronization of a variety of behaviors and emotions. Emotional contagion (also referred to as synchronization of emotions) has been defined as "the tendency to catch" (experience or express) another person's subjective feelings, expressions, physiological processes, action tendencies, and instrumental behaviors (Hatfield, Cacioppo, & Rapson, 1992, p. 153). Thus, the hypothesis was that the participants' degree of mutual social interactions and of friendship would be positively correlated with their menstrual synchrony.

Method

Setting and Participants

A Bedouin registered nurse living in one of the Bedouin villages in northern Israel collected the data from 27 families, 21 families from her own village and 6 families from another village. The sample consisted of 8 families with two sisters older than 13 years of age, 12 families with three sisters, 2 families with four sisters, 2 families with five sisters, 2 families with six sisters, and 1 family with seven sisters. In 23 families the sisters slept in the same room, in 3 families the sisters slept in two bedrooms, and in 1 family the sisters slept in three bedrooms. The mean (*SD*) age of the daughters was 20.6 years (5.6), the mean (*SD*) age of the mothers was 46 (7.89) years.

The living arrangements were similar to those described in another Bedouin town (Jakubowska, 1988). The space allotted for the family's use within the house is standard. Parents have separate bedrooms from their children. For sleeping, children are grouped according to sex, with each sex occupying a separate room, called "the boys room" and "the girls room." The eldest son often has a separate room. Larger houses do not imply more privacy. Larger houses have larger rooms, especially the living room and more hallways, but there is no fundamental change in the housing structure. In the present study, there were 4 families in which there was more than one bedroom for the daughters. In the other 23 families, all the daughters slept in one room. All the daughters sleep on individual beds or on individual mattresses.

All the women in the 27 families participated in the study, in contrast to the <50% median participation rate in prospective studies of synchrony (L. Weller & Weller, 1993a). Five other families refused to participate in the study, either because of the intimacy of the requested information or apprehension that the information collected was to be used by the tax authorities.

The 8 perimenopausal women (50-year-old or older) were excluded from the study. All women younger than 50 years old were cycling menstrually. The number of women who used oral contraceptives was minimal (4 mothers and 1 daughter). One of these women was excluded because she was over 50. The other 4 women were not excluded.

The respondents were all sisters above age 13 and the mother in these families. Each of these women were asked to complete a questionnaire and to record the dates of their next three menstrual onsets on a calendar supplied to them. All of the women in all the families completed the questionnaires and the menstrual calendars. Three subgroups were studied: (a) sisters sharing the same room (*roommates–sisters*); (b) a participant and her roommate with whom she reported spending most of her time (*close friends–roommates*); and (c) all the women in the family 13–50 years old (*family*). This definition has been used in previous studies (e.g., Graham & McGrew, 1980; McClintock, 1971; Quadagno et al., 1981). *Close friends–roomates* expressed a greater degree of closeness and friendship than roommates who did not spend most of their time together ($p < .001$) on a friendship score that is described in the next section.

Instruments

The cover page of the questionnaire explained that the major purpose of the research was the determination of menstrual symptoms, an extension of research performed previously in the United States. Confidentiality was assured. The questionnaire, which consisted primarily of closed-ended questions, included demographic data, questions on friendship, activities, menstruation, and related issues. Questions on menstruation included age of menarche, dates of the last and next to last period, average duration of menstruation, usual length of time between periods, regularity of the period, type of sanitary method (tampon, sanitary napkins), and use of contraceptives. Also included was a 21-item menstrual symptom questionnaire (Chesney & Tasto, 1975), in which women were asked to indicate which symptoms they suffer from during their menstrual cycle (e.g., backache, cramps, fatigue).

The friendship questions were as follows: What is the quality of your relationship with your sister/mother? How close do you feel to her? and To what extent are you friends? For each question, the participant responded on 4- or 5-point scale, ranging from 1 = *poor/not close relationship* to 4 (or 5) = *a very good/very close relationship*. Additional friendship questions dealt with mutual candidness, support, understanding one another, holding same opinions, sharing personal problems, and concern with the other's appearance and behavior. The questions on joint activities were as follows: To what extent do you and she: eat together? learn in the same school? go together to school? study together? wear each other's clothes? watch television together? do house work together? have the same hobbies? spend most of your time together? speak together for long periods of time? and do most things together? For each question, the participant responded on a 4-point scale, ranging from 1 = *no shared activities* to 4 = *many shared activities*. Each respondent answered all these friendship and activity questions for each of her sisters and for her mother. The one exception was that in the mothers' questionnaire, the first three friendship questions were omitted because of their possible sensitivity: What is the quality of your relationship with your daughter? How close do you feel to her? and To what extent are you friends?

Chronbach's alpha coefficients of reliability (Nunnally, 1977), a measure of item internal consistency, for the 11 joint activity questions were .82, .86, and .88, and for the 9 friendship questions were .86, .88, and 90 for roommates–sisters, roommates who are best friends, and family, respectively. For each participant, a mean friendship score and a mean activity score were computed.

Data Analysis

We followed the recommendation of a recent methodological article on menstrual synchrony (L. Weller & Weller, in press) which recommended that, for women living together for a considerable amount of time, menstrual onsets should be compared for each of 3 months. If synchrony is found for 2 of these months, the phenomenon of menstrual synchrony can be regarded as being substantiated. The reason for this is that there is wide variation in cycle length both among women and within the same women as shown by three major longitudinal studies (Chiazze, Brayer, Macisco, Parker, & Duffy, 1968; Treloar et al., 1967; Vollman, 1977). The commonly observed interval between menstrual periods is approximately 24–32 days (Wentz, 1988, p. 378) or 24–35 days (Speroff, Glass, & Kase, 1994, p. 219), with less than one sixth averaging 28 days (Vollman, 1977). Consequently, even after living together for a period of time, the couples' synchrony could be affected by cycle variability.

Menstrual synchrony scores were calculated according to Wilson's (1992, pp. 571–572) guidelines. Accordingly, the first recorded onset date of Participant A is compared with the first and second recorded onset dates of Participant B, and then the first recorded onset date of Participant B is compared with the second recorded onset date of Participant A. The least of the three values is the correct absolute onset difference between the participants' initial onset dates. For example, if the onset dates of Participant A are June 1 and June 29 and the onset dates of Participant B are June 5 and July 6, then the correct absolute onset difference between the participants' initial onset dates is 4 days, the least of the three comparisons. However, if the onset dates of Participant A are June 12 and July 13 and the onset dates of Participant B are June 30 and July 29, then the correct onset absolute difference is 13 days (June 30–July 13).

Table 1
Menstrual Synchrony and Expected Scores (by Days)

Group/month	*N*	Synchrony score	Expected score	Difference	*SD*	*t*(1)	*p*
Roommates–sisters							
Month 1	30	6.32	7.76	1.44	3.40	2.27	.011
Month 2	30	6.24	7.76	1.52	3.08	2.66	.004
Month 3	29	7.40	7.76	0.36	3.08	0.57	.28
Close friends–roommates							
Month 1	39	5.73	7.75	2.02	3.84	3.25	<.000
Month 2	39	6.01	7.75	1.74	4.25	2.52	.006
Month 3	31	7.44	7.75	0.31	4.61	0.88	.19
Families							
Month 1	18	5.80	7.70	1.90	2.74	2.86	<.000
Month 2	18	6.09	7.70	1.61	1.89	3.52	<.000
Month 3	17	7.19	7.70	0.51	2.71	0.75	.23

To calculate synchrony scores for more than 2 women, we again followed Wilson's (1992) guidelines, whereby for each woman we computed her minimal absolute onset difference with every other woman. A woman's mean synchrony score was her mean difference score based on the difference between her onset date and the date of every other woman. The group synchrony score (e.g., three or more sisters in a room, all the sisters and their mother) was the mean of each woman's mean synchrony score.

When the unit of analysis was 2 women, the smallest absolute intracouple difference could range from 0 (both women have the same onset days) to 14 days, assuming both women have a 28-day cycle. For example, if one woman reported her onset days on July 1 and July 29, and the second woman on July 15, the absolute difference would be 14 days. Had the second woman reported her onset day on either July 12 or July 18, the absolute difference would be 11 days. With a mean cycle of 32 days, the range would be 0 to 16 days.

Cycle length was calculated by counting the number of days between two onsets. For each participant's three recorded menstrual onset dates, there are two cycle lengths. For each pair or group of women, we calculated the overall mean cycle length. The cutoff point of the mean cycle length (mean cycle length divided by 4) separates synchronous onsets from nonsynchronous onsets, because onset differences based on random onset occurrence would be expected to average at this cutoff point, as shown by a computer simulation (50,000 runs) based on randomly generated numbers ($N = 2–7$). Thus, for a couple or unit with a mean cycle of 28, 29, 30, 31, or 32 days, the cutoff point (and expected onset difference) would be 7, 7.25, 7.5, 7.75, and 8 days, respectively. Onset differences below these cutoff points indicate synchrony. Onset differences above these cutoff points indicate no synchrony (as in A. Weller & Weller, 1995a).

To determine whether menstrual synchrony exists, we compared each pair or unit synchrony score with its cutoff-point cycle score, by means of one-sample *t* tests. Thus, if the couple had an onset difference score of 6 days and both women had a 28-day cycle, for that couple we compared 6 (observed) with 7 (cutoff point indicating no synchrony) days. If the couple had a 4-day onset difference and one woman had a 30-day cycle and the other woman had a 32-day cycle, we compared 4 (observed) with 7.75 (cutoff point indicating no synchrony) days. This was done for each couple or unit. If no synchrony occurs, a difference score of 0 would be expected. For example, if 2 women had a 7-day onset difference and both had a 28-day cycle, then the difference between the 7 days observed and the 7 days expected would be 0.

Finally, we analyzed the impact of activity and degree of friendship by means of multiple regression analyses. The dependent variable was the synchrony score, and the independent variables were the mean friendship score and the mean activity score for each participant. Three multiple regressions were undertaken: for the roommates–sisters ($n = 29$); for the close friends–roommates ($n = 42$); and for the family ($n = 27$). For the roommate–sister sample, the friendship and activity scores represented the mean of the participant's reports regarding her friendship and activities with each of her sisters–roommates. For the family sample, the friendship and activity scores were the mean of the participant's reports regarding each of her sisters and her mother.

To assess the impact of menstrual factors on synchrony, we conducted another multiple regression analysis. The dependent variable was the synchrony score of the participant, and the independent variables were the participant's age, age of menarche, reported cycle regularity, flow duration, type of sanitary method, and length of time between periods.

For each analysis as well as for the individual analysis of the menstrual factors, the multiple regressions were calculated for each month separately; that is, three multiple regressions for each analysis.

Results

Table 1 shows the mean synchrony score and the expected synchrony score for each of the 3 months according to the three analyses: roommates–sisters, close friends–roommates, and families. Evidence for synchrony was found for all three groups; that is, for each analysis, synchrony was found for 2 out of the 3 months with high levels of statistical confidence ranging from $p = .01$ to $p < .0001$.

We next examined whether the above findings might be explained, in part, by the interaction between the mother and her daughters. To this end, for each family we computed the onset differences between the mother and each of her daughters (but not between the daughters themselves) and compared these synchrony scores with their cycle midpoints (as in the previous analyses). No significant difference was obtained.

To determine how much synchrony exists for those months in which synchrony was found, we adopted a formula used in a previous review (L. Weller & Weller, 1993a). Each synchrony score was subtracted from the expected onset difference (the cutoff point of the mean cycle length, as explained in the Method section). As shown in Table 1, for the roommates–sisters the mean difference for the last 2 months was 1.44 and 1.52, respectively. When divided by their expected cycle score (7.76), the shift toward synchrony for this group is 19% and 20%, respectively. For close friends–roommates, the mean of the months with significant synchrony is 2.02 and 1.74, respectively. When divided by the expected cycle score (7.75), the shift toward synchrony for this group is 26% and 22%, respectively. For the families, the significant means were 1.90 and 1.61. When divided by their expected cycle score, the shift toward synchrony for this group is 25% and 21%, respectively. Overall, we found a 20%–25% trend toward synchrony in the months for which a significant degree of synchrony is found.

To examine the effects of activities and friendship on degree of synchrony, we performed multiple regressions for each month separately. In each of the multiple regressions, the dependent variable was degree of synchrony and the independent variables were the degree of activity (based on the 11 activity questions discussed in the Method section) and the degree of friendship (based on the 9 friendship questions discussed in the Method section). As shown in Table 2, all the multiple regressions produced nonsignificant R^2s (ranging from $R^2 = .01$ to $R^2 = .23$; *p*s from .11 to .90). We conclude therefore that within each group examined, neither degree of mutual activity nor degree of friendship affects menstrual synchrony. In addition, the menstrual-related variables did not affect synchrony. For the sister–roommates, the R^2s were .27 ($p = .13$), .31 ($p = .07$), and .20 ($p = .31$). For the roommates–friends, the R^2s were .25 ($p = .37$), .19 ($p = .61$), and .13 ($p = .80$).

Table 2
Influence of Mutual Activity and Friendship on Degree of Menstrual Synchrony

	Roommates–sisters		Close friends–roommates		Families	
Month	R^2	*p*	R^2	*p*	R^2	*p*
1st	.01	.90	.05	.37	.17	.22
2nd	.04	.58	.11	.11	.23	.15
3rd	.03	.67	.04	.46	.18	.23

Note. Mutual activity is based on 11 activity questions; friendship is based on 9 friendship questions.

Discussion

This study demonstrates the existence of menstrual synchrony among Bedouin roommates–sisters, among roommates–sisters who are close friends, and among all women 13–50 years old in the family. Although the magnitude of the effect was only moderate, we believe this is the definitive study of menstrual synchrony. This is because the unique sample, Bedouin women, enabled us to examine synchrony under the optimal conditions of women who have not only lived together for a prolonged period of time (starting much before the daughters' menarche) but also whose daily living consists of intensive contact with one another, where most of their daily living is confined within the village, and whose physical housing conditions are similar. Furthermore, this particular sample obviated two additional methodological problems that have beset many of the previous studies: Only a few women used oral contraceptives (which determine the onset of the period), and it is extremely unlikely that any of them engaged in premarital sex.

Previous studies have shown that frequency of sexual behavior affects the length of the women's cycle (Cutler et al., 1985; Veith et al., 1983). Thus, if one woman has frequent sex and her roommate has infrequent sex, their cycle lengths may be differentially affected, and this could be a confounding factor in the establishment of synchrony. It is indeed possible that differential sexual behavior by each of the women and inclusion of women who use oral contraceptives may be responsible for some of the negative findings reported in the literature on menstrual synchrony.

Had the study only determined synchrony based on 1 month's onsets, then the conclusion would have depended on whether the data were collected during the first or second month (where synchrony was demonstrated) or during the third month (where the trend toward synchrony was not significant). We see no particular relevance in that synchrony was not found for the third month. We do see relevance in the fact that synchrony was not evident in *one* of these months. This validates our recent suggestion (L. Weller & Weller, in press) that because of the inherent variability of women's cycle length, studies of menstrual synchrony should separately analyze their data for at least two if not three menstrual onsets. The variable pattern of our results is in accordance with the variable pattern of estrous synchrony in the rat, where it is "common to find 50–75% of the group synchronized, with fluctuations over time" (McClintock, 1983, p. 196).

The present findings also reveal synchrony among roommates–sisters who are close friends. This is in accordance with most other studies in the literature in which close friendship is typically associated with synchrony (L. Weller & Weller, 1993a), often even when the total sample is not synchronous (e.g., Goldman & Schneider, 1987; A. Weller & Weller, 1995b; L. Weller et al., 1995).

In the present study, the amount of shift toward synchrony (when synchrony occurred) among the roommates who are close friends is higher (24%) than among all roommates (about 20%), a difference of about 4% or an increase of about 20% over the roommates–sisters. Because the two groups were not independent samples but one consisted of an overlapping subset of the other, statistical tests could not be applied. However, this absolute difference of 4% seems to be in accordance with previous studies, some which showed larger differences in synchrony between roommates and roommates who are close friends (Goldman & Schneider, 1987; L. Weller et al., 1995) whereas others reported nonsignificant differences between these two groups (McClintock, 1971; L. Weller & Weller, 1993b).

The 20% shift toward synchrony among roommates is lower than the mean 33% shift estimated (L. Weller & Weller, 1993a, p. 437) for studies in which synchrony was found. However, this 33% assessment does not consider the number of studies that failed to find synchrony. Overall, it would seem that the degree of synchrony found in the present sample is within the range of that found in other studies. This suggests that the factors for which the study controlled may not be so important as we had thought. However, it is still unclear why a larger magnitude of effect was not found under this study's carefully controlled conditions.

Most studies have examined synchrony among two women who shared their room with each other. Other than her roommate, each woman may not have many intensive contacts with other women, causing the roommate to be the major source for most of the putative pheromonal interchange. In contrast, the Bedouin woman has intensive contact with all the other women in her family and with a number of other women in the village, subjecting her to more competing pheromonal influences than the woman living in a dormitory. In addition, the regular (eccrine gland) sweating during the hot summer months (when the study was undertaken) may have diluted the pheromonal signal from the axillary secretions that have been suggested to be the source of the pheromones (Preti, 1987; Russell, Switz, & Thompson, 1980).

This is the first study that examined menstrual synchrony of the entire family (mother with two or more daughters), and again we found the existence of synchrony. On one hand, because of the intensity of family living and the high sexual segregation in Bedouin societies (Kressel, 1992), this is expected. On the other hand, most of the studies of synchrony have been conducted on college women, that is, women whose mean age is about 19 and who are of similar ages. It is by no means certain that women of diverse ages would synchronize. Moreover, if they do synchronize, it may be the result of the mother's greater influence on her daughter. A separate analysis was undertaken in which for each family synchrony between the mother and each of her daughters was computed, omitting the synchrony among the sisters themselves. These results were not significant. Thus, we conclude that the mother has an equal share in the occurrence of synchrony and that family synchrony is not a result of the particular mother–daughter interaction, at least in the present sample. We note that one study (A. Weller & Weller, 1993) reported synchrony among mothers and daughters residing in the city, but that sample focused on a daughter–mother dyad living at home (other sisters living at home were not studied). Another research (L. Weller & Weller, 1993b) reported no synchrony between a mother–daughter dyad in the kibbutz, but synchrony was not expected as the daughters studied were not living at home but in the kibbutz dormitories with their age-mates.

A number of studies have attempted to distinguish between feelings of friendship and activities spent together (e.g., A. Weller & Weller, 1992, 1993), although the emotional and physical aspects of friendship are highly interdependent, as discussed above. In general, the participant is asked to rate the degree of closeness felt toward a roommate and to what extent she participates with this roommate in a number of specific activities. In the present research, in consultations with the Bedouin nurse who lived in the village, we included additional activities. This resulted in a comprehensive list of 11 activities, more inclusive than in previous studies. Similarly, most previous research limited the measurement of friendship to three questions (quality of relationship, closeness, and extent of friendship). In this research, again in consultation with the nurse, we added six questions (e.g., mutual candidness). Our measurement of friendship is therefore quite comprehensive. The high degree of item consistency shows that the two measurements are quite reliable. We have thus been able to examine the influence of both emotional closeness (friendship) and shared activities on synchronization. Although no study, including this one, has documented details on physical closeness between the women studied, the present study has largely controlled for this factor. The structure of the housing arrangements in the Bedouin homes is similar: usually only one bedroom for the daughters, no matter how many women; only one bedroom for the sons to sleep in (although the eldest son may have a bedroom to himself); a bedroom for the parents; and a living room. Thus, although the bedrooms and living room may vary by size, this study examined a sample living in standardized, controlled physical conditions.

Significant associations among degree of activity, degree of friendship, menstrual-related factors, and synchrony were not found. This is consistent with some of the previous reports. A review of the menstrual synchrony literature (L. Weller & Weller, 1993a) reported inconsistent findings with regard to the results of multiple regressions examining the effects of activity, friendship, and menstrual-related factors on synchrony. Sometimes the independent variables explained a high degree of variance in menstrual synchrony (e.g., 72%; A. Weller & Weller, 1992) and sometimes very little or none at all (e.g., 4%; A. Weller & Weller, 1993). It is possible that the close, intensive, and prolonged relationships within the Bedouin families together with the synchrony among the families, roommates–sisters, and close friends–roommates may have resulted in restricting the range (and predictability) of variables such as degree of friendship. Ethological or anthropological observations of the relationships between the women might be preferable than relying on the participants' reports of their friendship and joint activities.

Explanations for the evolution of reproductive synchrony in animals include reduced risk of predation (Low, 1976); social improvement of foraging efficiency of adults while feeding young (Emlen & Demong, 1975), or communal rearing (Bertram, 1975). Communal rearing is the only explanation that could be conceivably applicable to humans (Kiltie, 1982).

A number of hypotheses have been offered for the function of human menstrual synchrony. For example, one suggestion is that it heightens the probability of conception of polygynous families, for if the woman cycled out of synchrony the male would be "inundated with contradictory information" (Burley, 1979, p. 853). Another suggestion is that in the past, when women needed food to be supplied by men, it was to the women's advantage to bring as many men into the breeding community as possible. Menstrual synchrony served the women by preventing men from impregnating several women in turn (Turke, 1984). Knight (1991) suggested the hypothesis that at a later stage in human development it became advantageous for women to encourage men to leave them and hunt for meat. This would have been an unproductive strategy if one woman would discourage a man whereas another woman encouraged him, hence, the development of menstrual synchrony—a collective signaling of "yes" or "no" to men. It has also been suggested that menstrual synchrony may not have an adaptive significance but may be a side effect of some other adaptation (Kiltie, 1982; McClintock, 1981).

All these explanations focus on polygynous families, one-husband with two or more wives, or with a cohort of women. They do not address family synchrony, namely, among daughters and among mothers and daughters. Our data suggest that the adaptive mechanism that presumably produced synchrony among co-wives may not have been able to discriminate among all the women in the family. It thus may have included the daughters as well, even though this was without a reproductive advantage.

Human menstrual synchrony can serve as an important example of sociopsychological factors affecting the timing of neuroendocrinological events. This is in accordance with similar phenomena such as estrous synchrony, better characterized in other animals (McClintock, 1983; Wallis, 1985). Furthermore, human menstrual synchrony can be viewed as one instance of a more general phenomenon: biological synchronization of coupled oscillators (Schank & McClintock, 1992; Strogatz & Stewart, 1993). As such, the phenomenon provides another unifying theme with biological processes in other animals and at other levels of biological analysis: synchrony of timing between interacting agents.

References

Asso, D. (1983). *The real menstrual cycle*. London: Wiley.

Bell, P. A., Kline, L. M., & Barnard, W. A. (1988). Friendship and freedom of movement as moderators of sex differences in interpersonal distancing. *Journal of Social Psychology, 128*, 305–310.

Ben-David, Y. (1988). The process of adjustment to a new Bedouin town. In Y. Aini & E. Orion (Eds.), *The Bedouins* (pp. 343–356). Beer-Sheva, Israel: Beer-Sheva University Press. (in Hebrew)

Bertram, B. C. R. (1975). Social factors influencing reproduction in wild lions. *Journal of Zoology, 177*(London), 463–482.

Burleson, M. H., Gregory, W. L., & Trevathan, W. A. (1995). Heterosexual activity: Relationship with ovarian function. *Psychoneuroendocrinology, 20*, 405–421.

Burley, N. (1979). The evolution of concealed ovulation. *American Naturalist, 114*, 835–858.

Chesney, M. A., & Tasto, D. L. (1975). The development of a menstrual symptom questionnaire. *Behavioral Research and Therapy, 13*, 237–244.

Chiazze, L., Jr., Brayer, F. T., Macisco, J. J., Jr., Parker, M. P., & Duffy, B. J. (1968). The length and variability of the menstrual cycle. *Journal of the American Medical Association, 203*, 89–92.

Cutler, W. B., Garcia, C. R., & Kreiger, A. M. (1979). Sexual behavior frequency and menstrual cycle length in mature premenopausal women. *Psychoneuroendocrinology, 4*, 297–309.

Cutler, W. B., Preti, G., Huggins, G. R., Erickson, B., & Garcia, C. R. (1985). Sexual behavior frequency and ovulatory biphasic menstrual cycle patterns. *Physiology and Behavior, 34*, 805–810.

Doty, R. L., & Silverthorne, C. (1975). Influence of menstrual cycle on volunteering behaviour. *Nature, 254*, 139–140.

Ebbesen, E. B., Kjos, G. L., & Konecni, V. J. (1976). Spatial ecology: Its effects on the choice of friends and enemies. *Journal of Experimental Social Psychology, 12*, 505–518.

Emlen, S. T., & Demong, N. J. (1975, June 6). Adaptive significance of synchronized breeding in a colonial bird: A new hypothesis. *Science, 188*, 1029–1031.

Forrest, J. D., & Fordyce, R. R. (1993). Women's contraceptive attitudes and use in 1992. *Family Planning Perspectives, 24*, 175–179.

Goldman, S. E., & Schneider, H. G. (1987). Menstrual synchrony: Social and personality factors. *Journal of Social Behavior and Personality, 2*, 243–250.

Graham, C. A. (1991). Menstrual synchrony: An update and review. *Human Nature, 2*, 293–311.

Graham, C. A., & McGrew, W. C. (1980). Menstrual synchrony in female under-graduates living on a coeducational campus. *Psychoneuroendocrinology, 2*, 45–252.

Handelmann, G., Ravizza, R., & Ray, W. J. (1980). Social dominance determines estrous entrainment among female hamsters. *Hormones and Behavior, 14*, 107–115.

Hatfield, E., Cacioppo, J. T., & Rapson, R. L. (1992). Primitive emotional contagion. In M. S. Clark (Ed.), *Review of personality and social psychology* (Vol. 14, pp. 151–177). London: Sage.

Hayduk, L. A. (1983). Personal space: Where we stand. *Psychological Bulletin, 94*, 293–335.

Jarett, L. R. (1984). Psychological and biological influences on menstruation: Synchrony, cycle length, and regularity. *Psychoneuroendocrinology, 9*, 21–28.

Jakubowska, L. A. (1988). The Bedouin family in Rahat: Perspectives on social changes. In Y. Aini & E. Orion (Eds.), *The Bedouins* (pp. 139–156). Beer-Sheva, Israel: Beer-Sheva University Press.

Jung, J. (1971). *The experimenter's dilemma*. New York: Harper & Row.

Kiltie, R. A. (1982). On the significance of menstrual synchrony in closely associated women. *American Naturalist, 119*, 414–419.

Knight, C. (1991). *Blood relations: Menstruation and the origin of culture*. New Haven, CT: Yale University Press.

Kressel, G. M. (1992). Shame and gender. *Anthropological Quarterly, 65*, 34–46.

Low, B. S. (1976). The evolution of amphibian life histories in the desert. In D. W. Goodall (Ed.), *Evolution of desert biota* (pp. 149–196). Austin: University of Texas Press.

Matteo, S. (1987). The effect of job stress and job interdependency on menstrual cycle length, regularity and synchrony. *Psychoneuroendocrinology, 12*, 467–476.

McClintock, M. K. (1971). Menstrual synchrony and suppression. *Nature, 229*, 244–245.

McClintock, M. K. (1978). Estrous synchrony in the rat and its mediation by airborne chemical communication (*Rattus norvegicus*). *Hormones and Behavior, 10*, 264–276.

McClintock, M. K. (1981). Social control of the ovarian cycle and the function of estrous synchrony. *American Zoologist, 21*, 243–256.

McClintock, M. K. (1983). Pheromonal regulation of the ovarian cycle: Enhancement, suppression, and synchrony. In J. G. Vandenberg (Ed.), *Pheromones and reproduction in mammals* (pp. 113–149). New York: Academic Press.

McFarland, C., Ross, M., & DeCourville, N. (1989). Women's theories of menstruation and biases in recall of menstrual symptoms. *Journal of Personality and Social Psychology, 57*, 522–531.

Medugorac, I., & Lindauer, M. (1967). Das Zeigedachtuis der Bienen unter dem Einfluss von Narkose und von sozialen Zeitgebern [The behavior of bees and the influence of narcosis and of social zeitgebers]. *Zeitschrist fuer Vergleichende Physiologie, 55*, 450–474.

Nisbett, R. E., & Wilson, T. D. (1977). Telling more than we can know: Verbal reports on mental processes. *Psychological Review, 84*, 231–259.

Nunnally, J. (1977). *Psychometric theory*. New York: McGraw Hill.

Preston, F. S., Bateman, S. C., Short, R. V., & Wilkinson, R. T. (1974). The effects of flying and of time changes on menstrual cycle length and on performance in airline stewardesses. In M. Ferin, F. Halberg, R. M. Richart, & R. L. VandeWiele (Eds.), *Biorhythms and human reproduction* (pp. 501–512). New York: Wiley.

Preti, G. (1987). Reply to Wilson. *Hormones and Behavior, 21,* 547–550.

Quadagno, D. M., Shubeita, H. E., Deck, J., & Francoeur, D. (1981). Influence of male social contacts, exercise and all-female living conditions on the menstrual cycle. *Psychoneuroendocrinology, 3,* 239–244.

Rohles, F. H. (1971). Social entrainment of the feeding behavior in monkeys. *Folia Primatologica, 15,* 58–64.

Russell, M. J., Switz, G. M., & Thompson, K. (1980). Olfactory influences on the human menstrual cycle. *Pharmacology, Biochemistry and Behavior, 13,* 737–738.

Schank, J. C., & McClintock, M. K. (1992). A coupled-oscillator model of ovarian-cycle synchrony among female rats. *Journal of Theoretical Biology, 13,* 737–738.

Sommer, B. (1978). Stress and menstrual distress. *Journal of Human Stress, 4*(3), 5–10, 41–47.

Speroff, L., Glass, R. H., & Kase, G. (1994). *Clinical gynecologic endocrinology and infertility* (5th ed.). Baltimore: Williams & Wilkins.

Strogatz, S., & Stewart, I. (1993). Coupled oscillators and biological synchronization. *Scientific American, 269,* 68–75.

Treloar, A. E., Boynton, R. E., Borghild, G. B., & Brown, B. W. (1967). Variations in the human menstrual cycle through reproductive life. *International Journal of Fertility, 12,* 77–126.

Trevathan, W. R., Burleson, M. H., & Gregory, W. L. (1993). No evidence for menstrual synchrony in lesbian couples. *Psychoneuroendocrinology, 18,* 425–435.

Turke, P. W. (1984). Effects of ovulatory concealment and synchrony on protohominid mating systems and parental roles. *Ethology and Sociobiology, 5,* 33–44.

Veith, J. L., Buck, M., Getzlaf, S., Van Dalfsen, P., & Slade, S. (1983). Exposure to men influences the occurrence of ovulation in women. *Physiology and Behavior, 31,* 313–315.

Vollman, R. F. (1977). The menstrual cycle. In E. Friedman (Ed.), *Major problems in obstetrics and gynecology* (pp. 56–101). Philadelphia: Saunders.

Wallis, J. (1985). Synchrony of estrous swelling in captive group-living chimpanzees (*Pantroglodytes*). *International Journal of Primatology, 6,* 335–350.

Weller, A., & Weller, L. (1992). Menstrual synchrony in female couples. *Psychoneuroendocrinology, 17,* 171–177.

Weller, A., & Weller, L. (1993). Menstrual synchrony between mothers and daughters and between roommates. *Physiology and Behavior, 53,* 173–179.

Weller, A., & Weller, L. (1995a). Examination of menstrual synchrony among women basketball players. *Psychoneuroendocrinology, 20,* 613–622.

Weller, A., & Weller, L. (1995b). The impact of social interaction factors on menstrual synchrony in the workplace. *Psychoneuroendocrinology, 20,* 21–31.

Weller, L., & Weller, A. (1993a). Human menstrual synchrony: A critical assessment. *Neuroscience and Biobehavior Reviews, 17,* 427–439.

Weller, L., & Weller, A. (1993b). Multiple influences of menstrual synchrony: Kibbutz roommates, their best friends, and their mothers. *American Journal of Human Biology, 5,* 173–179.

Weller, L., & Weller, A. (1995). Menstrual synchrony: Agenda for future research. *Psychoneuroendocrinology, 20,* 377–384.

Weller, L., & Weller, A. (in press). Menstrual variability and the measurement of menstrual synchrony. *Psychoneuroendocrinology.*

Weller, L., Weller, A., & Avinir, O. (1995). Menstrual synchrony: Only in roommates who are close friends? *Physiology and Behavior, 58,* 883–889.

Wentz, A. C. (1988). Abnormal uterine bleeding. In H. W. Jones, A. C. Wentz, & L. S. Burnett (Eds.), *Novak's textbook of gynecology* (11th ed., pp. 378–393). Baltimore: Williams & Wilkins.

Wilson, H. C. (1992). A critical review of menstrual synchrony. *Psychoneuroendocrinology, 17,* 565–591.

Wilson, H. C., Kiefphaber, S. H., & Gravel, V. (1991). Two studies of menstrual synchrony: Negative results. *Psychoneuroendocrinology, 16,* 353–359.

Received January 26, 1996
Revision received September 24, 1996
Accepted September 25, 1996

Sleep and Biological Rhythms

One-third of our lives is spent sleeping, assuming we sleep an average of 8 hours a day. Is sleep really necessary? We know that practically all animals experience it. What, then, is the function of sleep?

Observe your pet cat for a day. Domestic cats spend about 15 hours napping. Are they really so busy during their waking moments that they need to rest that much? Feline species in the wild sleep for long hours in order to conserve the energy they need for catching prey. Your pet cat has probably kept this ancient evolutionary trait. Other animals go to the extreme of hibernation, characterized by a temporary suspension of most physiological processes when the food supply is low.

Do humans need sleep for the same purpose of conserving energy? Or do humans sleep for the purpose of rejuvenation after a hard day's work? A number of studies have given us answers that are not straightforward.

Sleep reduction studies reveal that the 8-hour sleep regimen may be more than necessary. Subjects asked to progressively decrease their sleeping hours achieved an optimum length of sleep of about 5 hours only. This was the duration of sleep sufficient to function effectively during the day. The subjects in these studies became efficient in their sleeping patterns, that is, spending less time tossing and turning in bed before going to sleep, and reaching deep sleep much more quickly. Certainly adjusting our sleeping habits can save a significant number of waking hours, but the optimum amount of sleep varies among individuals.

Can humans manage without sleep at all? Sleep deprivation studies reveal that lack of sleep does not significantly affect cognitive functioning. A college student went without sleep for 10 days and performed well on cognitive tests. His behavior was not significantly affected either. His performance on boring and monotonous tasks, however, declined. It seems that sleep deprivation simply causes the subjective experience of sleepiness.

Sleep could be the time when the brain is processing information it has acquired during the waking hours. Babies sleep much longer than adults because the sudden exposure to a host of novel stimuli during development requires a good amount of time to process. Babies who do not exhibit the normal pattern of sleep tend to develop some cognitive deficiencies. Anecdotes from adults also support the processing theory of sleep. Some report finding solutions to their problems by the time they wake up.

The cycle of sleep and wakefulness is an example of a circadian rhythm, a biological rhythm that occurs every 24 hours. Cues from the environment, called zeitgebers, can set the occurrence of circadian rhythms. For example, we can cue in to the availability of light or temperature changes during the day to set our sleep and waking pattern.

Since circadian rhythm operates on a temporal frame, a biological clock is believed to exist in the body to maintain the rhythm. The biological clock is believed to be a structure in the hypothalamus called the suprachiasmatic nucleus. Neurons in this brain area receive visual information from the receptor cells of the retina. The connection between the eye and the brain explains how light can control the sleep/wake cycle.

Some human behaviors that we see today were handed to us through the course of evolution. Some of these behaviors appear irrelevant or require modification to suit the contingencies of modern times. In the past, our ancestors probably needed sleep to save energy for hunting food or as a mechanism of safety during the night. With the advent of modern technology, human lifestyles and working conditions have changed. Can we adapt our biological rhythms to these changes without any adverse consequences? The question is difficult to answer, but it is worthwhile to consider that evolutionary changes in

UNIT 7

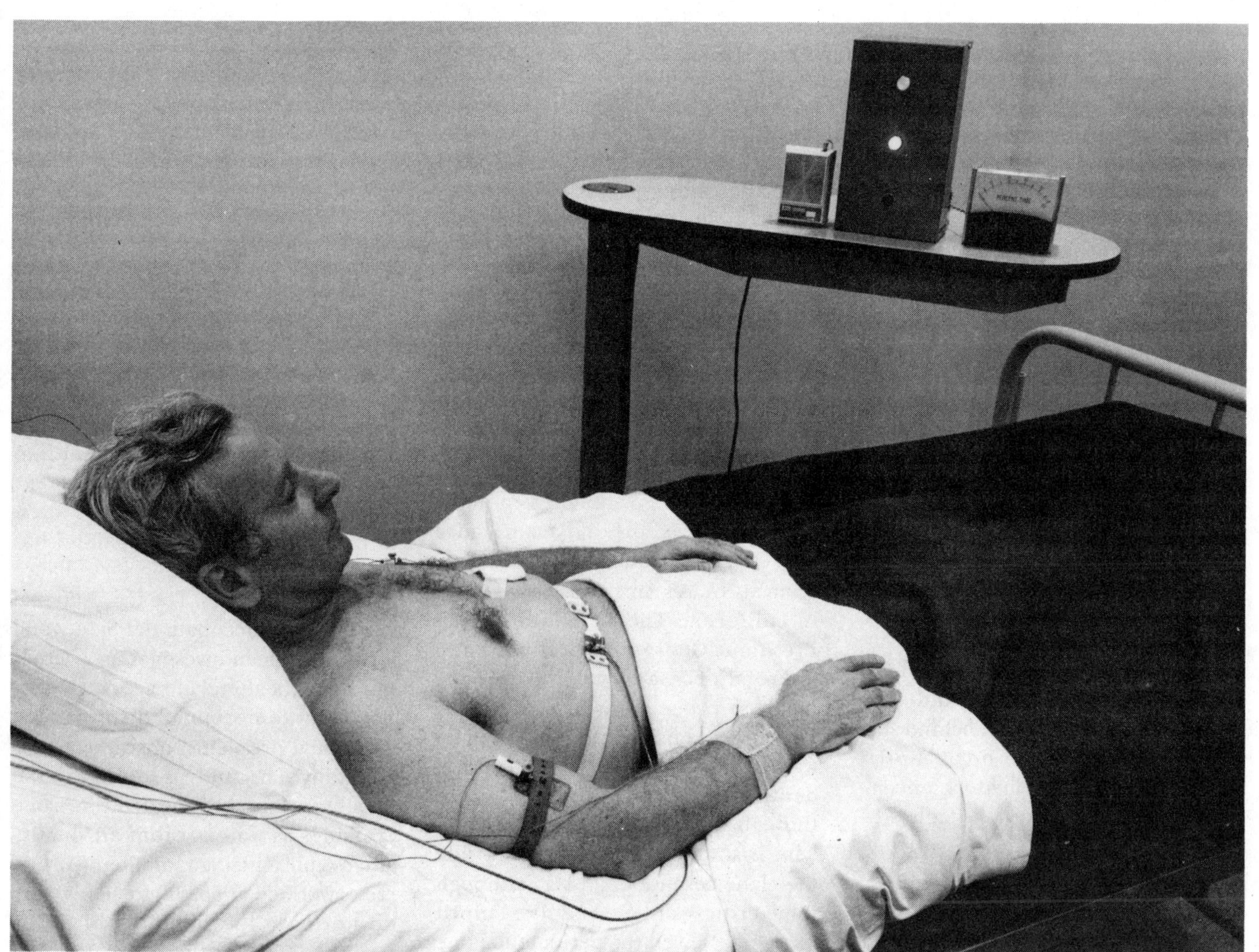

biological systems tend to be slow in catching up with abrupt and dramatic changes in the environment.

Looking Ahead: Challenge Questions

Cite examples of circadian biological rhythms. What is a biological clock and where is it located? Describe how the biological clock works at the molecular level. What is the role of melatonin in sleep? Can we modify our sleep patterns by using this substance? Under what circumstances would you consider taking a melatonin pill?

Why do we feel sleepy after prolonged wakefulness? Discuss the possible neurochemical event that induces such an experience.

'Traveling light' has new meaning for jet laggards

From light therapy to melatonin, research into our bodies' daily rhythms has led to promising treatments for weary travelers

By Edwin Kiester jr.

It was 6 P.M. in Helsinki, with stars shining brightly outside the restaurant. Unfortunately, my body insisted it was 8 o'clock in the morning and skies should be sunny. From San Francisco, we had flown for 17 hours, with three plane changes. Now we were sitting down to a hearty, traditional Finnish dinner even though my insides were proclaiming, "Time for breakfast!" Those weren't bacon and eggs in front of me, but a steaming plate of reindeer stew accompanied by a large mug of beer.

My wife and our host, her colleague from the Helsinki University of Technology, began an earnest conversation about engineering education. I listened and ate dutifully, but the dinner plate seemed to be dimming before my eyes. My lids drooped. My head slumped. My wife coughed and shot me alarming glances from behind her napkin. I straightened up abruptly. Then, little by little, my fork uncontrollably dropped toward the table. My head followed. Eyes closed, snoring gently, I came softly to rest in the plate of stew—another victim of the traveler's malady known as jet lag.

More than 425 million persons will fly internationally in 1997, and it's a safe bet that of these, a fair number of transoceanic and transcontinental travelers will suffer from the disorientation of hearing Big Ben strike noon when the body screams that it is 4 A.M. Indeed, one estimate says that more than 90 percent of long-distance travelers are stricken with jet lag, including "mega-laggers" who log so many frequent-flier miles that their bodies never get into sync with their wristwatches. The traveler's refrain, said while covering a yawn with a rueful smile, goes, "Excuse me. I'm still on Hong Kong time."

Jet lag is not always a laughing matter, though, nor is it limited to those of us jammed together in tourist class.

"How many bad decisions are made by jet-lagged businessmen who fly 12 hours and then go straight to a meeting?" asks Mark Rosekind, team leader of the Fatigue Countermeasures Program at NASA's Ames Research Center in California. The incident in which President George Bush fainted at a Tokyo dinner and vomited on the Japanese prime minister was initially blamed on Halcion, a sleeping pill he was taking for jet leg. Russian president Boris Yeltsin claimed he slept through an airport stop in Ireland and kept Irish dignitaries waiting outside the plane because of jet lag (although some critics contend that the culprit was vodka). Even the peripatetic Pope John Paul II is said to have been afflicted by jet lag.

Jet lag is a particular worry for the airlines, NASA and the military. In the post-Cold War world, rapid response forces may suddenly be called upon to fly halfway around the globe and then be thrown immediately into action. "It obviously wouldn't do for infantrymen to go on duty half asleep," says physiologist John French of the Air Force Sustained Operations Branch at Brooks Air Force Base in Texas. French has been directing a study of troops deployed to the Middle East, seeking ways to help them acclimate quickly to their new time zones.

The possible long-term health consequences to airline personnel repeatedly backing and forthing across multiple time zones have been a concern since the first jet transports went into service in the 1950s. Since almost any flight from New Zealand crosses several time zones, Air New Zealand has been conducting ongoing surveillance of its crew members. The U.S. National Institute for Occupational Safety and Health has been investigating whether female flight attendants are particularly subject to hormonal disturbances, menstrual problems, miscarriages or infertility. The study is looking at the possible effects of repeated time-zone crossings as well as cabin air quality and cosmic ionizing radiation. (Airline crews working at 35,000 to 40,000 feet do not have the shielding of six or seven miles of air that people on the ground have.)

A survey conducted by British Airways compared death rates of 446 retired pilots, most of them long-haul fliers, with others of their age group. The pilots had fewer heart attacks than their contemporaries but were more likely to die of brain tumors and

From *Smithsonian,* April 1997, pp. 110-119. © 1997 by Edwin Kiester, Jr. Reprinted by permission.

melanoma, a virulent form of skin cancer. "The increase in melanoma could simply be caused by increased exposure to the sun," says Ronald A. Pearson of the British Civil Aviation Authority, which is sponsoring an expanded version of the study. Still, he adds, "there was some suggestion that the higher incidence of melanoma and other cancers might be related to disturbances of the pineal [gland]"—the tiny light-sensitive gland in the brain that plays a central role in regulating the body's clock.

It is 9 P.M. and raining in London. On the stage of the Royal National Theater, Vanessa Redgrave and Paul Scofield are shouting at each other in an Ibsen play. Their angry voices may be one reason why I remain wide awake in a hot theater after 12 hours of flying across eight time zones. Another reason may be that before departure, determined to fight off the demons of jet lag, I placed myself in the hands of Dr. Al Lewy, professor of psychiatry at the Oregon Health Sciences University in Portland. Guided by more than a decade of jet-lag research, Dr. Lewy had carefully charted a program for me to follow, coming and going. "I won't say we can completely eliminate jet lag," Dr. Lewy had told me cautiously. "But we may be able to reduce its duration by half."

While at the National Institutes of Health in the late 1970s, Lewy and his colleagues made a landmark discovery concerning how the daily cycle of sunup and sundown influences our bodies and our behavior. They found that intense light—like sunlight—can turn off the production of melatonin, a hormone that regulates our daily rhythms, including the sleep-wake cycle. Later, Lewy discovered that light can be used to treat Seasonal Affective Disorder, or SAD, a form of depression brought on by the shorter days of winter (SMITHSONIAN, June 1985).

It is now firmly established that darkness and daylight help synchronize many body functions into clockwork tempos, known as circadian ("about a day") rhythms. The sleep-wake cycle is only the most obvious of these biological rhythms. Body temperature, hormone secretion and digestive functions also follow a daily schedule. For instance, body temperature reaches its peak at 5 P.M. and falls to its low for the day about 12 hours later, between 3 and 5 o'clock in the morning. And performance tests have shown that humans are their least competent just before dawn.

The human pacemaker, Lewy explains, is located in the suprachiasmatic nucleus, or SCN, two tiny bundles of neurons in the hypothalamus portion of the brain. Light falling on the retina of the eye travels directly to the SCN, which keeps time for many of our biological rhythms. The SCN sends a signal to the pineal gland, which produces melatonin, a hormone that is released only with the advent of darkness and that stops flowing with the first rosy fingers of dawn.

Best-selling books have made melatonin, which is available without a prescription, the miracle-drug-of-the-month. Extravagant claims have been made for its antiaging, sex-enhancing, disease-fighting powers, but Lewy and other specialists in pineal research are skeptical. They believe melatonin is simply the body's darkness signal. Its secretion tells the body's internal systems that night has come and it's time to curtail operations (or, for some systems—like the release of human growth hormone—that it's time to kick into gear). A drop in melatonin tells the body that morning is here.

"When you fly across multiple time zones, you knock all these light-influenced rhythms out of kilter," Lewy says, noting that shift workers suffer a similar topsy-turvy problem. "The body has to struggle to adapt to the new schedule, but it can't make that adjustment overnight. If travelers could be patient, they would gradually adapt, but as a rule of thumb it takes one day of adjustment for every time zone crossed." No one traveling from San Francisco to Paris, Lewy points out, wants to patiently wait out nine days of a two-week vacation in order to adjust to local time.

That's the textbook explanation for jet lag. On both the theoretical and practical sides, certain other basic facts have emerged. Jet lag more commonly strikes on eastbound flights than on the westbound leg, perhaps because eastbound flights shorten the day while westbound trips lengthen it, and it's often easier to stay up late than to go to sleep before we're ready. Symptoms are worse on the second day after a trip than the first. Experiments have suggested that women, extroverts and night owls have less jet lag than their counterparts, while older people have more than younger folks. And jet lag is clearly highly individual and subjective. In many studies of jet-lag cures, at least 15 percent of "controls" reported they overcame jet lag just fine, even though they received no treatment. "I never heard anyone complain of jet lag on a Caribbean vacation," says a leading researcher, Josephine Arendt of the University of Surrey in England.

Because there is "no single magic bullet that works for everyone," as NASA's Mark Rosekind says, every passenger swears by his or her own pet remedy, including President Clinton. According to the White House press office, the President protects himself against jet lag by drinking plenty of water before and during the flight, and taking frequent naps on Air Force One. For the rest of us, there are special eyeshades to be worn en route, special diets, swearing off alcohol and caffeine, aromatherapy and homeopathy, and, in keeping with the times, computer software that calculates the precise hours you should sleep or go to the beach after arrival, tailored to your flight schedule. In fact, in her book *Jet Smart*, Diana Fairechild, a former flight attendant, offers "200 tips for beating jet lag," a certain indication that there is no single surefire, universally accepted miracle.

Although scientists respect many of these home remedies, especially the value of naps and copious amounts of water, they have primarily focused on the relationships between light and darkness and the body chemistry.

In Boston, Charles Czeisler and his colleagues at Harvard Medical School and Brigham and Women's Hospital have been demonstrating how alternating periods of bright light and darkness can manipulate the body clock. In 1978, Czeisler demonstrated the effects of light and total darkness on biological rhythms. In the '80s, he began to work out the precise amount, duration and scheduling of light exposure that could reset the human pacemaker, charting what is known as a circadian phase response curve, or PRC—scientific jargon for a graph that shows the shift in an organism's 24-hour clock as the result of exposure to clock-setting cues, like bright light, at different points of the day or night. The first scientists to plot a circadian PRC for humans, Czeisler and his colleagues found that by using bright-light treatments at certain times, they could quickly reset the body clock. In a few sessions of exposure to bright light the equivalent intensity of sunshine on a clear day, Czeisler's colleague Richard Kronauer has said, they can put a New Yorker on Bombay time.

More recently, Czeisler's group has shown that even ordinary room light can affect the body's pacemaker. By constantly measuring body temperatures in volunteers kept in relatively dim light, Czeisler concluded that even light from a hotel-room lamp may reset the body clock. According to Czeisler, this suggests that people in modern society may be forced by artificial light into a constant state of jet lag, without crossing any time zones. By the same token, he notes, if timed properly, artificial light may be used to alleviate jet lag—though not as effectively as bright light or sunshine.

In 1984, Al Lewy and his colleague Serge Daan published a paper recommending strategically avoiding light at certain times and going out in bright sunshine at others to lessen the effects of jet lag. En route to London from the United States on a typical overnight flight, for example, one might wear an eye mask on the plane, change to sunglasses on arrival and repair immediately to one's hotel room for a nap followed by several hours outdoors in bright sunshine.

Others have since followed up on the bright-light and sunglasses treatment, resulting, for instance, in a jet-lag visor that can be switched on at the correct time to shine incandescent light into the eyes, and the use of thick welder's goggles to block out light on cue. This last approach has never been popular because, as Wesley Seidel of Stanford University says, "most people would rather have jet lag than walk around Paris in goggles."

Even without the cumbersome goggles, relying on bright, natural light is not wholly practical. On my trip to London, for instance, how could I have soaked up three hours of bright outdoor sunshine when I arrived in a steady drizzle?

While still "pushing light," for the past few years Lewy has been experimenting with melatonin to move the body clock ahead or turn it back, depending on when the pill is given. "When you give melatonin in the afternoon," he explains, "the body says 'Aha! Dusk has come!' and advances the internal clock. Or, if you take it in the morning, it tricks the body into believing that dawn hasn't come yet."

Like Czeisler, Lewy is also looking at phase response curves. But rather than charting the effect of light, he has been trying to determine the exact timing and dosage of melatonin that will move the clock backward or forward. Lewy's goal, at least partly accomplished, is to work out a formula that can help us poor souls leaping sleeplessly across time zones.

Thus, before my takeoff from California, Lewy reviewed my flight schedule and carefully calibrated the timing and amounts of melatonin that might help me fight my old nemesis. After ascertaining that I was in good health and had consulted my doctor, he recommended six days of melatonin over the outbound leg of my trip and the same for the homeward leg.

On the afternoon before the departure day, I was to take a half-milligram of melatonin, followed by another half-milligram on the day itself. Arriving in London, I was to take three milligrams at bedtime, another three milligrams the next night, and still another three at 8 P.M. the following night. The next two days I was to take a half-milligram at 5 P.M. one afternoon and at 3 P.M. the next. Returning, I was to take a half-milligram upon waking on the day before departure and on the day of departure itself, three milligrams at bedtime back in San Francisco, and three milligrams at bedtime the following night. If I woke in the night after midnight over the next several days, I was to take a half-milligram, but not after 5 A.M.

My wife, who has never been as roundly victimized by jet lag, was to avoid melatonin and serve as a control. We would compare results when our trip was over.

It is 9 A.M. in the English countryside and two days before our return flight to the United States. In compliance with Lewy's directions, I have swallowed a half-milligram of melatonin on arising, as I will again tomorrow. But seated across from me in her spartan laboratory office at the University of Surrey is a scientist who firmly disagrees with Lewy's advice. "I think Al's much too cautious," says Josephine Arendt of her friend and colleague. "I don't think a half-milligram has much effect. I'd recommend five milligrams on the day of departure. I know why he's doing it, though. People are usually dashing around running errands and things on the day they leave. And five milligrams makes about 10 percent of people feel very draggy."

Arendt is a genial woman who clearly enjoys her work. She sometimes wears a T-shirt with a melatonin molecule on the front, and she keeps two of her passport photographs on her bulletin board: one from 1985 and one from 1995. "So much for the antiaging effects of melatonin," she smiles.

Arendt began giving melatonin to humans in the 1980s, after studying its effect on sheep. In the best tradition of old-fashioned science, she chose herself as her first subject, secure in the knowledge—based on studies of melatonin as a treatment for Parkinson's patients—that it was safe. In 1983 she published a scientific paper suggesting that, based on animal evidence, the hormone might be used to reset the human body clock. "Let us say," she says with a twinkle, "that the idea was greeted with a certain amount of disbelief." In 1985 she published the results of experiments that supported the notion, but that paper, too, was greeted with skepticism. Nevertheless, she persevered, curious to see if melatonin could be used to prevent jet lag.

"Our first efforts were a bit unorthodox," she says. "We advertised in the *Financial Times* for sponsors. British Caledonian Airways agreed to donate round-trip tickets from London to San Francisco, and the Grand Metro Hotels offered to donate rooms. We managed to obtain a $20,000 grant. Then we sent 17 quite willing, mostly middle-aged volunteers off to your West Coast where, poor lambs, they were forced to stay a fortnight in order to adjust to San Francisco time before returning to beautiful Surrey.

"Eight of them received melatonin and nine a harmless placebo, given on the eastbound return trip for three days before leaving and four days after arrival in London, a total of seven days. They wore wrist actigraphs that monitored their activity levels; we collected their urine to measure for hormonal levels, and we had them self-rate their sleep quality and mood. I sent my husband with them, but I stayed here to pull the strings and harass them the moment they stepped off the plane.

"The results were very pleasing. By every measure, the melatonin group had significantly less jet lag and of shorter duration than the controls. They reported that they slept better, and that they were much more alert. Seven days after arrival, we asked them to rate their jet lag on a scale of 1 to 100. Six of the placebo group rated theirs higher than 50. The eight melatonin takers rated theirs from 2 to 17."

It is noon in the shadow of the cavernous wind tunnel at NASA's Ames Research Center south of San Francisco. Mark Rosekind, of the NASA Fatigue Countermeasures Program, greets me amiably and gestures around his office. "Our program doesn't have a laboratory," he grins. "We do field studies in the real world. Our laboratory is at 41,000 feet."

Under Congressional mandate, NASA has been investigating jet lag and its possible effects on airline crews and passenger safety since 1980. Research has focused on the interaction between jet lag and simple loss of sleep. "Fatigue is a combination of sleep loss, upsets of the circadian clock and the flight operations schedule," Rosekind says of the studies. "It's difficult to distinguish how much of what we feel after a long flight is due to crossing time zones and how much is sleep deprivation," Lewy had told me earlier. "After all, what happens before you start off on a long trip? You probably stay up late packing, maybe cleaning the house, then you probably start early for the airport. And not many of us sleep well on planes. If our eyes close for a few hours, we're lucky. And the atmosphere in the cabin is dehydrating, they keep serving you food and alcohol and caffeine, you don't get any exercise. So when you drag around Amsterdam, who can say it's all because your clock is out of sync?"

In one experiment, NASA researchers wired pilots on the three-person 747 flight decks of two major airlines to measure their brain waves during flight. Among other things, they recorded what Rosekind calls "microsleeps," his head bobbing quickly and then righting itself to demonstrate. Without adjusting the data for individual differences, the patterns showed that crew members nodded or closed their eyes briefly an average of ten times per crew during the last 90 minutes of a long flight, including two during the critical period of descent and landing. When NASA prescribed 40-minute naps for each pilot during flight, they recorded an average of only two microsleeps per crew during the last 90 minutes and none during descent and landing. While this procedure has not been sanctioned for U.S. airlines, in-flight naps for three-person long-distance crews have since been adopted by six major foreign airlines.

NASA also advises pilots that both jet lag and fatigue can be reduced by two nights of sound sleep before departure or during stopovers. "If I were to extrapolate for passengers what we've learned from pilots," Rosekind says, "I'd say, get a couple of good nights' sleep, and take short naps on the plane. After arrival, follow a good sleep schedule and learn how to use bright lights and caffeine strategically. And don't go to important meetings or make important decisions as soon as you arrive."

"Not all the questions have been answered and the mysteries solved," Arendt had told me earlier. One of the questions is the link, if any, between food intake and jet lag. Several years ago, a researcher at the Argonne National Laboratory in Illinois developed an anti-jet-lag diet that President Ronald Reagan, among others, followed. The diet consisted mainly of alternating between high-protein and high-carbohydrate meals as a way to manipulate sleep cycles. Unfortunately, at least one major study of the program found it had no effect on jet lag.

It is 11 A.M. in California. I have been home for three days, feel bright-eyed and alert, and am back on my regular schedule. Yesterday I took my last three milligrams of melatonin. I call Lewy to report. In London I managed to follow the local clock, but I confess to some mid-afternoon droopiness and some 3 A.M. wakenings. At one particularly alarming moment, I felt myself nodding over the Indian curry, but I managed to fight it off. The second day after our return, I had faded a bit in mid-afternoon but managed to stay awake until my normal bedtime. Also, the melatonin had triggered some vivid dreams, as Lewy had warned it might. On Arendt's 1-100 scale, I calculated my jet lag was somewhere around 15.

Meanwhile, my wife—in spite of being female, an extrovert and a night owl, and thus presumably less vulnerable—had been unable to conquer drowsiness the second day in London and had succumbed to a long nap at 3 P.M.

Lewy reminds me that he had never predicted a complete cure. The results of my trial, we agree, are encouraging but not conclusive. Obviously more research is needed. This summer we are invited to Helsinki again, and this time I hope to eat the reindeer stew.

A Mouse Helps Explain What Makes Us Tick

By NICHOLAS WADE

"Oh dear, oh dear, I shall be too late," the White Rabbit exclaimed as he examined his pocket watch.

The rabbit overheard by Lewis Carroll's Alice in her adventures in Wonderland now has a real-life counterpart: a mouse whose biological clock has been genetically reset to run at a 28-hour cycle instead of 24.

Deranging the daily rhythm of a mouse is not some perverse goal of modern science but rather a means to a larger end, the understanding of the biological clocks that govern the daily lives of everything from microbes to man.

The biological clock in humans governs rhythms like the sleep-wake cycle, the daily ebb and flow of many hormones, and the variations in mental alertness. It resets itself daily according to the amount of light perceived. Without a well-adjusted clock, the human condition can get very jagged, as is evident when changing a work shift or flying through too many time zones for the clock to keep pace.

The biological clock has long defied analysis, in part because the basic rhythmicity is generated at the deepest levels of the cell. In mammals, the master clock is in the suprachiasmatic nucleus of the brain, just above where the optic nerves from each eye cross over. The nucleus, about the size of a pinhead, consists of some 10,000 nerve cells, each containing a tiny clock at the level of its genes and proteins.

Biologists have identified a few individual components of the clocks used by fruit flies and by a microbe called Neurospora, which makes bread mold. But possession of the genes for these components did not, as is often the case, help fish out the counterpart genes in mice or humans.

In frustration, a bold new approach was conceived seven years ago by Dr. Joseph S. Takahashi of Northwestern University in Evanston, Ill. In fact it was a bold old approach, that of trying to find time-keeping genes in mice with the same mass screening method that was used to find the gene in fruit flies in 1971. But mice are far harder to work with than fruit flies.

The method is to serve meals laced with a heavily mutagenic chemical that randomly changes DNA all along the genome. By screening enough fruit flies or mice for defects in their biological clock, the researcher can hope to find one with an aberrant clock, and then rummage around in its genome to see which gene was disrupted.

A large site was built to watch—for a month—hundreds of mice running on wheels. Wheel-running affords an accurate signal of the animal's internal clock since laboratory mice like to take exercise regularly and will start punctually to the minute at the same time each night.

Dr. Takahashi and his team expected to have to screen several thousand mice before hitting on one with a broken clock. But fortune smiled upon their mouse-deranging endeavors, and it was mouse No. 25 [that] turned up incurably tardy. No other seriously clock-deranged mouse has yet shown up.

"We were incredibly lucky," Dr. Takahashi said.

The mutant mouse had a basic daily rhythm about an hour longer than normal mice, caused by a single defective gene, which Dr. Takahashi named the Clock gene. Descendants bred to have two defective copies of the Clock gene, one from each parent, had a daily rhythm four hours longer than normal.

Dr. Takahaski and his team discovered the clock-deranged mouse three years ago and then set about trying to identify the damaged gene, a snippet of genetic material hiding somewhere within the three billion units of DNA that make up the mouse's genome. The project took a 10-member team three years.

In today's issue of the journal Cell, the researchers report having laid hands on the gene and describe the molecular features of the protein it specifies. Dr. David P. King led efforts to pinpoint the location of the gene. Dr. Marina P. Antoch directed a clever method of proving the gene's function: she fixed the clock in mutant mice by substituting a correct piece of DNA.

Of great interest to specialists is the finding that one stretch of the protein, known as a domain, resembles a domain seen in the clock proteins of the fruit fly and the bread mold, even though the overall protein structures have little similarity. This bolsters the expectation, hitherto unsupported, that since circadin rhythms are an ancient behavior in all living creatures they should have a common basic mechanism.

The common domain is one that enables the protein to activate certain genes strung along the cell's DNA, though the target genes have not yet been identified. Just how this constitutes the mechanism of a clock remains to be determined. From what is known of the fruit fly and bread mold clocks, ingenious schemes have been suggested in which a Clock gene makes a protein, which links up with another protein and then turns off the gene in a daily feedback loop.

A team reports finding the gene that controls the biological clock.

Dr. Steven M. Reppert, who studies circadian rhythms at Massachusetts General Hospital, said the Takahashi team's work was "really a tour de force," adding, "This is the first molecular entry into the mammalian clock."

Dr. Charles A. Czeisler, a neuroendocrinolgist at Brigham and Women's Hospital in Boston, described the finding as "a landmark discovery which holds great promise for understanding the underpinnings" of the human biological clock.

Some people are night owls, others are alert in the mornings, a difference that may have a genetic basis.

"Given that a Clock gene has now been identified in mice, one can begin to tease apart whether these differences in human behavior may have a genetic basis," Dr. Czeisler said.

Dr. Takahashi's team found that the normal version of the Clock gene in mice is made up of 24 sections, known as exons. In the mutant mouse they created, a single unit of DNA was changed, causing one of the exons to be lost from the processed version of the gene. Loss of the exon resulted in a protein with one part missing, which slowed the clock.

Progress in Clock gene research has been gathering pace after a slow start. The two Clock genes so far known in the fruit fly are called Period, found in 1971, and Timeless, found in 1994. The bread mold gene Frequency was discovered in 1978. Two more bread mold genes, dubbed White collar-1 and White collar-2, were reported earlier this month by a team led by Jay C. Dunlap and Jennifer J. Loros at the Dartmouth Medical School in Hanover, N.H.

Adenosine: A Mediator of the Sleep-Inducing Effects of Prolonged Wakefulness

Tarja Porkka-Heiskanen, Robert E. Strecker, Mahesh Thakkar, Alvhild A. Bjørkum, Robert W. Greene, Robert W. McCarley*

Both subjective and electroencephalographic arousal diminish as a function of the duration of prior wakefulness. Data reported here suggest that the major criteria for a neural sleep factor mediating the somnogenic effects of prolonged wakefulness are satisfied by adenosine, a neuromodulator whose extracellular concentration increases with brain metabolism and which, in vitro, inhibits basal forebrain cholinergic neurons. In vivo microdialysis measurements in freely behaving cats showed that adenosine extracellular concentrations in the basal forebrain cholinergic region increased during spontaneous wakefulness as contrasted with slow wave sleep; exhibited progressive increases during sustained, prolonged wakefulness; and declined slowly during recovery sleep. Furthermore, the sleep-wakefulness profile occurring after prolonged wakefulness was mimicked by increased extracellular adenosine induced by microdialysis perfusion of an adenosine transport inhibitor in the cholinergic basal forebrain but not by perfusion in a control noncholinergic region.

Abundant experimental evidence supports the commonsense notion that prolonged wakefulness decreases the degree of arousal, which is usually measured as electroencephalographic activation (EEG arousal). Both the propensity to sleep and the intensity of delta EEG waves upon falling asleep have been demonstrated to be proportional to the duration of prior wakefulness (*1*). What might be the neural mediator of this effect of prior wakefulness? Our laboratory has provided evidence that the basal forebrain and mesopontine cholinergic neurons whose discharge activity plays an integral role in EEG arousal (*2*) are under the tonic inhibitory control of endogenous adenosine, an inhibition that is mediated postsynaptically by an inwardly rectifying potassium conductance and by an inhibition of the hyperpolarization-activated current (*3*). Adenosine is of particular interest as a putative sleep-wakefulness neuromodulator (*4*) because (i) the production and concentration of adenosine in the extracellular space have been linked to neuronal metabolic activity (*5*); (ii) neural metabolism is much greater during wakefulness (W) than during delta slow wave sleep (SWS) (*6*); and (iii) caffeine and theophylline are powerful blockers of electrophysiologically relevant adenosine receptors, promoting both subjectively and EEG-defined arousal while suppressing recovery sleep after deprivation (*7*). Our laboratory has recently demonstrated that microdialysis perfusion of adenosine in the cholinergic basal forebrain and the mesopontine cholinergic nuclei reduces wakefulness and EEG arousal (*8*).

Although the preceding evidence is consistent with adenosine as a neural sleep factor mediating the somnogenic effects of prolonged EEG arousal and wakefulness, key questions relevant to a demonstration of this role have remained unaddressed. (i) Are brain extracellular adenosine concentrations higher in spontaneous W than in SWS? (ii) Do adenosine concentrations increase with increasing duration of W and then decline slowly as recovery sleep occurs after W? (iii) Do pharmacological manipulations increasing brain adenosine concentrations produce changes in sleep and wakefulness that mimic those seen during recovery from prolonged wakefulness? (iv) Are adenosine sleep-wakefulness effects mediated selectively by neurons implicated in EEG arousal, such as cholinergic neurons, rather than stemming from widespread neuronal populations, each with relatively similar influence?

Under pentobarbital anesthesia, cats were implanted with electrodes for recording EEG, electromyogram, electro-oculogram, and ponto-geniculo-occipital waves for determination of behavioral state (*9*) and with guide cannulae for insertion of microdialysis probes (*10*). Probes were targeted to the cholinergic basal forebrain and, as a control region, to the thalamic ventroanterior/ventrolateral (VA/VL) complex, which was selected for contrast because it is not cholinergic and, as a relay nucleus, does not have cortical projections as widespread as those of the basal forebrain cholinergic neurons (*11*).

Brain extracellular adenosine concentrations were measured in the basal forebrain and the thalamus with the use of high-performance liquid chromatography and ultraviolet (UV) detection from samples collected by in vivo microdialysis (Fig. 1A) (*12*). Adenosine concentrations in consecutive samples over one complete sleep cycle [that is, a cycle containing W, SWS, rapid eye movement

T. Porkka-Heiskanen, Department of Psychiatry, Harvard Medical School, Brockton Veterans Administration Medical Center (VAMC), 116 A, 940 Belmont Street, Brockton, MA 02401, USA, and Institute of Biomedicine, University of Helsinki, Helsinki, Finland.
R. E. Strecker, M. Thakkar, A. A. Bjørkum, R. W. Greene, R. W. McCarley, Department of Psychiatry, Harvard Medical School, Brockton VAMC, 116 A, 940 Belmont Street, Brockton, MA 02401, USA.

*To whom correspondence should be addressed. E-mail: mccarley@warren.med.harvard.edu

(REM) sleep, and W again at the end] are shown in Fig. 1B. The initial cluster of successive W episodes has consistently high values, whereas the following cluster of sleep states has generally much lower SWS values, especially as SWS becomes more consolidated. In some experiments (Fig. 1B), samples were collected during REM sleep episodes, and the adenosine concentrations measured appeared similar to the concentrations seen in adjacent SWS samples. However, we did not pursue the analysis of REM sleep samples, because the focus of the present study was not on REM sleep. Furthermore, it was relatively difficult to get pure REM samples, and there was some evidence that the short-duration REM episodes did not allow full equilibrium of adenosine with the extracellular fluid. As predicted, adenosine concentrations were less in SWS than in W, being significantly reduced by 21% in both regions [paired t test, $t(4) = 6.53$ and $P < 0.01$ for the basal forebrain and $t(4) = 2.80$ and $P < 0.05$ for the thalamus]. The grand mean (±SEM) of adenosine concentrations was 30.6 ± 5.1 nM during W versus 24.1 ± 4.4 nM during SWS (*13*).

To study the effect of prolonged wakefulness on brain extracellular adenosine concentrations, we atraumatically kept the cats awake by playing with or handling them. During the 6-hour waking period and the 3-hour subsequent recovery sleep period, EEG activity was continuously monitored, and three 10-min microdialysis samples were analyzed per hour from the basal forebrain site. The mean adenosine concentrations for six animals for each hour of the experiment were expressed as a percentage of the second-hour values (adenosine concentration at 2 hours was 30.0 ± 9.5 nM) (Fig. 2). As predicted, during the extended waking period, the extracellular adenosine concentration increased progressively with increasing duration of waking, reaching, at 6 hours, about twice that (58.9 ± 15.7 nM) seen at the onset of the experiment (Fig. 2, $P < 0.05$). During the 3-hour recovery period, adenosine declined slowly, and, at the end of the 3-hour recording window, it still had not declined to the values at the experiment's onset, although values approximated the baseline value in one cat that was recorded for 6 hours of recovery sleep.

We next addressed the question of whether there was site specificity for adenosine effects on sleep and wakefulness. To achieve local increases in adenosine that would allow comparison of the sleep-wakefulness effects of elevated adenosine in the basal forebrain and in the thalamus, we used unilateral microdialysis perfusion of the adenosine transport inhibitor S-(4-nitrobenzyl)-6-thioinosine (NBTI, 1 μM) (*14*), in the basal forebrain and thalamus. NBTI increased adenosine concentrations about equally (to about twice the control values) in both the basal forebrain and thalamus (Fig. 3A). Despite the similar NBTI-induced increases in adenosine in the basal forebrain and thalamus, only the adenosine increases in the basal forebrain induced a decrease in wakefulness and an increase in SWS (Fig. 3B). Similarly, a power spectral analysis of the EEG revealed that the relative power in the delta band (0.3 to 4 Hz) was increased and the relative power in the gamma band was decreased after NBTI infusion in the basal forebrain but not in the thalamus (*15*) (Fig. 3C). NBTI perfusion in the basal forebrain also increased REM sleep, a finding similar to the effects of microdialysis perfusion of adenosine (*8*) (Fig. 3B).

Our final analysis examined how closely the increase of basal forebrain adenosine con-

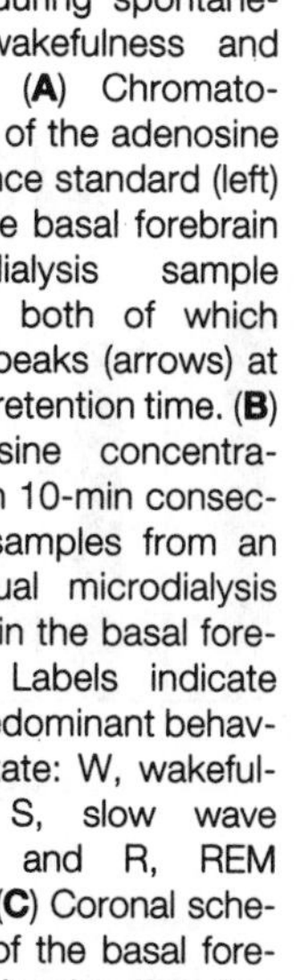

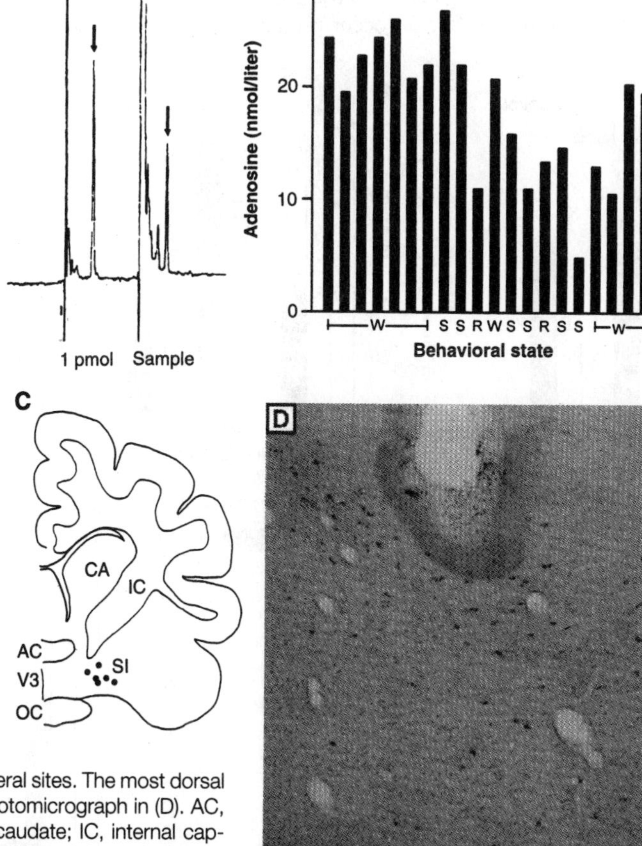

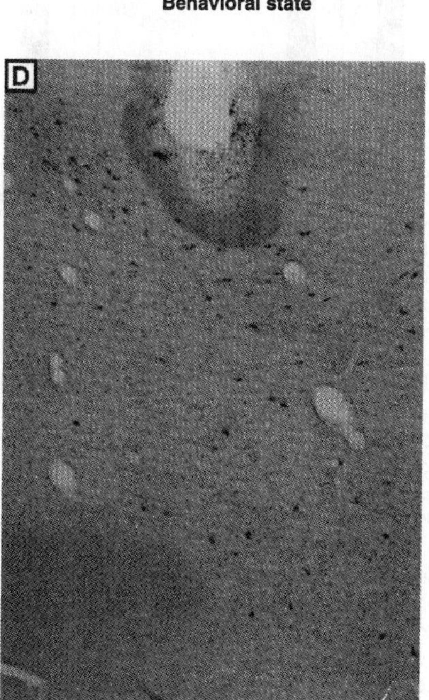

Fig. 1. Extracellular adenosine concentrations during spontaneous wakefulness and sleep. (**A**) Chromatograms of the adenosine reference standard (left) and the basal forebrain microdialysis sample (right), both of which show peaks (arrows) at 8-min retention time. (**B**) Adenosine concentrations in 10-min consecutive samples from an individual microdialysis probe in the basal forebrain. Labels indicate the predominant behavioral state: W, wakefulness; S, slow wave sleep; and R, REM sleep. (**C**) Coronal schematic of the basal forebrain showing the sites of the tips of the six probes used for the prolonged wakefulness and NBTI perfusion experiments. All sites are mapped onto this one section, including homotopic mapping for contralateral sites. The most dorsal site is that shown in the photomicrograph in (D). AC, anterior commissure; CA, caudate; IC, internal capsule; OC, optic chiasm; SI, substantia innominata; V3, third ventricle. (**D**) Photomicrograph showing choline acetyltransferase–positive (ChAT+) neurons (dark spots) surrounding a probe tip site (top); this illustration was selected because the relatively superficial location of the tip in the substantia innominata allows clear visualization of ChAT+ neurons.

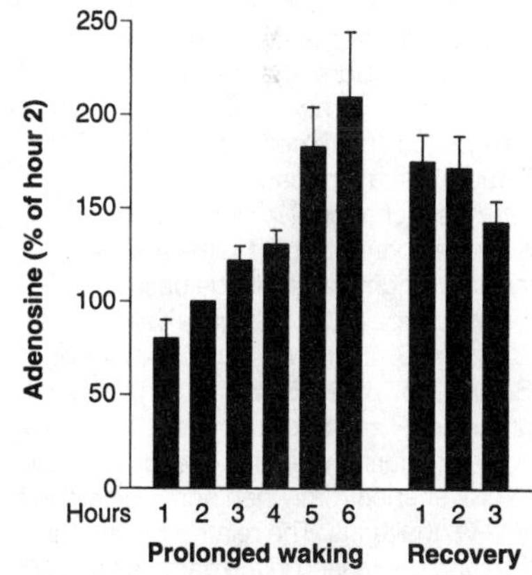

Fig. 2. Prolonged wakefulness and recovery sleep. Mean extracellular adenosine values increased in the basal forebrain during 6 hours of prolonged wakefulness [0900 to 1500; repeated measures of the analysis of variance (ANOVA) between treatments gave values of $F(8, 5) = 7.0$ and $P < 0.0001$, and the paired t test between the second and the last hour of wakefulness gave values of $t(5) = 3.14$ and $P < 0.05$]. The adenosine values decreased in the subsequent 3 hours of spontaneous recovery sleep ($n = 6$). Values are normalized relative to the second hour of deprivation (due to technical problems, three first-hour values were missing).

centrations by NBTI mimicked the sleep-wakefulness changes associated with the increased basal forebrain adenosine concentrations caused by prolonged wakefulness. Prolonged wakefulness and NBTI infusion in the basal forebrain induced adenosine increases in the basal forebrain of almost the same magnitude, which were slightly more than twice the control values (*16*) (Figs. 2 and 3A). We noted that this congruence of adenosine concentrations afforded a useful opportunity (i) to determine if the same increase in adenosine, whether from NBTI or prolonged wakefulness, produced similar sleep-wakefulness changes, a finding that would be compatible with adenosine's acting as a sleep factor modulating the somnogenic effects of prolonged wakefulness, and (ii) to determine how closely a local basal forebrain increase in adenosine produced the same sleep-wakefulness effects as the presumptively global adenosine increases induced by deprivation, thus allowing an estimate of the potency of local, unilateral, basal forebrain changes. Both prolonged wakefulness and NBTI infusion in the basal forebrain produced the same pattern of sleep-wakefulness changes, with a reduction in wakefulness and an increase in SWS (Fig. 3D). Power spectral analysis showed that both prolonged wakefulness and NBTI infusion, compared with control values of spontaneous sleep-wakefulness states with artificial cerebrospinal fluid (ACSF) perfusion, produced the same pattern of relative power changes, as discussed in the previous paragraph (*17*).

What might be the mechanism of the observed changes in extracellular concentrations of adenosine that occur in association with sleep-wakefulness changes? Mechanisms that influence extracellular adenosine concentrations include modulation of adenosine anabolic and catabolic enzyme activity and adenosine transport rate constants or activities (*18*). For example, increases in metabolic activity during wakefulness could increase intracellular adenosine concentrations and, by altering the transmembrane adenosine gradient, reduce or even reverse the direction of the inward diffusion of adenosine via its facilitated nucleoside transporters (*19*). Similar adenosine increases may occur in other central nervous system regions, and diurnal variations of adenosine concentrations in the frontal cortex and hippocampus have indeed been reported, although these studies did not measure behavioral state–related changes (*20*). We suggest that adenosine's powerful state-altering effects in the cholinergic basal forebrain region occur primarily because of the cholinergic neurons' widespread and strategic efferent targets in the thalamic and cortical systems that are important for the control of EEG arousal (*21*). Increased adenosine concentrations in the cholinergic basal forebrain zone would thus decrease EEG arousal, increase drowsiness, and promote EEG delta wave activity during subsequent sleep. We suggest that extracellular adenosine concentrations decrease in SWS because of the reduced metabolic activity of sleep, especially in delta wave sleep, when cholinergic neurons are relatively quiescent. This postulate is congruent with the observed declining exponential time course of delta wave activity over a night's sleep (*1*).

Taken together, these results suggest that adenosine is a physiological sleep factor that mediates the somnogenic effects of prior wakefulness. The duration and depth of sleep after wakefulness appear to be profoundly modulated by the elevated concentrations of adenosine.

REFERENCES AND NOTES

1. A. A. Borbély, *Hum. Neurobiol.* **1**, 195 (1982); I. Feinberg *et al.*, *Electroencephalogr. Clin. Neurophysiol.* **61**, 134 (1985).

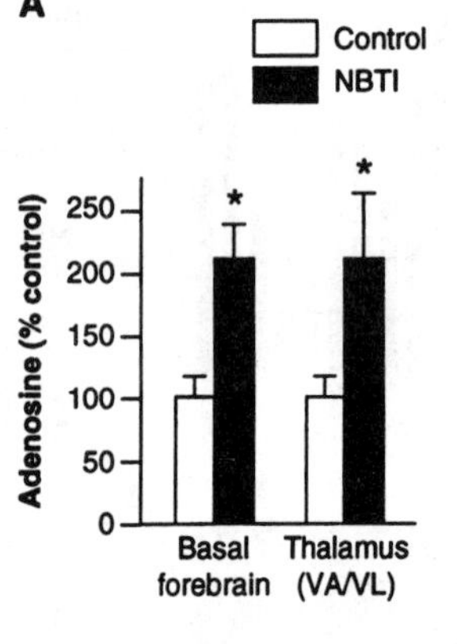

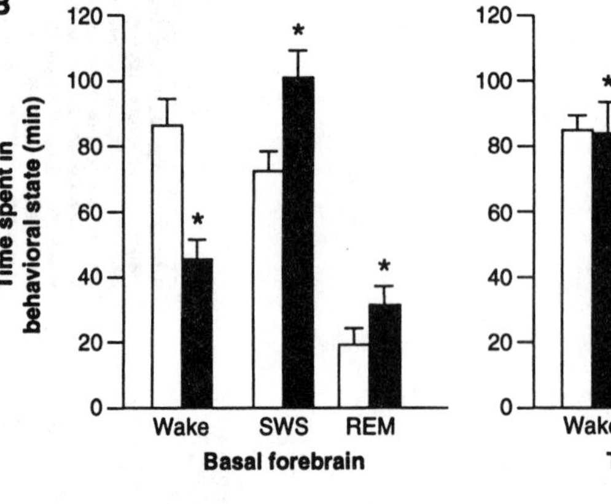

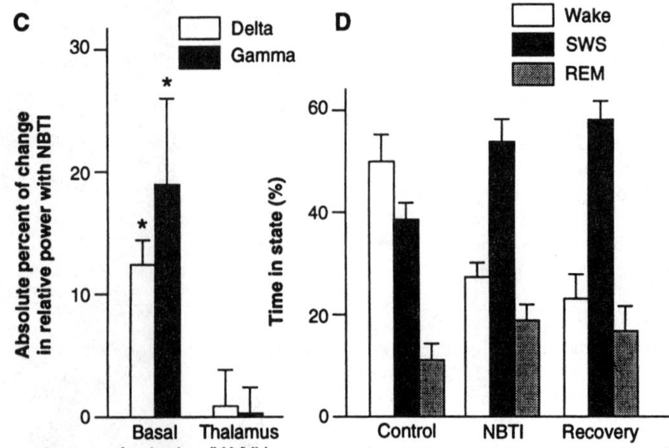

Fig. 3. Effects of local perfusion of the adenosine transport inhibitor NBTI (1 μM). (**A**) Microdialysis perfusion of NBTI increases adenosine concentrations in both the basal forebrain (paired *t* test, $t(5) = 4.79$ and $P < 0.01$) and the thalamus (paired *t* test, $t(4) = 3.92$ and $P < 0.05$) by about twofold (the means of the last three samples before and the means of the first three samples after onset of NBTI perfusion are compared). (**B**) NBTI administration causes sleep-wakefulness changes in the basal forebrain (left panel) but not in the VA/VL thalamus (right panel). In the basal forebrain, the paired *t* test gave values of $t(5) = 3.47$ and $P < 0.05$ for waking, $t(5) = 3.78$ and $P < 0.05$ for SWS, and $t(5) = 2.76$ and $P < 0.05$ for REM sleep. Changes in the thalamus are P = NS for all states. The ordinate shows the minutes spent in each state during the 3-hour recording period. (**C**) NBTI causes changes in the power spectrum when administered in the basal forebrain but not in the VA/VL thalamus. The relative power is increased in the delta band (0.3 to 4 Hz) and decreased in the gamma band (35 to 55 Hz) with NBTI infusion in the basal forebrain ($P < 0.04$; nonparametric Wilcoxon tests were used because of nonnormality of data) but is unchanged with NBTI infusion in the thalamus. (**D**) Comparison of the effects of prolonged wakefulness and NBTI perfusion in the basal forebrain on the percent of time spent in each behavioral state. During both the NBTI treatment and the recovery sleep conditions, SWS was increased as compared with control sleep [40 and 50%, respectively; $n = 5$; repeated measures of ANOVA between treatments gave values of $F(2, 4) = 5.92$ and $P < 0.05$], and this increase in SWS did not differ between the NBTI and recovery sleep conditions (post hoc Neuman Keul). Wakefulness was decreased in both experimental conditions as compared to control sleep [45 and 50%, respectively; repeated measures of ANOVA between treatments gave values of $F(2, 4) = 9.41$ and $P < 0.01$], whereas the two experimental conditions did not differ from each other. REM sleep in the NBTI-treated and recovery sleep groups had similar percentage increases (65 and 50%).

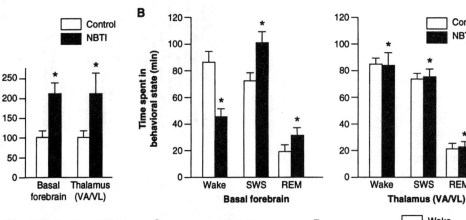

2. M. Steriade, S. Datta, D. Paré, G. Oakson, R. C. Dossi, *J. Neurosci.* **10**, 2541 (1990); M. Steriade, *Science* **272**, 225 (1996); B. E. Jones, *Prog. Brain Res.* **98**, 61 (1993).
3. D. G. Rainnie, H. C. R. Grunze, R. W. McCarley, R. W. Greene, *Science* **263**, 689 (1994).
4. M. Radulovacki, *Rev. Clin. Basic Pharmacol.* **5**, 327 (1985).
5. I. Pull and H. McIlwain, *Biochem. J.* **126**, 965 (1972); H. R. Winn, J. E. Welsh, R. Rubio, R. M. Berne, *Circ. Res.* **47**, 568 (1980); J. Schrader, M. Wahl, W. Kuschinsky, G. W. Kreutzberg, *Pfluegers Arch. Eur. J. Physiol.* **387**, 245 (1980); R. M. Berne, in *Cerebral Hypoxia in the Pathogenesis of Migraine*, F. C. Rose and W. K. Amery, Eds. (Pitman, London, 1982), pp. 82–91; D. G. Van Wylen, T. S. Park, R. Rubio, R. M. Berne, *J. Cereb. Blood Flow Metab.* **6**, 522 (1986); H. McIlwain and J. D. Poll, *Neurochem. Int.* **7**, 103 (1985).
6. In humans, a 44% reduction in the cerebral metabolic rate (CMR) of glucose during delta wave sleep, compared with that during wakefulness, was determined by P. Maquet *et al.* [*Brain Res.* **571**, 149 (1992)], and a 25% reduction in the CMR of O_2 was determined by P. L. Madsen *et al.* [*J. Appl. Physiol.* **70**, 2597 (1991)].
7. T. V. Dunwiddie, B. J. Hoffer, B. B. Fredholm, *Naunyn-Schmiedeberg's Arch. Pharmacol.* **316**, 326 (1981); R. W. Greene, H. L. Haas, A. Hermann, *Br. J. Pharmacol.* **85**, 163 (1985); A. Zwyghuisen-Doorenbos, T. A. Roehrs, L. Lipschutz, V. Timms, T. Roth, *Psychopharmacology* **100**, 36 (1990); D. Penetar *et al.*, *ibid.* **112**, 359 (1993). B. Schwierin, A. A. Borbély, and I. Tobler [*Eur. J. Pharmacol.* **300**, 163 (1996)] showed that caffeine given at the beginning of 6-hour sleep deprivation decreased delta power during rebound sleep.
8. C. M. Portas, M. Thakkar, D. G. Rainnie, R. W. Greene, R. W. McCarley, *Neuroscience*, in press. This study also demonstrated a concentration-response relation over a four-log-unit concentration range between adenosine perfused into the cholinergic basal forebrain and the extent of reduction of wakefulness.
9. R. Ursin and M. B. Sterman, *A Manual for Standardized Scoring of Sleep and Waking States in the Adult Cat* (Brain Information Service, Brain Research Institute, University of California, Los Angeles, 1981). EEG activation was scored in 20-s epochs.
10. Intracerebral guide cannulae (CMA 10 guide; CMA/Microdialysis, Stockholm, Sweden) were implanted 12 mm above the target. The coordinates for the basal forebrain (substantia innominata) were AP 15.5, ML 5, and DV −1.5, for the thalamus they were (VA/VL) AP 11, ML 5, and DV 2.5 [A. L. Berman and E. G. Jones, *The Thalamus and Basal Telencephalon of the Cat* (Univ. of Wisconsin Press, Madison, WI, 1982)]. After surgery, the animals were allowed to recover for 2 weeks. Histological processing was on 40-μm sections of formaldehyde-fixed brain tissue processed for immunohistochemistry with an antibody for choline acetyltransferase [P. J. Shiromani, S. Winston, R. W. McCarley, *Mol. Brain Res.* **38**, 77 (1996)].
11. We wished to test the hypothesis that adenosine exerts a selectively stronger influence on neurons that are intimately related to sleep-wakefulness control; we chose cholinergic neurons for study because our in vitro data indicate that adenosine exerts powerful inhibitory effects on them.
12. The mobile phase consisted of 8 mM NaH_2PO_4 in 8% methanol (pH = 4), with a flow rate of 80 μl/min produced by a Bioanalytical Systems (BAS, West Lafayette, IN) PM-80 pump. Separation was achieved by a BAS microbore column (MF-8949; 1 × 100 mm, with C18 packing of 3-μm particle size), which was attached directly to the injector (Rheodyne 9125) and to the UV detector (Waters 486 UV detector, outfitted with a Waters microbore cell kit). Adenosine was detected at a wavelength of 258 nm. Chromatographic data were recorded on a chart recorder, and the peak heights of microdialysis samples were compared to the peak heights of adenosine standards (1 pmol/10 μl) for quantification. The detection limit of the assay was 50 fmol (based on a signal-to-noise ratio of 3:1). Repeated assays of standards and pooled samples showed less than 10% variability. Custom-made CMA 10 probes from CMA/Microdialysis had a polycarbonate membrane (20,000-dalton cutoff), a 500-μm outer diameter, a 2-mm microdialysis membrane length, and a 35-mm shaft length. During the experiment, ACSF (composed of 147 mM NaCl, 3 mM KCl, 1.2 mM $CaCl_2$, and 1.0 mM $MgCl_2$, at a pH of 6.6) was pumped through the probe at a flow rate of 1.5 μl/min, the same flow rate used for drug perfusion. Consecutive 10-min dialysis samples were collected throughout the day via tubing with a low dead space volume (1.2 μl per 10 cm, FEP tubing; CMA/Microdialysis) and correlated with electrographically defined sleep-wakefulness states. Adenosine from a microdialysis sample produced a sharp chromatogram peak with a high signal-to-noise ratio and the same 8-min retention time as the adenosine standard (Fig. 1A).
13. For the analysis of the group data, a sleep cycle was defined as a continuous period that contained all of the behavioral states (W, SWS, and REM sleep), and began and ended with waking periods; the validity of comparisons over time was ensured by rejection of any cycles where there were suggestions of nonstationarity (adenosine values with >25% change between the first and last waking epochs). Of the samples in this comparison of W and SWS, 65% were 100% in a single state, and the remaining 35% had less than 20% of another state. The mean cycle duration was not different in the basal forebrain and thalamus samples.
14. NBTI actions are discussed in G. Sanderson and C. N. Scholfield [*Pfluegers Arch. Eur. J. Physiol.* **406**, 25 (1996)] and H. L. Haas and R. W. Greene [*Naunyn-Schmiedeberg's Arch. Pharmacol.* **337**, 561 (1988)]. These references and our preliminary data confirmed 1 μM as the lowest dose producing maximal effect. To ensure the presence of normal sleep, the 3-hour baseline period was not started until 30 min after the first REM episode (typically 1 to 2 hours after the animal was connected to the polygraph and microdialysis lines). Basal extracellular concentrations of adenosine were determined during the 3-hour baseline period that preceded the drug administration.
15. EEG power spectral analysis was performed during ACSF perfusion, during perfusion with 1 μM NBTI in the basal forebrain and thalamus, and during recovery sleep after 6 hours of wakefulness. Parietal EEG screw electrodes were used for EEG acquisition. The data were filtered at 70 Hz (low-pass filter) and 0.3 Hz (high-pass filter) with a Grass electroencephalograph and were continuously sampled at 128 Hz by a Pentium microprocessor computer with a Data-Wave (Data-Wave Technology, Longmont, CO) system. Absolute total power was calculated for the frequency range between 0.3 and 55 Hz. Five different frequency bands were used to calculate the relative power: delta, 0.3 to 4 Hz; theta, 4.1 to 9 Hz; alpha, 9.1 to 15 Hz; beta, 15.1 to 25 Hz; and gamma, 25.1 to 55 Hz. After basal forebrain NBTI perfusion, the relative power was significantly increased in the delta and decreased in the theta, alpha, beta, and gamma bands ($P < 0.04$; nonparametric Wilcoxon matched pairs signed-ranks test, used because of nonnormality of data). There was no change in power in any frequency band after NBTI infusion in the thalamus.
16. In evaluating the physiological relevance of adenosine at various concentrations, it is important to note that in vitro data from our laboratory (*3*) demonstrated that endogenous adenosine had a consistent inhibitory effect on cholinergic neurons. These data imply that adenosine's physiological effects in vivo are to be expected at baseline that is, without sleep deprivation or NBTI. Rainnie *et al.* (*3*) did not measure endogenous adenosine concentrations, and thus the precise in vitro effects of doubling adenosine concentrations have not yet been specified, although it is known that there are progressive increases in inhibition of cholinergic neurons (beyond that seen from the endogenous inhibitory effect) with increasing concentrations of exogenously applied adenosine. Furthermore, we believe that the actions of adenosine that we have found in animal studies apply also to humans. First, the increase in EEG sleepiness with increasing duration of wakefulness has been documented in humans (*1*). Second, the adenosine physiology and pharmacology of experimental animals and of humans appear to be comparable [see reviews in (*4*–*7*) and also L. J. Findley, M. Boykin, T. Fallon, L. Belardinelli, *J. Appl. Physiol.* **65**, 556 (1988); and H. L. Haas, R. G. Greene, M. G. Yasargil, V. Chan-Palay, *Neurosci. Abstr.* **13**, 155 (1987)]. Finally, the adenosine antagonist caffeine increases wakefulness in formal experimental studies [see (*7*) and H. P. Landolt, D. J. Dijk, S. E. Gaus, A. A. Borbely, *Neuropsychopharmacology* **12**, 229 (1995)] and, as with the adenosine antagonist theophylline, constitutes the sleep-delaying ingredient in coffee and tea.
17. Changes in the entire relative power spectrum with NBTI infusion and in recovery sleep after prolonged wakefulness were, for each band, in the same direction (n = four animals).
18. P. H. Wu, R. A. Barraco, J. W. Phillis, *Gen. Pharmacol.* **15**, 251 (1984); R. Padua, J. D. Geiger, S. Dambock, J. I. Nagy, *J. Neurochem* **54**, 1169 (1990); J. G. Gu and J. D. Geiger, *ibid.* **58**, 1699 (1992). Both *N*-methyl-D-aspartate receptor agonists [C. G. Craig and T. D. White, *J. Pharmacol. Exp. Ther.* **260**, 1278 (1992); *J. Neurochem.* **60**, 1073 (1993)] and agonists that increase adenosine 3′,5′-monophosphate [R. W. Gereau and P. J. Conn, *Neuron* **12**, 1121 (1994); P. A. Rosenberg, R. Knowles, Y. Li, *J. Neurosci.* **14**, 2953 (1994)] might also increase extracellular adeonosine concentrations by increasing extracellular adenine nucleotides that are catabolized to adenosine by 5′-ectonucleotidase (also a potential modulatory target).
19. This possibility has recently been reviewed by J. M. Brundege and T. V. Dunwiddie [*J. Neurosci.* **16**, 5603 (1996)], who also provided direct evidence for the possibility that an increase in intracellular adenosine (either by exogenous adenosine or inhibiting metabolism of endogenous adenosine) could lead to an increase in extracellular adenosine and its actions on receptors.
20. V. C. de Sánchez *et al.*, *Brain Res.* **612**, 115 (1993); J. P. Huston *et al.*, *Neuroscience* **73**, 99 (1996). Adenosine appears to have a tighter linkage to sleep after wakefulness than do other putative SWS factors [see review by J. M. Krueger and J. Fang, in *Sleep and Sleep Disorders: From Molecule to Behavior*, O. Hayaishi and S. Inoue, Eds. (Academic Press and Harcourt Brace, Tokyo, Japan, in press)].
21. It is also possible that adenosine's effects in the neocortex may be directly attenuated by cholinergic receptor activation, as has been shown in the hippocampus [P. F. Worley, J. M. Baraban, M. McCarren, S. H. Snyder, B. E. Alger, *Proc. Natl. Acad. Sci. U.S.A.* **84**, 3467 (1987)]. Thus, adenosine's direct inhibitory effects on cholinergic somata might be enhanced by a consequent disinhibition of adenosine's effects on neocortical neurons. The specificity of sleep-wakefulness effects of NBTI does not support the idea that adenosine's effects result from a global action on brain neurons, as suggested by J. H. Benington and H. C. Heller [*Prog. Neurobiol.* **45**, 347 (1995)].
22. We thank P. Shiromani, D. Rainnie, and D. Stenberg for their advice during this work; L. Camara and M. Gray for technical assistance; and C. Portas for her preliminary work on this project. Supported by National Institute of Mental Health, grant R37 MH39, 683 and awards from the Department of Veterans Affairs to R.W.M.

3 March 1997; accepted 15 April 1997

Emotions

Imagine that you really are attracted to this "friend" at school. You always want to sit next to this person in class and engage in a conversation. Every time this person smiles at you from across the hallway, your heart starts to beat so fast that you feel almost giddy. You gave your phone number to this person to call you about homework. Sometimes the person calls, and you have developed a habit of waiting by the telephone. When this person does not call, you feel so disappointed.

One day you see this friend at the cafeteria having an animated conversation with a member of the opposite sex, and it makes you so angry that you storm out of the room. Later on you learn from the grapevine that it was just an innocent encounter, and it makes you feel better. Now you are back to the same state of excitement.

This scenario is quite familiar to most of us. The situation consists of an array of experiences that we call emotions. We all experience emotions, but how are these experiences defined? Artists and writers convey emotions, using their craft. For example, the smile of Michaelangelo's "Mona Lisa" conveys positive emotions, and Shakespeare's "Romeo and Juliet" presents the power of emotions.

These aesthetic renditions are effective in giving us attributes of emotions, but do not really provide us with a systematic way of understanding the experience. Biologists and psychologists have investigated emotions from the biological and cognitive perspectives. Charles Darwin, for example, considered emotions as adaptive characteristics of the species. Fear, for example, is one emotion that may have been conserved through the course of evolution because of its adaptive value.

The direct roles of physiology and cognition in the occurrence of emotions are debatable. Can physiological responses to emotion-provoking stimuli elicit the subjective experience of emotion? In other words, will an increase in your heart rate and body temperature lead to the experience of love? Or can it be that these bodily responses are consequences of the experience? Our cognitive appraisal of the situation can also affect the kind of emotion we experience. Two people can evaluate the same stimulus but experience totally different emotional responses.

Several techniques have been used to investigate the biology of emotions. One example is the use of a "lie detector." Presumably when a person is lying, the emotion of fear develops and is manifested through certain physiological responses, such as increased heart rate and sweating. The machine then measures these physiological responses. Evidence shows, however, that lie detectors are fallible. If anything, these machines do not detect lying, but only physiological responses.

Neuroimaging techniques have also been used to study the physiology of emotions. Certain areas of the brain are seen to light up when a person experiences a particular emotion. These techniques are valuable in assessing brain activity in patients suffering from affective or emotional disorders.

Looking Ahead: Challenge Questions

What factors can you identify that have potential effects on an individual's experience of happiness? What do recent studies show with regards to these factors in relation to happiness? Do you believe that there is a genetic basis for happiness? Explain.

Discuss the neurobiological correlates of affiliative behavior and decision-making cognitive process. Are emotions bad for the decision-making process? Explain.

How do you define violence in the context of emotions? Is there a neural mechanism in humans that can explain such behavior? Discuss a neurobiological theory proposed to explain this behavior.

UNIT 8

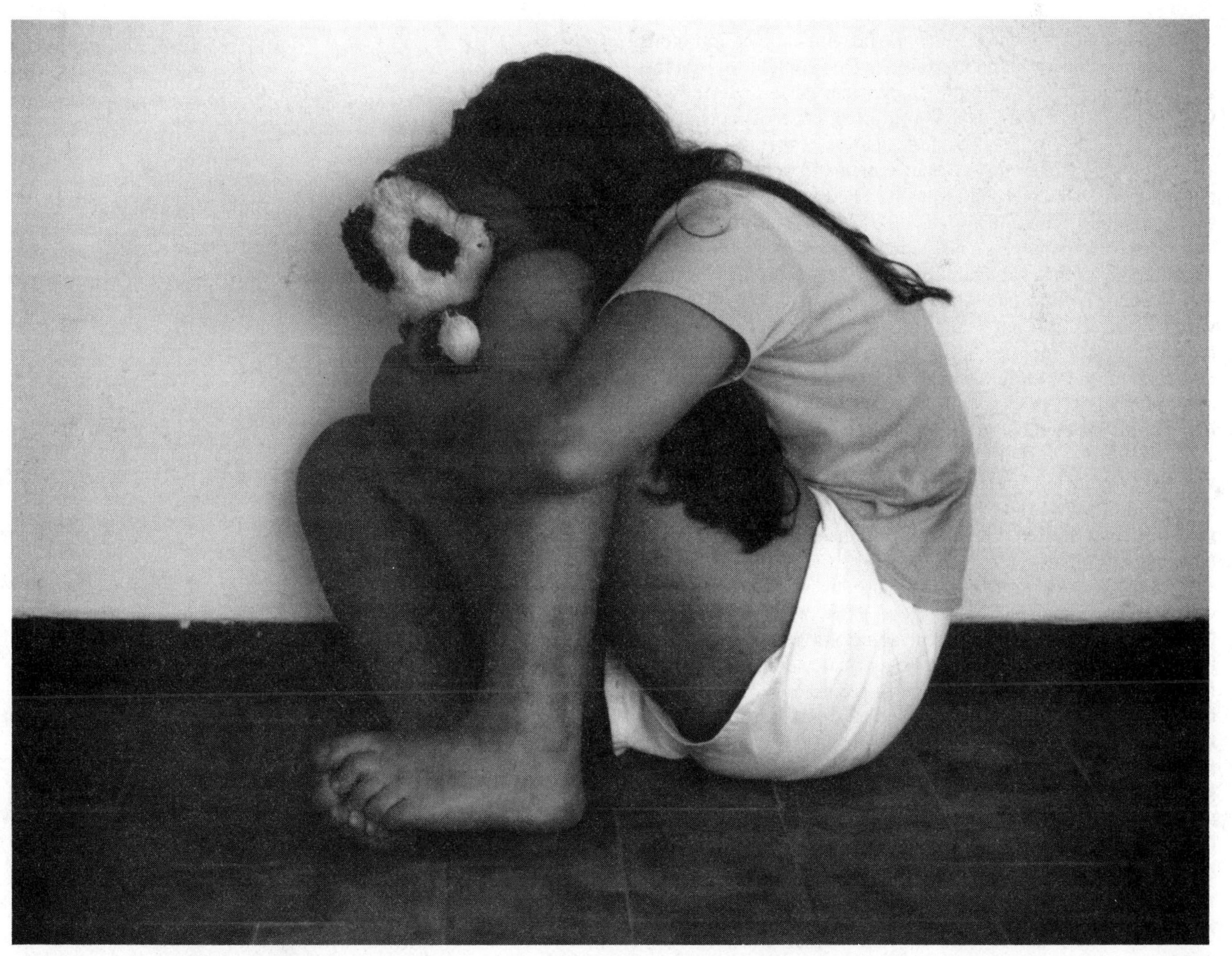

Article 28

HAPPINESS IS A STOCHASTIC PHENOMENON

David Lykken and Auke Tellegen

University of Minnesota

Abstract—*Happiness, or subjective well-being, was measured on a birth-record-based sample of several thousand middle-aged twins using the Well-Being (WB) scale of the Multidimensional Personality Questionnaire. Neither socioeconomic status, educational attainment, family income, marital status, nor an indicant of religious commitment could account for more than about 3% of the variance in WB. From 44% to 52% of the variance in WB, however, is associated with genetic variation. Based on the retest of smaller samples of twins after intervals of 4.5 and 10 years, we estimate that the heritability of the stable component of subjective well-being approaches 80%.*

Happiness depends, as Nature shows, less on exterior things than most suppose.

—William Cowper

Are those people who go to work in suits happier and more fulfilled than those who go in overalls? Do people higher on the socioeconomic ladder enjoy life more than those lower down? Can money buy happiness? As a consequence of racism and relative poverty, are black Americans less contented on average than white Americans? Because men still hold the reins of power, are men happier than women? The survey in this journal by Myers and Diener (1995) indicated that the answer to these questions, surprisingly, is "no." These authors pointed out that people have a remarkable ability to adapt, both to bad fortune and to good, so that one's life circumstances, unless they are very bad indeed, do not seem to have lasting effects on one's mood.

Yet some people do seem to be happier on average than other people are. Although people adapt surprisingly quickly to both good news and bad, the set point around which happiness varies from time to time apparently differs from one person to another. Myers and Diener considered personal relationships, religious faith, and the "flow" of working toward achievable goals as possible determiners of individual differences in the happiness set point.

We had already collected demographic and questionnaire data on a large sample of adults, and it seemed appropriate to try to replicate and perhaps extend some of Myers and Diener's findings. The Minnesota Twin Registry (Lykken, Bouchard, McGue, & Tellegen, 1990) is a birth-record-based registry of middle-aged twins born in Minnesota from 1936 to 1955. We know how far these twins went in school, their approximate family income, their marital status, and their socioeconomic status (SES), based on their occupations. These twins provide an unusually representative sample of the white population (during the 20 birth years searched, fewer than 2% of Minnesota births were to African or Native Americans). Some of the twins did not reach the eighth grade, whereas others have doctorates; they live on farms, in small towns, in big cities, and in foreign lands; their socioeconomic levels are representative of Minnesota-born adults.

Address correspondence to David Lykken, Department of Psychology, University of Minnesota, Minneapolis, MN 55455-0344.

METHOD

A self-rating questionnaire was administered to 2,310 members of this twin registry. One of the questionnaire items read as follows:

Contentment: Taking the good with the bad, how happy and contented are you on the average now, compared with other people?

The twins were asked to make their ratings on a 5-point scale: 1 = *the lowest 5% of the population*, 2 = *the lower 30%*, 3 = *the middle 30%*, 4 = *the upper 30%*, and 5 = *the highest 5%*.

Figure 1 shows that these seem to be contented people by and large and that the women are at least as happy as the men. More than 86% of these twins rated themselves as among the upper 35% in overall contentment. Most people (at least people born in Minnesota) believe that they are above average on most positive traits, but this pleasant illusion is strongest for the trait of contentment. Only 42% of the twins in this sample rated themselves in the upper 35% on intelligence, for example. We interpret these ratings to mean that most people are in fact reasonably happy most of the time. One is tempted to speculate that natural selection tended to favor happy people because they were more likely to mate and raise children and thus to become our ancestors.

Figure 2 displays the mean contentment ratings for the twins in each of the seven categories of the Hollingshead and Redlich system for classifying socioeconomic status. There is remarkably little reduction in self-rated contentment as one moves from the highest, or professional, category (SES = 1) down even to unskilled labor (SES = 6) and unemployed (SES = 7). Both of these findings corroborate Myers and Diener. These results led us to examine a measure of happiness having better psychometric properties than this single rating item.

The Well-Being (WB) scale of the Multidimensional Personality Questionnaire (MPQ; Tellegen, 1982; Tellegen & Waller, 1994) appears to be a reliable and valid measure of the condition that its name denotes, the disposition to feel good about oneself and one's own corner of the world. The 30-day retest reliability of the WB scale is .90, and its alpha reliability is .92. We have MPQ scores, corrected for age and sex and expressed in *T*-score units (M = 50, SD = 10), on 5,945 twins in the Minnesota Twin Registry.

Figure 3 shows the distribution of MPQ-WB scores for the 2,486 twins from whom we also had contentment ratings. For purposes of comparability with the ratings distribution, *T* scores for the WB distribution were divided into five intervals: <33,

From *Psychological Science,* May 1996, pp. 186–189.

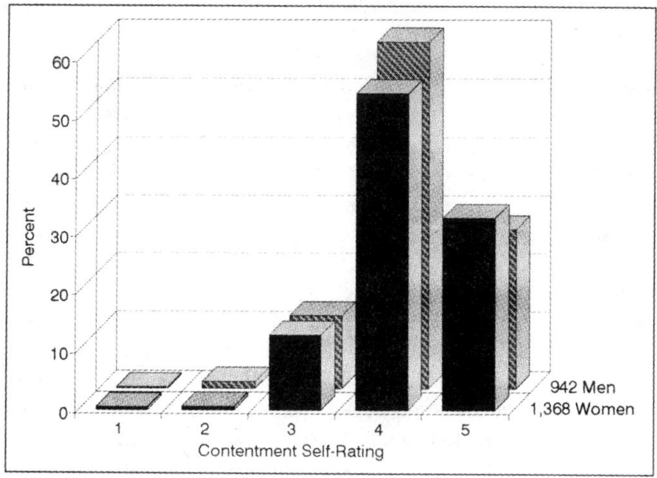

Fig. 1. Contentment ratings by gender for 2,310 Minnesota-born twins. Ratings are on a self-report scale from 1 (*the lowest 5% of the population*) to 5 (*the highest 5%*).

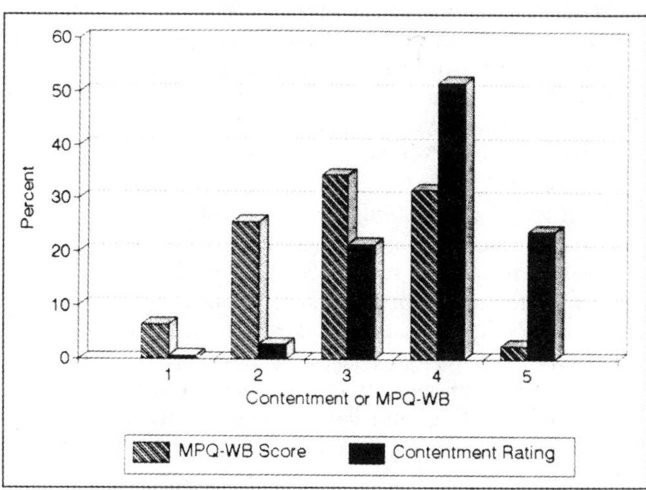

Fig. 3. Contentment self-ratings and Well-Being scores on the Multidimensional Personality Questionnaire (MPQ-WB) for 2,310 twins.

33–45, 46–54, 55–67, and >67; if the WB distribution were normal, these categories would have frequencies of 5%, 30%, 30%, 30%, and 5%, respectively, the same percentages that were specified for ratings on the contentment scale. As can be seen in the figure, the WB distribution is reasonably symmetrical, unlike the contentment self-ratings, presumably because the sum of the responses to the WB items measures variations in happiness around a mean value that represents a generally positive (rather than a negative or neutral) state of mind.

Myers and Diener (1995) suggested that their definition of subjective well-being (SWB) includes both the "presence of positive affect" and the "absence of negative affect" (p. 11). There is indeed substantial evidence that positive and negative emotions do not behave as merely the opposite poles of the same continuum. Positive and negative affect (PA and NA) emerge reliably as two largely independent superordinate state dimensions (e.g., Watson & Tellegen, 1985). The trait variables corresponding to these PA and NA state variables are the higher order Positive and Negative Emotionality (PE and NE) personality factors, both represented in the MPQ. In addition to the WB scale, which is a PE indicator, the MPQ includes a corresponding marker of NE, the Stress Reaction (SR) scale. WB and SR scores were correlated −.45 in the present sample of middle-aged twins. We estimated SWB simply as the difference between the two scores (i.e., SWB = WB − SR).

Because the predictors, years of education, SES, marital status, and current family income, were measured categorically, we computed eta coefficients, separately for men and women, and the proportion of the total variance in WB and in SWB accounted for by each of the predictors. In the case of married people, SES was defined as the status associated with either the subject's occupation or the subject's spouse's occupation, whichever was higher. To estimate the influence of religious commitment on happiness, we computed the correlation between WB and the Traditionalism scale of the MPQ. Finally, we estimated the heritability of WB on a large sample of middle-aged twins and the heritability of the stable component of happiness on a sample of twins who had been tested at about age 20 and then tested again some 10 years later.

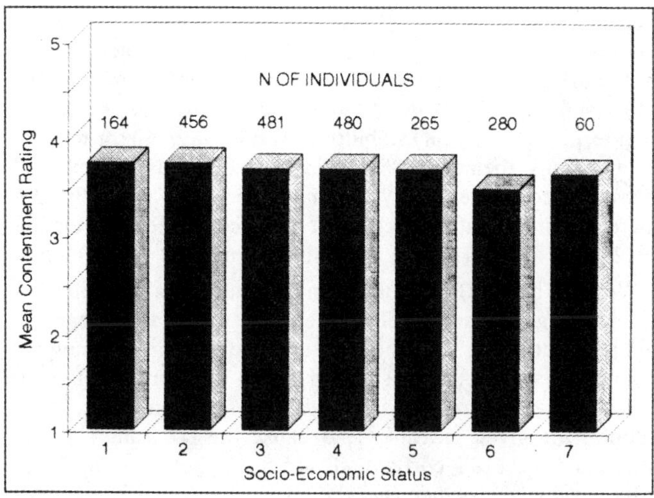

Fig. 2. Mean self-ratings for contentment of 2,186 middle-aged twins distributed among the seven categories of socioeconomic status from the professional class (1) to unskilled labor (6) and unemployed (7).

RESULTS

Demographic Status

Educational attainment accounted for less than 2% of the variance in WB for women, and less than 1% of the variance for men. For both men and women, SES accounted for less than 2% of the variance in general well-being. The data for income mirror those for SES: Income category accounted for less than 2% of the variance in feelings of well-being.

Even if one cannot predict happiness from the components of worldly success, such as education, income, or SES, maybe marital status has a stronger impact. Myers and Diener (1995, p.

15) cited meta-analyses indicating that there is a "happiness gap" between the married and the never-married, and we found one also, but it was trivial. The mean *T* score on WB for 3,571 married (and never divorced) twins was 50.1 (±0.16), and the mean for 337 never-married twins was 48.3 (±0.61). Less than 1% of the variance in WB was associated with marital status for men or women.

When these computations were repeated for our SWB estimate in place of WB, the relationships with the demographic variables were slightly stronger. Educational attainment and SES accounted for about 3% of the variance in SWB, and income for about 2%, but marital status still accounted for less than 1% of the variance. Thus, it appears that positive mood states are not much more frequent or intense for people with high social status or wealth and that people at the lower end of the social ladder are only slightly more vulnerable to negative mood states.

Traditional Values

The Traditionalism scale of the MPQ is moderately correlated (.49 ± .015) with religious commitment as measured by Waller, Kojetin, Lykken, Tellegen, and Bouchard (1990) but very weakly correlated (.05 ± .016) with scores on WB. Figure 4 shows that, whereas mean WB scores increase consistently, while SR scores decrease, from the lowest to the highest self-rating on contentment, contented people score no higher on Traditionalism than discontented people. Although these results do not refute the findings cited by Myers and Diener, they at least suggest that individual differences in religiousness cannot account for much of the variance in happiness. The same human adaptability that Myers and Diener invoked to explain why status and income do not determine happiness must apply here as well; religious conversion or being "born again" is said to be a joyful experience, but its effect on mood may not be more lasting than being promoted or winning the lottery.

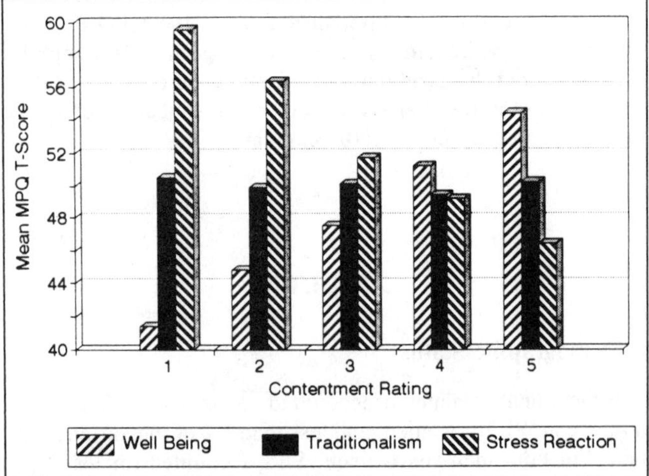

Fig. 4. Mean Well-Being, Stress Reaction, and Traditionalism scores on the Multidimensional Personality Questionnaire (MPQ) plotted against self-rated contentment. The MPQ scores have been converted into *T*-score form with mean = 50 and *SD* = 10.

The Heritability of Happiness

The MPQ was administered twice to a sample of younger twins who averaged 20 years of age at the first testing and 30 years at the second (McGue, Bacon, & Lykken, 1993). This sample included 79 monozygotic (MZ) twin pairs and 48 dizygotic (DZ) twin pairs, 254 individuals altogether. Scale scores were corrected for quadratic regression on age, separately for men and women. The retest correlation for the WB scale was .50, indicating, as one would expect, that there is considerable fluctuation in one's sense of well-being, especially perhaps during the important transitional period from age 20 to 30. These variations in subjective well-being no doubt are determined by the individual vicissitudes of life but not, apparently, by one's SES, income, educational achievement, marital status, or religious commitment (although it seems likely that marked and sudden changes in any of these would produce at least transitory changes in feelings of well-being).

For these younger twins who were retested after 10 years, we correlated Twin A's score on WB at Time 1 with Twin B's score at Time 2 (and, similarly, Twin B's score at Time 1 with Twin A's score at Time 2). For the 48 DZ pairs, this cross-twin, cross-time correlation for WB was essentially zero (.07); for the 79 MZ pairs, it equaled .40, or 80% of the retest correlation of .50. This disattenuated MZ correlation suggests that the stable component of well-being (i.e., trait happiness) is largely determined genetically. The negligible DZ correlation suggests that this stable and heritable component of happiness is an emergenic trait (Lykken, 1982; Lykken, Bouchard, McGue, & Tellegen, 1992), that is, a trait that is determined by a configural rather than an additive function of components. Emergenic traits, although determined in part genetically, do not tend to run in families, as do traits that are polygenic-additive.

A similar result was reported in an earlier study of 217 MZ and 114 DZ pairs of middle-aged Minnesota Registry twins, plus 44 MZ and 27 DZ pairs who were separated in infancy and reared apart (Tellegen et al., 1988). The best estimate of the heritability of WB in that study was .48 (±.08) and, as we found in the present study, a model involving only additive genetic effects did not fit the data. We assume that the 10-year retest reliability of WB for these older twins would be higher than the .50 reported for the age span from 20 to 30 years. Twenty-six pairs of the middle-aged twins reared apart were in fact retested on the MPQ by mail about 4.5 years after their first testing; the retest stability of WB for these 52 individuals was .67. If the long-term (e.g., 10 year) stability of WB is, say, .60 for middle-aged persons, then the 1988 data indicate that the heritability of the stable component of well-being is about .80 (.48/.60). Unshared environmental effects must then account for the remaining 20% of the variance in the stable component of happiness.

We now have MPQ results from both members of 1,380 pairs of middle-aged Minnesota Twin Registry twins (reared together and represented as MZT or DZT twins) and from a somewhat augmented sample of twins reared apart (MZA or DZA twins). The intraclass correlations for the WB scale on these larger samples are given in Table 1. Because the DZ values are so small, and the MZT correlations are not larger than the MZA values, we can conclude that the effects of shared home environment on SWB were negligible after the twins reached middle age. This conclusion means that the variance in adult happiness is determined about equally by genetic factors and by the effects of experiences unique to each individual.

Table 1. *Intraclass correlations on the Well-Being scale of the Multidimensional Personality Questionnaire for middle-aged twins reared together and reared apart*

Type of twin pair	Number of pairs	Intraclass *R*
Twins reared together:		
Monozygotic	647	.44 (±.03)
Dizygotic	733	.08 (±.04)
Twins reared apart:[a]		
Monozygotic	75	.52 (±.10)
Dizygotic	36	−.02 (±.17)

[a]We are indebted to T.J. Bouchard, Jr., for providing these data from the Minnesota Study of Twins Reared Apart.

No one doubts that making the team, being promoted at work, or winning the lottery tends to bring about an increment in happiness, just as flunking out, being laid off, or a disastrous investment would be likely to diminish one's feelings of well-being. As Myers and Diener (1995) suggested, however, the effects of these events appear to be transitory fluctuations about a stable temperamental set point or trait that is characteristic of the individual. Middle-aged people whose life circumstances have stabilized seem to be equally contented regardless of their social status or their income. The reported well-being of one's identical twin, either now or 10 years earlier, is a far better predictor of one's self-rated happiness than is one's own educational achievement, income, or status.

Is It "Happy Is as Happy Does" or the Other Way Around?

Myers and Diener suggested that people who enjoy close personal relationships, who become absorbed in their work, and who set themselves achievable goals and move toward them with determination are happier on the whole than people who do not. We agree, but we question the direction of the causal arrow. We know that when people with bipolar mood disorder are depressed, they tend to avoid intimate encounters or new experiences and tend to brood upon depressing thoughts rather than concentrating on their work. Then, when their mood swings toward elation, these same people tend to do the things that happy people do. There is undoubtedly a James-Lange feedback effect: Dysfunctional behavior exacerbates depression, whereas the things happy people do enhance their happiness. We argue, however, that the impetus is greater from mood to behavior than in the reverse direction. It may be that trying to be happier is as futile as trying to be taller and therefore is counterproductive.

CONCLUSIONS

If the transitory variations of well-being are largely due to fortune's favors, whereas the midpoint of these variations is determined by the great genetic lottery that occurs at conception, then we are led to conclude that individual differences in human happiness—how one feels at the moment and also how happy one feels on average over time—are primarily a matter of chance.

REFERENCES

Lykken, D.T. (1982). Research with twins: The concept of emergenesis. *Psychophysiology, 19,* 361–373.

Lykken, D.T., Bouchard, T.J., Jr., McGue, M., & Tellegen, A. (1990). The Minnesota Twin Registry: Some initial findings. *Acta Geneticae Medicae et Gemmellologiae, 39,* 35–70.

Lykken, D.T., Bouchard, T.J., Jr., McGue, M., & Tellegen, A. (1992). Emergenesis: Genetic traits that may not run in families. *American Psychologist, 47,* 1565–1577.

McGue, M., Bacon, S., & Lykken, D.T. (1993). Personality stability and change in early adulthood: A behavioral genetic analysis. *Developmental Psychology, 29,* 96–109.

Myers, D.G., & Diener, E. (1995). Who is happy? *Psychological Science, 6,* 10–19.

Tellegen, A. (1982). *Brief manual for the Multidimensional Personality Questionnaire.* Unpublished manuscript, University of Minnesota, Minneapolis.

Tellegen, A., Lykken, D.T., Bouchard, T.J., Jr., Wilcox, K., Segal, N., & Rich, S. (1988). Personality similarity in twins reared apart and together. *Journal of Personality and Social Psychology, 54,* 1031–1039.

Tellegen, A., & Waller, N. (1994). Exploring personality through test construction: Development of the Multidimensional Personality Questionnaire. In S.R. Briggs & J.M. Cheek (Eds.), *Personality measures: Development and evaluation* (Vol. 1, pp. 133–161). Greenwich, CT: JAI Press.

Waller, N., Kojetin, B., Lykken, D., Tellegen, A., & Bouchard, T. (1990). Religious interests, personality, and genetics: A study of twins reared together and apart. *Psychological Science, 1,* 138–142.

Watson, D., & Tellegen, A. (1985). Toward a consensual structure of mood. *Psychological Bulletin, 98,* 219–235.

(Received 4/4/95; Accepted 7/12/95)

On the Neurobiological Basis of Affiliation

New York Academy of Sciences conference examines social behavior from evolutionary and biological perspective

Two things caused a group of psychologists and neuro scientists to come together recently at Georgetown University in Washington, DC: neurobiology and affiliation. Convened for a New York Academy of Sciences conference, titled The Integrative Neurobiology of Affiliation, the group sought to examine the anatomy and physiology of the complex social interaction called affiliation.

The conference was supported in part by the National Institute of Mental Health, and the proceedings are scheduled to be published by the Academy in December of this year.

Focussing on only a sampling of the 29 total invited presentations, we highlight here the research of two of the five APS member presenters: Stephen W. Porges (University of Maryland-College Park) and David Crews (University of Texas-Austin). The other APS members included on the program of distinguished speakers were: Steven E. Brauth (Univ. of Maryland-College Park), Mary Carlson (Harvard Medical School), and William S. Hall (Univ. of Maryland-College Park).

Evolution's Quirky Logical Legacy

Both Porges and Crews study the evolution of the parts of the nervous system, and how those evolving parts function within the context of social behavior. To some degree, mammalian neural structures and functions can be traced to their ancient reptilian origins, and the ancient functional origins of modern behaviors and brain structures can elucidate the rather quirky logic that evolution bestows on neural systems underlying current-day mammalian social behavior.

The evolution of behavior must usually be inferred, rather than observed, because ancestral species are usually extinct, but David Crews finds among whiptail lizards a unique opportunity for the study of the evolution of sexual behavior; an ancestor and a descendant species live side by side, and can be directly compared.

Crucial to this evolutionary process is "exaptation," the process whereby an old structure is recruited to perform a new function. To put it another way, an old part of the nervous system is coopted for use in a new function, and the modern structure and function bear the stamp of both the logic of the ancient function it evolved from and the logic of the new function it now performs. While some aspects of the old function may be present, it is far from obvious in advance what part will be conserved and what aspect will be changed. Lest you think that behavior linked to the basic biological functions must remain boringly affixed to the system it first evolved to serve, here are two tales of exaptation.

Emotions and the Vagal Nerve Theory

Stephen W. Porges

Psychological study of the emotions can be a puzzling business. It often seems that all emotions are characterized as activations of the sympathetic nervous system, and the specific emotions are differentiated from each other on the basis of their cognitive components. Stephen Porges has developed the "polyvagal theory of the emotions," a new way of looking at our feelings. Porges's theory, elaborately detailed in the April 30 issue of the *New York Times*, resurrects the role of the parasympathetic nervous system and analyzes its multiple functions in light of evolutionary changes.

His contribution to the symposium, "Emotion: An Evolutionary By-Product of the Neural Regulation of the Autonomic Nervous System" could provide a way to put more "guts" into emotion research. Rather than concentrating on the sympathetic nervous system, which releases adrenaline in response to stress and activates the "fight-or-flight" response, Porges emphasizes the other half of the autonomic nervous system—the parasympathetic system—which basically mediates immobilization, and the conservation of metabolic energy.

Scared to Death

The single most important nerve in this system is the vagus nerve, or tenth cranial nerve. When strongly activated, the vagus nerve slows heart rate, slows or stops respiration (depending on species), and causes the digestive tract to empty. These are the hallmarks of complete terror, which essentially causes homeostatic systems to shut down. If severe enough, this response causes one to literally die of fright.

David Crews

How can this make evolutionary sense? This extreme response is, for humans and for all warm-blooded animals, a vestigial remnant of an ancient response that serves the cold-blooded vertebrates quite well: When all else fails, a reptile can "play dead" for a few minutes, during which time the danger just might go away. However, once mammals became warm-blooded, they lost the ability to survive oxygen deprivation for more than a few seconds.

So what happened to the vagal system for shutting down homeostatic systems to facilitate "playing dead"? Part of it survives as this vestigial system that has the power to cause death from fright, but the rest of it became modified into our complex system of control over our organs of emotional expression—the facial muscles and the larynx, for example—and into a finely adjustable "brake" that allows us to rapidly adjust our metabolic output, for example to rapidly switch from speaking to listening, without involving the sympathetic nervous system at all. In short, an old system for regulating one of the most basic needs (i.e., oxygen intake) has been exapted to enable us to get what we need from other individuals (e.g., by smiling, frowning, talking), and in the process has created a whole new universe of physiological responses. The graded interplay of the ancient vagal "play dead" response, the sympathetic "fight or flight" activation pathway, and the newest vagal modulatory pathways, plus the visceral afferents by which we sense our bodies' responses, combine to create the emotional component of our experience.

Neurogenic Evidence

A crucial piece of physical evidence Porges advances to support this interpretation is that the muscles and nerves involved in the expression of complex emotions (i.e., the facial and laryngeal muscles and the nerves that control them) all develop from the branchial arches of the embryo. These are the structures that become gills in fish, the structures originally dedicated to the regulation of oxygen supply. Known as the "vagabond" of the cranial nerves because of its wide, wandering path of innervation throughout the body, the vagal nerve appears to suffer from an ever-wandering function, as well!

On Pseudo-Sex, Lizards, and Evolution

The evolution of behavior must usually be inferred, rather than observed, because ancestral species are usually extinct, but David Crews finds among whiptail lizards a unique opportunity for the study of the evolution of sexual behavior; an ancestor and a descendant species live side by side, and can be directly compared. In this case, the descendants are parthenogenic (i.e., all the individuals are females), and they reproduce without sperm.

The loss of sexual reproduction in these animals must be relatively recent, because the immediate ancestor species (confirmed by genetic analysis) has both males and females and reproduces in the usual way. Although the parthenogenic lizards can reproduce without any sexual behavior if housed in isolation, they normally "go through the motions," alternating between male-like behavior (mounting) and female-like behavior (being mounted). In the bisexual species, male sexual behavior is stimulated by testosterone, acting on the anterior hypothalamus-preoptic area (AHPOA), and the AHPOA is larger in males than in females.

One might expect that this same brain nucleus, which is involved in the pseudo-male behavior of the parthenogenic lizards, would be enlarged since the pseudo-copulatory behaviors very closely resemble male behavior in the bisexual species. But it is not, and the sexual behaviors are not stimulated by androgen. Instead, progesterone has been coopted to play a role in initiation of male-like behaviors, and the AHPOA remains small and inactive, regardless of which pseudo-sexual phase the individual is going through. What's more, the typically "female" part of the hypothalamus, the ventromedial hypothalamus, is as well-developed in these animals as it is in the females of the ancestral species.

How did this behavior and its hormonal trigger evolve? Individual males of the ancestral bisexual species vary in their response to progesterone; some show typical courtship behavior in response to progesterone just as they do to testosterone. This preexisting variation in hormone response was therefore probably present in the individuals that gave rise to the new species and was incorporated as an essential part of its behavioral repertoire.

It may seem unexceptional to say, as did many participants at this conference, that behavior can be at the leading edge of evolutionary change. Perhaps what is most surprising is to uncover the ways in which complex behaviors have been cobbled together form bits and pieces of the most basic biology.

To order the full proceedings of the conference, contact the New York Academy of Sciences toll-free (800-843-6927 ext. 341). **Paul M. Rowe**

Paul M. Rowe is a freelance science writer based in Washington, DC.

Deciding Advantageously Before Knowing the Advantageous Strategy

Antoine Bechara, Hanna Damasio, Daniel Tranel, Antonio R. Damasio*

Deciding advantageously in a complex situation is thought to require overt reasoning on declarative knowledge, namely, on facts pertaining to premises, options for action, and outcomes of actions that embody the pertinent previous experience. An alternative possibility was investigated: that overt reasoning is preceded by a nonconscious biasing step that uses neural systems other than those that support declarative knowledge. Normal participants and patients with prefrontal damage and decision-making defects performed a gambling task in which behavioral, psychophysiological, and self-account measures were obtained in parallel. Normals began to choose advantageously before they realized which strategy worked best, whereas prefrontal patients continued to choose disadvantageously even after they knew the correct strategy. Moreover, normals began to generate anticipatory skin conductance responses (SCRs) whenever they pondered a choice that turned out to be risky, before they knew explicitly that it was a risky choice, whereas patients never developed anticipatory SCRs, although some eventually realized which choices were risky. The results suggest that, in normal individuals, nonconscious biases guide behavior before conscious knowledge does. Without the help of such biases, overt knowledge may be insufficient to ensure advantageous behavior.

In a gambling task that simulates real-life decision-making in the way it factors uncertainty, rewards, and penalties, the players are given four decks of cards, a loan of $2000 facsimile U.S. bills, and asked to play so that they can lose the least amount of money and win the most (*1*). Turning each card carries an immediate reward ($100 in decks A and B and $50 in decks C and D). Unpredictably, however, the turning of some cards also carries a penalty (which is large in decks A and B and small in decks C and D). Playing mostly from the disadvantageous decks (A and B) leads to an overall loss. Playing from the advantageous decks (C and D) leads to an overall gain. The players have no way of predicting when a penalty will arise in a given deck, no way to calculate with precision the net gain or loss from each deck, and no knowledge of how many cards they must turn to end the game (the game is stopped after 100 card selections). After encountering a few losses, normal participants begin to generate SCRs before selecting a card from the bad decks (*2*) and also begin to avoid the decks with large losses (*1*). Patients with bilateral damage to the ventromedial prefrontal cortices do neither (*1*, *2*).

A. Bechara and D. Tranel, Department of Neurology, Division of Behavioral Neurology and Cognitive Neuroscience, University of Iowa College of Medicine, Iowa City, IA 52242, USA.
H. Damasio and A. R. Damasio, Department of Neurology, Division of Behavioral Neurology and Cognitive Neuroscience, University of Iowa College of Medicine, Iowa City, IA 52242, and The Salk Institute of Biological Studies, La Jolla, CA 92186, USA.

*To whom correspondence should be addressed.

To investigate whether subjects choose correctly only after or before conceptualizing the nature of the game and reasoning over the pertinent knowledge, we continuously assessed, during their performance of the task, three lines of processing in 10 normal participants and in 6 patients (*3*) with bilateral damage of the ventromedial sector of the prefrontal cortex and decision-making defects. These included (i) behavioral performance, that is, the number of cards selected from the good decks versus the bad decks; (ii) SCRs generated before the selection of each card (*2*); and (iii) the subject's account of how they conceptualized the game and of the strategy they were using. The latter was assessed by interrupting the game briefly after each subject had made 20 card turns and had already encountered penalties, and asking the subject two questions: (i) "Tell me all you know about what is going on in this game." (ii) "Tell me how you feel about this game." The questions were repeated at 10-card intervals and the responses audiotaped.

After sampling all four decks, and before encountering any losses, subjects preferred decks A and B and did not generate significant anticipatory SCRs. We called this period pre-punishment. After encountering a few losses in decks A or B (usually by card 10), normal participants began to generate anticipatory SCRs to decks A and B. Yet by card 20, all indicated that they did not have a clue about what was going on. We called this period pre-hunch (Fig. 1). By about card 50,

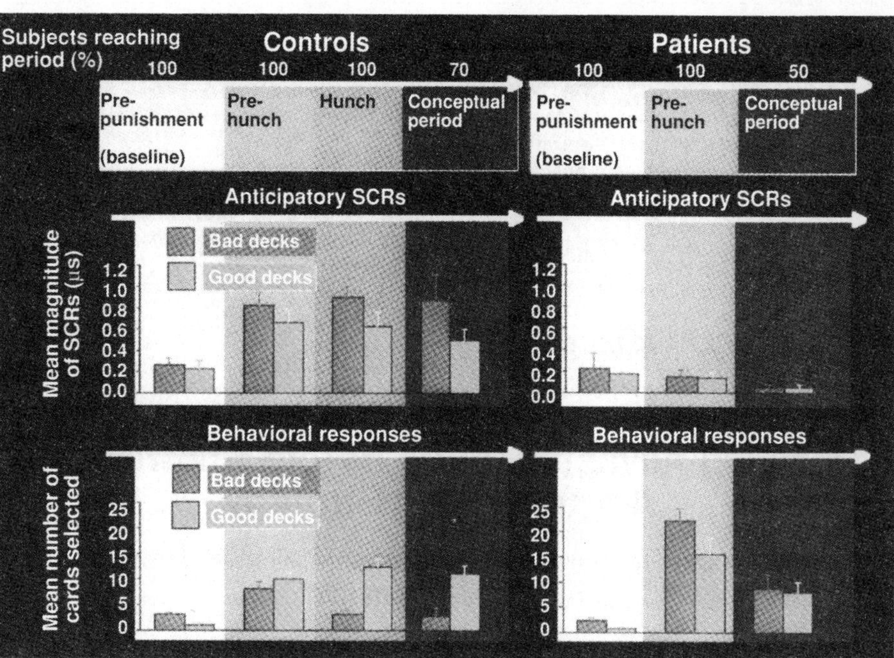

Fig. 1. Presentation of the four periods in terms of average numbers of cards selected from the bad decks (A and B) versus the good decks (C and D), and the mean magnitudes of anticipatory SCRs associated with the same cards. The pre-punishment period covered the start of the game when subjects sampled the decks and before they encountered the first loss (that is, up to about the 10th card selection). The pre-hunch period consisted of the next series of cards when subjects continued to choose cards from various decks, but professed no notion of what was happening in the game (on average, between the 10th (range: 7 to 13) and the 50th card (range: 30 to 60) in normals, or between the 9th (3 to 10) and the 80th card (60 to 90) in patients. The hunch period (never reached in patients) corresponded to the period when subjects reported "liking" or "disliking" certain decks, and "guessed" which decks were risky or safe, but were not sure of their answers [on average, between the 50th (30 to 60) and 80th card (60 to 90) in normals]. The conceptual period corresponded to the period when subjects were able to articulate accurately the nature of the task and tell for certain which were the good and bad decks, and why they were good or bad [on average, after the 80th card (60 to 90) in both normals and patients]. (Top panels) Bars represent means (±SEM) of the mean magnitude of anticipatory SCRs generated before the selection of cards from the bad decks versus the good decks. Anticipatory SCRs are generated in the time window before turning a card from any given deck, that is, during the time the subject ponders from which deck to choose (2). SCRs in association with the good and bad decks from normal controls or patients were not significantly different during the pre-punishment (baseline) period. However, there was a significant increase in the magnitude of these SCRs during the pre-hunch period, but only for normal controls. During the next two periods, SCR activity in normal subjects was sustained in the case of the bad decks, but it began to subside in the case of the good decks (8). (Bottom panels) Bars in the "Behavioral responses" plots represent means (±SEM) of the mean number of cards selected from the bad decks versus those selected from the good decks. Normal controls selected more cards from the good decks during the pre-hunch, hunch, and conceptual periods. In contrast, prefrontal patients selected more cards from the bad decks during these periods (9).

all normal participants began to express a "hunch" that decks A and B were riskier and all generated anticipatory SCRs whenever they pondered a choice from deck A or B. We called this period hunch. None of the patients generated anticipatory SCRs or expressed a "hunch" (Fig. 1). By card 80, many normal participants expressed knowledge about why, in the long run, decks A and B were bad and decks C and D were good. We called this period conceptual. Seven of the 10 normal participants reached the conceptual period, during which they continued to avoid the bad decks, and continued to generate SCRs whenever they considered sampling again from the bad decks. Remarkably, the three normal participants who did not reach the conceptual period still made advantageous choices (4). Just as remarkably, the three patients with prefrontal damage who reached the conceptual period and correctly described which were the bad and good decks chose disadvantageously. None of the patients generated anticipatory SCRs (Fig. 1). Thus, despite an accurate account of the task and of the correct strategy, these patients failed to generate autonomic responses and continued to select cards from the bad decks. The patients failed to act according to their correct conceptual knowledge.

On the basis of these results, we suggest that the sensory representation of a situation that requires a decision leads to two largely parallel but interacting chains of events (Fig. 2). In one, either the sensory representation of the situation or of the facts evoked by it activate neural systems that hold nondeclarative dispositional knowledge related to the individual's previous emotional experience of similar situations (5). The ventromedial frontal cortices are among the structures that we suspect hold such dispositional knowledge, the activation of which, in turn, activates autonomic and neurotransmitter nuclei (such as those that deliver dopamine to selected cortical and subcortical forebrain regions), among other regions. The ensuing nonconscious signals then act as covert biases on the circuits that support processes of cognitive evaluation and reasoning (6). In the other chain of events, the representation of the situation generates (i) the overt recall of pertinent facts, for example, various response options and future outcomes pertaining to a given course of action; and (ii) the application of reasoning strategies to facts and options. Our experiment indicates that in normal participants, the activation of covert biases preceded overt reasoning on the available facts. Subsequently, the covert biases may have assisted the reasoning process in cooperative manner, that is, biases would not decide per se, but rather facilitate the efficient processing of knowledge and logic necessary for

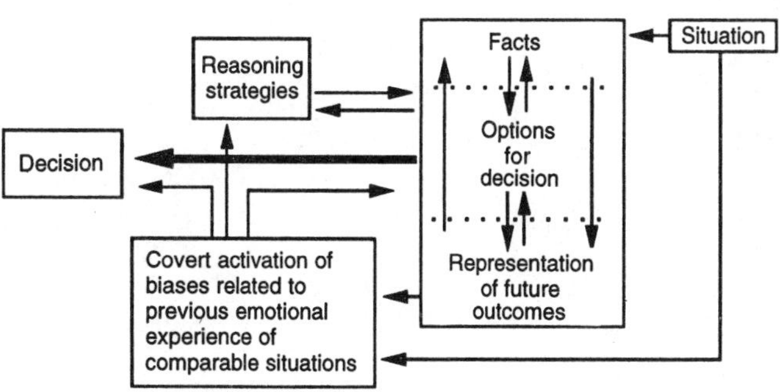

Fig. 2. Diagram of the proposed steps involved in decision-making.

conscious decisions (7). We suspect that the autonomic responses we detected are evidence for a complex process of nonconscious signaling, which reflects access to records of previous individual experience—specifically, of records shaped by reward, punishment, and the emotional state that attends them. In this light, damage to ventromedial cortices acts by precluding access to a particular kind of record of previous and related individual experience.

REFERENCES AND NOTES

1. A. Bechara, A. R. Damasio, H. Damasio, S. W. Anderson, *Cognition* **50**, 7 (1994).
2. A. Bechara, D. Tranel, H. Damasio, A. R. Damasio, *Cereb. Cortex* **6**, 215 (1996).
3. The patients who participated in the experiment were drawn from the Division of Cognitive Neuroscience's Patient Registry and have been described previously (*1*, *2*). Three are female (ages 53, 63, and 64), and three are male (ages 51, 52, and 65). All have stable focal lesions. Years of education: 13 ± 2 (mean ± SEM); verbal IQ: 111 ± 8 (mean ± SEM); performance IQ: 102 ± 8 (mean ± SEM).
4. The results in this group of normal participants are similar to the results described previously in other normal participants (*2*).
5. A. R. Damasio, *Descartes' Error: Emotion, Reason, and the Human Brain* (Grosset/Putnam, New York, 1994).
6. We envision these biases to act as markers or qualifiers in the manner suggested by A. Damasio [in (*5*), chap. 8] and by A. R. Damasio, D. Tranel, and H. Damasio [in *Frontal Lobe Function and Dysfunction*, H. S. Levin, H. M. Eisenberg, A. L. Benton, Eds. (Oxford Univ. Press, New York, 1991), pp. 217]. See also P. R. Montague, P. Dayan, C. Person, T. J. Sejnowski, *Nature* **377**, 725 (1995). This action might occur both at the cortical level and in subcortical structures such as basal ganglia.
7. On the basis of a series of related studies [A. Bechara, D. Tranel, H. Damasio, S. W. Anderson, A. R. Damasio, *Soc. Neurosci. Abstr.* **21**, 1210 (1995); D. Tranel, A. Bechara, H. Damasio, A. R. Damasio, *ibid.* **22**, 1108 (1996)], we believe that the bias mechanism identified here is distinct from other neural mechanisms whose integrity is crucial for decision- making. Such mechanisms include response inhibition [J. M. Fuster, *The Prefrontal Cortex: Anatomy, Physiology, and Neuropsychology of the Frontal Lobe* (Raven, New York, ed. 3, 1996); R. Dias, T. W. Robbins, A. C. Roberts, *Nature* **380**, 69 (1996); A. Diamond, in *The Development and Neural Bases of Higher Cognitive Functions*, A. Diamond, Ed. (New York Academy of Sciences, New York, 1990), vol. 608, pp. 637–669], working memory [P. S. Goldman-Rakic, in *Handbook of Physiology; The Nervous System*, F. Plum, Ed. (American Physiological Society, Bethesda, MD, 1987), vol. 5, pp. 373–401], and selective attention [M. I. Posner and S. Dehaene, *Trends Neurosci.* **17**, 75 (1994)]. In other words, we propose an addition to mechanisms already recognized as necessary for proper reasoning rather than an alternative to those mechanisms.
8. A three-way analysis of variance (ANOVA) on the anticipatory SCRs generated by normal participants and patients (between group), during the pre-punishment and pre-hunch periods (within group), and in association with the bad and good decks (within group) revealed, most importantly, a significant two-way interaction of group with period [$F(1,14) = 16.24, P < 0.001$]. Subsequent Newman-Keuls tests on these SCRs revealed that, during the pre-punishment (baseline) period, the SCRs associated with the good or bad decks of normals or patients were not significantly different. However, there was a significant increase in the magnitude of these SCRs during the pre-hunch period, relative to the pre-punishment period, but only for normals ($P < 0.01$). The SCRs from normals during pre-hunch were also significantly higher than the SCRs of patients during both pre-punishment and pre-hunch ($P < 0.01$). Because all normals generated anticipatory SCRs, whereas all patients did not, Fisher's exact test, based on the hypergeometric distribution, yielded a one-sided $P < 0.001$. SCRs from normals who selected cards from the bad decks during the hunch period were compared to the SCRs associated with sampling the good decks. The same comparisons of SCRs were done for the conceptual period. Although SCRs from the bad decks during the hunch or the conceptual period were generally higher than those from the good decks, the difference did not reach statistical significance. However, Newman-Keuls tests comparing SCRs from the hunch or the conceptual period to those from the pre-punishment period revealed significant differences in the case of the bad decks ($P < 0.01$) but not the good decks. This suggests that SCR activity was sustained in the case of the bad decks, but may have been subsiding in the case of the good decks.
9. A similar ANOVA in which mean number of cards selected was used instead of SCRs revealed, most importantly, a significant three-way interaction of group with period with decks [$F(1,14) = 6.9, P < 0.02$]. With subsequent Newman-Keuls tests, the most relevant comparison was that patients selected significantly more cards from the bad decks relative to the good decks during the pre-hunch period ($P < 0.01$). By contrast, controls selected more from the good decks relative to the bad decks (the difference was not statistically significant). During the hunch and conceptual periods, controls selected significantly more cards from the good decks relative to the bad decks ($P < 0.01$). By contrast, patients still selected more cards from the bad decks relative to the good decks during the conceptual period (the difference was not statistically significant).

10. Supported by the National Institute of Neurological Diseases and Stroke grant PO1 NS19632.

29 October 1996; accepted 30 January 1997

ADDENDUM to Bechara et al. (1997):

Since its publication, this article has been interpreted as providing a neural foundation for the phenomenon of intuition and for a number of phenomena regarding nonconscious processing in the realm of social psychology. This is a broader context than the one we had originally considered, but that broader context is in keeping with the main thrust of the work. Key references in regard to this other context are Kilhstrom (1987), Lewicki et al. (1992), Reber (1989), and Roediger (1990).

Kihlstrom J. (1987). The cognitive unconscious. *Science,* **237,** 1445–1452.

Lewicki, P., Hill, T., & Czyzewska, M. (1992). Nonconscious acquisition of information. *American Psychologist,* **47,** 796–801.

Reber, A. S. (1989). Implicit learning and tacit knowledge. *Journal of Experimental Psychology: General,* **118,** 219–235.

Roediger, H. L. (1990). Implicit memory: Retention without remembering. *American Psychologist,* **45,** 1043–1056.

Something Snapped

A SCIENTIST FIGHTS TO ESTABLISH A NEW THEORY THAT EXPLAINS, AND MAY HELP TO PREVENT, SUDDEN AND SEEMINGLY INEXPLICABLE ACTS OF VIOLENCE.

BY PHILIP LOPICCOLO

As she read through police reports of the bizarre homicide, Anneliese Pontius, the forensic psychiatrist assigned to the case, was as puzzled as everyone else. On paper, the alleged killer, whose mental status she was to assess, seemed unremarkable. A handsome male in his early twenties, Ian Walter (not his real name) had no criminal record and no history of violence. In fact, acquaintances described him as reclusive and shy. But a few days earlier, this mild-mannered social loner had gone berserk.

❖ While picnicking with a companion, Walter is suddenly overcome by a strange feeling. He imagines seeing two large white male dogs fighting but is puzzled because he knows only one such dog is really present. Intrigued, he chases them, but the dogs run away and vanish "into nothing" as they jump over a river. ❖ In their place, Walter sees a fisherman in waders holding out a fly rod. Suddenly, Walter charges the man—a total

Reprinted with permission from *Technology Review,* October 1996, pp. 52-61. © 1996 by the Association of Alumni and Alumnae of the Massachusetts Institute of Technology.

stranger toward whom he harbored no ill feelings—and pushes him underwater, saying, "I'll teach you how to fish like a bear." The man, in his forties, finds a rock and tries to hit Walter in the face. Meanwhile, Walter's picnic companion arrives , grabs his head, and shouts, "No! No! Don't do it!" But Walter, seemingly emotionless, bites her finger and holds the man under until he drowns. He then tries to drown his companion too, but he suddenly comes to his senses and lets her go.

Next, hallucinating that he hears the sound of bloodhounds, Walter takes off his bright red shirt and hides it, thinking he won't be as easily detected. He goes home, takes a shower, and, when the police arrive, readily confesses not only to the drowning but also to murdering a shopkeeper, which turns out to be a complete fabrication. He feels so remorseful that he later tries to hang himself in his jail cell, but the bootlaces he uses break.

By the time she finished examining the file, Pontius, a psychiatrist at Massachusetts General Hospital and associate clinical professor of psychiatry at Harvard University, suspected that the case might not be as inexplicable as it seemed. In thousands of interviews with convicted felons over the past 36 years, she recalled seeing this precise pattern several times before. In fact, she reached a point 15 years ago when she decided to begin documenting these odd cases. And since then, from examinations of more than 200 alleged killers, she has recorded the details of some 20 examples of social loners like Walter who committed eerily similar brief psychotic acts.

From her analysis of these cases, she has proposed a radical new theory: that certain shy and lonely people who ruminate about stresses and traumas that most people vent to family members or friends may be at risk of a type of brain seizure that can produce extreme and potentially lethal behavior. Her research could have profound legal implications if used as a new insanity defense. Perhaps more significantly, it could change our attitudes about long-term loneliness and lend support to the notion that some form of intervention is vital, particularly at an early age.

Motiveless Murders

As Pontius began studying each odd new case in greater depth, she was struck by how incongruous they all seemed with respect to typical homicides. Indeed, most murderers have both a motive and a plan. They tend to have strong feelings of rage, jealousy, and greed. They usually kill people they know, often members of their own families. And they normally do not experience sudden brief psychotic episodes.

Pontius's cases appeared vastly different from one another in their specific details, but she found on closer examination that each was fundamentally the same in at least a dozen significant ways. All featured reasonably healthy young men who were social loners with no plan or motive for committing a homicide. Just before the attack, each felt puzzled by strange hallucinations or feelings about suddenly revived past memories. The murder itself was carried out without rage or feeling, much like an animal kills its prey. During the act, the perpetrator felt spontaneous visceral responses—such as nausea, racing heart, and incontinence—and experienced escalating psychotic hallucinations or delusions, often of grandeur. When the killer snapped out of his altered state, which usually lasted only a few minutes, he had almost total recall of the homicidal act. Still, he made no reasonable attempt to conceal it but rather often acted "stupidly" and felt overwhelming remorse, frequently turning himself over to the police or attempting suicide.

Because of these remarkable similarities, Pontius believed, the cases could not be written off as mere anomalies or coincidences. Nor could these symptoms be adequately classified by vague labels such as "atypical psychosis" or "brief psychosis not otherwise specified" or "organic delusional disorder." "Those are just wastepaperbasket terms," she maintains, "with no explanatory value and therefore no potential remedial value."

A New Syndrome

In search of a more specific and useful diagnosis, Pontius ruled out the well-established disorders that share some of the same symptoms. For example, while some epileptic seizures can cause sudden hallucinations, they cloud consciousness, often to the point of a total blackout, leaving the victim both incapable of performing a complex act like murder and unable to remember much about any activities performed during the episode. Likewise, schizophrenia causes delusions and hallucinations, usually auditory, but it is a recurring, long-term condition characterized by specific thought disturbances and lifelong coping problems. Post-traumatic stress disorder, which is caused by traumas experienced during war, natural catastrophes, or other violent encounters, can be accompanied by visceral reactions, but the condition persists for years, usually without psychosis or violence. Panic attacks, which also entail spontaneous visceral responses, result in recurring avoidant behavior, not aggression.

Pontius also eliminated several other well-known but less-common disorders that researchers have recently suggested to explain the behavior. Some argue, for example, that temporal-lobe epilepsy, which occasionally leaves its victims irritable and aggressive between seizures, might be responsible for such explosive actions. But Pontius thinks this does not apply. As evidence she points to a recent study of between-seizure aggression in some 5,400 cases that found only one instance of mildly aggressive behavior that was nowhere near the level of violence evinced by her subjects.

Philip LoPiccolo is a senior editor of Technology Review.

Finally, others suggest that homicidal behavior might occur during a dissociative state, in which a person with multiple personalities takes on the identity of a dangerously aggressive self. But Pontius notes that behavioral changes in people with dissociative or multiple personality disorders are usually recurring and much longer lasting than the fleeting changes demonstrated by her subjects.

Unable to apply a known diagnosis, Pontius began to explore whether the dozen or so symptoms that each perpetrator exhibited could be caused by a malfunction in a mysterious part of the brain—the limbic system—where aggressive drives originate. Experiments in which scientists observed the behavior of animals whose limbic systems have been damaged have shown that it is a center of emotion and memory and is responsible for aggressive behavior—such as predatory or defense killing—that has helped ensure the survival of the individual or the species.

In humans, limbic drives are usually held in check by the highly developed frontal-lobe system, which composes fully one-third of the brain. Indeed, we know from positron emission tomography (PET) scans, functional magnetic resonance imaging (FMRI), and other modern brain-imaging techniques that the frontal lobes are most active when the brain is performing so-called executive functions, such as planning ahead, postponing gratification, and considering the consequences and implications of actions, which essentially define socialized behavior.

But if the limbic system becomes overstimulated, Pontius theorizes, it might temporarily overwhelm the frontal lobes—with which it has an intimately reciprocal relationship—and thus the ability to control animalistic urges. Such an imbalance, she believes, could produce the very symptoms exhibited by the specific subgroup of felons she has been studying.

One way the limbic system could become hyperstimulated, Pontius suggests, is by undergoing the same kind of electrical storm that causes seizures. But unlike seizures that attack the frontal lobes or other highly advanced brain systems—thus clouding or impairing a victim's reasoning ability, consciousness, and memory—a limbic seizure might be more selective, she says. Such a "partial" seizure might leave the rest of the brain largely intact and functioning, albeit impaired, as it is temporarily unable to control the supercharged aggressive drives.

In Search of a Trigger

Pontius is convinced that she has identified a cluster of unique symptoms and a probable underlying cause—a brain seizure—that together define a new syndrome, which she has termed limbic psychotic trigger reaction. When it comes to explaining what the "trigger" would be for such an extreme response—the all-important next step in the process of determining how to help people suffering from the affliction—she offers what she feels is the most likely cause but admits that it is both preliminary and as yet unproven.

As she began searching for a trigger—or, more formally, an engendering neurophysiological mechanism—Pontius reviewed the medical records of her subjects and asked them to undergo electroencephalogram (EEG) studies, computed tomography (CT) scans, or magnetic resonance imaging (MRI) studies. She found scattered abnormalities in some of the cases but no evidence of a common brain affliction. Yet when she once again employed the analytic tools of her trade, detailed clinical observations and patient interviews, she discovered in each case a powerful, highly individualized external stimulus—a specific event that revived the memory of a stressful experience from the past—that she believes "kindled" a limbic seizure capable of causing homicidal episodes.

Pontius points to neurophysiological research to support this notion of seizure kindling. In fact, over the past three decades researchers have induced brain seizures in a wide range of mammals, "from rats to monkeys," she says, with no evidence of structural brain damage merely by subjecting them to harmless, repetitive, intermittent stimuli—electrical shocks or periods of isolation, for example.

Pontius found that Ian Walter's psychological history correlates with the kindled-seizure concept. The initial stimulus in Walter's case, an unforgotten experience from his childhood, she believes, was that his father died suddenly when Walter was five years old. According to his mother's account, Walter did not express any sadness over the death. He had argued with his father just before his fatal heart attack and did not attend his funeral. "Good riddance," he had said. "After all, I was mad at Father anyhow."

After his father's death, Walter became isolated. He apparently wasn't close to his well-to-do mother, since he was raised by her servants—a married couple he described as disciplinarians. Nor was he close to his three brothers who were one to two decades his senior. Throughout his childhood, adolescence, and early adult years, it seemed that he had failed to develop a lasting and trusting relationship with anyone but rather had only fleeting, superficial relationships. When Pontius asked him which animal he identified with, he responded, "The bear resembles me most. He is strong, isolated, and he hibernates."

In the interview, Walter spontaneously recalled memories of his father teaching him to fish. Most significantly, he said that for as long as he could remember, he would frequently see a photograph in his older brother's living room of his father in fishing gear in a specific posture. "I have a very clear picture of it in my mind," he said. "He is looking back sideways, a fly rod in his hand, holding it out and smiling." When Pontius asked him to draw a picture of his fisherman-victim, he drew what she describes as "a man in fishing gear, with waders, in half-body profile, full face, holding a fly rod into a river."

Pontius suggests that Walter's inability to share his thoughts and feelings with anyone about his father's death prevented him from "laying them to rest." As Walter was growing up, he was frequently reminded of his father, especially when he saw his brother's photo of him. Many such stresses may have contributed to Walter's precarious mental state. But Pontius assumes that the sight of a man in waders with a fishing rod striking his father's familiar pose was the trigger stimulus that vividly revived Walter's memories about his father and kindled a partial limbic-system seizure that finally pushed him over the brink.

The first signs that the seizure was creating an imbalance between the limbic system and frontal lobes, Pontius says, was Walter's puzzlement and hallucination about two large white dogs fighting and his distorted sense of time (he believed he stalked the dogs for "only a few paces," while witnesses said the chase lasted at least several minutes).

In the next phase of the seizure, during which Walter drowned the fisherman, the frontal lobes weren't able to contain the aggressive impulses coming from the limbic system, but Walter was able to continue functioning on most other levels. For instance, he remained conscious but behaved completely out of character and illogically, as evidenced by the act itself and his telling the victim he would teach him to "fish like a bear." He also had full control of his motor skills, which enabled him to carry out the attack, and was able to find his way home and retain a detailed memory of the events when he began to recover some 15 or 20 minutes later.

In the final stage of the seizure, the frontal lobes were regaining control over the limbic system but had not yet fully recovered. During this period, Walter suddenly abandoned drowning a second victim but experienced auditory hallucinations of bloodhounds barking and acted inefficiently in his attempts to conceal the crime by hiding his shirt and simply going home to take a shower after having sweated profusely. His false confession of having killed a shopkeeper was also a likely sign of lingering frontal-lobe dysfunction.

Where's the Proof?

Pontius's theory has generated a storm of controversy in the psychiatric community, and not just concerning her proposed trigger of a kindled limbic seizure—which she admits is debatable—but also about whether she has even defined a new syndrome.

Unfortunately, Pontius points out, proof is hard to come by, just as it is for most other partial seizures such as temporal-lobe epilepsy, which, despite being recognized as a syndrome for half a century, is still mainly a diagnosis based on behavior. For one thing, the EEG studies she has conducted on her subjects could not be definitive, even if by some chance a seizure were triggered during testing. That's because the EEG is merely a crude way of recording electrical activity from the surface of the brain, she explains, and is not nearly sensitive enough to detect readings from structures residing as deeply as the limbic system. Furthermore, even the most advanced deep-brain imaging technologies, such as PET, FMRI, and single proton emission computed tomography (SPECT), are not sophisticated enough to prove that a limbic seizure causes homicidal behavior, she says, even if these brain-scanning techniques could be performed during the act.

But Pontius points to physical evidence that she thinks does support her hypothesis, at least indirectly. Rather than trying to recreate settings that might trigger bizarre behavior (which, even if permitted, would be difficult as well as dangerous), and then trying to identify any abnormal electrical discharges in the limbic system, she wondered what would happen if the scenario were reversed. In other words, if the limbic system were purposely overstimulated, what perceptual and behavioral changes would a subject exhibit?

Obviously, inserting electrodes into someone's brain would pose both practical and ethical problems. But in 1982, a team led by Pierre Gloor, a neurologist at the University of Montreal, conducted just such experiments on about 45 subjects—albeit not to test new theories about the behavioral effect from partial seizures of the limbic system. Rather, his group was attempting to pinpoint the source of seizures in patients with severe temporal-lobe epilepsy so neurosurgeons could excise the smallest possible portion of the brain necessary to short-circuit the neural surges.

Gloor's group surgically inserted electrodes at various points in each patient's brain and, because brain tissue lacks pain receptors, left the electrodes in place for several days, even while the patients remained conscious. As Gloor electrically stimulated a portion of the limbic system called the amygdala in the patients, each described symptoms that correlated remarkably with the specific experiences recalled by the felons Pontius had assessed—including visual or auditory hallucinations, strange indescribable feelings, unusual visceral sensations, time distortions, and revived memories.

Though Pontius believes Gloor's study provides compelling evidence, many remain skeptical. "It certainly fits in with the anatomy and behavioral physiology of the syndrome that she proposes," says Joseph Coyle, chair of the psychiatry department at Harvard. "But for all we know, Gloor's results could be coincidental," he says. "What still needs to be demonstrated is that the behavior she describes is related to abnormal electrical activity in the brain, and that the electrical activity is triggered by a particular percept."

One of those who do find Pontius's theory persuasive is Bernhard Fox, a professor of psychiatry and behavioral sciences at Boston University School of Medicine. First of all, he says, while journals usually demand eight cases before they will accept claims of a new syndrome or disease entity, Pontius has already identified more than twice that many. Second, he points out, she has listed about a dozen specific criteria common to each of the cases—more than enough to define the syndrome. "I find that just a few of the criteria—that the murderers did not act deliberately, had no plan or motive, did not try to conceal the crime, and felt extreme remorse—to be very powerful evidence for a new syndrome." Overall, he says, "I would say that this stands a good chance of being cross-validated by other people, once they take a good look at it."

Another aspect of Pontius's theory that Fox and others find significant is that limbic seizures may appear in degrees. The researchers speculate therefore that they may be much more common and varied than might otherwise be expected. Indeed, Pontius points out that not all of her cases entailed homicides; some involved other limbic survival drives such as acquisition and sex.

Consider the experience of the devout 55-year-old monk living in a monastery in New England who was on an outing to the city. When he reaches into his pocket for the money he thought he had been given, he finds he has none. Suddenly, he decides to rob a nearby bank. He walks up to the teller and convinces her to give him $100. He takes the money, goes to a topless club, and starts fondling the performers, telling them his sudden delusional belief that he is a greater painter than Rembrandt and a better writer than Thomas Merton, a renowned monk and author. Suddenly, he snaps out of it and goes straight to the police and confesses. At first they don't believe him. But when the bank confirms his story, they arrest him and send him to the hospital, where Pontius examined him and suggested he be returned to the monastery and kept under closer surveillance.

During the interview with the monk, Pontius learned that he had grown up very poor during the Depression and was distraught during his childhood that his mother had to work as a domestic servant. Several years later, when he entered the monastery, he took a vow of poverty. Pontius maintains that the stresses associated with his family's poverty during his childhood may have been repeated many times during the monk's years in the monastery. The fact that he lived a lonely life in which he did not share his memories about these often-repeated experiences, she says, may have contributed to the limbic seizure, which may have been triggered by reaching into a pocket for money and finding none.

"Less extreme cases might not ordinarily come to the attention of anyone," says Pontius. But a specific, personalized trigger may frequently cause limbic overactivation in some social loners who harbor their emotions over a long period. As a result, they may suddenly do "irrational things that ruin their whole lives."

The Pain of Separation

Pontius stresses that not all loners are prone to committing violent acts or manifesting other uncontrolled limbic drives. In fact, unlike the extremely isolated subjects she has been studying, most lonely or shy people have at least one close friend or family member with whom to share thoughts and feelings about even normal stresses.

Jerome Kagan, a professor of psychology at Harvard and a prominent expert in shyness, is quick to agree. "Occasionally we get a shy person who loses it," he says. For instance, John Hinckley, the would-be assassin of President Reagan, was "a shy boy," as was Theodore Kaczynski, the suspected Unabomber. But most shy people obviously don't kill, he says. In fact, studies have shown that "the more shy you are, the *less* likely you are to do anything aggressive."

Nevertheless, one researcher who agrees that extreme social isolation has the power to trigger seizures is Paul MacLean, author of *The Triune Brain in Evolution*—a seminal work that explores how the human forebrain evolved and expanded to its great size while retaining an ancestral relationship to reptiles, early mammals, and late mammals through the limbic system. "The worst thing that can happen to a mammal is separation," he says. "The need for socialization can probably be traced to the early evolution of mammals, when the nursing call developed—in the newest part of the limbic system, incidentally—to help prevent separation of mother and infant," explains MacLean, a senior research scientist in the National Institute of Mental Health and former head of the NIMH Laboratory of Brain Evolution and Behavior. He points out that only three things distinguish mammals from reptiles and other vertebrates: the development of nursing and maternal care, the vocal communication for maintaining maternal-offspring contact, and playful behavior. "When the very things that make us mammals, as opposed to birds or reptiles, are denied us," he says, "this can have devastating effects."

Pontius believes that in some cases severe limbic seizures might be prevented if social loners were provided with at least one friendly person to talk to, especially in their early years, perhaps by teachers who look out for very lonely children. They should have a steady friend they can trust, she says.

Trust is particularly vital during the first three to five years of life, says Pontius, who is also trained in child psychiatry. If it is not established or is broken through separation or loss during that time, "children can withdraw into themselves and never trust anyone again, ever." Psychotherapy later in life may only partially alleviate such lack of trust.

If parents cannot provide steady friendship, options for helping lonely children include finding other adults, such as scout leaders or participants in the Big Brother and Big Sister programs, or peers for them to talk to, Pontius says. Unfortunately, peers usually shun loners, which only makes matters worse, she says.

Recommending help for distrustful or otherwise troubled social loners is one aspect of Pontius's work about which most everyone agrees. But it's important to know the cause, says David Bear, professor of psychiatry at the University of Massachusetts Medical School. "With Pontius's patients, if you could get them to a therapist and let them start talking about this disturbing event and not make it so private and mysterious, then catharsis, one of the oldest psychiatric tools, could work." With schizophrenics, he says, an antipsychotic medication might be appropriate in addition to some kind of supportive therapy.

In either case, Bear says it's important to stress that intervention is critical. Someone might be at risk of committing suicide or of becoming violent, even of committing multiple murders, he says, so the key is to open a channel of communication. As an example, he cites the case of John Salvi, who was convicted in March of killing two women at an abortion clinic in Brookline, Mass. "The only thing Salvi asked for was to get his statement out to the world about how Catholics are persecuted and how he has a scheme to prevent it," says Bear, who testified as an expert psychiatric witness for the defense in the trial. "If someone had talked to him or if he had gotten any psychiatric attention, then the whole thing might not have happened."

MacLean says intervention is also beneficial because it helps ease the pain of loneliness and separation, which creates the kind of tension that can trigger seizures. In fact, he recalls conducting trials of drugs to reduce epileptic seizures and finding that by "just sitting down and talking to the patients," both those in the control group and those treated with the new medication improved. "People have all this stuff going on internally that they are not aware of, and most doctors are not aware of, that can precipitate seizures."

Finally, some researchers, including Kenneth Blum, a professor of pharmacology at the University of Texas at San Antonio, who has reviewed Pontius's work, thinks that medications could be effective in treating limbic-seizure disorders. "We know that we can treat certain violent tendencies with an anticonvulsant drug called Carbamazepine, or Tegretol," he says.

Alternative Explanations

While Pontius vigorously defends her definition of a new syndrome and believes that reminders of even minor repetitive stresses can kindle psychotic limbic seizures, she is eager to explore theories about other possible engendering mechanisms. For example, she recently began collaborating with Blum, who has also been working with social loners suffering from aberrant behaviors that purportedly stem from limbic-system dysfunction. Blum believes he has found a genetic root to such problems—specifically, he claims to have discovered a genetic deficiency in a group of receptors that accept a chemical messenger called dopamine that elicits pleasant feelings in the limbic system.

Blum suggests that what Pontius is talking about are people who suffer from this so-called reward-deficiency syndrome. "Her limbic psychotic trigger mechanism is essentially the failure of the brain in these people to carry the proper genetic messages to allow them to feel good," he says. Without realizing why, they engage in dopamine-producing behaviors, such as sex or gambling, he says, while others go to the extreme of committing acts of violence and murder.

Pontius disagrees that her patients committed homicide for pleasure or for *any* purpose, and thinks that her patients and Blum's probably suffer from different types of limbic dysfunctions. Still, she is curious about the role of genetic factors in limbic-system dysfunctioning, as they may provide the hard physical evidence that her skeptics have been clamoring for. Indeed, Pontius has begun sending Blum DNA samples from her subjects so he can look for defects in the genes associated with the dopamine receptors.

Pontius is also in contact with Paul MacLean of NIMH, who believes that lesions in the limbic system may be responsible for aberrant behaviors. "I think there must be lesions of some kind in most of Pontius's cases; we just haven't seen them yet," says MacLean. He thinks such lesions could result from malformations that occur in the developing cortex before birth or soon after, or during the stress to the brain as the head passes through the birth canal. Other head traumas or even viral diseases could also cause lesions in the limbic system.

Pontius is eager to explore this theory as well, especially considering that about half of her patients reported they had suffered head injuries at some point in their lives. She also notes that animal research has shown that lesions or dysfunctions in the hippocampus, which is also in the limbic system, inhibit the ability to let go of old thought patterns or, more precisely, to learn new, more efficient ways to complete tasks. She is curious to learn whether such lesions might make it difficult for some people to put aside certain memories, which might trigger the bizarre behavior, or whether lesions may even cause someone to become a social outcast, which may lead to the same result.

It is not possible, of course, for Pontius to probe for lesions in her subjects. But in an attempt to gain some insight into the brain-lesion hypothesis, she plans to collaborate with Guy Pigeon, a doctor of veterinary medicine and director of research at the Animal Medical Center in New York City. At Pontius's suggestion, Pigeon's group will conduct postmortem examinations on a rare group of pet dogs who suddenly attack or kill their owners. She believes that because these animals are often isolated from normal socialization with a pack and from their owners for long periods at a time, they may be somewhat analogous to social loners who have succumbed to a limbic psychotic trigger reaction.

Legal Implications

Pontius continues to gather clinical documentation of both her syndrome and its suggested trigger largely through referrals from legal professionals in contact with people who commit emotionless, motiveless, unplanned felonies during a brief psychosis. In fact, since reports of her work have begun to appear in both the professional and popular press, she has received numerous calls and letters about other possible cases from defense attorneys who believe their clients might have had limbic seizures. "I read your article," one public defender told Pontius. "We have 50 people on death row, and several of them might fit your description."

That Pontius's syndrome could be used as a new legal defense is exactly what frightens some observers. In fact, it has been successful in all but one of the cases where it has been employed, at least in getting patients sent to maximum-security hospitals rather than to prison. "The first time I read about this limbic-seizure disorders theory, I thought, 'Oh my God, somebody could go out and kill people serially and use this as a defense to get away with it,'" says Jarrod Barnhill, a psychiatrist at the University of North Carolina who reviewed Pontius's theory before it appeared in the *Bulletin of the American Academy of Psychiatry and Law*.

Ralph Slovenko, a professor of law and psychiatry at Wayne State University who finds Pontius's theory convincing, likewise fears that one of the "hazards of the biological approach is that an overly aggressive lawyer might use it as a last-ditch defense." For example, in the trial of John Hinckley, the defense was able to introduce a CT scan of Hinckley's brain, he says. "The CT scan doesn't meet the test of scientific reliability in court, and it showed some abnormality that you could find on almost anybody," he says. "But they found him not guilty by reason of insanity."

It might seem that the limbic psychotic trigger reaction could be similarly used. After all, since there's no physical proof of the disorder, couldn't someone who committed a grisly murder simply fake having had a limbic seizure? If a person claimed he had experienced hallucinations just prior to his homicidal attack, that he hadn't really tried to conceal the crime, that he did indeed feel remorse, how would we know if he were telling the truth?

Pontius isn't worried. "With a dozen symptoms each present in all my cases so far, faking is very difficult," she says. For instance, if someone falsely claims there was no motive or planning, that is easily disproved by the evidence. "Frequently, there are witnesses, because a seizure is never planned or under volitional control," she says, "and witnesses can observe the absence of emotion during the irrational act or see behavior with visceral symptoms—or the police see it in the underwear." Finally, she says, the perpetrators assume full responsibility, do not blame anybody but themselves, and virtually ask to be punished. If not, they may try suicide or they may plead guilty even before their case is presented at trial."

Judge William Nicholas, a family court judge in Kent County, Del., and formerly a defense attorney in one of Pontius's cases that did go to trial, also sees no danger that this defense could be misused. "It would be pretty hard to fool anybody with this sort of defense unless it were true," he says, "and even then it would be a difficult sell." In fact, Nicholas finds that mental-illness defenses in general are usually a last resort and not particularly persuasive to juries.

Some observers share Pontius's view: that fears about freeing the guilty are misplaced, and that society should rather be more concerned about providing appropriate detention or treatment of those in prison or on death row who truly were not responsible for their actions. "The greater danger is that we wind up punishing people who could not control their actions," says James Hannon, associate professor of sociology and director of the graduate program in Criminal Justice at Suffolk University in Boston.

No one can estimate at this point how many people might have suffered from limbic seizures, only to be judged as being responsible for a crime. But Hannon, who finds the evidence for limbic seizure disorder syndrome "very strong," believes the number could be significant. "We have 1.4 million people behind bars in America, and even if limbic seizure disorders are responsible for one-tenth of 1 percent of all crimes, that's 1,400 people," he says. Moreover, he says, that percentage represents the entire prison population. He estimates that it could be much higher for people who have committed murder, many of whom may be on death row, and for those who have attempted murder.

Of the 25,000 homicides committed each year, about 10 percent are unexplained, irrational killings of complete strangers, Hannon says. He estimates that about 10 percent of those, or some 250 in all, could be attributed to limbic seizure disorders. He also thinks that the number of people suffering from limbic seizure disorders who have *attempted* murder may be at least three or four times the number who have actually completed a homicidal act. After all, he says, because these attacks are unplanned, they probably do not involve the use of firearms and are committed in public, so victims can often defend themselves, or bystanders can come to their rescue.

Hannon agrees, however, that a limbic-seizure defense or other insanity defenses, even when used appropriately, tend to fall on deaf ears. The reason, he believes, is that our criminal justice system has become increasingly "retributive"—the courts pass a sentence not as a deterrent but to punish someone. But what happens, he asks, if we discover that the aggression of many of these murderers is due to a brain dysfunction that could be treated or cured, and that a murderer could be rehabilitated? "We sacrifice the offender whether he is damaged or not in order to fulfill the social function," he says, "which is to preserve a sense of an ordered world and of our ability to safeguard ourselves, and to support our belief that individuals are responsible for all of life's outcomes." But research such as Pontius's may eventually reveal that individuals are often not fully responsible for all outcomes, and "the attempts to punish or execute them for sociological reasons will look increasingly foolish and unjust," he says, "That is why her work is so important."

Learning and Memory

Perhaps the most important survival ability that organisms possess is the ability to learn new information and remember its meaning. For example, in order for a mouse to survive, it must learn the consequences of getting attacked by a predator and remember to avoid it next time. Imagine the consequences of our not learning, or failing to remember, the meaning of red and green traffic lights!

Learning and memory are psychological processes that go hand in hand. One way to evaluate these processes is to use behavioral measures. Students are very familiar with one technique used to measure learning and memory: examinations. But besides the behavioral responses, learning and memory are also manifested as physical changes in the nervous system.

One of the early investigations on the neurobiology of learning and memory was conducted by Karl Lashley in the early 1900s. Lashley hypothesized that memories are stored in certain areas in the brain. To test this hypothesis, several brain areas in the rat were lesioned, and performance on memory tasks was later assessed. The results of the study proved disappointing, for the memory of the subjects was not significantly affected. Lashley concluded that memory traces, or engrams, are not localized in any one part of the brain.

In spite of Lashley's negative findings, the study provided significant insights into memory research. Memory can be viewed as a process or functional activity in the brain that develops after exposure to sensory stimuli. Damage to certain areas of the brain affects memory due to destruction of the neural network that processes memory, not because of the loss of the memory trace.

At the cellular level, changes in the structure and function of neurons occur during learning and memory. Increase in synaptic branching occurs in neurons "taught" to respond to certain stimuli. The pattern of release of certain neurotransmitters, such as dopamine, is also correlated with these processes. Recently, the drug nicotine was implicated to have an enhancing effect on learning and memory.

Although some argue that complex behaviors cannot be explained simply by neurotransmitters and activities of the neurons, neurological studies conducted on humans with disorders of learning and memory strongly support the biological basis for these psychological processes. Alzheimer's disease, a condition characterized by severe memory deterioration, is associated with the death of neurons in certain areas of the brain, including the hippocampus. A deficiency in the neurotransmitter acetylcholine activity is also evident in the hypothalamus. It is also postulated that the hippocampus in a developing child is important in learning language, and in adults it is essential for conceptual learning. In some autistic individuals, hippocampal activity is dysfunctional.

Looking Ahead: Challenge Questions

Describe some types of memories stored in the brain. What structures of the brain are significantly involved in memory processing? At the cellular level, describe how learning and memory can occur. How can glucose affect these processes?

What are the different levels of memory processing? Discuss the significance of working memory. Where in the brain could working memory reside?

UNIT 9

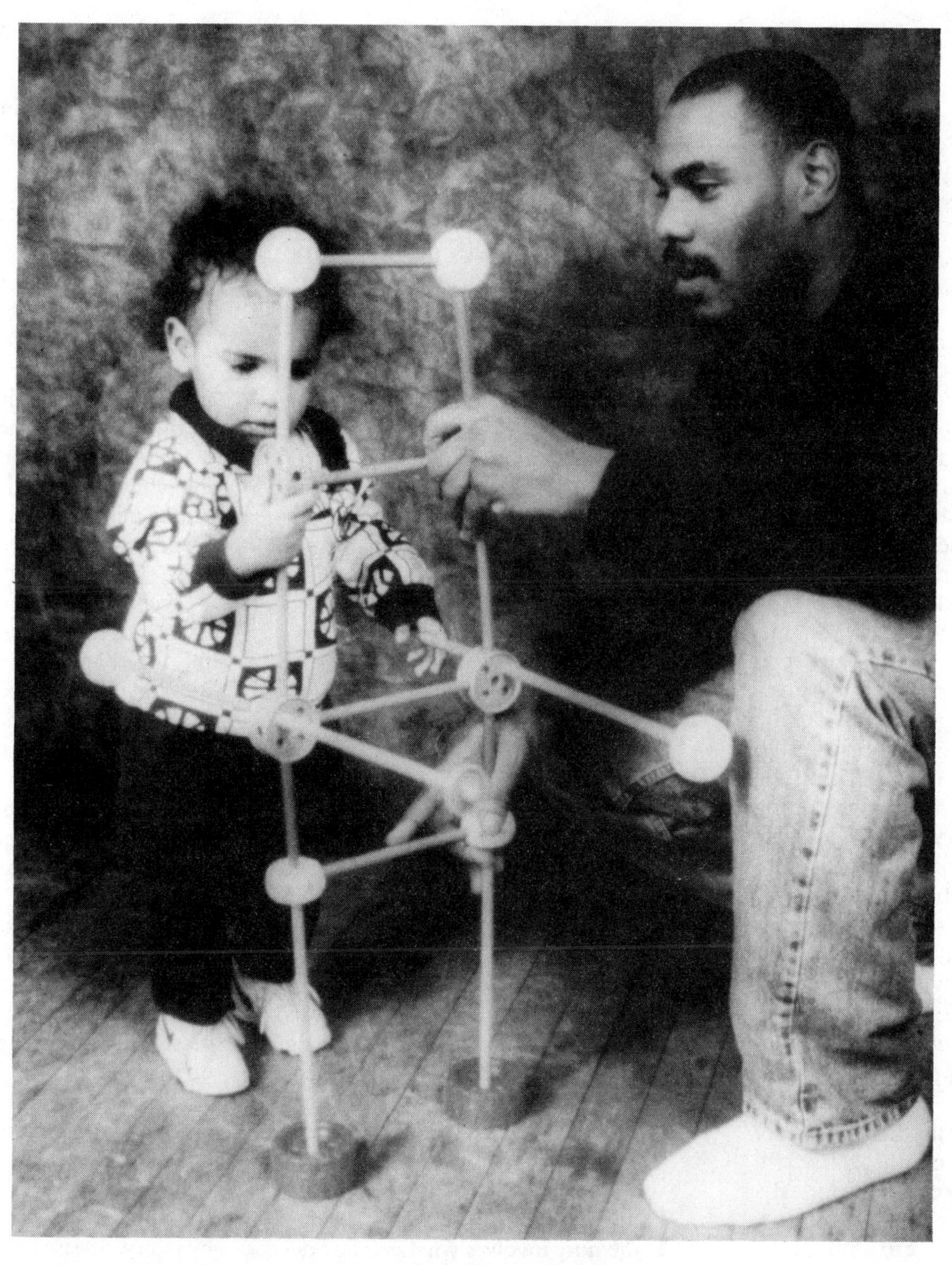

TRENDS IN NEUROSCIENCE

The Machinery of Thought

Studies of the brains of monkeys and, more recently, of humans are revealing the neural underpinnings of working memory, one of the mind's most crucial functions

by **Tim Beardsley,** *staff writer*

In a darkened basement laboratory on the campus of the National Institutes of Health in Bethesda, Md., volunteers earn $100 by lying for two hours with their head inside a huge magnetic resonance imaging (MRI) machine while they gaze at a screen reflected in a mirror. The screen periodically displays black-and-white pictures: some are faces, others scrambled blocks of light and shade. When a face appears on the screen, the subject signals by pressing buttons whether the face is a new one or the same as one that was shown a few seconds earlier as a "target" to be remembered.

As the test proceeds, the MRI machine bombards the volunteer's brain with radio-frequency waves that excite hydrogen atoms in the bloodstream, causing the atoms to emit signals of their own. Later, the machine transforms the resulting electromagnetic cacophony into color-coded maps of oxygen consumption levels throughout the subject's brain. Because increased oxygen consumption results from heightened neural activity, researchers can analyze these brain maps to learn what parts of the brain work hardest when a person recognizes a face.

With experiments such as these, researchers are beginning to fathom the neural processes underlying "working memory"—the limited, short-term store of currently relevant information that we draw on when we comprehend a sentence, follow a previously decided plan of action or remember a telephone number. When we bring to mind the name of Russia's president, for instance, that information is temporarily copied from long-term memory into working memory.

Psychological studies have demonstrated that working memory is fundamental to the human ability to reason and make judgments that rely on remembered contextual information. There are compelling humanitarian reasons for understanding working memory. Schizophrenia, one of the most devastating mental illnesses, is believed to be caused in part by a defect of this system. Studies of the molecular basis of working memory "have implications for drug treatment in mental illness," says Patricia Goldman-Rakic of Yale University, one of the most prominent investigators of working memory.

An intensive research effort has started to produce detailed information about the areas of the brain involved when we engage this vital intellectual faculty and is illuminating the patterns of neural activity that allow it to operate. The important role of specific brain chemicals in working memory is also becoming clear. Yet for all the progress, researchers have still to agree on how working memory is controlled and organized.

From Electrodes to Fast MRI

The prototypical test for working memory involves what is called delayed choice. An animal or a person signals where some specific cue was previously seen, before an imposed period of waiting. Thus, a monkey might be given a choice of two jars in separate positions and be rewarded for pointing to the one in which it previously saw food placed.

The task provides no clue to the correct response at the time of testing, so the monkey must rely on its recollection of the correct location. A related challenge rewards an animal for remembering which of several images it saw presented initially as a target. The NIH volunteers who were recalling faces were engaged in a variant of this test.

Technological advances have greatly enhanced researchers' ability to probe the neural underpinnings of such capacities. Investigators began studying cerebral activity in working memory some 40 years ago by inserting electrodes into individual neurons within the brains of monkeys. This method has its limits, however. Although monkey brains have clear anatomical similarities to human brains, the animals' behavior is vastly simpler, making detailed comparisons with human thinking problematic. Lacking language, the animals must be patiently trained over a period of weeks to master tasks that a person would pick up in a minute.

Electrode-recording techniques are also ethically unacceptable for use on people. Researchers try to learn which parts of our species' brain do what by studying the effects of damage caused by injury, disease or therapeutic surgery.

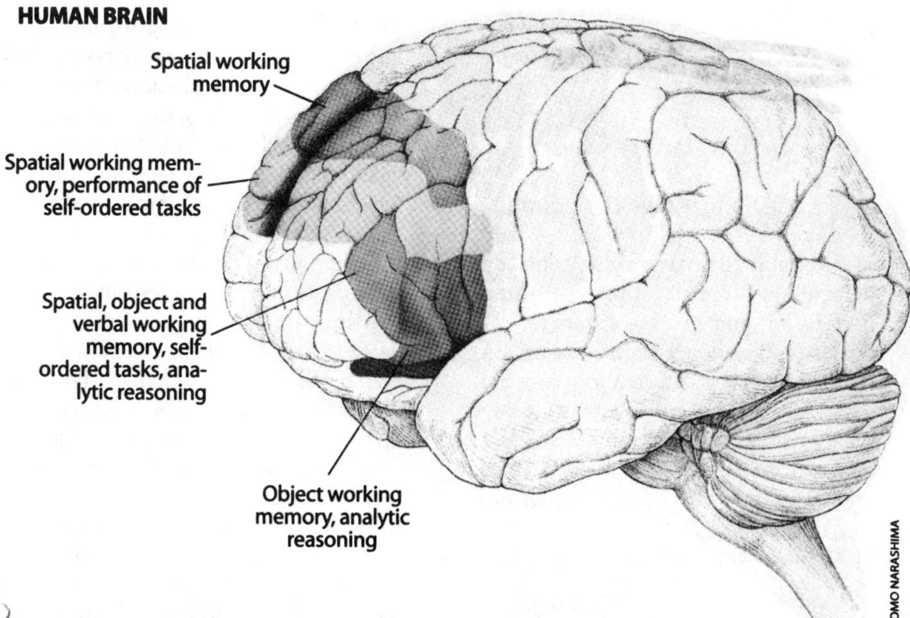

PREFRONTAL CORTEX is vital for maintaining in humans and in monkeys the temporary store of information known as working memory. Different tasks excite subregions within the prefrontal cortex, although details are controversial.

Yet patients have different medical histories—and their brains vary in exact shape—so interpreting this clinical data is tricky at best.

Earlier this decade, positron emission tomography, or PET scanning, made enormous strides by showing which parts of the human brain are busiest when performing different tasks, such as hearing words or speaking. But PET requires exposing the human subjects to radioactive tracers, and to keep radiation doses within acceptable levels, researchers have to use techniques that can resolve brain areas only about a centimeter apart. Also, during a delayed-choice task, PET scans are too slow to distinguish between the neural activity pattern of a target being held in mind and the pattern that follows a few seconds later when the target is recognized.

The new technique used at NIH and elsewhere, called functional MRI, can resolve the position of active neurons to about two millimeters and is fast enough to study activity before and after the brain recognizes a cue on a screen. The rapidly improving technique has over the past two years become the state of the art for functional brain imaging.

Monkey Puzzle

Experiments involving electrodes implanted in monkeys still provide crucial information, however, because they reveal in fine detail and on a millisecond-by-millisecond timetable what happens as these primates respond to cues and rewards. When animals perform such feats of working memory, several brain regions can play a role, but as Joachín M. Fuster of the University of California at Los Angeles showed in the 1970s, one area that is always involved is the prefrontal cortex.

The prefrontal cortex is a layer of tissue that lies just behind the forehead. With neural connections to almost all the areas of the brain that process sensory information, it is well situated to maintain a flexible store of information relevant to any task at hand. It is also the part of the brain that has grown the most in humans, as compared with monkeys. Monkeys missing some parts of their prefrontal cortex preserve their long-term memory but perform miserably on delayed-choice tests. Humans similarly afflicted suffer a reduced attention span and ability to plan.

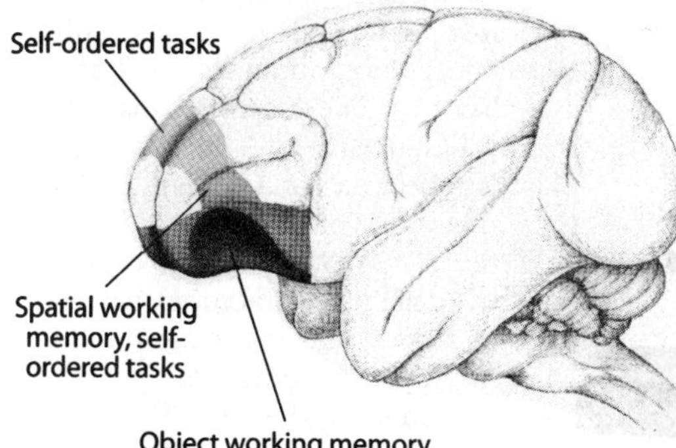

Fuster and, separately, Kisou Kubota and Hiroaki Niki of the Kyoto Primate Center made electrical recordings from a variety of neurons in the monkey prefrontal cortex, including some that apparently were active only while the animals were holding information in working memory. Subsequently, Goldman-Rakic and her colleagues have explored working memory in monkeys with more sophisticated tests. They established that prefrontal neural activity during a delayed-choice task indeed corresponds well to the functioning of working memory.

Goldman-Rakic and her associate Graham Williams have taken the analysis all the way to the subcellular level, showing that receptors for the neurotransmitter dopamine pivotally influence the responsiveness of cells in the prefrontal cortex and their actions in working memory. "There is no other example I know" of research that spans the gulf between behavior and subcellular function, Goldman-Rakic notes. She and her colleagues have recently shown that administering antischizophrenic drugs to monkeys for six months leads to specific changes in the numbers of two different types of dopamine receptors in that region, further evidence that schizophrenia—or its treatment—alters normal function there.

Research by other scientists supports the view that the prefrontal cortex could sustain working memory. Robert Desimone of the National Institute of Mental Health, along with Earl K. Miller, Cynthia Erickson and others, has discovered in the monkey's prefrontal cortex neurons that fire at different rates during the delayed-choice task, depending on the target the animal saw previously. Neurons in other parts of the brain generally "forget" the target when a distracting stimulus appears—their rate of firing changes. Prefrontal neurons detected by Desimone and his colleagues, in contrast, maintain their rate of activity during a delayed-choice task even after the animal is presented with irrelevant, distracting stimuli.

Activity in some prefrontal neurons, then, appears to embody directly the temporary working memory of the appearance of a target the animal is seeking. Other researchers have found prefrontal neurons that seem to maintain locations in working memory: Giuseppe Di Pellegrino of the University of Bologna and Steven Wise of the National Institute of Mental Health have found prefrontal neurons that are busiest when an animal has to remember where it saw a cue. Stimuli fail to excite the same frenzy unless they are in the location that is the current target for the task.

Neurons in the prefrontal cortex could thus apparently control how animals respond in a delayed-choice task. Fuster, one of the pioneers in the field, says the prefrontal cortex "serves the overarching function of the temporal organization of behavior" by driving networks that maintain currently important information in an active state. And neurons in the prefrontal cortex might exert their influence in more subtle ways, too.

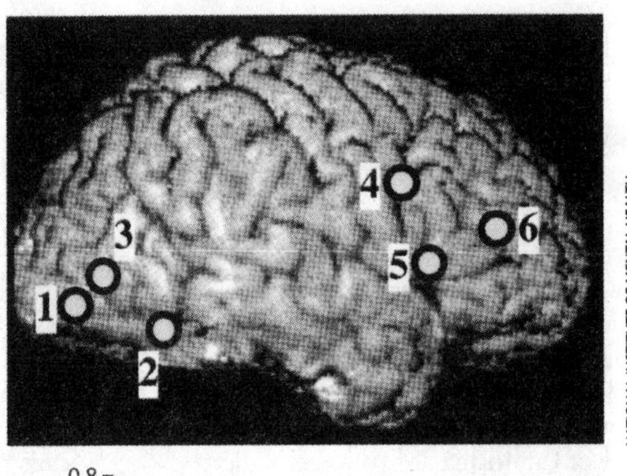

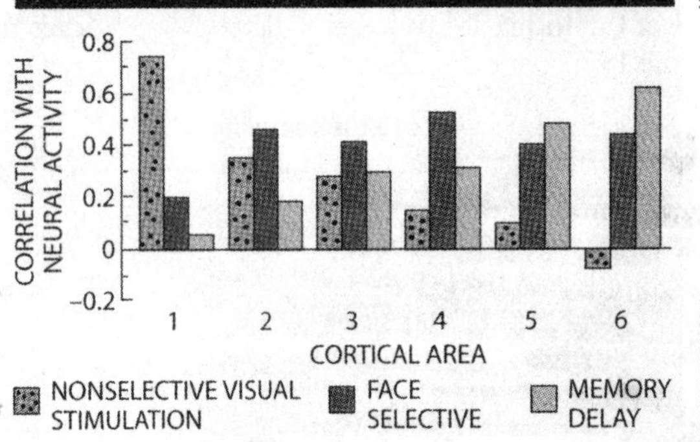

MRI shows that parts of the prefrontal cortex (*4, 5, 6*) are active while a face is remembered. Other areas (*1, 2, 3*) respond to seen faces and patterns.

Besides controlling directly the responses in delayed-choice tests, Desimone believes, the prefrontal cortex might tune the visual and possibly other perceptual systems to the task at hand. "What's loaded into working memory goes back to sensory processing," he suggests. Hundreds of experiments with both animals and people have shown that organisms are far more likely to perceive and react to cues relevant to their current needs than to irrelevant stimuli. This effect explains why we are more likely to notice the aroma wafting from a neighbor's grill when we are hungry than just after eating. If Desimone is right, the prefrontal cortex could be responsible for focusing an animal's attention and thus possibly steering awareness.

Imaging studies with PET and functional MRI corroborate the evidence from brain injuries that the human prefrontal cortex, like that of monkeys, is central to working memory. Several research groups have now imaged activity in the prefrontal cortex when people remember things from moment to moment. Different tasks may also require various other brain regions closer to the back of the head, but for primates in general, the prefrontal cortex always seems to be busy when target information is kept "in mind."

The Devil in the Details

Having shown that the prefrontal cortex is crucial to working memory, investigators naturally want to understand its internal structure. Goldman-Rakic and her associates at Yale have found evidence that when an animal retains information about a spatial location, the prefrontal activity is confined to a specific subregion. A separate area below it is most active when an animal is remembering the appearance of an object. These findings, together with observations of the anatomy of neural pathways, led Goldman-Rakic to propose that the prefrontal cortex is organized into regions that temporarily store information about different sensory domains: one for the domain of spatial cues, one for cues relating to an object's appearance and perhaps others for various types of cues.

There are, moreover, some indications that the human prefrontal cortex may be organized along similar domain-specific lines. A PET study reported last year by Susan M. Courtney, Leslie G. Ungerleider and their colleagues at the National Institute of Mental Health found that in humans, as in the monkeys studied earlier by Goldman-Rakic, certain brain areas are especially active during exercises that challenge working memory for visual details and for locations. Moreover, the most active brain regions lie in similar relative positions in both species.

Goldman-Rakic's proposal about the organization of the prefrontal cortex argues against the standard view of the various components of working memory. The British psychologist Alan Baddely proposed in 1974 that working memory has a hierarchical structure, in which an "executive system" in the prefrontal cortex allocates processing resources to separate "slave" buffers for verbal and spatial information. The memory buffers were supposed to be well behind the prefrontal cortex. But Goldman-Rakic is unconvinced that the brain's executive processes are confined to any particular location. Moreover, in the traditional model, memories organized by domain would lie somewhere behind the prefrontal cortex, not within it.

The high-speed imaging capability of functional MRI is now able to help resolve the question. A study that Courtney and Ungerleider and their colleagues published in April in *Nature* pinpoints the part of the brain that is liveliest while working memory holds an image of a face. That region—the middle part of the prefrontal cortex—has been fingered as the crux of working memory in a variety of studies.

Yet the face-recognition task Courtney and company used does not involve any obviously executive functions, Ungerleider notes. Their findings thus contradict the view that only executive functions reside within the prefrontal cortex, but they do fit with Goldman-Rakic's scheme. Similarly, Jonathan D. Cohen of Carnegie Mellon University and his co-workers found a region of the prefrontal cortex partly overlapping the one identified by Courtney that is active while subjects remember letters seen in a sequence. The more the subjects had to remember in the Cohen experiment, the more active their prefrontal regions. So Cohen's result also suggests that working memories are actually stored, in part, in the prefrontal cortex. Domain-specific organization "is the dominant view" of the prefrontal cortex, Wise says.

Wise himself does not subscribe to

that dominant view, however. He points, for example, to a study reported in *Science* in May by Miller and his associates at the Massachusetts Institute of Technology. The researchers recorded from neurons in the prefrontal cortex of monkeys while they solved delayed-choice tasks that required them to remember information about both the appearance and spatial locations of objects. Over half the neurons from which Miller recorded were sensitive to both attributes, a result not expected if domain-specific organization prevails. "It argues against Goldman-Rakic's view that identity and location are processed in different parts of the prefrontal cortex," Miller says.

Goldman-Rakic responds that she and her colleagues have recently found hundreds of cells in part of the prefrontal cortex that respond selectively even in untrained animals to objects or faces—further evidence, she asserts, that the information in that area is organized in part by sensory domain. "We do feel the evidence is overwhelming that the functions of neurons in the prefrontal cortex are dictated in large part by the neurons' sensory inputs," she says. Moreover, Goldman-Rakic believes technical problems cast doubt on Miller's experiment. She maintains the targets he used were too close to the center of the visual field, which could produce spurious firings.

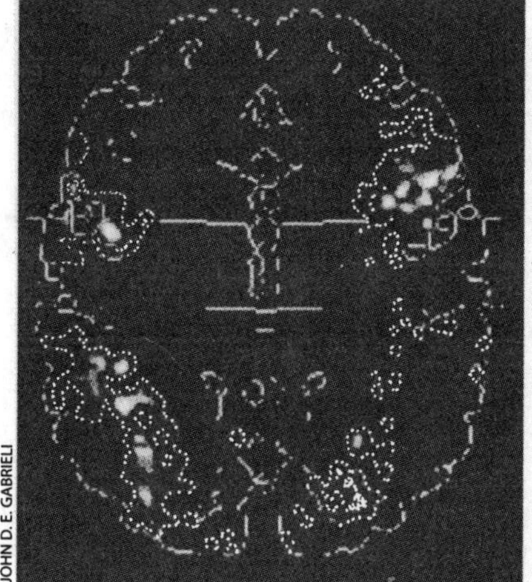

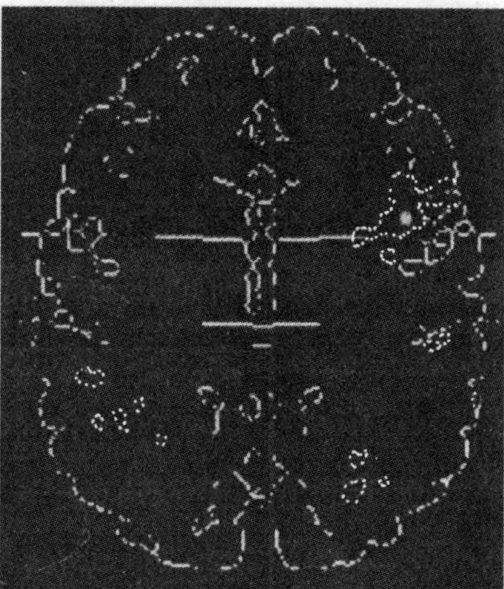

JOHN D. E. GABRIELI

BOTH SIDES of the prefrontal cortex (*top*) are very active when volunteers perform hard analytical tasks (*left image*). During more moderate reasoning, the activity is reduced and concentrated on the right side (*right image*).

Keeping Self-Control

Michael Petrides of McGill University, another leading figure in the field, has mounted a different challenge to the standard view. Petrides's studies point to two distinct levels of processing, both within the prefrontal cortex. In his view the levels are distinguished primarily not by whether they maintain information about place or objects, as Goldman-Rakic holds, but rather by the abstractness of the processing they perform. The lower level in the hierarchy—physically lower in the brain as well as conceptually lower—retrieves data from long-term memory storage elsewhere. The higher "dorsolateral" level, in contrast, monitors the brain's processes and enables it to keep track of multiple events. This higher monitoring level is called on when subjects are asked, for example, to articulate a random list of each number from 1 to 10, with no repetition: a subject has to remember each digit already chosen.

Petrides finds that both humans and monkeys with lesions in the dorsolateral part of the prefrontal cortex are crippled in their ability to monitor their own mental processes: they perform badly on special tests he has devised that require subjects to remember their earlier responses during the test. He also cites PET studies of healthy humans that find heightened activity in the same region when subjects are performing the tasks he uses. The finding is the same whether the tasks involve spatial cues or not. "The material does not seem to matter—the process is crucial," Petrides says.

Other researchers have found evidence to support the notion that the higher parts of the prefrontal cortex are key for self-monitoring. In an experiment by Mark D'Esposito and his associates at the University of Pennsylvania, volunteers performed either one or both of two tasks that, separately, did not require working memory. One task required subjects to say which words in a list read aloud were the names of vegetables, whereas the other asked them to match a feature of a geometric figure seen in different orientations. Functional MRI showed that the dorsoventral prefrontal cortex became active only when subjects attempted both tasks simultaneously. And in April at a meeting of the Cognitive Neuroscience Society, D'Esposito presented a meta-analysis of 25 different neuroimaging studies. The analysis supported Petrides's general notion that tasks involving more computation involve higher regions of the prefrontal cortex. "It was amazing that this came out," D'Esposito says.

D'Esposito's analysis also confirmed earlier indications that humans, far more than monkeys, represent different types of information in different halves of the brain. The meta-analysis did not, however, detect the upper/lower distinction between spatial and object working memory that Goldman-Rakic espouses.

Asymmetry of the human hemispheres is becoming apparent to other researchers as well. John D. E. Gabrieli and his colleagues at Stanford University have used functional MRI to study the brains of volunteers who were solving pictorial puzzles such as those often found on intelligence tests. The puzzles were of three types. One group was trivial, requiring the subject simply to select a symbol identical to a sample. A second group was a little harder: people had to select a figure with a combination of features that was absent from an array of sample figures. The third group contained more taxing problems that required analytical reasoning.

Gabrieli's study sheds some light on the debate over the organization of the prefrontal cortex. When volunteers pondered the intermediate class of tasks, which most resembled the tasks other investigators have used when studying working memory, the right side of the higher part of the prefrontal cortex was prominently active. Moreover, the activity was in areas that other researchers have found to be used when cues about spatial location are stored. This result fits Goldman-Rakic's idea that working memory for spatial location is stored in the higher regions of the prefrontal cortex, because these intermediate tasks all demanded that subjects visualize features in different locations.

When the volunteers in Gabrieli's experiment worked on the hard problems, however, the prefrontal cortices of the subjects became even more active, on the left as well as the right side. The added complexity produced a pattern of activation like that Petrides has found during his tests of self-monitoring.

Gabrieli's data thus provide some support for Petrides's theory of a higher executive level in the prefrontal cortex, as well as for Goldman-Rakic's view that domain-specific regions exist there. "There are definitely domain-specific places," Gabrieli says. "And there are others that rise above that." In other words, both sides in the debate over domain-specific organization of the prefrontal cortex may have a point. Yet in June, Matthew F. S. Rushworth of the University of Oxford and his colleagues reported in the *Journal of Neuroscience* that monkeys with large lesions in their lower prefrontal cortex could still perform well on delayed-choice tests. The finding casts new doubt on the theory that object working memory resides there and seems to support Petrides.

It may take years before the outstanding questions about the prefrontal cortex are settled and the operation of the brain's executive functions are pinned down to everyone's satisfaction. "If you put a theory out, people will attack it," Goldman-Rakic muses. "Everyone is contributing." And the modus operandi of the brain's decision-making apparatus is slowly becoming visible. "We are getting," Goldman-Rakic observes, "to the point where we can understand the cellular basis of cognition."

Further Reading

COGNITIVE NEUROSCIENCE. Special section in *Science,* Vol. 275, pages 1580–1610; March 15, 1997.

DOWN-REGULATION OF THE D_1 AND D_5 DOPAMINE RECEPTORS IN THE PRIMATE PREFRONTAL CORTEX BY CHRONIC TREATMENT WITH ANTIPSYCHOTIC DRUGS. Michael S. Lidow, John D. Elsworth and Patricia S. Goldman-Rakic in *Journal of Pharmacology and Experimental Therapeutics,* Vol. 281, No. 1, pages 597–603; April 1997.

TEMPORAL DYNAMICS OF BRAIN ACTIVATION DURING A WORKING MEMORY TASK. J. D. Cohen, W. M. Perlstein, T. S. Braver, L. E. Nystrom, D. C. Noll, J. Jonides and E. E. Smith in *Nature,* Vol. 386, pages 604–608; April 10, 1997.

TRANSIENT AND SUSTAINED ACTIVITY IN A DISTRIBUTED NEURAL SYSTEM FOR HUMAN WORKING MEMORY. S. M. Courtney, L. G. Ungerleider, K. Keil and James V. Haxby, *ibid,* pages 608–611.

INTEGRATION OF WHAT AND WHERE IN THE PRIMATE PREFRONTAL CORTEX. S. Chenchal Rao, Gregor Rainer and Earl K. Miller in *Science,* Vol. 276, pages 821–824; May 2, 1997.

NEUROSCIENCE

How Does the Brain Organize Memories?

Howard Eichenbaum

Cognitive neuroscientists agree that there are multiple forms of memory, each mediated by distinct brain pathways (*1*, *2*). There is not such ready agreement, however, as to the critical distinctions among types of memory and the contributions of specific anatomical structures to each. On page 377 of this issue, Vargha-Khadem *et al.* (*3*) address both of these issues by analyzing the memory deficits in three individuals who had sustained brain lesions very early in life. Their results show that the hippocampus, a structure located within the medial temporal lobe of the brain and long associated with memory function (*4*), is critical for everyday episodic memory (our record of personal events), but is not necessary for semantic memory (our lifetime accumulation of universal factual knowledge). Although the hippocampus has been argued to function in episodic memory before (*5*), these new case studies offer a particularly impressive example that can be attributed to selective focal hippocampal damage early in life.

Striking as the findings are, they are also consistent with the possibility that both types of learning are impaired in these cases. Directly comparing new episodic and semantic learning in the laboratory turns out to be quite difficult, because normal subjects can take advantage of their episodic memory to recall new semantic material. This problem in separating performance of the two types of memory has led some to eschew the episodic-semantic distinction, focusing instead on amnesics' characteristic failure in conscious recollection of both events and facts. Such a deficit in so-called declarative memory is contrasted with fully spared acquisition of biases, skills, and habits expressed unconsciously through changes in performance speed or choice (*6*). Using this account, the seemingly selective deficit in these amnesics' memory for unique episodes, as well as their forgetting of a story or drawing, can be attributed to a partially compromised declarative capacity doing especially poorly on any type of complex material experienced only once.

Recognizing this interpretive stand-off, Vargha-Khadem *et al.* turned to nonconventional tests modeled after measures that in animals distinguish the memory functions of the hippocampus itself from that of the immediately surrounding parahippocampal cortical region (see the figure). Monkeys and rats with selective hippocampal damage do surprisingly well at stimulus recognition and stimulus association learning, but have severe deficits after parahippocampal damage (*7*). Likewise, the individuals with hippocampal lesions showed intact recognition memory in similar tests with words and faces, and even normal learning of verbal or face associations, as contrasted with the reports of more extensive impairment in these measures in a patient with identified damage in both the hippocampus and parahippocampal region (*4*, *8*). Animals with selective hippocampal damage are impaired in memory for spatial location or spatial context (*9*), a deficit similar to that of the individuals described by Vargha-Khadem in associating an object with the place where it was seen, as well as a face with its voice. These parallels led Vargha-Khadem *et al.* to suggest an anatomically feasible model of complementary memory functions in which representations formed in the cerebral cortex are bound together into semantic associations by the parahippocampal region, and then further processed by the hippocampus to add the contextually rich episodic or spatial information (see the figure).

More detailed neurobiological observations offer another perspective and a degree of reconciliation between the episodic and declarative accounts. One source of data comes from neuropsychological studies showing that the hippocampal deficit observed in animals requires a deeper explanation than attribution to a (spatial) contextual factor (*10*). Thus, when animals with selective hippocampal damage acquire stimulus associations, they fail on novel queries in which the stimuli are only indirectly related through other stimulus elements (*11*). Drawing an even closer parallel with the human studies, animals with hippocampal damage seem to acquire a complex "semantic" structure involving an orderly hierarchy of stimuli. But the nature of their

The author is at the Laboratory of Cognitive Neurobiology, Department of Psychology, Boston University, Boston, MA 02215, USA. E-mail: hbe@bu.edu knowledge structure, or access to it, is abnormal in that these animals lack the flexibility of expression that supports inferences between stimulus elements that are only indirectly related within the hierarchy (*12*). A similar dissociation can be observed between their successful, albeit gradual, place learning contrasted with failure when challenged to navigate to the place by a novel route or when previous experiences can interfere with new place learning (*13*). Both rigidity of access and sensitivity to interference are hallmarks of human amnesics' difficulty in conscious recollection, suggesting a connection between hippocampal function in declarative memory and in flexibility of memory expression across species (*5, 14*).

Complementary evidence from studies on neural activity in the hippocampal area provides further clues about the distinct memory functions of the hippocampus and parahippocampal region. In a recent functional magnetic resonance imaging study, a part of the hippocampus was maximally activated when human subjects indirectly accessed the memory of a word cued by a picture of the corresponding object, whereas the parahippocampal region was maximally activated during simple differentiation and encoding of novel pictures for later recognition (*15*). Similarly, single-cell recordings in both rats and monkeys have shown that cortical areas, including those in the parahippocampal region, encode specific memory cues and can sustain and regenerate these item-specific representations (*16*). By contrast, the activity of hippocampal neurons reflects myriad combinations of items or abstract relations between stimuli, as observed in so-called place cells, whose activity reflects the position of a rat with respect to the configuration of spatial cues (*17*), and in cells whose activity reflects configurations of nonspatial cues and actions (*18*), including combinations of faces and gender or emotional expression in humans (*19*). In addition, a potentially telling property of hippocampal cells is their propensity to dramatically change representations, even across highly similar situations that vary only in the task contingencies or subtle variations in the stimuli (*20*). These findings have led to the suggestion that the hippocampus seeks to differentiate potentially ambiguous patterns and, at the same time, to capture the relevant contingencies in each of them.

These observations begin to fill in the mechanistic details of the model shown in the figure (*21*). Functionally specific cortical representations converge onto the parahippocampal region, which might support a binding of simultaneously experienced contiguities through feedback onto the cortex. When the items are in the same modality or are closely contiguous, this could lead to an overly rigid binding of the items, making them inaccessible when the elements are later separated (for example, we meet someone in a conference but can't recognize the person later on the street outside). The physiological data, as well as computational models (*22*), suggest that the hippocampus is suited to promote more flexible associations by recognizing relations among items and differentiating overlapping patterns (separating where one sees the person from the places and times of the events). This could contribute to the encoding of each unique episode, as well as relating the context-free information into semantic knowledge. The data from animals with amnesia, as well as computational modeling, indicate that the hippocampus may also interleave patterns within the memory network so as to provide access to the whole knowledge structure from any point. Within this scheme, episodic and declarative memory are not alternative types of memory, but rather are two powerful benefits of the networking of cortical memories supported by the hippocampus.

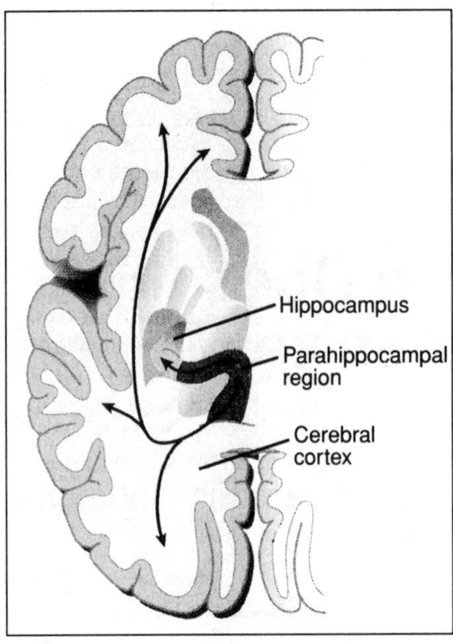

The human brain: wired for memory. Widespread regions of the cerebral cortex, the repositories of highly specific representations, are bidirectionally connected to the parahippocampal region. Interactions among these areas could underlie memories of some associations between cortical representations without hippocampal involvement. The parahippocampal region is then bidirectionally connected with the hippocampus, which can provide an additional influence on memory processing by the preceding areas.

References and Notes

1. N. J. Cohen and H. Eichenbaum, *Memory, Amnesia, and the Hippocampal System* (MIT Press, Cambridge MA, 1993).
2. D. L. Schacter and E. Tulving, Eds., *Memory Systems* (MIT Press, Cambridge, MA, 1994).
3. F. Vargha-Khadem *et al.*, *Science* **277**, 377 (1997).
4. W. B. Scoville and B. Milner, *J. Neurol. Neurosurg. Psychiatry* **20**, 11 (1957).
5. For example, E. Tulving, C. A. G. Hayman, C. A. MacDonald, *J. Exp. Psychol. Learn. Mem. Cogn.* **17**, 595 (1991); S. B. Hamann and L. R. Squire, *Behav. Neurosci.* **109**, 1027 (1995). For discussion of childhood amnesia see also, F. B. Wood, I. S. Brown, R. H. Felton, *Brain Cogn.* **10**, 76 (1989); A. Ostergard and L. R. Squire, *ibid.* **14**, 127 (1990).
6. N. J. Cohen and L. R. Squire, *Science* **210**, 207 (1980); L. R. Squire, B. Knowlton, G. Musen, *Annu. Rev. Psychol.* **44**, 453 (1993).
7. H. Eichenbaum, T. Otto, N. J. Cohen, *Brain Behav. Sci.* **17**, 449 (1994); E. A. Murray, *Sem. Neurosci.* **8**, 13 (1996).
8. S. Corkin, D. G. Amaral, R. G. Gonzáles, K. A. Johnson, B. T. Hyman, *J. Neurosci.* **17**, 3964 (1997).
9. R. G. M. Morris, P. Garrud, J. P. Rawlins, J. O'Keefe, *Nature* **297**, 681 (1982); R. G. Phillips and J. E. LeDoux, *Learn. Mem.* **1**, 34 (1994).
10. H. Eichenbaum, *Curr. Opin. Neurobiol.* **6**, 187 (1996).
11. M. Bunsey and H. Eichenbaum, *Nature* **379**, 255 (1996).
12. J. A. Dusek and H. Eichenbaum, *Proc. Natl. Acad. Sci. U.S.A.* **94**, 7109 (1997).
13. H. Eichenbaum, C. Stewart, R. G. M. Morris, *J. Neurosci.* **10**, 3531 (1990); I. Q. Whishaw, J.-C. Cassel, L. E. Jarrard, *ibid.* **15**, 5779 (1995); M. L. Shapiro and D. S. Olton, in (*2*), pp. 87–118.
14. D. L. Schacter, in *Memory Systems of the Brain*, N. M. Weinberger, J. L. McGaugh, G. Lynch, Eds. (Guilford, New York, 1985), pp. 351–380; P. J. Reber, B. J. Knowlton, L. R. Squire, *Behav. Neurosci.* **110**, 861 (1996).
15. J. D. E. Gabrieli, J. B. Brewer, J. E. Desmond, G. H. Glover, *Science* **276**, 264 (1997).
16. E. K. Miller and R. Desimone, *ibid.* **263**, 520 (1994); K. Sakai and Y. Miyashita, *Nature* **354**, 152 (1991); B. J. Young, T. Otto, G. D. Fox, H. Eichenbaum, *J. Neurosci.* **17**, 5183 (1997).
17. J. A. O'Keefe, *Exp. Neurol.* **51**, 78 (1976).
18. E. T. Rolls *et al.*, *J. Neurosci.* **9**,1835 (1989); I. P. Riches, F. A. W. Wilson, M. W. Brown, *ibid.* **11**, 1763 (1991); T. Ono, K. Nakamura, H. Nishijo, S. Eifuku, *J. Neurophysiol.* **70**, 1516 (1993); B. J. Young, G. D. Fox, H. Eichenbaum, *J. Neurosci.* **14**, 6553 (1994); S. A. Deadwyler, T. Bunn, R. E. Hampson, *ibid.* **16**, 354 (1996); K. M. Gothard, W. E. Skaggs, K. M. Moore, B. L. McNaughton, *ibid.* **16**, 823 (1996).
19. I. Fried, K. A. MacDonald, C. L. Wilson, *Neuron* **18**, 753 (1997).
20. S. I. Wiener, C. A. Paul, H. Eichenbaum, *J. Neurosci.* **9**, 2737 (1989); E. J. Markus, Y.-L. Qin, B. Leonard, W. E. Skaggs, B. L. McNaughton, *ibid.* **15**, 7079 (1995); H. Tanila, P. Sipila, M. Shapiro, H. Eichenbaum, *ibid.* **17**, 5167 (1997).
21. H. Eichenbaum, *Annu. Rev. Psychol.* **48**, 547 (1997).
22. Special issue, *Computational Models of Hippocampal Function in Memory*, M. Gluck, Ed., *Hippocampus* **6**, 643 (1996).

BRIEF COMMUNICATIONS

Estradiol Is Related to Visual Memory in Healthy Young Men

Diane L. Kampen and Barbara B. Sherwin
McGill University

The influence of testosterone and estrogen on memory was investigated in 33 healthy young men. Tests of visual memory, visuospatial ability, verbal memory, and attention were administered, and circulating levels of estradiol and free testosterone were measured. Participants with high levels of estradiol performed better on 2 measures of visual memory than did those with normal but lower levels. There were no differences between individuals with high and low levels of testosterone on any cognitive measure. These results support the contention that estradiol influences memory in young men.

Circulating levels of the gonadal hormones have been related to a variety of cognitive functions in humans. In men, the androgens, especially testosterone (T), have been related to performance on tasks with a spatial component. For example, in healthy men from industrialized countries, positive relationships have been demonstrated between measured circulating T levels and visuospatial orientation (Gordon & Lee, 1986), spatial form comparison (Christiansen & Knussmann, 1987), and composite visuospatial scores (Errico, Parsons, Kling, & King, 1992). Male !Kung San hunter–gatherers from Namibia exhibited positive correlations between tactual–spatial measures and T levels (Christiansen, 1993). Also, older men given exogenous T performed better on a visuospatial task than did age-matched placebo controls, although visual memory performance did not differ between groups (Janowsky, Oviatt, & Orwoll, 1994).

Diane L. Kampen and Barbara B. Sherwin, Department of Psychology, McGill University, Montreal, Quebec, Canada.

This study was supported by Operating Grant MT-11623 awarded by the Medical Research Council of Canada. We thank Robert Madan and Sara Grey for help with data collection, Michelle Prostak, Laura Schliefer, Linda Carlson, Mary C. Olmstead, and Norman White for helpful comments regarding drafts of this article, and Naomi Epstein for drawing the blood samples.

Correspondence concerning this article should be addressed to Diane L. Kampen, who is now at the Department of Psychology, St. Thomas University, Fredericton, New Brunswick, Canada EB 5G3. Electronic mail may be sent via Internet to kampen@stthomasu.ca.

On the other hand, some investigators have reported no association between visuospatial ability and either endogenous T (McKeever, Rich, Deyo, & Connor, 1987), exogenous T (Gordon, Corbin, & Lee, 1986), or DHEAS (an adrenal androgen; Barrett-Connor & Edelstein, 1994). Others reported better performance on spatial ability tasks by men with low levels of T (Gouchie & Kimura, 1991; Shute, Pellegrino, Hubert, & Reynolds, 1983), or complicated relationships between dihydrotestosterone (a T metabolite) and spatial task performance (McKeever & Deyo, 1990). Thus, the relationship between circulating levels of T and performance on a variety of visual and/or spatial ability tasks in healthy men is inconclusive.

Relatively fewer studies have examined the relationship between the estrogens (E) and cognition in men. The available evidence suggests no relationship in North American men on composite visuospatial or verbal ability scores (Errico et al., 1992), or on simple repetitive tasks, tasks requiring inhibition, or a test of spatial visualization (Komnenich, Lane, Dickey, & Stone, 1978). Similarly, no effect of E was seen on either spatial or verbal ability in !Kung San men (Christiansen, 1993).

In contrast to the negative findings reported with men, in women E is positively associated with performance on verbal tasks (Hampson, 1990), fine motor tasks (Graham, 1980; Hampson, 1990), and verbal memory (Kampen & Sherwin, 1994; Phillips & Sherwin, 1992a, 1992b; Sherwin, 1988). We therefore thought it was possible that E levels in men might be related to performance on tasks measuring these or other cognitive abilities.

From *Behavioral Neuroscience*, June 1996, pp. 613-617.

The relationship between memory and the gonadal hormones in men has received relatively little attention compared to other cognitive functions (e.g., Errico et al., 1992; Janowsky et al., 1994). We therefore conducted a pilot investigation to test possible associations between endogenous levels of E and T and performance on a variety of memory tasks in young adult men.

Method

Participants

Thirty-seven healthy, English-speaking men (mean age = 21.1 years, range 18 to 29 years) were recruited at a large university with posters and class announcements. Potential participants were screened by telephone and were told that they would be tested on a variety of cognitive tests to serve as a control group for other studies being conducted with elderly persons in the same laboratory. They were also told a blood sample would be taken and that the reason for this would be further explained at the conclusion of the testing session. Exclusion criteria precluded the participation of anyone who had not learned English before the age of five, had a recent head injury or psychiatric illness, had a history of substance abuse, or had ever participated in a similar cognitive study.

Data from four individuals were excluded from all analyses: One had a previously undisclosed psychiatric problem, another was extremely anxious and nervous prior to and during collection of the blood sample, a third had ingested a significant amount of alcohol the evening before the test session, and the fourth did not have his blood drawn due to a technical problem. Therefore, 33 respondents provided a complete set of data for analysis.

Paper-and-Pencil Questionnaires

The Personal Information Form (PIF) was used to gather information about the participants' sociodemographic characteristics and current health, including any medications being taken. They were not, however, specifically asked about steroid hormone use. In addition, respondents were asked to rate their alertness, the stressfulness of recent life events, and to estimate their caffeine, nicotine, and alcohol intake both 2 and 24 hr prior to testing, as well as how much they had eaten during the morning prior to testing.

Because mood fluctuations have been related to changes in T levels (Mazur & Lamb, 1980), mood was measured using the Multiple Affect Adjective Checklist (Zuckerman & Lubin, 1985) and the Profile of Mood States—Bipolar Form (Lorr & McNair, 1982). These self-report paper-and-pencil tests measure current mood and recent mood, respectively, and have good psychometric properties.

Neuropsychological Measures

Four cognitive domains were assessed with the neuropsychological battery: visual memory, visuospatial ability, verbal memory, and attention. The visual memory tasks included assessment of memory for different types of visual stimuli. Two tests of visual recall of designs (Lezak, 1985) were administered, the Benton Visual Retention Test (Form D, Administration C, 20-s delay; Sivan, 1992) and the visual reproduction (VR) subtest of the Wechsler Memory Scale—Revised (WMS–R; Wechsler, 1987). Both require the respondent to study a design and then draw it from memory. Two additional subtests of the WMS–R were also administered, figural memory and visual paired associates. Figural memory requires that the participant remember three abstract visual designs and immediately identify them from an array of nine designs. For the visual paired-associates test, participants learn pairs of colors and abstract line drawings over 6 learning trials.

A general measure of visuospatial ability was provided by a mental rotation test (Vandenberg & Kuse, 1978). Verbal memory was assessed with the paragraph-recall and paired-associates subtests of the Wechsler Memory Scale (Wechsler, 1945; Russell, 1975). Digit span (Wechsler Adult Intelligence Scale—Revised, WAIS–R; Wechsler, 1981) and a block span test (Milner, 1971) provided measures of attention.

Four of the memory tests were administered both immediately and after a 30-min delay (visual reproduction, visual paired associates, paragraph recall, verbal paired associates), to test for immediate and longer-term memory. Participants were not told of the delay component at the time of initial testing.

Procedure

Participants were tested individually in the laboratory for approximately 90 min between 10:30 a.m. and 1:30 p.m., to control for normal circadian T fluctuations (Nieschlag, 1974). After signing a consent form approved by a university research committee, participants completed the PIF and mood questionnaires. Next the cognitive tests were administered in the same order to all respondents. Following testing, a nurse drew a 10-ml sample of blood for assay of plasma T and estradiol (E2, the most bioactive estrogen). Each individual was then debriefed and paid for his participation.

Plasma T and E Assays

The 10-ml blood sample was collected by venipuncture into heparinized Vacutainer tubes. Each sample was centrifuged, divided into two vials, and stored at −50 °C for later analysis. A hospital endocrine laboratory used radioimmunoassay techniques to measure levels of E2 (Sorin Biomedica, Saluggia, Italy) and free T (Diagnostics Product Corporation, Los Angeles, CA). Normal ranges for these hormones were supplied by the companies in the assay kit information packages. T was assayed in two batches, and the average T level for each participant was used for all data analyses. E2 was assayed in one batch only. For both the T and E2 assays, each batch included samples from all participants, to control for interassay variability.

Data Analyses

To determine the effects of E on cognition, participants were divided into two groups using a median split. Participants whose E2 level equaled the median were dropped from further analysis. Within the cognitive domains of visual memory, verbal memory, and attention, separate multivariate analyses of variance (MANOVAs) were conducted. If a MANOVA was significant at the $p < .05$ level, individual t tests were used to evaluate group differences. A t test was used to test for differences in mental rotation. For analyses to determine possible correlations between E2 levels and test scores, the significance was set at $p < .01$ to control for the increased possibility of a Type I error when conducting multiple comparisons.

On the basis of their plasma T levels, participants were also divided into high and low T groups to investigate possible effects of T on performance. The statistical analyses were identical to those used with the E2 groups. In all cases, if the data were not normally distributed, they were either transformed, or the appropriate nonparametric tests were used.

Results

Hormone Levels

Plasma E2 levels ranged from 38 to 179 pmol/L (normal male range for this assay: 37 to 220 pmol/L) with a median of 69 pmol/L. Two men whose E2 levels were 69 pmol/L were dropped from further analysis of E effects, leaving 15 men in the high E2 group (HE2) and 16 in the low E2 group (LE2). The difference between E2 levels in the two groups was significant, $t(29) = 8.45, p < .001$ (see Table 1).

Table 1
Hormone Levels of Healthy Males in High and Low Hormone Groups Formed By a Median Split

Hormone	Group: High	Low	*p*
E2 (pmol/L)			
M	81.1	58.5	<.001
SD	7.6	7.3	
T (pmol/L)			
M	86.6	62.9	<.001
SD	8.8	9.4	

Note. E2 = estradiol; T = free testosterone.

The E2 level for one participant (179 pmol/L) was more than seven standard deviations above the next highest individual's level (94 pmol/L), although it was within the normal range. This participant was included in the HE2 group. Prior to all analyses, his hormone level was transformed to 95 (one more than the second highest E2 score; Tabachnick & Fidell, 1989).

Average T levels ranged from 47 to 111 pmol/L (normal male range for this assay, 28 to 156 pmol/L), with a median of 78.5 pmol/L. One participant's average T level was identical to the median level, and he was dropped from further analysis of T effects. This left 16 men in the high T group (HT) and 16 men in the low T group (LT). The difference between T levels in the HT and LT groups was significant, $t(30) = 7.34, p < .001$ (see Table 1).

Demographic and Neuropsychological Measures

None of the demographic variables differed between either the two E groups or the two T groups ($ps > .05$). Performances on both the delayed-verbal and visual paired-associates tests were at ceiling level and were not further analyzed ($Ms = 13.9$ out of a possible 14 and 5.9 out of a possible 6, respectively). A MANOVA showed that the two E2 groups differed significantly on overall visual memory, $F(5, 25) = 3.35, p < .05$. The HE2 group performed significantly better on immediate visual paired associates, $t(29) = 2.62, p < .05$, and immediate visual reproduction, $t(29) = 3.49, p < .01$. The scores on the other visual memory tests were not significantly different ($ps > .10$). No effect of E2 level was seen on verbal memory or attention (MANOVA $Fs < 2.21, ps > .10$), or mental rotation, $t(29) = .96, p > .10$. None of the correlations between E2 and any cognitive measure were significant ($rs < .33, ps > .05$). Mean untransformed scores and standard deviations of the HE2 and LE2 groups on the cognitive tests analyzed are shown in Table 2.

There were no significant correlations between E levels and any mood subscale scores ($rs < .34, ps > .05$), nor were there any significant between-groups differences on any subscales ($ps > .05$).

None of the MANOVAs conducted using the two T groups were significant in any cognitive domain ($Fs < 1.37, ps > .10$). Nor were the mental rotation scores significantly different, $t(30) = 1.19, p > .10$. There were no significant correlations between free T and any of the neuropsychological measures ($rs < .28, ps > .05$) or the mood scores ($rs < .24, ps > .05$). Neither were there between-groups differences on any of the mood measures ($ps > .05$). Mean untransformed scores and standard deviations of the HT and LT groups on the cognitive tests analyzed are shown in Table 2.

Discussion

The results of this study suggest that, in healthy young men, higher plasma E2 is associated with significantly better performance on two measures of immediate visual memory: visual paired associates and visual reproduction. These findings occurred in the absence of differences in mood, demographic variables, or attention between the high and low E groups. The apparent absence of an effect of T on the cognitive performance of young men in the present study suggests that circulating levels of T have no relationship with the cognitive abilities examined. However, it must be recalled that our respondents exhibited a limited range of T levels: Their range

Table 2
Mean Performance Scores on the Cognitive Tests by Men in the High and Low Hormone Groups

Test	HE2 *M*	HE2 *SD*	LE2 *M*	LE2 *SD*	HT *M*	HT *SD*	LT *M*	LT *SD*
Visual memory								
Visual PA (18)	17.1_a	1.2	15.6_a	1.9	16.8	1.7	16.1	1.3
VR immediate (41)	38.7_b	1.6	35.7_b	3.1	37.4	3.2	36.9	2.6
VR delayed (41)	34.6	4.6	32.7	4.9	33.8	4.8	34.5	4.3
Figural memory (10)	8.5	1.2	8.1	1.5	8.6	1.2	7.9	1.5
Benton VRT (10)	8.7	1.0	8.1	1.5	8.7	1.1	8.1	1.5
Verbal memory								
PR immediate (60)	34.3	7.4	32.3	5.5	33.1	7.2	33.4	5.7
PR delayed (60)	29.8	6.7	27.3	6.0	28.6	7.3	28.6	5.0
Verbal PA (42)	39.9	2.6	38.9	3.9	38.6	3.7	40.0	3.2
Attention								
Digit span (28)	20.3	2.8	18.3	2.9	19.1	3.7	19.2	2.6
Block span (28)	16.2	3.0	15.6	3.5	15.7	3.2	16.1	3.5
Mental rotation (40)	30.2	9.6	26.6	11.2	29.9	9.6	25.6	11.2

Note. Numbers in parentheses indicate the highest possible score for each test. Within rows, means with the same subscript differ significantly (a = $p < .05$, b = $p < .01$). HE2 = High estradiol group, LE2 = Low estradiol group; HT = High testosterone group, LT = Low testosterone group; PA = paired associates; VR = visual reproduction; VRT = visual retention test; PR = paragraph recall.

(64 pmol/L) was half of the total range of normal values for this particular hormone assay (128 pmol/L). This restricted range may have precluded detection of significant relationships between performance on the cognitive tasks and T levels. In addition, performance seems to have been at or near ceiling level on some of the visual (delayed visual paired associates, and possibly figural memory and Benton visual retention) and verbal (delayed verbal paired associates) memory tests. If more sensitive tests of these abilities had been used, an association between T levels and performance may have emerged. However, scores on other visual and verbal memory tests were well below ceiling level and were not related to T levels.

One possible explanation of the finding that E, but not T, enhances visual memory may relate to the fact that plasma E2 and free T levels were highly correlated in these individuals ($r = .80, p < .001$). It is possible that the association between cognition and T reported in previous investigations may have occurred as a result of positive effects of E2, with T appearing influential only because of its correlation with E2. If that is indeed the case, it will be important for future studies to include measurement of both T and E levels. Of course, it may also be the case that E2 appears influential in this study because of its association with T, and that with a larger sample or a broader range, T levels would have been related to performance. However, neither the multivariate nor univariate analyses of T-group differences approached significance.

No association was found between E2 and verbal memory in our sample of young men, although a positive relationship has been reported in women. This could have occurred because E truly does not affect verbal memory in men. It is also possible that the limited range of the E2 levels of our respondents (spanning only the lower 1/3 of the normal range) again may have precluded detection of an association between E2 and verbal memory. The ceiling effect on delayed verbal paired associate memory may also have concealed an association between E2 levels and performance on this task.

In this investigation E2 levels were related to performance only on immediate visual memory tasks. In women, a specific association has been found between E levels and verbal but not visual memory (e.g., Kampen & Sherwin, 1994; Phillips & Sherwin, 1992a). Whether a similar specificity exists between E and visual memory in men can only be ascertained by replicating this study using a variety of memory tasks at the appropriate level of difficulty in both the visual and verbal domains. In addition, investigation of this phenomenon should be conducted with other, nonuniversity, populations.

The apparent positive effect of E on measures of visual memory found in this study stands in contrast to a report of suppressed E and elevated T levels being associated with better visuospatial ability in men (Janowsky et al., 1994). In that study, exogenous T was administered to elderly men and measured at two different time points, both before and after cognitive testing, whereas E was measured only once (before cognitive testing). Although the reported finding appears to contradict the present results, there are numerous differences between the two studies: the populations tested (untreated young men vs. hormone-treated elderly men), the sources of hormone (endogenous vs. exogenous T), and the abilities measured (visuospatial ability vs. visual memory). In addition, the time of blood sampling differed in the two studies. In the Janowsky study, E measurements were taken at a time when T levels were also suppressed in the T-treated group. It would be interesting to determine if E was also elevated 4 hr later, at the second blood sampling time, when T levels were elevated. It is possible that such an E elevation might have occurred in these men, given the relatively rapid conversion of T to E by aromatase in various body tissues (Handelsman, 1995), including the brain (Naftolin et al., 1975). Further research is needed to resolve this issue.

The neural mechanisms that might mediate hormonal effects on memory are currently unknown. One brain area important for normal memory is the hippocampus (Squire, 1992), and there is evidence that both E and T can affect the hippocampus. For example, E but not T increases hippocampal cell excitability within 20 min of administration in adult male rats, whereas hippocampal cells of female rats respond to the application of T but not E (Teyler, Vardaris, Lewis, & Rawitch, 1980). In male rats, replacement of E after gonadectomy and adrenalectomy was more effective than T replacement in restoring hippocampal outgrowth after entorhinal cortex ablation (Morse, DeKosky, & Scheff, 1992). Both of these findings support the observation that E can influence areas of the male brain that are relatively less affected by T. Additionally, E and T have different effects in male and female brains, and estrogenic influences on cognition may thus be manifested differently in males and females.

In fact, such sex differences in performance do occur. For example, gonadectomized male rats given E performed better on a delayed-choice version of the radial arm maze than did untreated, gonadectomized males, whereas no such improvement was seen in treated vs. control gonadectomized female rats (Luine & Rodriguez, 1994). This raises the possibility that E might enhance aspects of cognitive functioning in both men and women, although the effects may occur in different domains.

In summary, the animal literature provides tentative support for our finding of an estrogenic enhancement of visual memory in healthy, young adult, male students. Continued investigation is required to more firmly establish the effects of E on men's cognitive functioning. Further studies of the brain effects of E and T in both male and female animals are also needed to provide additional information about the specific sites in the human brain where these hormones may act to influence cognition.

References

Barrett-Connor, E., & Edelstein, S. L. (1994). A prospective study of dehydroepiandrosterone sulfate and cognitive function in an older population: The Rancho Bernardo Study. *Journal of the American Geriatrics Society, 42,* 420–423.

Christiansen, K. (1993). Sex hormone-related variations of cognitive performance in !Kung San hunter-gathers of Namibia. *Neuropsychobiology, 27,* 97–107.

Christiansen, K., & Knussmann, R. (1987). Sex hormones and cognitive functioning in men. *Neuropsychobiology, 18,* 27–36.

Errico, A. L., Parsons, O. A., Kling, O. R., & King, A. C. (1992). Investigation of the role of sex hormones in alcoholics' visuospatial deficits. *Neuropsychologia, 30,* 417–426.

Gordon, H. W., Corbin, E. D., & Lee, P. A. (1986). Changes in specialized cognitive function following changes in hormone levels. *Cortex, 22,* 399–415.

Gordon, K., & Lee, P. A. (1986). A relationship between gonadotropins and visuospatial function. *Neuropsychologia, 24,* 563–576.

Gouchie, C., & Kimura, D. (1991). The relationship between testosterone levels and cognitive ability patterns. *Psychoneuroendocrinology, 16,* 323–334.

Graham, E. A. (1980). Cognition as related to menstrual cycle phase and estrogen level. In A. Dan, E. Graham, & C. Beecher (Eds.), *The menstrual cycle: A synthesis of interdisciplinary research* (pp. 190–208). New York: Springer.

Hampson, E. (1990). Estrogen-related variations in human spatial and articulatory-motor skills. *Psychoneuroendocrinology, 15,* 97–111.

Handelsman, D. J. (1995). Testosterone and other androgens: Physiology, pharmacology, and therapeutic use. In L. J. DeGroot, Besser, M, H. G. Burger, J. L. Jameson, E. L. Loriaux, J. C. Marshall, W. D. Odell, J. T. Potts, Jr., & A. H. Rubenstein (Eds.) *Endocrinology* (3rd ed., pp. 2351–2361). Philadelphia: W. B. Saunders Company.

Janowsky, J. S., Oviatt, S. K., & Orwoll, E. S. (1994). Testosterone influences spatial cognition in older men. *Behavioral Neuroscience, 108,* 325-332.

Kampen, D. K., & Sherwin, B. B. (1994). Estrogen use and verbal memory in healthy postmenopausal women. *Obstetrics and Gynecology, 83,* 979–983.

Komnenich, P., Lane, D. M., Dickey, R. P., & Stone, S. C. (1978). Gonadal hormones and cognitive performance. *Physiological Psychology, 6,* 115–120.

Lezak, M. (1985). *Neuropsychological Assessment* (2nd ed.). New York: Oxford University Press.

Lorr, M., & McNair, D. (1982). *Profile of Mood States: Bi-Polar Form.* San Diego: Educational and Industrial Testing Service.

Luine, V., & Rodriguez, M. (1994). Effects of estradiol on radial arm maze performance of young and aged rats. *Behavioral and Neural Biology, 62,* 230–236.

Mazur, A., & Lamb, T. A. (1980). Testosterone, status, and mood in human males. *Hormones and Behavior, 14,* 236–246.

McKeever, W. F., & Deyo, R. A. (1990). Testosterone, dihydrotestosterone, and spatial task performances of males. *Bulletin of the Psychonomic Society, 28,* 305–308.

McKeever, W. F., Rich, D. A., Deyo, R. A., & Conner, R. L. (1987). Androgens and spatial ability: Failure to find a relationship between testosterone and ability measures. *Bulletin of the Psychonomic Society, 25,* 438–440.

Milner, B. (1971). Interhemispheric differences in the localization of psychological processes in man. *British Medical Bulletin, 27,* 272–277.

Morse, J. K., DeKosky, S. T., & Scheff, S. W. (1992). Neurotrophic effects of steroids on lesion-induced growth in the hippocampus. II. Hormone replacement. *Experimental Neurology, 118,* 47–52.

Naftolin, F., Ryan, K. J., Davies, I. J., Reddy, V. V., Flores, F., Petro, Z., Kuhn, M, White, R. J., Takaoka, Y., & Wolin, L. (1975). The formation of estrogens by central endocrine tissues. *Recent Progress in Hormone Research, 31,* 295–315.

Nieschlag, E. (1974). Circadian rhythm of plasma testosterone. In J. Aschoff, F. Ceresa, & F. Halberg (Eds.), *Chronobiological aspects of endocrinology* (pp. 117–136). New York: F. K. Schattauer Verlag.

Phillips, S. M., & Sherwin, B. B. (1992a). Effects of estrogen on memory function in surgically menopausal women. *Psychoneuroendocrinology, 17,* 485–495.

Phillips, S. M., & Sherwin, B. B. (1992b). Variations in memory function and sex steroid hormones across the menstrual cycle. *Psychoneuroendocrinology, 17,* 497–506.

Russell, E. W. (1975). A multiple scoring method for the assessment of complex memory functions. *Journal of Consulting and Clinical Psychology, 43,* 800–809.

Sherwin, B. B. (1988). Estrogen and/or androgen replacement therapy and cognitive functioning in surgically menopausal women. *Psychoneuroendocrinology, 13,* 345–357.

Shute, V. J., Pellegrino, J. W., Hubert, L., & Reynolds, R. W. (1983). The relationship between androgen levels and human spatial abilities. *Bulletin of the Psychonomic Society, 21,* 465–468.

Sivan, A. B. (1992). *Manual for the Benton Visual Retention Test.* New York: Psychological Corporation.

Squire, L. R. (1992). Memory and the hippocampus: A synthesis from findings with rats, monkeys, and humans. *Psychological Review, 99,* 195–231.

Tabachnick, B. G., & Fidell, L. S. (1989). *Using multivariate statistics.* New York: HarperCollins.

Teyler, T. J., Vardaris, R. M., Lewis, D., & Rawitch, A. B. (1980, August 29). Gonadal steroids: Effects on excitability of hippocampal pyramidal cells. *Science, 209,* 1017–1019.

Vandenberg, S. G., & Kuse, A. R. (1978). Mental rotations, a group test of three-dimensional spatial rotation. *Perceptual and Motor Skills, 47,* 599–604.

Wechsler, D. (1945). A standardized memory scale for clinical use. *Journal of Psychology, 19,* 87–95.

Wechsler, D. (1981). *Manual for the Wechsler Adult Intelligence Scale—Revised.* New York: Psychological Corporation.

Wechsler, D. (1987). *Manual for the Wechsler Memory Scale—Revised.* New York: Psychological Corporation.

Zuckerman, M. & Lubin, B. (1985). *The Multiple Affect Adjective Check List Revised.* San Diego: Educational and Industrial Testing Service.

Received January 9, 1995
Revision received June 9, 1995
Accepted October 16, 1995

Glucose effects on declarative and nondeclarative memory in healthy elderly and young adults

CAROL A. MANNING, MICHAEL W. PARSONS, ELLEN M. COTTER, and PAUL E. GOLD
University of Virginia, Charlottesville, Virginia

Peripheral glucose ingestion enhances performance on explicit declarative verbal memory tasks in healthy elderly people. In the present experiment, healthy young and elderly adults were administered glucose (50 g) or saccharin followed by tests of declarative verbal memory (free recall and recognition of a word list) and a nondeclarative priming test (word-stem completion). In the elderly, glucose significantly enhanced performance on the declarative but not on the nondeclarative portions of the test. Performance by the young subjects was equivalent in the glucose and saccharin conditions. These findings, that glucose enhances memory for a declarative/explicit but not nondeclarative/implicit task, support the notion that declarative and nondeclarative memory systems are separate functional and anatomic systems.

Pharmacological enhancement of memory by glucose in rodents (Gold, 1991; White, 1991) and in healthy elderly people and people with Alzheimer's disease is now well established (Craft, Zallen, & Baker, 1992; Craft, Murphy, & Wenstrom, 1994; Hall, Gonder-Frederick, Chewning, Silveira, & Gold, 1989; Manning, Hall, & Gold, 1990; Manning, Parsons, & Gold, 1992; Manning, Ragozzino, & Gold, 1993; Wann, Ballard, & Lade, 1991; cf. Gold, 1995). In a series of double-blind experiments, performance on a variety of memory tasks was facilitated by glucose ingestion in individuals with memory deficits resulting from conditions including advanced age and Alzheimer's disease. In particular, these experiments demonstrated glucose enhancement of explicit (or declarative) memory. These explicit tests emphasize conscious recollection of recently learned material (Squire, Knowlton, & Musen,1993). For example, relative to saccharin performance, glucose ingestion facilitated performance in healthy elderly subjects on a test of memory for narrative prose (Hall et al., 1989) and improved performance on a variety of declarative memory tasks, including word and paragraph recall, but did not affect performance on other nonmemory neuropsychological measures such as attention or motor speed (Manning et al., 1990). Glucose ingestion also improved performance in healthy middle-aged people (age 40–55) on declarative verbal, visual, and associative memory tasks (Wann et al., 1991). Glucose improved paragraph recall, again a declarative task, in mildly demented probable Alzheimer patients (Craft et al., 1992). In moderately to severely demented probable Alzheimer patients, Manning et al. (1993) found that glucose improved performance on a variety of declarative tasks, including information learned in the experimental setting (paragraph recall) and general information (orientation) but not memory in the nondeclarative domain (word-stem completion).

There is mounting evidence for a separate memory system involving a category of learning that is distinct from explicit recall of semantic or episodic information (McAndrews, Glisky, & Schacter, 1987; Shimamura, Salmon, Squire, & Butters, 1987; Squire et al., 1993; Tulving & Schacter, 1990). This nonconscious memory, called priming, involves recall of information without the subject's being made aware that (s)he is explicitly recalling previously learned information. Priming is of particular interest because performance on such tasks can be dissociated from performance on more traditional explicit memory tasks; individuals with deficits on declarative semantic tasks may demonstrate intact priming abilities (McAndrews et al., 1987; Shimamura et al., 1987). For example, amnesic individuals who have impaired declarative memory demonstrate intact priming (Cave & Squire, 1992; Graf, Squire, & Mandler, 1984; Musen & Squire, 1992; Schacter, Cooper, Tharan, & Rubens, 1991). Further evidence for a dissociation of memory types includes experiments in which patients with Huntington's disease display normal priming but impaired performance on explicit memory tasks (Bylsma, Rebok, & Brandt, 1991; Christopher, 1991). In addition, healthy elderly people have been shown to have impaired word recall and recognition but intact priming relative to young subjects (Light & Singh, 1987). A second line of evidence suggesting a dissociation between declarative memory and priming comes from research indicating that varying the strength of declarative memory does not affect priming (see Squire et al., 1993). Recently, a double dissociation was found in healthy elderly in which

This research was supported by the Sandoz Foundation for Gerontological Research, the Alzheimer's Association, NIH Training Grant HD07232, NIA (AG 07648), ONR (NOOO1489-J-1216), NSF (BNS-9012239), and NINDS (NS 32914). Special thanks are extended to Michelle Eng and Belinda Conley for help in manuscript preparation.
Correspondence should be directed to C. A. Manning, Department of Neurology, Box 394, University of Virginia, Charlottesville, VA 22908 (e-mail: cm4r@virginia.edu).

From *Psychobiology,* June 1997, pp. 103-108.

different types of priming tasks (word-stem completion vs. word-fragment completion) correlated with performance on traditional neuropsychological tests associated with different brain areas (frontal lobes vs. hippocampus) (Winocur, Moscovitch, & Stuss, 1996).

To date, the effects of glucose on memory in healthy elderly individuals have been examined only in the declarative domain. The question of whether glucose facilitation of memory maps onto the declarative/nondeclarative organization of memory has yet to be examined. In severely demented Alzheimer's patients, glucose enhanced recognition of a word list but did not affect priming stem completion of the same word list (Manning et al., 1993). This dissociation suggests that glucose may promote performance on declarative tasks but not affect the separate memory system encompassing priming. Evidence that glucose does not facilitate priming in Alzheimer's patients, taken together with findings that glucose appears to be most effective as a memory modulator in healthy elderly on such tasks as memory for narrative prose and word-list recall in which there is a demonstrated age decline (unlike priming) (Craik, 1977; Drachman & Leavitt, 1972), suggests that glucose might not enhance priming performance in healthy elderly.

Examining the effects of glucose on declarative and nondeclarative memory tasks within the same individuals provides us with the opportunity to determine whether pharmacological enhancement of memory, as evidenced by glucose, will dissociate in the same fashion (declarative vs. nondeclarative) as found in amnesic patients. In other words, does the structure of memory split into different components when based on a drug-treatment/modulation design? If glucose facilitates both declarative and nondeclarative tasks, at least two explanations are possible: (1) glucose is broad acting and nonspecific to memory structure or (2) our current conceptualization of memory along declarative/nondeclarative lines needs modification. On the other hand, if glucose enhancement of memory dissociates along the declarative/nondeclarative distinction, this would provide additional evidence for separate memory systems.

The findings here indicate that in healthy elderly subjects, glucose enhances memory for word-list recall, a declarative verbal memory task, but not for word-stem completion, a priming task, focused on the same presentation of a word list.

METHOD

Subjects

This study used elderly and young subjects. Twenty-three elderly volunteers (8 males, 15 females) were recruited from the local senior citizens center, local churches, and newspaper announcements. They were between 61 and 80 years old (M = 67) and had an average of 15 years of education. All were in good health without evidence of dementia, as measured by Folstein mini-mental status scores of 26 or greater (Folstein, Folstein, & McHugh, 1975), and were community dwelling. None had a history of chronic health problems or neurological disease.

Twenty-four undergraduates (8 males, 16 females) comprised the young subject group. All were enrolled in an introductory psychology course and received credit toward fulfillment of a research requirement as compensation for participation. They were between 17 and 22 years old (M = 18.6) and had an average of 13 years of education.

Procedures

A repeated measures design was used in which each subject served as his or her own control. Testing took place on two mornings (0700–0900 h) separated by 1 week. All testing was carried out individually. All subjects refrained from eating or drinking during the 8 h preceding testing in order to ensure that all were tested with baseline blood glucose levels. After arriving at the testing center, medical and educational information was obtained from each subject. Next, baseline blood glucose measurements were recorded using a Glucoscan 2000 meter (Lifescan, Mountain View, CA). In this procedure, one drop of blood from a finger stick is placed on an enzyme pad that is read by a reflectance meter. This procedure is relatively pain free, and no discomfort was reported. Upon completion, the subjects ingested an 8-oz lemon-flavored beverage sweetened with either 50 g of glucose or 23.7 mg of saccharin. These beverages were taste matched for sweetness. Both subject and examiner were blind to condition. To maintain the double-blind status of the experiment, one examiner administered the memory measures and another obtained blood-glucose levels. Blood glucose levels were measured 15 min after beverage ingestion, which is the time required for significant rises in blood glucose (Hall et al., 1989; Manning et al., 1990), and twice more over the next 30 min.

Fifteen minutes after beverage ingestion, a priming task adapted from Squire, Shimamura, and Graf (1987) was administered. For this test, 72 target words with a mean frequency of occurrence of 67 per million (Francis & Kučera, 1982) and with between four and nine letters each were printed individually on index cards. The first three letters (the stems) were identical to at least 10 other dictionary entries, but each word had a stem unique from the other 71 target words.

First, subjects were shown 23 words (18 targets and 5 filler words), one at a time. They were asked to rate how well they liked each word on a 5-point scale. This was done twice with the word list presented in two different random orders. This procedure ensured that the words were semantically encoded. A card showing the choices from 1 (*like extremely*) to 5 (*dislike extremely*) was placed in front of the subject. The speed of presentation, which averaged about 5 sec per word, was determined by the subject.

Next, priming was tested through word completion in which subjects were shown, one at a time, 29 three-letter word stems each written on an index card. The subjects were asked to complete the stem, using the first word that came to mind, and were given 3 sec to do so. Any word except for a proper noun was acceptable. Eighteen of the stems could be completed from the list that they had just seen. Five of the 11 new stems were placed at the beginning of the list; the other 6 were spread throughout the 18 previously seen stems. The 11 new stems were used to assess baseline guessing rates—that is, to see how many words could be accurately completed despite no previous contact in the experimental context. No reference was made to the fact that this was a memory test and that some of these words could be completed by using previously seen words.

The recognition component of the task involved showing 36 words, 18 previously seen and 18 distractor words with a total possible correct of 36. The subjects were requested to specify whether or not they had seen the word in the liking task. Following this, a measurement of the blood glucose level was obtained.

The free-recall portion of the priming task was administered next. Here, the subject was asked to write down as many words from the liking task as he/she could recall. The subjects were given as much time as they wanted; this averaged about 4 min. A final blood glucose measurement was obtained and subjects were dismissed for the day.

One week later, the identical procedure was repeated using the alternate beverage and equivalent test forms. The alternate test forms used identical criteria—that is, in terms of word frequency of occurrence and number of letters. Different word lists constituted the two alternate forms. This was necessary because each subject received both forms. Within each form, however, studied versus unstudied words were interchanged across subjects; that is, the composition of the 11 unstudied words and the 18 studied words was changed in a random fashion to avoid target lists' being easier to complete. Note that a nontraditional design was used in which the same word list was used for recall, priming, and recognition within a given week. This was done in order to examine the possibility of different effects of glucose on the same words, depending on the constraints of the memory strategy (recall, priming, or recognition). Since the same procedure was used in both glucose and saccharin conditions, the effects of using a single word list within conditions should have been equivalent across conditions without a glucose effect. The beverage sweetener was counterbalanced across subjects to control for order and practice effects across weeks. The same procedures were used for the young and elderly subjects.

Statistical Analyses

Data were analyzed using Wilcoxon rank comparisons of two samples (Siegel, 1956) (two-tailed) for glucose versus saccharin

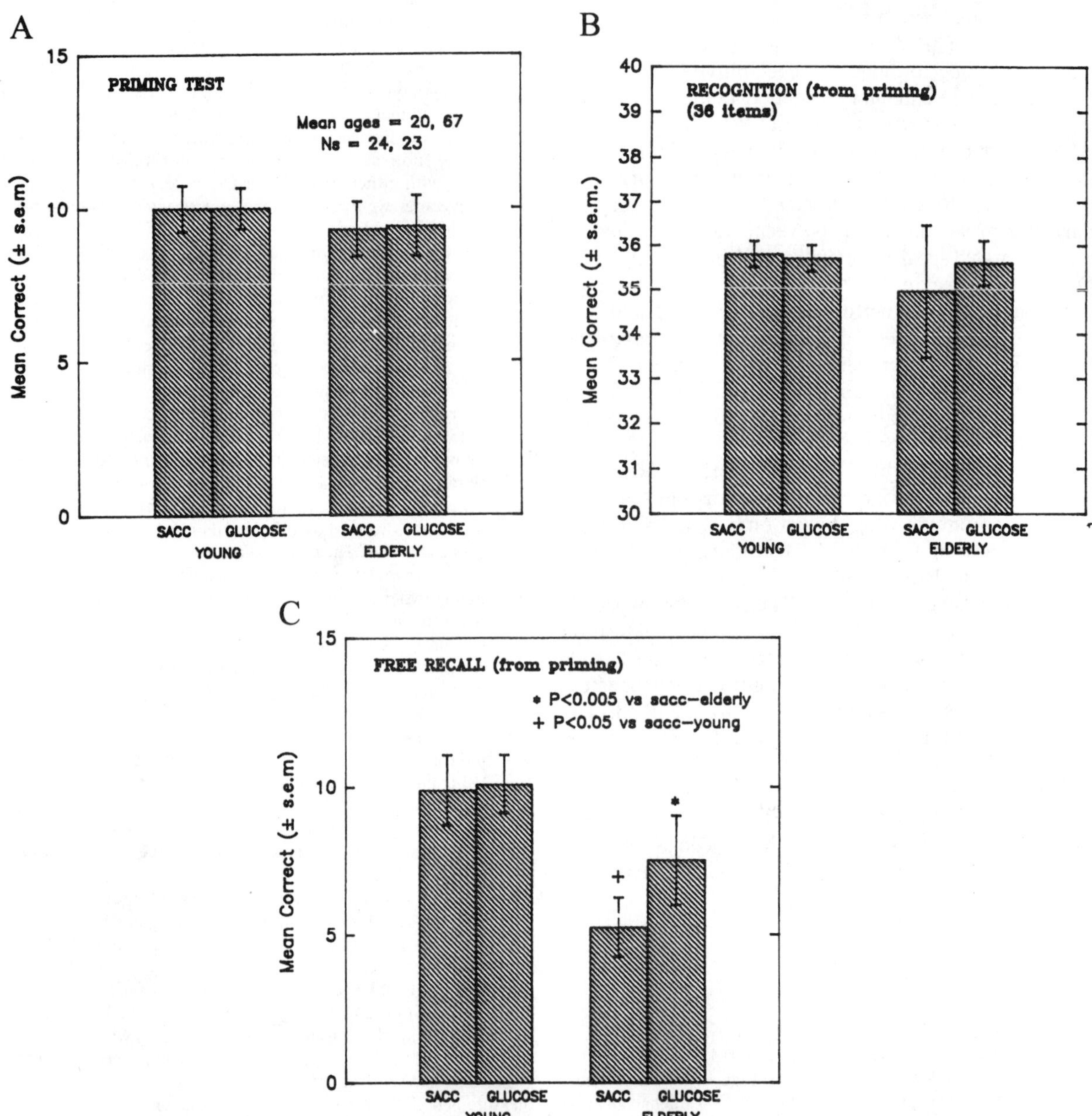

Figure 1. Mean number of items correct are presented for young and elderly in saccharin and glucose conditions in the (A) priming (stem completion), (B) word-recognition, and (C) free-recall portions of the test. Free recall was significantly ($p < .05$) improved after glucose ingestion in the elderly. Elderly subjects recalled significantly ($p < .05$) fewer words after saccharin ingestion than did young subjects after saccharin ingestion. Recognition (panel B) was nearly perfect for young and elderly subjects in both glucose and saccharin conditions.

performance. Spearman rank-order correlations were used to assess reliability of the tests across conditions.

RESULTS

Priming was determined by subtracting the number of correctly completed word stems for unstudied words from the total number of completed stems. In this way, only correct completion of stems for studied words were counted as primed. As can be seen in Figure 1A, the mean priming rate for young people was 10 (SD = 4.9) in both glucose and saccharin conditions. The mean priming rate for older subjects was 9.2 (8.7) and 9.3 (8.9) for saccharin and glucose, respectively. Mean baseline guessing rates, computed as the number of correctly completed stems for unstudied words, were 3.5 (1.2) and 3.3 (1.4) for saccharin and glucose, respectively, in the young people, and 3.0 (2.5) and 3.8 (2.9) in the older subjects.

In the elderly, glucose significantly improved free recall of the priming task word list relative to performance after saccharin ingestion (Figure 1B). Although recognition of the priming word list improved in the glucose condition, it was not statistically significant (p = .07). However, performance on this portion of the test was nearly perfect (correct recognition of 35.6 and 34.96 out of 36 for glucose and saccharin, respectively) (Figure 1C). In the young subjects, performance was equivalent across conditions (glucose and saccharin) within each memory task—priming, recognition, and recall.

As expected, blood glucose levels rose significantly after ingestion of the glucose beverage (Figure 2). In addition, blood glucose levels were significantly higher in the elderly than in the young on both glucose and saccharin days at all measurements except for the baseline measurement on the saccharin day. Thus, glucose regulation was poorer in the elderly subjects than in the young, as noted by generally higher blood glucose levels and larger increases in blood glucose after glucose ingestion in the elderly.

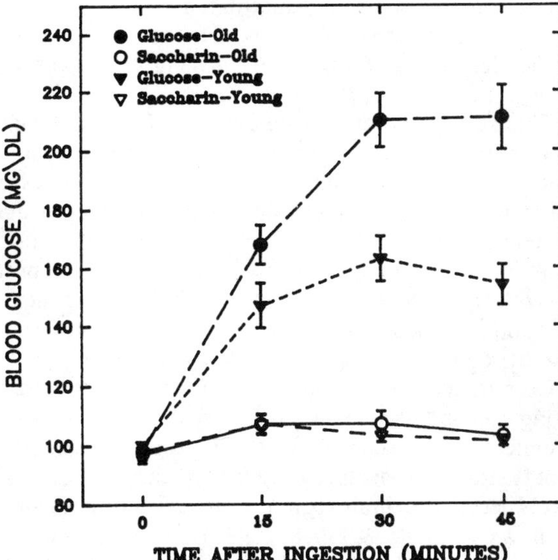

Figure 2. Mean blood glucose levels at baseline were comparable in young and elderly subjects in glucose and saccharin conditions. Mean blood glucose levels were significantly higher at all subsequent measurements when the beverage was sweetened with glucose rather than saccharin.

DISCUSSION

The present results indicate that glucose enhances performance in explicit declarative verbal memory in healthy elderly people, but that glucose does not affect word-stem completion. The dissociation between glucose facilitation of explicit recall but not of priming supports the hypothesis that priming is independent of explicit memory (Tulving & Schacter, 1990). This is particularly evident when taking into account that the word list for the explicit and the implicit conditions of the test comprised a single list learned at the same time. Thus, since the words were learned only once, the difference in glucose facilitation of explicit but not of implicit memory cannot be explained by different learning conditions. Likewise, glucose was administered only once during the testing protocol, eliminating administration differences as a source of enhancement of declarative but not of nondeclarative performance. Equivalent word-stem completion was seen in glucose and saccharin conditions without floor or ceiling effects. Therefore, there was room for improvement in priming performance if glucose had proven effective. It is also possible that glucose enhances explicit and implicit memory at different doses, a possibility that would require a full dose–response curve to evaluate; task-related dose–response differences for memory enhancement with glucose, as with other pharmacological treatments, are quite common in experiments with rodents (e.g., Gold, Vogt, & Hall, 1986; Packard & White, 1990).

These findings provide at least a third line of evidence indicating that implicit memory, as measured by a stem-completion task, is a memory system distinct from declarative memory. The current results can be added to findings from studies with amnesic patients in which deficits exist in declarative but not in nondeclarative domains (Cave & Squire, 1992; Graf et al., 1984; Musen & Squire, 1992; Schacter et al., 1991) and from experiments in which increasing the degree of recall ability does not affect priming (Squire et al., 1993). The current cognitive conceptualization of memory into declarative/nondeclarative domains appears to remain stable across at least three types of experiments involving (1) naturally occurring pathologies, (2) manipulation of memory strength, and now (3) a drug treatment/memory modulation design.

Glucose facilitated performance on declarative verbal recall in the elderly group, providing a replication in principle of previous studies (Hall et al., 1989; Manning et al., 1990). Despite being an explicit/declarative verbal memory task, the word-recognition component of the test was not significantly facilitated by glucose. This may be attributed to the nearly perfect recognition scores in the elderly (34.96 out of 36), leaving little room for improvement.

This study did not provide evidence for glucose enhancement of memory in young adults. These negative findings may be a result of age-related differences in susceptibility to glucose enhancement of memory, to age differences in glucose regulation resulting in an adjustment of the glucose dose necessary for facilitation, or to age-related differences in test difficulty. Experiments using multiple doses of glucose together with tests of varying difficulty would be necessary to address this issue.

Current neurobiological evidence suggests that circulating glucose levels may interact with specific neurochemical and neuroanatomical systems in the brain. Recent findings in rodents suggest that extracellular glucose levels decrease in brain regions activated during learning (Fellows, Boutelle, & Fillenz, 1993), suggesting that exogenous administration of glucose might ameliorate this decrease. In addition, circulating glucose levels might contribute to regulation of brain acetylcholine synthesis in aged rodents by serving as a precursor for acetyl-CoA, a substrate in acetylcholine synthesis (Gibson & Peterson, 1981; Ricny, Tucek, & Novakova, 1992). Such findings fit well with evidence that glucose injections augment several effects of cholinergic agonists and attenuate effects of cholinergic antagonists (cf. Gold, 1994). Glucose also attenuates the effects on memory and other behavioral measures of systemic or direct brain injections of the opiate agonist morphine (Ragozzino & Gold, 1994; Ragozzino, Parker, & Gold, 1992; Stone, Walser, Gold, & Gold, 1991). Recent evidence (Ragozzino, Unick, & Gold, 1996) indicates that glucose injections augment release of acetylcholine in the hippocampus of rats while the animals are performing a memory task; glucose had no effect on acetylcholine release in rats kept in holding cages, suggesting that glucose may act somewhat selectively when neural systems are engaged by memory tasks, and perhaps differentially so, depending on the nature of the behavioral task. While neurobiological measures such as these may contribute to the effects of glucose on cognitive functions, it is important to note that parallel information about neurotransmitters other than acetylcholine in brain regions other than the hippocampus is not available.

One interpretation of the findings of the present experiment is that activation of the neural systems mediating explicit memory creates a demand for glucose in these neural systems, while activation of the neural systems mediating implicit memory does not create such a demand in these, other, neural systems. A similar interpretation can be applied to differences in neural systems activated by retrieval of information via explicit or implicit mechanisms. The present experiment cannot distinguish effects of glucose on acquisition from those on retrieval because glucose was present at both the times of acquisition and the times of retrieval of information. However, the findings of other experiments in both humans and rodents indicate that glucose administration at the time of *either* acquisition or retrieval enhances learned performance (Manning, Stone, Korol, & Gold, 1997; Stone, Rudd, & Gold, 1990).

This study examined only one form of priming: stem completion. Future experiments examining other types of priming, in addition to procedural memory tests, are in order. These experiments would further clarify the extent of glucose's ability to facilitate memory, as well as provide information on the cognitive and neurobiological underpinnings of memory formation. Utilization of multiple implicit and explicit tasks might provide evidence for a double dissociation, thus strengthening the idea of separate memory systems.

Taken together, these findings suggest that glucose enhancement of acquisition and/or recall is subject to the nature of the method used to assess memory. This study provides replication of evidence that glucose enhances performance on explicit verbal memory tasks in healthy elderly people. However, implicit memory, as measured by word-stem completion, was unchanged after glucose ingestion in the same subjects. This dissociation between types of recall-task demand suggests that the two types of tasks may (1) utilize different neural pathways and (2) be independent of each other, although direct confirmation of separate memory systems is beyond the scope of this paper. This study did not provide evidence that glucose potentiates memory in healthy young adults. Differences in age-related susceptibility to glucose may be associated with increased difficulties with peripheral glucose regulation with aging and the inability of aged subjects to regulate optimally the neuroendocrine systems responsible for memory storage.

REFERENCES

Bylsma, F. W., Rebok, G. W., & Brandt, J. (1991). Long-term retention of implicit learning in Huntington's disease. *Neuropsychologia*, **29**, 1213-1221.

Cave, C. B., & Squire, L. R. (1992). Intact and long-lasting repetition priming in amnesia. *Journal of Experimental Psychology: Learning, Memory, & Cognition*, **18**, 509-520.

Christopher, R. (1991). Implicit, explicit, and semantic memory functions in Alzheimer's disease and Huntington's disease. *Journal of Clinical & Experimental Neuropsychology*, **13**, 479-494.

Craft, S., Murphy, C., & Wenstrom, J. (1994). Glucose effects on complex memory and nonmemory tasks: The influence of age, sex, and glucoregulatory response. *Psychobiology*, **22**, 95-105.

Craft, S., Zallen, G., & Baker, L. D. (1992). Glucose in mild senile dementia of the Alzheimer type. *Journal of Clinical & Experimental Neuropsychology*, **14**, 253-267.

Craik, F. I. M. (1977). Age differences in human memory. In J. E. Birren & K. W. Schaie (Eds.), *Handbook of the psychology of aging* (pp. 384-420). New York: Van Nostrand Reinhold.

Drachman, D. A., & Leavitt, J. (1972). Memory impairment in the aged: Storage versus retrieval deficit. *Journal of Experimental Psychology*, **93**, 302-308.

Fellows, M., Boutelle, G., & Fillenz, M. (1993). Physiological stimulation increases nonoxidative glucose metabolism in the brain of the freely moving rat. *Journal of Neurochemistry*, **60**, 1258-1263.

Folstein, M. F., Folstein, S. E., & McHugh, P. R. (1975). "Mini-mental state": A practical method for grading the cognitive state of patients for the clinician. *Journal of Psychiatric Research*, **12**, 189-198.

Francis, W. N., & Kučera, H. (1982). *Frequency analysis of English usage: Lexicon and grammar*. Boston: Houghton-Mifflin.

Gibson, G. E., & Peterson, C. (1981). Aging decreases oxidative metabolism and the release and synthesis of acetylcholine. *Journal of Neurochemistry*, **37**, 978-984.

Gold, P. E. (1991). An integrated memory regulation system: From blood to brain. In R. C. A. Frederickson, J. L. McGaugh, & D. L. Felten (Eds.), *Peripheral signaling of the brain: Role in neural-immune interactions, learning and memory* (pp. 391-419). Toronto: Hogrefe & Huber.

Gold, P. E. (1994). Modulation of emotional and non-emotional memories: Same pharmacological systems, different neuroanatomical systems. In J. L. McGaugh, N. M. Weinberger, & G. S. Lynch (Eds.), *Brain and memory: Modulation and mediation of neural plasticity* (pp. 41-74). New York: Oxford University Press.

Gold, P. E. (1995). The role of glucose in regulating brain and cognition. *American Journal of Clinical Nutrition*, **61**, S987-S995.

Gold, P. E., Vogt, J., & Hall, J. L. (1986). Posttraining glucose effects on memory: Behavioral and pharmacological characteristics. *Behavioral & Neural Biology*, **46**, 145-155.

Graf, P., Squire, L. R., & Mandler, G. (1984). The information that amnesic patients do not forget. *Journal of Experimental Psychology: Learning, Memory, & Cognition*, **10**, 164-178.

Hall, J. L., Gonder-Frederick, L. A., Chewning, W. W., Silveira, J., & Gold, P. E. (1989). Glucose enhancement of memory in young and aged humans. *Neuropsychologia*, **27**, 1129-1138.

Light, L. L., & Singh, A. (1987). Implicit and explicit memory in young and older adults. *Journal of Experimental Psychology: Learning, Memory, & Cognition*, **13**, 531-541.

Manning, C. A., Hall, J. L., & Gold, P. E. (1990). Glucose effects on memory and other neuropsychological tests in elderly humans. *Psychological Science*, **5**, 307-311.

Manning, C. A., Parsons, M. W., & Gold, P. E. (1992). Anterograde and retrograde enhancement of 24-hour memory by glucose in elderly humans. *Behavioral & Neural Biology*, **58**, 125-130.

Manning, C. A., Ragozzino, M. E., & Gold, P. E. (1993). Glucose enhancement of memory in patients with probable senile dementia of the Alzheimer's type. *Neurobiology of Aging*, **14**, 523-528.

Manning, C. A., Stone, W. S., Korol, D. L., & Gold, P. E. (1997). *Glucose enhancement of 24-hour memory retrieval in healthy elderly humans*. Manuscript in preparation.

McAndrews, M. P., Glisky, E. L., & Schacter, D. (1987). When priming persists: Long-lasting implicit memory for a single episode in amnesic patients. *Neuropsychologia*, **25**, 497-506.

Musen, G., & Squire, L. R. (1992). Nonverbal priming in amnesia. *Memory & Cognition*, **20**, 441-448.

Packard, M. G., & White, N. M. (1990). Effect of posttraining injections of glucose on acquisition of two appetitive learning tasks. *Psychobiology*, **18**, 282-286.

Ragozzino, M. E., & Gold, P. E. (1994). Task-dependent effects of intra-amygdala morphine injections: Attenuation by intra-amygdala glucose injections. *Journal of Neuroscience*, **14**, 7478-7485.

Ragozzino, M. E., Parker, M. E., & Gold, P. E. (1992). Memory impairments with morphine injections into the medial septum: Attenuation by glucose administration. *Brain Research*, **597**, 241-249.

Ragozzino, M. E., Unick, K. E., & Gold, P. E. (1996). Hippocampal acetylcholine release during memory testing in rats: Augmentation by glucose. *Proceedings of the National Academy of Sciences*, **93**, 4693-4698.

Ricny, J., Tucek, S., & Novakova, J. (1992). Acetylcarnitine, carnitine and glucose diminish the effect of muscarinic antagonist quinuclidinyl benzilate on striatal acetylcholine content. *Brain Research*, **576**, 215-219.

Schacter, D. L., Cooper, L. A., Tharan, M., & Rubens, A. B. (1991). Preserved priming of novel objects in patients with memory disorders. *Journal of Cognitive Neuroscience*, **3**, 118-131.

Siegel, S. (1956). *Nonparametric statistics for the behavioral sciences*. New York: McGraw-Hill.

Shimamura, A. P., Salmon, D. P., Squire, L. R., & Butters, N. (1987). Memory dysfunction in dementia and amnesia. *Behavioral Neuroscience*, **101**, 347-351.

Squire, L. R., Knowlton, B., & Musen, G. (1993). The structure and organization of memory. *Annual Review of Psychology*, **44**, 453-495.

Squire, L. R., Shimamura, A. P., & Graf, P. (1987). Strength and duration of priming effects in normal subjects and amnesic patients. *Neuropsychologia*, **25**, 195-210.

Stone, W. S., Rudd, R. J., & Gold, P. E. (1990). Amphetamine, epinephrine, and glucose enhancement of memory retrieval. *Psychobiology*, **18**, 227-230.

Stone, W. S., Walser, B., Gold, S. D., & Gold, P. E. (1991). Scopolamine- and morphine-induced impairments of spontaneous alternation performance in mice: Reversal with glucose and cholinergic and adrenergic agonists. *Behavioral Neuroscience*, **105**, 264-271.

Tulving, E., & Schacter, D. L. (1990). Priming and human memory systems. *Science*, **247**, 301-306.

Wann, P. A., Ballard, L. A., & Lade, B. J. (1991). Sweet recall: Glucose enhancement of memory in middle-aged humans. *Journal of Clinical & Experimental Neuropsychology*, **13**, 18.

White, N. (1991). Peripheral and central memory-enhancing actions of glucose. In R. C. A. Frederickson, J. L. McGaugh, & D. L. Felten (Eds.), *Peripheral signaling of the brain: Role in neural-immune interactions and learning and memory* (pp. 421-441). Toronto: Hogrefe & Huber.

Winocur, G., Moscovitch, M., & Stuss, D. T. (1996). Explicit and implicit memory in the elderly: Evidence for double dissociation involving medial temporal- and frontal-lobe functions. *Neuropsychology*, **10**, 57-65.

(Manuscript received June 10, 1996;
revision accepted for publication December 17, 1996.)

Disorders of Behavior and the Nervous System

The ancient Egyptians and Greeks inferred the biological basis of behavioral disorders thousands of years ago. Circa 1900 B.C., the Egyptians believed that conversion disorder, which is a condition characterized by persistent complaint of physical dysfunction without any apparent physical cause, was due to the uterus wandering aimlessly within a woman's body. Even the wise Hippocrates, hundreds of years later, believed this to be the case. He called the disorder "hysteria," which means "uterus" in Greek. His advice for women suffering from hysteria was to get married. Hippocrates attributed other behavioral disorders to imbalance of bodily fluids called "humors." Certainly most of these explanations were erroneous, but they have directed our focus to the biological basis of behavioral disorders.

The brain became the organ most associated with behavioral disorders by the twentieth century. One evidence is the development of psychosurgery at that time. Patients suffering from uncontrollable seizures and restlessness underwent lobotomy, a surgery in which the frontal lobe of the cerebral cortex was separated from the rest of the brain. The results were dramatic. Patients became calm, mellow, and their moods more docile. Psychosurgery is rarely applied now because of unwanted side effects and for ethical reasons as well.

Progress in the neurosciences provides systematic ways to understand, diagnose, assess, and treat behavioral disorders. Brain imaging techniques, for example, can locate areas of dysfunction in the brain associated with particular behavioral disorders. Techniques in neurochemistry can identify abnormal fluctuations in neurotransmitter concentration in the brain of patients with certain disorders. Quantitative genetics can trace the heritability of certain behavioral disorders, and molecular genetics can identify the abnormal genes that set the occurrence of the disorder.

It is popular nowadays to treat behavioral disorders using the biomedical approach, that is, treatment using drugs, neurosurgery, or more recently, gene therapy. Parkinson's disease is a good example. Parkinson's disease is characterized by a progressive loss of the ability to control movement, eventually leading to death. Drugs such as L-Dopa have been used in some patients. Correcting for the defective gene for this condition is now being considered.

Several neurological disorders are better understood today with the help of sophisticated techniques such as neuroimaging. We now can determine areas within the brain that are afflicted by the disorder. We have also identified the major neurotransmitters involved in various disorders such as drug addiction and attention deficit hyperactivity disorder (ADHD). Knowing these factors will help us develop strategies in combating these illnesses.

Looking Ahead: Challenge Questions

What are the behavioral symptoms of Parkinson's disease? Which regions of the brain are affected in patients with the disease? Discuss the neurotransmitter system involved in this disorder. What is the possible role of the brain's immune system in Parkinson's disease?

Is drug addiction a brain disorder? Discuss why you agree or disagree. Describe the role of dopamine in mediating the effects of psychoactive drugs. Can you speculate on a biopsychological model to treat drug addiction?

Describe the symptoms of ADHD in children. Can this condition occur in adults, too? What is the current belief with regards to the pathogenesis of ADHD?

UNIT 10

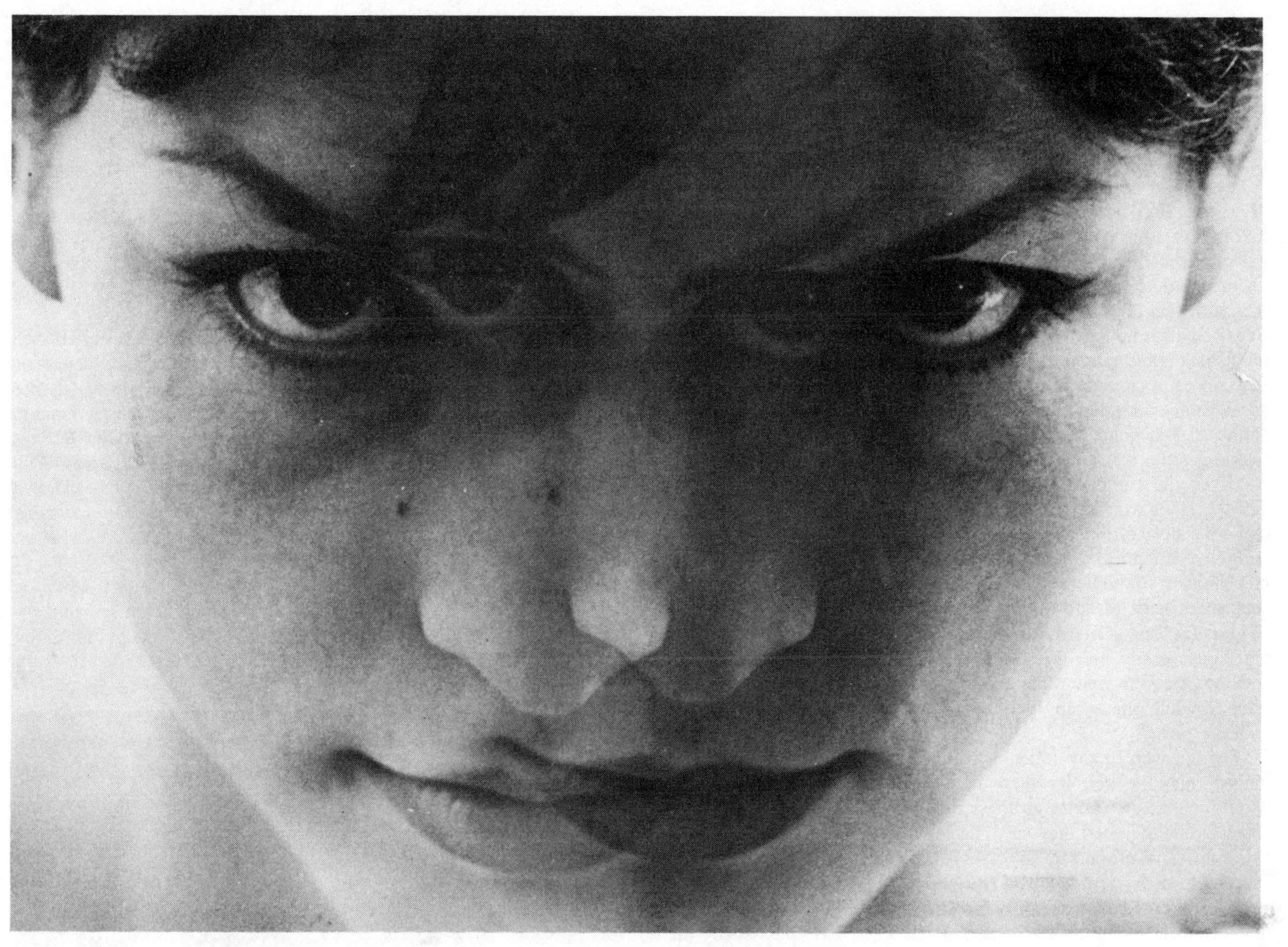

ADDICTED

Why do people get hooked? Mounting evidence points to a powerful brain chemical called dopamine

By J. MADELEINE NASH

IMAGINE YOU ARE TAKING A SLUG OF WHISKEY. A puff of a cigarette. A toke of marijuana. A snort of cocaine. A shot of heroin. Put aside whether these drugs are legal or illegal. Concentrate, for now, on the chemistry. The moment you take that slug, that puff, that toke, that snort, that shot, trillions of potent molecules surge through your bloodstream and into your brain. Once there, they set off a cascade of chemical and electrical events, a kind of neurological chain reaction that ricochets around the skull and rearranges the interior reality of the mind.

Given the complexity of these events—and the inner workings of the mind in general—it's not surprising that scientists have struggled mightily to make sense of the mechanisms of addiction. Why do certain substances have the power to make us feel so good (at least at first)? Why do some people fall so easily into the thrall of alcohol, cocaine, nicotine and other addictive substances, while others can, literally, take them or leave them?

The answer, many scientists are convinced, may be simpler than anyone has dared imagine. What ties all these mood-altering drugs together, they say, is a remarkable ability to elevate levels of a common substance in the brain called dopamine. In fact, so overwhelming has evidence of the link between dopamine and drugs of abuse become that the distinction (pushed primarily by the tobacco industry and its supporters) between substances that are addictive and those that are merely habit-forming has very nearly been swept away.

The Liggett Group, smallest of the U.S.'s Big Five cigarette makers, broke ranks in March and conceded not only that tobacco is addictive but also that the company has known it all along. While RJR Nabisco and the others continue to battle in the courts—insisting that smokers are not hooked, just exercising free choice—their denials ring increasingly hollow in the face of the growing weight of evidence. Over the past year, several scientific groups have made the case that in dopamine-rich areas of the brain, nicotine behaves remarkably like cocaine. And late last week a federal judge ruled for the first time that the Food and Drug Administration has the right to regulate tobacco as a drug and cigarettes as drug-delivery devices.

Now, a team of researchers led by psychiatrist Dr. Nora Volkow of the Brookhaven National Laboratory in New York has published the strongest evidence to date that the surge of dopamine in addicts' brains is what triggers a cocaine high. In last week's edition of the journal *Nature* they described how powerful brain-imaging technology can be used to track the rise of dopamine and link it to feelings of euphoria.

Like serotonin (the brain chemical affected by such antidepressants as Prozac), dopamine is a neurotransmitter—a molecule that ferries messages from one neuron within the brain to another. Serotonin is associated with feelings of sadness and well-being, dopamine with pleasure and elation. Dopamine can be elevated by a hug, a kiss, a word of praise or a winning poker hand—as well as by the potent pleasures that come from drugs.

The idea that a single chemical could be associated with everything from snorting cocaine and smoking tobacco to getting good

PRIME SUSPECT

They don't yet know the precise mechanism by which it works, but scientists are increasingly convinced that dopamine plays a key role in a wide range of addictions, including those to heroin, nicotine, alcohol and marijuana

DOPAMINE MAY BE LINKED TO GAMBLING, CHOCOLATE AND EVEN SEX

grades and enjoying sex has electrified scientists and changed the way they look at a wide range of dependencies, chemical and otherwise. Dopamine, they now believe, is not just a chemical that transmits pleasure signals but may, in fact, be the master molecule of addiction.

This is not to say dopamine is the only chemical involved or that the deranged thought processes that mark chronic drug abuse are due to dopamine alone. The brain is subtler than that. Drugs modulate the activity of a variety of brain chemicals, each of which intersects with many others. "Drugs are like sledgehammers," observes Dr. Eric Nestler of the Yale University School of Medicine. "They profoundly alter many pathways."

Nevertheless, the realization that dopamine may be a common end point of all those pathways represents a signal advance. Provocative, controversial, unquestionably incomplete, the dopamine hypothesis provides a basic framework for understanding how a genetically encoded trait—such as a tendency to produce too little dopamine—might intersect with environmental influences to create a serious behavioral disorder. Therapists have long known of patients who, in addition to having psychological problems, abuse drugs as well. Could their drug problems be linked to some inborn quirk? Might an inability to absorb enough dopamine, with its pleasure-giving properties, cause them to seek gratification in drugs?

Such speculation is controversial, for it suggests that broad swaths of the population may be genetically predisposed to drug abuse. What is not controversial is that the social cost of drug abuse, whatever its cause, is enormous. Cigarettes contribute to the death toll from cancer and heart disease. Alcohol is the leading cause of domestic violence and highway deaths. The needles used to inject heroin and cocaine are spreading AIDS. Directly or indirectly, addiction to drugs, cigarettes and alcohol is thought to account for a third of all hospital admissions, a quarter of all deaths and a majority of serious crimes. In the U.S. alone the combined medical and social costs of drug abuse are believed to exceed $240 billion.

FOR NEARLY A QUARTER-CENTURY the U.S. has been waging a war on drugs, with little apparent success. As scientists learn more about how dopamine works (and how drugs work on it), the evidence suggests that we may be fighting the wrong battle. Americans tend to think of drug addiction as a failure of character. But this stereotype is beginning to give way to the recognition that drug dependence has a clear biological basis. "Addiction," declares Brookhaven's Volkow, "is a disorder of the brain no different from other forms of mental illness."

That new insight may be the dopamine hypothesis' most important contribution in the fight against drugs. It completes the loop between the mechanism of addiction and programs for treatment. And it raises hope for more effective therapies. Abstinence, if maintained, not only halts the physical and psychological damage wrought by drugs but in large measure also reverses it.

HIGH AND LOWS

Drug	Number who used in the past month
Heroin Triggers release of dopamine; acts on other neurotransmitters	200,000
Amphetamines Stimulate excess release of dopamine	800,000
Cocaine/Crack Blocks dopamine absorption	1.5 million
Marijuana Binds to areas of brain involved in mood and memory; triggers release of dopamine	10 million
Alcohol Triggers dopamine release; acts on other neurotransmitters	11 million abusers
Nicotine Triggers release of dopamine	61 million
Caffeine May trigger release of dopamine	130 million*

Sources: SAMHSA, National Coffee Association *coffee drinkers

Genes and social forces may conspire to turn people into addicts but do not doom them to remain so. Consider the case of Rafael Rios, who grew up in a housing project in New York City's drug-infested South Bronx. For 18 years, until he turned 31, Rios, whose father died of alcoholism, led a double life. He graduated from Harvard Law School and joined a prestigious Chicago law firm. Yet all the while he was secretly visiting a shooting gallery' once a day. His favored concoction: heroin spiked with a jolt of cocaine. Ten years ago, Rios succeeded in kicking his habit—for good, he hopes. He is now executive director of A Safe Haven, a Chicago-based chain of residential facilities for recovering addicts.

How central is dopamine's role in this familiar morality play? Scientists are still trying to sort that out. It is no accident, they say, that people are attracted to drugs. The major drugs of abuse, whether depressants like heroin or stimulants like cocaine, mimic the structure of neurotransmitters, the most mind-bending chemicals nature has ever concocted. Neurotransmitters underlie every thought and emotion, memory and learning; they carry the signals between all the nerve cells, or neurons, in the brain. Among some 50 neurotransmitters discovered to date, a good half a dozen, including dopamine, are known to play a role in addiction.

The neurons that produce this molecular messenger are surprisingly rare. Clustered in loose knots buried deep in the brain, they number a few tens of thousands of nerve cells out of an estimated total of 100 billion. But through long, wire-like projections known as axons, these cells influence neurological activity in many regions, including the nucleus accumbens, the primitive structure that is one of the brain's key pleasure centers. At a purely chemical level, every experience humans find enjoyable—whether listening to music, embracing a lover or savoring chocolate—amounts to little more than an explosion of dopamine in the nucleus accumbens, as exhilarating and ephemeral as a firecracker.

Dopamine, like most biologically important molecules, must be kept within strict bounds. Too little dopamine in certain areas of the brain triggers the tremors and paralysis of Parkinson's disease. Too much causes the hallucinations and bizarre thoughts of schizophrenia. A breakthrough in addiction research came in 1975, when psychologists Roy Wise and Robert Yokel at Concordia University in Montreal reported on the remarkable behavior of some drug-addicted rats. One day the animals were placidly dispensing cocaine and amphetamines to themselves by pressing a lever attached to their cages. The next they were angrily banging at the lever like someone trying to summon a stalled elevator. The reason? The scientists had injected the rats with a drug that blocked the action of dopamine.

In the years since, evidence linking dopamine to drugs has mounted. Amphetamines stimulate dopamine-producing cells to pump out more of the chemical. Cocaine keeps dopamine levels high by inhibiting the activity of a transporter molecule that would ordinarily ferry dopamine back into the cells that produce it. Nicotine, heroin and alcohol

WHAT ELSE?

Preliminary evidence suggests that dopamine may be involved even when we form dependencies on things—like coffee or candy—that we don't think of as drugs at all

trigger a complex chemical cascade that raises dopamine levels. And a still unknown chemical in cigarette smoke, a group led by Brookhaven chemist Joanna Fowler reported last year, may extend the activity of dopamine by blocking a mopping-up enzyme, called MAO B, that would otherwise destroy it.

The evidence that Volkow and her colleagues present in the current issue of *Nature* suggests that dopamine is directly responsible for the exhilarating rush that reinforces the desire to take drugs, at least in cocaine addicts. In all, 17 users participated in the study, says Volkow, and they experienced a high whose intensity was directly related to how extensively cocaine tied up available binding sites on the molecules that transport dopamine around the brain. To produce any high at all, she and her colleagues found, cocaine had to occupy at least 47% of these sites; the "best" results occurred when it took over 60% to 80% of the sites, effectively preventing the transporters from latching onto dopamine and spiriting it out of circulation.

SCIENTISTS BELIEVE THE DOPAMINE system arose very early in the course of animal evolution because it reinforces behaviors so essential to survival. "If it were not for the fact that sex is pleasurable," observes Charles Schuster of Wayne State University in Detroit, "we would not engage in it." Unfortunately, some of the activities humans are neurochemically tuned to find agreeable—eating foods rich in fat and sugar, for instance—have backfired in modern society. Just as a surfeit of food and a dearth of exercise have conspired to turn heart disease and diabetes into major health problems, so the easy availability of addictive chemicals has played a devious trick. Addicts do not crave heroin or cocaine or alcohol or nicotine per se but want the rush of dopamine that these drugs produce.

Dopamine, however, is more than just a feel-good molecule. It also exercises extraordinary power over learning and memory. Think of dopamine, suggests P. Read Montague of the Center for Theoretical Neuroscience at Houston's Baylor College of Medicine, as the proverbial carrot, a reward the brain doles out to networks of neurons for making survival-enhancing choices. And while the details of how this system works are not yet understood, Montague and his colleagues at the Salk Institute in San Diego, California, and M.I.T. have proposed a model that seems quite plausible. Each time the outcome of an action is better than expected, they predicted, dopamine-releasing neurons should increase the rate at which they fire. When an outcome is worse, they should decrease it. And if the outcome is as expected, the firing rate need not change at all.

As a test of his model, Montague created a computer program that simulated the nectar-gathering activity of bees. Programmed with a dopamine-like reward system and set loose on a field of virtual "flowers," some of which were dependably sweet and some of which were either very sweet or not sweet at all, the virtual bees chose the reliably sweet flowers 85% of the time. In laboratory experiments real bees behave just like their virtual counterparts. What does this have to do with drug abuse? Possibly quite a lot, says Montague. The theory is that dopamine-enhancing chemicals fool the brain into thinking drugs are as beneficial as nectar to the bee, thus hijacking a natural reward system that dates back millions of years.

The degree to which learning and memory sustain the addictive process is only now being appreciated. Each time a neurotransmitter like dopamine floods a synapse, scientists believe, circuits that trigger thoughts and motivate actions are etched onto the brain. Indeed, the neurochemistry supporting addiction is so powerful that the people, objects and places associated with drug taking are also imprinted on the brain. Stimulated by food, sex or the smell of tobacco, former smokers can no more control the urge to light up than Pavlov's dogs could stop their urge to salivate. For months Rafael Rios lived in fear of catching a glimpse of bare arms—his own or someone else's. Whenever he did, he remembers, he would be seized by a nearly unbearable urge to find a drug-filled syringe.

Indeed, the brain has many devious tricks for ensuring that the irrational act of taking drugs, deemed "good" because it enhances dopamine, will be repeated. PET-scan images taken by Volkow and her colleagues reveal that the absorption of a cocaine-like chemical by neurons is profoundly reduced in cocaine addicts in contrast to normal subjects. One explanation: the addicts' neurons, assaulted by abnormally high levels of dopamine, have responded defensively and reduced the number of sites (or receptors) to which dopamine can bind. In the absence of drugs, these nerve cells probably experience a dopamine deficit, Volkow speculates, so while addicts begin by taking drugs to feel high, they end up taking them in order not to feel low.

PET-scan images of the brains of recovering cocaine addicts reveal other striking changes, including a dramatically impaired ability to process glucose, the primary energy source for working neurons. Moreover, this impairment—which persists for up to 100 days after withdrawal—is greatest in the prefrontal cortex, a dopamine-rich area of the brain that controls impulsive and irrational behavior. Addicts, in fact, display many of the symptoms shown by patients who have suffered strokes or injuries to the prefrontal cortex. Damage to this region, University of Iowa neurologist Antonio Damasio and his colleagues have demonstrated, destroys the emotional compass that controls behaviors the patient knows are unacceptable.

Anyone who doubts that genes influence behavior should see the mice in Marc Caron's lab. These tireless rodents race around their cages for hours on end. They lose weight because they rarely stop to eat, and then they drop from exhaustion because they are unable to sleep. Why? The mice, says Caron, a biochemist at Duke University's Howard Hughes Medical Institute laboratory, are high on dopamine. They lack the genetic mechanism that sponges up this powerful stuff and spirits it away. Result: there is so much dopamine banging around in the poor creatures' synapses that the mice, though drug-free, act as if they were strung out on cocaine.

CRACK

Prolonged cocaine use deadens nerve endings in the brain's pleasure-regulation system. A brain scan of a cocaine abuser, shows a marked drop in the number of functioning dopamine receptors

For years scientists have suspected that genes play a critical role in determining who will become addicted to drugs and who will not. But not until now have they had molecular tools powerful enough to go after the prime suspects. Caron's mice are just the most recent example. By knocking out a single gene—the so-called dopamine-transporter gene—Caron and his colleagues may have created a strain of mice so sated with dopamine that they are oblivious to the allure of cocaine, and possibly alcohol and heroin as well. "What's exciting about our mice," says Caron, "is that they should allow us to test the hypothesis that all these drugs funnel through the dopamine system."

Several dopamine genes have already been tentatively, and controversially, linked to alcoholism and drug abuse. Inherited variations in these genes modify the efficiency

COKE'S HIGH IS DIRECTLY TIED TO DOPAMINE LEVELS

A.A.'S PATH TO RECOVERY STILL SEEMS THE BEST

with which nerve cells process dopamine, or so the speculation goes. Thus, some scientists conjecture, a dopamine-transporter gene that is superefficient, clearing dopamine from the synapses too rapidly, could predispose some people to a form of alcoholism characterized by violent and impulsive behavior. In essence, they would be mirror images of Caron's mice. Instead of being drenched in dopamine, their synapses would be dopamine-poor.

The dopamine genes known as D2 and D4 might also play a role in drug abuse, for similar reasons. Both these genes, it turns out, contain the blueprints for assembling what scientists call a receptor, a minuscule bump on the surface of cells to which biologically active molecules are attracted. And just as a finger lights up a room by merely flicking a switch, so dopamine triggers a sequence of chemical reactions each time it binds to one of its five known receptors. Genetic differences that reduce the sensitivity of these receptors or decrease their number could diminish the sensation of pleasure.

The problem is, studies that have purported to find a basis for addiction in variations of the D2 and D4 genes have not held up under scrutiny. Indeed, most scientists think addiction probably involves an intricate dance between environmental influences and multiple genes, some of which may influence dopamine activity only indirectly. This has not stopped some researchers from promoting the provocative theory that many people who become alcoholics and drug addicts suffer from an inherited condition dubbed the reward-deficiency syndrome. Low dopamine levels caused by a particular version of the D2 gene, they say, may link a breathtaking array of aberrant behaviors. Among them: severe alcoholism, pathological gambling, binge eating and attention-deficit hyperactivity disorder.

The more science unmasks the powerful biology that underlies addiction, the brighter the prospects for treatment become. For instance, the discovery by Fowler and her team that a chemical that inhibits the mopping-up enzyme MAO B may play a role in cigarette addiction has already opened new possibilities for therapy. A number of well-tolerated MAO B inhibitor drugs developed to treat Parkinson's disease could find a place in the antismoking arsenal. Equally promising, a Yale University team led by Eric Nestler and David Self has found that another type of compound—one that targets the dopamine receptor known as D1—seems to alleviate, at least in rats, the intense craving that accompanies withdrawal from cocaine. One day, suggests Self, a D1 skin patch might help cocaine abusers kick their habit, just as the nicotine patch attenuates the desire to smoke.

Like methadone, the compound that activates D1 appears to be what is known as a partial agonist. Because such medications stimulate some of the same brain pathways as drugs of abuse, they are often addictive in their own right, though less so. And while treating heroin addicts with methadone may seem like a cop-out to people who have never struggled with a drug habit, clinicians say they desperately need more such agents to tide addicts—particularly cocaine addicts—over the first few months of treatment, when the danger of relapse is highest.

REALISTICALLY, NO ONE BELIEVES better medications alone will solve the drug problem. In fact, one of the most hopeful messages coming out of current research is that the biochemical abnormalities associated with addiction can be reversed through learning. For that reason, all sorts of psychosocial interventions, ranging from psychotherapy to 12-step programs, can and do help. Cognitive therapy, which seeks to supply people with coping skills (exercising after work instead of going to a bar, for instance), appears to hold particular promise. After just 10 weeks of therapy, before-and-after PET scans suggest, some patients suffering from obsessive-compulsive disorder (which has some similarities with addiction) manage to resculpt not only their behavior but also activity patterns in their brain.

In late 20th century America, where drugs of abuse are being used on an unprecedented scale, the mounting evidence that treatment works could not be more welcome. Until now, policymakers have responded to the drug problem as though it were mostly a criminal matter. Only a third of the $15 billion the U.S. earmarks for the war on drugs goes to prevention and treatment. "In my view, we've got things upside down," says Dr. David Lewis, director of the Center for Alcohol and Addiction Studies at Brown University School of Medicine. "By relying so heavily on a criminalized approach, we've only added to the stigma of drug abuse and prevented high-quality medical care."

Ironically, the biggest barrier to making such care available is the perception that efforts to treat addiction are wasted. Yet treatment for drug abuse has a failure rate no different from that for other chronic diseases. Close to half of recovering addicts fail to maintain complete abstinence after a year—about the same proportion of patients with diabetes and hypertension who fail to comply with their diet, exercise and medication regimens. What doctors who treat drug abuse should strive for, says Alan Leshner, director of the National Institute on Drug Abuse, is not necessarily a cure but long-term care that controls the progress of the disease and alleviates its worst symptoms. "The occasional relapse is normal," he says, "and just an indication that more treatment is needed."

Rafael Rios has been luckier than many. He kicked his habit in one lengthy struggle that included four months of in-patient treatment at a residential facility and a year of daily outpatient sessions. During that time, Rios checked into 12-step meetings continually, sometimes attending three a day. As those who deal with alcoholics and drug addicts know, such exertions of will power and courage are more common than most people suspect. They are the best reason yet to start treating addiction as the medical and public health crisis it really is.

—With reporting by Alice Park/New York

Gene Therapy for the Nervous System

Inserting genes into brain cells may one day offer doctors a way to slow, or even reverse, the damage from degenerative neurological disease

by Dora Y. Ho and Robert M. Sapolsky

The prospect of acquiring any chronic illness is disturbing. But for most people, the threat of neurological impairment evokes a special dread. Afflictions such as Parkinson's disease or amyotrophic lateral sclerosis (Lou Gehrig's disease) progressively rob control of the body. Damage to the spinal cord can create equal misery in just an instant. And Alzheimer's disease attacks the very essence of one's personality as it destroys the mind.

Unfortunately, physicians and medical researchers have made only limited progress in the battle against such diseases, in large part because the brain and spine are so vulnerable. Unlike many types of cells, neurons (nerve cells) in the central nervous system of adults are typically unable to divide. That fact of life creates the central tragedy of neurological illness or injury: under normal circumstances, neurons that are lost are gone for good, and injured nerve tissue of the brain and spinal cord cannot be expected to repair itself.

But scientific advances might yet change that grim situation. Some of the most ambitious research in neurology aims to replace lost cells in damaged tissue by transplanting neurons or by delivering growth factors—chemicals that can stimulate surviving neurons to extend their reach or that can awaken the cells' dormant ability to regenerate. Such therapies would be immensely beneficial, but it will probably take many years before they become routine. Preventing neuron loss in the first place is a more modest goal—one that is perhaps not so distant.

In the past few years, researchers have learned a great deal about how neurons die after a sudden medical insult such as a stroke, seizure or head injury, as well as during progressive diseases such as Parkinson's or Alzheimer's. Some attempts to take advantage of these recent discoveries suggest that administering certain drugs may protect threatened neurons or even that lowering the temperature of the brain can avert the death of fragile cells during a neurological crisis. What is more, new knowledge about how neurons succumb to various diseases has raised the exciting possibility of protecting these cells by modifying their genes.

Reprogramming for Survival

Genes instruct cells to make specific proteins, such as the enzymes that catalyze various chemical reactions. Nerve cells, for example, produce enzymes that synthesize neurotransmitters—substances that carry chemical signals across the tiny gaps (synaptic spaces) between one neuron and another. Gene therapy targeted to failing neurons could potentially provide them with a gene specifying a protein that is able to shield these cells from whatever threat may loom.

To create such remedies, researchers must first decide what kinds of proteins would be most helpful. In some cases, the goal would be to augment the production of a particular brain protein when the naturally occurring version is dysfunctional or made in inadequate amounts. Or, in theory, one might want to add a novel protein, found in a different type of tissue—or even in a different organism entirely.

Another strategy, called the antisense approach, also constitutes a form of gene therapy [see "The New Genetic Medicines," by Jack S. Cohen and Michael E. Hogan; SCIENTIFIC AMERICAN, December 1994]. Antisense tactics aim to limit the manufacture of proteins that are doing damage. Some types of amyotrophic lateral sclerosis and certain other neurological diseases result from the destructively intense activity of a normal protein or from the action of an abnormal protein that works in an injurious manner. Antisense therapies might also help when neurons synthesize proteins that (for reasons that are still inexplicable) exacerbate a neurological crisis. To that end, many researchers are now trying to find ways to block the production of so-called death proteins, which induce endangered neurons to commit cellular suicide.

Once the basic understanding of a particular neurological disease is in place, it does not take great imagination to come up with a list of genes that might save neurons from destruction. The challenge is in figuring out how to deliver those genes. In principle, one can insert a gene into brain tissue by directly injecting appropriately coded segments of pure DNA. Unfortunately, this brute-force method is rarely successful, because neurons are not particularly efficient at picking up such "naked" DNA. A better technique is to encase the gene in a fatty bubble called a liposome. Because of the chemical nature of these tiny containers, liposomes easily transport DNA into target neurons by fusing with the cell membrane and releasing their contents into the interior. The cell, for reasons not entirely understood, will then incorporate some of this material into its nucleus, where its own DNA resides, and will use the gene as a blueprint for making the therapeutic protein [see "Nonviral Strategies for Gene Therapy," by Philip L. Felgner, *Scientific American*, June 1997].

An even better tool for putting genes into cells is a virus. In the course of a typical infection, viruses insert their genetic material into cells of the victim, where this added genetic code directs the synthesis of various molecules needed to make new viral particles. Although natural viruses can be immensely destructive, scientists can tame and convert some of them into microscopic Trojan horses, which then can carry a therapeutic gene and quietly deposit it inside a cell without causing damage. For gene therapy in the central nervous system, investigators are focusing much of their effort on just a few viral types, including adenoviruses and herpesviruses.

Combating Parkinson's

Experiments with these viral vectors, as such delivery vehicles are called, have provided the first hints that gene therapy in the nervous system can work. One promising area of research is directed against Parkinson's disease. This devastating disorder arises because a part of the brain, known as the substantia nigra, degenerates over time. This region helps to regulate motor control, and its destruction makes it hard for a person to initiate movements or execute complex coordinated motion. The loss also brings on the classic parkinsonian tremor [see "Understanding Parkinson's Disease," by Moussa B. H. Youdim and Peter Riederer; Scientific American, January].

Parkinson's disease ensues after the death of nigral neurons that secrete the neurotransmitter dopamine. For complex reasons, these neurons also generate

ROBERT M. SAPOLSKY (*photograph*); SLIM FILMS (*virus*); TOMO NARASHIMA (*rat brain*)

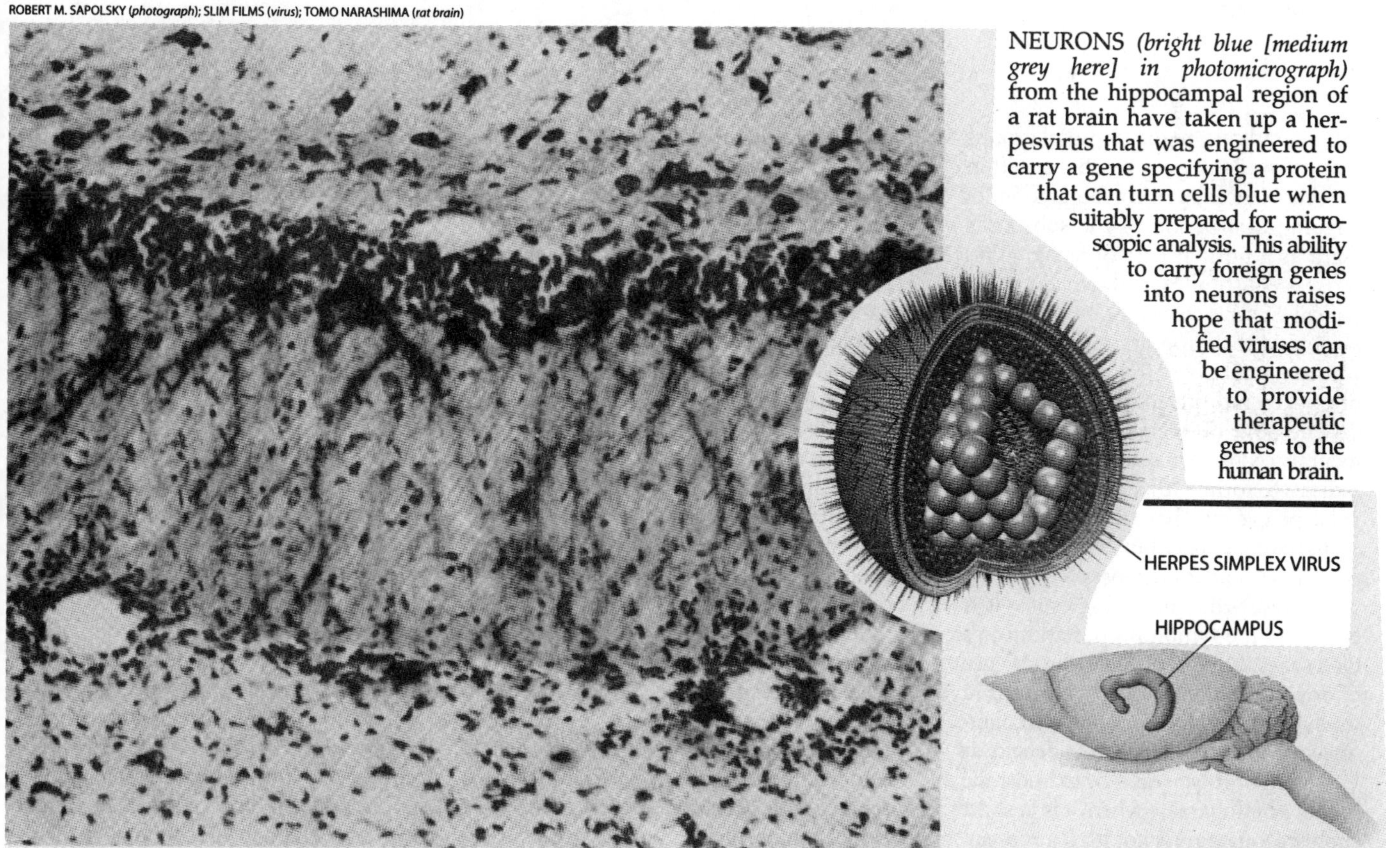

NEURONS *(bright blue [medium grey here] in photomicrograph)* from the hippocampal region of a rat brain have taken up a herpesvirus that was engineered to carry a gene specifying a protein that can turn cells blue when suitably prepared for microscopic analysis. This ability to carry foreign genes into neurons raises hope that modified viruses can be engineered to provide therapeutic genes to the human brain.

A Toolbox of Gene Delivery Agents for Nerve Cells

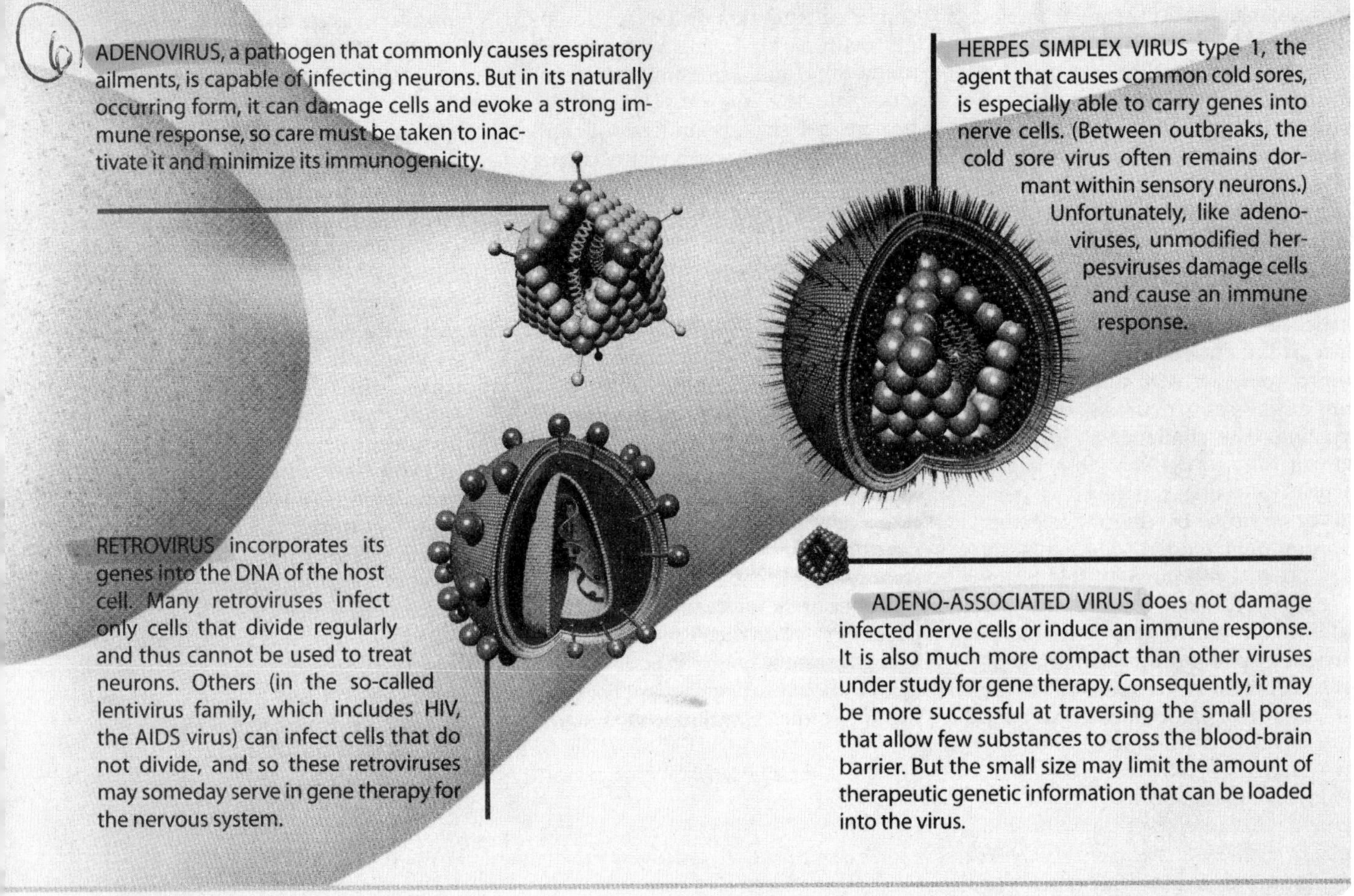

ADENOVIRUS, a pathogen that commonly causes respiratory ailments, is capable of infecting neurons. But in its naturally occurring form, it can damage cells and evoke a strong immune response, so care must be taken to inactivate it and minimize its immunogenicity.

HERPES SIMPLEX VIRUS type 1, the agent that causes common cold sores, is especially able to carry genes into nerve cells. (Between outbreaks, the cold sore virus often remains dormant within sensory neurons.) Unfortunately, like adenoviruses, unmodified herpesviruses damage cells and cause an immune response.

RETROVIRUS incorporates its genes into the DNA of the host cell. Many retroviruses infect only cells that divide regularly and thus cannot be used to treat neurons. Others (in the so-called lentivirus family, which includes HIV, the AIDS virus) can infect cells that do not divide, and so these retroviruses may someday serve in gene therapy for the nervous system.

ADENO-ASSOCIATED VIRUS does not damage infected nerve cells or induce an immune response. It is also much more compact than other viruses under study for gene therapy. Consequently, it may be more successful at traversing the small pores that allow few substances to cross the blood-brain barrier. But the small size may limit the amount of therapeutic genetic information that can be loaded into the virus.

TOMO NARASHIMA (*neuron*); SLIM FILMS (*viruses*)

oxygen radicals, rogue chemical groups that cause damaging reactions within the cell. Hence, there is a fair amount of ongoing destruction in the substantia nigra as a normal part of aging. (This process contributes to the mild tremor typical of senescence.) Sometimes Parkinson's disease appears to strike people who are predisposed to having an excess of oxygen radicals in their brain tissue or who have been exposed to environmental toxins that cause these oxygen radicals to form. Other cases seem to involve people who have normal amounts of these chemicals but who have impaired antioxidant defenses.

Whatever the underlying cause, it is clear that the symptoms of Parkinson's disease result primarily from the absence of dopamine after too many neurons in the substantia nigra die. Thus, a straightforward way to correct this deficit, at least temporarily, would be to boost the amount of dopamine where it is in short supply. Dopamine is not itself a protein, but the enzymes that synthesize this neurotransmitter are. So increasing the manufacture of one enzyme critical to that process (tyrosine hydroxylase) should enhance the synthesis of this much needed brain chemical for as long as the dopamine-producing cells of the substantia nigra survive.

Although administering a chemical precursor to dopamine—a substance called L-dopa—also works to augment levels of this neurotransmitter, the drug reacts throughout the brain, causing serious side effects. The lure of gene therapy in this context is that corrective changes would take effect just within the substantia nigra.

Several scientists have been working hard to exploit this possibility. In a pair of recent collaborative studies, five research teams reported success using herpesviruses as gene vectors to correct symptoms in rats that were surgically treated in a way that caused them to exhibit some of the manifestations of Parkinson's disease. Application of gene therapy increased the production of the corrective enzyme, raised the level of dopamine near the cells that had been deprived of this neurotransmitter and partially eliminated the movement disorders in these animals.

Dale E. Bredesen and his colleagues at the Burnham Institute in La Jolla, Calif., recently explored an even more sophisticated scheme. Investigators had shown previously that transplanting neurons from the substantia nigra of fetal rats corrected some of the parkinsonian defects that were surgically induced in adult rats. This strategy worked because the robust young neurons were able to grow and produce dopamine for the nearby cells in need. A problem emerged, however. For some reason, the grafted neurons tended to activate an internal suicide program (a process termed apoptosis) and died after a while. So Bredesen and his co-workers carried out gene therapy on the fetal neurons before transplanting them; the researchers hoped to coax these cells to produce large quantities of a protein called bcl-2, which suppresses cell suicide.

The result was dramatic: four weeks later the rats that had received standard grafts were only marginally better, whereas the creatures that obtained the added gene in their grafts were substantially improved. Treatment for Parkinson's disease would require a longer period of effectiveness still—one would want the grafts to survive for years. Physicians have already carried out human fetal cell transplants to help patients with severe Parkinson's disease, but these attempts have met with mixed results. Perhaps one or two clever gene modifications to the human fetal cells before they are transplanted would make that procedure work much better.

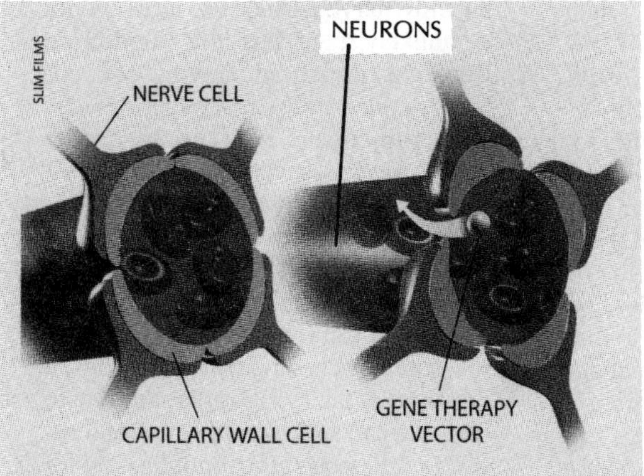

BLOOD-BRAIN BARRIER consists of tightly packed cells that line the capillaries within the brain (*left*). The tiny spaces between these cells allow only small molecules to reach this organ's many neurons. It is possible that certain treatments could be devised that would widen these gaps temporarily (*right*), permitting larger substances (such as therapeutic viral vectors) to pass into brain neurons.

Battling Stroke

The success of current research with animals indeed sparks hope that new treatments will eventually emerge for Parkinson's and other progressive degenerative diseases of the brain. Gene therapy also offers the prospect of stemming tissue damage during such acute neurological crises as the overstimulation of a seizure or the loss of oxygen and nutrients that occurs during a stroke.

Under these conditions, the most vulnerable cells in the brain are the many neurons that respond to an extremely powerful neurotransmitter called glutamate. Glutamate normally induces recipient neurons to take up calcium, which causes long-lasting changes in the excitability of synapses stimulated by this neurotransmitter. This process may, in fact, be the cellular basis of memory.

But during seizure or stroke, neurons are unable to mop up glutamate from synapses or clear the tidal wave of calcium that floods into many brain cells. Instead of fostering mild changes in the synapses, the glutamate and calcium do serious damage: the cellular architecture of the affected neurons crumbles, and newly generated oxygen radicals create further havoc. This destruction then kills cells directly or signals the initiation of internal suicide programs that will cause the swift demise of the flagging neurons.

Our group has examined the possibility that gene therapy could interrupt this calamitous sequence of events. For our first experiments, we extracted some brain cells from a rat and cultured them in a petri dish. We then subjected these neurons to a modified herpesvirus engineered to carry a gene for a protein that transports energy-rich glucose molecules across the cell membrane. In a patient suffering a neurological crisis, a similar type of therapy might increase the influx of glucose just when the beleaguered neurons would benefit most from extra energy (which is needed, among other tasks, to pump the excess calcium out of these cells).

Early experiments showed that our treatment enhanced the uptake of glucose and helped to maintain proper metabolism in neurons subjected to the test-tube equivalent of seizure or stroke. We later found that we could lessen the damage from stroke in rats by injecting the viral vector into the vulnerable region of the brain before an injurious event occurred. It is obviously not possible for a person to forecast when a seizure or a stroke will happen. But, as Matthew S. Lawrence and Rajesh Dash discovered when they worked in our laboratory, there is a window of a few hours after a seizure when the gene treatment to these rats still helps to protect neurons from additional damage—which suggests that humans, too, might one day benefit from a similar kind of therapy.

Another form of potential gene therapy for stroke and trauma targets the activation of suicide programs. Howard J. Federoff and his colleagues at the University of Rochester, and Lawrence, working with our group, independently constructed herpes-virus vectors that included the suicide-suppressing *bcl*-2 gene. Application of this vector tends to shield the

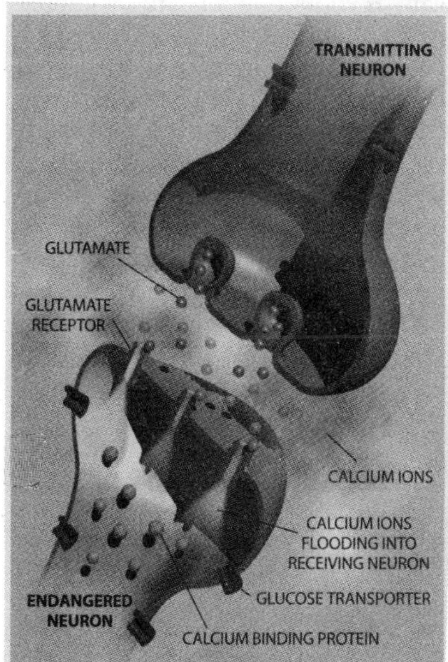

CRISIS CONDITIONS ensue during a seizure or stroke when too much of the neurotransmitter glutamate accumulates in the synaptic gap between neurons. Specialized molecules, called glutamate receptors, on the receiving cell then allow calcium ions, which are normally present in high concentration only on the outside, to flood into the cell's interior and cause permanent damage. Future genetic therapies could augment the amount of calcium binding protein (which safely sequesters these ions) or increase the number of glucose transporters (which would bring more energy-rich molecules to fuel the endangered neuron).

brain cells of rats from damage when crisis conditions occur, even if the treatment begins only after the insult.

Investigators also report advances that might one day prevent the so-called lipid storage diseases—genetic disorders that cause defects in certain enzymes and lead to a fatal accumulation of fatty molecules in the brain. To explore such therapies, researchers have produced mice that carry a mutation in the gene encoding the enzyme beta-glucoronidase. (People suffering from a rare malady called Sly syndrome have the same gene mutation.) John H. Wolfe and his colleagues at the University of Pennsylvania transplanted into an afflicted mouse fetal nuerons engineered to produce beta-glucoronidase. These researchers found that the implants were able to dispose of damaging lipids throughout the animal's brain.

Despite the many encouraging first steps in applying gene therapy to the nervous system, sundry hurdles remain. For example, significant problems persist in engineering viral vectors. Cripple the virus too much, and it becomes difficult to maintain sufficient potency to infect cells. Strip away too little, and the virus will damage the host neurons. Because the viral vectors now available each suffer from one or the other of these shortfalls, a great deal of refinement will be needed before scientists can safely begin testing gene therapies in people with neurological disease.

Another difficulty emerges simply because the brain—a vital but delicate organ—is encased in a relatively impregnable skull. Thus, injecting a therapeutic drug directly into the affected tissue is rather difficult. Most researchers conducting animal studies resort to neurosurgery: drilling a hole in the skull and injecting the vector directly into the endangered part of the brain. But, clearly, human patients would require something less invasive for routine treatment. Although one could give a vector intravenously (if it could be designed to enter only nerve tissue), the virus would be unlikely to get past the blood-brain barrier, a specialized network of capillaries that lets only small molecules pass into brain tissue. So, without further special measures, virtually all of the viral vector would wastefully end up in places other than the brain.

Even if these obstacles could be overcome, some final stumbling blocks would still stand in the way. After a viral vector reaches a patch of neurons, it does not go far. (Viruses that are able to replicate can spread readily in brain tissue, but these agents cannot be used for gene therapy, because they invariably provoke a damaging immune response.) A safe viral vector traverses a limited area, where it infects only a small percentage of neurons. Hence, these viruses are not particularly effective in reaching diseased tissue. Furthermore, for most of the vectors tried so far, activity persists for a few weeks at most—too brief a period to combat slow but relentless degenerative illnesses. So researchers will need to find ways to improve the spread, efficiency and duration of these engineered infections.

Future Shocks?

Despite the many challenges, studies of gene therapy for diseases of the nervous system—like most ambitious efforts that have shown some initial successes—have generated an aura of optimism. Perhaps with adequate effort, gene therapy for the brain will eventually be commonplace.

A glimpse of the possibilities ahead comes from the work of Anders Björklund and his colleagues at the University of Lund in Sweden. These researchers, who pioneered methods to transplant fetal neurons, have engineered grafts to produce large quantities of a nerve growth factor. They implanted some of these engineered cells into mature rats, targeting a region of the brain that is critical for learning and memory—an area that, not surprisingly, slowly degenerates during normal aging. Remarkably, this maneuver reversed cognitive decline in aged rats.

That success suggests that gene therapy might serve not just to blunt the edges of disease but to improve memory, sensation and coordination in older people. At present, scientists have enormous strides to make before they can hope to aid geriatric patients in this way. But ultimately, gene therapists may be able to offer powerful medicines for rejuvenating aging brains.

Such treatments might also be able to make younger people's minds work "better than well," to borrow a now popular phrase describing the effects of Prozac. Few areas of medical research pry at such a Pandora's box as does work on improving normal brain function. But this prospect—and its possible abuses—will be difficult to sidestep if scientists are to continue to pursue genetic treatments directed at specific neurological diseases. So further research on applying gene therapy to the nervous system, like some other swiftly moving currents in the flow of biomedical inquiry, will surely force vexing ethical questions to float to the surface.

The Authors

DORA Y. HO and ROBERT M. SAPOLSKY have worked together for almost seven years. Ho, a researcher in the department of biological sciences at Stanford University, investigated the genetics of the herpes simplex virus during her Ph.D. studies, which she completed in 1990. Since that time, she has focused her work on developing herpesviruses for gene therapy and understanding the molecular biology of diseases of the central nervous system. Sapolsky, a professor of biological sciences and neuroscience at Stanford, initially concentrated his research on the physiology of stress, an enterprise that at times takes him to Kenya to study baboons in the wild. In 1990 he shifted part of his research effort from stress hormones in the brain toward gene therapy for disorders of the nervous system.

Understanding Parkinson's Disease

The smoking gun is still missing, but growing evidence suggests highly reactive substances called free radicals are central players in this common neurological disorder

by Moussa B. H. Youdim and Peter Riederer

One of the more emotional moments of the 1996 summer Olympics in Atlanta occurred at the opening ceremonies, even before the games started. Muhammad Ali—the former world heavyweight boxing champion and a 1960 Olympic gold medal winner—took the torch that was relayed to him and, with trembling hands, determinedly lit the Olympic flame. His obvious effort reminded the world of the toll Parkinson's disease and related disorders can take on the human nervous system. Ali, who in his championship days had prided himself on his ability to "float like a butterfly, sting like a bee," now had to fight to control his body and steady his feet.

Ali's condition also highlighted the urgent need for better treatments. We cannot claim that a cure is around the corner, but we can offer a glimpse into the considerable progress investigators have made in understanding Parkinson's disease, which afflicts more than half a million people in the U.S. alone. Although still incomplete, this research has recently begun suggesting ideas not only for easing symptoms but, more important, for stopping the underlying disease process.

Parkinson's disease progressively destroys a part of the brain critical to coordinated motion. It has been recognized since at least 1817, when James Parkinson, a British physician, described its characteristic symptoms in "An Essay on the Shaking Palsy." Early on, affected individuals are likely to display a rhythmic tremor in a hand or foot, particularly when the limb is at rest. (Such trembling has helped convince many observers that Pope John Paul II has the disorder.) As time goes by, patients may become slower and stiffer. They may also have difficulty initiating movements (especially rising from a sitting position), may lose their balance and coordination and may freeze unpredictably, as their already tightened muscles halt altogether.

Nonmotor symptoms can appear as well. These may include excessive sweating or other disturbances of the involuntary nervous system and such psychological problems as depression or, in late stages, dementia. Most of the problems, motor or otherwise, are subtle at first and worsen over time, often becoming disabling after five to 15 years. Patients typically show their first symptoms after age 60.

The motor disturbances have long been known to stem primarily from destruction of certain nerve cells that reside in the brain stem and communicate with a region underlying the cortex. More specifically, the affected neurons are the darkly pigmented ones that lie in the brain stem's substantia nigra ("black substance") and extend projections into a higher domain called the striatum (for its stripes).

As Arvid Carlsson of Gothenburg University reported in 1959, the injured neurons normally help to control motion by releasing a chemical messenger—the neurotransmitter dopamine—into the striatum. Striatal cells, in turn, relay dopamine's message through higher motion-controlling centers of the brain to the cortex, which then uses the information as a guide for determining how the muscles should finally behave. But as the dopamine-producing neurons die, the resulting decline in dopamine signaling disrupts the smooth functioning of the overall motor network and compromises the person's activity. Nonmotor symptoms apparently result mainly from the elimination of other kinds of neurons elsewhere in the brain. What remains unknown, however, is how the various neurons that are lost usually become injured.

Because damage to the substantia nigra accounts for most symptoms, investigators have concentrated on that area. Some 4 percent of our original complement of dopamine-producing neurons disappears during each decade of adulthood, as part of normal aging. But Parkinson's disease is not a normal feature of aging. A pathological process amplifies the usual cell death, giving rise to symptoms after approximately 70 percent of the neurons have been destroyed. Whether this process is commonly triggered by something in the environment, by a genetic flaw or by some combination of the two is still unclear, although a defect on chromosome 4 has recently been implicated as a cause in some cases.

Drawbacks of Existing Therapies

Research into the root causes of Parkinson's disease has been fueled in part by frustration over the shortcomings of the drugs available for treatment. Better understanding of the nature of the disease process will undoubtedly yield more effective agents.

The first therapeutics were found by chance. In 1867 scientists noticed that extracts of the deadly nightshade plant eased some symptoms, and so doctors began to prescribe the extracts. The finding was not explained until about a century later. By the mid-1900s pharmacologists had learned that the medication worked by inhibiting the activity in the striatum of acetylcholine, one of the chemical molecules that carries messages between neurons. This discovery implied that dopamine released into the striatum was normally needed, at least in part, to counteract the effects of acetylcholine. Further, in the absence of such moderation, acetylcholine overexcited striatal neurons that projected to higher motor regions of the brain.

Although the acetylcholine inhibitors helped somewhat, they did not eliminate most symptoms of Parkinson's disease; moreover, their potential side effects included such disabling problems as blurred vision and memory impairment. Hence, physicians were delighted when, in the 1960s, the more effective drug levodopa, or L-dopa, proved valuable. This agent, which is still a mainstay of therapy, became available thanks largely to the research efforts of Walter Birkmayer of the Geriatric Hospital Lainz-Vienna, Oleh Hornykiewicz of the University of Vienna, Theodore L. Sourkes and Andre Barbeau of McGill University and George Cotzias of the Rockefeller University.

These and other workers developed L-dopa specifically to compensate for the decline of dopamine in the brain of Parkinson's patients. They knew that dopamine-producing neurons manufacture the neurotransmitter by converting the amino acid tyrosine to L-dopa and then converting L-dopa into dopamine. Dopamine itself cannot be used as a drug, because it does not cross the blood-brain barrier—the network of specialized blood vessels that strictly controls which substances will be allowed into the central nervous system. But L-dopa crosses the barrier readily. It is then converted to dopamine by dopamine-making neurons that survive in the substantia nigra and by nonneuronal cells, called astrocytes and microglia, in the striatum.

When L-dopa was introduced, it was hailed for its ability to control symptoms. But over time physicians realized it was far from a cure-all. After about four years, most patients experience a wearing-off phenomenon: they gradually lose sensitivity to the compound, which works for shorter and shorter increments. Also, side effects increasingly plague many people—among them, psychological disturbances and a disabling "on-off" phenomenon, in which episodes of immobility, or freezing, alternate unpredictably with episodes of normal or involuntary movements. Longer-acting preparations that more closely mimic dopamine release from neurons are now available, and they minimize some of these effects.

As scientists came to understand that L-dopa was not going to be a panacea, they began searching for additional therapies. By 1974 that quest had led Donald B. Calne and his co-workers at the National Institutes of Health to begin treating patients with drugs that mimic the actions of dopamine (termed dopamine agonists). These agents can avoid some of the fluctuations in motor control that accompany extended use of L-dopa, but they are more expensive and can produce unwanted effects of their own, including confusion, dizziness on standing and involuntary motion.

In 1975 our own work resulted in the introduction of selegiline (also called deprenyl) for treatment of Parkinson's disease. This substance, invented by a

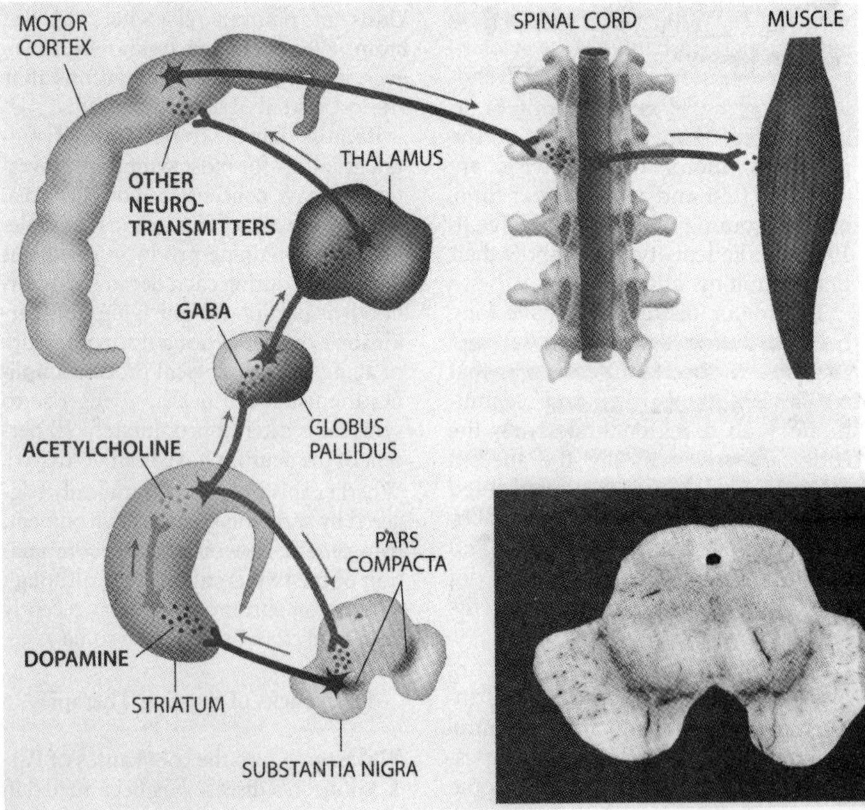

NEURONAL CIRCUIT disrupted in Parkinson's disease is shown schematically. When dopamine-producing neurons die, loss of dopamine release in the striatum causes the acetylcholine producers there to overstimulate their target neurons, thereby triggering a chain reaction of abnormal signaling leading to impaired mobility. The pars compacta region of the substantia nigra in the normal brain appears dark (*left photograph*) because dopamine-producing neurons are highly pigmented; as neurons die from Parkinson's disease, the color fades (*right photograph*).

LAURIE GRACE

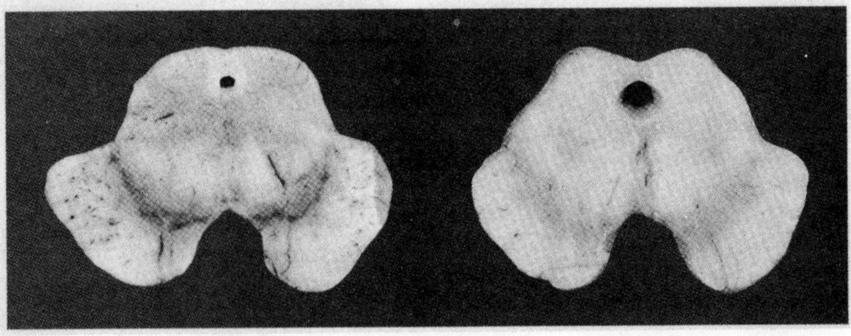

DANIEL P. PERL *Mount Sinai School of Medicine*

Hungarian scientist, had failed as a therapy for depression and was almost forgotten. But it can block the breakdown of dopamine, thus preserving its availability in the striatum. Dopamine can be degraded by the neurons that make it as well as by astrocytes and microglia that reside near the site of its release. Selegiline inhibits monoamine oxidase B, the enzyme that breaks down dopamine in the astrocytes and microglia.

Selegiline has some very appealing properties, although it, too, falls short of ideal. For example, it augments the effects of L-dopa and allows the dose of that drug to be reduced. It also sidesteps the dangers of related drugs that can block dopamine degradation. Such agents proved disastrous as therapies for depression, because they caused potentially lethal disturbances in patients who ate certain foods, such as cheese. In fact, we began exploring selegiline as a treatment for Parkinson's disease partly because studies in animals had implied it would avoid this so-called cheese effect.

Tantalizingly, some of our early findings suggested that selegiline could protect people afflicted with Parkinson's disease from losing their remaining dopamine-producing neurons. A massive study carried out several years ago in the U.S. (known as DATATOP) was unable to confirm or deny this effect, but animal research continues to be highly supportive. Whether or not selegiline itself turns out to be protective, exploration of that possibility has already produced at least two important benefits. It has led to the development of new kinds of enzyme inhibitors as potential treatments not only for Parkinson's disease but also for Alzheimer's disease and depression. And the work has altered the aims of many who study Parkinson's disease, causing them to seek new therapies aimed at treating the underlying causes instead of at merely increasing the level or activity of dopamine in the striatum (approaches that relieve symptoms but do not prevent neurons from degenerating).

Key Role for Free Radicals

Of course, the best way to preserve neurons is to halt one or more key steps in the sequence of events that culminates in their destruction—if those events can be discerned. In the case of Parkinson's disease, the collected evidence strongly implies (though does not yet prove) that the neurons that die are, to a great extent, doomed by the excessive accumulation of highly reactive molecules known as oxygen free radicals. Free radicals are destructive because they lack an electron. This state makes them prone to snatching electrons from other molecules, a process known as oxidation. Oxidation is what rusts metal and spoils butter. In the body the radicals are akin to biological bullets, in that they can injure whatever they hit—be it fatty cell membranes, genetic material or critical proteins. Equally disturbing, by taking electrons from other molecules, one free radical often creates many others, thus amplifying the destruction.

The notion that oxidation could help account for Parkinson's disease was first put forward in the early 1970s by Gerald Cohen and the late Richard E. Heikkila of the Mount Sinai School of Medicine. Studies by others had shown that a synthetic toxin sometimes used in scientific experiments could cause parkinsonian symptoms in animals and that it worked by inducing the death of dopamine-producing neurons in the substantia nigra. Cohen and Heikkila discovered that the drug poisoned the neurons by inducing formation of at least two types of free radicals.

Some of the most direct proof that free radicals are involved in Parkinson's disease comes from examination of the brains of patients who died from the disorder. We and others have looked for "fingerprints" of free radical activity in the substantia nigra, measuring the levels of specific chemical changes the radicals are known to effect in cellular components. Many of these markers are highly altered in the brains of Parkinson's patients. For instance, we found a significant increase in the levels of compounds that form when fatty components of cell membranes are oxidized.

Circumstantial evidence is abundant as well. The part of the substantia nigra that deteriorates in Parkinson's patients contains above-normal levels of substances that promote free radical formation. (A notable example, which we have studied intensively, is iron.) At the same time, the brain tissue contains unusually low levels of antioxidants, molecules involved in neutralizing free radicals or preventing their formation.

Researchers have also seen a decline in the activity of an enzyme known as complex I in the mitochondria of the affected neurons. Mitochondria are the power plants of cells, and complex I is part of the machinery by which mitochondria generate the energy required by cells. Cells use the energy for many purposes, including ejecting calcium and other ions that can facilitate oxidative reactions. When complex I is faulty, energy production drops, free radical levels rise, and the levels of some antioxidants fall—all of which can combine to increase oxidation and exacerbate any other cellular malfunctions caused by an energy shortage.

Early Clues from Addicts

What sequence of events might account for oxidative damage and related changes in the brains of people who suffer from Parkinson's disease? Several ideas have been proposed. One of the earliest grew out of research following up on what has been called "The Case of the Frozen Addicts."

In 1982 J. William Langston, a neurologist at Stanford University, was astonished to encounter several heroin addicts who had suddenly become almost completely immobile after taking the drug. It was as if they had developed severe Parkinson's disease overnight. While he was exploring how the heroin might have produced this effect, a toxicologist pointed him to an earlier, obscure report on a similar case in Bethesda, Md. In that instance, a medical student who was also a drug abuser had become paralyzed by a homemade batch of meperidine (Demerol) that was found, by Irwin J. Kopin and Sanford P. Markey of the NIH, to contain an impurity called MPTP. This preparation had destroyed dopamine-making cells of his substantia nigra. Langston, who learned that the drug taken by his patients also contained MPTP, deduced that the impurity accounted for the parkinsonism of the addicts.

His hunch proved correct and raised the possibility that a more common substance related to MPTP was the triggering cause in classical cases of Parkinson's disease. Since then, exploration of how MPTP damages dopamine-rich neurons has expanded understanding of the disease process in general and has uncovered at least one pathway by which a toxin could cause the disease.

Scientists now know that MPTP would be harmless if it were not altered by the body. It becomes dangerous after passing into the brain and being taken up by astrocytes and microglia. These cells feed the drug into their mitochondria, where it is converted (by monoamine oxidase B) to a more reactive molecule and then released to do mischief in dopamine-making neurons of the substantia nigra. Part of this understanding comes from study in monkeys of selegiline, the monoamine oxidase B inhibitor. By preventing MPTP from being altered, the drug protects the animals from parkinsonism.

In the absence of a protective agent, altered MPTP will enter nigral neurons, pass into their mitochondria and inhibit the complex I enzyme. This action will result, as noted earlier, in an energy deficit, an increase in free radical production and a decrease in antioxidant activity—and, in turn, in oxidative damage of the neurons.

In theory, then, an MPTP-like chemical made naturally by some people or taken up from the environment could cause Parkinson's disease through a similar process. Many workers have sought such chemicals with little success. Most recently, for instance, brain chemicals known as beta carbolines have attracted much attention as candidate neurotoxins, but their levels in the brains of Parkinson's patients appear to be too low to account for the disease. Given that years of study have not yet linked any known toxin to the standard form of Parkinson's disease, other theories may more accurately describe the events that result in excessive oxidation in patients with this disorder.

Are Immune Cells Overactive?

Another hypothesis that makes a great deal of sense places microglia—the brain's immune cells—high up in the destructive pathway. This concept derives in part from the discovery, by Patrick L. McGeer of the University of British Columbia and our own groups, that the substantia nigra of Parkinson's patients often contains unusually active microglia. As a rule, the brain blocks microglia from becoming too active, because in their most stimulated state, microglia produce free radicals and behave in other ways that can be quite harmful to neurons [see "The Brain's Immune System," by Wolfgang J. Streit and Carol A. Kincaid-Colton; SCIENTIFIC AMERICAN, November 1995]. But if something, perhaps an abnormal elevation of certain cytokines (chemical messengers of the immune system), overcame that restraint in the substantia nigra, neurons there could well be hurt.

Studies of dopamine-making neurons conducted by a number of laboratories have recently converged with research on microglia to suggest various ways that activated microglia in the substantia nigra could lead to oxidative damage in neurons of the region. Most of these ways involve production of the free radical nitric oxide.

For example, overactive microglia are known to produce nitric oxide, which can escape from the cells, enter nearby neurons and participate in reactions that generate other radicals; these various radicals can then disrupt internal structures [see "Biological Roles of Nitric Oxide," by Solomon H. Snyder and David S. Bredt; SCIENTIFIC AMERICAN, May 1992]. Further, nitric oxide itself is able to inhibit the complex I enzyme in mitochondria; it can thus give rise to the same oxidative injury that an MPTP-like toxin could produce.

If these actions of nitric oxide were not devastating enough, we have found that both nitric oxide and another free radical (superoxide) emitted by overactive microglia can free iron from storehouses in the brain—thereby triggering additional oxidative cascades. We have also demonstrated that iron, regardless of its source, can react with dopamine and its derivatives in at least two ways that can further increase free radical levels in dopamine-synthesizing cells.

In one set of reactions, iron helps dopamine to oxidize itself. Oxidation of dopamine converts the molecule into a new substance that nigral cells use to construct their dark pigment, neuromelanin. When iron levels are low, neuromelanin serves as an antioxidant. But it becomes an oxidant itself and contributes to the formation of free radicals when it is bound by transition metals, especially iron. In support of the possibility that the interaction of iron and neuromelanin contributes to Parkinson's disease, we and our colleagues have shown that the pigment is highly decorated with iron in brains of patients who died from the disease; in contrast, the pigment lacks iron in brains of similar individuals who died from other causes.

In the other set of dopamine-related reactions, iron disrupts the normal sequence by which the neurotransmitter is broken down to inert chemicals. Neurons and microglia usually convert dopamine to an inactive substance and hydrogen peroxide, the latter of which becomes water. When iron is abundant, though, the hydrogen peroxide is instead broken down into molecular oxygen and a free radical. Dopamine's ability to promote free radical synthesis may help explain why dopamine-making neurons are particularly susceptible to dying from oxidation. This ability has also contributed to suspicion that L-dopa, which increases dopamine levels and eases symptoms, may, ironically, damage nigral neurons. Scientists are hotly debating this topic, although we suspect the concern is overblown.

In brief, then, overactive microglia could engender the oxidative death of dopamine-producing neurons in the substantia nigra by producing nitric oxide, thereby triggering several destructive sequences of reactions. And iron released by the nitric oxide or other free radicals in the region could exacerbate the destruction. As we have noted, brain cells do possess molecules capable of neutralizing free radicals. They also contain enzymes that can repair oxidative damage. But the protective systems are less extensive than those elsewhere in the body and, in any case, are apparently ill equipped to keep up with an abnormally large onslaught of oxidants. Consequently, if the processes we have described were set off in the substantia nigra, one would expect to see ever more neurons fade from the region over time, until finally the symptoms of Parkinson's disease appeared and worsened.

Actually, any trigger able to induce an increase in nitric oxide production or iron release or a decrease in complex I activity in the substantia nigra would promote Parkinson's disease. Indeed, a theory as plausible as the microglia hypothesis holds that excessive release of the neurotransmitter glutamate by neurons feeding into the striatum and substantia nigra could stimulate nitric oxide production and iron release. Excessive glutamate activity could thus set off the same destructive cascade hypothetically induced by hyperactive microglia. Overactive glutamate release has been implicated in other brain disorders, such as stroke. No one yet knows whether glutamate-producing neurons are overactive in Parkinson's disease, but circumstantial evidence implies they are.

Other questions remain as well. Researchers are still in the dark as to whether Parkinson's disease can arise by different pathways in different individuals. Just as the engine of a car can fail through any number of routes, a variety of processes could presumably lead to oxidative or other damage to neurons of the substantia nigra. We also have few clues to the initial causes of Parkinson's disease—such as triggers that might, say, elevate cytokine levels or cause glutamate-emitting cells to be hyperactive. In spite of the holes, ongoing research has suggested intriguing ideas for new therapies aimed at blocking oxidation or protecting neurons in other ways.

Therapeutic Options

If the scenarios we have discussed do occur alone or together, it seems reasonable to expect that agents able to quiet microglia or inhibit glutamate release in the substantia nigra or striatum would protect neurons in at least some patients. The challenge is finding compounds that are able to cross the blood-brain barrier and produce the desired effects without, at the same time, disturbing other neurons and causing severe side effects. One of us (Riederer) and his colleague Johannes Kornhuber of the University of Würzburg have recently demonstrated that amantadine, a long-standing anti-Parkinson's drug whose mechanism of action was not known, can block the effects of glutamate. This result suggests that the compound might have protective merit. Another glutamate blocker—dextromethorphan—is in clinical trials at the NIH.

Drugs could also be protective if they halted other events set in motion by the initial triggers of destruction. Iron chelators (which segregate iron and thus block many oxidative reactions), inhibitors of nitric oxide formation and antioxidants are all being considered. Such agents have been shown to protect dopamine-producing neurons of the substantia nigra from oxidative death in animals. On the other hand, the same human DATATOP trial that cast doubt on selegiline's protective effects found that vitamin E, an antioxidant, was ineffective. But vitamin E may have failed because very little of it crosses the blood-brain barrier or because the doses tested were too low. Antioxidants that can reach the brain deserve study; at least one such compound is in clinical trials at the NIH.

Regardless of the cause of the neuronal destruction, drugs that were able to promote regeneration of lost neurons would probably be helpful as well. Studies of animals suggest that such substances could, indeed, be effective in the human brain. Researchers at several American facilities are now testing putting a molecule called glial-derived neurotrophic factor (GDNF) directly into the brain of patients. Efforts are also under way to find smaller molecules that can be delivered more conveniently (via pill or injection) yet would still activate neuronal growth factors and neuronal growth in the brain. One agent, Rasagiline, has shown promise in animal trials and is now being tested in humans. Some studies imply that the nicotine in tobacco might have a protective effect, and nicotinelike drugs are being studied in the laboratory as potential therapies. Patients, however, would be foolish to take up smoking to try to slow disease progression. Data on the value of smoking to retard the death of dopamine neurons are equivocal, and the risks of smoking undoubtedly far outweigh any hypothetical benefit.

As work on protecting neurons advances, so does research into compensating for their decline. One approach being perfected is the implantation of dopamine-producing cells. Some patients have been helped. But the results are variable, and cells available for transplantation are in short supply. Further, the same processes that destroyed the original brain cells may well destroy the implants. Other approaches include surgically destroying parts of the brain that function abnormally when dopamine is lost. This surgery was once unsafe but is now being done more successfully.

The true aim of therapy for Parkinson's disease must ultimately be to identify the disease process long before symptoms arise, so that therapy can be given in time to forestall the brain destruction that underlies patients' discomfort and disability. No one can say when early detection and neural protection will become a reality, but we would not be surprised to see great strides made on both fronts within a few years. In any case, researchers cannot rest easy until those dual objectives are met.

The Authors

MOUSSA B. H. YOUDIM and PETER RIEDERER have collaborated since 1974. Youdim, a pioneer in the development of monoamine oxidase inhibitors for the treatment of Parkinson's disease and depression, is professor of pharmacology at Technion-Israel Institute of Technology in Haifa, Israel. He is also director of the Eve Topf and U.S. National Parkinson's Disease Foundation's Centers of Excellence for Neurodegenerative Diseases, both at Technion, and a Fogarty Scholar in Residence at the U.S. National Institutes of Health, where he spends three months every year. Riederer heads the Laboratory of Clinical Neurochemistry and is professor of clinical neurochemistry at the University of Würzburg in Germany. The authors shared the Claudius Galenus Gold Medal for the development of the anti-Parkinson's drug selegiline.

Further Reading

JAMES PARKINSON: HIS LIFE AND TIMES. A. D. Morris. Edited by F. Clifford Rose. Birkhauser, 1989.

EMERGING STRATEGIES IN PARKINSON'S DISEASE. Edited by H. L. Klawans. Special issue of *Neurology,* Vol. 40, No. 10, Supplement 3; October 1990.

IRON-MELANIN INTERACTION AND PARKINSON'S DISEASE. M.B.H. Youdim, D. Ben Shacher and P. Riederer in *News in Physiological Sciences,* Vol. 8, pages 45–49; February 1993.

PARKINSON'S DISEASE: THE L-DOPA ERA. M. D. Yahr in *Advances in Neurology,* Vol. 60, pages 11–17; 1993.

ALTERED BRAIN METABOLISM OF IRON AS A CAUSE OF NEURODEGENERATIVE DISEASES? M. Gerlach, D. Ben Shacher, P. Riederer and M.B.H. Youdim in *Journal of Neurochemistry,* Vol. 63, No. 3, pages 793–807; September 1994.

NEURODEGENERATION AND NEUROPROTECTION IN PARKINSON'S DISEASE. Edited by C. W. Olanow et al. Academic Press, 1996.

Looking Beyond The Reading Difficulties In Dyslexia, A Vision Deficit

Guinevere F. Eden* and Thomas A. Zeffiro**

***Abstract**: Dyslexia is an impairment in reading that can result from an abnormal developmental process, in the case of developmental dyslexia, or a cerebral insult, in the case of acquired dyslexia. It has long been known that the clinical manifestations of developmental dyslexia are varied. In addition to having reading difficulties, individuals with developmental dyslexia exhibit impairments in their ability to process neurologically the phonetic properties of written or spoken language. Recently, it has been demonstrated through a variety of experimental approaches that these individuals also have trouble performing several visual tasks, including visual-motion processing. The results of these studies, as well as the anatomical and physiological abnormalities seen in the brains of individuals with dyslexia, suggest that the pathophysiology of developmental dyslexia is more complex than originally thought, extending beyond the classically defined language areas of the brain to the vision-processing areas and perhaps even to areas controlling eye movements. Functional neuroimaging is a useful tool for more precisely delineating the pathophysiology of this reading disorder. Studies relying on such techniques have led us to speculate that a vision disorder may be just as much a component of dyslexia as the language-disorder problem.*

BY DEFINITION, DEVELOPMENTAL DYSLEXIA is a reading disorder, diagnosed by observing a discrepancy between an individual's reading ability and that person's predicted reading potential. (In this article, as in the field, "dyslexic" and "reading-disabled" are used interchangeably.) However, this discrepancy has never been useful as a sole diagnostic criterion, because the estimation of reading ability and intelligence can vary depending on the tools used to measure them and the formula used to quantify the discrepancy between performance and expectation. Despite the difficulty in reliably identifying individuals with developmental dyslexia, the consensus is that this reading disability affects between 4 and 10 percent of children in the United States.

Most clinicians and investigators believe that dyslexia is primarily a disorder of phonological processing—the isolation and manipulation of sounds within the brain. Dyslexic individuals have difficulty matching the sounds within words, called phonemes, to their written alphabetic forms[1]. For example, Richard Olson[2] has shown that pig Latin, a word game most of us are familiar with from our childhoods, in which "pig" becomes "igpay" and "research" becomes "esearchray," can be used to demonstrate the phonological impairments of dyslexic individuals because they often make errors translating words into pig Latin.

Studies focusing on the phonological abilities of dyslexic people have identified deficits in the performance of a variety of tasks thought to engage processing of the phonological features of language. There is growing evidence, for example, that being slow to name shown objects is a characteristic of dyslexia[3]. Already at the kindergarten level, children who later become

Guinevere Eden is an Assistant Professor at the Institute for Cognitive and Computational Sciences, at Georgetown University Medical Center in Washington, D.C., and a Special Volunteer in the Section on Functional Brain Imaging at the National Institute of Mental Health (NIMH) in Bethesda, Md. Thomas Zeffiro is the Vice President and Medical Director at Sensor Systems Inc., in Sterling, Va., and a Special Volunteer at the Laboratory of Diagnostic Radiology Research at NIMH.

*Georgetown Institute for Cognitive and Computational Sciences, Georgetown University Medical Center, Washington, DC 20007.
**Sensor System Systems Inc., 103A Carpenter Dr., Sterling, VA 20164-4423.

From *The Journal of NIH Research,* November 1996, pp. 31-34. © 1996 by Guinevere F. Eden and Thomas A. Zeffiro. Reprinted by permission.

reading-disabled are slower at naming aloud letters, numbers, colors, and objects from a chart[4].

On the basis of this and other evidence, most investigators and clinicians interested in developmental dyslexia favor the view that disordered language processing is the main cause of reading problems in dyslexia. And most investigators have favored the view that reading disability results from a specific language impairment such as the ability to analyze the component phonemes of words (phonological awareness)[5,6].

Properties Of The Parvocellular And Magnocellular Layers Of The Lateral Geniculate Nucleus

Physiological Property	Parvocellular (P-cells)	Magnocellular (M-cells)
Color Sensitivity	Yes	No
Contrast Sensitivity	Low	High
Spatial Resolution	High	Lower
Temporal Resolution	Slow	Fast

Source: M. Livingstone et al., *Neurosci.* **7**, 3468 (1987).

Nevertheless, there have always been alternative hypotheses concerning the pathophysiology of this disorder. Historically, there was early interest in potential visual-system deficits in dyslexia. In 1925, Samuel Orton, a pioneer in this field, described an impairment of visual processing[7]. The evidence in support of visual-system dysfunction accumulated in the past two decades includes a wide variety of studies that have shown visual and oculomotor abnormalities, in addition to language deficits, in subjects with dyslexia[8,9]. Visual-perception studies have demonstrated that individuals with dyslexia process visual information more slowly than others. It is obvious that reading (and writing) make heavy demands on the visual system[10]. For this reason, many kinds of reading errors—ranging from visuospatial scanning errors to incorrect visual-linguistic integration—can result from impaired visual processing. The former occurs when a child skips a line of words and the latter when the child reads "dog" as "god."

Investigators have been able to show that the underlying processes impaired in these various visual abilities linked to dyslexia may have some common attributes. The initial work along this line focused on early processing of sequences of visual stimuli given over a time period (temporal sequences). These experiments investigated visual persistence, in which an image appears to persist even though its stimulus has been removed, the result of continuing neural activity. In 1980, William Lovegrove and colleagues at the University of Wollongong in Australia found differences in visual persistence between children with and without dyslexia[11]. Reading-disabled children exhibited longer visual persistence when viewing wide, grayish bars (as opposed to narrow bars) on a computer screen. Furthermore, reading-disabled children were less sensitive to the contrast between bars than were nondyslexic children[12].

Lovegrove and colleagues explained these differences as selective impairments of the sustained and transient channels of the visual pathway in the brain. Because both contrast sensitivity and visual persistence varied from normal in reading-disabled children, the researchers concluded that these children have disturbances in the transient system, which mediates perception of movement and other qualities related to the temporal characteristics of the visual world. One way in which such a visual deficit could influence the reading process would be by preventing a person from acquiring the accurate visual information needed to form spelling-to-sound correspondences.

Unlike studies of language, studies of human visual processing have had the benefit of a more detailed understanding of the anatomy and physiology of the visual system gained from experiments with nonhuman primates. In the nonhuman-primate brain, anatomical analysis and single-unit recordings from cells of the parvocellular ("small-cell") and magnocellular ("large-cell") subdivisions of the lateral geniculate nucleus (LGN), which is in the thalamus, have shown that these cells exhibit distinctive anatomical and physiological properties[13]. Neurons in the two ventral magnocellular layers (M-cells) are larger and more myelinated than are those in the four dorsal parvocellular layers (P-cells).

In general, M-cells have a brief response to visual stimuli and are relatively more sensitive to brightness contrast, whereas P-cells have a more sustained response to visual stimuli and are relatively more responsive to color. (Differences between cells from these two systems are summarized in the table on this page). The outputs from the M-cell and P-cell layers of the LGN are thought to partially segregate to extrastriate cortical areas specialized for processing color and

Most clinicians and investigators believe that dyslexia is primarily a disorder of phonological processing—the isolation and manipulation of sounds within the brain.

form (receiving projections from P-cells) versus motion (receiving projections from M-cells)[14–16]. In macaques, cells in the posterior bank of the superior temporal sulcus—named area V5 or area MT (middle temporal area, part of the magnocellular system)—will fire in response to a motion stimulus as long as the stimulus is in that cell's "sight" and is moving in the direction the cell "likes"[17]. The nature of the connections of area V5/MT has led to this area's description as the "funnel for the motion pathway"[18]. In humans, M-cell and P-cell systems have been identified on the basis of anatomical, behavioral, and clinical evidence. With the addition of recent functional neuroimaging studies, several researchers now have demonstrated specialized visual-motion processing in the V5/MT area in humans[19–21].

It has been postulated that poor operation of the visual M-cell system—also referred to as the transient system—interferes with normal reading in persons with dyslexia. In one study, 75 percent of reading-disabled children exhibited a sensory deficit demonstrated by greater visual persistence at low spatial frequencies[11,22]. This means that their visual systems' processing of the images was too slow and persistent and therefore not able to capture the visual detail of rapidly flickering wide bars (a combination of characteristics to which the M-cell system usually responds well). Because reading-disabled children do not abnormally process information involving the P-cell system, which mediates the analysis of structural detail—also called the sustained system—it has been postulated that only the fast-processing transient pathway, or magnocellular pathway, is abnormal in dyslexic subjects. This is the system that is believed to predominantly project onto area V5/MT.

There have also been studies on the temporal and spatial aspects of reading in dyslexics. One of us (G.E.) and colleagues at Oxford University in Oxford, England, and the Bowman Gray School of Medicine in Winston-Salem, N.C., showed that dyslexic children performed significantly worse than controls in tasks that involved processing visual information presented temporally (e.g., figuring out how many dots were shown one after another) but were only mildly impaired when the same kind of visual information was presented spatially (e.g., figuring out how many dots were presented on a screen simultaneously)[23]. It is the speed of processing required for the temporal dot task that makes this task more challenging for the dyslexic subjects than the static visuospatial dot task. Subtle visuospatial impairments in dyslexics can be detected in some other tasks, such as making a judgment about the angle of a line[24]. Taken together, these findings support the hypothesis that a deficit in rapid visual processing—or a magnocellular deficit that possibly extends into the parietal area—underlies dyslexia, and that the disorder is associated with visuoperceptual and visuospatial deficits.

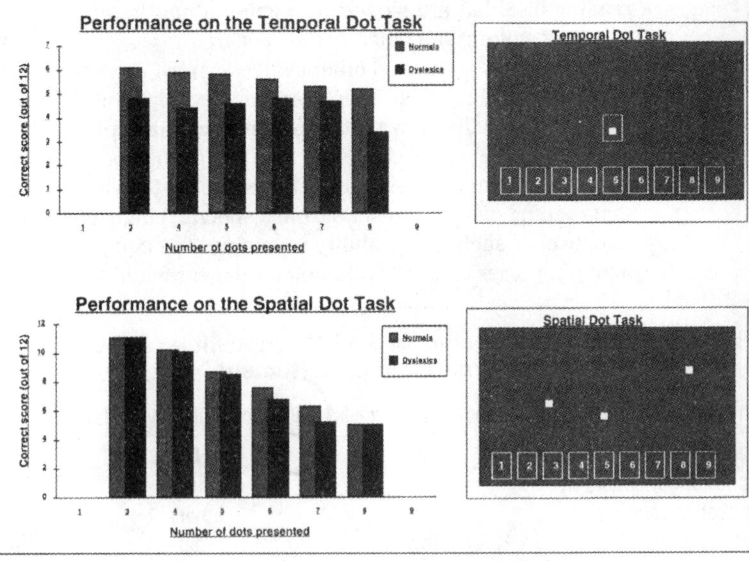

***Summary of the task and results** in the temporal and spatial dot task. In the temporal dot task, subjects were asked to match the number of dots that appeared sequentially with a number at the bottom of the screen. In the spatial dot task, subjects were asked to indicate the number of dots appearing on the screen at one time. Dyslexic children perform worse than controls at both tasks, but their deficit is more striking for the temporal dot task. [Reprinted with permission from G. Eden et al.,* Cortex ***31**, 451 (1995).]*

Anatomical studies of the visual system have revealed abnormalities in the magnocellular layers of the LGN of dyslexic brains[25]. Nissl-stained sections from the LGN of the postmortem brains of dyslexic individuals showed magnocellular neuron cell bodies to be smaller than normal (on average 27 percent smaller) and to have a disorganized appearance.

In light of these findings, the proposed defect in the M-cell pathway in dyslexic individuals might be detectable as impaired activation in V5/MT during the perception of moving visual stimuli. In a recent study we conducted with our colleagues John VanMeter, Judith Rumsey, José Maisog, and Roger Woods at the National Institute of Mental Health in Bethesda, Md., we investigated this possibility by studying visual-motion processing in nondyslexic and dyslexic men[26]. We used functional magnetic resonance imaging (fMRI) to measure local blood-oxygenation levels while the subjects viewed dot patterns. Changes in the fMRI signal were compared when subjects were shown a moving pattern and a stationary pattern (the latter designed to engage more of the parvocellular system) to ensure that any differences between the nondyslexic and dyslexic subjects were not due to a general deficit in visual processing. As part of the same study, the subjects also were given a task of judging the velocity of stimulus motion. Our study found a significant performance difference between controls and dyslexics. When the dyslexics were shown the moving patterns during the fMRI scans, they failed to produce the same activation in area V5/MT observed in controls. This deficit was observed only in area V5/MT. In contrast, the presentation of stationary patterns resulted in equivalent activations in the visual cortical area V1/V2 in both groups of subjects. Responses in V5/MT and other motion-sensitive visual cortical areas in the anterior portion of the temporal lobes can be seen in the axial sections of the brain in the figure on the following page. These results demonstrate the feasibility of using fMRI as a tool to detect and localize abnormal neuronal processing in dyslexia.

The motion-perception task used in our fMRI study involved passive perception rather than active decision-making. Thus, the differences observed between the normal and dyslexic groups are unlikely to be explained by differences in effort. This effort difference has plagued studies of dyslexia that utilize tests such as phonological awareness because dyslexic subjects have greater difficulty with this task. Further, individuals with dyslexia have phonological impairments, yet the reciprocal relationship between this language impairment and the visual deficit has made it difficult in the past to isolate the visual deficit. Functional neuroimaging directly examines visual-system function, so the results cannot be explained with reference to abnormal verbal strategies.

***Functional magnetic resonance images** of task-related signal change during the perception of motion in a dyslexic (right) and in a control (left). Unlike the control, the dyslexic shows no activation in area V5/MT, an area of the visual cortex sensitive to motion.*

These findings provide a neurophysiological basis for previously observed visual-perceptual–processing deficits in dyslexia that have implicated the M-cell system. However, the interpretation of absence of motion-sensitivity in V5/MT in dyslexia is complex and still speculative. Because of the presence of other motion-sensitive areas in the brain, which appear to be somewhat preserved in dyslexia, the physiological absence of V5/MT and the accompanying behavioral deficits in dyslexia could be the result of disrupted interaction among the motion-processing areas of the brain. Whatever the cause, disruption of V5/MT activity will most likely interfere with signals to other visual cortical areas (particularly V1/V2), as well as to the oculomotor apparatus, which controls movements of the eyes. This interference with the oculomotor system would offer one explanation for the eye-movement abnormalities reported in dyslexics, because the mismatch between retinal signals and cortical signals (from V5/MT) could result in inappropriate eye movements. The degree to which abnormal eye movements are a reflection of dysfunction in V5/MT is not clear, and to what extent the dysfunction possibly interferes with the reading process has been an area of debate. But abnormal eye movements could explain why, for example, a child with dyslexia will tell you that "it looks like the words are walking" when he or she tries to read.

Further research will be needed to determine where in the brain lies the culprit that causes confusion in the M-cell system. Comparisons with studies of motion-detection deficits in humans with destructive lesions involving area V5/MT[27,28] and surrounding structures are of limited utility, because the dyslexics' motion-detection deficit is far more subtle. Detecting motion-sensitivity deficits in dyslexic people requires psychophysical testing, and motion insensitivity generally is not a symptomatic complaint. More useful is a comparison with the visual-motion–detection deficit seen in nonhuman primates after recovery from focal V5/MT lesions. Ibotenic acid injection into V5/MT causes severe acute motion-detection deficits, but motion sensitivity recovers over days to weeks. The animals eventually show only minimal motion-detection impairment, despite complete absence of neurons in area V5/MT[29]. It is possible that the latent effect of an ibotenic acid lesion better reflects the difficulties in motion processing seen in the developmental lesions of dyslexia.

Another interpretation of our data could be that the visual-system abnormalities may be one component, or only a marker, of a disorder with numerous constituent disorders, including the well-studied deficit in phonological awareness (the ability to isolate the component sounds within words)[7,30]. The joint appearance of these disorders in dyslexia may be due to an underlying deficit of the brain pathways that process temporal stimuli. Paula Tallal and colleagues at Rutgers University in New Brunswick, N.J., showed that dyslexic children with concomitant oral-language disabilities performed no differently from normal children in distinguishing linguistic and nonlinguistic auditory stimuli, as long as they were presented slowly[31]. When the same stimuli were presented rapidly, however, the dyslexic children performed much worse than nondyslexic children. It has been postulated that these findings could be interpreted as a "transient" auditory-processing deficit that may be responsible for the phonological-processing deficits repeatedly observed in dyslexics. The temporal phonological and visual deficits may be explained in the framework of a common temporal information-processing deficit. Perhaps a range of system impairments—all involving temporal processing—is responsible for the range of sensory, motor, and cognitive deficits exhibited by reading-disabled children. This explanation would account for the heterogeneity observed in the dyslexic population. However, much of this is still speculative.

Abnormal eye movements could explain why, for example, a child with dyslexia will tell you that "it looks like the words are walking" when he or she tries to read.

In summary, many studies of dyslexia have provided strong evidence for deficits in the left hemisphere related to disordered language functions, such as naming and phonological awareness. We have reviewed the evidence that a more widespread constellation of other dyslexia-related abnormalities is detectable in the visual domain of the brain, manifested as disorders of rapid naming, rapid visual processing, and motion detection. However, it is not clear whether both the language and visual problems arise from the same etiology or whether one problem is the result of the other. Further development of this line of research utilizing functional neuroimaging may result in more accurate techniques for the earlier diagnosis and characterization of developmental dyslexia.

References

1. L. Bradley and P. Bryant, "Categorizing sounds and learning to read—a casual connection," *Nature* **301**, 419 (1983).
2. R. Olson, B. Wise, F. Conners, J. Rack, and D. Fulker, "Measurement of word recognition, orthographic, and phonological skills," *J. Learn. Disabil.* **22**, 339 (1989).
3. M. Denckla and R. Rudel, "Rapid 'automized' naming (RAN): Dyslexia differentiated from other learning disabilities," *Neuropsychologia* **14**, 471 (1976).
4. M. Wolf and H. Goodglass, "Dyslexia, dysnomia, and lexical retrieval: A longitudinal investigation," *Brain Lang.* **28**, 154 (1986).
5. I. Y. Liberman, D. Shankweiler, F. W. Fischer, and B. Carter, "Explicit syllable and phoneme segmentation in the young child," *J. Exp. Child Psychol.* **18**, 201 (1974).
6. L. Bradley and P. Bryant, "Difficulties in auditory organisation as a possible cause of reading backwardness," *Nature* **271**, 746 (1978).
7. S. T. Orton, " 'Word-blindness' in school children," *Arch. Neurol. Psychiatr.* **14**, 581 (1925).
8. G. Eden, J. Stein, H. Wood, and F. Wood, "Differences in eye movements and reading problems in dyslexic and normal children," *Vision Res.* **34**, 1345 (1994).
9. O. Zangwill and C. Blakemore, "Dyslexia: reversal of eye movements during reading." *Neuropsychologia* **10**, 371 (1972).
10. D. Willows, in *Learning about Learning Disabilities*, B.Y.L. Wong, Ed. (Academic Press Inc., New York, 1991), pp. 163–192.
11. W. J. Lovegrove, M. Heddle, and W. Slaghuis, "Reading disability: spatial frequency specific deficits in visual information store," *Neuropsychologia*, **18,** 111 (1980).
12. F. Martin and W. Lovegrove. "The effect of field size and luminance on contrast sensitivity differences between specifically reading disabled and normal children," *Neuropsychologia* **22**, 73, (1984).
13. R. Shapley and V. Perry, "Cat and monkey retinal ganglion cells and their visual functional roles," *Trends Neurosci.* **9**, 229 (1986).
14. S. M. Zeki, "Colour coding in rhesus monkey prestriate cortex," *Brain Res.* **53**, 422 (1973).
15. L. G. Ungerleider and M. Mishkin, in *Analysis Of Visual Behavior*, D. J. Ingle, M. A. Goodale, and R. J. W. Mansfield, Eds. (MIT Press, Cambridge, Mass. 1982). pp. 549–586.
16. M. Livingstone and D. Hubel, "Segregation of form, colour, movement and depth: anatomy, physiology, and perception," *Science* **240**, 740 (1988).
17. S. M. Zeki, "Functional organisation of visual area in the posterior bank of the superior temporal sulcus in the rhesus monkey," *J. Physiol. (Land)* **236**, 549 (1974).
18. S. M. Zeki, in *Vision, Coding and Efficiency,* C. Blakemore, Ed. (University Press, Cambridge, 1990), pp. 321–345.
19. J. D. G. Watson, R. Meyers, R. S. J. Frackowiak, J. V. Hajinal, R. P. Woods, J. C. Mazziotta et al., "Area V5 of the human brain: evidence froma combined study using positron emission tomography and magnetic resonance imaging," *Cereb. Corter.* **3**, 79 (1993).
20. K. Cheng, H. Fujita, I. Kanno, S. Miura, and K. Tanaka. "Human cortical regions activated by a wide-field visual motion: an H2 150 study," *J. Neurophysiol.* **74**, 413 (1995).
21. R. Tootell, J. Reppas, R. Kwong, R. Malach, R. Born, T. Brady et al., "Functional analysis of human MT and related visual corticla areas using magnetic resonance imaging." *J. Neurosci.* **15**, 3215 (1995).
22. W. J. Lovegrove, F. Martin, and W. Slaghius, "A theoretical and experimental case for visual deficit in specific reading difficulty." *Cognit. Neuropsychol.* **3**, 225 (1986).
23. G. Eden, J. F. Stein, H. M. Wood, and F. B. Wood, "Temporal and spatial processing in reading-disabled and normal children," *Cortex* **31**, 451 (1995).
24. G. Eden, J. F. Stein, H. M. Wood, and F. B. Wood, "Visuospatial judgment in reading disabled and normal children," *Percept. Mot. Skills.* **82**, 155 (1996).
25. M. Livingstone, G. Rosen, F. Drislane, and A. Galaburda, "Physiological and anatomical evidence for a magnocellular deficit in developmential dyslexia," *Proc. Natl. Acad. Sci. USA* **80**, 7943 (1991).
26. G. F. Eden, J. W. vanMeter, J. Rumsey, J. M. Maisog, R.P. Woods, and T. A. Zeffiro, "Abnormal processing of visual motion in dyslexia revealed by functional brain imaging," *Nature* **382**, 66, (1992).
27. S. M. Zeki, "Cerebral akinetopsia (visual motion blindness): a review," *Brain* **114**, 811 (1991).
28. J. Zihl, "Selective disturbance of movement vision after bilateral brain damage," *Brain* **106**, 313 (1983).
29. W. T. Newsome and E. B. Pare, "A selective impairment of motion perception following lesions of the middle temporal visual area (MT)," *J. Neurosci.* **8**, 2201 (1988).
30. M. Snowling, "Phonemic deficits in developmental dyslexia," *Psychol. Res.* **43**, 219 (1981).
31. P. Tallal, "Auditory temporal perception, phonics, and reading disabilities in children," *Brain Lang.* **9**, 182 (1980).

Attention Deficit: Nature, Nurture, or Nicotine?

Unable to concentrate at work? Start projects and never finish them? You may have adult attention-deficit disorder, or you may be just another of the thousands of fidgety people who have convinced themselves that they have it.

Estimates of the number of adults who have the psychiatric malady known as attention-deficit disorder or, more recently, attention-deficit-hyperactivity disorder (ADHD), range from almost none to two in every 100 people. The problem with determining who has ADHD, which affects about one in 25 children, is that it is a subjective diagnosis made by a physician in consultation with parents and teachers. ADHD is most often diagnosed between the ages of 6 and 11, with boys outnumbering girls by about three to one.

Now, researchers are beginning to tease apart the physiological hallmarks and risk factors for ADHD. In the September issue of the *American Journal of Psychiatry*, Sharon Milberger, Joseph Biedennan, and their colleagues at Massachusetts General Hospital in Boston report a striking connection between maternal smoking and ADHD in children. In the same journal, John Hill and Eugene Schoener of Wayne State University School of Medicine in Detroit estimate that as ADHD children grow up, the disorder declines sharply to affect two adults in every 1,000 by age 30, and just five in 10,000 adults overall by age 40.

And in the most comprehensive magnetic resonance imaging (MRI) study of ADHD children to date, Xavier Castellanos, Jay Giedd, Judith Rapoport, and their colleagues at the National Institute of Mental Health (NIMH) in Bethesda, Md., report in the July issue of *Archives of General Psychiatry* that the portions of ADHD boys' brains that control movement and that focus attention are indeed structurally different from those of normal boys. Ongoing studies with girls and identical twins (one with ADHD, one without) may enable psychiatrists to determine which adults have a disorder that could benefit from psychostimulant treatment, Castellanos says.

Milberger, Biederman, and their colleagues turned up the ADHD-smoking link in a study of 140 mothers of children with ADHD and 120 normal controls. They found that 22 percent of the mothers of ADHD children smoked a pack of cigarettes per day during at least three months of pregnancy; only 8 percent of the mothers of children without ADHD smoked. The difference remained statistically significant when the researchers controlled for social class, genetic risk, parental ADHD, and parental IQ.

"We were surprised by the strength of this effect," says Biederman. "This should sound an alarm with the public and may have significant public health implications," he says.

However, the results are based solely on the mothers' recollections of their smoking patterns. The researchers acknowledge that the mothers of ADHD children may have been more likely to report smoking during pregnancy out of a desire to blame the disorder on a concrete cause, possibly skewing the results. Biederman says that the study simply raises a red flag and must be confirmed epidemiologically.

Nevertheless, he and his colleagues suggest that nicotinic receptors on dopamine-producing neurons, which are located in the caudate nucleus and elsewhere in the brain, may be affected in the fetus by maternal smoking.

From *The Journal of NIH Research,* November 1996, pp. 24-26.

Animal studies by several groups have indicated that chronic nicotine exposure increases the overall number of nicotine receptors in the brain, increases dopamine release in striatal structures, and produces hyper-active animals.

Dopamine is the primary inhibitory neurotransmitter in the striatal structures, although it can also be stimulatory. Dopamine concentrations in the striatum are known to affect movement and emotions. Both Parkinson's disease, a movement disorder, and schizophrenia, a psychotic disorder that involves exaggerated emotional responses, are known to involve the striatal dopamine system.

The prevailing theory about which parts of the brain are malfunctioning in ADHD involves a dysfunction of what's known as the cortical-striatal loop. This circuit originates in the prefrontal cortex, which can only produce excitatory signals. The cortical-striatal loop involves signaling through middle-brain structures, such as the caudate nucleus and putamen. These structures process signals and send output to the globus pallidus, where signals are further refined and shuttled to the thalamus, the main sensory relay station in the brain. The thalamus feeds signals back to the prefrontal cortex and ultimately determines whether cortical commands (both motor and emotional) will be excitatory or inhibitory.

In their MRI study, Castellanos and his colleagues at NIMH's child-psychiatry branch found differences in the size of some of the components of the cortical-striatal loop between ADHD and normal children. The researchers measured the cortical-striatal structures of 57 boys diagnosed with ADHD and 55 normal controls, all of whom were between 5 and 18 years old. The five-year study revealed that in normal children, the right prefrontal cortex, caudate-nucleus, and globus-pallidus regions are nearly always bigger than the corresponding regions on the left, but in ADHD children, the two sides are equal in size. However, the researchers were unable to replicate the findings of previous studies, including some of their own, which showed size differences in the corpus-callosum, the structure that connects the two cerebral hemispheres of the brain.

Castellanos says that he and his colleagues are reexamining the corpus callosum data and that they are not yet convinced that no differences in the size of this structure exist between normal and ADHD children. Such measurements are difficult, he says, because there is so much variability in the sizes of the brain structures, and many of the structures are minuscule.

"Among the most important structures are the globus pallidus and caudate nucleus," Castellanos says. All neural signals in the cortical-striatal loop eventually pass through these areas, but [in children] the caudate nucleus volume is equivalent to one teaspoon, and the globus pallidus is a quarter teaspoon," he says. Moreover, says Castellanos, he and his colleagues only detected size differences of less than 10 percent between the structures of ADHD and non-ADHD children.

Yet the significance of the size variation is not well understood, says Castellanos. He hopes to find more answers in follow-up work, which is now underway. He and his colleagues are remeasuring the prefrontal cortex, globus-pallidus, and caudate-nucleus regions of the children from the first study as they grow up, hoping to reveal whether the structures change as the children mature. And new tools such as functional MRI, which directly measures blood flow in the brain, may provide even more definitive results, says Castellanos. Such findings may also shed light on adult ADHD, he says.

For decades, ADHD had been thought of almost exclusively as a childhood disorder that diminished as a child grew up. Then, in the Nov. 15, 1990, issue of the *New England Journal of Medicine,* a group of scientists led by Alan Zemetkin of NIMH reported a positron emission tomography (PET) study of adults who had children diagnosed with ADHD and who themselves currently had ADHD symptoms. These people had lower-than-normal levels of activity in the prefrontal cortex, as measured by glucose utilization, an indirect indicator of blood flow.

The article caught the attention of the popular press, and suddenly thousands of fidgety, easily distractible adults began showing up in their doctors' offices with self-diagnoses, demanding treatment with Ritalin (methylphenidate hydrochloride). Ritalin, the psychostimulant drug often used to treat children, is a mild central-nervous-system stimulant that inhibits the synaptic reuptake of dopamine. But the number of adults who are affected severely enough to require treatment with such psychostimulants, which can cause loss of appetite, insomnia, and—more rarely—cardiac arrhythmias, remains controversial.

"Part of the issue is semantic," says Biederman. "It depends on how you define the boundaries of illness." He estimates that between 1 and 2 percent of adults have ADHD.

Zemetkin, however, believes the number of adults with true ADHD is much lower. He warns that prescribing psychostimulant drugs for patients who might not have any real disorder, or who might have more severe mental illnesses, such as schizophrenia or depression, could be harmful. "I am very skeptical when an adult patient comes to me saying he has ADHD," says Zemetkin. "I go through an exhaustive checklist of every possible psychiatric disorder to rule out everything else first," he says.

Hill and Schoener also come in at the low end. To calculate their estimate of adult ADHD, they reviewed nine prospective studies published over the past 25 years, five of which came from Salvatore Mannuzza's group at Columbia University in New York City. The combined studies followed 718 children who were between 6 and 12 years old initially and in their middle to late teens at follow-up. In only one study was the mean follow-up age more than 20 years old, the average follow-up age being 25.5. Hill and Schoener formulated a mathematical model that predicts a 50 percent decline in ADHD every five years beyond childhood. They predicted the incidence of ADHD at age 30 and 40 by extrapolating from this model.

Several studies have shown that the overall number of neurons in the midbrain decreases with age, a change that could account for the decrease in ADHD symptoms in adults, Zemetkin says. So if you are still fidgety and distractible in mid-life, don't despair: You might be able to chalk it up to a youthful brain.

—KARYN HEDE GEORGE

Ethical Issues

A humanitarian society is measured by its ethical standards. Ethics are prescribed norms of character that represent a society's view of what is right or wrong, or what is moral or immoral. Ethical standards vary among civilizations and societies across different time periods.

Scientific activities are not devoid of ethical concerns. Scientists who deal directly with the manipulation of human beings, either at the physical or psychological level, are aware of the ethical dilemmas that often involve the procedures adopted or findings of a study. Although scientific investigations may start out with good intentions, the consequences are not always positive.

Research in the biomedical field often involves live subjects in the course of the study. The kind of subjects used in an experiment is an important concern. Should human or animal subjects be used? If human subjects are chosen, who among the population will be selected, and how? Can the study guarantee the safety of the subjects? Are the adverse side effects of the manipulation known and controllable? It is debatable whether or not animals should be used at all. If animals are used in research, the issue becomes how to avoid causing them unnecessary harm or pain.

The other controversial issue is the pervasive use of genetic explanations for behaviors. Indeed the genetic variable may account for some variability in behaviors, but it is fallacious to believe that the genes completely determine our behavioral attributes. Human nature is far more complex and sensitive to a host of factors, not only within the individual, but also to those factors that are ever-present in the environment.

Looking Ahead: Challenge Questions

What ethical issues concern the use of animals for research? Under what conditions is the use of animals for research acceptable? Cite some examples as to how the use of animal subjects have been relevant to biopsychology. Describe some alternative strategies to the use of animals for research.

What are the historical roots of eugenics? What is the controversy that surrounds this system? Can you identify some of present-day society's behaviors that may suggest a revival of this perspective? How do you relate genetic screening to the concept of eugenics?

What is your opinion as to the underlying basis of behaviors such as violence, mental illness, or homosexuality? Is it based solely on the nature or nurture factors?

UNIT 11

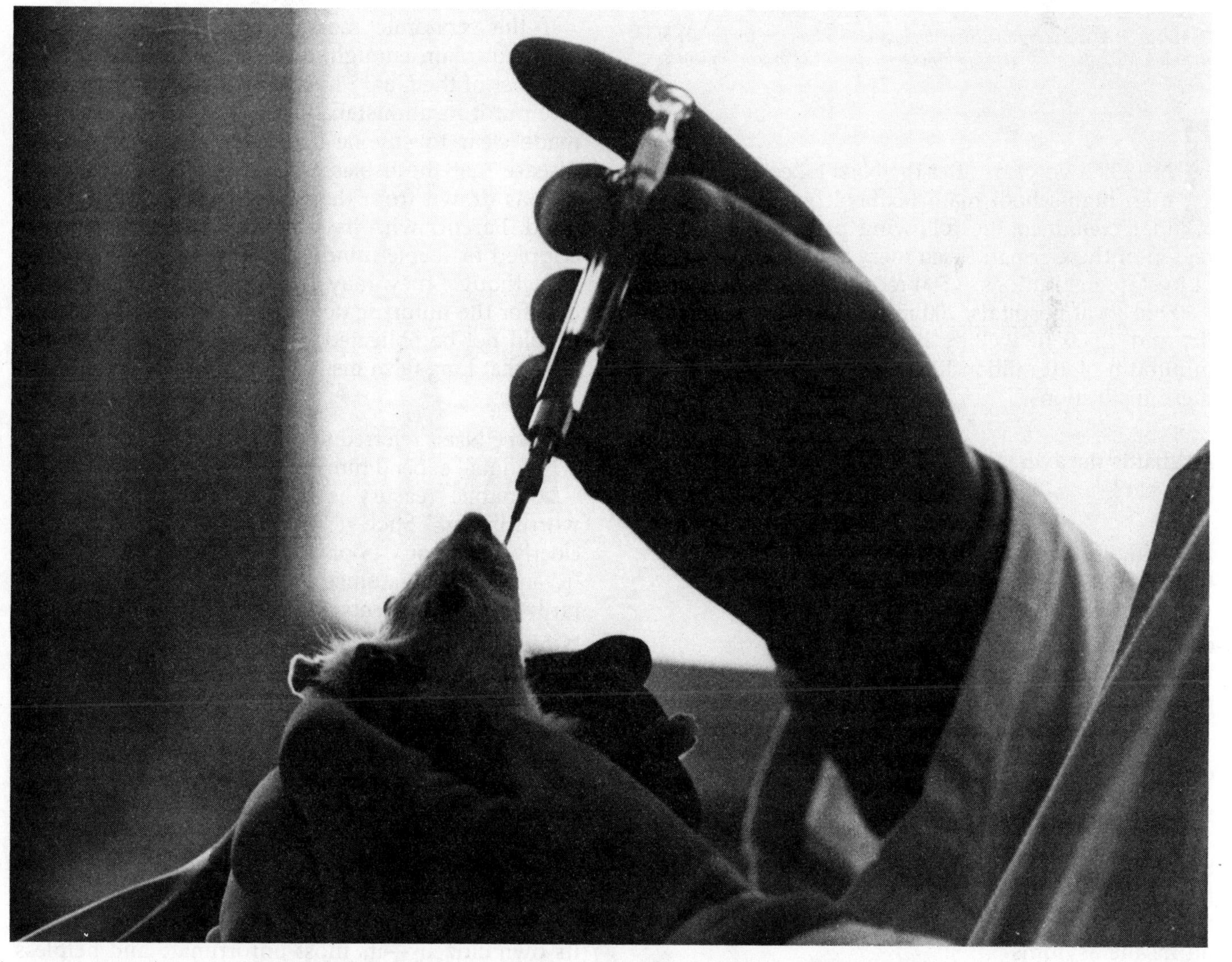

Science Misapplied: The Eugenics Age Revisited

Seeking relief from extreme economic hardships after the First World War, Nazi Germany based its misguided campaign to eliminate "unproductive" members from its society on the fledgling field of genetics. Given similar economic pressures and a renewed search for genetic roots to social problems, what's to stop us from following a similar course today?

Garland E. Allen

GARLAND E. ALLEN *is a professor of biology at Washington University in St. Louis, Mo., and a historian of science who specializes in genetics issues.*

IN 1935, two years after the Nazi takeover, a German high-school math textbook was published that contained the following problem: "In one region of the German Reich there are 4,400 mentally ill in state institutions, 4,500 receiving state support, 1,600 in local hospitals, 200 in homes for the epileptic, and 1,500 in welfare homes. The state pays a minimum of 10 million RM [Reich Marks]/year for these institutions.

I. What is the average cost to the state per inhabitant per year?

II. Using the result calculated from I, how much does it cost the state if:

a. 868 patients stay longer than 10 years?

b. 260 patients stay longer than 20 years?

c. 112 patients stay longer than 2 years?"

Another problem asked the students: If the construction of an insane asylum requires 6 million RM, how many housing units for normal families could be built at 15,000 RM apiece for the amount spent on insane asylums?

If the economic message from these problems were not plain enough, a pamphlet published by a member of the Nazi Physician's League the year before put it in unmistakably blunt terms: "It must be made clear to anyone suffering from an incurable disease that the useless dissipation of costly medications drawn from the public store cannot be justified. Parents who have seen the difficult life of a crippled or feeble-minded child must be convinced that, though they may have a moral obligation to care for the unfortunate creature, the broader public should not be obligated . . . to assume the enormous costs that long-term institutionalization might entail."

The Nazis referred to those who required the continual expenditure of medical resources from the public treasury as "useless eaters" or "lives not worth living." Such terms were also applied to the elderly, the chronic poor, and the crippled. These "misfit" individuals, assumed to be the offspring of hereditarily defective parents, were deemed a burden on the rest of society.

In 1933 these concepts had been given legal status when the Reich Cabinet passed the "Law on Preventing Hereditarily Diseased Progeny," calling for involuntary sterilization of all those identified as bearers of hereditary disease. These "diseases" included not only clinically definable conditions, such as Huntington's disease, hereditary blindness, deafness, and epilepsy, but also more nebulous social and behavioral traits such as "feeblemindedness," "pauperism," and alcoholism.

What would bring a nation to the point of viewing its own citizens—its most unfortunate and helpless members at that—as useless lives, as nothing more than an economic burden on society? More important for us today, was this a phenomenon unique to fascist Germany, or could it happen in the United States?

To understand whether such attitudes could flourish here, it is instructive to examine the history of the science—in particular a branch of biology that came to be known as eugenics—that served as the foundation for the German ideology of "lives not worth living." Such a review will reveal, first of all, that a similar movement not only could, but in fact *did* occur in the United States. More significant, it will also show that the forces driving the original eugenics movement—a mentality that blames the victim for shrinking economic resources and a misguided faith in genetic science to label and formulate social policy about so-called unproductive members of society—may be at play once again today.

Breeding Better People

The term eugenics was coined in 1883 by Sir Francis Galton, Charles Darwin's cousin and an early pioneer of statistics, to refer to those born "good in stock, hereditarily endowed with noble qualities." More directly, according to Galton's U.S. disciple, Charles Davenport, eugenics was the science of "the improvement of the human race by better breeding." To both men, better breeding implied improving the quality of the human species using the findings of modern science, particularly the science of heredity. Eugenics was thus viewed as the human counterpart of modern scientific animal and plant husbandry. In fact, it seemed ironic to eugenicists that people paid so much attention to the pedigrees of their farm and domestic stock while they ignored the pedigrees of their children.

The purpose of eugenics, Galton wrote, "is to express the science of improving stock, which is by no means confined to questions of judicious mating, but which, especially in the case of man, takes cognizance of all influences that tend in however remote a degree to give the more suitable races or strains of blood a better chance of prevailing over the less suitable than they otherwise would have had." In this brief definition, Galton lays out all the dimensions that came to characterize eugenics as an ideology and social/political movement during the first half of the twentieth century:

- A firm trust in the methods of selective breeding as an effective means of improving the overall quality of the human species.
- A strong conviction of the power of heredity to directly determine physical, physiological, and mental (including personality) traits in adults.
- An inherent belief in the inferiority of some races and superiority of others—a view extended to ethnic groups and social classes as well.
- A faith in the power of science, rationally employed, to solve pressing social problems, including ones so seemingly intractable as urban and labor violence, and to eliminate various forms of mental disease, including manic depression, schizophrenia, and feeblemindedness.

Steeped in such grandiosity and ethnocentrism, U.S. eugenicists pursued research on the inheritance of a variety of physical, mental, and personality traits. But since they primarily used family-pedigree charts, which were often based on highly subjective and impressionistic data collected from family members, the eugenicists' understanding of genetics was often simplistic and naive, even for the early decades of this century. For example, in a 1919 study based on analysis of pedigrees, Davenport claimed that thalassophilia, or "love of the sea," was a sex-linked Mendelian recessive trait appearing in families of prominent U.S. naval officers. That the trait must be sex-linked seemed clear, since in pedigree after pedigree only males in the various families observed ever became naval officers.

U.S. EUGENICIST CHARLES DAVENPORT CONCLUDED IN 1921 THAT GERMANS RANKED HIGHEST IN LEADERSHIP, HUMOR, GENEROSITY, SYMPATHY, AND LOYALTY, WHILE IRISH PEOPLE WERE THE MOST "SUSPICIOUS" AND JEWISH PEOPLE THE MOST "OBTRUSIVE."

Other traits such as alcoholism, pauperism, prostitution, rebelliousness, criminality, feeblemindedness, ability to excel in chess, and even forms of industrial sabotage such as "train wrecking" were all claimed to be determined by one or two pairs of Mendelian genes. When one of Davenport's friends, a professional psychiatrist, criticized him for lumping complex human behaviors into single categories such as insanity, he dismissed the criticism as being "uninformed."

Such simplistic models for complex behaviors were extended to explain the differences between racial, ethnic, and national groups. In a study of the "Comparative Social Traits of Various Races" in 1921 (based on a series of questionnaires given to school children), Davenport concluded that Germans ranked highest on qualities such as leadership, humor, generosity, sympathy, and loyalty, while on these same traits Irish, Italian, and in two cases (loyalty and generosity) British people ranked lowest. The Irish ranked highest in "suspiciousness," while Jewish people ranked highest in "obtrusiveness." Davenport assumed, of course, that most if not all such traits were genetically determined, and the social behaviors of not only individual family members, but also whole nations, were genetically fixed at birth.

Not surprisingly, eugenicists also developed close ties with the newly emerging profession of psychometrics, the psychological theory of mental measurement, which was eagerly being employed to develop standardized IQ tests. Prominent psychometricians—such as Lewis Terman, who created the Stanford-Binet IQ test for preschool children, and Robert Yerkes, the psychologist from Harvard who designed and directed the administration of the Army IQ tests during World War I—believed the mental functions they were measuring were innate, or genetically determined, and therefore that training and education could accomplish only as much for certain social and ethnic groups as the "raw material" of their mental capacity would allow.

For their part, eugenicists welcomed the IQ test as an objective and quantitative tool for measuring innate mental ability. For example, on the basis of IQ tests given to immigrants arriving at Ellis Island, eugenicist Henry H. Goddard "discovered" that more than 80 percent of the Jewish, Hungarian, Polish, Italian, and Russian immigrants were mentally defective, or feebleminded. Goddard believed that such a defect was "a condition of the mind or brain which is transmitted as regularly and surely as color of hair or eyes."

Meanwhile, a host of organizations were formed to support eugenics research. In 1910, Davenport established the first major eugenics institution in the United States, the Eugenics Records Office (ERO), which served until 1940 as both a center for eugenics research, complete with an office staff and a battery of field workers, and as a repository for eugenic data (mostly family pedigrees). In 1913, the Eugenics Research Association was founded to bring together those interested in the latest eugenical investigations. In 1918, the Galton Society began meeting monthly at the American Museum of Natural History in New York to hear papers on eugenics and related subjects. And in 1923, the American Eugenics Society, which grew to include more than 1,200 members and branch organizations in 29 states by the end of the decade, was formally launched as a result of a proposal drawn up at the International Congress of Eugenics in New York in 1921. Elsewhere, J.H. Kellogg, the cereal magnate from Battle Creek, Mich., founded the Race Betterment Foundation in the years just before World War I, while eugenics education societies formed in Illinois, Missouri, Wisconsin, Minnesota, Utah, and California.

Pursuing the educational front, eugenicists promoted the science through popular accounts such as *Mankind at the Crossroads* by E.G. Conklin (1914), *Passing of the Great Race* by Madison Grant (1916), *The Rising Tide of Color Against White World Supremacy* by Lothrop Stoddard (1920), *Applied Eugenics* by Paul Popenoe and Roswell Johnson (1923), and *The Fruit of the Family Tree* by Alfred E. Wiggam (1924). These and other works presented the spectre of race degeneration and the takeover of modern society by degenerates and "foreigners" who were all out-breeding the staunch, established white Anglo-Saxon stock.

Finally, several textbooks, including *Genetics and Eugenics* by W.E. Castle (1916, 1923) and *Evolution, Genetics, and Eugenics* by H.H. Newman (1921, 1925, 1932), took the technical message of eugenics to the classroom. By 1928, the American Genetics Association boasted that there were 376 college courses devoted exclusively to eugenics. High-school biology textbooks followed suit by the mid-1930s, with most containing material favorable to the idea of eugenical control of reproduction. It would thus have been difficult to be an even moderately educated reader in the 1920s or 1930s and not have known, at least in general terms, about the claims of eugenics.

The Search for Order

Though the eugenics movement eventually became a worldwide phenomenon—with contributions from scientists and laypeople in England, France, Italy, Scandinavia, Latin America, and Russia—by far the most work occurred in Germany and the United States, whose eugenicists had formed a particularly strong and direct bond, especially after the Nazis came to power in 1933. As early as the mid-1920s, American eugenicists such as Davenport and Harry H. Laughlin, superintendent of the Eugenics Records Office, were already well known to German authorities such as Fritz Lenz, professor of racial hygiene at the University of Munich. Indeed, in 1928 Lenz requested permission from Laughlin to reprint his article "Eugenical Sterilization" in the *Archiv für Rassen und Gesellschaftsbiologie (Archive for Race and Social Biology)*. Laughlin responded enthusiastically: "I should feel highly honored to have this paper appear in the *Archiv*. Your many American friends trust that some time in the near future you will be able to visit the centers of eugenical interest in this country."

More directly, the Nazis used a model Laughlin had devised as the basis for their own sterilization law in 1933. In recognition of this critical role, Laughlin was given an honorary doctorate of medicine degree from Heidelberg University in 1936, which he enthusiastically accepted at the time of the university's 550th anniversary celebration. Meanwhile, Davenport, a Harvard alumnus, arranged for a delegation of German eugenicists to participate in Harvard's 300th celebration later the same year.

Other U.S. eugenicists were keenly interested in how the Nazis were progressing with eugenical programs, from sterilization legislation to popular education. In fact, a number of Americans visited Germany in the 1930s to meet with their colleagues and visit the "eugenic courts," which the Nazis had set up to pass judgment on cases where compulsory sterilization was recommended. The visitors included the secretary of the American Public Health Association, the president of the Eugenics Research Association, and a representative of the Sterilization League of New Jersey, as well as geneticist T.U.H. Ellinger and racial theorist Lothrop Stoddard, who met with leading eugenicists such as Lenz and high-ranking Nazi officials such as Heinrich Himmler.

Frederick Osborn, the secretary of the American Eugenics Society who also followed eugenical developments in Germany with great interest, wrote a report in 1937 summarizing developments in the German sterilization program. His memo is instructive in demonstrating the general enthusiasm American eugenicists felt for the Nazi program: "Germany's rapidity of change with respect to eugenics was possible only under a dictator....The German sterilization program is apparently an excellent one...recent developments in Germany constitute perhaps the most important experiment which has ever been tried."

Nazi eugenicists and their American counterparts shared more than a set of scientific beliefs and social programs; indeed, the most fundamental basis of eugenic arguments in both countries grew from a common economic and social experience. The period between the World Wars brought considerable upheaval to most of the countries in the capitalist West. The task of gearing down from a wartime economy was superimposed on a set of problems that had been developing long before the onset of World War I itself: boom-and-bust economic cycles, periods of raging inflation, rising unemployment, sagging rates of profit, and labor unrest. To many, the traditional fabric of society appeared to be unraveling.

In both Europe and the United States, the response to these conditions by those with economic and political power was to search for ways to bring a *laissez-faire* economy (which operates with relatively little governmental interference), and the political and social practices attached to it, under control. Historian Robert Wiebe of Northwestern University has termed the period from 1890 to 1930 as "the search for order."

In the United States, this search was tied to a movement known as "progressivism" and its political incarnation, the Progressive Party, whose representative, Theodore Roosevelt, held the presidency from 1901 to 1909. Progressive ideology, which called for rational planning and scientific management of every phase of society, was seen as the new and "modern" approach, and hence "progressive" by the standards of the day. For *laissez-faire* views it substituted an emphasis on state intervention and promoted the use of trained experts in setting economic and social regulatory policies. And it preached the doctrine of efficiency, which applied cost-benefit analysis and emphasized solving problems at their root, rather than after a crisis has arisen, for example, as in preventive medicine.

Eugenics was first embraced politically as a scientific means of halting the rising stream of "defective" immigrants who came to the United States from 1880 to 1914 seeking relief from the economic problems besetting Europe. These new immigrants arrived principally from Eastern and Southern Europe, the Balkans, and Russia. Many were Jewish. And all were ethnically and culturally distinct from earlier waves of foreigners, such as those in the mid-nineteenth century who had migrated mostly from Anglo-Saxon countries of Western Europe such as Germany, England, Ireland, and Scotland. To many Americans these new immigrants were considered "the dregs of humanity," unassimilable, mentally deficient (as confirmed by tests such as those Goddard administered at Ellis Island), socially radical (many had been involved in trade-union activities in Europe), and willing to work for low wages, thus taking jobs away from hard-working Americans.

Calls for restricting immigration grew so dramatically after the war that in 1921 Albert Johnson, head of the House Committee on Immigration and Naturalization, held a series of hearings preparatory to introducing a bill that would seriously limit immigration, especially from the areas characterized by the new immigrant groups. Because any restriction had to appear to be fair, not singling out particular countries or ethnic groups as targets, Johnson appointed Laughlin of the Eugenics Records Office as "expert eugenics witness." In this capacity, Laughlin testified twice before the House Committee on Immigration and Naturalization. In 1922, he cited IQ data, Army test results, and family pedigree analyses of instutionalized persons to demonstrate the defective biological nature of the new immigrants. His message was that biology, specifically genetics, was crucial in considering such social and political questions as those surrounding immigration, and that little or no attention had been paid to this in the past.

Laughlin's point seemed eminently rational: it was inefficient and wasteful of taxpayers' money to care for the world's socially inadequate all their lives; better simply to prevent them from entering the country in the first place. For legislators worried about the nation's budget and facing staggering social problems of rising unemployment, labor strikes, and inflation, Laughlin's emphasis on the eugenical point of view as rational and efficient management was seductive.

In his second official testimony—in 1924, shortly before the immigration bill went to the floor of Congress—Laughlin presented data showing that prisons and mental asylums housed a disproportionate number of immigrants from the very geographic areas that many nativists wanted to restrict. Two committee members, representing largely immigrant constituencies, protested that Laughlin's information was subject to a variety of interpretations, and in response another biologist, Herbert Spencer Jennings from Johns Hopkins University, was called to comment on Laughlin's data and conclusions. Jennings thought Laughlin's analysis of the immigration data was grossly overstated, but Jennings was given only five minutes to testify on the last day of the hearings, and thus had almost no impact on the subsequent immigration legislation.

The Johnson Act, as it was called, duly passed in 1924, restricted annual immigration from any region to 2 percent of the number of residents from that region already living in the United States as of the 1890 census. Since the vast bulk of the new immigrants had arrived after that date, the Johnson Act, as hoped, restricted these groups most heavily. Immigration from Eastern Europe fell from 75 percent of the total immigration in 1914 to 15 percent after 1924. Laughlin and U.S. eugenicists in general considered the passage of the immigration act a great political triumph.

Managing Reproduction

Eugenicists similarly argued that if unemployment and crime resulted from the behavior of genetically inadequate persons, then clearly the most rational solution was to prevent those types from being born in the first place. It was inefficient, they contended, to allow the biologically degenerate and unfit to reproduce, merely to fill the insane asylums, hospitals, and prisons with defective people that the state must support the rest of their lives.

Such efficiency arguments permeated eugenic literature. For example, eugenicists pointed out that it would have cost less than $150 in 1790 for the state of New York to have sterilized Ada Juke (the pseudonym of a young woman whose impoverished descendants were the subject of one of the first eugenic studies by American sociologist Richard Dugdale in 1874), while the estimated cost of caring for her descendants by the 1920s had topped $2 million.

Using the argument for national efficiency, eugenicists successfully lobbied for the passage of a number of state eugenical sterilization laws in the 1920s and 1930s. Eugenical sterilization was aimed specifically at those individuals in mental or penal institutions who, from family-pedigree analysis, were considered likely to give birth to socially defective children. Sterilization could be ordered any time after a patient had been examined by a eugenics committee, usually composed of a lawyer or family member representing the individual, a judge, and a doctor or other eugenic "expert."

In the end, more than 30 states had enacted such compulsory sterilization laws by 1940. And between 1907 (when the first such law was put into effect in Indiana) and 1941, more than 60,000 eugenical sterilizations were performed in the United States. Moreover, most state sterilization laws were not repealed until after the 1960s.

Logical Conclusions

Other countries—most notably England, France, and Italy—had their own versions of progressivism, but nowhere did the ideology of efficiency and scientific planning hold greater sway than in Germany. After World War I, restrictions imposed on the defeated nation in the Treaty of Versailles, enormous public and private pre- and postwar debt, the loss of overseas colonies and of the iron- and coal-rich regions of the Rhineland, and heavy reparations payments all converged to heighten the already existing problems of prewar inflation, unemployment, and the growing strength of organized labor. When the terms of Versailles became known, Germany experienced a series of upheavals that threatened to equal or surpass those of the Bolshevik revolution in Russia in 1917. General strikes and immense loss of morale made Germany a more-than-likely candidate for another communist assumption of state power.

In the face of such upheaval, the newly established Weimar Republic, without a Kaiser and modeled on British-style parliamentary rule, was relatively ineffective. During its 15-year reign following the first World War, the Weimar government seemed increasingly unable to take the strong steps necessary to bring the economy under control. And the stock market crash of 1929 hit a more vulnerable Germany perhaps hardest of all. Tough management was the order of the day, and if fascists stood for nothing else, it was strong-arm control.

Facing drastic state budget cuts, the newly installed Nazi government viewed "wards of the state" as both costly and expendable and thus took eugenics to its ultimate end—sterilization and genocide. In fact, during the whole of the Nazi period, somewhere around 400,000 institutionalized persons were involuntarily sterilized; the majority of these were during the first four years of the sterilization law's existence (1933-1937). In some areas, such as the state of Baden-Wurttemberg, more than 1 percent of the entire population was sterilized. However, as the war effort accelerated and resources became tighter, "euthanasia" was increasingly substituted for sterilization.

Sheila Weiss, a historian at Clarkson University,

emphasized recently that from an efficiency standpoint, a racial policy such as the euthanasia program is not without its logic, as morally perverse as that logic may appear. "Throughout its history, race hygiene was a strategy aimed at boosting national efficiency through the rational management of population," she says. "Although the extermination of millions of European Jews cannot really be viewed as a measure designed to boost national efficiency, the interpretation of the Jews as an unfit, surplus, and disposable group is not unrelated to the emphasis implicit in German race hygiene regarding 'valuable' and 'valueless' people. Hence, when all is said and done, it is the *logic* of eugenics far more than its racism that proved to be the most unfortunate legacy of the German race hygiene movement for the Third Reich."

Researchers are unable to verify claims that biology is to blame for complex social behaviors—such as violence in inner-city youth—because the genes affecting behavioral traits are the most influenced by the environment.

The advent of eugenic solutions showed that under varieties of emotional and financial duress, ordinary individuals, not just misguided or demagogic political figures, can succumb to the logic of what can be seen in a calmer light as an abhorrent solution. Indeed, according to Oxford historian Michael Burleigh, many individual families hardest hit by economic conditions in Germany were sometimes "relieved" to have their mentally ill or dependent relatives committed to institutions, sterilized, or even subjected to euthanasia, rather than persist in the expensive and emotionally draining experience of maintaining them in home care.

The whole Nazi eugenical and sterilization effort, of course, was misguided from the outset, based as it was on a simplistic notion that complex behavioral and personality traits could be reduced to single labels or categories. It could not have worked even if the "thousand-year Reich" had lived out its millennium. Germany's problems were hardly the result of a significant increase in deleterious genes within its population.

Meanwhile, in the United States the eugenics movement declined somewhat in importance by the mid-1930s, for reasons that are complex and controversial. Most scholars of the subject agree that failure of eugenicists to keep abreast of rapid developments in Mendelian genetics was not, as formerly claimed, a major factor. Similarly, apparent links between American and Nazi eugenics in the 1930s appear to have played only a minor role in bringing eugenics into disrepute.

My own view is that the older, harsher, more simplistic eugenics of Davenport and his generation declined because it had outlived its political usefulness. With immigration restrictions in place and sterilization laws on the books in many states, the eugenics movement had achieved about as much as could be expected at that time.

Eugenics Today?

How close are we today to embracing a modern form of eugenics? Will we in the United States someday soon re-walk those paths of trying to solve our social problems with scientific panaceas? I am sorry to say that I think the answer may be yes. A new eugenics movement would, of course, be called by a different name, but an era of similar economic and social conditions and a similar political response—our current philosophy of "cost-effectiveness" or "the bottom line"—has already arrived.

Witness the decline in our own economic and social conditions in the past two decades as an indicator of our potential to find eugenical arguments (clothed in the updated language of molecular genetics) attractive once again: Average weekly earnings have fallen 16 percent since 1973, and median income of families with children (under 18) has declined 32 percent. Meanwhile, the top 1 percent of the population controls almost 48 percent of household wealth and income, while the top 20 percent controls 94 percent. Unemployment has hovered at the 5 to 7 percent figure for the past four years, and analysts complain that these figures fail to include a whole category of "underemployed" (part-time, occasional) workers, or those who have simply given up on the job market and no longer report to unemployment offices.

A parallel between the economic and social milieu of the United States today and that of Germany in the Weimar and especially Nazi periods emerges in the debates over health care. Then as now, the discussions centered on decisions about who should receive what kind of health care and for how long. Indeed, in Germany medicine was considered a national resource to be used only for those individuals who showed the greatest prospect of recovery and future productivity.

In the "cutback" atmosphere that dominates our discussions of other social policies, the mood seems similarly exclusionary and bitter. For example, legislation that proposes to limit welfare recipients to five years over a lifetime, the suggestion that welfare mothers with more than two children be given Norplant (an antifertility drug), the idea of "three strikes and you're out" (three convictions mean a life sentence), and increasing calls for the death penalty—all run a striking parallel to the mood in late Weimar and Nazi Germany that called for reduction of rations for, and later elimination of, the aged, those with terminal diseases, repeat offenders, and the mentally impaired. Such extreme measures were justified in Germany by the policy of efficiency and scarcity of resources. Our current focus on "tough love" may be just a euphemism for what may somewhere down the road become "lives not worth living."

It is important not to underestimate the degree to which economic and social stress can lower our sensitivity to each other and to moral and ethical values. To a family already stressed by pay cuts, increased workload, rising costs of living and reduction in benefits, the use of tax dollars to maintain what is portrayed as a large population of dependent, nonproductive citizens is not likely to engender much sympathy. Witness the success of California's Proposition 187, which denies public services—health care and schooling, for example—to "illegal aliens."

If we are willing to contemplate severely restricting public assistance now, leaving a whole segment of the population to live at less-than-subsistence levels, is it too far a step to consider such people "expendable"? Historian of science Diane Paul of the University of Massachusetts puts it succinctly: "One clear lesson from the history of eugenics is this: what may be unthinkable when times are flush may come to seem only good common sense when they are not. In the 1920s, most geneticists found the idea of compulsory sterilization repugnant. In the midst of the Depression, they no longer did....Over time, noble sentiments came increasingly to clash with economic demands. Charitable impulses gave way to utilitarian practices."

I do not want to sound alarmist. We are not, after all, in anything like the severe stage of economic decline Weimar Germany experienced in the 1920s. But it would also be unwise to fail to anticipate how we might respond if we found ourselves in such dire straits. Contemplating our potential for accepting fascist solutions is particularly important at a time when it might be possible to alter our course.

On another front, genetic determinism—the notion that genes have the power to determine social and personality traits such as criminality and aggressiveness—is becoming as rampant today in both scientific and lay circles as it was in Weimar Germany in the 1920s. The United States has devoted considerable resources to research on the genetic basis of many such traits. For example, the National Institute of Alcoholism and Alcohol Abuse has allocated $25 million for research on the genetic origins of alcoholism. The National Institute of Mental Health has awarded even larger sums for the study of the genetics of schizophrenia and manic depression. Three years ago, the National Institutes of Health (NIH) proposed bringing much of the criminality research under the umbrella of a $400 million, government-funded "Violence Initiative" that would coordinate studies on the biological basis of violence in inner-city youth. Other recent studies have attempted to find a specific genetic basis for conditions such as shyness, novelty seeking, risk taking, proneness to anger, impulsivity, attention deficit disorder, and the like.

Meanwhile, the publicity given to each new or preliminary report on the genetics of human behavioral traits has grown even faster than the research itself. Every major popular magazine—*Time, Newsweek, U.S. News and World Report*, and the *Atlantic Monthly*, to name only a few—as well as most major newspapers have carried stories about the newest discovery of a gene for a given disease or trait. Moreover, all the accounts have been presented against the backdrop of the Human Genome Project, whose legitimate discoveries about the location of DNA segments for Huntington's disease and cystic fibrosis, among other conditions, have lent an aura of authenticity and prestige to the general field of human genetics that further validates the more hyperbolic popular reports.

Lessons from History

What can we do to prevent a resurgence of a Nazi-like mentality? One of the most important weapons we have is the knowledge that Nazism did occur once in recent history. Our understanding of that experience can provide powerful lessons, if we are willing to learn from them, about how simplistic science can be perverted to socially destructive ends.

We also have a far more sophisticated understanding of genetics today than did our counterparts in the 1920s and 1930s. While this knowledge does not guarantee that simplistic claims of a genetic basis for our social behavior will not be put forward, it does mean we can counter such arguments with modern facts. Indeed, researchers have had great difficulty establishing any satisfactory claim that specific genes cause complex human social behaviors. Virtually none of the studies claiming such links have been duplicated by independent researchers. And many have been withdrawn after the first flurry of excitement surrounding their publication in professional journals.

One reason for the difficulty in verifying such claims is that the process by which embryos grow suggests that genes are not rigid bits of information that invariably lead to the same outcome. Changes in the chemical, physical, and biological conditions can turn genes on or off or change their degree of expression at critical periods in the developmental process. In this respect, the genes affecting human behavioral and personality traits, the most plastic to begin with, are the most influenced by environmental input.

The fact that today's researchers have had no greater success in rigorously establishing the genetic basis for social behaviors than did their counterparts 70 or 80 years ago suggests that the whole question is misconstrued. Although simplistic claims are still being and probably will continue to be made, trying to sort out how much genes as opposed to environment shape human behavior is ultimately a scientifically meaningless undertaking.

Such studies would be virtually impossible, given our unwillingness to subject ourselves and our children to the rigorously controlled, multigenerational experimentation that would be necessary to begin to tease apart the relative contributions of heredity and environment in the development of special behavioral traits. If the environment cannot be controlled—if we cannot know clearly what influences acted with what intensities at all periods of development—then we have no real way of determining the relative influence of heredity and environment in the interaction.

Defining human behaviors also involves a high level of subjectivity. What is a "criminal" or "violent" act? What is alcoholism? We can make up arbitrary definitions for legal, psychiatric, or clinical purposes, but this does not mean we are dealing with behaviors that have the same causal roots. If researchers cannot agree on the nature or definition of a trait, they have little hope of rigorously studying its genetics.

Yet another advantage we have at the moment is experience, both in the scientific and lay communities, showing that open opposition to genetic determinist ideas can affect the degree to which they are accepted. Geneticists and other biologists did not stand up publicly to oppose eugenical claims in the 1920s and 1930s the way some of their counterparts are doing today. The NIH Violence Initiative might have moved into place unnoticed had not Maryland psychiatrist Peter Breggin, who is head of the Center for the Study of Psychiatry and Psychology in Bethesda, Md., made a cause célèbre of the Institute's proposal to study the biological basis of violence in innercity youth. The claims of Arthur Jensen, Richard Herrnstein, and William Shockley 20 years ago about a genetic basis for racial difference in IQ might have become quietly incorporated into mainstream biology, sociology, psychology, and educational theory had not the scientific claims been disputed publicly by knowledgeable geneticists such as Richard Lewontin and psychologists such as Leon Kamin.

Finally, and most fundamentally, if economic and social conditions ultimately determine the support and the publicity awarded to genetically deterministic ideas, then it is clear we must also work to change those conditions and create an economically more humane and egalitarian society—a desirable goal in its own right. Only by exposing the flaws of naive genetic determinism, while also attending to basic problems in our economic and social system, can we avoid repeating the worst errors of our predecessors.

Trends in Animal Research

Increased concern for animals, among scientists as well as the public, is changing the ways in which animals are used for research and safety testing

by Madhusree Mukerjee, *staff writer*

There is no question about it: the number of animals used in laboratory experiments is going down. In the U.K., the Netherlands, Germany and several other European countries, the total has fallen by half since the 1970s. In Canada, mammals have largely been replaced by fish. The figures for the U.S. are unclear. The U.S. uses between 18 and 22 million animals a year, but exact numbers are unknown for roughly 85 percent of these—rats, mice and birds. Primate use has stayed constant, whereas the use of dogs and cats is down by half since the 1970s.

No one reason accounts for the decline, but several factors are obvious. In 1975 the animal-rights movement exploded onto the scene with the publication of *Animal Liberation* by the Australian philosopher Peter Singer. The book's depiction of research, and a series of exposés by suddenly vigilant activists, threw a harsh spotlight on scientists. In the following years, public perceptions of animals became increasingly sympathetic. Dian Fossey, Jane Goodall and other ethologists related to an enthralled audience tales of love, sorrow, jealousy and deceit among primates. Although not so popular with scientists, such anthropomorphic views of animals fueled the passage of laws regulating experimentation.

And the scientists have changed. Those entering the biomedical profession in recent decades have imbibed at least some of the concerns of the movement, if not its ideals; many are willing to acknowledge the moral dilemmas of their craft. Some experiments that were applauded in the 1950s would not be done today, because they would be deemed to cause too much suffering. Oftentimes biotechnology is allowing test tubes to be substituted for animals. And a few researchers, cognizant that only their expertise can help reduce the need for animals, are avidly seeking alternatives. All these efforts are bearing fruit.

The Philosophers

The underlying force behind these changes appears to be society's evolving views of animals. These perceptions owe a great deal to philosophy and to science—and very little to religion. The Bible is unequivocal about the position of animals in the natural order: God made man in his image and gave him dominion over all other creatures. And although Hinduism and Buddhism envisage a hierarchy of organisms rather than a sharp division, their influence on the animal-rights movement is limited to vague inspiration and vegetarian recipes. The real roots lie in secular philosophy. In 1780 the English barrister Jeremy Bentham asked what "insuperable line" prevented humans from extending moral regard to animals: "The question is not, Can they reason? nor, Can they talk? but, Can they suffer?"

The question became more poignant in 1859 with the advent of Charles Darwin's theory of evolution. The theory provided a scientific rationale for using animals to learn about humans, and Darwin endorsed such use. But he also believed in an emotional continuum between humans and animals and was troubled by the suffering that experimentation could cause. This dichotomy inspired clashes between animal lovers and experimenters in 19th-century England, culminating in the 1876 British

The Evolution of Animal Use in Research

1822
British anticruelty act
introduced by Richard Martin
He later founded the RSPCA

1859
Charles Darwin
publishes the theory of evolution

1866
Henry Bergh
founds ASPCA in U.S.

1876
British Cruelty to Animals Act
regulates animal experimentation

1885
Louis Pasteur
develops rabies vaccine

Cruelty to Animals Act regulating animal experimentation. But the phenomenal success of medicine in the next century made the animal-protection movement recede into the background.

It rebounded in the 1970s, with Singer's attack. A philosopher in the utilitarian tradition of Bentham, Singer holds that in all decisions the total amount of good that results—human and animal—should be weighed against the suffering—human and animal—caused in the process. Not that to him the interests of humans and animals have equal weight: life is of far greater value to a human than, for example, to a creature with no self-awareness. But if there is something one would not do to, say, a severely incapacitated child, then neither should one do it to an animal that would suffer as much. Ignoring the interests of an animal just because it is not human is, to Singer, "speciesism," a sin akin to racism. Invoking the connections between humans and the great apes, Singer, Goodall and others have issued a call for these creatures, at least, to be freed from experimentation.

Although Singer started the modern animal-rights movement, it takes its name and its most uncompromising ideas from Tom Regan's *The Case for Animal Rights* (University of California Press, 1983). Regan believes that all humans and most animals have inherent rights, which he describes as invisible "no trespassing" signs hung around their necks. They state that our bodies may not be transgressed, no matter how much good might thereby result. Regan does not equate humans with animals—to save survivors in a lifeboat, a dog could be thrown overboard before a human would—yet he states that animals cannot be experimented on, because they are not merely means to an end.

Many other philosophers have lent their voices to the animals, but few have come to the aid of researchers. One who did so, Michael A. Fox, author of *The Case for Animal Experimentation* (University of California Press, 1986), later declared himself convinced by his critics and became an advocate for animals. Attempts to refute Singer and Regan usually involve pointing to morally relevant criteria that separate humans from animals. Raymond G. Frey of Bowling Green State University has written that animals cannot have interests, because they cannot have desires, because they cannot have beliefs, because they do not have language. Regan counters that a dog may well believe "that bone is tasty" without being able to formulate the phrase and that a human infant would never learn to speak unless it could acquire preverbal concepts to which it could later assign words, such as "ball."

Another supporter of research, Carl Cohen of the University of Michigan, has argued that rights are not inherent: they arise from implicit contracts among members of society, and they imply duties. Because animals cannot reciprocate such duties, they cannot have rights. This argument meets with the retort that infants and the mentally ill cannot fulfill such obligations either but are not left out of the realm of rights: Why omit animals? (One response is that human rights are based on characteristics of "typical" humans, not on borderline cases, prompting animal advocates to ask what these special qualities are—and so on and on.)

Some research proponents also note that nature is cruel: lions kill zebras, cats play with mice. Evolution has placed humans on top, so it is only natural for us to use other creatures. This argument, which some say elevates "survival of the fittest" to a moral philosophy, falls prey to a proposition called the naturalistic fallacy. To paraphrase the 18th-century philosopher David Hume, what "is" cannot dictate what "ought to be." So natural history may well illuminate why human morals evolved into their present form, but humans can transcend their nature. One animal advocate declares: "Killing and eating [meat] is an integral part of the evolution of human beings. Not killing and not eating [meat] is the next step in our evolution."

Many philosophers fall into the troubled middle, arguing for interests or rights to be ordered in a hierarchy that allows some uses of animals but bars others. Such distillations of animal-liberation ideas have been finding their way into legislation. The U.K., Australia, Germany and several other nations require a utilitarian cost-benefit analysis to be performed before an animal experiment can proceed. And in November 1996 the Netherlands passed into law the statement that animals have "intrinsic value": they are sentient beings, entitled to the moral concern of humans.

The Public

Not that, of course, all the Dutch are vegetarians. Rational argumentation may have influenced public opinion, but as Harold A. Herzog, Jr., a psychologist at Western Carolina University, remarks, the average person's stance on animal issues remains wildly inconsistent. In one survey, questions phrased in terms of rats yielded a far more pro-

1891
Diphtheria antitoxin produced

Tetanus antitoxin found

1951
Christine Stevens founds Animal Welfare Institute in U.S.

1952
Jonas Salk develops killed-virus polio vaccine

1953
Albert Sabin develops live, attenuated polio vaccine

1954
Humane Society of the U.S. founded

vivisection outcome than those mentioning dogs. Jesse L. Owens, a neuroscientist at the University of Alaska, protests that medical research is "the only use of animals that is essential" and like other researchers is bewildered by people who eat meat and in the same gulp condemn experimentation.

Not surprisingly, the animal-liberation movement has coincided with society's becoming increasingly distant from farms—and shielded from the reality behind dinner. Those who grew up on farms often see animals as objects to be used, whereas those who had pets tend to express more sympathy. One line along which attitudes divide is gender. In all countries surveyed, women are more pro-animal and antivivisectionist than men, and three quarters of American animal-rights activists are women. Also noticeable is a generation gap. Surveys by Stephen R. Kellert of Yale University find that those who are older or less educated are more likely to see animals as resources, whereas those who are younger or more educated tend to view animals with compassion.

Public support of animal experimentation, though higher in the U.S. than in Europe, has been slowly declining. In 1985, 63 percent of American respondents agreed that "scientists should be allowed to do research that causes pain and injury to animals like dogs and chimpanzees *if* it produces new information about human health problems"; in 1995, 53 percent agreed. Even in disciplines that have traditionally used animals, the trend is unmistakable. A survey by Scott Plous of Wesleyan University finds that psychologists with Ph.D.'s earned in the 1990s are half as likely to express strong support for animal research as those with Ph.D.'s from before 1970. (Part of this result comes from the increased presence of women, but there is a significant drop among men as well.)

Opposition to animal experimentation is often said to derive from antiscience sentiments, aggravated by poor public knowledge of science. But according to a 1994 survey led by Linda Pifer of the Chicago Academy of Sciences, negative attitudes toward animal experimentation in the U.S. correlate only weakly with lack of knowledge about science. And in Belgium, France and Italy, for instance, greater scientific literacy is connected with an increased rejection of animal experimentation.

Sociologists agree that opposition to vivisection derives primarily from sympathy for animals. Almost all animal rightists are vegetarians; many are "vegans," eschewing milk, eggs, leather and other animal products. "My philosophy of living as softly on the earth as I can is my life," one activist told Herzog. In striving to cause the least suffering possible, these individuals labor under a heavy moral burden that sits lightly on the rest of us. Some activists have indulged in threatening researchers, breaking into laboratories or even arson. But the number of such illegal acts, listed by the U.S. Department of Justice, dropped from about 50 a year in 1987 to 11 in 1992. (More recent figures are unavailable but are believed to be small.)

Many animal experimenters are also animal lovers. Surveys by Harold Takooshian, a sociologist at Fordham University, reveal that biomedical researchers have the same mixed feelings about animals and animal research as does the general public. (The groups that gave animals the lowest rating and vivisection the highest were farmers, hunters and the clergy.) Thomas M. Donnelly, a veterinarian at the Rockefeller University's animal center, also runs a shelter to which he takes cats that are no longer needed for research. Almost all the toxicologists and pharmacologists at a 1996 meeting on alternatives to animal experimentation had experience with using animals and were moved enough by it to seek substitutes. Scientists choose to use animals because they feel it is the only way to help humans. Donald Silver, who did cancer studies on mice at Sloan-Kettering Hospital in the 1970s, recounts that whenever he had doubts about his work, he had only to think about the terminally ill patients in the children's ward.

The Scientists

Of course, scientists' perceptions of animals have evolved as well. In the early 20th century Darwinian worries about emotions were dispelled by the rise of behaviorism. Because thoughts cannot be measured, but behavior can, practitioners such as C. Lloyd Morgan and, later, B. F. Skinner sought to describe animals purely in terms of their responses to stimuli. Bernard Rollin, author of *The Unheeded Cry* (Oxford University Press, 1989), argues that at some point, the animal psyche went from being impossible to measure to being nonexistent. The test of a good theory, "Morgan's canon," required all actions to be interpreted in terms of the lowest psychological faculties possible. In practice, this meant that a rat would not be feeling pain even if its "writhes per minute" were being used to test the efficacy of an analgesic. Its neurochemistry was

1959
William M. S. Russell and Rex L. Burch state **three Rs** of animal experimentation

1966
Animal Welfare Act (AWA) passed in the U.S.

1969
Dorothy Hegarty founds Fund for the Replacement of Animals in Medical Experiments in U.K.

1970
Amendments to AWA cover warm-blooded animals and require pain relief

1975
Peter Singer publishes animal-liberation philosophy

merely inducing a physiological reflex.

"We were taught as undergraduates not to think of animals as other than stimulus-response bundles," asserts Melanie Stiassney, an ichthyologist at the American Museum of Natural History. "The dogma is you can't credit them with feelings." In turn, it is often thought undesirable for a researcher to have feelings about the animal under study: emotions can impair professional judgment and also make it hard to perform certain procedures. Arnold Arluke, a sociologist at Northeastern University who studied animal laboratories from 1985 to 1993, reports that some technicians were deeply disturbed when a playful dog or a roomful of mice had to be put down. Such distress was officially discouraged and therefore kept secret. But after being "burned" by the death of a favorite animal, laboratory workers learned to avoid emotional connections with the creatures.

The resulting dissociation, which is often likened to that of a surgeon from a patient, allows a researcher to function with a minimum of stress. But given the emotional separation, a scientist may not realize when an animal is in pain—especially if the very existence of pain is in doubt. Nowadays, many researchers are aware of dissociation and seek objective ways to detect distress. And animal pain has come into its own. At a 1996 meeting on the *Guide to the Care and Use of Laboratory Animals*—a collection of guidelines that all researchers funded by the National Institutes of Health have to follow—veterinarian Gerald F. Gebhart of the University of Iowa stated that the pain-sensing apparatus is the same throughout the vertebrate kingdom and offered this rule of thumb: "If it hurts you, it probably hurts the animal."

Increasingly, animal experimenters try to balance scientific imperatives with humaneness. Keith A. Reimann, a veterinarian at Harvard University's animal facility, does AIDS-related research in monkeys. He insists that a macaque be euthanized as soon as it becomes sick, even if additional information might be gained by following the course of the illness. Franz P. Gruber of the University of Konstanz in Germany, who serves on a board overseeing animal experimentation, says his committee does not allow "death as an end point"—studies in which the animal dies of the disease or procedure being studied. Instead the committee works with the researcher to define a stage at which the creature can be put out of its misery.

One area of concern to American veterinarians involves paralytic drugs. These agents immobilize an animal for surgery, for six or more hours at a time; anesthesia, however, may wear off in an hour or two. A few researchers are reportedly reluctant to administer additional anesthetics for fear that an overdose could kill the animal before the experiment is over, leading to a loss of data. But without such "topping up," the animal may become conscious during the operation and not be able to convey, by twitch or cry, that it is in agony. And some scientists object to using painkillers because they do not want to introduce a new variable into the experiment.

Compassionate feelings for animals also influence studies, although researchers rarely admit to such unscientific, if creditable, motivations. When asked about their choice of species subjects, for example, three neuroscientists—working on monkeys, rats and frogs, respectively—replied unhesitatingly that it was determined by the scientific question at hand. But later in the conversation, the frog experimenter confided that he, personally, could not work on "a furry animal," and the rat experimenter said he would not work with a cat or even with a rat in a more painful protocol.

The Three Rs

Scientists' concern for animals first became visible professionally in the 1950s, when the behavioristic paradigm came under attack. British zoologist William M. S. Russell and microbiologist Rex L. Burch published *The Principles of Humane Experimental Technique* (Methuen, London, 1959), in which they put forth the "three Rs." This principle sets out three goals for the conscientious researcher: replacement of animals by in vitro, or test-tube, methods; reduction of their numbers by means of statistical techniques; and refinement of the experiment so as to cause less suffering. Although they took some decades to catch on, the three Rs define the modern search for alternatives.

Starting in the 1960s, humane organizations and governments began to fund studies in alternative methods. European governments, especially, have invested considerable resources. For the past 15 years, Germany has been giving out about $6 million a year in research grants alone; the Netherlands spends $2 million a year (including overheads for its alternatives center). The European Center for the Validation of Alternative Methods, a body set up in 1992 by the European Commission, requires another $9 million annually. In the U.S., governmental interest has been com-

1981
Center for Alternatives to Animal Testing founded in U.S.

1985
Amendments to AWA result from Silver Spring, Md., and Pennsylvania primate exposés

1992
European Center for the Validation of Alternative Methods founded

1993
First World Congress on Alternatives held in the U.S.

1996
Second World Congress on Alternatives held in the Netherlands

paratively low; the National Institute of Environmental Health Sciences (NIEHS) is now offering $1.5 million worth of grants a year, for three years. And industry provides the $1 million a year that the Center for Alternatives to Animal Testing (CAAT) at Johns Hopkins University disburses in grants. (Although 15 federal agencies have recently formed the Interagency Coordinating Committee for Validation of Alternative Methods, this venture is as yet unfunded.)

All this effort has yielded a variety of means for reducing animal use. Statistical sophistry, for example, is allowing the classical LD50 (or lethal dose 50 percent) test for acute toxicity to be eliminated. This test requires up to 200 rats, dogs or other animals to be force-fed different amounts of a substance, to determine the dose that will kill half a group. Although in vitro alternatives are still far away—because the mechanisms underlying toxicity are poorly understood—protocols currently accepted worldwide call for a tenth the number of animals. The Organization for Economic Cooperation and Development, for example, asks for between three and 18 animals to be used: if the substance kills the first three, it need be tested no further.

Another unpleasant procedure is the LD80 test for vaccines. Experimental animals are vaccinated against a disease; they and a control group are then exposed to it. The vaccine passes only if at least 80 percent of the experimental group remains healthy and if 80 percent of the control group dies. Again using statistics, Coenraad Hendriksen of the National Institute of Public Health and the Environment in the Netherlands found a way of testing diphtheria and tetanus vaccines that requires simply checking the level of antibodies. Apart from greatly reducing the suffering, it uses half the number of animals.

"Data mining"—the sifting of mountains of information for relevant new findings—has also proved astonishingly helpful. Horst Spielmann of ZEBET, the German center for alternatives to animal testing, surveyed decades of industry data on pesticides and concluded that if mice and rats prove sensitive to a chemical, it does not have to be tested on dogs. Spielmann anticipates that 70 percent of the dog tests can be dispensed with. Klaus Cussler of the Paul Ehrlich Institute in Langen, Germany, reviewed data on the "abnormal safety test" for vaccines (called the "mouse and guinea pig safety test" in the U.S.), which involves vaccinating mice and guinea pigs and watching for untoward reactions. Their findings led to the test being dropped for vaccines checked in other standard ways. "It was so senseless," Cussler shakes his head.

In 1989, after observing that production of monoclonal antibodies in mice with tumors causes much suffering, ZEBET funded industry research into test-tube alternatives. Consequently, the antibodies, used in cancer therapy, are now rarely manufactured in mice in Europe (although mice remain the norm in the U.S.). Production of polio vaccines is another success story. In the 1970s the Netherlands used 5,000 monkeys a year; now kidney cell cultures from just 10 monkeys provide enough vaccine for everyone. Hormones or vaccines manufactured in cell cultures are also purer than those made in vivo (that is, in the animals themselves), so each batch need not be tested as before for safety and efficacy.

In 1993 the Department of Transportation became the first U.S. agency to accept in vitro tests, for skin corrosivity. The traditional test requires placing a substance on a rabbit's shaved back to see how far it eats in. The test's replacement uses reconstructed human skin or a biomembrane such as Corrositex—testimony to the role played by venture capital in finding alternatives. Several cosmetics manufacturers have entirely eliminated animal testing: they rely on in-house substitutes or use ingredients that have been tested in the past.

As yet, most researchers in the basic sciences see little hope of replacing animals. They stick to reduction or refinement, such as using an animal lower on the phylogenetic tree. The next spate of cuts in animal use, Spielmann predicts, will come in the field of medical education, for which alternative teaching tools have been devised. British surgeons, in fact, have not trained on animals since the 1876 act banned such use; instead they practice on human cadavers and later assist experienced surgeons in actual operations. In the U.S., more than 40 of the 126 medical schools do not use animals in their regular curricula.

The most significant change has been in mind-set. Since 1985 in the Netherlands, every scientist starting research on animals has been required to take a three-week course. They learn hands-on procedures, proper anesthesia, specifications of inbred strains and so on—as well as the three Rs. First the students design an animal experiment; then they are asked to find ways of answering the same question without animals. The resulting discussion and hunt for information induces a new way of thinking. "It gives them time for reflection," says Bert F. M. van Zutphen of Utrecht University, who pioneered the course. "It's of utmost importance. To know how far I can go for my own conscience."

The Laws

Another source of change in scientists' attitudes has been legislation. In the U.S., laws tend to derive from isolated incidents. The Animal Welfare Act of 1966—the federal law regulating animal use—came into being because of Pepper, a Dalmatian believed by its owners to have been stolen and sold to a lab, and a *Life* magazine article depicting starving dogs in dealers' pens. Perhaps the most significant change came in 1985, in the wake of two exposés involving primates. In Silver Spring, Md., macaques belonging to Edward Taub of the Institute for Behavioral Research were found to be chewing on their limbs, to which the nerves had been cut. And in 1984 videotapes from the University of Pennsylvania Medical Center displayed laboratory personnel mocking baboons whose heads had been smashed in during experiments on head trauma. The outcry following these revelations allowed Senator Robert Dole of Kansas to bring an amendment to the act. It established institutional animal care and use committees (IACUCs) at each facility using regulated animals and required laboratories to exercise dogs and to ensure the psychological well-being of primates.

The "well-being" clause can be considered an instance of the public's imposing a scientific paradigm on scientists. An inspector from the U.S. Department of Agriculture, which administers the Animal Welfare Act, sought expert advice at that time on primate psychology. There was no such thing, he was told. Now, just 10 years later, primates have emotions. At the 1996 NIH meeting, Gebhart listed fear, anxiety, boredom, separation and isolation as conditions to which experimenters should attend in their subjects. And a few labs are even trying to enrich the lives of their rabbits.

The laws have generally had the effect of driving up the costs of animal re-

The Numbers of Research Animals

Use of animals in European laboratories has been slowly declining (*a*). In the U.S., the available statistics (*b*) include primates, dogs, cats, guinea pigs, rabbits, hamsters and others but exclude rats, mice and birds—an estimated 17 million additional animals per year. Primate use is roughly constant, although the numbers of cats and dogs (*c*) is declining. (In many instances, dogs are being replaced by pigs, calves and other farm animals. These have been counted since 1990 but are not included in the chart.) The National Institutes of Health supports research into invertebrate models (*d*); however, funding has been increasing more steeply for vertebrate (and human) studies. In Canada, animal numbers (*e*) have hovered at around two million a year, but fish have replaced mammals in many areas, especially toxicology.

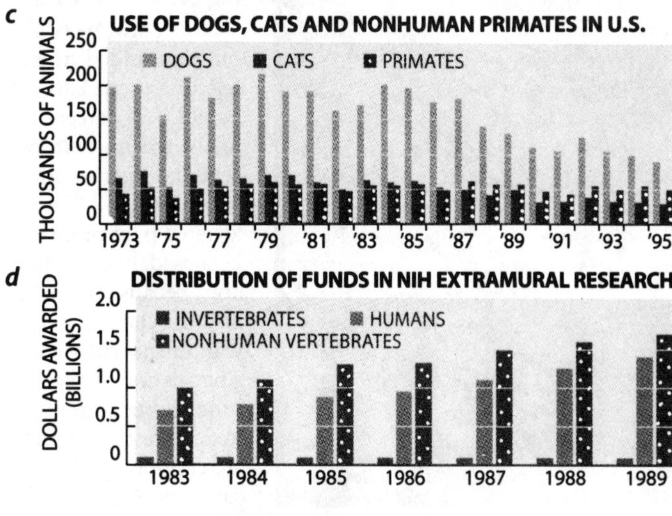

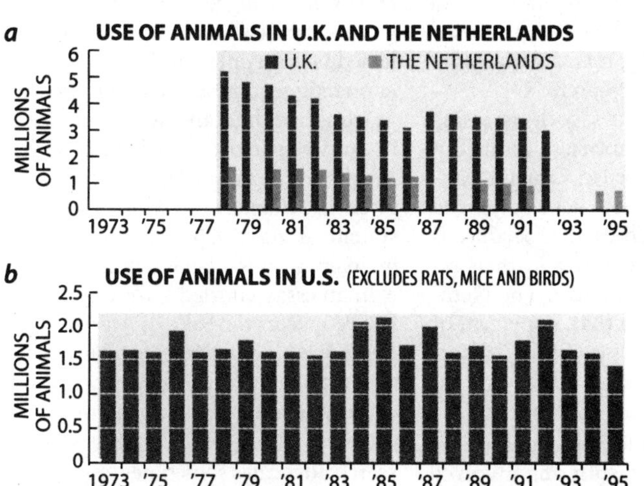

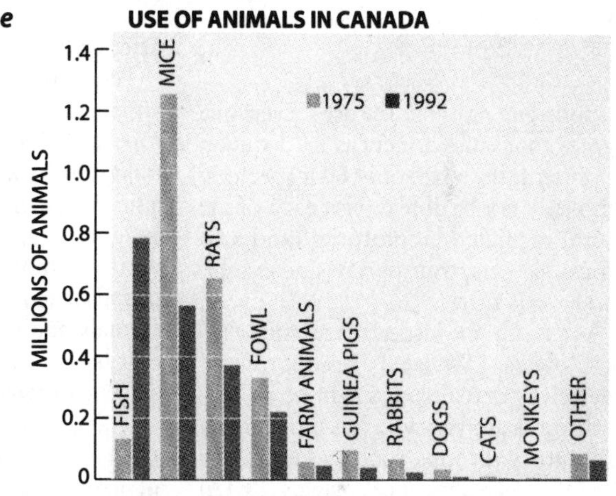

BRYAN CHRISTIE; SOURCES: USDA (*a–c*); NATIONAL CENTER FOR RESEARCH RESOURCES, NIH (*d*); CANADIAN COUNCIL ON ANIMAL CARE (*e*)

search. Animal protectionists complain, however, that the Animal Welfare Act and its amendments invariably get diluted at the implementation stage. The act, for instance, refers to warm-blooded animals, but the regulations written by the USDA exclude rats, mice and birds. The agency says it does not have funds for inspecting the laboratories that use these creatures, which is true; animal welfarists, however, say the omission originally came from lobbying by the biomedical community. In 1990 humane organizations sued to have these animals included. Although they initially won, the suit was thrown out on appeal, on the grounds that animal protectionists have no legal standing: only those who are injured—that is, the rats, mice and birds—can bring a civil suit. Dale Schwindaman of the USDA has promised, however, to include these animals within the next five years.

Another controversy has to do with so-called performance standards. When writing regulations for the 1985 amendments, the USDA refrained, for example, from stating how many times a week the dogs had to be walked. Such specifics are referred to as engineering standards. Instead the agency allowed each facility to come up with its own plans for dog and primate well-being, the "performance" of which was to be evaluated. (Because these plans are kept in-house, and not with the USDA, the public cannot obtain them through the Freedom of Information Act.)

Researchers are enthusiastic about the flexibility of performance standards, whereas Martin L. Stephens of the Humane Society of the U.S. calls them "euphemisms for no standards." USDA inspectors are divided. Some argue that the standards are vague and unenforceable. Among others, Harvey McKelvey of the USDA's northwestern region says they let him use his judgment: "If I see an animal is bored with its toy, I can write that it needs a new one. I couldn't do that with engineering standards." The new NIH guide also embraces performance standards.

The animal care committees have empowered those scientists who wish to cut down on wastage and improve conditions for animals. "If you have an institution with conscientious people, the IACUC system works fairly well," says Ralph A. Meyer of Carolinas Medical Center. Cathy Liss of the Animal Welfare Institute in Washington, D.C., agrees that some committees do far better than the law. But there is concern about the remainder. In 1992 an audit of the USDA's enforcement activities by the Office of the Inspector General revealed that out of 26 institutions selected at random, 12 "were not adequately fulfilling their

PETA

ANTIVIVISECTION POSTER attacks the rationales behind animal research.

responsibilities under the act." Everyone agrees that enforcement is inadequate: at present, there are only 69 inspectors, who may not be able to visit each of the 1,300 regulated laboratories (and also animal dealers, transporters and exhibitors) every year.

As a result, the inspectors rely on whistle-blowers. "We need eyes out there," McKelvey explains. It might be an animal-rights activist who has infiltrated a laboratory: groups such as People for the Ethical Treatment of Animals (PETA) prepare detailed case histories that they present to the USDA or the NIH. Or it might be a researcher or technician.

Still, the USDA can offer few reassurances to informants. A former member of the animal care committee at New York University Medical Center claims to have been fired in August 1995 for protesting irregularities in N.Y.U.'s labs and cooperating with the USDA's investigations. The university states that his position became redundant. But the scientist, along with an administrator who was also dismissed, is suing N.Y.U., as well as the USDA—which, he says, failed to provide whistle-blower protection. (The agency did fine N.Y.U. $450,000 for assorted violations of the Animal Welfare Act.) Several USDA inspectors express frustration with their agency's provisions on informants. "We can't protect a whistle blower," McKelvey says. "The regulation is weak." Unlike civil-discrimination suits, which require only a concatenation of circumstances, the USDA needs to prove that the person was fired because of having blown the whistle.

Also controversial are the statistics on pain and distress provided by the IACUCs to the USDA. They indicate that in 1995, 54 percent of the regulated animals had no pain or distress, 37 percent had distress alleviated by painkillers, and only 8.8 percent suffered unalleviated pain or distress. The data have been widely criticized for being unreliable, because the USDA does not specify how to classify pain. Andrew N. Rowan of the Tufts University Center for Animals and Public Policy has noted that some rather painful procedures, such as toxicity testing or antibody production, are commonly placed in the nonpainful category. Although the USDA proposed a pain scale in 1987, it was withdrawn after objections by researchers.

There are difficulties with assessing animal distress. Nevertheless, many European nations, as well as Canada, Australia and New Zealand, have developed pain scales in which each procedure is assigned a grade. As a result, their reports are more informative. The Netherlands listed in 1995 that 54 percent of animals had minor discomfort, 26 percent had moderate discomfort, and 20 percent suffered severe discomfort.

A pain scale would make it easier for IACUCs to rate the suffering involved in different schemes for doing an experiment. At present, the committees are required to certify that the animal researcher has looked for alternatives and that the number of animals used is reasonable. Alan M. Goldberg of CAAT wishes that they would also evaluate the experimental design. "Right now, using method A, they check: Is it the right number of animals? They don't look at method B or C"—which could involve in vitro techniques. Nor—unlike committees in Germany, Australia and elsewhere—are they required to weigh the benefits of research against the suffering or to include representatives of animal-welfare organizations in the review process. (The IACUCs do have to include someone unaffiliated with the institution, but who fills that position is again a source of controversy.)

The Propaganda

Change in the U.S. has been slow and painful. Notwithstanding some evolution of practices, the ferocity of the attacks by the most fervent animal rightists has led to a sense of moral outrage and an unwillingness to compromise—on both sides. Almost all activists insist that animal research is unnecessary; to them, investigators using animals are cruel and corrupt, consumed by a desire for ever more papers and grants. One antivivisection tract is entitled *Slaughter of the Innocent,* and the cover of another features splashes of blood. To animal liberators, the killing of more than six billion animals a year, mostly for food, represents a holocaust, and Adolf Hitler's doctors are proof that experimenters can be inhumane.

Many animal researchers, in turn, think of animal rightists as being brainless "bunny huggers" at best and dangerous fanatics at worst. Leaflets published by the American Medical Association represent the animal-rights position as equating humans with animals; a quote from Ingrid Newkirk of PETA, "A rat is a pig is a dog is a boy," is offered as evidence. (Newkirk claims her statement was "When it comes to feeling pain, a rat is a pig is a dog is a boy.")

In an essay entitled "We Can't Sacrifice People for the Sake of Animal Life," Frederick K. Goodwin, former head of the National Institute of Mental Health, has argued that the issue of animal rights threatens public health. In this vein, research advocates sometimes portray proposals to control animal research as being attacks on human life. For instance, one organization advises this response to a query about experimentation on pound animals: "How would you feel if the one research project that may save your child's life was priced out of existence because pound animals were banned?" Some writers invoke Hitler as proof that animal advocates are antihuman: he was an animal lover who passed anticruelty laws in 1930s Germany.

Finding itself under moral—and sometimes physical—siege, the research community has often retreated behind electronic surveillance systems—and an ethical code that frequently denounces internal dissent as treason, "giving ammunition to the enemy." One scientist interviewed for this article said that if his criticisms became known, he would be fired. In 1991 two animal researchers, John P. Gluck and Steven R. Kubacki of the University of New Mexico, wrote a treatise deploring the lack of ethical introspection in their field. Gluck testifies that the article quickly changed his status from an insider to a distrusted outsider. Arluke's studies revealed an absence of discussion about ethics: in 33 of 35 laboratories, moral positions were defined institutionally. Newcomers were given to understand that senior scientists had answered all the difficult questions, leaving them little to worry about.

The insulation has made it difficult for changes in other branches of the life sciences—or from across the Atlantic—to filter in. Primatologists, for instance, have been discussing complex emotions in their subjects for decades. But many American experimenters still refuse to use the word "suffering," because it suggests an animal has awareness. Even the word "alternatives" is suspect; instead the NIH describes these as "adjuncts" or "complements" to animal research. Some researchers seem to regard the three Rs as an animal-rights conspiracy. Robert Burke of the NIH has stated: "To argue that we must refine our methods suggests that they are currently inadequate or unethical.... In my view, it is intellectually dishonest and hypocritical to continue to advocate the original three Rs as a goal for science policy. It is also, without question, dangerous to give our enemies such useful tools with which to pervert the scientific enterprise."

Of the 17 institutes included in the NIH, only the NIEHS has been active in researching alternatives. Following a directive by Congress, the NIH awarded about $2.5 million in earmarked grants between 1987 and 1989. But F. Barbara Orlans of the Kennedy Institute of Ethics at Georgetown University charges that the money did not constitute a special allocation for alternatives: 16 of the 17 grants went to studies that had traditionally been funded. (Like other public health agencies worldwide the NIH supports research into invertebrate, in vitro and computer models that are not billed as alternatives.)

In 1993 Congress directed the NIH to come up with a plan for implementing the three Rs. The resulting document, entitled "Plan for the Use of Animals in Research," is an overview of biomedical models, with some emphasis on nonmammalian systems. "The central message of the plan," explains Louis Sibal of the NIH, "is that scientists have to decide for themselves what the best method of solving their problem is." Whereas the European Union plans to cut animal use in half by the year 2000, a 1989 NIH report stated that animal use is not likely to decrease.

One arena in which the propaganda battles have been especially fierce is the classroom: both sides see dissection as the key to the next generation's sympathies. Animal advocates say dissection in schools is unnecessary and brutalizing and that the 5.7 million vertebrates (mostly wild frogs, but also cats, fetal pigs, pigeons and perch) used every year are procured in inhumane ways. Research advocates fear that without dissection, instruction will be inadequate, and fewer students will be attracted to or equipped for the life sciences.

In 1989, when the National Association of Biology Teachers (NABT) announced a new policy encouraging alternatives, it provoked a violent reaction. Barbara Bentley of the State University of New York at Stony Brook, for instance, denounced the monograph on implementing the policy as "an insidiously evil publication—evil because it is a barely disguised tract produced by animal rightists." An intense campaign followed, and in 1993 the NABT issued a new policy statement, warning teachers to "be aware of the limitations of alternatives." There is no high school dissection in most European countries.

"It is possible to be both pro research and pro reform," Orlans says. She and others in the troubled middle have a simple message: the impasse must end. Animal liberators need to accept that animal research is beneficial to humans. And animal researchers need to admit that if animals are close enough to humans that their bodies, brains and even psyches are good models for the human condition, then ethical dilemmas surely arise in using them. But the moral burden is not for scientists alone to bear. All of us who use modern medicine and modern consumer products need to acknowledge the debt we owe to our fellow creatures and support science in its quest to do better by the animals.

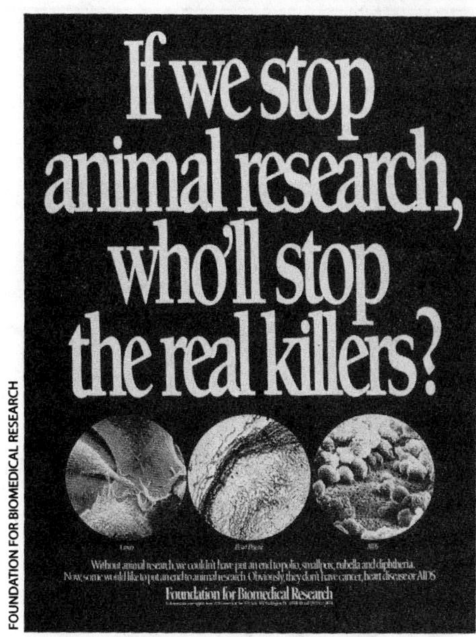

MEDICAL NECESSITY of animal experiments is emphasized in a pro-research poster.

FOUNDATION FOR BIOMEDICAL RESEARCH

Further Reading

IN THE NAME OF SCIENCE: ISSUES IN RESPONSIBLE ANIMAL EXPERIMENTATION. F. Barbara Orlans. Oxford University Press, 1993.

THE MONKEY WARS. Deborah Blum. Oxford University Press, 1994.

THE ANIMAL RESEARCH CONTROVERSY: PROTEST, PROCESS AND PUBLIC POLICY. Andrew N. Rowan and Franklin M. Loew, with Joan C. Weer. Center for Animals and Public Policy, Tufts University School of Veterinary Medicine, 1995.

More coverage of the animal-rights debate is available on-line at http://www.sciam.com

POLITICS OF BIOLOGY

How the nature vs. nurture debate shapes public policy—and our view of ourselves

BY WRAY HERBERT

Laurie Flynn uses the technology of neuroscience to light up the brains of Washington lawmakers. As executive director of the National Alliance for the Mentally Ill, she marshals everything from cost analysis to moral pleading to make the case for laws banning discrimination against people with mental illness. But her most powerful advocacy tool by far is the PET scan. She takes a collection of these colorful brain images up to Capitol Hill to put on a show, giving lawmakers a window on a "broken" brain in action. "When they see that it's not some imaginary, fuzzy problem, but a real physical condition, then they get it: 'Oh, it's in the brain'."

The view of mental illness as a brain disease has been crucial to the effort to destigmatize illnesses such as schizophrenia and depression. But it's just one example of a much broader biologizing of American culture that's been going on for more than a decade. For both political and scientific reasons—and it's often impossible to disentangle the two—everything from criminality to addictive disorders to sexual orientation is seen today less as a matter of choice than of genetic destiny. Even basic personality is looking more and more like a genetic legacy. Nearly every week there is a report of a new gene for one trait or another. Novelty seeking, religiosity, shyness, the tendency to divorce, and even happiness (or the lack of it) are among the traits that may result in part from a gene, according to new research.

This cultural shift has political and personal implications. On the personal level, a belief in the power of genes necessarily diminishes the potency of such personal qualities as will, capacity to choose, and sense of responsibility for those choices—if it's in your genes, you're not accountable. It allows the alcoholic, for example, to treat himself as a helpless victim of his biology rather than as a willful agent with control of his own behavior. Genetic determinism can free victims and their families of guilt—or lock them in their suffering.

On the political level, biological determinism now colors all sorts of public-policy debates on issues such as gay rights, health care, juvenile justice, and welfare reform. The effort to dismantle social programs is fueled by the belief that government interventions (the nurturing side in the nature-nurture debate) don't work very well—and the corollary idea that society can't make up for every unfortunate citizen's bad luck. It's probably no coincidence that the biologizing of culture has accompanied the country's shift to the political right, since conservatives traditionally are more dubious about human perfectability than are liberals. As Northeastern University psychologist Leon Kamin notes, the simplest way to discover someone's political leanings is to ask his or her view on genetics.

Even so, genetic determinism can have paradoxical consequences at times, leading to disdain rather than sympathy for the disadvantaged, and marginalization rather than inclusion. Cultural critics are beginning to sort out the unpredictable politics of biology, focusing on four traits: violence, mental illness, alcoholism, and sexual orientation.

The nature of violence. To get a sense of just how thorough—and how politicized—the biologizing of culture has been, just look at the issue of urban gang violence as it is framed today. A few years ago, Frederick Goodwin, then director of the government's top mental health agency, was orchestrating the so-called Federal Violence Initiative to identify inner-city kids at biological risk for criminal violence, with the goal of intervening with drug treatments for what are presumed to be nervous-system aberrations. Goodwin got himself fired for comparing aggressive young males with primates in the jungle, and the violence initiative died in the resulting furor. But even to be proposing such a biomedical approach to criminal justice shows how far the intellectual pendulum has swung toward biology.

The eugenics movement of the 1930s was fueled at least in part by a desire to get rid of habitual criminals, and many attempts have been made over the years to identify genetic roots for aggression, violence, and criminality. A 1965 study, for instance, found that imprisoned criminals were more likely than other people to have an extra Y chromosome (and therefore more male genes). The evidence linking this chromosomal aberration to crime was skimpy and tenuous, but politics often runs ahead of the evidence: Soon after, a Boston hospital actually started screening babies for the defect, the idea being to intervene early with counseling should personality problems become apparent. The screening was halted when further study showed that XYY men, while slightly less intelligent, were not unusually aggressive.

As with many psychopathologies, criminal aggression is difficult to define precisely for research. Indeed, crime and alcohol abuse are so entangled that it's often difficult to know whether genetic markers are associated with drinking, criminality—or something else entirely, like a personality trait. A 1993 National Research Council study, for example, reported strong evidence of genetic influence on antisocial personality disorder, but it also noted that many genes are probably involved. Getting from those unknown genes to an actual act of vandalism or assault—or a life of barbaric violence—requires at this point a monstrous leap of faith.

Yet it's a leap that many are willing to make. When geneticist Xandra Breakefield reported a possible genetic link to violent crime a few years ago, she immediately started receiving phone inquiries from attorneys representing clients in prison; they were hoping that such genetic findings might absolve their clients of culpability for their acts.

Mutations and emotions. Just two decades ago, the National Institute of Mental Health was funding studies of economic recession, unemployment, and urban ills as possible contributors to serious emotional disturbance. A whole branch of psychiatry known as "social psychiatry" was dedicated to helping the mentally ill by rooting out such pathogens as poverty and racism. There is no longer much evidence of these sensibilities at work today. NIMH now focuses its studies almost exclusively on brain research and on the genetic underpinnings of emotional illnesses.

The decision to reorder the federal research portfolio was both scientific and political. Major advances in neuroscience methods opened up research that wasn't possible a generation ago, and that research has paid off in drugs that very effectively treat some disorders. But there was also a concerted political campaign to reinterpret mental illness. A generation ago, the leading theory about schizophrenia was that this devastating emotional and mental disorder was caused by cold and distant mothering, itself the result of the mother's unconscious wish that her child had never been born. A nationwide lobbying effort was launched to combat such unfounded mother blaming, and 20 years later that artifact of the Freudian era is entirely discredited. It's widely accepted today that psychotic disorders are brain disorders, probably with genetic roots.

But this neurogenetic victory may be double edged. For example, family and consumer groups have argued convincingly that schizophrenia is a brain disease like epilepsy, one

VIOLENCE. How can an act of vandalism or a bank robbery be rooted in DNA? There are a lot of choices involved in living a life of crime.

piece of evidence being that it is treatable with powerful antipsychotic drugs. Managed-care companies, however, have seized upon the disease model, and now will rarely authorize anything but drug treatment; it's efficient, and justified by the arguments of biological psychiatry. The American Psychiatric Association just this month issued elaborate guidelines for treating schizophrenia, including not only drugs but an array of psychosocial services—services the insurance industry is highly unlikely to pay for.

The search for genes for severe mental disorders has been inconclusive. Years of studies of families, adoptees, and twins separated at birth suggest that both schizophrenia and manic-depressive illness run in families. But if that family pattern is the result of genes, it's clearly very complicated, because most of the siblings of schizophrenics (including half of identical twins, who have the same genes) don't develop the disorder. Behavioral geneticists suspect that several genes may underlie the illness, and that some environmental stress—perhaps a virus or birth complications—also might be required to trigger the disorder.

On several occasions in the past, researchers have reported "linkages" between serious mental illness and a particular stretch of DNA. A well-known study of the Amish, for example, claimed a link between manic-depression and an aberration on chromosome 11. But none of these findings has held up when other researchers attempted to replicate them.

Even if one accepts that there are genetic roots for serious delusional illnesses, critics are concerned about the biologizing of the rest of psychiatric illness. Therapists report that patients come in asking for drugs, claiming to be victims of unfortunate biology. In one case, a patient claimed he could "feel his neurons misfiring"; it's an impossibility, but the anecdote speaks to the thorough saturation of the culture with biology.

Some psychiatrists are pulling back from the strict biological model of mental illness. Psychiatrist Keith Russell Ablow has reintroduced the idea of "character" into his practice, telling depressed patients that they have the responsibility and capacity to pull themselves out of their illness. Weakness of character, as Ablow sees it, allows mental illness to grow. Such sentiment is highly controversial within psychiatry, where to suggest that patients might be responsible for some of their own suffering is taboo.

Besotted genes. The best that can be said about research on the genetics of alcoholism is that it's inconclusive, but that hasn't stopped people from using genetic arguments for political purposes. The disease model for alcoholism is practically a secular religion in this country, embraced by psychiatry, most treatment clinics, and (perhaps most important) by Alcoholics Anonymous. What this means is that those seeking help for excessive drinking are told they have a disease (though the exact nature of the disease is unknown), that it's probably a genetic condition, and that the only treatment is abstinence.

But the evidence is not strong enough to support these claims. There are several theories of how genes might lead to excessive drinking. A genetic insensitivity to alcohol, for example, might cause certain people to drink more; or alcoholics might metabolize alcohol differently; or they may have inherited a certain personality type that's prone to risk-taking or stimulus-seeking. While studies of family pedigrees and adoptees have on occasion indicated a familial pattern for a particular form of alcoholism (early-onset disorder in men, for example), just as often they reveal no pattern. This shouldn't be all that surprising, given the difficulty of defining alcoholism. Some researchers identify alcoholics by their drunk-driving record, while others focus on withdrawal symptoms or daily consumption. This is what geneticists call a "dirty phenotype"; people drink too much in so many different ways that the trait itself is hard to define, so family patterns are all over the place, and often contradictory.

Given these methodological problems, researchers have been trying to locate an actual gene (or genes) that might be involved in alcoholism. A 1990 study reported that a severe form of the disorder (most of the subjects in the study had cirrhosis of the liver) was linked to a gene that codes for a chemical receptor for the neurotransmitter dopamine. The researchers even developed and patented a test for the genetic mutation, but subsequent attempts to confirm the dopamine connection have failed.

The issues of choice and responsibility come up again and again in discussions of alcoholism and other addictive disorders. Even if scientists were to identify a gene (or genes) that create a susceptibility to alcoholism, it's hard to know what this genetic "loading" would mean. It certainly wouldn't lead to alcoholism in a culture that didn't condone drinking—among the Amish, for example—so it's not deterministic in a strict sense. Even in a culture where drinking is common, there are clearly a lot of complicated choices involved in living an alcoholic life; it's difficult to make the leap from DNA to those choices. While few would want to return to the time when heavy drinking was condemned as strictly a moral failing or character flaw, many are concerned that the widely accepted disease model of alcoholism actually provides people with an excuse for their destructive behavior. As psychologist Stanton Peele argues: "Indoctrinating young people with the view that

MENTAL ILLNESS. Are psychiatric disorders diseases? The answer influences everything from insurance coverage to new research funding.

they are likely to become alcoholics may take them there more quickly than any inherited reaction to alcohol would have."

Synapses of desire. It would be a mistake to focus only on biological explanations of psychopathology; the cultural shift is much broader than that. A generation ago, the gay community was at war with organized psychiatry, arguing (successfully) that sexual orientation was a lifestyle choice and ought to be deleted from the manual of disorders. Recently the same community was celebrating new evidence that homosexuality is a biological (and perhaps genetic) trait, not a choice at all.

Three lines of evidence support the idea of a genetic basis for homosexuality, none of them conclusive. A study of twins and adopted siblings found that about half of identical twins of homosexual men were themselves gay, compared with 22 percent of fraternal twins and 11 percent of adoptees; a similar pattern was found among women. While such a pattern is consistent with some kind of genetic loading for sexual orientation, critics contend it also could be explained by the very similar experiences many twins share. And, of course, half the identical twins did not become gay—which by definition means something other than genes must be involved.

A well-publicized 1991 study reported a distinctive anatomical feature in gay men. Simon LeVay autopsied the brains of homosexual men and heterosexual men and women and found that a certain nucleus in the hypothalamus was more than twice as large in heterosexual men as in gay men or heterosexual women. Although LeVay couldn't explain how this neurological difference might translate into homosexuality, he speculates that the nucleus is somehow related to sexual orientation. The hypothalamus is known to be involved in sexual response.

The only study so far to report an actual genetic connection to homosexuality is a 1993 study by Dean Hamer, a National Institutes of Health biologist who identified a genetic marker on the X chromosome in 75 percent of gay brothers. The functional significance of this piece of DNA is unknown, and subsequent research has not succeeded in duplicating Hamer's results.

Homosexuality represents a bit of a paradox when it comes to the intertwined issues of choice and determinism. When Hamer reported his genetic findings, many in the gay community celebrated, believing that society would be more tolerant of behavior rooted in biology and DNA rather than choice. LeVay, himself openly gay, says he undertook his research with the explicit agenda of furthering the gay cause. And Hamer testified as an expert witness in an important gay-rights case in Colorado where, in a strange twist, liberals found themselves arguing the deterministic position, while conservatives insisted that homosexuality is a choice. The argument of gay-rights advocates was that biological status conveyed legal status—and protection under the law.

History's warning. But history suggests otherwise, according to biologist and historian Garland Allen. During the eugenics movement of the 1920s and 1930s, both in the United States and Europe, society became less, not more, tolerant of human variation and misfortune. Based on racial theories that held Eastern Europeans to be genetically inferior to Anglo-Saxon stock, Congress passed (and Calvin Coolidge signed) a 1924 law to restrict immigration, and by 1940 more than 30 states had laws permitting forced sterilization of people suffering from such conditions as "feeblemindedness," pauperism, and mental illness. The ultimate outcome of the eugenics craze in Europe is well known; homosexuals were not given extra sympathy or protection in the Third Reich's passion to purify genetic stock.

Allen is concerned about the possibility of a "new eugenics" movement, though he notes that it wouldn't be called that or take the same form. It would more likely take the form of rationing health care for the unfortunate. The economic and social conditions today resemble conditions that provided fertile ground for eugenics between the wars, he argues; moreover, in Allen's view, California's Proposition 187 recalls the keen competition for limited resources (and the resulting animosity toward immigrants) of the '20s. Further, Allen is quick to remind us that eugenics was not a marginal, bigoted movement in either Europe or the United States; it was a Progressive program, designed to harness science in the service of reducing suffering and misfortune and to help make society more efficient.

ALCOHOLISM. Heredity might be involved in some kinds of alcoholism. But no gene can make you buy a bottle of Scotch, pour a glass, and toss it down.

These concerns are probably justified, but there are also some signs that we may be on the crest of another important cultural shift. More and more experts, including dedicated biologists, sense that the power of genetics has been oversold and that a correction is needed. What's more, there's a glimmer of evidence that the typical American may not be buying it entirely. According to a recent *US. News*/Bozell poll, less than 1 American in 5 believes that genes play a major role in con-

U.S. News/Bozell poll of 1,000 adults conducted by KRC Research Feb. 6–9, 1997. Margin of error: plus or minus 3.1 percent.

trolling behavior; three quarters cite environment and society as the more powerful shapers of our lives. Whether the behavior under question is a disorder like addiction, mental illness, or violence, or a trait like homosexuality, most believe that heredity plays some role, but not a primary one. Indeed, 40 percent think genes play no role whatsoever in homosexuality, and a similar percentage think heredity is irrelevant to drug addiction and criminality. Across the board, most believe that people's lives are shaped by the choices they make.

These numbers can be interpreted in different ways. It may be that neurogenetic determinism has become the "religion of the intellectual class," as one critic argues, but that it never really caught the imagination of the typical American. Or we may be witnessing a kind of cultural self-correction, in which after a period of infatuation with neuroscience and genetics the public is becoming disenchanted, or perhaps even anxious about the kinds of social control that critics describe.

Whatever's going on, it's clear that this new mistrust of genetic power is consonant with what science is now beginning to show. Indeed, the very expression "gene for" is misleading, according to philosopher Philip Kitcher, author of *The Lives to Come.* Kitcher critiques what he calls "gene talk," a simplistic shorthand for talking about genetic advances that has led to the widespread misunderstanding of DNA's real powers. He suggests that public discourse may need to include more scientific jargon—not a lot, but some—so as not to oversimplify the complexity of the gene-environment interaction. For example, when geneticists say they've found a gene for a particular trait, what they mean is that people carrying a certain "allele"—a variation in a stretch of DNA that normally codes for a certain protein—will develop the given trait in a standard environment. The last few words—"in a standard environment"—are very important, because what scientists are *not* *saying* is that a given allele will necessarily lead to that trait in every environment. Indeed, there is mounting evidence that a particular allele will not produce the same result if the environment changes significantly; that is to say, the environment has a strong influence on whether and how a gene gets "expressed."

It's hard to emphasize too much what a radical rethinking of the nature-nurture debate this represents. When most people think about heredity, they still think in terms of classical Mendelian genetics: one gene, one trait. But for most complex human behaviors, this is far from the reality that recent research is revealing. A more accurate view very likely involves many different genes, some of which control other genes, and many of which are controlled by signals from the environment. To complicate matters further, the environment is very complicated in itself, ranging from the things we typically lump under nurture (parenting, family dynamics, schooling, safe housing) to biological encounters like viruses and birth complications, even biochemical events within cells.

The relative contributions of genes and the environment are not additive, as in such-and-such a percentage of nature, such-and-such a percentage of experience; that's the old view, no longer credited. Nor is it true that full genetic expression happens once, around birth, after which we take our genetic legacy into the world to see how far it gets us. Genes produce proteins throughout the lifespan, in many different environments, or they don't produce those proteins, depending on how rich or harsh or impoverished those environments are. The interaction is so thoroughly dynamic and enduring that, as psychologist William Greenough says, "To ask what's more important, nature or nurture, is like asking what's more important to a rectangle, its length or its width."

The emerging view of nature-nurture is that many complicated behaviors probably have some measure of genetic loading that gives some people a susceptibility—for schizophrenia, for instance, or for aggression. But the development of the behavior or pathology requires more, what National Institute of Mental Health Director Stephen Hyman calls an environmental "second hit." This second hit operates, counterintuitively, through the genes themselves to "sculpt" the brain. So with depression, for example, it appears as though a bad experience in the world—for example, a devastating loss—can actually create chemical changes in the body that affect certain genes, which in turn affect certain brain proteins that make a person more susceptible to depression in the future. Nature or nurture? Similarly, Hyman's own work has shown that exposure to addictive substances can lead to biochemical changes at the genetic and molecular levels that commandeer brain circuits involving volition—and thus undermine the very motivation needed to take charge of one's destructive behavior. So the choice to experiment with drugs or alcohol may, in certain people, create the biological substrate of the addictive disorder. The distinction between biology and experience begins to lose its edge.

HOMOSEXUALITY. Gay-rights advocates once argued that homosexuality was a matter of lifestyle choice. Now they stress genes and destiny.

Nurturing potentials. Just as bad experiences can turn on certain vulnerability genes, rich and challenging experiences have the power to enhance life, again acting through the genes. Greenough has shown in rat studies that by providing cages full of toys and complex structures that are continually rearranged—"the animal equivalent of Head Start"—he can increase the number of synapses in the rats brains by 25 percent and blood flow by 85 percent. Talent and intelligence appear extraordinarily malleable.

Child-development experts refer to the life circumstances that enhance (or undermine) gene expression as "proximal processes" a term coined by psychologist Urie Bronfenbrenner. Everything from lively conversation to games to the reading of stories can potentially get a gene to turn on and create a protein that may become a neuronal receptor or messenger chemical involved in thinking or mood. "No genetic potential can become reality," says Bronfenbrenner, "unless the relationship between the organism and its environment is such that it is *permitted* to be expressed." Unfortunately, as he details in his new book, *The State of Americans,* the circumstances in which many American children are living are becoming more impoverished year by year.

If there's a refrain among geneticists working today, it's this: The harder we work to demonstrate the power of heredity, the harder it is to escape the potency of experience. It's a bit paradoxical, because in a sense we end up once again with the old pre-1950s paradigm, but arrived at with infinitely more-sophisticated tools: Yes, the way to intervene in human lives and improve them, to ameliorate mental illness, addictions, and criminal behavior, is to enrich impoverished environments, to improve conditions in the family and society. What's changed is that the argument is coming not from left-leaning sociologists, but from those most intimate with the workings of the human genome. The goal of psychosocial interventions is optimal gene expression.

So assume for a minute that there is a cluster of genes somehow associated with youthful violence. The kid who carries those genes might inhabit a world of loving parents, regular nutritious meals, lots of books, safe schools. Or his world might be a world of peeling paint and gunshots around the corner. In which environment would those genes be likely to manufacture the biochemical underpinnings of criminality? Or for that matter, the proteins and synapses of happiness?

Junior Comes Out Perfect

Genetic screening will give privileged parents heightened capacity to shape the destinies of their children. What about the other parents? By Philip Kitcher

The pace and extent of the genetic revolution makes it tempting to speculate about life at the end of the 21st century. Will sex become completely recreational, with the serious business of reproduction going on in carefully monitored tubes? Will the main form of medical treatment consist of gene therapy, designed to replace defective DNA at the squeeze of a syringe?

Probably not. Doubtless in the decades to come gene therapy will become more exact, but unless numerous difficult problems are solved, the possibility of precisely engineering people who carry mutant genes into people who are genetically normal is minute. Yet our understanding of the genetics of human disease does promise to transform medical practice. One hundred years from now, we shall know the molecular structures of virtually all human genes, the functions of a significant percentage of them and the molecular mechanisms at work in a large number of human afflictions. Fantasies aside, the chief novelty of late-21st-century medicine will lie in its powerful ability to predict and prevent.

Philip Kitcher is a philosopher of science at the University of California, San Diego. He is the author most recently of "The Lives to Come: The Genetic Revolution and Human Possibilities."

Disease, it should be remembered, even hereditary disease, does not always have to be treated by replacing genes. A proper understanding of how a particular genetic mutation leads to illness or disability can sometimes provide clues about how to put it right, through dietary modifications, medicines or surgery. Looking into the next century, we can foresee a continuum of cases. At one extreme are the diseases for which genetic knowledge will lead to successful treatment. Many biomedical researchers draw inspiration from the case of phenylketonuria, or PKU. Children with PKU carry genes that render them unable to metabolize the amino acid phenylalanine. Left untreated, they build up large amounts of phenylalanine in their cells (and lack sufficient amounts of another amino acid, tyrosine) and become severely mentally retarded. By testing a baby just after birth, however, a doctor can prescribe a diet low in phenylalanine and high in tyrosine that enables an afflicted child to develop normally.

At the opposite pole are diseases that, despite enormous molecular insight, we are at a loss to treat. For example, the structure of the crucial protein implicated in sickle-cell anemia has been known for decades, but for almost 40 years (at least), that knowledge inspired no significant improvements in treatment. In between lie diseases like cystic fibrosis, where scientists have made some progress but so far have not achieved total success. Investing in molecular genetic research today is like buying tickets in a huge number of lotteries: we would be exceptionally unfortunate not to win the jackpot in some, but we cannot tell in advance how many prizes we will obtain or exactly what they will be.

Given the trajectory of genetic technology, it is fairly easy to envisage what a visit to the doctor may be like in 2096. The patient, let's call her Baby K, has her first checkup when she is an 8-week old fetus. A technician removes a few fetal cells. Several days later, interviews with the doctor and a genetic counselor provide a detailed picture: a 250-page printout sums up information about the DNA at 50,000 regions of the fetal chromosomes—all those regions whose functions in human development are at last understood.

The first pages of the printout are devoted to rare but dreadful disruptions of early development. To their relief, the parents of Baby K learn that she will not suffer tragic neural diseases like Tay-Sachs, neurofibromatosis or Lesch-Nyhan syndrome: at the genetic loci affecting these and hundreds of less familiar diseases, the sequences in the fetal DNA are reassuringly normal. With luck, more common genetic diseases—cystic fibrosis and fragile X syndrome—are also ruled out. Baby K's susceptibility to the major diseases that develop later in life, which depend on numerous environmental variables, is described in probabilistic terms: it turns out she is at average or at low risk for the vast majority of diseases, the principal exceptions being juvenile diabetes and a form of breast cancer that usually develops late in middle age. Fortunately, the molecular underpinnings of these diseases are well understood by the 21st century; by making mild changes in Mrs. K's diet before she gives birth and prescribing medicine to Baby K in early childhood, doctors can reduce Baby K's risk of diabetes to the normal range. As she grows into early adulthood, she will be well advised to receive regular breast-tissue checks.

The printout continues with a detailed preview of Baby K's immune system. The sequencing of bacterial and viral genomes began in the 1990's and will be elaborated on a grand scale in the coming decades. The resultant knowledge, combined with enhanced understanding of the workings of the immune system, will surely offer doctors in 2096 new clues for fortifying a young child against infectious diseases: changes in diet perhaps, or a schedule of injections designed to bolster the immune response. Baby K's parents will also learn something about the looks of their child-to-be: brown eyes and curly hair, say, maybe slightly over-average height and slender.

The session concludes with a review of the printout's last pages, the "behavioral tendencies." The counselor emphasizes the importance of environmental variables: the probability that Baby K will develop a particular personality trait might vary quite widely. But, thanks in part to advances made in neurochemistry in the late 20th century, Mr. and Mrs. K can learn a few things about their daughter: she does not carry any of the known markers for same-sex preference; there is no reason to think she will have less-than-average intelligence; she is not very likely to be hyperactive or suffer from an attention deficit, and she displays no abnormal propensity for depression. If the K's are particularly fortunate, the only cause for worry might be a possible tendency toward alcohol addiction—another predictive diagnosis stemming from the pioneering investigations of the 1990's and another case in which forewarned is forearmed.

The K's leave the interview with a vivid picture of their child and the contours of her life. Genetic testing has issued no guarantee against the ravages of birth trauma, childhood accidents, urban violence, earthquakes or other acts of God. Yet they don't have to worry about many potential threats to their child's well-being, and they have been told how to cope with certain aspects of her genetic inheritance—aspects that, in an earlier era, would have been recognized too late.

That is what we can hope genetic technology will bring. But the real value of biomedical research will depend not just on what scientists do but on the ways in which social policy is framed to make use of their contributions. Even in 2096, the news that genetic counselors deliver will not always be good. The story of Baby K was optimistic partly because her genetic abnormalities could be addressed with preventive strategies. What options will be available for parents and patients, and what pressures will they feel, when problems do not come with solutions?

Suppose Baby K's parents had learned she has a propensity for muscular degeneration, which could not be halted, or a tendency to depression, which only crude therapies could treat, or that she would be blind or deaf. Under these circumstances, they would have been left pondering a different group of questions: not the practical details of raising a healthy daughter but wondering whether they should allow the pregnancy to continue. Although the K's cannot ask for a baby engineered to their specifications, they can decide, to some extent—and to a far greater degree than is currently possible—what kinds of children they will have, provided they are prepared to abort fetuses with characteristics at odds with their wishes.

So far, the consequences of genetic foreknowledge have been very largely benign. In the past 20 years, prenatal genetic screening has greatly reduced the incidence of Tay-Sachs disease, both in the United States and in many other countries, and the incidence of types of thalassemia (a disease similar to sickle-cell anemia) in various Mediterranean countries where it once was prevalent. All except the most devout opponents of abortion should view these developments as merciful, sparing the parents of a Tay-Sachs child, for example, the anguish of watching an apparently healthy infant degenerate beyond help. By 2096, it will be possible to spread mercy more widely, forestalling births that would have revealed grossly disordered development or would have brought pain without hope of improvement. But it will be possible to do many other things as well—terminate a pregnancy because, say, the fetal genes indicate high risk for a heart attack in middle age, or a predisposition to obesity or blue eyes or a disease that can only be treated at great expense.

This is precisely the point at which social pressure comes to bear. We can rest comfortably I think, in assuming that our descendants will not institute some centrally directed eugenics program. Medicine in 2096 will continue to leave choices in the hands of parents. But reproductive decisions will not be entirely free: compulsory sterilization and the storm-trooper's gun are only the least subtle ways of controlling birth. Thousands, perhaps millions, of women in some parts of the world are already aborting female fetuses because they believe that their daughters, growing up in cultures heavily biased toward males, will not lead healthy and happy lives.

American parents of the late-21st century are unlikely to be pressured into aborting a healthy female fetus, but unless there are large social changes, other prejudices could permeate their society. For some, news that their child will be extremely short, obese or learning-disabled will be received with distaste or even revulsion. Many others simply may fear their neighbors' attitudes and believe that a child with one of these characteristics will face an uphill struggle. Knowing the personal and career difficulties confronted by those who are very short or obese, the menial jobs often delegated to school dropouts, otherwise unprejudiced parents may decide, with great reluctance, to end the pregnancy. "It just wouldn't be fair," they may say, "to bring a child like that into a world like this." Intense competition and social inequality already drive middle-class parents to register newborn infants for elite schools, to select the "right" preschool enrichment programs. Tomorrow the struggle for advancement may begin in the womb.

Genetic discoveries already underscore old prejudices and create new ones. As news reports were hailing the mapping and sequencing of the first genes implicated in breast cancer, women from high-risk families were discovering that the new ability to test had devastating consequences: many who carry abnormal genes at the pertinent loci have found that some insurance companies will not cover prophylactic mastectomies, that insurance coverage abruptly stops, that employers dismiss them. Genetic discrimination has already begun, and it is likely to become more extensive unless measures are taken to protect people whose draw in the genetic lottery has been unlucky. Several states have passed legislation to limit genetic discrimination, but these are only timid and hesitant first steps. Universal health coverage is necessary to protect the 5 to 10 percent of the population who will find themselves uninsurable because of accidents in conception.

Far more is required to insure that the reproductive choices made in 2096 are free from harsh constraints. Children born with genetic disabilities not only need the same access to health care and employment as other members of their society; they also need special support that will enable them to realize their potential. Unless prospective parents can rely on tolerance and respect for those who are different, unless they are assured that their community will do what it can to aid the disabled, then the pressure to view reproduction as a process in which the "right" products are stamped with social approval and the "wrong" ones discarded will be irresistible.

Baby K will surely exist. The pressing question is: How many Baby K's will there be? In the gloomiest vision of the future, the parents of Baby K are simply privileged members of a callous society. They have access to sophisticated medical testing and the results do not pose any hard choices for them. As middle-class citizens, well-educated and comfortable, they take the standard course of finding out if the fetus is "defective." Their child's place in the meritocracy depends on their doing all they can to produce a "perfect" baby—and, luckily, they receive good news.

As long as there is a wide gap in social and economic status, many middle-class parents will feel compelled only to have children who satisfy the genetic requirements for success.

Economic and genetic differences amplify each other, reinforcing pressure on the affluent to produce only "genetically correct" children. As long as there is a wide difference in social and economic status between those who succeed by the prevailing standards and those who do not, many middle-class parents will feel compelled only to have children who satisfy the genetic requirements for success. At the other social extreme will be people whose genetic misfortunes doom them to unemployment, the people with disabilities whose lives are cramped by inadequate support, those whose limited insurance coverage or minimal education denies them the chance to benefit from the new preventive medicines. Some genetic disabilities, virtually eliminated in the middle class, will persist at significant frequency in this segment of the population, but because they lack any powerful constituency, the disabled will find that services to help them are underfinanced. If we simply extrapolate from today's social attitudes, from the growing inequality between rich and poor, from the merciless individualism and competitiveness characteristic of most affluent societies, it is not farfetched to predict that the medical practices of 2096 will follow suit. Socioeconomic inequalities will turn victims of the quirks of conception into a true genetic underclass.

There are brighter possible futures. The K's might come from any stratum of society, from any ethnic group: the resources of preventive medicine would be available to all. Inhabiting a more egalitarian society—in which people with many different characteristics are valued and have productive lives, in which the highly educated surgeon and the manual laborer do not inhabit different economic and social spheres—the K's do not have to measure their child against a standard of "genetic correctness." As they await the detailed report from their doctor, they know that if the news is less than exceptional, they will face a genuine choice: government and community support will help them do the best for their child; prejudice will not sharply constrain the life of a child who is different from the majority.

This future is not beyond reach. In recent years, some Mediterranean countries have shown that it is possible to combat thalassemia while retaining a compassionate attitude toward those who are afflicted with it. The incidence of the disease has declined in Sardinia and Cyprus, but those Governments have continued to invest heavily in treatment and support for sufferers so that the crucial blood transfusions that are needed are now much more widely available than before. These countries point a way forward. Prenatal testing need not be a substitute for the costly business of nurturing those born with diseases and disabilities: it can be part of a comprehensive community investment in all citizens.

It is not easy, of course, to extend policies that work for small, homogeneous societies to a large, multiethnic nation. But that is the challenge. The tools for probing the human genome give us the responsibility of deciding how much to learn about embryonic lives and what to do with that knowledge. The medicine of the future will be a vivid portrait of our social priorities. The character of our choices will be measured by the number of people who will live the fortunate story of Baby K.

Evolutionary Perspectives

When Charles Darwin announced his theory of evolution to the world, a paradigm shift happened in the field of biology. More importantly, the theory has also affected our understanding of human nature. The theory of evolution quickly spread to several intellectual disciplines, including psychology. One of the major American psychologists, William James, was triggered to shift the focus of psychology from the structuralist mode developed by Wilhelm Wundt in Germany to what he called the "functionalist" movement. Functionalism in psychology restated the Darwinian perspective of evolution in terms of behavior: that individuals possess certain behaviors because these behaviors help them adapt to their environment and hence enhance their chances of survival.

Such a view has since been extended to biopsychology. One of the ways to understand behavior is to evaluate its significance to the survival of the individual and the propagation of its genetic potential for generations to come. It is almost inevitable nowadays not only to study the biological mechanisms within the individual that facilitates the behavior (e.g., hormones and other chemical messengers in the body), but also to ask the "survival value" of such behavior. Incorporating the evolutionary context of behaviors makes the understanding of behavior holistic in approach, thus seemingly more complete.

Although interpreting behavior from the evolutionary perspective seems like a good thing to do, one must be cautious of biological determinism. Just because the behavior is observable in nature does not always mean that the behavior is good for the individual. More often, behaviors evolve much slower than changes in the environment. It is possible that the behavior may no longer be adaptive to the individual, but that the genetic machinery within has not yet modified itself to adjust to these changes.

One grave error in the utilization of evolutionary theory is the establishment of eugenics, that is, a perspective that subscribes to the notion that some groups of people are more "superior" than others and that this superiority is inscribed in their genes. Indeed, an individual's genetic material plays a role in that person's behavioral and physical characteristics, but the environment also has a significant effect in shaping the development of the individual. Genetic determinism when used as a paradigm must be guarded, not only because it is scientifically unsound, but also because it is capable of corrupting a person's intellectual reasoning.

The set of articles in this section present major views in and applications of evolutionary biology relevant to biopsychology. One of the current debates in the field is whether the organism possesses characteristics for the survival of the "individual," or whether these characteristics are present for the survival of the "group." One can see how easy it is to take sides in this debate, because when we look at our own behaviors, we may have been motivated to behave either "selfishly" or "altruistically" on some occasions.

Looking Ahead: Challenge Questions

Are our behaviors really controlled exclusively by instructions kept in our genes? How does this view have an impact on our basic concept of human nature? Or are we motivated to act in such a way that we, as a group, will survive against the odds generated by our environment? Is altruism biologically significant?

Explain the following complex human behaviors from the evolutionist's perspective: gender difference in gender roles; jealousy; and violence against wives. Describe some other perspectives that have been offered to explain these behaviors.

UNIT 12

God's Utility Function

Humans have always wondered about the meaning of life. According to the author, life has no higher purpose than to perpetuate the survival of DNA

Richard Dawkins

RICHARD DAWKINS, an Englishman, was born in Kenya in 1941. Educated at the University of Oxford, he completed his doctorate in zoology under the Nobel Prize–winning ethologist Niko Tinbergen. After two years on the faculty of the University of California, Berkeley, Dawkins returned to Oxford, where he is now a reader in zoology and a fellow of New College. Dawkins is well known for his books The Selfish Gene *and* The Blind Watchmaker. *His latest book,* Climbing Mount Improbable, *was published by W. W. Norton in 1996. Dawkins will soon take up the newly endowed Charles Simonyi Chair of Public Understanding of Science at Oxford.*

In his many books on evolution and natural selection, Richard Dawkins examines the topics not from the perspective of individual organisms (as Charles Darwin did) but instead from what he has termed "the gene's-eye view." The genes in living creatures today are, he claims, the "selfish" ones that ensured their own survival by enabling their hosts—what Dawkins calls "survival machines"—to live long enough to reproduce. Dawkins argues that the complexity of life can be explained by the extraordinary contest among genes for survival, rather than by any grand purpose in the universe.

In his recently published book, River Out of Eden: A Darwinian View of Life, *Dawkins explains how the struggle of genes to replicate might account for some of the central mysteries of life, including "How did life begin?" and "Why are we here?" The article that follows is adapted from a chapter of* River Out of Eden *(BasicBooks, 1995).*

"I cannot persuade myself," Charles Darwin wrote, "that a beneficent and omnipotent God would have designedly created the Ichneumonidae with the express intention of their feeding within the living bodies of Caterpillars." The macabre habits of the Ichneumonidae are shared by other groups of wasps, such as the digger wasps studied by the French naturalist Jean Henri Fabre.

Fabre reported that before laying her egg in a caterpillar (or grasshopper or bee), a female digger wasp carefully guides her sting into each ganglion of the prey's central nervous system so as to paralyze the animal but not kill it. This way, the meat stays fresh for the growing larva. It is not known whether the paralysis acts as a general anesthetic or if it is like curare in just freezing the victim's ability to move. If the latter, the prey might be aware of being eaten alive from inside but unable to move a muscle to do anything about it. This sounds savagely cruel, but, as we shall see, Nature is not cruel, only pitilessly indifferent. This lesson is one of the hardest for humans to learn. We cannot accept that things might be neither good nor evil, neither cruel nor kind, but simply callous: indifferent to all suffering, lacking all purpose.

We humans have purpose on the brain. We find it difficult to look at anything without wondering what it is "for," what the motive for it or the purpose behind it might be. The desire to see purpose everywhere is a natural one in an animal that lives surrounded by machines, works of art, tools and other designed artifacts—an animal, moreover, whose waking thoughts are dominated by its own goals and aims.

Although a car, a tin opener, a screwdriver and a pitchfork all legitimately warrant the "What is it for?" question, the mere fact that it is possible to frame a question does not make it legitimate or sensible to do so. There are many things about which you can ask "What is its temperature?" or "What color is it?" but you may not ask the temperature question or the color question of, say, jealousy or prayer. Similarly, you are right to ask "Why?" of a bicycle's mudguards or the Kariba Dam, but at the very least you have no right to assume that the question deserves an answer when posed about a boulder, a misfortune, Mount Everest or the universe. Questions can be simply inappropriate, however heartfelt their framing.

Somewhere between windscreen wipers and tin openers on the one hand, and rocks and the universe on the other, lie living creatures. Living bodies and their organs are objects that, unlike rocks, seem to have purpose written all over them. Notoriously, of course, the apparent purposefulness of living bodies has dominated the reasoning of theologians from Thomas Aquinas to William Paley. For example, Paley, the 18th-century English theologian, asserted that if an object as comparatively simple as a watch requires a watchmaker, then far more complicated living creatures must certainly have been divinely designed. Modern "scientific" creationists also support this "argument from design."

The true process that has endowed wings, eyes, beaks, nesting instincts and everything else about life with the strong illusion of purposeful design is now well understood. It is Darwinian natural selection. Darwin realized that the organisms alive today exist because their ancestors had traits allowing them and their progeny to flourish, whereas less fit individuals perished with few or no offspring. Our understanding of evolution has come astonishingly recently, in the past century and a half. Before Darwin, even educated people who had abandoned the "Why" question for rocks, streams and eclipses still implicitly accepted the legitimacy of the "Why" question where living creatures were concerned. Now only the scientifically illiterate do. But "only" conceals the unpalatable truth that we are still talking about an absolute majority of the world's population.

Engineering a Cheetah

Darwin assumed that natural selection favored those individuals best fitted to survive and reproduce. This statement is equivalent to saying that natural selection favors those genes that replicate through many generations. Although the two formulations are comparable, the "gene's-eye view" has several advantages that become clear when we consider two technical concepts: reverse engineering and utility function. Reverse engineering is a technique of reasoning that works like this: you are an engineer, confronted with an artifact you have found and do not understand. You make the working assumption that it was designed from some purpose. You dissect and analyze the object with a view to working out what problem it would be good at solving: "If I had wanted to make a machine to do so and so, would I have made it like this? Or is the object better explained as a machine designed to do such and such?

The slide rule, talisman until recently of the honorable profession of engineer, is as obsolete in the electronic age as any Bronze Age relic. An archaeologist of the future, finding a slide rule and wondering about it, might note that it is handy for drawing straight lines or for buttering bread. But a mere straightedge or butter knife would not have needed a sliding member in the middle. Moreover, the precise logarithmic scales are too meticulously disposed to be accidental. It would dawn on the archaeologist that, in an age before electronic calculators, this pattern would constitute an ingenious trick for rapid multiplication and division. The mystery of the slide rule would be solved by reverse engineering, using the assumption of intelligent, economical design.

"Utility function" is a technical term not of engineers but of economists. It means "that which is maximized." Economic planners and social engineers are rather like architects and physical engineers in that they strive to optimize something. Utilitarians strive for "the greatest happiness of the greatest number." Others avowedly increase their own happiness at the expense of the common welfare. If you reverse-engineer the behavior of one country's government, you may conclude that what is being optimized is employment and universal welfare. For another country, the utility function may turn out to be the continued power of the president, the wealth of a particular ruling family, the size of the sultan's harem, the stability of the Middle East or the maintenance of the price of oil. The point is that more than one utility function can be imagined. It is not always obvious what individuals, firms or governments are striving to achieve.

Let us return to living bodies and try to extract their utility function. There could be many, but it will eventually turn out that they all reduce to one. A good way to dramatize our task is to imagine that living creatures were made by a Divine Engineer and try to work out, by reverse engineering, what the Engineer was trying to maximize: God's Utility Function.

Cheetahs give every indication of being superbly designed for something, and it should be easy enough to reverse-engineer them and work out their utility function. They appear to be well designed to kill gazelles. The teeth, claws, eyes, nose, leg muscles, backbone and brain of a cheetah are all precisely what we would expect if God's purpose in designing cheetahs was to maximize deaths among gazelles. Conversely, if we reverse-engineer a gazelle, we shall find equally impressive evidence of design for precisely the opposite end: the survival of gazelles and starvation among cheetahs. It is as though cheetahs were designed by one deity, gazelles by a rival deity. Alternatively, if there is only one Creator who made the tiger and the lamb, the cheetah and the gazelle, what is He playing at? Is He a sadist who enjoys spectator blood sports? Is He trying to avoid overpopulation in the mammals of Africa? Is He maneuvering to boost David Attenborough's television ratings? These are all intelligible utility functions that might have turned out to be true. In fact, of course, they are all completely wrong.

The true utility function of life, that which is being maximized in the natural world, is DNA survival. But DNA is not floating free; it is locked up in living bodies, and it has to make the most of the levers of power at its disposal. Genetic sequences that find themselves in cheetah bodies maximize their survival by causing those bodies to kill gazelles. Sequences that find themselves in gazelle bodies increase their chance of survival by promoting opposite ends. But the same utility function—the survival of DNA—explains the "purpose" of both the cheetah and the gazelle.

This principle, once recognized, explains a variety of phenomena that are otherwise puzzling—among them the energetically costly and often laughable struggles of male animals to attract females, including their investment in "beauty." Mating rituals often resemble the (now thankfully unfashionable) Miss World pageant but with males parading the catwalk. This analogy is seen most clearly in the "leks" of such birds as grouse and ruffs. A lek is a patch of ground used by male birds for displaying themselves in front of females. Females visit the lek and watch the swaggering demonstrations of a number of males before singling one out and copulating with him. The males of lekking species often have bizarre ornamentation that they show off with equally remarkable bowing or bobbing movements and strange noises. The words "bizarre" and "remarkable," of course, reflect subjective value judgments. Presumably, lekking male black grouse, with their puffed-up dances accompanied by cork-popping noises, do not seem strange to the females of their own species, and this is all that matters. In some cases, female birds' idea of beauty happens to coincide with ours, and the result is a peacock or a bird of paradise.

The Function of Beauty

Nightingale songs, pheasant tails, firefly flashes and the rainbow scales of tropical reef fish are all maximizing aesthetic beauty, but it is not, or is only incidentally, beauty for human delectation. If we enjoy the spectacle, it is a bonus, a by-product. Genes that make males attractive to females automatically find themselves passed down to subsequent generations. There is only one utility function that makes sense of these beauties: the quantity that is being diligently optimized in every cranny of the living world is, in every case, the survival of the DNA responsible for the feature you are trying to explain.

This force also accounts for mysterious excesses. For example, peacocks are burdened with finery so heavy and cumbersome that it would gravely hamper their efforts to do useful work—if they felt inclined to do useful work, which, on the whole, they don't. Male songbirds use dangerous amounts of time and energy singing. This certainly imperils them, not only because it attracts predators but also because it drains energy and uses time that could be spent replenishing that energy. A student of wren biology claimed that one of his wild males sang itself literally to death. Any utility function that had the long-term welfare of the species at heart, or even the individual survival of a particular male, would cut down on the amount of singing, the amount of displaying, the amount of fighting among males.

Yet when natural selection is also

considered from the perspective of genes instead of just the survival and reproduction of individuals, such behavior can be easily explained. Because what is really being maximized in singing wrens is DNA survival, nothing can stop the spread of DNA that has no beneficial effect other than making males beautiful to females. If some genes give males qualities that females of the species happen to find desirable, those genes, willy-nilly, will survive, even though the genes might occasionally put some individuals at risk.

Humans have a rather endearing tendency to assume that "welfare" means group welfare, that "good" means the good of society, the well-being of the species or even of the ecosystem. God's Utility Function, as derived from a contemplation of the nuts and bolts of natural selection, turns out to be sadly at odds with such utopian visions. To be sure, there are occasions when genes may maximize their selfish welfare by programming unselfish cooperation or even self-sacrifice by the organism. But group welfare is always a fortuitous consequence, not a primary drive.

The realization that genes are selfish also explains excesses in the plant kingdom. Why are forest trees so tall? Simply to overtop rival trees. A "sensible" utility function would see to it that they were all short. Then they would get exactly the same amount of sunlight with far less expenditure on thick trunks and massive supporting buttresses. But if they all were short, natural selection could not help favoring a variant individual that grew a little taller. The ante having been upped, others would have to follow suit. Nothing can stop the whole game from escalating until all trees are ludicrously and wastefully tall. But it is ludicrous and wasteful only from the point of view of a rational economic planner thinking in terms of maximizing efficiency rather than survival of DNA.

Homely analogies abound. At a cocktail party, everybody talks themselves hoarse. The reason is that everybody else is shouting at the top of their voices. If only everyone could agree to whisper, they would hear one another exactly as well, with less voice strain and less expenditure of energy. But agreements like that do not work unless they are policed. Somebody always spoils it by selfishly talking a bit louder, and, one by one, everybody has to follow suit. A stable equilibrium is reached only when everybody is shouting as loudly as they physically can, and this is much louder than they need from a "rational" point of view. Time and again, cooperative restraint is thwarted by its own internal instability. God's Utility Function seldom turns out to be the greatest good for the greatest number. God's Utility Function betrays its origins in an uncoordinated scramble for selfish gain.

A Universe of Indifference

To return to our pessimistic beginning, maximization of DNA survival is not a recipe for happiness. So long as DNA is passed on, it does not matter who or what gets hurt in the process. Genes don't care about suffering, because they don't care about anything.

It is better for the genes of Darwin's wasp that the caterpillar should be alive, and therefore fresh, when it is eaten, no matter what the cost in suffering. If Nature were kind, She would at least make the minor concession of anesthetizing caterpillars before they were eaten alive from within. But Nature is neither kind nor unkind. She is neither against suffering nor for it. Nature is not interested in suffering one way or the other unless it affects the survival of DNA. It is easy to imagine a gene that, say, tranquilizes gazelles when they are about to suffer a killing bite. Would such a gene be favored by natural selection? Not unless the act of tranquilizing a gazelle improved that gene's chances of being propagated into future generations. It is hard to see why this should be so, and we may therefore guess that gazelles suffer horrible pain and fear when they are pursued to the death—as many of them eventually are.

The total amount of suffering per year in the natural world is beyond all decent contemplation. During the minute that it takes me to compose this sentence, thousands of animals are being eaten alive, many others are running for their lives, whimpering with fear, others are being slowly devoured from within by rasping parasites, thousands of all kinds are dying of starvation, thirst and disease. It must be so. If there is ever a time of plenty, this very fact will automatically lead to an increase in population until the natural state of starvation and misery is restored.

In a universe of electrons and selfish genes, blind physical forces and genetic replication, some people are going to get hurt, other people are going to get lucky, and you won't find any rhyme or reason in it, nor any justice. The universe that we observe has precisely the properties we should expect if there is, at bottom, no design, no purpose, no evil and no good, nothing but pitiless indifference. As that unhappy poet A. E. Housman put it:

> For nature, heartless, witless nature
> Will neither care nor know

DNA neither cares nor knows. DNA just is. And we dance to its music.

Evolution's New Heretics

A growing number of evolutionary biologists think that the interests of groups sometimes supersede those of individuals

Roger Lewin

A native of England, Roger Lewin earned a Ph.D. in biochemistry from Liverpool University. He now lives in Cambridge, Massachusetts, where he is a freelance writer (specializing in evolution and ecology) and an associate at Harvard's Peabody Museum. Lewin is the author of several books, including In the Age of Mankind: A Smithsonian Book of Human Evolution *(Smithsonian Institution Press, 1989) and* The Sixth Extinction, *which he coauthored with Richard Leakey and which was published by Doubleday.*

Like an old-time preacher, David Sloan Wilson has the appearance of a man with a mission. An evolutionary biologist at the State University of New York at Binghamton, Wilson is given to marching up and down, flailing his arms, and proclaiming passionately, even in informal conversation. His message is as clear as it is bold: A whole generation of evolutionary biologists has been misled into believing that natural selection grinds inexorably at the level of individual interests, and only at that level. Instead, Wilson argues, biologists must recognize that groups of organisms have evolutionary interests, too, and that natural selection sometimes operates at this "higher" level. "Group selection" means that, occasionally, individuals within a group—for instance, an ant colony, a baboon troop, a nomadic band of human hunter-gatherers, or even a human population united by a common culture—may sacrifice their own reproductive future if, by doing so, the group benefits. This benefit comes through increased fitness, that is, through contributing more offspring to the next generation than do other, competing groups. Similarly, individuals may cooperate if the common end enhances the group's fitness.

For more than twenty years, Wilson has been working unceasingly—initially very much as a loner, but now with a growing band of supporters—advocating a theory that has been viewed by some as nothing less than heretical. Although much of his writing is couched in the arcane language of mathematical models, Wilson is concerned with a form of behavior that is very basic and, intuitively anyway, easily understood: altruism.

Humans may pride themselves on being genuinely altruistic, selflessly helping others, whether it is by dying for one's country or giving a couple of dollars to a homeless person on the street. But, modern evolutionary biologists ask, can animals other than humans be described as sometimes acting altruistically? Is the honeybee that dies in the act of stinging an intruder to the hive being altruistic? And what of a lioness that suckles the young of others in the pride as well as her own? Humans think of altruism as doing good for its own sake, but most of us would deny such motives to other animals. Two decades ago, Harvard biologist Edward O. Wilson proclaimed in his important and controversial book *Sociobiology: The New Synthesis* that altruism is "the central theoretical problem" of evolutionary biology in a social context.

Darwin was aware of apparently altruistic behaviors in nature. His theory of evolution by natural selection is principally about the survival of individuals in their "struggle for existence," in which they are always seeking ways of promoting their own reproductive success. Nevertheless, he recognized that individuals might sometimes act selflessly if, as a result, the success of the group is promoted instead. In *The Descent of Man,* Darwin used this line of argument to explain the evolution of morality. If this sounds uncannily like David Sloan Wilson's position, it is. So why has Wilson been called a heretic for championing something that Darwin expressed a century ago? How is it, as Wilson recently noted, that "the rejection of group selection was treated as a scientific advance comparable to the rejection of Lamarckism, and like Lamarckism, its memory was kept alive as an example of how not to think?"

During the century following the publication of *The Descent of Man*, Darwin's clear vision of group selection was superseded by a fuzzy view of life as a harmonious enterprise, with individuals acting toward a collective good. Most scientists, for instance, saw territoriality as individuals acting to control the density of the population for the good of all. Similarly, dominance hierarchies—the pecking orders so common among social animals—were seen as a means of reducing wasteful conflicts within the group.

This naïve version of group selection culminated in the 1962 publication of V. C. Wynne-Edwards's classic book, *Animal Dispersion in Relation to Social Behaviour*. Wynne-Edwards proposed that attributes of *all* social groups were subject to the forces of natural selection. His book was the target of immediate and blistering attack, for by then a new generation of evolutionary biologists had arisen. These scientists, building on a foundation of mathematical population genetics that increasingly emphasized the importance of individual selection, demolished the credibility of group selection at that time.

Prominent among the opponents was George C. Williams, of the State University of New York at Stony Brook, who took on group selection in his 1966 book, *Adaptation and Natural Selection*. Williams argued that, although a theoretical possibility, selection at the level of the group was an insignificant evolutionary force compared with individual selection. One reason was that the rate of evolution is far higher at the level of the individual than at that of the group; another was that, for the most part, groups are rather fluid, with members often moving between them, thus diluting the group as an evolving entity. Moreover, a group of altruists could easily be exploited by a sneakily selfish individual bent on boosting its own reproductive output at the expense of others holding back for the sake of the group.

If group selection were important, reasoned Williams, we would expect populations of sexually reproducing species to contain more females than males. This is because the number of reproductively active females—not the number of males—ultimately determines the number of offspring in the population; and, in evolutionary terms, the more successfully reared offspring there are in a group, the more successful that group is. Under individual selection, an even sex ratio is predicted (as a result of a balance in the struggle by individuals to maximize their own reproductive success through their offspring). And, Williams observed, an even ratio of males to females is what is most often seen in the world.

With the publication of *The Selfish Gene* in 1976, Oxford University biologist Richard Dawkins moved the focus of natural selection even further away from the group. For Dawkins, it is not just individuals but the genes within them that matter. More ammunition against group selection came with the development of kin selection and game theory, mathematical models that were designed to explain altruism and cooperative behavior.

The theory of kin selection has deep roots, going back principally to the insights of another Oxford biologist, William Hamilton, and fellow Brit John Maynard Smith, of the University of Sussex. Maynard Smith and Hamilton pointed out that when an apparently altruistic individual sacrifices a measure of its reproductive opportunity to enhance that of another, the donor—or at least some of its genes—may actually benefit if it is a relative of the recipient of the favor.

Game theory (originally a method developed by mathematicians to examine economic cooperation and conflict among humans) showed that even unrelated individuals cooperate while looking to their own interests. Robert Trivers, then at Harvard University, used this approach in developing the notion of reciprocal altruism, or "I'll scratch your back now because you scratched mine a while ago and I expect you to scratch mine again."

The era of the individual in evolutionary biology was thus firmly established and was apparently unassailable. Ethologists entered field studies confident that this theoretical perspective would powerfully inform what they would observe, particularly among primate species. "It's true. It was powerful," says Barbara Smuts, a primatologist at the University of Michigan, who has studied chimpanzees and baboons in East Africa. "But sometimes you had to stretch it and that made me uneasy." For instance, she doubted that a short-term, narrow view of self-interests could explain some features of alliances between males and females, because even after a long period of devotion to a female, a male has no guarantee that he will enjoy her mating favors in the future. Like many others, though, Smuts says, "I just thought that when I had more data it would be okay. I never thought about group selection. . . . No one did."

Frans de Waal, of the Yerkes Primate Center in Atlanta, recalls someone once describing a primate society as being like a transparent organism. "It was a powerful metaphor," he now says, "thinking of the group as an organism. But we weren't allowed to talk like that." A generation of field researchers felt the same: most accepted that group selection was discredited, and a few nursed curiosity about it but kept quiet for fear of appearing intellectually unsound.

To qualify as a "vehicle" of selection, says evolutionary biologist David Sloan Wilson, animals living in a group must share a common evolutionary fate and be in competition with other such groups.

Meanwhile, David Sloan Wilson had been laboring at his theoretical last since the mid-1970s, fashioning a theory of group selection that he believed eschewed the naïvete of earlier models. Wilson argues that the fundamental issue is the "vehicle" of selection. An individual, for instance, consists of a population of cells, but insofar as those cells share a common fate, in an evolutionary sense, the individual—and not the cells—is properly seen as the vehicle of selection. Similarly, a long-term alliance, or friendship, between a male and female baboon can be considered a vehicle because they share a common fate in the reproductive success that stems from the alliance. The female members of a pride of lions may also be a vehicle because their fitness depends on the fitness of their group, in terms of hunting success and protection against outside attack. An entire social group of vervet monkeys, for instance, may be a vehicle in their joint foraging and defense.

Group selection works, Wilson says, when groups are competing but not when they are in isolation. Suppose an individual within an isolated group provisions the offspring of other adults in the group, thus increasing their Darwinian fitness. Even though the overall fitness of the group is enhanced, the behavior will not be selected because it is not to the advantage of the individual doing it. However, Wilson argues, if the group is in competition with other such groups, the behavior will be selected because the group as a whole has an advantage relative to other groups.

One of the most persuasive examples of group selection in nature, argues Wilson, is the evolution of virulence in parasites. It is in a parasite's Darwinian interest to reproduce as bountifully as is compatible with high transmission to other hosts. A strain that multiplies too fast may rapidly kill off its host, thereby reducing its chances of transmission to other hosts.

Imagine two mice, each infected with a different strain of a certain parasite. Multiplying rapidly, the more virulent strain will have greater reproductive success than the less virulent one. Because its host-mouse soon expires, however, transmission to other mice will be lower than that of the less virulent parasite population. Natural selection therefore favors high virulence within hosts but lower virulence between them. "If group selection were a negligible force in disease evolution, then parasites would evolve to maximize their virulence and the notion of optimal virulence would be irrelevant," observe David Wilson and University of Wisconsin philosopher Elliot Sober. Further support for group selection comes from the group behavior of social insects and the discovery of female-biased sex ratios in a variety of organisms, including fig wasps, hummingbird flower mites, and social spiders.

The main body of evolutionary biologists, however, remains convinced that individual-level selection is the key to understanding social organization and behavior and rejects group selection as wrongheaded thinking. Dawkins is blunt in his response to Wilson's version of group selection, writing recently that he is "baffled by . . . the sheer, wanton, head-in-bag perversity of the position." Williams points out that from his calculations and observations, group selection occupies only a tiny corner of the world of evolution. "It's not a matter of logical correctness," he says. "It's a matter of importance, and Wilson greatly overstates the importance of group selection." Maynard Smith is critical of Wilson for causing "more confusion than clarity by using the term group selection in many different ways," but he also praises him for being "one of the few who has made the subject interesting again."

Meanwhile, Wilson is making converts. "My resistance crumbled immediately, as soon as I saw what he was saying," recalls Smuts, who was witness to one of Wilson's informal, passionate expositions at a 1994 gathering of the Human Behavior and Evolution Society. "The logic of the vehicle of selection, at different levels, is very persuasive." She was particularly drawn to the shifts in focus from within-group competition to within-group cooperation that might occur for an individual at different times and under different circumstances, particularly in intelligent species. "Male chimpanzees are a good example," Smuts explains. "At any time, the community might be challenged by another group, so that individual interest in competing with other males for access to females will be temporarily suspended in favor of collective group protection."

De Waal finds himself sympathetic to group selection but is still waiting to see how it might be a more powerful explanatory perspective than individual selection. He recently published *Good Natured*, a book on the evolution of morality in human and nonhuman primates. "Human morality is a classic case of something imposed on individuals for the well-being of the community," he explains. "Individuals benefit from a strong, united community, and that is why the community is valued so highly in our moral system." This might be seen as an example of what some anthropologists call cultural group selection.

Like humans, de Waal says, chimpanzees appear to value harmony in their social group. When peace is disrupted, often by bouts between competing males, a female acting as mediator may bring the two males together—sometimes diffusing the rising tension, sometimes effecting a reconciliation after an all-out fight. For instance, she might begin grooming one of the combatants, gradually luring him closer to his adversary; once the males have been drawn together, she will use her considerable, subtle social skills to get the two males to groom each other. Such intervention is a tricky and sometimes risky business. "It is a striking example of an individual taking care of relationships in which the mediator is not herself directly involved," observes de Waal. "This is what moral systems do all the time." Nevertheless, de Waal sees such cases of rudimentary morality "as an outcome of individual-level selection because the female benefits from a harmonious social context." Can human morality also be viewed as a result of individual-level selection, although expressed more generally and with more force because of language? "I suspect there is an interplay between individual and group selection in primate social systems," de Waal speculates, "but we haven't worked out what it is yet."

Some scientists believe passionately in group selection; others view it as an example of wrong-headed thinking. Still others are curious about the idea but unconvinced. If group selection does exist, altruism may be one result, but genocide would be another, less welcome outcome.

Anthropologists are deeply split over the place of group selection in human society. Some, such as Christopher Boehm of the University of Southern California, believe it has played a large role, much more than in nonhuman societies. "The egalitarian social structure you see in a foraging society is the result of the group's preventing its leaders from becoming dominant," argues Boehm. Richard Alexander, of the University of Michigan, points out that nobody "knows if group selection has been important in determining the genetic makeup of modern humans. . . . If it has been important, it has likely involved direct intergroup competition and hostility of the sort we've seen all across history."

The foray into the human realm inevitably muddies the waters of the group selection debate because of the thick overlay of culture. When one anthropologist points out that humans readily die for their country, supposedly demonstrating altruism for the good of the group, another reminds us that it is usually the poor who fight wars for the benefit of the rich and that if the poor choose not to fight, they may be flung in jail. Moreover, recent studies reveal that a person is much more likely to, say, give money to beggars when accompanied by a friend (particularly one of the opposite sex) than when alone. The motive here seems to be to enhance the social standing of the giver.

Donald Campbell, of Lehigh University, speaks for many when he says he expects there is a biological underpinning to many aspects of human social behavior as a result of group selection. An admirer of Wilson and Sober's work, he is disappointed that their arguments don't yet illuminate the way. He would like to see group selection in the human realm made "more explicitly plausible."

Finally, the sociological dimension of the group selection debate cannot be ignored, as psychiatrist Randolph Nesse, of the University of Michigan, observes. "It's not surprising that Wilson and Sober want to see human altruism as the result of group selection," he says. "Many people do. The discovery that some altruism isn't genuinely altruistic but is instead fundamentally selfish is deeply disturbing. Some would find comfort if we were able to reconcile our moral feelings with biological reality, but unfortunately it seems we can't." Nesse argues that we have to accept this reality and not seek to change the science to suit our feelings.

Not surprisingly, Wilson rejects this line of argument. "One of the great insights that is going to come out of group selection is that morality will be justified at face value," he says. "That is, it's a system designed to benefit the common good. But, you shouldn't think I'm a hopeless romantic, because a lot of nasty things are the result of group selection as well, including the ability to inflict genocide."

Sex Differences in Social Behavior

Are the Social Role and Evolutionary Explanations Compatible?

John Archer
University of Central Lancashire

The competing claims of two explanations of sex differences in social behavior, social role theory, and evolutionary psychology are examined. The origin and scope of research on sex differences in social behavior are outlined, and the application of social role theory is discussed. Research that is based on modern sexual selection theory is described, and whether its findings can be explained by social role theory is considered. Findings associated with social role theory are weighed against evolutionary explanations. It is concluded that evolutionary theory accounts much better for the overall pattern of sex differences and for their origins. A coevolutionary approach is proposed to explain cross-cultural consistency in socialization patterns.

The purpose of this article is to examine whether sex differences in social attributes are better explained by the dominant social science view, *social role theory*, or by a Darwinian perspective and to discuss whether they are alternative or complementary explanations. I begin by outlining the historical background of research on sex differences in social behavior, which led to the development of social role theory. The scope of the sex differences covered by this largely laboratory based research can be widened by examining some other areas in which findings are consistent with social role theory. I then consider the Darwinian principle of sexual selection, which has informed research on differences between men and women in sexuality, mate choice, and aggression. The issues of whether these findings can be explained by social role theory and research associated with social role theory, or by evolutionary theory, are then considered.

I conclude that the Darwinian perspective provides a more plausible account of the origins of sex differences in social behavior, in that the specific content of sex differences fits the different fitness requirements, or reproductive strategies, of males and females, and the interaction between them. However, this does not mean that cultural influences play no part in the generation of these differences. *Socialization*, one of the major processes identified by social role theory, can be viewed as reflecting the adaptive requirements of men and women. Gendered socialization practices can be understood in terms of coevolutionary processes, originating not from historically developed societal roles but from different selection pressures on men and women during the course of human and prehuman evolution.

Historical Background of Sex Differences in Social Behavior

The investigation of sex differences in psychological attributes and behavior arose from the tradition of individual differences research. It originally concentrated on cognitive and perceptual attributes for which there was a considerable amount of descriptive data. In earlier reviews

I thank David Buss, Anne Campbell, Alice Eagly, and Barry McCarthy for helpful discussion and comments on this article.

Correspondence concerning this article should be addressed to John Archer, Department of Psychology, University of Central Lancashire, Preston PR1 2HE, Lancashire, England. Electronic mail may be sent via Internet to j.archer@uclan.ac.uk.

From *American Psychologist*, September 1996, pp. 909-917. © 1996 by the American Psychological Association. Reprinted by permission.

(e.g., Anastasi, 1958; Garai & Scheinfeld, 1968; Maccoby, 1967), the relative skills and abilities of the two sexes formed the main agenda. Nevertheless, even here there was some consideration of the social realm, in the form of interests and attitudes and emotion and aggressiveness. The extensive summary by Maccoby and Jacklin (1974) likewise considered both cognitive and social sex differences.

Essentially, this research tradition was atheoretical in origin. Later, explanations were provided for these sex differences, but they were largely an exercise in the nature–nurture debate, with traditional socialization views involving reinforcement and imitation (Kagan & Moss, 1962; Mischel, 1967) vying with physiological explanations involving brain development or hormonal differences (e.g., Gray & Buffery, 1971; Hutt, 1972). They were mainly applied to cognitive abilities, and the physiological explanations were often regarded as implying that the two sexes possessed natural abilities fitting them for traditional roles (Archer, 1976), whereas the content of socialization was viewed as arising from sociohistorical forces.

The Application of Meta-Analysis

Since this time, several important developments have occurred in the methodology and theory that have been brought to bear on sex differences in psychological attributes and behavior. One was the introduction of meta-analytic techniques to the review of research evidence (see Eagly, 1995). There have been several consequences of the increased precision this entailed. The decision about which sex differences are "real" was much less a matter of impression and personal judgment, as it was when Maccoby and Jacklin's (1974) review was published. Increased quantification also brought the realization that many of the sex differences that had been extensively discussed and argued over were relatively small in terms of overall effect size: For example, that for spatial performance showed a point biserial correlation of .22 and that for verbal skills showed .10 (Hyde, 1981). One practical implication of such quantification was to question the logic of regarding these sex differences as strong influences on the numbers of women entering traditionally masculine occupational roles such as science and engineering (Hyde, 1981; but see Feingold, 1995, for an analysis that questions this conclusion).

A second development, beginning with Hall (1978) but later associated with the work of Eagly and her colleagues, was the extension of the meta-analytic approach to social behavior. Eagly and Carli (1981) examined influenceability, concluding that women were more persuadable than men, but with the proviso that the effect size was small and that there may have been (male) bias in the selection of studies that were published. Hall (1984) analyzed 125 studies of nonverbal communication and found comparatively large differences between men and women. Smaller differences were found for helping behavior (Eagly, 1987) and for aggression (Eagly & Steffen, 1986), although in the second case the data came exclusively from experimental social psychological studies, which had a number of limitations (Archer, 1989). The issue of the magnitude of such differences and their implications is the continued subject of debate (Eagly, 1995; Hyde & Plant, 1995).

John Archer
Copyright by University of Central Lancashire.

The Importance of Social Context

The older reviews of cognitive differences tended to view them as individual attributes—either the product of biology or of social learning. This was, however, an oversimplification even for cognitive attributes. For example, if the same task is presented to boys and girls as either a measure of needlework or of electronics, the effect of the labeling is to reverse the direction of sex difference in performance (Davies, 1986; Hargreaves, Bates, & Foot, 1985). Thus, social context is important even for supposedly internalized skills. For social behavior, it is essential to consider the context in which it is manifest, and this led to changes of emphasis in the way that sex differences were conceptualized. Instead of being viewed as residing in the individual, what Deaux (1984) called "sex as a subject variable" (p. 105), they became viewed as the product of an interaction between people in a wider social setting. Consequently, explanations of such sex differences became more concerned with social processes. For example in their model, Deaux and Major (1987) identified first the gender-related beliefs that people brought to an interaction, and second the extent to which a specific situation activated these beliefs: Sex differences arose from the extent to which these beliefs influenced the specific interactions of the people concerned. The emphasis had therefore shifted to processes such as gender-stereotypic beliefs and the salience of these beliefs for those people in a given situation. Sex differences were consequently viewed as flexible, context-dependent outcomes of social processes.

Societal Roles

Deaux and Major (1987) concentrated on sex differences in terms of dyadic interactions. In her social role theory, Eagly (1987) was concerned with a different level of analysis, that of societal roles. This is both a theory of origins and of process. Sex differences in social behavior are viewed as having arisen historically from the societal position of women and men—their division of labor into homemakers and full-time paid employees. The different roles evoke expectancies about the characteristics associated with these roles. These have been summarized as communal (i.e., features such as nurturance and yielding) in the case of the homemaker role, and agentic (i.e., features such as assertive and instrumental) in the case of the paid employee role. Such features are also viewed as forming the basis of gender stereotypes (e.g., Williams & Best, 1982).

According to social role theory, expectancies are transformed into sex differences in social behavior through two processes: The first is the learning of sex-typed skills and beliefs (i.e., through socialization processes) and the second is a more direct influence of expectancies associated with gender roles on people's behavior and dispositions. The second process was emphasized in the earlier research on influenceability (Eagly, 1983), thus making the social role view similar to that of Henley (1977), who explained sex differences in nonverbal behavior as directly stemming from societal power relations. Nevertheless, in her subsequent book, Eagly (1987) characterized this as an *oppression theory,* and distanced the social role view from it, leaning more toward an overlap with socialization theory. Essentially, the distinction between the two processes depends on whether internal dispositions or situational contingencies control behavior (House, 1981). Internal dispositions will have been built up over a period of time through learning and could only be changed gradually, whereas for situational contingencies, a change in behavior would follow fairly closely any change in societal roles.

Although social role theory incorporates socialization as an important process in generating sex differences, it differs from traditional socialization accounts of sex differences (e.g., Mischel, 1967) in that it specifies (or, more accurately, implies) the form this socialization will take. From the perspective of social role theory, we should expect socialization to involve learning communal and agentic traits.

Another important aspect of any approach that views societal structures and roles as primary is that it necessarily includes the concept of power. A power explanation could be viewed as an alternative to one that emphasizes the specific content of roles, and Henley's explanation of nonverbal behavior (see above) provides an example of this. However, Eagly (1987) incorporated the higher status of men in social role theory through evidence that status is associated with agentic characteristics. Power therefore provides an additional reason for men to be agentic. The reader should keep in mind that this is distinct from explanations, such as Henley's, which involve a more direct influence of power on people's behavior.

One important aspect of the social role view of sex differences is its inclusiveness. All aspects of men's and women's social behavior can be characterized as arising from their agency and communion. However, as we have just noted, there could be a more direct influence of status differences on some characteristics, for example, assertiveness. Other sex differences might be attributed to aspects of socialization that are better characterized in terms other than agency and communion: Male emotional inexpressiveness, which arises from the emphasis on toughness and avoidance of femininity in boys' peer groups (Archer, 1992a), is one possibility.

The Scope of Social Role Theory

Eagly's (1987) application of social role theory was informed by the available experimental social psychological literature and therefore covered topics such as helping, influenceability, nonverbal behavior, and behavior in small groups. However, the scope of the sex differences in social behavior that can be characterized in terms of agency and communion is wider than Eagly's analysis suggested. This is partly because further data have become available but also because her meta-analyses mainly covered experimental social psychological evidence.

More recent studies include an analysis of women's lower physical and psychological well-being (Helgeson, 1994), women's greater emotional sensitivity and responsiveness (Grossman & Wood, 1993), and a meta-analysis of sex differences in personality (Feingold, 1994). In each case, the findings can be explained in terms of the agency–communion distinction identified by social role theory. Feingold found that men were more assertive and women more tenderminded, trusting, and anxious. It is again worth noting that some of these, such as assertiveness, anxiety, and well-being, might be the direct consequence of status inequalities, and others, such as well-being, emotion, and anxiety, might result from socialization specifically concerned with male inexpressiveness.

Other important sex differences, which did not form part of analyses that were based on experimental social psychological studies, include same-sex friendship patterns, the meanings attached to material possessions, attachment styles in close relationships, and coping with the loss of a relationship. These are also consistent with the overall pattern predicted by social role theory of women being more communal and men more agentic. But, again, the more specific pattern of male inexpressiveness can be identified.

Rubin (1985) studied men's and women's friendship patterns in North America and found that, compared with women, men tended to form less disclosing relationships, which were based on shared activities. Most of the men in Rubin's sample could not name a best friend. Those who did have close friends avoided speaking about personal matters, so as not to appear vulnerable. Women formed closer, more intimate friendships that were based on sharing feelings and experiences, and most of the women in the sample (single, ages 25 to 55 years) were able to name a best friend.

Many other studies (e.g., Wright, 1988) have confirmed these differences between men's and women's friendships in Western samples, and the different patterns have been characterized as agentic and communal, respectively, clearly fitting them to social role theory. Nevertheless, in contrast to the meta-analytic syntheses, these conclusions arise from impressions gained from a variety of studies using a variety of methods, and as with all sex differences, they hide within-sex variations (Duck & Wright, 1993; Wright, 1988). There is also a controversy over whether the difference lies in the underlying structure of friendship, as Rubin suggested, or in the method of communication used (Dosser, Balswick, & Halverson, 1986; Duck & Wright, 1993). If it is the second of these, the sex difference would be more specifically connected to male inexpressiveness rather than the overall agentic–communal distinction.

Dittmar (1989) found that the reasons women and men gave for valuing material possessions tended to be different, and these could be characterized in terms of a symbolic–functional dimension. Women viewed possessions more in terms of emotional and relational connotations, whereas men viewed them more instrumentally. Again, the distinction fits the more general communal–agentic dimension.

Research on adult attachment has shown that more men fit the *dismissing style* (Bartholomew & Horowitz, 1991; Brennan, Shaver, & Tobey, 1991) that involves not wanting to depend on others, whereas more women fit the *preoccupied style,* which involves a heightened desire for intimacy with others (Bartholomew & Horowitz, 1991; Brennan et al., 1991). These differences can also be viewed in terms of agency and communion, or alternatively as resulting from male inexpressiveness (Dosser et al., 1986).

Stroebe and Schut (1995) have characterized the typical ways in which women and men cope with bereavement as *loss-oriented* (i.e., facing the loss) and *restoration-oriented* (i.e., avoiding or denying it). According to their Dual Process model (DPM) of coping with grief, both coping styles are usually necessary for successful resolution, but there are sex differences in the degree to which the styles are adopted. This view is supported by several findings, including those of Schut, Stroebe, van den Bout, and de Keijser (in press) that widows benefit more from behaviorally oriented therapy, whereas widowers benefit more from therapy emphasizing emotional expression. These different coping styles are perhaps more marked in the case of death of a child, with fathers showing more intense denial (Bohannon, 1990–1991) and trying to control or hide their feelings (Cook, 1988). A study of children's grief (Silverman & Worden, 1993) indicated that coping styles begin during childhood. Again, the differences can be explained both in terms of social role theory and male inexpressiveness.

Social role theory can account for these additional sex differences in terms of agency and communion, yet the alternative, more specific explanation of socialization for male inexpressiveness is applicable in most cases. We return to this issue after considering the main alternative approach to social role theory—sexual selection.

Evolutionary Psychology and Sexual Selection

Over the last 10 years, there have been numerous other studies of sex differences in social behavior that have been informed by a very different perspective than social role theory or socialization. This is *evolutionary psychology,* which has formed an important theoretical development in the social sciences over this time (Archer, 1996; Buss, 1995a; Daly & Wilson, 1988, 1994). Evolutionary psychology incorporates the revolutionary change in Darwinian thinking that has occurred in the last 30 years and was characterized as modern Darwinism by Cronin (1991). She described its two main features as, first, a primary interest in the evolution of social behavior (rather than structures) and, second, the realization that it is the genes—as opposed to the individual or the group—that are the units of natural selection. This eventually enabled human social behavior to be viewed in an entirely different way. Instead of being concerned with immediate causes or the individual's developmental history, a modern Darwinian explanation would ask how a particular type of social behavior had originated (in terms of its contribution to successfully perpetuating the genes of the animals displaying it). The particular emphasis in evolutionary psychology has been to explain the present-day human psyche (its biases and dispositions) in terms of adaptations that were successful in evolutionary history. In other words, the past is also seen as explaining present-day psychological mechanisms. Like social role theory, this explanation therefore concerns both origins and current psychological processes.

Darwin (1871) described the differences in form and behavior of the two sexes in the animal world in terms of sexual selection, which he viewed as a result of competition for access to preferred mates among the males and choice between available mates by females. Why this should be so was not realized until the article by Trivers (1972), which formed one of the foundations of modern Darwinian thinking. The sex (usually the female) that contributes most to the future offspring becomes a resource sought after by the sex (usually the male) contributing less. Another way of putting this is that the female is limited in the number of potential offspring she can produce as a result of her larger contribution to each one. This leads to different selection pressures on the two sexes: Females are better able to maximize fitness (i.e., gene frequency in subsequent generations) by being more discriminating, so as to obtain a male with good genes, resources, and parental skills; males are better able to maximize fitness by seeking to mate with many females, but in doing so they have to possesses features attractive to females and to compete with other males. Intermale aggression is viewed as being more overt and damaging than interfemale aggression for this reason.

Whenever there is internal fertilization combined with paternal care (as there is in humans), there will also be selection for maximizing paternity. Some aspects of male aggression can be seen in terms of sexual jealousy and possessiveness originating from the evolutionary advantage of paternity certainty.

Sexual Selection Applied to the Psychology of Men and Women

Trivers's analysis predicts that in social mammals such as human beings, the sexes are likely to show different dispositions underlying their social behavior, principally their sexual and courtship behavior and their aggression. Because men are also limited by the evolved dispositions of women, which makes them more discriminating when choosing a mate, there is also a conflict of interests between the two sexes in terms of the behavior that would maximize their fitness. The consequences of this for human sex differences have been analyzed by Smuts (1992, 1995), who argued that the patriarchy—men's domination over women—has evolved from this conflict of reproductive interests. The reasons why men have gained the advantage are, first, that they have the size and strength to do so and, second, that they can gain more than women would lose. By overcoming female choice, a man can mate with a large number of women; by resisting this, women gain a much smaller advantage in the form of a more adaptive set of genes.

The sexual conflict of interests can be regarded as an evolutionary arms race (Dawkins & Krebs, 1979), where one side—the male—has an inherent advantage. In addition to these general considerations, during the course of human evolution, additional factors, such as dispersal from natal groups by women and the ability of some men to monopolize essential resources, have combined to make inequality both marked and institutionalized (Smuts, 1995).

There is now a large body of research on human sex differences that has been informed by the evolutionary perspective (see Buss, 1994, 1995b). It has involved features of male behavior such as aggression and dominance, both to other men and to women; sexual aggression; sex differences in preferred numbers of partners; mate selection criteria; and strategies for obtaining and keeping a mate. I offer four illustrative examples: discrimination in mate choice, mate selection criteria, sexual jealousy, and intermale aggression.

Sexual selection theory identifies women as the discriminating sex when it comes to mate selection. The other side of the coin is that men will show a greater preference for sex without commitment and for multiple partners. The impact of these preferences on overt behavior is likely to be partly hidden by societal constraints and lack of opportunity for most men. Yet it is clear from several lines of ethnographic and historical evidence (e.g., Betzig, 1992; Symons, 1979) that when men do have the opportunity for sexual access with little or no cost, they do indeed have many partners. Social psychological studies show the same dispositions among young men in North America. Symons and Ellis (1989) asked U.S. students various questions, including whether they would have intercourse with an anonymous member of the opposite sex who was as attractive as their current partner, if there were no risks attached and no chance of forming a relationship. Men were four times more likely than women to answer that they certainly would and women two and a half times more likely to say that they certainly would not. Ehrlichman and Eichenstein (1992) asked samples of young Americans to select preferred wishes from a long list or to rate 20 specified wishes. Overall, the two sexes were similar, but men showed a much stronger preference for the statement "to have sex with anyone I choose," and for having sex without a relationship. In terms of an overall effect size, the meta-analysis of Oliver and Hyde (1993) found the sex difference in such attitudes to casual sex to be large (d = .81).

Other research has focused on the characteristics that women and men look for in a potential partner. Sexual selection theory predicts that men will value features indicative of health and reproductive potential, whereas women will value features indicating genetic fitness and the ability to provide resources and protection for the woman and the offspring. To test these hypotheses, Buss (1989b, 1992) obtained ratings of the desirability of characteristics for a potential mate from over 10,000 respondents in 37 cultures from six continents. Across all cultures, men consistently rated youth and looks as more important than did women, in agreement with findings from U.S. college students (Buss & Schmitt, 1993; Feingold, 1990). Buss found that in nearly all the cultures, women preferred men with higher earning capacity, and in three fourths of them women rated ambition and industriousness higher than did men,. This was again consistent with findings that were based on both questionnaires and overt behavior among U.S. samples (e.g., Buss & Schmitt, 1993; Ellis, 1992; Feingold, 1990).

An important evolutionary pressure that has influenced the behavior of males in species with internal fertilization and paternal care is the avoidance of *cuckoldry,* rearing another male's offspring. One widespread tactic for reducing this is to behave so as to discourage the female's interest in other males and other males' interest in the female. Men's sexual jealousy has been viewed in this light (Daly, Wilson, & Weghorst, 1982; Symons, 1979), with the prediction that it will focus on sexual access to the partner, because it is this that ensures paternity. Women's jealousy, on the other hand, is predicted to be more concerned with the diversion of time and resources to a rival. Buss, Larsen, Westen, and Semmelroth (1992) tested this hypothesis with American undergraduates, using written and auditory material depicting their partner forming an emotional attachment, or having sexual intercourse, with another partner. As predicted, men rated the sexual cue and women the emotional cue as more distressing. Physiological measures were consistent with these ratings. Other studies have replicated these findings (see Buss, 1995b).

Aggression has been considered from both the evolutionary and the social role perspectives, although the material used to study it has been different. Eagly and Steffen's (1986) meta-analytic review, which was confined to laboratory studies, found a small overall effect size for greater male aggressiveness. Daly and Wilson (1988) carried out an extensive analysis of sex differences in human aggression that was based on homicide figures across cultures. Using this measure, which they viewed as lacking the biases inherent in self-reports, revealed enormous differences between the sexes, which were even more pronounced when only same-sex victims were concerned.

When considering aggression, it is important to separate same-sex exchanges, which are linked to sexual selection, from those between the sexes, which are linked to the sexual conflict of interests, as outlined above. Smuts (1992, 1995) showed that attempts by males to control females, often by force, are widespread among nonhuman primates. Although these are often resisted, the effectiveness of the resistance is variable (and as indicated above, selection for resistance would generally be less than that for male coercion). The same conflict of interests has been played out during human evolution and history, particularly after the coming of agriculture, when men—especially the more powerful ones—controlled resources necessary for women to survive and reproduce (Smuts,

1995). Rape and violence toward women can be viewed as originating from these selection pressures.

Overall, the pattern of sex differences found in characteristics associated with sexuality, mate choice, and aggression fits that predicted by Darwinian theory (Buss, 1995b). It is what we should expect if these differences originated from sexual selection and an evolutionary conflict of interests between the sexes, rather than from another source such as the division of labor between the sexes or historically produced power inequalities.

Can Social Role Theory Explain These Findings?

Although both the Darwinian and the social role perspective have offered explanations for sex differences in aggression, those differences in sexuality, mate choice, and the triggers for sexual jealousy have not generally been addressed by social role theory, which would be hard-pressed to explain the particular pattern of results.

A possible exception is one aspect of mate choice criteria, female preference for high earning potential in a man. Caporael (1989) suggested that this represents an attempt by women to reduce their own powerlessness (i.e., it was a consequence of status inequalities between men and women). However, the preference for high earning potential is maintained (and even strengthened) when the woman herself has a high earning potential (Buss, 1989a; Wiederman & Allgeier, 1992). This shows that the prediction derived from sexual selection is maintained irrespective of the woman's own access to resources, thus supporting the Darwinian explanation over that based on structural powerlessness.

The social role interpretation of sex differences in aggression again views these as derived from gender roles, although with certain reservations about contextual variations and the type of aggression involved (Eagly, 1987). More recent findings that men's beliefs about aggression tend to be instrumental and women's tend to be expressive (Archer & Haigh, in press; Campbell & Muncer, 1994) are consistent with the social role view (although they would not contradict evolutionary predictions).

Nevertheless, the detailed pattern of findings for sex differences in aggression towards same-sex others are better explained by sexual selection. For example, homicide shows a much larger sex difference than is the case for less damaging acts of aggression, and this is maintained in societies differing widely in absolute homicide rates (Daly & Wilson, 1990). A Darwinian approach predicts that the sex difference would lie not in the overall extent of aggressive feelings but in the greater risks that men would be prepared to engage in when in conflicts with other men (Daly & Wilson, 1988), in other words, in the extent of escalation of dispute. The data for homicides clearly support this. Furthermore, sexual selection theory also predicts that it is young men, particularly those with little access to resources, who will engage in the most damaging disputes. Again, homicide data support this prediction across different societies (Wilson & Daly, 1993), a pattern that is difficult to explain in terms of social role and other standard social science explanations (Archer, 1995). Social role theory would find it particularly difficult to explain age-related differences in aggression.

One final point is that similar sex differences in aggression are found in a wide range of other species (Archer, 1988; Trivers, 1972). Social role theory, which views all sex differences as having originated in the timespan of human history, cannot explain these findings. Male competition not only explains the existence of sex differences in aggression but also the pattern of cross-species variation.

Can Darwinian Theory Account for Findings Explained by Social Role Theory?

I conclude that social role theory accounts very poorly, if at all, for the pattern of sex differences identified by evolutionary psychologists. Does evolutionary theory fare any better when applied to the sex differences most closely associated with social role theory? These differences were reviewed in an earlier section, where I noted that although sex differences were consistent with the social role interpretation, many could alternatively be viewed in terms of either male inexpressiveness or a direct effect of status inequalities.

Male inexpressiveness, which underlies several important sex differences (friendship, attachment styles, and coping with loss), can be viewed as originating from intermale competition, rather than characteristics associated with the division of labor. It is necessary for men to avoid signs of vulnerability in a masculine competitive environment that emphasizes the importance of toughness and reputation. To show feelings of vulnerability is to open oneself to exploitation. Cross-cultural surveys of socialization patterns (e.g., Gilmore, 1990; Low, 1989) reveal the generality of such social environments for boys and men. Viewed in this way, many of women's social characteristics, such as greater disclosure in same-sex friendships, more vulnerable attachment styles, and more loss-oriented ways of coping with grief, reflect the absence of inexpressiveness.

Other features of women's social behavior identified by research from the social role perspective—for example, nonverbal behavior associated with deference and influenceability, together with aspects of female socialization such as obedience, responsibility, and social restraint—can be attributed to the male domination of women. We have already discussed an evolutionary explanation for why men generally dominate women rather than vice versa, in terms of the conflict of interests between male and female reproductive strategies. Smuts (1995) argued that the patriarchy is "a human manifestation of a sexual dynamic that is played out over and over again, in many different ways, in other animals" (p. 22).

It is apparent that the Darwinian perspective, in the form of male competition and the reproductive conflict of interests between men and women, can provide alternative explanations for the origin of the sex differences identified by research associated with social role theory. We therefore need to ask whether the division of labor between the sexes—the main feature of social role theory—does provide a more plausible alternative. In contrast to the features identified by evolutionary theory, division of labor is unique to human evolution and history. Male domination of female reproductive life occurs more widely among nonhuman primates (Smuts, 1992, 1995). For this reason, it provides a more plausible explanation than that offered by social role theory. Whether male inexpressiveness or the more general features of agency and communion better explain the other sex differences cannot be answered so readily.

Gendered Socialization as a Coevolutionary Process

Overall, the evidence indicates that the pattern of sex differences in social behavior is better explained by a Darwinian than a social role perspective: What we observe at the present time is more likely to have originated from selection pressures during human and prehuman evolution than as a consequence of the human division of labor.

Does this mean that the same pattern of sex differences would arise independently of the cultural setting? The social role perspective is fairly clear that this would not be the case. Eagly and Steffen (1986) argued that women and men would show similar levels of aggression if they were treated identically in their rearing. Daly and Wilson (1994), on the other hand, argued that the two sexes have different dispositions, which would be manifest under a wide range of conditions irrespective of gendered socialization.

These predictions are difficult to test empirically. In practice, it is almost impossible to remove the influence of culture or to provide an environment in which no form of gendered socialization operates. The removal of the influence of culture would take away so much that is characteristic of growing up in any human society that any individual subject to such a process would inevitably be deprived of other important aspects of social learning. It is now apparent from animal research that the nature–nurture issue has not been well served by using the deprivation experience to identify either what is learned or what is innate (Archer, 1992b).

Debate over this issue may turn attention away from the important connections between evolution and culture. Focusing on evolved dispositions or lack of them neglects the degree to which a consistent pattern of both gender stereotypes and gendered social learning is found in most cultures. For example, toughness and a willingness to fight are a crucial part of boys' early socialization and are maintained as important features of masculine self-definition in most cultural contexts (Archer, 1992a, 1994; Gilmore, 1990), although they are learned alongside rules regarding restraint and when it is appropriate to act out aggressiveness. An analysis of 93 societies from the ethnographic record by Low (1989) found that boys are generally taught to be more aggressive, show more fortitude, and to be more self-reliant than are girls. Girls are consistently taught to be more industrious, responsible, obedient, and sexually restrained than are boys.

The social role explanation for this consistency is that it follows from consistency in the division of labor and power inequalities across cultures. We have already concluded that the pattern of observed sex differences better fits an analysis derived from Darwinian theory. Various theoretical writings have highlighted the importance of gene–culture interactions. For example, Durham (1991) concluded from his analysis of the coevolution of genetic and cultural systems that "genetic selection and cultural selection are generally expected to co-operate in the evolution of attributes that, from the point of view of their selectors, are adaptively advantageous" (p. 457).

Gendered socialization provides a clear example of such coevolution. A possible scenario is that cultural traditions encouraging aggressiveness, courage, fortitude, and dominance among men arose in the rearing patterns of our hominid and ape ancestors. These would have enhanced such traits that would have in any case tended to be present to a greater degree in males than females and would have been important for fitness in males, as a result of sexual selection. These characteristics would have later become articulated by language into ideologies that justified their perpetuation. Boys then came to learn the reasons why they should be tough and myths about male heroes.

Smuts (1995) proposed a similar process in relation to male domination of women. She suggested that

> Men's use of language and ideology to keep women down is not a departure from pre-linguistic forms of male control but, rather, a natural extension and elaboration of these forms. If male chimpanzees could talk, they would probably develop rudimentary myths and rituals that increased male political solidarity and control over females and that decreased female tendencies toward autonomy and rebellion. (p. 19)

The coevolutionary approach regards socialization not as something new and separate from human nature. Instead, it provides a distinct contribution to the development of present-day sex differences in social behavior that can at the same time be viewed as arising from evolved dispositions. The present-day contributions to once-adaptive ends are both genes and culture, and the two are closely interrelated. The biosocial model of the socialization of personality by Harris (1995), which emphasizes major contributions from inherited dispositions and from peer-group socialization, is consistent with this view.

Cross-cultural differences in gender socialization can also be viewed from a coevolutionary perspective as representing ways in which gendered socialization is adapted to the more specific requirements of different social environments. Low (1989) found that in societies where there is an opportunity for greater polygyny, male competitive training is exaggerated. Thus, socialization reflects the future fitness requirements for men in that society. The modification of dispositions in response to the rearing environment so as to produce adult characteristics that fit that environment is termed an *alternative reproductive strategy* by evolutionary biologists (e.g., Dominey, 1984).

According to this analysis, the consistency in the content of gender socialization represents not the imposition of roles that arose by historical accident from one source but the way that cultural learning interacts with biological dispositions to produce individuals who are able to pursue the reproductive strategies appropriate for their own sex. Furthermore, the variation in gender socialization represents ways in which these strategies can be modified according to the more specific requirements of different social environments.

It is unclear whether this analysis can be extended to forms of behavior discouraged by mainstream socialization, such as the high-risk behavior of young men, which is associated with violence, and other delinquent activities. These might be attributable to evolved dispositions that persist despite society's attempts to discourage them, or they may be explained in coevolutionary terms as the result of peer group influences (Archer, 1992a; Harris, 1995).

Conclusions

The social role view and evolutionary theory both predict that there will be widespread differences in the social behavior and dispositions of women and men. The reason for such wide-ranging predictions is that they are both theories of origins. Social role theory views sex differences as arising from the division of labor between the sexes through agentic and communal patterns of behavior. Evolutionary theory attributes many of the same sex differences to the consequences of sexual selection and the conflict between the different reproductive strategies of men and women. Such features are widespread in other mammals, and evolutionary theory best accounts for both the origins of most sex differences in social behavior and their observed pattern at the present time.

At the level of the processes that currently generate these sex differences, the consistent pattern of gendered socialization can best be viewed as a coevolutionary process that accentuates evolved dispositions. Sexual selection theory predicts a pattern that fits men for the social world of intermale competition—for example, assertiveness, toughness, and not showing emotion—and seeking to control the reproductive decisions of women; it predicts a pattern for women that would foster interpersonal networks and exercising choice over their own reproductive decisions. This prediction better fits the evidence from cross-cultural studies of socialization patterns than one that is simply characterized in terms of agency and communion, as is social role theory. Gendered socialization is therefore viewed as playing an important part in maintaining behavior consistent with the different fitness interests of men and women.

REFERENCES

Anastasi, A. (1958). *Differential psychology* (3rd ed.). New York: Macmillan.

Archer, J. (1976). Biological explanations of psychological sex differences. In B. B. Lloyd & J. Archer (Eds.), *Exploring sex differences* (pp. 241–266). London: Academic Press.

Archer, J. (1988). *The behavioural biology of aggression.* Cambridge, England: Cambridge University Press.

Archer, J. (1989). From the laboratory to the community: Studying the natural history of human aggression. In J. Archer & K. Browne (Eds.), *Human aggression: Naturalistic approaches* (pp. 25–41). London: Routledge.

Archer, J. (1992a). Childhood gender roles: Social context and organization. In H. McGurk (Ed.), *Childhood social development: Contemporary perspectives* (pp. 31–61). Hillsdale, NJ: Erlbaum.

Archer, J. (1992b). *Ethology and human development.* Savage, MD: Barnes & Noble.

Archer, J. (1994). Violence between men. In J. Archer (Ed.), *Male violence* (pp. 121–140). London: Routledge.

Archer, J. (1995). What can ethology offer the study of human aggression? *Aggressive Behavior, 21,* 243–255.

Archer, J. (1996). Evolutionary social psychology. In M. Hewstone, W. Stroebe, & G. Stephenson (Eds.), *Introduction to social psychology: A European perspective* (pp. 25–45). Oxford, England: Blackwell.

Archer, J., & Haigh, A. (in press). Do beliefs about aggressive feelings and actions predict reported levels of aggression? *British Journal of Social Psychology.*

Bartholomew, K., & Horowitz, L. M. (1991). Attachment styles among young adults: A test of a four-category model. *Journal of Personality and Social Psychology, 61,* 226–244.

Betzig, L. (1992). Roman polygyny. *Ethology and Sociobiology, 13,* 309–349.

Bohannon, J. R. (1990–1991). Grief responses of spouses following the death of a child: A longitudinal study. *Omega, 22,* 109–121.

Brennan, K. A., Shaver, P. R., & Tobey, A. E. (1991). Attachment styles, gender and parental problem drinking. *Journal of Social and Personal Relationships, 8,* 451–466.

Buss, D. M. (1989a). Conflict between the sexes: Strategic interference and the evocation of anger and upset. *Journal of Personality and Social Psychology, 56,* 735–747.

Buss, D. M. (1989b). Sex differences in human mate preferences: Evolutionary hypotheses tested in 37 cultures. *Behavioral and Brain Sciences, 12,* 1–49.

Buss, D. M. (1992). Mate preference mechanisms: Consequences for partner choice and intrasexual competition. In J. H. Barkow, L. Cosmides, & J. Tooby (Eds.), *The adapted mind: Evolutionary psychology and the generation of culture* (pp. 249–266). New York: Oxford University Press.

Buss, D. M. (1994). *The evolution of desire: Strategies of human mating.* New York: Basic Books.

Buss, D. M. (1995a). Evolutionary psychology: A new paradigm for psychological science. *Psychological Inquiry, 6,* 1–30.

Buss, D. M. (1995b). Psychological sex differences: Origins through sexual selection. *American Psychologist, 50,* 164–168.

Buss, D. M., Larsen, R. J., Westen, D., & Semmelroth, J. (1992). Sex differences in jealousy: Evolution, physiology and psychology. *Psychological Science, 3,* 251–255.

Buss, D. M., & Schmitt, D. P. (1993). Sexual strategies theory: An evolutionary perspective on human mating. *Psychological Review, 100,* 204–232.

Campbell, A., & Muncer, S. (1994). Men and the meaning of violence. In J. Archer (Ed.), *Male violence* (pp. 332–351). London: Routledge.

Caporael, L. R. (1989). Mechanisms matter: The difference between sociobiology and evolutionary psychology [Commentary on Buss, 1989b]. *Behavioral and Brain Sciences, 12,* 17–18.

Cook, J. (1988). Dad's double binds: Rethinking fathers' bereavement from a men's studies perspective. *Journal of Contemporary Ethnography, 17,* 285–308.

Cronin, H. (1991). *The ant and the peacock.* Cambridge, England: Cambridge University Press.

Daly, M., & Wilson, M. (1988). *Homicide.* New York: Aldine de Gruyter.

Daly, M., & Wilson, M. (1990). Killing the competition: Female/female and male/male homicide. *Human Nature, 1,* 87–107.

Daly, M., & Wilson, M. (1994). Evolutionary psychology of male violence. In J. Archer (Ed.), *Male violence* (pp. 253–288). London: Routledge.

Daly, M., Wilson, M., & Weghorst, S. J. (1982). Male sexual jealousy. *Ethology and Sociobiology, 3,* 11–27.

Darwin, C. (1871). *The descent of man and selection in relation to sex.* London: Murray.

Davies, D. R. (1986). Children's performance as a function of sex-typed labels. *British Journal of Social Psychology, 25,* 173–175.

Dawkins, R., & Krebs, J. R. (1979). Arms races between and within species. *Proceedings of the Royal Society of London B, 205,* 489–511.

Deaux, K. (1984). From individual differences to social categories: Analysis of a decade's research on gender. *American Psychologist, 39,* 105–116.

Deaux, K., & Major, B. (1987). Putting gender into context: An interactive model of gender-related behavior. *Psychological Review, 94,* 369–389.

Dittmar, H. (1989). Gender identity-related meanings of personal possessions. *British Journal of Social Psychology, 28,* 159–171.

Dominey, W. J. (1984). Alternative mating tactics and evolutionarily stable strategies. *American Zoologist, 24,* 385–396.

Dosser, D. A., Balswick, J. O., & Halverson, C. F., Jr. (1986). Male inexpressiveness and relationships. *Journal of Social and Personal Relationships, 3,* 241–258.

Duck, S., & Wright, P. H. (1993). Reexamining gender differences in same-gender friendships: A close look at two kinds of data. *Sex Roles, 28,* 709–727.

Durham, W. C. (1991). *Co-evolution: Genes, culture and human diversity.* Stanford, CA: Stanford University Press.

Eagly, A. H. (1983). Gender and social influence: A social psychological analysis. *American Psychologist, 38,* 971–981.

Eagly, A. H. (1987). *Sex differences in social behavior: A social role interpretation.* Hillsdale, NJ: Erlbaum.

Eagly, A. H. (1995). The science and politics of comparing women and men. *American Psychologist, 50,* 145–158.

Eagly, A. H., & Carli, L. L. (1981). Sex of researchers and sex-typed communications as determinants of sex differences in influenceability: A meta-analysis of social influence studies. *Psychological Bulletin, 90,* 1–20.

Eagly, A. H., & Steffen, V. J. (1986). Gender and aggressive behavior: A meta-analytic review. *Psychological Bulletin, 100,* 309–330.

Ehrlichman, H., & Eichenstein, R. (1992). Private wishes: Gender similarities and differences. *Sex Roles, 26,* 399–422.

Ellis, B. J. (1992). The evolution of sexual attraction: Evaluative mechanisms in women. In J. H. Barkow, L. Cosmides, & J. Tooby (Eds.), *The adapted mind: Evolutionary psychology and the generation of culture* (pp. 267–288). New York: Oxford University Press.

Feingold, A. (1990). Gender differences in effects of physical attractiveness on romantic attraction: A comparison across five research paradigms. *Journal of Personality and Social Psychology, 59,* 981–993.

Feingold, A. (1994). Gender differences in personality: A meta-analysis. *Psychological Bulletin, 116,* 429–456.

Feingold, A. (1995). The additive effects of differences in central tendency and variability are important in comparisons between groups. *American Psychologist, 50,* 5–13.

Garai, J. E., & Scheinfeld, A. (1868). Sex differences in mental and behavioral traits. *Genetic Psychology Monographs, 77,* 169–299.

Gilmore, D. D. (1990). *Manhood in the making.* New Haven, CT: Yale University Press.

Gray, J. A., & Buffery, A. W. H. (1971). Sex differences in emotional and cognitive behaviour in mammals including man: Adaptive and neural bases. *Acta Psychologica, 35,* 89–111.

Grossman, M., & Wood, W. (1993). Sex differences in intensity of emotional experience: A social role interpretation. *Journal of Personality and Social Psychology, 65,* 1010–1022.

Hall, J. A. (1978). Gender effects in decoding nonverbal cues. *Psychological Bulletin, 85,* 845–857.

Hall, J. A. (1984). *Non-verbal sex differences.* Baltimore, MD: Johns Hopkins University Press.

Hargreaves, D. J., Bates, H. M., & Foot, J. M. C. (1985). Sex-typed labelling affects task performance. *British Journal of Social Psychology, 24,* 153–155.

Harris, J. (1995). Where is the child's environment? A group socialization theory of development. *Psychological Review, 102,* 458–489.

Helgeson, V. S. (1994). Relation of agency and communion to well-being: Evidence and potential explanations. *Psychological Bulletin, 116,* 412–428.

Henley, N. M. (1977). *Body politics: Power, sex and non-verbal communication.* Englewood Cliffs, NJ: Prentice-Hall.

House, J. (1981). Social structure and personality. In M. Rosenberg & R. H. Turner (Eds.), *Social psychology: Sociological perspectives* (pp. 525–561). New York: Basic Books.

Hutt, C. (1972). *Males and females.* Harmondsworth, England: Penguin.

Hyde, J. S. (1981). How large are cognitive gender differences? A meta-analysis using w^2 and *d*. *American Psychologist, 36,* 892–901.

Hyde, J. S., & Plant, E. A. (1995). Magnitude of psychological gender differences: Another side to the story. *American Psychologist, 50,* 159–161.

Kagan, J., & Moss, H. A. (1962). *Birth to maturity.* New York: Wiley.

Low, B. S. (1989). Cross-cultural patterns in the training of children: An evolutionary perspective. *Journal of Comparative Psychology, 103,* 311–319.

Maccoby, E. E. (1967). Sex differences in intellectual functioning. In E. E. Maccoby (Ed.), *The development of sex differences* (pp. 25–55). London: Tavistock.

Maccoby, E. E., & Jacklin, C. N. (1974). *The psychology of sex differences.* Stanford, CA: Stanford University Press.

Mischel, W. (1967). A social learning view of sex differences in behavior. In E. E. Maccoby (Ed.), *The development of sex differences* (pp. 56–81). London: Tavistock.

Oliver, M. B., & Hyde, J. S. (1993). Gender differences in sexuality. A meta-analysis. *Psychological Bulletin, 114,* 29–51.

Rubin, L. (1985). *Just friends: The role of friendship in our lives.* New York: Harper & Row.

Schut, H., Stroebe, M. S., van den Bout, J., & de Keijser, J. (in press). Intervention for the bereaved: Gender differences in the efficacy of the two counselling programs. *British Journal of Clinical Psychology.*

Silverman, P. R., & Worden, J. W. (1993). Children's reactions to the death of a parent. In M. S. Stroebe, W. Stroebe, & R. O. Hansson (Eds.), *Handbook of bereavement: Theory, research and intervention* (pp. 300–316). New York: Cambridge University Press.

Smuts, B. (1992). Male aggression against women: An evolutionary perspective. *Human Nature, 3,* 1–44.

Smuts, B. (1995). The evolutionary origins of patriarchy. *Human Nature, 6,* 1–32.

Stroebe, M. S., & Schut, H. A. W. (1995, June). *The dual process model of coping with loss.* Paper presented at the International Work Group on Death, Dying and Bereavement, Oxford, England.

Symons, D. (1979). *The evolution of human sexuality.* New York: Oxford University Press.

Symons, D., & Ellis, B. (1989) Human male–female differences in sexual desire. In A. S. Rasa, C. Vogel, & E. Voland (Eds.), *The sociobiology of sexual and reproductive strategies* (pp. 131–146). London: Chapman & Hall.

Trivers, R. L. (1972). Parental investment and sexual selection. In B. Campbell (Ed.), *Sexual selection and the descent of man* (pp. 136–179). Aldine: Chicago.

Wiederman, M. W., & Allgeier, E. R. (1992). Gender differences in mate selection criteria: Sociobiological or socioeconomic explanation? *Ethology and Sociobiology, 13,* 115–124.

Williams, J. E., & Best, D. L. (1982). *Measuring sex stereotypes: A thirty-nation study.* Beverly Hills, CA: Sage.

Wilson, M., & Daly, M. (1993). Lethal confrontational violence among young men. In N. J. Bell & R. W. Bell (Eds.), *Adolescent risk taking* (pp. 84–106). Newbury Park, CA: Sage.

Wright, P. H. (1988). Interpreting research on gender differences in friendship: A case for moderation and a plea for caution. *Journal of Social and Personal Relationships, 5,* 367–373.

SEX DIFFERENCES IN JEALOUSY IN EVOLUTIONARY AND CULTURAL PERSPECTIVE:
Tests From the Netherlands, Germany, and the United States

Bram P. Buunk,[1] Alois Angleitner,[2] Viktor Oubaid,[3] and David M. Buss[4]

[1]University of Groningen, the Netherlands, [2]University of Bielefeld, Germany, [3]University of Heidelberg, Germany, and [4]University of Texas

Abstract—*As predicted by models derived from evolutionary psychology, men within the United States have been shown to exhibit greater psychological and physiological distress to sexual than to emotional infidelity of their partner, and women have been shown to exhibit more distress to emotional than to sexual infidelity. Because cross-cultural tests are critical for evolutionary hypotheses, we examined these sex differences in three parallel studies conducted in the Netherlands (*N = 207*), Germany (*N = 200*), and the United States (*N = 224*). Two key findings emerged. First, the sex differences in sexual jealousy are robust across these cultures, providing support for the evolutionary psychological model. Second, the magnitude of the sex differences varies somewhat across cultures—large for the United States, medium for Germany and the Netherlands. Discussion focuses on the evolutionary psychology of jealousy and on the sensitivity of sex differences in the sexual sphere to cultural input.*

Social scientists have frequently[1] observed that sexual jealousy can be a strikingly strong emotion. In his classic work on the natives of the Trobriand Islands, for example, Malinowski (1932) noted that "jealousy, with or without adequate reason, and adultery are the two factors in tribal life which put most strain on the marriage tie" (p. 97). The sociologist Davis (1948) noted that jealousy is a "fear and rage reaction fitted to protect, maintain, and prolong the intimate association of love" (p. 183). Despite the potentially powerful impact of sexual jealousy, emotion researchers have devoted relatively little attention to it. According to most emotion researchers, jealousy is not a primary emotion. Instead, it is considered a derivative or blend of the more basic, central, primary emotions (Frank, 1988; Hupka, 1984; Plutchik, 1980). As a consequence, it has been relatively ignored by mainstream emotion researchers, who focus their efforts on emotions deemed more basic, such as fear, disgust, and sadness.

Recently, however, jealousy has received increasing attention (e.g., Buss, 1994; Buunk & Hupka, 1987; Salovey, 1991; White & Mullen, 1989). For example, cumulating evidence indicates that male sexual jealousy is a major cause of wife battering and homicide across a large number of cultures (e.g., Daly & Wilson, 1988; Daly, Wilson, & Weghorst, 1982). The two times when a woman faces the greatest risk of harm from a husband or boyfriend are when he suspects her of a sexual infidelity and when the woman decides to terminate the relationship (Daly & Wilson, 1988). Given an emotion powerful enough to provoke violent and sometimes lethal reactions, sexual jealousy can hardly be considered to be a peripheral emotion from the perspectives of the magnitude of arousal, the coherence of events that trigger its activation, and the magnitude of impact on people's lives. Indeed, from these perspectives, a compelling case can be made for the primacy of sexual jealousy as a basic human emotion and for the urgency of understanding its nature and functioning.

Address correspondence to David M. Buss, Department of Psychology, University of Texas, Austin, TX 78712; e-mail: dbuss@psy.utexas.edu.

Although in anthropological records, most acts of violent sexual jealousy are committed by men (Daly et al., 1982), studies in Western cultures find few sex differences in sexual jealousy (Salovey, 1991; White & Mullen, 1989). When researchers have asked global questions such as "Do you consider yourself a jealous person?" or "How often do you get jealous?" men and women have typically responded identically (Bringle & Buunk, 1985). Moreover, research has thus far not convincingly shown that either sex responds more negatively than the other when confronted with the possibility of the partner's sexual involvement with someone else. When differences are found, women usually report more negative feelings than men in response to extradyadic involvement of the partner (Buunk, 1986, 1995; Guerrero, Eloy, Jorgensen, & Andersen, 1993; de Weerth & Kalma, 1993).

Until recently, there was not a theory that could predict or explain sex differences in jealousy. Fifteen years ago, however, evolutionary psychologists predicted that, psychologically, the cues that trigger sexual jealousy should be weighted differently in men and women (Daly et al., 1982; Symons, 1979). The evolutionary rationale stems from an asymmetry between the sexes in a fundamental aspect of their reproductive biology: Fertilization occurs internally within the woman. This is not a biological law. There is nothing in evolutionary theory that dictates that fertilization must occur internally within the woman. Although it is a widespread trait, occurring in all 220 species of primates, 4,000 species of mammals, and countless insect species, it is not universal. Fertilization occurs internally within the male in some species (females literally implant their eggs within the male), and it occurs external to both sexes in some species, notably certain fish (Trivers, 1985).

The fact that fertilization occurs internally within women, however, means that over human evolutionary history, men have faced a profound adaptive problem that has not been faced by women: uncertainty in their parenthood of children. Some cultures have sayings to describe this phenomenon, such as "mama's baby, papa's maybe." Studies using blood samples or DNA fingerprinting are rare, but estimates based on existing evidence suggest that approximately 9% to 13% of children today have putative fathers that are not their genetic fathers

From *Psychological Science*, November 1996, pp. 359-363.

(Baker & Bellis, 1995). Paternity uncertainty, in short, is not just a hypothetical possibility. It is a reality and probably has been throughout human evolutionary history.

From a man's perspective, in the evolutionary past, a sexual infidelity on the part of his mate would have been tremendously damaging in reproductive currencies because of compromises in paternity certainty. First, the man would risk losing the mating effort he expended, including time, energy, risk, and nuptial gifts devoted to attracting and courting the woman. Second, he would suffer mating opportunity costs lost through foregone chances to attract and court other women. Third, the man would risk losing the woman's parental effort because it might be channeled to a competitor's child and not his own. Fourth, and perhaps most important, if the man would invest in the child, he would risk investing resources in a genetic vehicle that did not contain his genes. Because of the large costs linked with compromises in paternity, evolutionary psychologists have predicted that men's sexual jealousy will be triggered centrally by cues to sexual infidelity.

Women have faced a different set of adaptive challenges. A mate's sexual infidelity does not jeopardize a woman's certainty in parenthood. The child is her own regardless of her mate's sexual philandering. Nonetheless, if her mate becomes interested in another women, she risks losing his time, energy, resources, parental investment, protection, and commitment—all of which could get diverted to a rival woman and her children. Because the emotional involvement of a man with another woman is a reliable leading indicator of the potential diversion and loss of the man's investment, evolutionary researchers have proposed that cues to emotional infidelity would be central triggers of women's jealousy (Buss, Larsen, Westen, & Semmelroth, 1992).

The predicted sex differences have been found within the United States. In a series of forced-choice experiments, men indicated greater distress to a partner's sexual than emotional infidelity, whereas women indicated greater distress to a partner's emotional than sexual infidelity (Buss et al., 1992). These findings have been replicated by other researchers within the United States (Wiederman & Allgeier, 1993), and show up in measures of physiological distress as reflected by increased electromyographic activity, increased electrodermal response, and elevated heart rate (Buss et al., 1992). In addition, some earlier studies offered findings in line with the evolutionary perspective. Francis (1977), for example, found that among men, sexual involvement with a third person was the most mentioned situation evoking jealousy, whereas among women, the partner spending time or talking with a third person turned out to be the most frequently mentioned triggers of jealousy.

Cross-cultural data, however, are crucial for testing this evolution-based hypothesis. First, because the sex-linked triggers are hypothesized to be species-typical characteristics of evolved human psychology, data from other cultures are required for adequate testing (see, e.g., Symons, 1979). Second, it is well documented that cultures differ tremendously in their attitudes toward aspects of sexuality such as premarital sex and extramarital affairs (see, e.g., Buss, 1989; Frayser, 1985). For example, whereas over 75% of the U.S. population unequivocally disapproves of extramarital sex, the comparable percentage in the Netherlands is less than 45% (Buunk & van Driel, 1989). Furthermore, cultures differ in their emphasis on sexual equality (Frayser, 1985). Cultures that emphasize sexual equality and have particularly liberal attitudes about sexuality for both women and men should provide an especially rigorous challenge for testing the hypothesized sex differences in sexual jealousy. Thus, we sought to conduct parallel studies in three countries with different cultures—the Netherlands, Germany, and the United States. In particular, including the Netherlands seems appropriate because the Dutch appear to downplay sex differences and emphasize equality between the sexes more than people from virtually any other culture for which reliable data exist (Hofstede, 1994).

STUDY 1: THE UNITED STATES

Subjects and Method

After reporting age (mean = 18.6, SD = 0.92) and sex (N = 115 men and 109 women), subjects at a large Midwestern university were presented with the following dilemmas, interspersed at different locations within a larger instrument:

> Please think of a serious or committed romantic relationship that you have had in the past, that you currently have, or that you would like to have. Imagine that you discover that the person with whom you've been seriously involved became interested in someone else. What would upset or distress you more (please circle only one):
>
> (A) Imagining your partner forming a deep emotional attachment to that person.
>
> (B) Imagining your partner enjoying passionate sexual intercourse with that other person.

Subjects completed additional questions, and then encountered the next dilemma, with the same instructional set, but followed by a different, but parallel, choice:

> (A) Imagining your partner trying different sexual positions with that other person.
>
> (B) Imagining your partner falling in love with that other person.

Results

Shown in Figure 1 are the percentages of women and men reporting more distress in response to sexual infidelity than to emotional infidelity for the first empirical probe. The first empirical probe, contrasting deep emotional attachment with passionate sexual intercourse, yielded a large and highly significant sex difference (t = 6.96, $p < .0001$). Furthermore, the effect size (gamma), signified by the difference between means in standard deviation units, was large (γ = .98), with the sexes differing by 43% in the responses to which infidelity scenario was more distressing. Cohen (1977) defined effect sizes as small if they are .20, medium if they are .50, and large if they are .80 or greater.

Shown in Figure 2 are the responses to the contrast between a partner trying different sexual positions with someone else versus falling in love with that other person. The sex difference again was highly significant (t = 5.45, $p < .0001$). The sexes

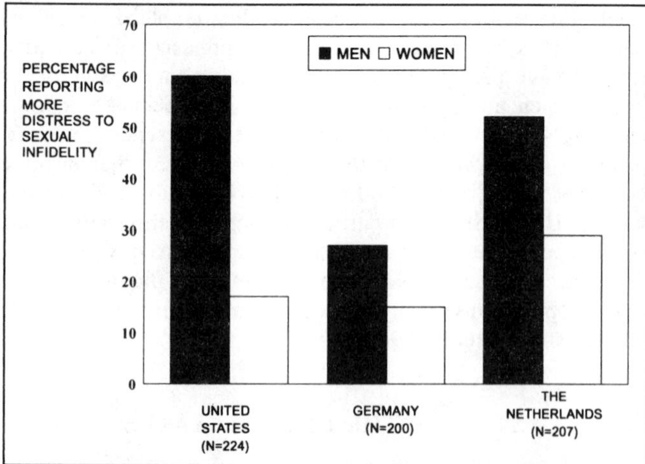

Fig. 1. Percentage of subjects reporting that they would be more distressed by imagining their partner enjoying passionate sexual intercourse with another person than by imagining their partner forming a deep emotional attachment to that person. Results are shown separately for men and women from the United States, Germany, and the Netherlands.

differed by 32% in their responses, with an effect size of .78, which is also considered large based on Cohen's (1977) criteria.

STUDY 2: GERMANY

Subjects and Method

A sample of 200 Germans from the city of Bielefeld participated in a parallel study. After reporting age (mean = 26.07, *SD* = 3.67) and sex (*N* = 100 men and 100 women), they responded to the same dilemmas as in the U.S. study. The German instructions for the first infidelity dilemma were as follows (female version):

> Bitte denken Sie an eine ernsthafte oder feste romantische Beziehung, die Sie in der Vergangenheit gehabt haben, die Sie gegenwärtig haben oder die Sie gerne hätten. Stellen Sie sich weiter vor, Sie würden entdecken, dass diese Person, mit der Sie eine solche ernsthafte Beziehung führen, beginnt, sich für jemand anderen zu interessieren. Was würde Sie mehr verletzen oder aufregen? Bitte kreuzen Sie eine der Alternativen an:
>
> (A) Die Vorstellung, dass Ihr Partner eine tiefe gefühlsmäßige Zuneigung zu dieser Person entwickeln würde.
>
> (B) Die Vorstellung, dass Ihr Partner leidenschaftlichen Geschlechtsverkehr mit dieser andersen Person ausubt.

Subjects completed additional questions, and then encountered the next dilemma, with the same instructional set, but followed by a different, but parallel, choice:

> (A) Die Vorstellung, dass Ihr Partner verschiedene sexuelle Stellungen mit dieser anderen Person ausprobiert.
>
> (B) Die Vorstellung, dass Ihr Partner sich in diese andere Person verliebt.

Results

Shown in Figure 1 are the percentages of women and men reporting more distress in response to sexual infidelity than to emotional infidelity in the first empirical probe which contrasted deep emotional attachment with passionate sexual intercourse. This probe yielded a significant sex difference (t = 2.06, $p < .02$). The effect size (gamma), however, was considerably smaller ($\gamma = .30$) than the comparable effect size for the U.S. sample, with the sexes differing by 12% in the responses to which infidelity scenario was more distressing. According to Cohen's (1977) criteria, this effect size is slightly larger than small.

Shown in Figure 2 are the responses to the contrast between a partner trying different sexual positions with someone else versus falling in love with that other person. The sex difference was again highly significant (t = 4.03, $p < .0001$). The sexes differed by 22% in their responses, with an effect size of .60, which is considered slightly above medium based on Cohen's (1977) criteria.

A comparison between Germany and the United States reveals that the percentages of women endorsing the sexual infidelity scenario were almost identical for the two cultures, differing by only 2% for the first infidelity scenario and 4% for the second scenario. In sharp contrast, the men from the two cultures differed considerably. Fully 33% more of the American men than the German men expressed greater distress to sexual than to emotional infidelity in the first dilemma, and 14% more American than German men expressed greater distress to sexual than to emotional infidelity in the second dilemma. Although the problematic nature of translation makes absolute comparisons of this sort of questionable interpretation, the results do suggest that the smaller sex difference in the German sample than in the U.S. sample may be due to differences in men's responses, rather than to differences in women's responses.

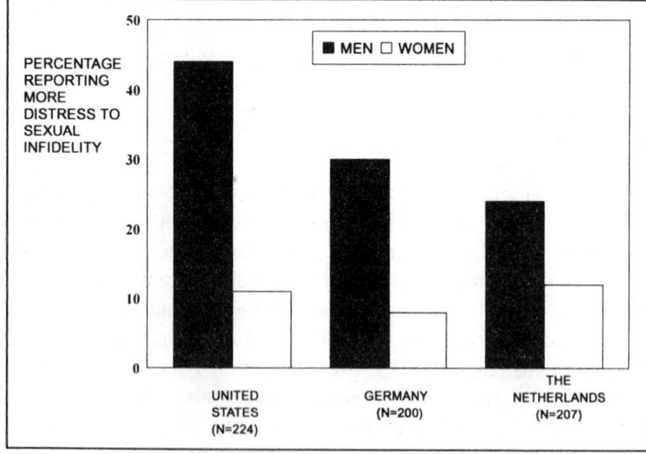

Fig. 2. Percentage of subjects reporting that they would be more distressed by imagining their partner trying different sexual positions with another person than by imagining their partner falling in love with that person. Results are shown separately for men and women from the United States, Germany, and the Netherlands.

STUDY 3: THE NETHERLANDS

Subjects and Method

A sample of 207 Dutch undergraduate students, 102 males and 105 females, participated in this study (mean age = 21.6, *SD* = 2.73). The same dilemmas were presented as in the U.S. and German studies. For both probes, the same introduction was presented as in both other countries.

The exact wording of the introduction and the first dilemma in Dutch was as follows:

De volgende vragen gaan over jaloezie. We willen je vragen te denken aan de serieuze intieme relatie die je nu hebt. Heb je nu niet een dergelijke relatie, denk dan aan een serieuze intieme relatie die je hebt gehad in het verleden, of stelt je voor hoe je je zou voelen wanneer je een dergelijke relatie zou hebben. Stel je nu voor dat je er achter komt dat je partner geinteresseerd raakt in een ander. Wat zou je erger vinden, wat zou je meer storen (kies een mogelijkheid):

(A) je voorstellen dat je partner een diepe, emotionele band met die ander ontwikkelt.

(B) je voorstellen dat je partner hartstochtelijk seksueel contact met die ander heeft.

The second dilemma read as follows in Dutch:

(A) je voorstellen dat je partner verschillende seksuele posities met die ander uitprobeert.

(B) je voorstellen dat je partner op die ander verliefd wordt.

Results

Shown on the right of Figure 1 are the percentages of women and men reporting more distress in response to sexual infidelity than to emotional infidelity in the first dilemma. This probe, contrasting deep emotional attachment with passionate sexual intercourse, yielded a significant sex difference (t = 3.41, $p <$ .001). The effect size (gamma) was medium (γ = .46), with the sexes differing by over 20% in their responses to which infidelity scenario was more distressing. This sex difference is larger than the sex difference found with the German sample, but smaller than the sex difference found with the American sample.

Shown in Figure 2 are the responses to the contrast between a partner trying different sexual positions with someone else versus falling in love with that other person. The sex difference again was significant (t = 2.11, $p <$ .04). The sexes differed by just over 10% in their responses, with an effect size of .29, which is considered slightly larger than small based on Cohen's (1977) criteria.

A comparison of the responses from the three cultures is revealing. First, responding to the same probes, the sexes differed in the same ways in all three cultures, providing support for the evolutionary psychological hypothesis about sex linkage in the weighting given to the triggers of sexual jealousy. Second, the results suggest that these cultures differ in the magnitude of this sex difference. The difference between males and females is consistently large within the American sample, but ranges from small to medium within both European samples.

DISCUSSION

This research makes two contributions to current knowledge about the nature of sex differences in jealousy. First, these studies provide the first systematic cross-cultural tests of the evolutionary psychological hypothesis that men and women differ in the weighting given to the triggers of sexual jealousy. Because the sexes have faced different adaptive problems caused by a mate's infidelity—compromised paternity confidence for men and the diversion of resources and investment for women—the sexes have been predicted to give different weighting to sexual acts of infidelity versus acts that signal emotional involvement and hence the potential diversion of resources over time.

The German and Dutch cultures provide especially rigorous tests of the hypothesis because these cultures have more relaxed attitudes about sexuality, including extramarital sex, than does the American culture; furthermore, these European cultures emphasize sexual equality, especially in the sexual domain, more than American culture does. The fact that the sex differences still emerged in these cultures provides support for the evolutionary psychological hypothesis. Even in the Netherlands, where values strongly deemphasize gender differences (Hofstede, 1994), and where a majority feels extramarital sexual relationships are acceptable under certain circumstances (Buunk & van Driel, 1989), men still tend to become more upset than women over their partner showing purely sexual interest in a third person, and women tend to become more upset than men over their partner expressing a desire for romantic and emotional involvement with someone else.

The second contribution of the present research is demonstrating that the magnitude of this sex difference differs across cultures. The Dutch and German samples showed small to moderate sex differences, whereas the American sample showed a large sex difference that was consistent across the empirical probes. Although the direction of the sex difference in jealousy is consistent across cultures, culture clearly matters in determining the magnitude of this sex difference. Further research may be directed more at identifying cultural features that account for such differences.

Several limitations qualify these results. First, although the German sample was selected in part from the adult population, the samples from the United States and the Netherlands were students. Thus, the results may not be representative of the entire cultures of these countries, and the results of the three studies are not completely comparable. Second, the vagaries of translation render exact comparisons of absolute percentages problematic; such comparisons should be interpreted with caution. Third, given that the individual probes undoubtedly contain some unreliability of measurement, the findings may actually underestimate the magnitude of the sex difference within each culture. The findings thus may regarded as lower-bound estimates of the magnitude.

Although some investigators (e.g., Hupka & Ryan, 1990) might interpret the cultural differences found in the present research as a disconfirmation of the evolutionary psychology framework, such an interpretation would be mistaken. Evolutionary hypotheses are sometimes misinterpreted as implying rigid, robotlike, instinctual behavior that suggests that the individual is oblivious to the social environment. In fact, evolutionary psychology postulates psychological mechanisms that were designed to respond to the social environment. Clearly, the jealousy mechanisms examined in these studies are sensitive to sociocultural conditions, even though the particulars of these cultural conditions are not yet known.

One explanation for the cross-cultural differences is that in sexually more liberal cultures where men may distribute their mating effort over a number of women, and hence devote less investment toward any one woman, men are less sexually jealous of any particular woman. Another possibility is that women in more sexually liberal cultures secure investments from a larger number of men, and hence are less jealous of any one partner's emotional involvement with other women. Still another possibility is that women in more sexually egalitarian cultures are more self-reliant for resources, and this self-reliance alters the intensity of jealousy they experience about a partner's emotional involvement with another woman.

Future research could profitably examine these and other features of the different cultures to pinpoint more precisely the causal locus of the cultural effect. Future research could also examine other cultures, including, at the other extreme, those that are more sexually conservative (e.g., perhaps China and Indonesia in the East, or Ireland within Western Europe) or that emphasize greater sexual inequality (e.g., Iran), to test the suggestion that these cultures might reveal even larger sex differences than those found within the United States. Given the importance of sexual jealousy in spousal violence and homicide, such studies might take an especially high priority.

Taken together, these studies suggest a complex portrait of human sexual psychology—one that is sex-differentiated, but also sensitive to cultural context. Whereas evolutionary psychology has been critical in guiding us to pose questions about sex differences in the triggers of jealousy and guiding a cross-cultural search for their existence, a cultural perspective has been valuable in uncovering variation in the magnitudes of those sex differences. Combining evolutionary and cultural perspectives may provide the most valuable models for exploring the mysteries of the uniquely human sexual psychology.

Acknowledgments—The authors thank John Kihlstrom and Todd Shackelford for helpful comments on an earlier version of this article.

REFERENCES

Baker, R.R., & Bellis, M.A. (1995). *Sperm competition: Copulation, masturbation, and infidelity*. London: Chapman and Hall.

Bringle, R.G., & Buunk, B.P. (1985). Jealousy and social behavior: A review of personal, relationship and situational determinants. In P. Shaver (Ed.), *Review of personality and social psychology* (Vol. 2, pp. 241–264). Beverly Hills, CA: Sage.

Buss, D.M. (1989). Sex differences in human mate preferences: Evolutionary hypotheses tested in 37 cultures. *Behavioral and Brain Sciences, 12,* 1–49.

Buss, D.M. (1994). *The evolution of desire: Strategies of human mating*. New York: Basic Books.

Buss, D.M., Larsen, R.J., Westen, D., & Semmelroth, J. (1992). Sex differences in jealousy: Evolution, physiology, and psychology. *Psychological Science, 3,* 251–255.

Buunk, B.P. (1986). Husband's jealousy. In R.A. Lewis & R. Salt (Eds.), *Men in families* (pp. 97–114). Beverly Hills, CA: Sage.

Buunk, B.P. (1995). Sex, self-esteem, and extradyadic sexual experience as related to jealousy responses. *Journal of Social and Personal Relationships, 12,* 147–153.

Buunk, B.P., & Hupka, R.B. (1987). Cross-cultural differences in the elicitation of sexual jealousy. *Journal of Sex Research, 23,* 12–22.

Buunk, B.P., & van Driel, B. (1989). *Variant lifestyles and relationships*. Newbury Park, CA: Sage.

Cohen, J. (1977). *Statistical power analysis for the behavioral sciences* (rev. ed.). San Diego: Academic Press.

Daly, M., & Wilson, M. (1988). *Homicide*. New York: Aldine de Gruyter.

Daly, M., Wilson, M., & Weghorst, S.J. (1982). Male sexual jealousy. *Ethology and Sociobiology, 3,* 11–27.

Davis, K. (1948). *Human society*. New York: MacMillan.

de Weerth, C., & Kalma, A.P. (1993). Female aggression as a response to sexual jealousy: A sex role reversal? *Aggressive Behavior, 19,* 265–279.

Francis, J.L. (1977). Towards the management of heterosexual jealousy. *Journal of Marriage and Family Counseling, 3,* 61–69.

Frank, R.H. (1988). *Passions within reason: The strategic role of the emotions*. New York: W.W. Norton.

Frayser, S. (1985). *Varieties of sexual experience: An anthropological perspective*. New Haven, CT: HRAF Press.

Guerrero, L.K., Eloy, S.V., Jorgensen, P.F., & Andersen, P.A. (1993). Her or his? Sex differences in the experience and communication of jealousy in close relationships. In P.J. Kalbfleish (Ed.), *Interpersonal communication: Evolving interpersonal relationships* (pp. 109–132). Hillsdale, NJ: Erlbaum.

Hofstede, G. (1994). *Culture's consequences: International differences in work-related values*. Beverly Hills, CA: Sage.

Hupka, R.B. (1984). Jealousy: Compound emotion or label for a particular situation? *Motivation and Emotion, 8,* 141–155.

Hupka, R.B., & Ryan, J.M. (1990). The cultural contribution to jealousy: Cross-cultural aggression in sexual jealousy situations. *Behavioral Science Research, 24,* 51–71.

Malinowski, B. (1932). *The sexual life of savages*. Boston: Beacon.

Plutchik, R. (1980). *Emotion: A psychoevolutionary synthesis*. New York: Harper & Row.

Salovey, P. (Ed.). (1991). *The psychology of jealousy and envy*. New York: Guilford Press.

Symons, D. (1979). *The evolution of human sexuality*. New York: Oxford University Press.

Trivers, R. (1985). *Social evolution*. Menlo Park, CA: Benjamin/Cummings.

White, G.L., & Mullen, P.E. (1989). *Jealousy: Theory, research, and clinical strategies*. New York: Guilford Press.

Wiederman, M.W., & Allgeier, E.R. (1993). Gender differences in sexual jealousy: Adaptationist or social learning explanation? *Ethology and Sociobiology, 14,* 115–140.

(RECEIVED 7/17/95; ACCEPTED 7/24/95)

Male Sexual Proprietariness and Violence Against Wives

Margo I. Wilson and Martin Daly

There is a cross-culturally ubiquitous connection between men's sexual possessiveness and men's violence.[1] We have studied accounts of uxoricides (wife killings) from a broad range of societies, and find that male sexual proprietariness—broadly construed to encompass resentment both of infidelity and of women's efforts to leave marriages—is everywhere implicated as the dominant precipitating factor in a large majority of cases.[2] The discovery of wifely infidelity is viewed as an exceptional provocation, likely to elicit a violent rage, both in societies where such a reaction is considered a reprehensible loss of control and in those where it is considered a praiseworthy redemption of honor. Indeed, such a rage is widely presumed to be so compelling as to mitigate the responsibility of even homicidal cuckolds.

Battered women nominate "jealousy" as the most frequent motive for their husbands' assaults, and their assailants commonly make the same attribution.[1,3] Moreover, assaulted wives often maintain that their husbands are not only violently jealous about their interactions with other men, but are so controlling as to curtail contacts with female friends and family. In a 1993 national survey, Statistics Canada interviewed more than 8,000 women currently residing with male partners. In addition to answering questions about their experiences of violence, the women indicated whether five statements about autonomy-limiting aspects of some men's behavior applied to their husbands. Autonomy-limiting behavior was especially likely to be attributed to those husbands who were also reported to have behaved violently, and women who had experienced relatively serious or frequent assaults were much more likely to affirm each of the five statements than were women who had experienced only lesser violence (Table 1).[4] These and other data suggest that unusually controlling husbands are also unusually violent husbands. Rather than being one of a set of alternative controlling tactics used by proprietary men, wife assault appears to go hand in hand with other tactics of control.

Margo I. Wilson and **Martin Daly** conduct research on interpersonal conflict and violence. Address correspondence to Margo Wilson, Department of Psychology, McMaster University, Hamilton, Ontario, Canada L8S 4K1; e-mail: wilson@mcmaster.ca.

EVOLUTIONARY PSYCHOLOGY, INTRASEXUAL COMPETITION, AND MARITAL ALLIANCE

Why should sexually proprietary feelings be linked with violence in this way? Although it is often supposed that wives are assaulted mainly because they are accessible, legitimate targets when men are frustrated or angry, mere opportunity cannot account for the differential risk of violent victimization within households. Wives are far more likely than other relatives to be murdered by an adult in their household (Fig. 1).[2] Wife assault has distinct motives. We propose that a satisfactory account of the psychological links between male sexual proprietariness and violence will depend on an understanding of the adaptive problems that men have faced in the course of human evolutionary history and the ways in which the psyche is organized to solve them. Those adaptive problems include both the risk of losing the wife, a valued reproductive resource, to a rival and the risk of directing paternal investments to another man's child.[1]

Adaptations are organismic attributes that are well "designed," as a result of a history of natural selection, to achieve functions that promoted reproductive success in ancestral environments.[5] Because organisms can usefully be analyzed into numerous distinct parts with complementary functions, investigation in the life sciences is almost invariably conducted in the shadow of (often inexplicit) adaptationist ideas. Sound hypotheses about what the heart or lungs or liver are "for" were essential first steps for investigating their physiology, for example. Psychological research is similarly (and equally appropriately) infused with adaptationist premises.

The goal of psychological science is and always has been the discovery and elucidation of psychological adaptations. Evolutionary thinking can help. By paying explicit attention to adaptive significance and selective forces, evolutionists are better able to generate hypotheses about which developmental experiences and proximate causal cues are likely to affect which aspects of behavior, and what sorts of contingencies, priorities, and combinatorial infor-

From *Current Directions in Psychological Science,* February 1996, pp. 2-7.

Table 1. *Association between violence against wives and husbands' autonomy-limiting behaviors, according to a national probability sample of Canadian wives*[4]

Statement	History of violence against wife		
	Serious violence N = 286	Relatively minor only N = 1,039	None N = 6,990
"He is jealous and doesn't want you to talk to other men"	39	13	4
"He tries to limit your contact with family or friends"	35	11	2
"He insists on knowing who you are with and where you are at all times"	40	24	7
"He calls you names to put you down or make you feel bad"	48	22	3
"He prevents you from knowing about or having access to the family income, even if you ask"	15	5	1

Note. Table entries are the percentages of respondents affirming that each item applied to their husbands. Violence was categorized as "serious" or "relatively minor" on the basis of the alleged assaultive acts; the validity of this distinction is supported by sample interviews indicating that an injury requiring medical attention occurred in 72% of the incidents that met the "serious" criterion versus 18% of the "relatively minor" violent incidents.

mation-processing algorithms are likely to be instantiated in the architecture of the mind.[6,7] Psychological constructs from self-esteem to color vision to sexual jealousy are formulated at a level of abstraction intended to be of panhuman (cross-cultural) generality. If these things exist and are complexly structured and organized, they almost certainly evolved to play some fitness-promoting role in our ancestors' lives. But although psychologists usually recognize that the phenomena they study have utility, jealousy in particular has often been dismissed as a functionless epiphenomenon or pathology. In light of what is known about evolution by selection, this is scarcely plausible.

In a sexual population, all the males are engaged in a *zero-sum game* in which the paternal share of the ancestry of all future generations is divided among them, while the females are engaged in a parallel contest over the maternal share of that ancestry. In a fundamental sense, then, one's principal competitors are same-sex members of one's own species. But although it is true for both females and males that selection entails a zero-sum competitive contest for genetic posterity, the evolutionary consequences are not necessarily similar in the two sexes. In particular, *sexual selection* (the component of selection that is attributable to differential access to mates) is generally of differential intensity, leading to a variety of sexually differentiated adaptations for intrasexual competition.[8]

In most mammals, the variance in male fitness is greater than the variance in female fitness, with the result that male mammals are generally subject to more intense sexual selection than females, and that the psychological and morphological attributes that have evolved for use in intrasexual competition are usually costlier and more dangerous in males than in

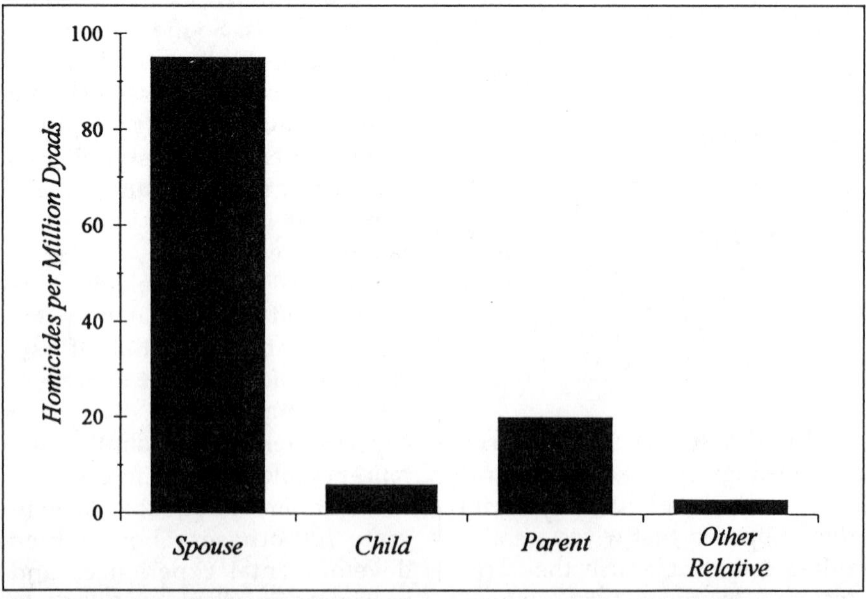

Fig. 1. Homicide victimization rates characteristic of different categories of co-residing relatives (considering only adults as potential perpetrators) in the city of Detroit, 1972.[2]

females. The human animal is no exception to these generalizations, and rivalry among men is a ubiquitous and sometimes deadly source of conflict. Where homicide rates are high, most victims are men, and their killers are mainly unrelated male acquaintances; the predominant motive is not robbery, but some sort of interpersonal conflict, especially a status or "face" dispute, with an overt element of sexual rivalry apparent in a substantial minority of the cases.[2] Of course, killing often oversteps the bounds of utility, but the circumstances under which dangerous violence is used in these cases bespeak its more typical functionality in its much more numerous nonlethal manifestations. And although the principal victims of men's lethal assaults are other men, violence is a coercive social tool that can be used on women, too, including wives.

From a selectionist perspective, the marital relationship has special properties. The fitnesses of genetic relatives overlap in proportion to genealogical proximity, a situation that engenders selection for altruistic and cooperative inclinations toward kin. Mates share genetic interests, too, but their solidarity is more fragile. By reproducing together, a monogamous couple may attain a state in which all exigencies affect their fitnesses identically, a situation conducive to consensus and harmony. However, the correlation between their expected fitnesses can be abolished or even rendered negative if one or both betray the relationship.[7]

Is it reasonable to propose the existence of an evolved social psychology specific to the marital relationship? Certainly, marital alliance is neither a sporadically distributed cultural option nor a modern discovery or invention, like agriculture or writing. Women and men everywhere enter into socially recognized unions, with a set of complementary sex-specific entitlements and obligations predicated on the complementarity of female and male sexual and reproductive roles, and they have done so for many millennia. We therefore expect that there are certain fundamental, universal sources of marital conflict, reflecting situations in which one marriage partner could have gained fitness in ancestral human environments at the other partner's expense. These situations would include conflicts over equity of contributions to the couple's joint endeavors (work sharing), over each partner's nepotistic interest in the welfare of his or her distinct kindred (in-law disputes), over asymmetrical temptations to abandon the union, and over sexual infidelity. In a pair-forming, biparental species, most of these conflicts can apply both ways, but the potential effects of infidelity are an exception: Males, unlike females, can be cuckolded and unwittingly invest their parental efforts in the service of rivals' fitness.

There is abundant contemporary, historical, and ethnographic evidence that even closely guarded women expend effort and incur risk to evade mates, especially when in marriages not of their own choosing.[1] But the proposition that the risk of misattributed paternity has been a distinct selective force on male psyches, over and above the effects of alienation of wives, implies that infidelity within undissolved marriages has been a threat to male fitness. Male sexual anatomy and physiology lend some support to this proposition. In cross-species comparisons, testis size closely tracks the degree to which females mate polyandrously in the short term, presumably because such matings engender *sperm competition* among rival ejaculates within the female reproductive tract, selecting for males who have high sperm counts and ejaculate volumes and who therefore get more of their own sperm into the contest.[9,10] Human male testis size suggests an ancestral level of polyandrous mating between the "promiscuity" of female chimpanzees and the monogamy of female gorillas. Moreover, if sperm competition has been a selective force, one might expect that men will exhibit contingently variable responses to cues that might indicate some risk of female infidelity. Results of one recent study support this expectation: The number of spermatozoa transferred in a given copulation in steady couples was better predicted by the proportion of time since the last copulation that the pair were out of contact than by the mere passage of time since the last ejaculation, an effect interpreted as a sophisticated psychophysiological adaptation to lapses in mate monitoring.[10] Some genuine risk of misattributed paternity would also appear to explain systematic biases of attention and attribution favoring allegations of paternal rather than maternal resemblances in babies.[7]

Undetected cuckoldry poses a major threat to a man's fitness, but for women the threat is slightly different: that a husband's efforts and resources will be diverted to the benefit of other women and their children. It follows that the arousal of men's and women's proprietary feelings toward their mates is likely to have evolved to be differentially attuned to distinct cues indicative of the sex-specific threats to fitness in past environments. Diverse evidence on feelings, reactions, and cultural practices supports the hypothesis that men are more intensely concerned with sexual infidelity per se and women more intensely concerned with the allocation of their mates' resources, affection, and attentions.[1,11]

CONTINGENT CUING OF MALE SEXUAL PROPRIETARINESS AND THE EPIDEMIOLOGY OF VIOLENCE AGAINST WIVES

If sexual proprietariness is aroused by cues of threats to sexual monopoly, and if use of violence is contingent on cues of its utility (including tolerable costs), then variations within and between societies in the frequency and severity of violence against wives may be largely attributable to variations in such cues.[1] Those relevant to the arousal of sexual proprietariness are likely to include cues of pressure from potential rivals and cues of one's partner's fertility and attractiveness to those rivals. Regarding the former issue, we would expect a husband to be sensitive to indicators of the local intensity of male competition and sexual poaching, and to indicators of the status, attractiveness, and resources of potential rivals relative to himself. Being part of a relatively large age cohort may also be expected to intensify male-male competition, especially if same-age women are unavailable; thus, cohort-size effects on intrasexual rivalry and hence on the coercive constraint of women may be especially evident where age disparities at marriage are large. Parameters like relative cohort size, local marital instability, and local prevalence of adultery clearly cannot be cued simply by stimuli immediately present, but must be induced from experience accumulated over large portions of the life span.

If men's violence and threats function to limit female autonomy, husbands may be motivated to act in these ways in response to probabilistic cues that their wives may desert them. Women who actually leave their husbands are often pursued, threatened, and assaulted; separated wives are even killed by their husbands at substantially higher rates than wives who live with their husbands (Fig. 2).[3] The elevation of uxoricide risk at separation is even more severe than the contrasts in Figure 2 suggest because the rate denominators include all separated wives regardless of the duration of separation, whereas when separated wives are killed, it is usually soon after separation. Of course, the temporal association between separation and violence does not necessarily mean that the former caused the latter; however, many husbands who have killed their wives had explicitly threatened to do so should their wives ever leave, and explain their behavior as a response to the intolerable stimulus of their wives' departure.

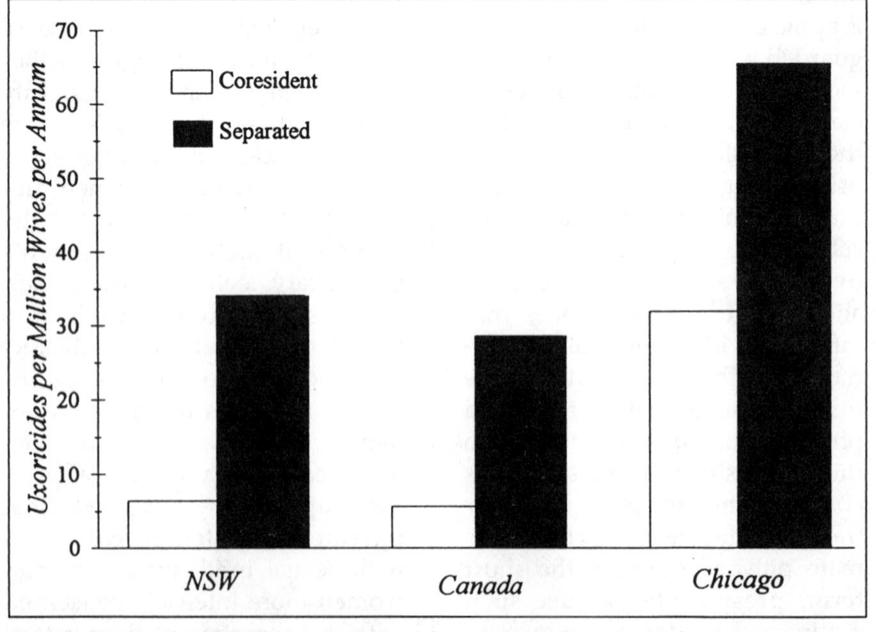

Fig. 2. Rates of uxoricides perpetrated by registered-marriage husbands, for coresiding versus estranged couples in New South Wales (NSW), Australia (1968–1986); Canada (1974–1990); and Chicago (1965–1989).[3]

Why are men ever motivated to pursue and kill women who have left them? Such behavior is spiteful in that it is likely to impose a net cost on its perpetrator as well as its victim, and therefore challenges the evolutionary psychological hypothesis that motives and emotions are organized in such a way as to promote the actors' interests. Moreover, if the adaptive function of the motivational processes underlying violence against wives resides in retaining and controlling one's mate, as we have suggested, killing is all the more paradoxical. The problem is akin to that of understanding vengeance.[2] A threat is an effective social tool, and usually an inexpensive one, but it loses its effectiveness if the threatening party is seen to be bluffing, that is, to be unwilling to pay the occasional cost of following through when the threat is ignored or defied. Such vengeful follow-through may appear counterproductive—a risky or expensive act too late to be useful—but effective threats cannot "leak" signs of bluff and may therefore have to be sincere. Although killing an estranged wife appears futile, threatening one who might otherwise leave can be self-interested, and so can pursuing her with further threats, as can advertisements of anger and ostensible obliviousness to costs.

Evolutionary psychologists have predicted and confirmed that men are maximally attracted to young women as sexual and marital partners.[12] This fact suggests that sexual proprietariness will be relatively intensely aroused in men married to younger women, and young wives indeed incur the highest rates of both lethal[2–4] (Fig. 3) and nonlethal[4] violence by husbands. (It might be suggested that male sexual jealousy cannot be an evolved adaptation because men remain sexually jealous of postmenopausal or otherwise infertile women, but adaptations can have evolved only to track ancestrally informative cues of fertility and not fertility itself. In a modern society with contraception, improved health, and diverse cosmetic manipulations, postmenopausal women are likely to exhibit fewer cues of age-related declining reproductive value than still-fertile women in ancestral societies.[12])

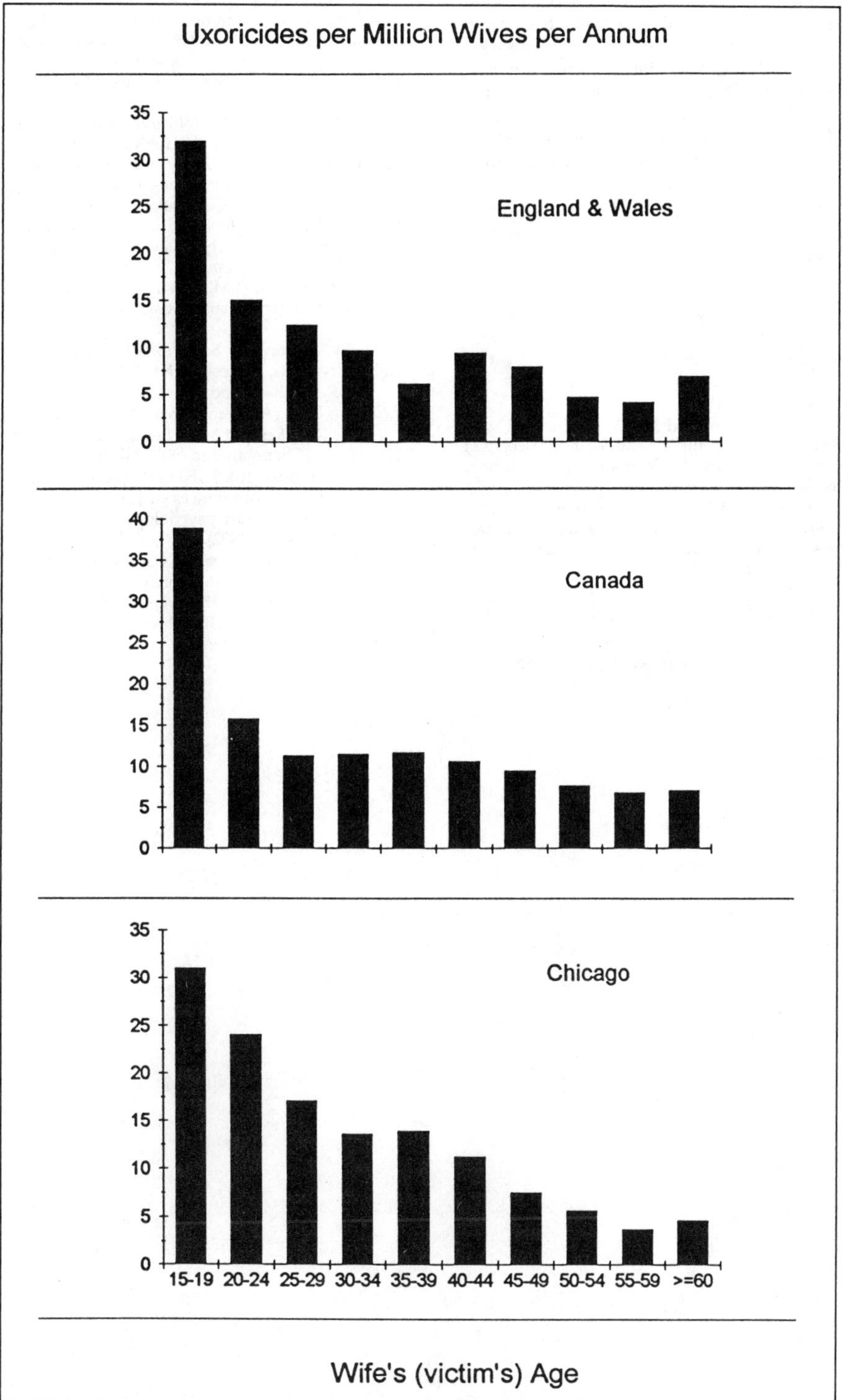

Fig. 3. Uxoricide rates as a function of the victim's age, in England and Wales (1977–1990), Canada (1974–1990), and Chicago (1965–1989).[3]

There are several reasons to suppose that husbands may be relatively insecure in their proprietary claims in *de facto* marriages, which have higher rates of dissolution and a weaker or more ambiguous legal status than registered unions. And, indeed, wives in *de facto* marital unions in Canada incur an eight times greater risk of uxoricide and a four times greater risk of nonlethal assault by husbands.[4] However, registered and *de facto* unions differ in many ways, and the higher risk of uxoricide and assault in the latter may be due to a complex combination of factors, including youth, poverty, parity, and the presence of stepchildren;[2,4,7] whether adultery and desertion are greater sources of conflict in *de facto* unions than in registered unions is unknown. Demographic risk markers such as type of marital union and age are undoubtedly correlated with several variables that may be more directly causal to the risk of violence; elucidation of their relative roles awaits further research. However, it was the logic of evolution by selection which suggested to us that these demographic variables are likely correlates of breaches of sexual exclusivity and hence of violence.

Evolution by selection offers a framework for the development of hypotheses about the functional design of motivational-emotional-cognitive subsystems of the mind such as male sexual proprietariness, providing hints about proximate causal cues, modulated expression, attentional priorities, and perceptual and informational processing. We have argued that the development and modulation of male sexual proprietariness is contingent on ecologically valid cues of threats to a sexually exclusive relationship. The link between male sexual proprietariness and violent inclinations has presumably been selected for because violence and threat work to deter sexual rivals and limit female autonomy. (This is not to say that violent capacities and inclinations were not also subject to selection pressures in other contexts, including intergroup warfare and hunting.) The expression of male sexual proprietariness, including violent manifestations, will depend not only on the presence and incidence of ecologically valid cues, but also on community, family, and person-specific factors that are likely to affect the thresholds and other parameter settings of the psychological mechanisms involved.

Acknowledgments—Our research on violence against wives has been supported by grants from the Social Sciences and Humanities Research Council of Canada, the Harry Frank Guggenheim Foundation, the Natural Sciences and Engineering Research Council of Canada, the North Atlantic Treaty Organization, and the McMaster University Arts Research Board. We thank J. Bannon, C.R. Block, R. Block, O. Fedorowycz, H. Johnson, C. Nuttall, A. Wallace, and M. Wilt for access to data.

Notes

1. M.I. Wilson and M. Daly, The man who mistook his wife for a chattel, in *The Adapted Mind*, J.H. Barkow, L. Cosmides, and J. Tooby, Eds. (Oxford University Press, New York, 1992); M.I. Wilson and M. Daly, An evolutionary psychological perspective on male sexual proprietariness and violence against wives, *Violence & Victims, 8*, 271–294 (1993).

2. M. Daly and M.I. Wilson, *Homicide* (Aldine de Gruyter, Hawthorne, NY, 1988).

3. M.I. Wilson, M. Daly, and J. Scheib, Femicide: An evolutionary psychological perspective, in *Evolutionary Biology and Feminism*, P.A. Gowaty, Ed. (Chapman and Hall, New York, in press).

4. M.I. Wilson, H. Johnson, and M. Daly, Lethal and nonlethal violence against wives, *Canadian Journal of Criminology, 37*, 331–361 (1995).

5. G.C. Williams, *Adaptation and Natural Selection* (Princeton University Press, Princeton, NJ, 1966).

6. J. Tooby and L. Cosmides, The psychological foundations of culture, in *The Adapted Mind*, J.H. Barkow, L. Cosmides, and J. Tooby, Eds. (Oxford University Press, New York, 1992); D.M. Buss, Evolutionary psychology: A new paradigm for psychological science, *Psychological Inquiry, 6*, 1–30 (1995).

7. M. Daly and M.I. Wilson, Discriminative parental solicitude and the relevance of evolutionary models to the analysis of motivational systems, in *The Cognitive Neurosciences*, M. Gazzaniga, Ed. (MIT Press, Cambridge, MA, 1995); M. Daly and M.I. Wilson, Evolutionary psychology and marital conflict: The relevance of stepchildren, in *Sex, Power, Conflict: Feminist and Evolutionary Perspectives*, D.M. Buss and N. Malamuth, Eds. (Oxford University Press, New York, in press).

8. M. Andersson, *Sexual Selection* (Princeton University Press, Princeton, NJ, 1994).

9. T.R. Birkhead and A.P. Møller, *Sperm Competition in Birds* (Academic Press, London, 1992).

10. R.R. Baker and M.A. Bellis, *Human Sperm Competition* (Chapman and Hall, London, 1995).

11. D.M. Buss, R.J. Larsen, D. Westen, and J. Semmelroth, Sex differences in jealousy: Evolution, physiology, and psychology, *Psychological Science, 3*, 251–255 (1992).

12. D.S. Symons, Beauty is in the adaptations of the beholder: The evolutionary psychology of human female sexual attractiveness, in *Sexual Nature/Sexual Culture*, P.R. Abramson and S.D. Pinkerton, Eds. (University of Chicago Press, Chicago, 1995).

Index

Credits/Acknowledgments

Cover design by Charles Vitelli.

1. Methods in Biopsychology
Facing overview—Card 12F from the *Thematic Apperception Test* by Henry A. Murray, Cambridge, MA: Harvard University Press. © 1943 by the President and Fellows of Harvard College; © 1971 by Henry A. Murray. Reprinted by permission of the publisher.

2. The Neuron and Regions of the Brain
Facing overview—Medical World News photo. 37—Illustration by Leigh Coriale Illustration & Design.

3. Neural Development and Plasticity
Facing overview—Dushkin/McGraw-Hill illustration by Mike Eagle.

4. Sensation and Perception
Facing overview—United Nations photo by W. A. Graham.

5. Motivation: Hunger and Aggression
Facing overview—© 1998 by PhotoDisc, Inc.

6. Reproductive Behavior
Facing overview—WHO photo.

7. Sleep and Biological Rhythms
Facing overview—NIH Gerontology Center photo. 112—Photos by Richard W. Wrangham.

8. Emotions
Facing overview—© 1998 by PhotoDisc, Inc.

9. Learning and Memory
Facing overview—© 1998 by Cleo Freelance Photography, Inc.

10. Disorders of Behavior and the Nervous System
Facing overview—WHO photo by Jean Mohr.

11. Ethical Issues
Facing overview—WHO photo by Jean Mohr.

12. Evolutionary Perspectives
Facing overview—WHO photo.

*PHOTOCOPY THIS PAGE!!!**

ANNUAL EDITIONS ARTICLE REVIEW FORM

■ NAME: ______________________________ DATE: ______________

■ TITLE AND NUMBER OF ARTICLE: ______________________________

■ BRIEFLY STATE THE MAIN IDEA OF THIS ARTICLE: ______________________________

____

■ LIST THREE IMPORTANT FACTS THAT THE AUTHOR USES TO SUPPORT THE MAIN IDEA:

____

____

____

____

____

■ WHAT INFORMATION OR IDEAS DISCUSSED IN THIS ARTICLE ARE ALSO DISCUSSED IN YOUR TEXTBOOK OR OTHER READINGS THAT YOU HAVE DONE? LIST THE TEXTBOOK CHAPTERS AND PAGE NUMBERS:

____

____

____

____

____

■ LIST ANY EXAMPLES OF BIAS OR FAULTY REASONING THAT YOU FOUND IN THE ARTICLE:

____

____

____

____

____

■ LIST ANY NEW TERMS/CONCEPTS THAT WERE DISCUSSED IN THE ARTICLE, AND WRITE A SHORT DEFINITION:

____

____

____

____

____

*Your instructor may require you to use this ANNUAL EDITIONS Article Review Form in any number of ways: for articles that are assigned, for extra credit, as a tool to assist in developing assigned papers, or simply for your own reference. Even if it is not required, we encourage you to photocopy and use this page; you will find that reflecting on the articles will greatly enhance the information from your text.

We Want Your Advice

ANNUAL EDITIONS revisions depend on two major opinion sources: one is our Advisory Board, listed in the front of this volume, which works with us in scanning the thousands of articles published in the public press each year; the other is you—the person actually using the book. Please help us and the users of the next edition by completing the prepaid article rating form on this page and returning it to us. Thank you for your help!

ANNUAL EDITIONS: BIOPSYCHOLOGY 98/99

Article Rating Form

Here is an opportunity for you to have direct input into the next revision of this volume. We would like you to rate each of the 49 articles listed below, using the following scale:

1. **Excellent: should definitely be retained**
2. **Above average: should probably be retained**
3. **Below average: should probably be deleted**
4. **Poor: should definitely be deleted**

Your ratings will play a vital part in the next revision. So please mail this prepaid form to us just as soon as you complete it.
Thanks for your help!

Rating	Article
____	1. Magnet on the Brain
____	2. Evolutions: The Human Cerebral Cortex
____	3. New Imaging Methods Provide a Better View into the Brain
____	4. Creating a Body of Knowledge
____	5. The Brain's Immune System
____	6. Tarzan's Little Brain
____	7. Stem Cells in the Central Nervous System
____	8. Why Oligodendrocytes Die in Spinal Cord Injury
____	9. Neurotrophins and the Neurotrophic Factor Hypothesis
____	10. Making Our Minds Last a Lifetime
____	11. Studies Show Talking with Infants Shapes Basis of Ability to Think
____	12. Nature, Nurture, Brains, and Behavior
____	13. For the Cortex, Neuron Loss May Be Less than Thought
____	14. The Smell of Love
____	15. The Senses
____	16. Visual Processing: More than Meets the Eye
____	17. Effects of Alcohol on Human Aggression: Validity of Proposed Explanations
____	18. Attenuation of the Obesity Syndrome of *ob/ob* Mice by the Loss of Neuropeptide Y
____	19. Aggressive Youth: Healing Biology with Relationship
____	20. Natural-Born Mothers
____	21. Rethinking Puberty: The Development of Sexual Attraction
____	22. Subtle, Secret Female Chimpanzees
____	23. Animals' Fancies: Why Members of Some Species Prefer Their Own Sex
____	24. Menstrual Synchrony under Optimal Conditions: Bedouin Families
____	25. 'Traveling Light' Has New Meaning for Jet Laggards

Rating	Article
____	26. A Mouse Helps Explain What Makes Us Tick
____	27. Adenosine: A Mediator of the Sleep-Inducing Effects of Prolonged Wakefulness
____	28. Happiness Is a Stochastic Phenomenon
____	29. On the Neurobiological Basis of Affiliation
____	30. Deciding Advantageously before Knowing the Advantageous Strategy
____	31. Something Snapped
____	32. The Machinery of Thought
____	33. How Does the Brain Organize Memories?
____	34. Estradiol Is Related to Visual Memory in Healthy Young Men
____	35. Glucose Effects on Declarative and Nondeclarative Memory in Healthy Elderly and Young Adults
____	36. Addicted
____	37. Gene Therapy for the Nervous System
____	38. Understanding Parkinson's Disease
____	39. Looking Beyond the Reading Difficulties in Dyslexia, A Vision Deficit
____	40. Attention Deficit: Nature, Nurture, or Nicotine?
____	41. Science Misapplied: The Eugenics Age Revisited
____	42. Trends in Animal Research
____	43. Politics of Biology
____	44. Junior Comes Out Perfect
____	45. God's Utility Function
____	46. Evolution's New Heretics
____	47. Sex Differences in Social Behavior: Are the Social Role and Evolutionary Explanations Compatible?
____	48. Sex Differences in Jealousy in Evolutionary and Cultural Perspective: Tests from the Netherlands, Germany, and the United States
____	49. Male Sexual Proprietariness and Violence against Wives

(Continued on next page)

ABOUT YOU

Name ______________________ Date ____________

Are you a teacher? ❑ Or a student? ❑

Your school name ______________________

Department ______________________

Address ______________________

City ______________________ State __________ Zip __________

School telephone # ______________________

YOUR COMMENTS ARE IMPORTANT TO US!

Please fill in the following information:

For which course did you use this book? ______________________

Did you use a text with this *ANNUAL EDITION*? ❑ yes ❑ no

What was the title of the text? ______________________

What are your general reactions to the *Annual Editions* concept?

Have you read any particular articles recently that you think should be included in the next edition?

Are there any articles you feel should be replaced in the next edition? Why?

Are there any World Wide Web sites you feel should be included in the next edition? Please annotate.

May we contact you for editorial input?

May we quote your comments?

No Postage
Necessary
if Mailed
in the
United States

ANNUAL EDITIONS: BIOPSYCHOLOGY 98/99

BUSINESS REPLY MAIL

First Class Permit No. 84 Guilford, CT

Postage will be paid by addressee

Dushkin/McGraw·Hill
Sluice Dock
Guilford, CT 06437